The Wiley Bicentennial–Knowledge for Generations

Each generation has its unique needs and aspirations. When Charles Wiley first opened his small printing shop in lower Manhattan in 1807, it was a generation of boundless potential searching for an identity. And we were there, helping to define a new American literary tradition. Over half a century later, in the midst of the Second Industrial Revolution, it was a generation focused on building the future. Once again, we were there, supplying the critical scientific, technical, and engineering knowledge that helped frame the world. Throughout the 20th Century, and into the new millennium, nations began to reach out beyond their own borders and a new international community was born. Wiley was there, expanding its operations around the world to enable a global exchange of ideas, opinions, and know-how.

For 200 years, Wiley has been an integral part of each generation's journey, enabling the flow of information and understanding necessary to meet their needs and fulfill their aspirations. Today, bold new technologies are changing the way we live and learn. Wiley will be there, providing you the must-have knowledge you need to imagine new worlds, new possibilities, and new opportunities.

Generations come and go, but you can always count on Wiley to provide you the knowledge you need, when and where you need it!

Peter Booth Wiley
Chairman of the Board

Networking Basics

Patrick Ciccarelli, Christina Faulkner, Jerry FitzGerald,
Alan Dennis, David Groth, and Tony Skandier

with Frank Miller

Credits

PUBLISHER
Anne Smith

PROJECT EDITOR
Brian B. Baker

MARKETING MANAGER
Jennifer Slomack

SENIOR EDITORIAL ASSISTANT
Tiara Kelly

PRODUCTION MANAGER
Kelly Tavares

PRODUCTION EDITOR
Kerry Weinstein

CREATIVE DIRECTOR
Harry Nolan

COVER DESIGNER
Hope Miller

COVER PHOTO
©Mike Watson/Corbis

Wiley 200th Anniversary Logo designed by: Richard J. Pacifico

This book was set in Times New Roman by Aptara, printed and bound by R. R. Donnelley. The cover was printed by R. R. Donnelley.

To order books or for customer service, please call 1-800-CALL WILEY (225-5945).

ISBN 978-0-470-11129-1

Printed in the United States of America

10 9 8 7 6 5 4 3 2 1

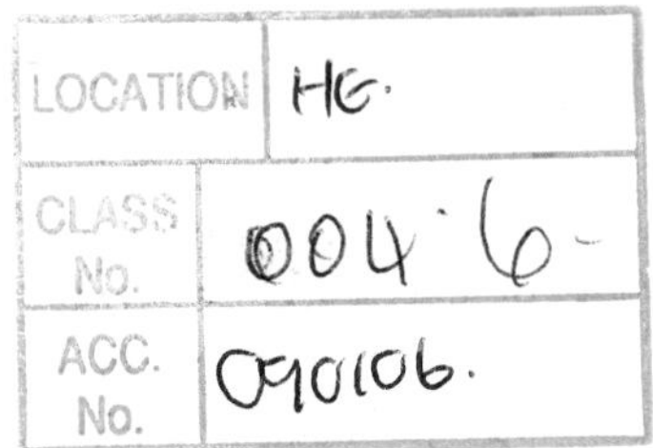

Christina Faulkner and **Patrick Ciccarelli** are instructors for the Cisco Networking Academy at San Francisco State University and founding partners of Nethos Inc., a Bay area technology consulting company serving education and small business markets. Both authors have Masters degrees in Instructional Design. Faulkner has more than 15 years of experience as an educator, and Ciccarelli previously worked in PC technical support for several years.

Jerry FitzGerald is the author of *Business Data Communications: Basic Concepts, Security and Design* and *Designing Controls into Computerized Systems*, among other books and numerous articles. He received a Ph.D. in business economics from the Claremont Graduate School and an MBA from the University of Santa Clara. He has extensive experience in risk analysis, computer security, audit and control of computerized systems, data communications, networks, and systems analysis. He is the principal in Jerry FitzGerald & Associates, a firm he started in 1977.

Alan Dennis is Professor of Information Systems and John T. Chambers Chair of Internet Systems in the Kelly School of Business at Indiana University. He is the author of *Networking in the Internet Age*, coauthor *of Systems Analysis and Design: An Applied Approach* with Barbara Haley Wixom, and coauthor of *Systems Analysis and Design: An Object-Oriented Approach with UML* with Barbara Haley Wixom and David Tegarden. He received a Ph.D. in management of information systems from the University of Arizona.

David Groth is a full-time author and consultant. He is the author of Sybex's best-selling *A+ Complete Study Guide, PC Chop Shop: Tricked Out Guide to PC Modding*, and is coauthor of *Cabling: The Complete Guide to Network Wiring, Network+ Study Guide: Exam N10-003, i-Net+ Study Guide: Exam IK0-002, CompTIA Network+ Certification Kit (Exam N10-003)*, and coeditor of *A+ Fast Pass.*

Toby Skandier is in technical education development and delivery for Sprint Corporation. He is the author of *CliffsTestPrep CompTIA A+, Network Administrator Street Smarts: A Real World Guide to CompTIA Network+ Skills*, and coauthor of *Network+ Study Guide: Exam N10-003, CompTIA A+ Complete Study Guide.*

Frank Miller has nearly 30 years experience designing, developing, and delivering technical training materials. He has worked with computer networking for nearly 20 years, with experience that includes Unix and Linux networks, AppleTalk, LAN Manager, various generations of Novell's NetWare, and every version of Microsoft Windows networking since the first days of Windows for Workgroups. He has written numerous books and training materials that are used by various schools and professional organizations in the United States and around the world.

College classrooms bring together learners from many backgrounds, with a variety of aspirations. Although the students are in the same course, they are not necessarily on the same path. This diversity, coupled with the reality that these learners often have jobs, families, and other commitments, requires a flexibility that our nation's higher education system is addressing. Distance learning, shorter course terms, new disciplines, evening courses, and certification programs are some of the approaches that colleges employ to reach as many students as possible and help them clarify and achieve their goals.

Wiley Pathways books, a new line of texts from John Wiley & Sons, Inc., are designed to help you address this diversity and the need for flexibility. These books focus on the fundamentals, identify core competencies and skills, and promote independent learning. Their focus on the fundamentals helps students grasp the subject, bringing them all to the same basic understanding. These books use clear, everyday language and are presented in an uncluttered format, making the reading experience more pleasurable. The core competencies and skills help students succeed in the classroom and beyond, whether in another course or in a professional setting. A variety of built-in learning resources promote independent learning and help instructors and students gauge students' understanding of the content. These resources enable students to think critically about their new knowledge and apply their skills in any situation.

Our goal with *Wiley Pathways* books—with their brief, inviting format, clear language, and core competencies and skills focus—is to celebrate the many students in your courses, respect their needs, and help you guide them on their way.

CASE Learning System

To meet the needs of working college students, *Networking Basics* uses a four-part process called the CASE Learning System:

- **C:** Content
- **A:** Analysis
- **S:** Synthesis
- **E:** Evaluation

Based on Bloom's taxonomy of learning, CASE presents key topics in networking basics in easy-to-follow chapters. The text then prompts analysis, synthesis, and evaluation with a variety of learning aids and assessment tools. Students move efficiently from reviewing what they have learned, to acquiring new information and skills, to applying their new knowledge and skills to real-life scenarios.

Using the CASE Learning System, students not only achieve academic mastery of networking basics *topics,* but they master real-world *skills* related to that content. The CASE Learning System also helps students become independent learners, giving them a distinct advantage in the field, whether they are just starting out or seeking to advance in their careers.

Organization, Depth, and Breadth of the Text

- ▲ **Modular format:** Research on college students shows that they access information from textbooks in a nonlinear way. Instructors also often wish to reorder textbook content to suit the needs of a particular class. Therefore, although *Networking Basics* proceeds logically from the basics to increasingly more challenging material, chapters are further organized into sections that are self-contained for maximum teaching and learning flexibility.
- ▲ **Numeric system of headings:** *Networking Basics* uses a numeric system for headings (e.g., 3.2.4 identifies the fourth subsection of Section 2 of Chapter 3). With this system, students and teachers can quickly and easily pinpoint topics in the table of contents and the text, keeping class time and study sessions focused.
- ▲ **Core content:** The topics in *Networking Basics* are organized into 12 chapters.

Chapter 1, "Networking Fundamentals," introduces PC networks and their importance to modern businesses. The chapter begins with an overview of the development of PC networks and the Internet. It compares and contrasts peer-to-peer, client/server, and directory service–based networking models and explains the roles of low- and high-level protocols in network communication. Students are also introduced to local area networks (LANs), metropolitan area networks (MANs), and wide area networks (WANs).

In Chapter 2, "Network Standards and Models," students are introduced to the standard models used to describe networking technologies and the standards bodies that produce them. Students are provided with a detailed look at the Open Systems Interconnection (OSI) model and learn why the model is important. The chapter also compares the OSI model to two other commonly used models: the Internet model and the TCP/IP, or Department of Defense (DoD), model. The chapter gives the students a baseline for understanding and comparing network technologies, software, and devices.

Chapter 3, "Network Architectures," provides students with a detailed look at common network architectures, including peer-to-peer, client/server, directory service, and hybrid architecture models. It includes an overview of the security models used in each of these network architectures and the relationship between logical and physical network models. Students learn the basics of developing a network design to meet an organization's operational requirements.

Chapter 4, "Network Topologies," compares and contrasts common logical and physical topologies. Students are given guidelines for selecting the most appropriate topology, based on network requirements, including when a hybrid topology is the best solution. As a way of discussing the technologies involved with each topology, students are introduced to the access methods used by each, including a detailed comparison of Carrier-Sense Multiple Access/Collision Detect (CSMA/CD) and Token Ring as representative access types.

Chapter 5, "Network Media and Devices," provides a detailed discussion of wired media types, network connection devices, and Internet connection devices. The chapter compares and contrasts the use of coaxial (coax), unshielded twisted-pair (UTP), shielded twisted-pair (STP), and fiber-optic cable in both legacy and current network applications. Students learn to recognize the various cable types and, given network requirements, how to choose the most appropriate cable types. Students also learn how to choose appropriate connection devices, based on network requirements, with a detailed look at bridge and router operations.

Chapter 6, "Network Protocols," looks at the Data Link layer and Network layer protocols in detail, including applicable published standards. It discusses protocols in the context of their role in network communications. The chapter looks first at lower-level protocols, focusing on and comparing the Ethernet and Token Ring protocols. It then moves on to network protocols, with a comparison of the TCP/IP, IPX/SPX, and AppleTalk protocol suites, which are the protocols that students are most likely to encounter in real-world networking applications.

Chapter 7, "Transmission Control Protocol/Internet Protocol (TCP/IP)," puts special and appropriate emphasis on the TCP/IP protocol suite. Students learn about the importance of TCP/IP as the de facto standard for nearly all current PC networking applications. The chapter looks at representative TCP/IP packets to introduce how addresses are used and then discusses addressing requirements. Students learn about the need for name resolution and the most common name resolution options. Students also learn about the requirements for configuring computers to support TCP/IP, using Microsoft Windows as a representative example operating system.

Chapter 8, "Wireless, Remote, and Wide Area Networking," broadens students' exposure to network environments by introducing additional networking options. Students learn about the current state of wireless networking standards and ways in which wireless networking can be integrated into a network design. The chapter compares the use of dial-in and Internet-based remote access configurations with the benefits and drawbacks of each. The chapter introduces WAN connectivity methods currently in use and how to make design choices based on network requirements.

Chapter 9, "Network Servers and Services Fundamentals," focuses on the role of the network operating system (NOS) in a network environment. Students compare and contrast popular options, looking at Novell NOS options, Microsoft Windows versions, as well as Unix, Linux, and Apple Macintosh, with a special focus on Mac OS X. The chapter includes a look at interoperability issues students might encounter in a heterogeneous networking environment.

In Chapter 10, "Wide Area and Enterprise Networking Services," the role of network servers is expanded to include larger network environments, including the Internet. The chapter discusses networking requirements in the context of network analysis and design. Students learn what questions they need to ask and what information they need to gather, as well as how to apply what they have learned to create a viable network design. The chapter takes a broad-based approach, showing the dependencies between technical requirements, user and manager requests, and budgetary constraints.

Chapter 11, "Network Management," describes management roles and requirements, as well as how these might be delegated in a large organization. The chapter focuses on key management and support areas, such as backup and restoration, network monitoring, performance tuning, and software change management. Students are introduced to several management tools and learn about the use of technologies based on Simple Network Management Protocol (SNMP).

Chapter 12, "Network Security," discusses issues critical to all networks. Students learn about the most common threats to network security and how to avoid them. They also learn about recovery requirements for after a network has been attacked. The chapter looks at both what can be done through network and client software, such as user and password management, and hardware devices that help protect a network, such as firewalls. Students learn about encryption and its use in data communications. They also learn about the threat that viruses pose and available antivirus tools and countermeasures.

Pre-reading Learning Aids

Each chapter of *Networking Basics* features the following learning and study aids to activate students' prior knowledge of the topics and orient them to the material:

▲ **Pre-test:** This pre-reading assessment tool in multiple-choice format not only introduces chapter material but also helps students anticipate the chapter's learning outcomes. By focusing students' attention on what they do not know, the self-test provides students with a benchmark against which they can measure their own progress. The pre-test is available at www.wiley.com/college/ciccarelli.

▲ **What You'll Learn in This Chapter:** This bulleted list focuses on subject matter that will be taught. It tells students what they will be learning in the chapter and why it is significant for their careers. It also helps students understand why the chapter is important and how it relates to other chapters in the text.

▲ **After Studying This Chapter, You'll Be Able To:** This list emphasizes capabilities and skills students will learn as a result of reading the chapter. It sets students up to synthesize and evaluate the chapter material and relate it to the real world.

Within-text Learning Aids

The following learning aids are designed to encourage analysis and synthesis of the material, support the learning process, and ensure success during the evaluation phase:

▲ **Introduction:** This section orients the student by introducing the chapter and explaining its practical value and relevance to the book as a whole. Short summaries of chapter sections preview the topics that follow.

▲ **"For Example" boxes:** Found within each section, these boxes tie section content to real-world examples, scenarios, and applications.

- **Figures and tables:** Line art and photos have been carefully chosen to be truly instructional rather than filler. Tables distill and present information in a way that is easy to identify, access, and understand, enhancing the focus of the text on essential ideas.
- **Self-Check:** Related to the "What You'll Learn in This Chapter" bullets and found at the end of each section, this battery of short-answer questions emphasizes student understanding of concepts and mastery of section content. Whether the questions are discussed in class or studied by students outside class, students should not go on before they can answer all questions correctly.
- **Key Terms and Glossary:** To help students develop a professional vocabulary, each key term appears in boldfaced when it first appears in the chapter. A complete list of key terms appears at the end of each chapter, and all the key terms, along with brief definitions, appear in a glossary at the end of the book. Knowledge of key terms is assessed through the book's assessment tools (see Evaluation and Assessment Tools Section).
- **Summary:** Each chapter concludes with a brief summary that reviews the major concepts in the chapter and links back to the "What You'll Learn in This Chapter" list.

Evaluation and Assessment Tools

The evaluation phase of the CASE Learning System consists of a variety of within-chapter and end-of-chapter assessment tools that test how well students have learned the material. These tools also encourage students to extend their learning into different scenarios and higher levels of understanding and thinking. The following assessment tools appear in every chapter of *Networking Basics*:

- **Summary Questions:** These questions help students summarize the chapter's main points by asking a series of multiple-choice and true/false questions that emphasize student understanding of concepts and mastery of chapter content. Students should be able to answer all of the Summary Questions correctly before moving on.
- **Applying This Chapter Questions:** These questions drive home key ideas by asking students to synthesize and apply chapter concepts to new, real-life situations and scenarios.
- **You Try It:** These examples are designed to extend students' thinking and so are ideal for discussion or writing assignments.

Using an open-ended format and sometimes based on web sources, they encourage students to draw conclusions using chapter material applied to real-world situations, which fosters both mastery and independent learning.

- **Post-test:** A student should take the post-test after completing the chapter. It includes all the questions in the pre-test so that students can see how their learning has progressed and improved.

Instructor Package

Networking Basics is available with the following teaching and learning supplements, all of which are available online at the text's companion website, located at www.wiley.com/college/ciccarelli:

- **Instructor's Resource Guide:** Provides the following aids and supplements for teaching a networking basics course:
  - *Sample syllabus:* A convenient template that instructors can use to create their own course syllabi.
  - *Teaching suggestions:* For each chapter, teaching suggestions include a chapter summary, learning objectives, definitions of key terms, lecture notes, answers to select text question sets, and at least three suggestions for classroom activities, such as ideas for speakers to invite, videos to show, and other projects.
- **PowerPoint slides:** Key information is summarized in 10 to 15 PowerPoint slides per chapter. Instructors can use these in class or may choose to share them with students for class presentations or to provide additional study support.
- **Test bank:** Includes one test per chapter, as well as a midterm and two finals: one cumulative, one noncumulative. Each includes true/false, multiple-choice, and open-ended questions. Answers and page references are provided for the true/false and multiple-choice questions, and page references are provided for the open-ended questions. Questions are available in Microsoft Word and computerized test bank formats.

Student Project Manual

The inexpensive *Networking Basics Project Manual* contains activities (an average of five projects per textbook chapter) designed to help students apply textbook concepts in a practical way. Easier exercises at the beginning graduate to more challenging projects that build critical-thinking skills.

A

Taken together, the content, pedagogy, and assessment elements of *Networking Basics* offer the career-oriented student the most important aspects of the information technology field as well as ways to develop the skills and capabilities that current and future employers seek in the individuals they hire and promote. Instructors will appreciate its practical focus, conciseness, and real-world emphasis.

We would like to thank the reviewers for their feedback and suggestions during the text's development. Their advice on how to shape *Networking Basics* into a solid learning tool that meets both their needs and those of their busy students is deeply appreciated.

We would especially like to thank the following reviewers for their significant contributions:

- Edwin Sloan, Hillsborough Community College
- Harold Lamson, ITT Technical Institute

We would also like to thank Carol Traver for all her hard work in formatting and preparing the manuscript for production.

BRIEF CONTENTS

CONTENTS

1 NETWORKING FUNDAMENTALS

Starting Point

Go to www.wiley.com/college/ciccarelli to assess your knowledge of networking fundamentals.
Determine where you need to concentrate your effort.

What You'll Learn in This Chapter

- ▲ The basic benefits and drawbacks of networks
- ▲ Network components and the roles of devices
- ▲ Network models
- ▲ Network types
- ▲ Data communication fundamentals
- ▲ Changes in network technologies

After Studying This Chapter, You'll Be Able To

- ▲ Describe the benefits of and potential concerns about PC networks
- ▲ Trace the development of PC networks and the Internet
- ▲ Identify network devices, communication components, computer types, and their roles
- ▲ Compare and contrast the client/server, directory services, and peer-to-peer network models
- ▲ Explain the roles of low-level and high-level protocols in network communications
- ▲ Compare and contrast basic features of local area, metropolitan area, and wide area networks
- ▲ Identify the roles of Internet technologies in intranets and extranets
- ▲ Describe the significance of pervasive networking, convergence, and information publishers in ongoing network development

INTRODUCTION

There was a time, not too long ago, when networked personal computers (PCs) were the exception. Now, not only have networks become the rule for businesses, home networks have become common. Why? In short, **networks**, which consist primarily of desktop computers connected together so that they can communicate, enhance both business and personal productivity by enabling users to share resources. Though not completely accurate, the term **personal computer (PC)** has come to refer generically to a personal desktop computer that includes its own processor, memory, and local storage.

This chapter explores the reasons behind the growth of networks, with a quick look at the roots of PC networks and the Internet, and some of the advantages and disadvantages of networks. Then you'll learn some fundamental network concepts, including the basic components of a network, the roles different network devices play, and the two primary network models in use today. Next, you'll be introduced to the topic of data communications and protocols. The chapter then turns to a discussion of the three main types of networks you are likely to encounter, and it concludes with a look at some of the major trends that are likely to affect the future of networking.

1.1 Understanding the Need for Networks

Modern networks grew out of what has been referred to as "mainframe sensibilities." Many of the earliest network designers and developers came from a mainframe background. In a traditional mainframe computer environment, like the one shown in Figure 1-1, "dumb" terminals connect to a central mainframe computer. A **dumb terminal** is effectively a screen and a keyboard, with all data storage, processing, and control occurring at the mainframe.

A PC network is similar to a mainframe setup in that the computers are electronically connected. Most networks have one or more specialized computers called **servers** that provide resources to the network, acting somewhat like the central mainframe. The biggest difference is that PCs are **smart terminals** that have their own processing and memory.

1.1.1 Networking Roots

To understand the need for a PC network, let's take a closer look at its roots. Mainframe computers brought computers from the realm of government-only to businesses, though only the biggest businesses could afford to take advantage of them.

The introduction of the PC led to a revolution in how businesses, and eventually homes, operated. Small businesses and individual users could now afford to obtain computers. However, information technology (IT) professionals coming

Figure 1-1

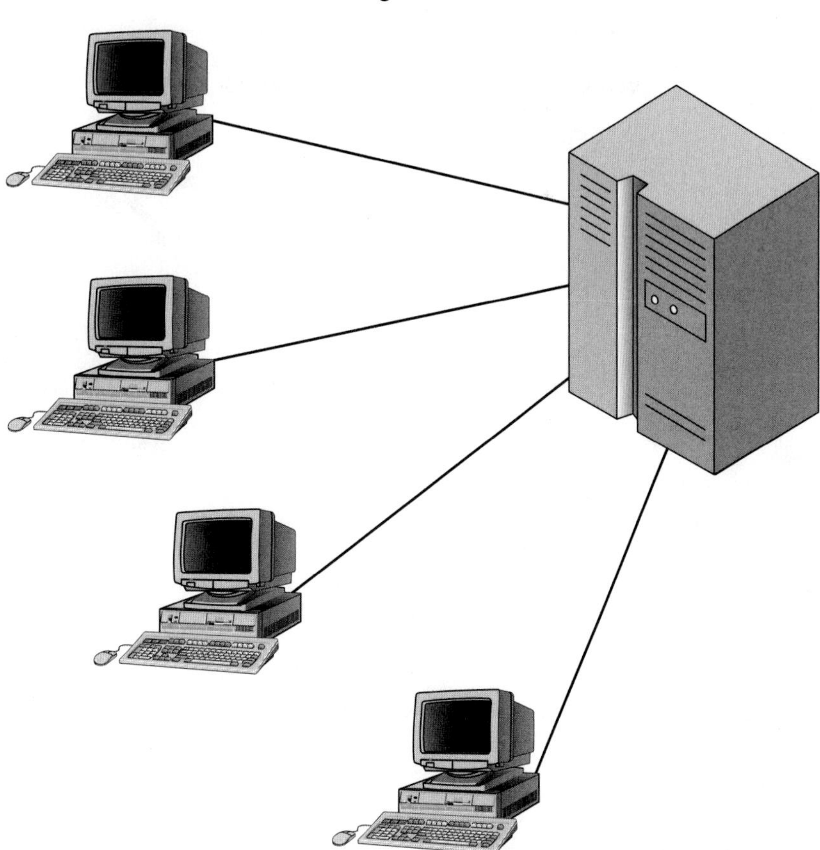

A mainframe computer and terminals.

from a mainframe background saw some fundamental problems. PCs represented isolated pockets of data, making it difficult for users to share information. They also saw them as a potential security risk because anyone who had physical access to a computer has access to its data.

The first PC networks grew out of a desire to resolve these problems. They provided for shared storage and, in most cases, centralized storage, enabling information sharing. Most also had centralized security to limit access to authorized personnel only.

Another driving factor in the creation of networks was that, before PC networks, any requests for changes, reporting requirements, or anything else to do with data went through the IT data center. Often, these data centers were slow to react, didn't have the necessary resources, or weren't always interested in making changes to meet end-user requests. PCs and PC networks brought to the desktop and the individual user applications and a much higher level of control over data.

Figure 1-2

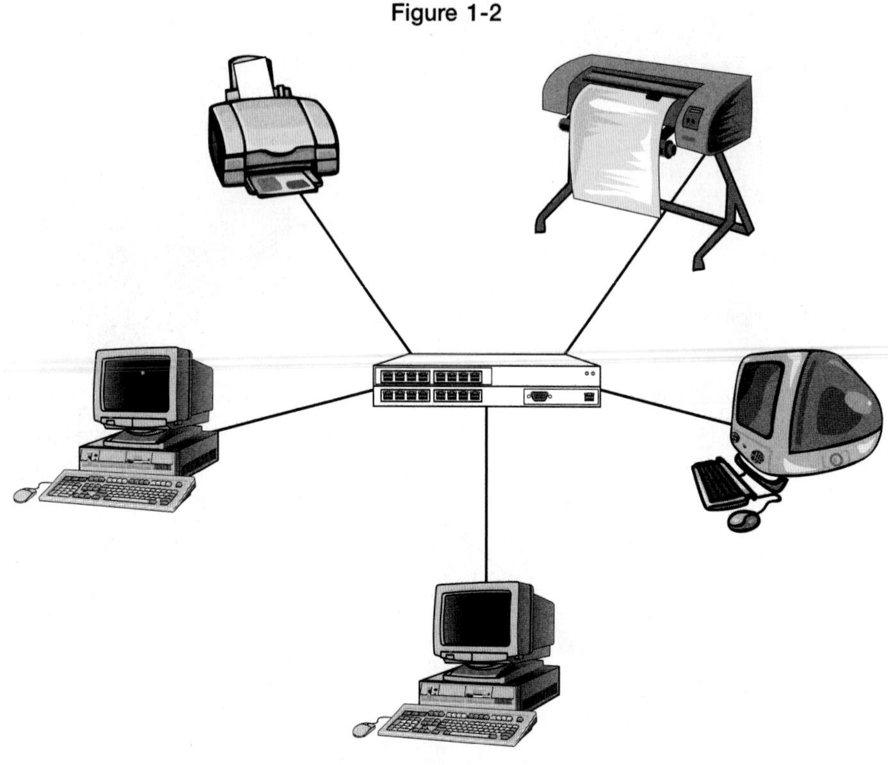

A sample network.

1.1.2 Network Benefits

A network, for our purposes, is a set of PCs and other devices connected so that they can communicate, as shown in Figure 1-2. The biggest benefit of PC networks is that they facilitate resource sharing. Primary among these shared resources are shared data; PC network users can easily share information and work together. In fact, for most business networks, the original justification for creating networks was consolidating and sharing data.

Network resources start with data, but they don't end there. Networks also let users share hardware resources, such as printers, so that each user doesn't need a separate printer. This has been a driving factor for both business and home networks. Another shared resource that has become more important in recent years, and is often the primary reason for home networks, is a high-speed Internet connection.

A network is also a communication and support tool. Most businesses would be lost without email, and in many cases, email is implemented internally as a network resource. Windows operating systems also have utilities to enable remote troubleshooting and even remote control of computers.

Other PC network benefits relate to security. Most networks have built-in **authentication methods**, which are ways that the network can validate who is and who isn't allowed access to the network. Most networks rely on usernames and passwords for authentication, but others use advanced methods, including **biometric devices** that authenticate a user based on physical features such as a fingerprint or retinal scan.

Not only does security control who can access the computer, it also lets a network administrator manage what the user can do once he or she connects to the network. This includes access to shared data and resources and also who can make changes to computer configurations or install new software.

1.1.3 Network Concerns

The greatest benefit of a network is also its greatest potential concern: Sharing information can be dangerous if the wrong person obtains access to that information. Business plans, materials costs, or customer lists getting into the wrong hands can be devastating. Personal information in the wrong hands can lead to identity theft. If you are going to have a network, you have to protect it.

Maintenance and support are also network concerns. Networks require ongoing support and regular maintenance. This includes both network hardware and software. It means keeping the network up-to-date and running and fixing problems as they occur. An important part of a network is the **network administrator**, an IT expert specializing in upkeep and support, such as ensuring that data is backed up on a regular basis because losing a computer that holds everyone's shared files can be much more serious than losing a single computer's data.

That brings us right back around to security. The security tools available depend on the type of network. Network maintenance involves reviewing and maintaining security. **Wired networks**, which are connected by physical cables, have different issues than **wireless networks**, which use radio transmissions to communicate. Different network models and different networking products have different ways of implementing security. It's critical that you know what is available and what is applicable to your situation and put it to use.

1.1.4 The Internet

The Internet plays a key role in many modern networking configurations. A case could be made that the Internet is one of the most important developments in the history of both information systems and communication systems. It has also been a breeding ground for the design and development of new information and communication technologies, with many PC network innovations tracing their roots directly to the Internet.

The Internet was started by the U.S. Department of Defense in 1969 as a network of four computers called ARPANET. By 1987, the U.S. Internet, joined to its Canadian equivalent, supported approximately 11,000 servers. Efforts were made by the United States in 1988 and Canada in 1989 to implement a high-speed **infrastructure** to address performance problems, and the combined U.S. and Canadian Internet grew to nearly 200,000 servers by the end of 1989.

By the early 1990s, most of the individual country networks were linked together in one worldwide network of networks. Each of these individual country networks was distinct, with its own name, access rules, and fee structures, but all the networks used the same standards as the U.S. Internet. Gradually, distinctions among the networks in each of the countries began to disappear, and the U.S. name, the **Internet**, began to be used to mean the entire worldwide

FOR EXAMPLE

The Need for Data Sharing

Depending on how long you've been around computers, you might see networks as simply a fact of life. It may be hard to understand the change resulting from the growth of PC networks if you've never worked in a non-networked environment.

Step back a few years to when networks were less common and consider this scenario: Your supervisor wants you to put together an end-of-quarter report. Different people in your department have worked on the different components, including text documents, charts, and graphs. All you have to do is put together the pieces, but this means physically going to each person and copying the required content to disk. Then you need to carry the disks back to your desk, copy the data to your computer, and put together the report. What if someone is out on vacation? Hopefully you can get access to that person's computer and figure out where the data are stored. This manual file sharing system was sometimes referred to as "sneaker-net."

How have networks changed this process? All the files can be stored in one central location, probably in a folder set up for that purpose. You never have to leave your desk; you can just connect to the network and access the files you need. Of course, you still have the put the report together, but at least you're not left dealing with a stack of disks.

One final problem with the sneaker-net was that after you were finished, the disks often ended up in a case in your desk drawer, if not just tossed loose on your desk. That meant that someone could easily walk by your desk, scoop up the disks, and walk out with a pocket full of confidential company information.

network of networks connected to the U.S. Internet. By the end of 1992, there were more than 1 million servers on the Internet.

Originally, commercial traffic was forbidden on the Internet. In the early 1990s, commercial networks began, and new commercial online services began offering access to anyone willing to pay. Connection into the worldwide Internet became an important marketing issue. Commercial growth quickly overshadowed the traditional government, university, and research use of the Internet. In 1994, with more than 4 million servers on the Internet (most of which were commercial), the U.S. and Canadian governments stopped funding their few remaining circuits and turned them over to commercial firms. Most other national governments soon followed. No one knows exactly how large the Internet has become, but estimates suggest that more than 500 million computers and 1 billion people are now on the Internet.

SELF-CHECK

1. Describe the original technology on which PC networks are based.
2. List some benefits and drawbacks of PC networks.

1.2 Understanding Network Basics

Networks are used to make work and communication more efficient. A network connects computers and can also connect other devices, such as shared printers, removable media drives, and scanners. In order to understand networks and how they work, you need to start with the basics.

1.2.1 Understanding Networks

As discussed already in this chapter, networks enable people to share resources. Printers, hard disks, and applications can be shared, greatly reducing the costs of providing these resources to each person who uses the network. Networks are built around this idea, connecting shared resources and their consumers. Several terms are used to describe these network devices, including *senders* and *receivers* and *servers* and *clients*. The sender, or source, is a computer that sends information to another computer, also commonly referred to as a network server. The receiver is the computer that the information is sent to, also known as the destination computer or client. A device capable of communicating on the network is also referred to generically as a **node**, which is a term used to describe any uniquely identifiable device.

1.2.2 Understanding Network Components

There are three basic hardware components in a typical network like the one shown in Figure 1-3: one or more servers or host computers (including microcomputers and mainframes), clients (PCs), and a **circuit**, or cable plant, which is the path over which the devices communicate. The term cable plant is becoming less descriptive of the network **transmission media** (i.e., the media carrying the network signal), however, as wireless networks become increasingly popular. In addition, servers and clients also need special-purpose network software that enables them to communicate.

The server stores data and software that can be accessed by the clients. Several servers can work together over the network with client computers to support the business application. The client is the interface, providing input to and output from

Figure 1-3

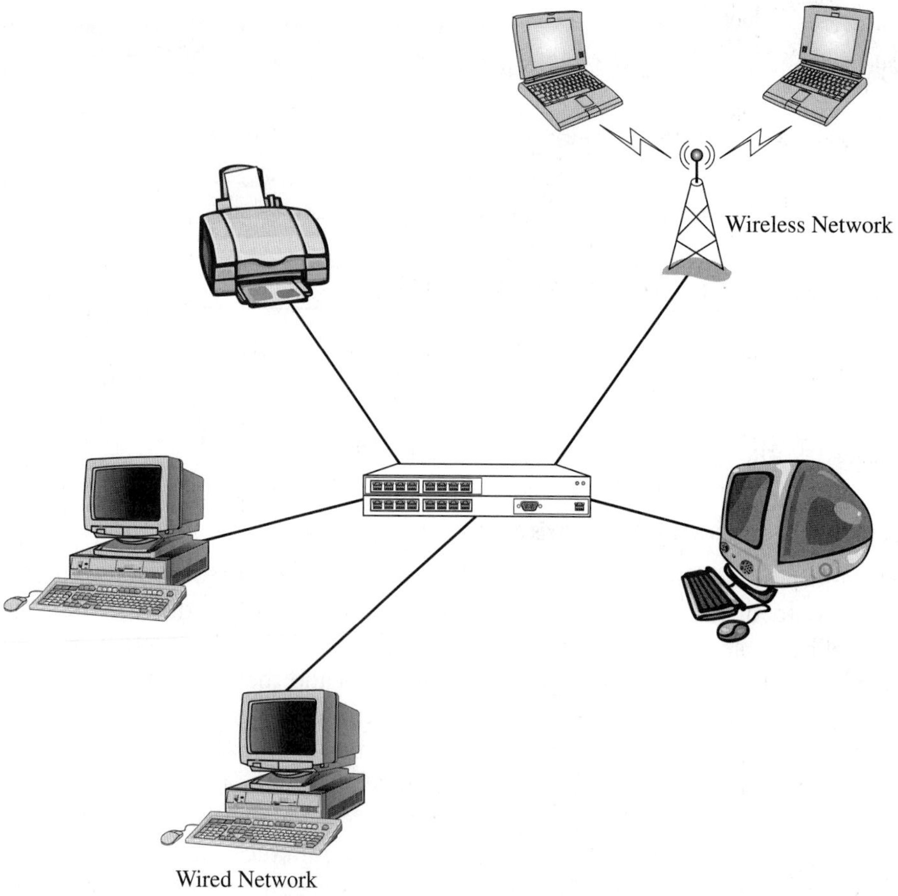

A typical network.

the server, at the user's end of a communication circuit. It provides users with access to the network, the data and software on the server, and other shared resources.

Strictly speaking, a network does not need a computer designated specifically as a server. Most modern client computers are designed to support the dual roles of both client and server, sharing resources to the network and, at the same time, accessing resources from the network.

The circuit (i.e., the cable plant or transmission media) is the pathway through which the messages travel. Traditional wired networks typically use copper wire, although **fiber-optic cable** and wireless transmission are common. *Fiber-optic cable* uses a light (laser) signal transmitted over transparent glass or plastic fibers. In addition, devices in the circuit such as hubs, switches, routers, bridges, and gateways perform special functions.

1.2.3 Understanding Network Device Roles

Figure 1-4 shows a small network that has four client PCs and three specialized server PCs connected by a hub and cables that make up the circuit. In this network, messages move through the hub, to and from the computers. All computers share the same circuit and take turns sending messages.

Each computer, client, or server has a **network adapter**, or **network interface card (NIC)**, which is the hardware that enables a computer to connect to a network. In the case of a wireless network, the network adapter sends and receives radio-frequency messages, not unlike a walkie-talkie or cell phone. The network adapter also determines the low-level protocol used by the computer to communicate on the network. The **protocol** defines things like signal strength and format. Network adapters running one protocol cannot communicate with network adapters running different protocols. There are also high-level protocols, implemented and managed through software, that control functions such as how computers recognize each other and how messages are formatted. Protocols are discussed further in Section 1.3.

A **hub** is a connection device. In many networks, hubs are used as central points where the cables leading out to network PCs come together. A hub is simply a connection point that does not provide any sophisticated control. In current networks, you are more likely to see a switch than a hub. From the outside, the two devices look much the same, but a **switch** is a more sophisticated communication device that helps control and manage the data passing between the PCs.

Figure 1-4 also shows a **router**, which is a special device that connects two or more networks. A router enables computers on one network to communicate with computers on other networks; at the same time, it provides a level of isolation between the networks. Routers are a key part of the Internet, which is, at its core, a massive set of interconnected networks.

A **bridge** is another device used to connect two or more physical networks. Bridges do not provide the same level of isolation as routers but can be used in

Figure 1-4

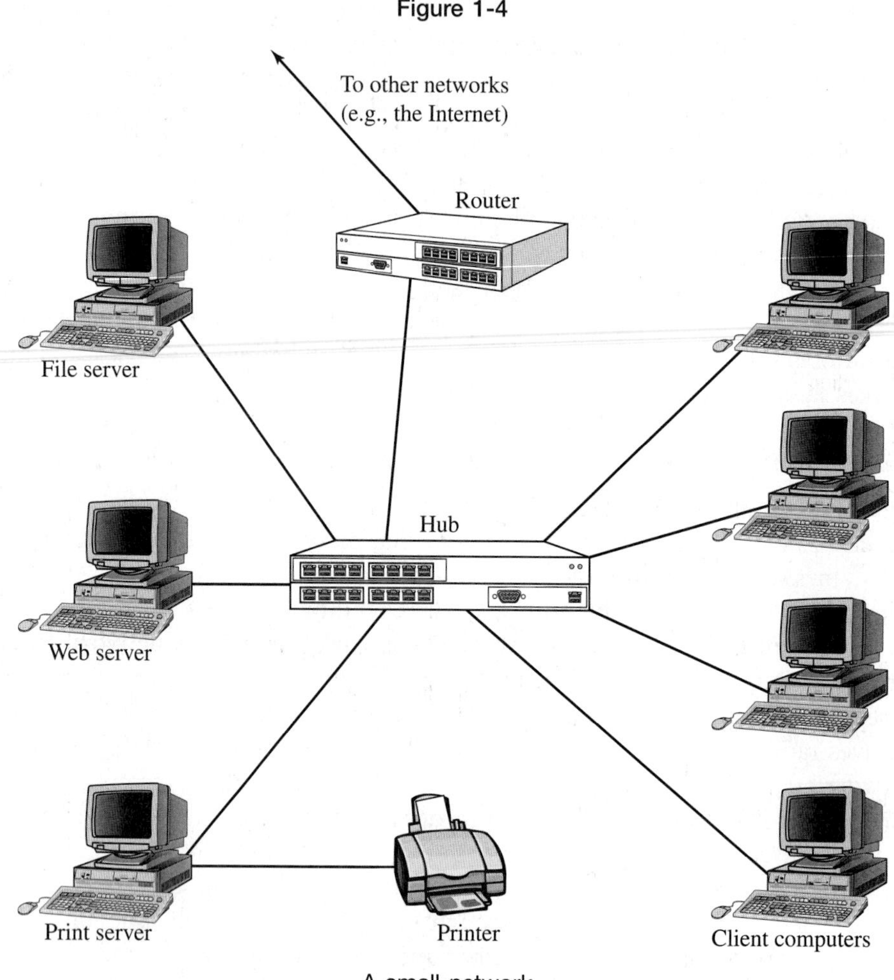

A small network.

some situations where routers cannot be used. Another device, called a **brouter**, combines the functionality of a bridge and a router in the same device.

A **gateway** is used to connect dissimilar networks and devices. For example, a gateway can be used to connect PCs on a **local area network (LAN)** to a mainframe computer.

1.2.4 Understanding Network Models and Software

There are two basic network models: the client/server and peer-to-peer models. Physically, there is little to differentiate the two. From the information you have so far, the network in Figure 1-4 could follow either model.

The **client/server network** model is the model that most closely matches the mainframe network model. One or more computers are designated as servers, providing resources to the network. The rest of the computers are clients, consuming those resources. The identifying feature of a client/server network is centralized control over network security. Clients or, more accurately, the user working at the client, must be authenticated and allowed access to the network. You can also control the resources to which the user has access, as well as the level of access. For example, some users might be able to read from or write to a server, while other users may be able to read data only.

An enhancement that grew out of the traditional client/server network is the directory services–based network. In a **directory services network**, everything on the network, including users, computers, and shared resources, is maintained in a centralized directory. These networks are designed to make it easier to manage today's rapidly growing networks, which can include hundreds or even thousands of clients, servers, and network users. Copies of the directory are usually maintained on multiple servers to provide redundancy in case of failure and to optimize network performance.

In a **peer-to-peer network**, you still have shared resources, but you don't have centralized control over access to the network or its resources. Also, peer-to-peer networks are, by design, small. Microsoft recommends that peer-to-peer networks (referred to as **workgroups** in Microsoft documentation) be limited to no more than 12 nodes. In a peer-to-peer network, the network client computers act as both clients and servers and are sometimes referred to as **peer servers**. Individual users control what is made available to the network and the level of access allowed. A possible point of confusion is that computers can be running a server operating system, such as Windows 2000 Server, but the network can still be configured as a peer-to-peer network, with the server operating system implemented in a peer server role.

1.2.5 Understanding Servers and Clients

The basic difference between clients (which include peer servers) and servers is the software they run. Clients, as you might guess, run a **client operating system**. It enables them to access the network and, in most current versions, to act as a peer server. Common client operating systems include Microsoft Windows 2000 Professional, Windows XP, and Windows Vista.

Servers run what is called either a **server operating system** or **network operating system**. Either one enables the computer to act as a server, including the software necessary for central security management. A server operating system typically includes a client interface and can be used as a network client, if necessary. Familiar examples are Windows Server systems, such as Windows 2000 Server and Windows Server 2003, as well as most Linux versions. Some older network operating systems enabled a computer to operate in the role of server only. The only interface provided was one for server configuration and network management. The best-known example of this type of server operating system is Novell's NetWare.

Take another look at Figure 1-4, and you can see that the network has three servers. The **file server** stores data and software that can be used by computers on the network. The **print server**, which is connected to a printer, manages all printing requests from the clients on the network. The **web server** stores documents and graphics that can be accessed from any **web browser**, the software needed to display information stored as webpages, such as Netscape Navigator or Microsoft Internet Explorer. However, there is nothing to indicate whether the servers are acting as servers only or if they are peer servers and also acting as clients. You don't have enough information to tell you whether this is a client/server, directory services, or peer-to-peer network.

It's important to understand that peer servers are not limited to peer-to-peer networks. You can deploy peer servers on client/server and directory services–based networks to provide additional resources. For example, you might configure client computers with attached printers as peer servers acting as print servers.

FOR EXAMPLE

The Growing Role of Networks

It's now generally assumed that a new computer is destined for a network. For instance, a network adapter is now considered standard computer hardware and, in most cases, is integrated into the computer. In addition, all current PC operating systems have client software, and usually have server software components, built in as a critical part of the operating system.

This is taken a step further in portable (laptop and notebook) computers. Not only does a laptop have a built-in wired network adapter, nearly all new laptops also come with a wireless network adapter, giving you the option of connecting to either type of network. Most also include a telephone **modem**, which is the device that lets a computer communicate over standard dial-up telephone lines.

Another key part of this increasingly connected environment is the Internet. The desire to connect to the Internet, which is itself a massive (and primarily PC-based) network, has been a major factor in home PC sales. If you have any doubt of the Internet's influence, think about this: When was the last time you saw an advertisement for a business or service that didn't include the address of its website?

SELF-CHECK

1. Compare the roles of network clients and network servers.
2. For what purpose is a router used in a network?
3. Compare the client/server, directory services, and peer-to-peer models.

1.3 Understanding Data Communications

Data communications is the movement of computer information from one point to another by means of electrical, optical, or radio-frequency transmission systems. Data communications networks facilitate more efficient use of computers and improve the day-to-day control of a business by providing faster information flow. They also provide message transfer services to allow computer users to talk to one another via email, chat, and video streaming. The broader term **telecommunications** includes the transmission of voice and video (images and graphics) as well as data and usually implies longer distances. The line between the two has tended to blur in recent years, with telecommunications often a key part of data communications.

1.3.1 Low-Level Protocols

Low-level protocols control the physical process of data communication. The first network protocols were **Token Ring**, **ARCNET**, and **Ethernet**. Each protocol used a different method for computers to access the network, and computers using one protocol could not (and still cannot) communicate directly with computers using a different protocol. The protocols also have an addressing method that ensures that each computer on the network is uniquely identifiable. This address is coded into the network adapter.

Ethernet has always been the most significant of the three protocols. Robert Metcalf, then a graduate student at Harvard University, first drew the concept for Ethernet on a piece of paper as part of his Ph.D. thesis. Today, Ethernet is the most widely used access method for computer networks.

1.3.2 High-Level Protocols

High-level protocols operate at the software level and control things such as message formatting, which is how messages are broken up into smaller pieces, known as packets, for transmission and then reassembled at the other end. These protocols control **addressing**, how computers are able to identify and recognize

Table 1-1: High-Level Protocols

Protocol	*Description*
AppleTalk	An Apple proprietary protocol also supported by some Windows versions.
IPX/SPX	A Novell proprietary protocol originally required on NetWare networks.
NetBEUI	A protocol originally used by MS-DOS and Windows network software.
TCP/IP	A protocol suite developed for use on the Internet and currently used on the Internet and PC networks, including Windows, Linux, and NetWare networks.

each other on a network. They also control the **handshaking** process used by computers for establishing connections with each other. Establishing a **connection** refers to the process of having two computers recognize each other and open a communication channel between them, which is similar to starting a conversation by placing a telephone call to another person.

Over the years, a number of high-level protocols have been developed (see Table 1-1), and this has led to some confusion and problems in getting different computers to communicate with each other. Apple used its own proprietary protocol, known as **AppleTalk**, on its networks. For several years, Novell exclusively used a protocol known as **IPX/SPX** on its networks, with the PC client software providing IPX/SPX support. Microsoft originally used a limited protocol known as **NetBEUI** but early on realized that to grow, Windows needed broader-based communication support; Microsoft therefore began including its own AppleTalk- and IPX/SPX-compatible protocols as part of its operating systems.

The Internet was based from the beginning on **Transmission Control Protocol/Internet Protocol (TCP/IP)**, which is actually a suite of different protocols, each supporting different communication roles. In the past several years, however, TCP/IP has become the de facto standard for all computer networking applications, including PC networks. Current versions of Microsoft Windows and Novell NetWare both default to installing TCP/IP as the only protocol in use on computers running their operating systems. Linux, on the other hand, has used TCP/IP since its inception.

A word of warning when discussing TCP/IP networks: In TCP/IP terms, a router is called a *gateway*. Because of this, when discussing network devices, you need to understand the network protocol used on the network and the context in which the term is used.

FOR EXAMPLE

How Protocols Work Together

Like so many other computer-related terms, the exact definition of the term *protocol* depends on its context. Are you taking about a low-level protocol or a high-level protocol? What's the difference, and why does it matter? As you have learned, low-level protocols handle the physical communication process. You can think, then, of high-level protocols handling the logical communication process.

To get a general idea of how the different types of protocols work, let's look at a relatively simple example. You want to retrieve a file from a file server. To do this, you have to locate the file server on the network, establish a connection with the file server, request the file, accept it from the server, and then close the connection when finished.

The whole process is handled through a series of standard messages, defined by the protocol (i.e., high-level protocol) used to communicate. Each of these messages is routed through the computer to the network adapter, where it is converted into an electronic signal, as shown in Figure 1-5. The computer at the other end receives the electronic signal and converts it back into data that can be recognized and used by the computer. Actually, every computer sees the data, but all the computers except the destination computer (identified through a unique address) ignore the data.

Figure 1-5

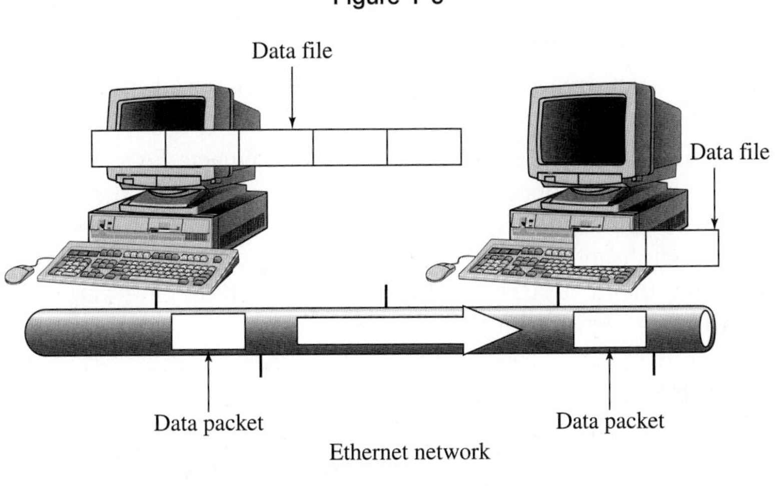

Network communication.

(continued)

Part of the problem is that the blocks of data, known as **packets**, that can be sent between the computers are subject to a specific size limit, defined by the low-level protocol used. There is also a limit set by the high-level protocol, which is no larger than the low-level protocol's physical limit. To get around this, the high-level protocol breaks the data (the file, in this case) into pieces small enough for transmission and formats them with all the control information needed before passing them to the network adapter. It also numbers the packets so that the receiving system knows the proper order and can reassemble them back into the original file.

SELF-CHECK

1. Define data communications.
2. Compare the roles of low-level and high-level protocols.

1.4 Comparing Types of Networks

There are three main categories of networks:

- A **local area network (LAN)** is a relatively small network of computers, printers, and other devices in a single building or floor.
- A **metropolitan area network (MAN)** is a high-speed internetwork of LANs across a metropolitan area.
- A **wide area network (WAN)** traditionally connects LANs using the public switched telephone network or, more commonly, the Internet.

There are significant differences between LANs, MANs, and WANs. In addition to covering different sizes of geographic areas, they have varying installation and support costs associated with them.

Devices used in LANs can be relatively inexpensive and easy to maintain. Larger networks require more sophisticated networking equipment and additional support. The investment in a MAN or WAN is not only based on installation and equipment costs but also on the costs of long-term support and on-site administration. Most larger networks require at least one full-time on-site administrator plus additional support staff. In many cases, a single person handles all LAN-related issues. Often, in very small offices, one person may take on the responsibilities of network support in addition to his or her regular work. Other small- to medium-size offices hire consultants to provide technical support they cannot provide themselves.

In addition to these network types, **backbone networks** work in something of a supporting role. These networks provide a high-bandwidth path for communicating between networks. There are also network technologies implemented as part of these networks and based on technologies developed initially for the Internet. In fact, the Internet has led to the demise of many traditional backbone networks. Today, because of the ease of access to the Internet and low costs for high-bandwidth Internet access, companies can connect to remote or distant locations without spending lots of money. A person working on a small local network with Internet access can share documents and files with people all over the planet and access servers at distant locations. The global reach of the Internet allows this kind of connectivity without the high cost of installation and support associated with private WANs. Security is provided through use of a **virtual private network (VPN)**, effectively a network within a network that provides a private communication path over the public Internet.

1.4.1 Local Area Networks (LANs)

LANs play an important part in the everyday functioning of schools, businesses, and government. LANs save people time, lower equipment costs by centralizing printers and other resources, and allow sensitive information to remain in a secure location. Recently, LANs have been used as tools to improve collaboration between employees and for job training using audio and video.

A LAN connects computers and other network devices so that the devices can communicate with each other to share resources. Devices on a wired LAN are connected using inexpensive cable. Due to limitations in distance, performance, and manageability, a LAN is usually confined to a single office or floor of a building. In Figure 1-6, for example, several computers are connected via a cable to a hub. The lines from the computers to the hub are the cables that allow data transmissions to pass from one computer to the others.

Many new LANs are being installed using wireless technologies. Wireless LANs allow users to connect to network resources without the need for cabling or wiring. Computers can be configured to communicate directly with each other so that no other connectivity equipment is required. Wireless networks commonly use an **access point**, which acts as a central access point (working similarly to a hub or switch) and can also connect a wireless network to a wired network. (Figure 1-3 shows an example of this.)

Figure 1-6

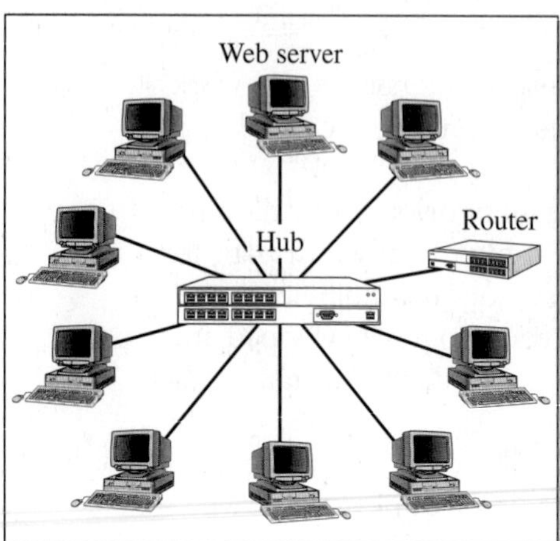

Local area network (LAN) at the Records Building— one node of the McClellan Air Force Base backbone network.

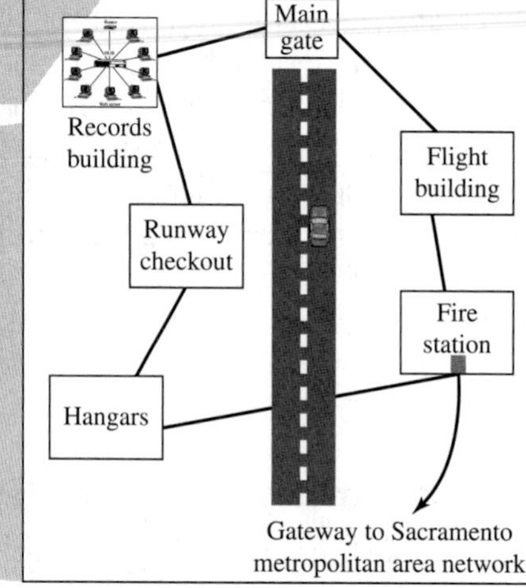

Backbone network at the McClellan Air Force Base—one node of the Sacramento metropolitan area network (MAN).

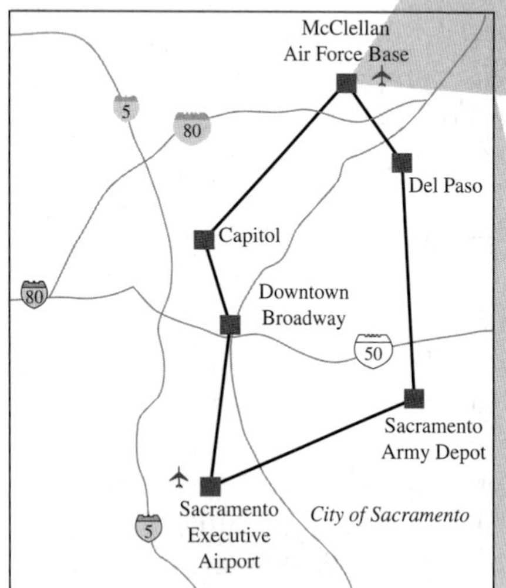

Metropolitan area network (MAN) in Sacramento—one node of the wide area network (WAN).

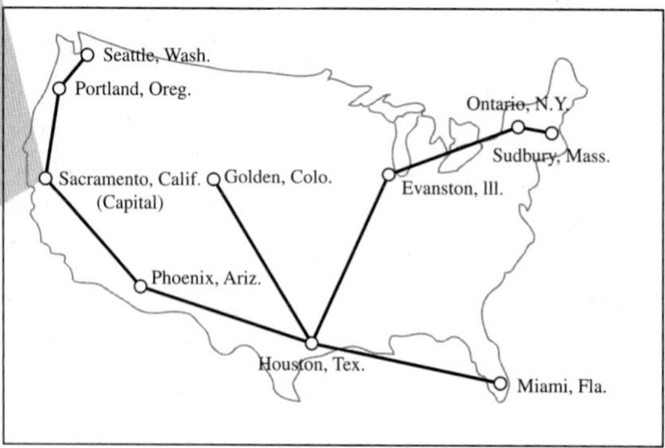

Wide area network (WAN) showing Sacramento connected to nine other cities throughout the U.S.

Comparing network types.

A company network might be configured as one or more LANs, depending on the size of the company and the building. A company that is located in a multistory building with hundreds of employees could have a LAN on each floor. Between each floor, a bridge or a router could be used to connect the LANs.

LANs have the following characteristics:

- ▲ They are used within small areas (such as in an office building).
- ▲ They offer high-speed communication—typically, 100Mbps or faster.
- ▲ They provide access for many devices.
- ▲ They use LAN-specific equipment such as hubs and NICs.

Many people are now installing home area networks (HANs), which are effectively identical to LANs. These networks allow home users to connect a variety of electronic devices, such as computers, peripherals, telephones, video games, "smart" appliances (i.e., computerized devices such as high-end cell phones), and home security systems. They also let all the computers share a single Internet connection.

1.4.2 Metropolitan Area Networks (MANs)

A MAN is made up of LANs that are interconnected across a city or metropolitan area, typically spanning up to 75 miles, like the one shown in Figure 1-6. Using a MAN is a popular way of allowing local governments to share valuable resources, communicate with one another, and provide a large-scale private phone service. MANs are also appealing to fairly large regional businesses that want to connect their offices for the same reasons. Although MANs are very expensive to implement, they offer a high-speed alternative to the slower connections often available in WANs because of the MAN's higher-performance cable plant and equipment.

Traditional MANs connect through a *backbone network,* a large, central network. A backbone network can be used to connect LANs to form MANs, and it can also connect other backbone networks, MANs, and even WANs. Backbone networks typically span up to several miles and provide high-speed communication, commonly up to 100Mbps to 1,000Mbps. The second diagram in Figure 1-6 shows a backbone network near Sacramento, California, that connects the LANs located in several buildings at McClellan Air Force Base.

Figure 1-7 takes a closer look at MAN configuration. The LANs are standard LANs, and a router is used to connect to the MANs, typically with just one connection to each site. Creating a new MAN connection requires purchasing or leasing existing cable from a telecommunications company (the least-expensive option)

Figure 1-7

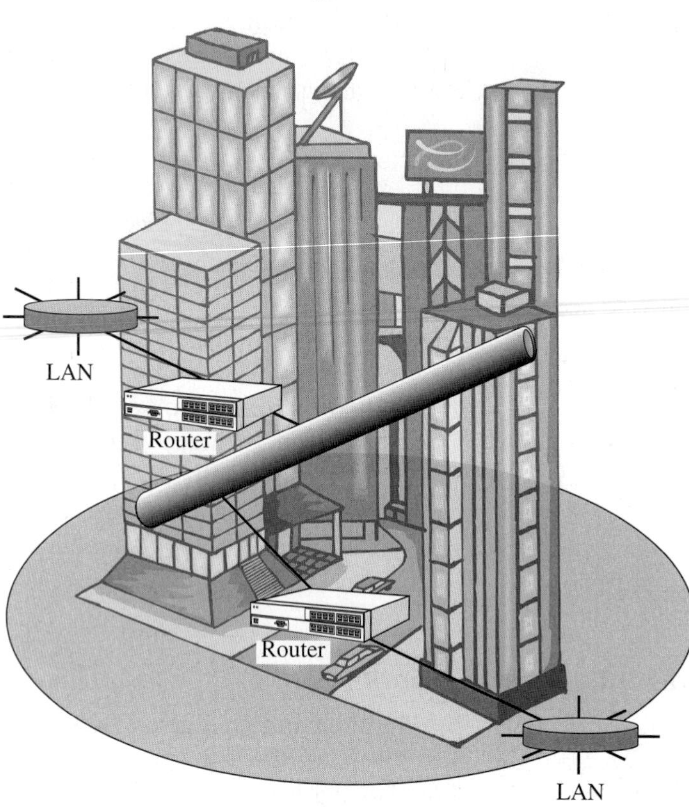

MAN connections.

or having new cables installed, which can cost hundreds of thousands of dollars. MANs can also use shared space on fiber-optic lines.

MANs have the following characteristics:

- ▲ Sites are dispersed across a city and perhaps the surrounding area as well.
- ▲ With the advent of MANs, historically slow connections (56Kbps–1.5Mbps) have given way to communication at hundreds of megabits per second and even gigabit speeds.
- ▲ They provide single points of connection between each LAN.
- ▲ They use devices such as routers, telephone switches, and microwave antennas as parts of their communication infrastructure.

In recent years, there has been a tendency toward linking LANs through high-bandwidth Internet connections instead of building or buying MANs.

FOR EXAMPLE

Choosing Your MAN Connection

There was a time when your only option for configuring a MAN was working with the regional carrier (i.e., the local telephone company) to lease the lines and connection equipment. That meant you only had one vendor available—a vendor who had few restrictions on the rates it charged for hooking up your LANs.

Things have changed in recent years. Most metropolitan areas have multiple communication carriers, including public and private telephone companies, data communication companies, and cable providers. In most cases, you are no longer required to purchase or lease your connection equipment from your carrier. The benefit of this competition is reduced costs for communication lines and connection equipment. The drawback is that you no longer have a single vendor to go to when you have problems. This means that the communication carrier can blame the connection equipment, the equipment vendor can blame the carrier, and they both can blame you (or your consultant) for not configuring the setup correctly.

All these factors have helped drive the Internet as a MAN connection option. **Internet service providers (ISPs)** are happy to lease the bandwidth, and the connection is made using stable, established, and well-understood technologies. When problems arise, most ISPs are willing to provide diagnostic and troubleshooting assistance, though sometimes at an added cost.

Another relatively common option is leasing space on communications satellites, such as those used for satellite TV transmissions, for MAN connectivity. The biggest problem with this solution is that connections can be sensitive to weather conditions, with the connection becoming degraded or even lost during heavy rains.

1.4.3 Wide Area Networks (WANs)

A WAN interconnects two or more LANs or MANs. Traditionally, a LAN becomes a WAN when it connects across the public telephone network, often using lines leased from local telephone companies. These connections often involve lines known as **long-haul transmission lines** because they are designed to carry traffic over long distances and require coordinating services from multiple **regional carriers** (i.e., regional telephone companies). They can also be connected through fiber-optic cabling or, less frequently, wireless technologies. WANs typically run over telephone cables because they cover a wide geographic area—they may span cities, states, or even countries, as shown in Figure 1-6.

Interconnecting LANs and MANs over great distances, often over both land and water, requires a lot of coordination and sophisticated equipment. In most cases, local telephone companies provide the physical cable connection. When connections are required across the globe, the network usually involves telecommunications companies providing satellite connectivity.

The majority of WANs communicate at speeds between 56Kbps and 1.5Mbps, although speeds up to 9.953Gbps are available. At one time, WANs were considered low-speed connections, but this is rapidly changing as the availability of high-bandwidth connections increases and the associated costs drop.

WANs have the following characteristics:

- They can cover a very large geographic area—even span the world.
- They usually communicate at slow speeds (compared to LANs).
- Access to the WAN is limited; a LAN usually has only one WAN link that is shared by all devices.
- They use devices such as routers, modems, and **WAN switches**, connectivity devices specific to LANs and used to connect to long-haul transmission media.

By connecting many LANs using WANs, organizations enable their users to share information. The Internet was created using WAN links, and they continue to make up the Internet today. Ironically, the Internet has been replacing more traditional connection methods, especially in new WAN implementations.

1.4.4 Internet Technologies

Technologies developed for the Internet have been a major evolutionary factor in how LANs are implemented and used. Two common terms are **intranets** and **extranets**.

An *intranet* is a LAN that uses the same technologies as the Internet, such as using web servers like the one shown in Figure 1-8, to facilitate internal communications, but is open to only those inside the organization. Sometimes an intranet includes a mix of private and public access. For example, although some pages on a web server may be open to the public and accessible by anyone on the Internet, some pages may be on an intranet and therefore hidden from those

Figure 1-8

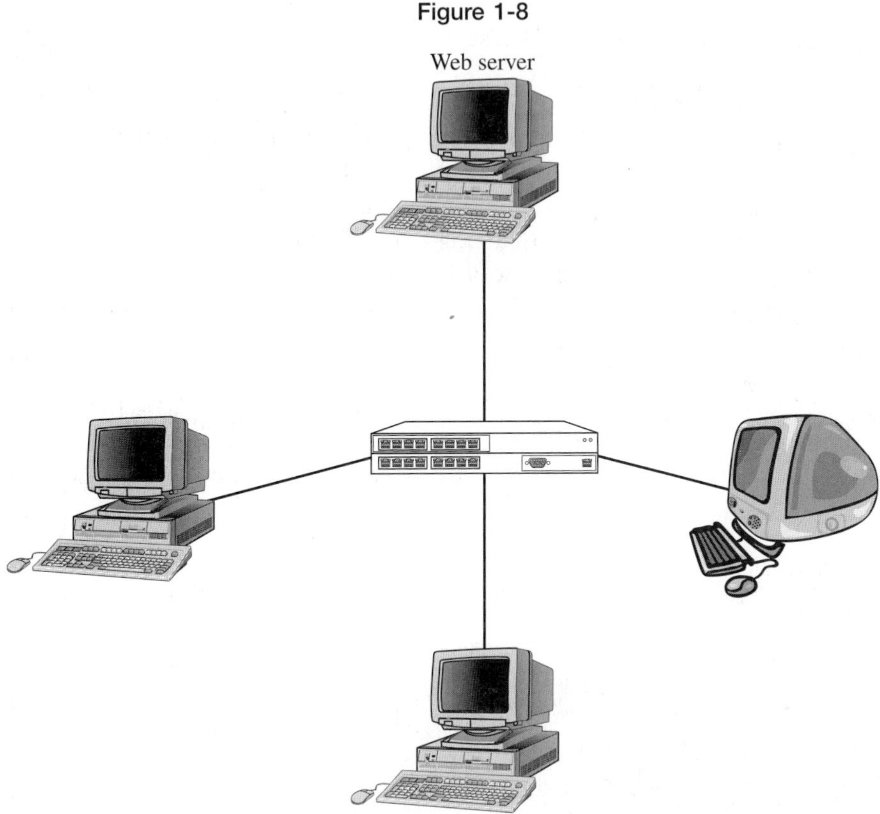

An intranet with a web server.

who connect to the web server from the Internet at large. Sometimes an intranet uses a completely separate web server hidden from the Internet. The intranet for the Information Systems Department at Indiana University, for example, provides information on faculty expense budgets, class scheduling for future semesters, and discussion forums.

An *extranet* is similar to an intranet in that it uses the same technologies as the Internet; however, it is provided to invited users outside the organization who access the network from the Internet. It can provide access to information services, inventories, and other internal organizational databases that are provided only to customers, suppliers, and those who have paid for access. Typically, users are given passwords to gain access, but more sophisticated technologies, such as smart cards or special software may also be required. Many universities provide extranets for web-based courses so that only those students enrolled in a course can access course materials and discussions.

FOR EXAMPLE

Growing Your Network

The basic network types are not the only network configuration options. The truth is that network configurations are very flexible, and a significant number of networks use some variation on or combination of network types. For example, a LAN is not necessarily a single, stand-alone network. LANs are usually described and drawn that way for simplicity's sake, but the key to describing a network as a LAN is the fact that it occupies a small geographic area.

Consider a situation in which a company occupies both floors in the building shown in Figure 1-9. The most common configuration is to have each floor as a semiautonomous network. A vertical backbone is used to connect the networks. A router on each floor is used to connect that floor's

Figure 1-9

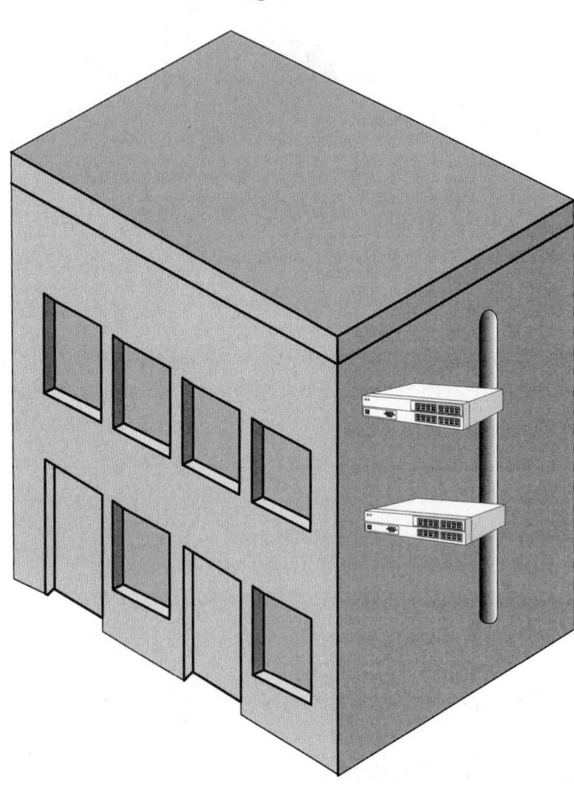

A vertical backbone.

network to the backbone. The network configuration as a whole would be referred to as a routed LAN. It is definitely a LAN, given the very small geographic region involved, but it is routed to provide a level of isolation between the floors while still enabling them to communicate.

Unlike the backbone in a MAN, a vertical backbone is not purchased or leased from a telecommunications company. Instead, it is installed by the company as part of its corporate network infrastructure. In many cases, the backbone is simply a fiber-optic cable run between the floors. The routers are designed so that they can connect both to the fiber-optic line and the wired network. By some definitions, the connection device would be called a brouter, rather than a router, but the term brouter is not commonly used in modern network descriptions. There are even some configurations in which the connection might be made with a bridge instead of a router.

SELF-CHECK

1. Compare the characteristics of LANs, MANs, and WANs.
2. How are intranets and extranets similar to one another? How are they different?

1.5 The Future of Networking

Data communications and computer processing go hand in hand, but many feel that we have moved from the computer era to the communications era. Three major interrelated trends are driving the future of communications and networking: pervasive networking; the integration of voice, video, and data; and new information services.

1.5.1 Pervasive Networking

Pervasive networking means that communication networks will one day be everywhere; virtually any device will be able to communicate with any other device in the world. This is true in many ways today. To see this, you don't need to look any further than today's cell phones. Not only can you place calls, you can browse the web, check email, and even check in with your PC. Media players, first designed as a replacement for portable tape or CD players, now support a full range of multimedia services. The boundary between a television tuner and computer is disappearing. Common household devices are being designed so that they can be networked with and controlled by a central computer, including heating and cooling systems, windows, light switches, water heaters, and even appliances such as dishwashers.

Helping to drive this change is the rate of increase in data transmissions, or the available bandwidth. For example, in 1980, the capacity of a traditional telephone-based dial-up communication was about 300 bits per second (bps). By the 1990s, data were routinely transmitted at 9,600bps, and by 2000, dial-up modems could transmit at 56Kbps and digital subscriber line (DSL) at 1.5Mbps over that same telephone line. Rates in multiple gigabit-per-second (Gbps) ranges are available on the most recent DSL lines and through cable television carriers. Rates of 10Gbps wireless transmission are also promised in the near future. As rates have gone up, the relative costs have gone down. A major benefactor has been the Internet, with ever-increasing Internet circuit bandwidths and subscriber connection speeds. In many regions, telephone and cable television companies are the primary *Internet service providers (ISPs),* the companies providing the doorway to the Internet.

Between 1980 and 2000, LAN and backbone technologies increased capacity from about 128Kbps to 10Mbps or 100Mbps. It's expected that soon backbones will routinely be running at 10Gbps. The changes in WANs have been even more dramatic, from a typical rate of 56Kbps in 1980 to 622Mbps over a high-speed circuit in 2000, with most experts now predicting a high-speed WAN or Internet circuit able to carry 25Tbps (25 terabits, or 25 trillion bits per second), or maybe even higher, in a few years.

The term *broadband communication* has been used to refer to the new high-speed communication circuits. Broadband is a technical term that refers to a specific type of data transmission that is used by one of these circuits, specifically DSL circuits, but its true technical meaning has become overwhelmed by its use in the popular press to refer to high-speed circuits in general.

1.5.2 The Integration of Voice, Video, and Data

A second key trend in networking is the integration of voice, video, and data communication, sometimes called **convergence**. In the past, the telecommunications systems used to transmit video signals (such as cable TV), voice signals (primarily telephone calls), and data (including computer data and email) were completely separate. One network was used for data, one for voice, and one for cable TV.

This began changing rapidly in the late 1990s. The integration of voice and data is largely complete in WANs. The carriers, such as AT&T, provide telecommunication services that support data and voice transmission over the same circuits, and hardware manufacturers provide the infrastructure needed the meet the changing definition of data. One of the fastest-growing consumer and business service areas is the cable television industry, with cable service providers offering cable television, Internet access, and telephone service all over the same lines.

The integration of video, voice, and data occurred somewhat more slowly in LANs and local telephone services than in WANs, but this is rapidly changing.

Most companies have successfully integrated voice and data on the same network, though some still lay two separate cable networks into offices: one for voice and one for computer access. Early roadblocks to the integration of video included legal restrictions and the bandwidth requirements.

1.5.3 New Information Services

A third key trend in networking is the provision of new information services on the rapidly expanding networks. The web has changed the nature of computing so that now, anyone with a computer can be an information publisher. You can find information on virtually anything on the web. Never before in the history of the human race has so much knowledge and information been available to ordinary citizens. As individuals and organizations, we face three main challenges:

- ▲ Assessing the accuracy and value of information.
- ▲ Assimilating the information we decide is useful.
- ▲ Using the information effectively.

FOR EXAMPLE

Future Shock?

Not only are networking technologies changing rapidly, the rate of change is increasing. One place you can see this is the integration of voice and video in computer operating systems and in PC networks. It's visible in Microsoft's release in 2005 of Windows XP Media Edition, which integrates multimedia services (including television reception and recording) into its Windows operating system. This means you can watch TV while you work or connect your computer as your television tuners and video recorder. Businesses use streaming video (i.e., video transmissions over the network) as an information tool and for employee training. Equipment for **Voice over IP (VoIP)**, the technical term for Internet-based telephone service, is both inexpensive and readily available from a wide variety of retailers, including chain discount stores. For many companies, their ISP is also their telephone company.

All the major news services now offer video clips along with traditional print stories, and many television networks let you watch recent programs that you might have missed on broadcast TV from their websites. You can purchase both audio and video files, including full-length theatrical movies, from commercial download services. You can even distribute your own audio and video files through **podcasts**, self-contained files that can be played back on a computer or media player.

Today, many companies are beginning to use application service providers (ASPs) rather than develop their own computer systems. An ASP develops a specific system (e.g., an airline reservation system or a payroll system), and a company purchases the service, without ever installing the system on its own computers. It uses the service, the same way you might use a web hosting service to publish your own webpages rather than attempt to purchase and operate your own web server. Some experts are predicting that by 2010, ASPs will have evolved into information utilities—that is, companies that provide a wide range of standardized information services, the same way that electric utilities today provide electricity or telephone utilities provide telephone service. Companies would simply purchase most of their information services (e.g., email, web, accounting, payroll, logistics) from these information utilities rather than attempt to develop their systems and operate their own servers. We are already starting to see some movement in this area with various services, such as file transfer and storage and public email services.

SELF-CHECK

1. What is convergence?
2. What is an information utility?
3. What challenges do organizations face in relation to the information made available by the Internet?

SUMMARY

This chapter introduced networks and some of the underlying technologies and terms. You learned a little about the roots of PC networks and the Internet. You also learned about network benefits and drawbacks, as well as the basic network models. Next, you learned about both low-level and high-level communication protocols. You also compared network models, including their underlying structure and characteristics of each. Finally, the chapter took a quick look at the future of networking.

KEY TERMS

Access point
Addressing
AppleTalk
ARCNET
Authentication method
Backbone network (BN)

Biometric device
Bridge
Brouter
Circuit
Client operating system
Client/server network
Connection
Convergence
Data communications
Directory services network
Dumb terminal
Ethernet
Extranet
Fiber-optic cable
File server
Gateway
Handshaking
High-level protocol
Hub
Infrastructure
Internet
Internet service provider (ISP)
Intranet
IPX/SPX
Local area network (LAN)
Long-haul transmission lines
Low-level protocol
Metropolitan area network (MAN)
Modem
NetBEUI
Network
Network adapter
Network administrator
Network interface card (NIC)
Network operating system
Node
Packet
Peer server
Peer-to-peer network
Personal computer (PC)
Podcast
Print server
Protocol
Regional carrier
Router
Server
Server operating system
Smart terminal
Switch
Telecommunications
Token Ring
Transmission Control Protocol/ Internet Protocol (TCP/IP)
Transmission media
Virtual private network (VPN)
Voice over IP (VoIP)
WAN switch
Web browser
Web server
Wide area network (WAN)
Wired network
Wireless network
Workgroup

ASSESS YOUR UNDERSTANDING

Go to www.wiley.com/college/ciccarelli to evaluate your knowledge of networking fundamentals.
Measure your learning by comparing pre-test and post-test results.

Summary Questions

1. Broadband is a technical term that refers to DSL data communications. True or false?
2. Which of the following refers to a network deployed in the smallest geographic area?
   (a) WAN
   (b) MAN
   (c) Backbone network
   (d) LAN
3. What is the primary shared resource on PC networks?
   (a) data
   (b) printers
   (c) scanners
   (d) none of the above
4. Which of the following is a device used to connect network devices such as computers and printers?
   (a) node
   (b) router
   (c) hub
   (d) gateway
5. Which of the following is a device used to connect two or more LANs?
   (a) node
   (b) router
   (c) hub
   (d) gateway
6. Which network model does not support centralized security?
   (a) client/server
   (b) directory services
   (c) peer-to-peer
7. Microsoft Internet Explorer is an example of a web server. True or false?
8. What is distinctive about fiber-optic cable compared to other transmission media types?

(a) It carries digital data.
(b) It uses radio-frequency communication transmissions.
(c) It contains copper wire.
(d) It uses glass or plastic to carry the data signal.

9. What is the term used to refer to any uniquely identifiable device on a network?
   (a) node
   (b) sender
   (c) receiver
   (d) gateway
10. What is the device that makes a physical connection between a computer and the network cable in a traditional wired network?
   (a) switch
   (b) NIC
   (c) brouter
   (d) access point
11. What is the most commonly used low-level protocol on PC networks?
   (a) ARCNET
   (b) Token Ring
   (c) Ethernet
   (d) NetBEUI
12. Which of the following is defined by a high-level protocol?
   (a) the physical connection to the network
   (b) signal strength
   (c) connection procedures
   (d) cable plant structure
13. Which protocol is the de facto standard for PC networking?
   (a) IPX/SPX
   (b) AppleTalk
   (c) NetBEUI
   (d) TCP/IP
14. What type of network would you use to connect various locations in San Francisco through existing phone company–owned cables?
   (a) HAN
   (b) LAN
   (c) MAN
   (d) WAN

15. An extranet is a network that uses Internet technologies to allow access to invited users from outside the organization. True or false?
16. Which of the following terms refers to the integration of voice, video, and data communications?
    (a) convergence
    (b) pervasive networking
    (c) information utility
    (d) extranet
17. What is an ASP?
    (a) a company that provides public access to the Internet.
    (b) a company that develops specific systems and services
    (c) a company that provides telecommunication infrastructure for purchase or lease
    (d) a company the designs and develops connection devices
18. Which of the following refers to a private communication path over a public network?
    (a) Backbone network
    (b) MAN
    (c) ASP
    (d) VPN
19. Which of the following is a device used to connect a wireless network and a wired network?
    (a) access point
    (b) switch
    (c) gateway
    (d) modem
20. Why would you deploy a peer server on a peer-to-peer network?
    (a) Peer servers provide centralized access authentication.
    (b) Peer servers are dedicated servers optimized for peer-to-peer use.
    (c) Peer servers act in the role of both server and client.
    (d) Peer servers cannot be used on other types of networks.

Applying This Chapter

1. You are working with a team, designing a network for a large organization. The team is gathering information about network requirements and trying to make some initial design specifications. The company has five

offices in St. Louis and additional offices in Dallas, Los Angeles, and Seattle.

(a) What issues will help determine the types of connections needed between the offices?

(b) Describe the general network design and the role of connectivity devices.

(c) Why would a directory services network more likely meet the organization's needs than a peer-to-peer network?

2. You have the job of justifying a network for your office. The office has 20 PCs, about one-third with attached printers, and most with modems. Users connect to the Internet through separate dial-up connections. Users use floppy disks and writable CDs to share data.

(a) What benefits would a network have for your office?

(b) What type of network would you recommend and why?

YOU TRY IT

Network Configuration

You are a consultant currently specializing in small-to-medium businesses. You want to expand your business to include home network design and implementation.

1. What network issues are similar in small businesses and home networks?
2. What additional issues might you need to deal with in a home network?
3. What is the potential impact of pervasive computing developments on home network design?
4. Why might you configure the network as an intranet?

2

NETWORK STANDARDS AND MODELS

Starting Point

Go to www.wiley.com/college/ciccarelli to assess your knowledge of network standards and models.
Determine where you need to concentrate your effort.

What You'll Learn in This Chapter

▲ The role of network standards
▲ The OSI model
▲ The TCP/IP (DoD) model
▲ The Internet model

After Studying This Chapter, You'll Be Able To

▲ Explain why network standards are important and how they are developed
▲ Identify major standards bodies and their general responsibilities
▲ Describe the purpose of the OSI model and why it is important
▲ List and describe each of the layers in the OSI model
▲ Compare and contrast the OSI, TCP/IP (or DoD), and Internet models

INTRODUCTION

This chapter discusses the role of network standards and introduces the major standards bodies. Perhaps the best known of these is the Open Systems Interconnection reference model (the OSI model), which helped change the face of network computing. However, it is not the only network standards model. Two other closely related models are the TCP/IP model, also called the DoD model, and the Internet model.

2.1 Understanding the Need for Standards

Standards are created through various means and for a variety of reasons. Some standards are carefully and clearly defined and documented. Examples of this type of standards include the specifications for how a NIC connects to a network cable plant. Other standards are more a description of accepted practices created after the fact. For example, there is a common look and feel among the user interfaces used by various desktop operating systems, but there is no general standard with guidelines that each vendor is required to follow.

The primary reason for network standards is to ensure that hardware and software produced by different vendors can work together. Thanks to standards, customers are not locked into one vendor. They can buy hardware and software from any vendor whose equipment meets a standard, as in the network shown in Figure 2-1. In this figure, you see a mix of software and hardware working together to form a small network and even connecting the network PCs to the Internet.

NICs from one vendor can communicate with NICs from another vendor. All modems that are built to the same standard are functionally the same. Standards help to promote more competition and hold down prices. You can focus on quality and cost instead of manufacturer when making your purchase decisions.

2.1.1 Understanding the Standards Process

There are two types of standards: formal and de facto. A **formal standard** is one that has been developed by an official industry or government body. For example, there are formal standards for applications (e.g., websites, email), for protocols, and for physical hardware. Formal standards typically take several years to develop. One potential problem is that technological innovations can outpace standards, reducing their usefulness.

De facto standards are standards that emerge in the marketplace and are supported by several vendors but have no official standing. For example, Microsoft Windows is a product of one company and has not been formally recognized by any standards organization, yet it is a de facto standard. In the

Figure 2-1

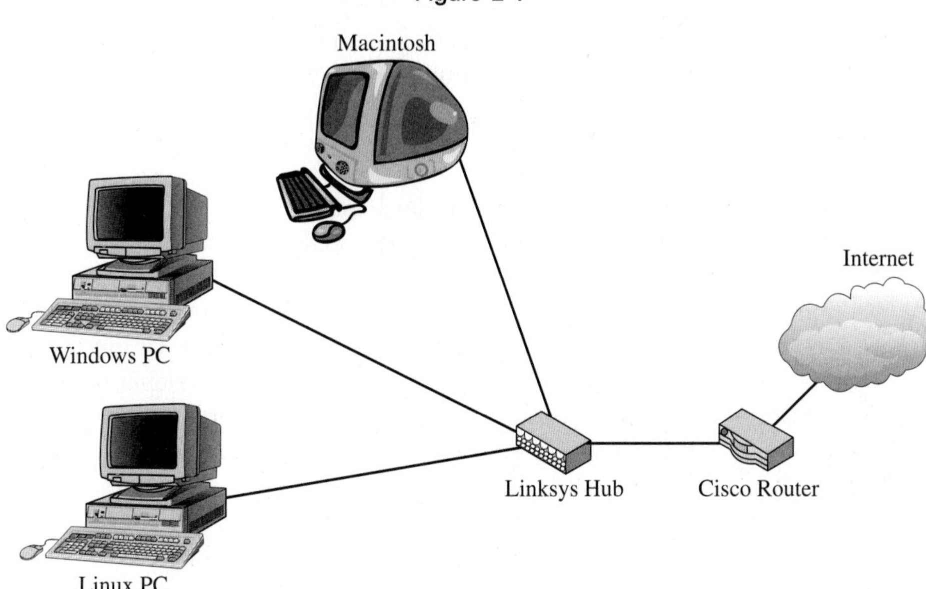

A mixed-vendor environment.

communications industry, de facto standards often become formal standards once they have been widely accepted.

In some cases, a standard can fall into both categories. For example, the TCP/IP protocol suite is based on formal standards, and it defines the standard for protocols used on the Internet. There is no formal standard, however, that defines which protocol should be used on PC networks. The fact that the vast majority of PC networks use TCP/IP makes it the de facto standard for that application.

The formal **standardization process** has three stages:

- **Specification stage:** The **specification stage** consists of developing a nomenclature and identifying the problems to be addressed.
- **Identification of choices stage:** In the **identification of choices stage**, those working on the standard identify the various solutions and choose the optimum solution from among the alternatives.
- **Acceptance stage:** The **acceptance stage**, which is the most difficult stage, consists of defining the solution and getting recognized industry leaders to agree on a single, uniform solution. Large investments of time, money, and products are often at stake. Because of this, the standards-making processes are not immune to corporate politics and the influence of national governments. Often, manufacturers release products based on **draft standards**, standards that have not yet made it through the full acceptance process.

2.1.2 Recognizing Standards Organizations

Formal standards are proposed, developed, and maintained through standards organizations. The major standards organizations have defined areas of responsibility. The following are some of the largest and most important standards organizations:

▲ **International Organization for Standardization (ISO):** The **ISO** makes technical recommendations about data communication. The ISO website homepage is shown in Figure 2-2. The ISO membership includes the national standards organization of each ISO member country. In turn, ISO is a member of the **International Telecommunications Union (ITU)**, whose task is to make technical recommendations about telephone, telegraph, and data communication interfaces on a worldwide basis.

▲ **International Telecommunications Union–Telecommunications Group (ITU-T):** The **ITU-T** is the technical standards-setting organization of the

Figure 2-2

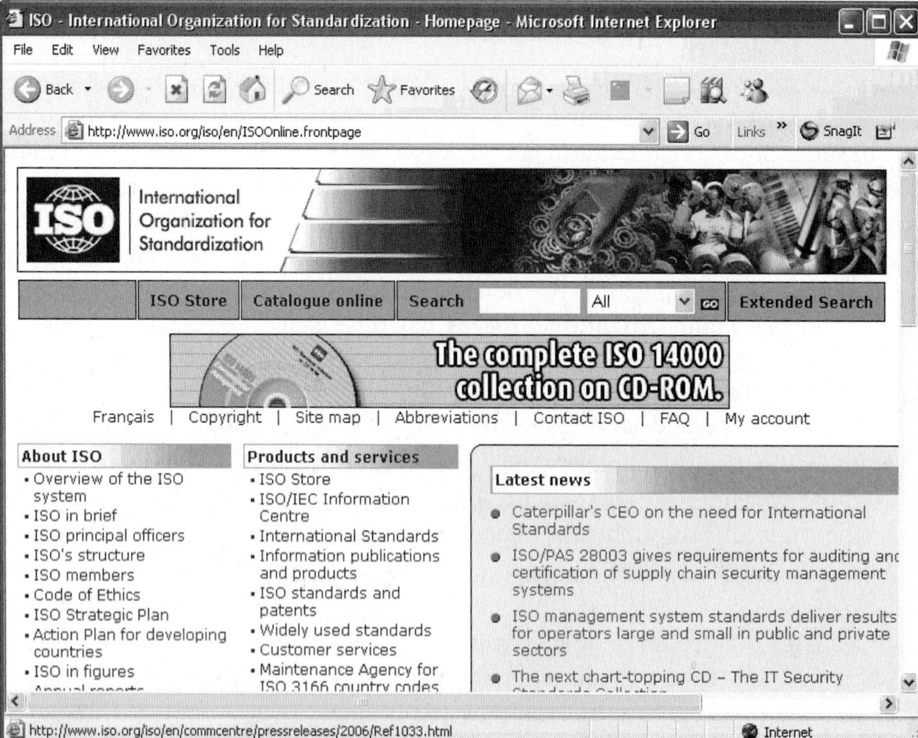

The ISO website homepage.

Source: ISO.org.

United Nations. ITU is composed of representatives from about 200 member countries. Membership was originally focused on just the public telephone companies in each country, but ITU now seeks members among public- and private-sector organizations that operate computer or communications networks or build software and equipment for them.

▲ **American National Standards Institute (ANSI): ANSI** is the coordinating organization for the U.S. national system of technical and nontechnical standards. ANSI has about 1,000 members from public and private

FOR EXAMPLE

Building an Industry on a De Facto Standard

Some 25 years ago, the PC industry was a very different world than it is today. There were a few manufacturers of home and hobby computers, most notably Apple, Radio Shack, and Commodore. Commodore had even made an attempt to get desktop computers into businesses, with its PET line of computers. The term *personal computer* had yet to be coined to describe these computers designed for individual use. This changed with the introduction of IBM's personal computer, nicknamed the PC. The IBM branding made companies suddenly take notice, and PCs began making their way to business desktops. At the time, rather than being the standard, IBM's PC was simply one standard among many. There was no formal desktop computer standard.

What IBM did when it released the PC was revolutionary. If IBM had patented the technologies in the PC as proprietary, then other companies would have had to license the technology to build their own versions. Instead, IBM decided to make the PC an open standard, released it publicly, and welcomed other companies to build their own versions of the PC, referred to at the time as *PC clones*.

The industry still didn't have a formal standard, but it had a de facto standard that manufacturers could agree upon in the IBM PC. Soon, a flood of PC-standard computers hit the market. Competition soon drove down prices and made computers readily affordable. Non-PC systems, such as the Apple Macintosh, had to drop their prices, too, just to remain competitive. It wasn't long before IBM became a minor player in a marketplace that it had helped invent.

Today's consumers continue to benefit from that early decision. Computers grow steadily more powerful while prices continue to drop. Computers are everywhere and a part of everyday life, thanks in no small part to a de facto standard.

organizations in the United States. ANSI is actually a standardization organization, not a standards-making body. It accepts standards developed by other organizations and publishes them as American standards and coordinates development of voluntary national standards that comply with international recommendations. ANSI is a voting participant in and the U.S. representative to the ISO and the ITU-T.

- **Institute of Electrical and Electronics Engineers (IEEE):** The **IEEE** is a professional society in the United States that includes the Standards Association (IEEE-SA), which develops various standards, but is best known for its standards for LANs. These include the most commonly used standards for wired networking (Ethernet/IEEE 802.5) and wireless networking (IEEE 802.11). Other countries have similar groups; for example, the British counterpart of the IEEE is the Institution of Electrical Engineers (IEE).
- **Internet Engineering Task Force (IETF):** The **IETF** sets the standards that govern the operation of much of the Internet. The IETF is unique in that it doesn't really have official membership, and anyone is welcome to join its mailing lists, attend its meetings, and comment on developing standards. Standards (including those that define TCP/IP) are developed and published through **Request for Comments (RFC)** documents.

SELF-CHECK

1. Compare formal and de facto standards.
2. Why are standards important to an industry segment such as networking?
3. List the major standards organizations related to data communications, networking, and the Internet.

2.2 Understanding the OSI Model

The **Open Systems Interconnection reference model (OSI model)** helped change the face of network computing. Before the OSI model, most commercial networks used by businesses were built using nonstandardized technologies developed by individual vendors. During the late 1970s, the ISO created the Open Systems Interconnection Subcommittee to develop a framework of standards for computer-to-computer communications, and this subcommittee completed the seven-layer OSI model in 1984. The use of a layered standard makes it much easier to develop software and hardware that link different networks because software and hardware can be developed one layer at a time.

You will probably never use a network based strictly on the OSI model because it never caught on commercially in North America. Some European networks use it, and most network components define their purpose and use based on this model.

So, why does the OSI model matter? It is used as a commonly accepted and understood frame of reference for discussing network equipment and network-related issues. Other models you are likely to encounter, such as the Internet model, are usually described in terms of the OSI model. Also, questions about the OSI model are on the network and network-related certification exams offered by Microsoft, Cisco, Novell, CompTIA, and other vendors. While most certifications focus primarily on specific vendor products, they do sometimes include questions related to industry standards that apply to a specific certification topic. For example, the OSI model is considered an appropriate topic on a Microsoft or Novell certification exam that includes networking basics.

2.2.1 Understanding How the OSI Model Works

The seven layers of the OSI model are the Application, Presentation, Session, Transport, Network, Data Link, and Physical layers. These layers make up a framework that defines the way in which information passes up and down between physical hardware devices and the applications running on user desktops. Figure 2-3 shows the relationship between the layers and a brief overview of the function of each.

Each layer of the OSI model is independent of every other layer in its purpose and responsibilities. Each must do its own job and must be able to move information between the layers above and below it. In this way, the model creates a modular system in which functions can be isolated to their respective layers. Each layer makes design and development easier and also aids developers and network engineers alike in the troubleshooting problems that arise in a network.

The movement of data through the OSI model is easy to follow. When two devices want to communicate with each other, data are sent from the Application layer of the source computer or device. The data, in the form of a packet, continues down the layers of the OSI model until it reaches layer 1, the Physical layer. From there, it begins its journey onto the network.

The Physical layer is where data join with the transmission media and are transmitted over wires or through the air. The transfer physically occurs as an electrical signal, modulated light, or radio waves. When the data reach the destination device, they travel back through the OSI model until they are fully processed and usable.

Figure 2-3

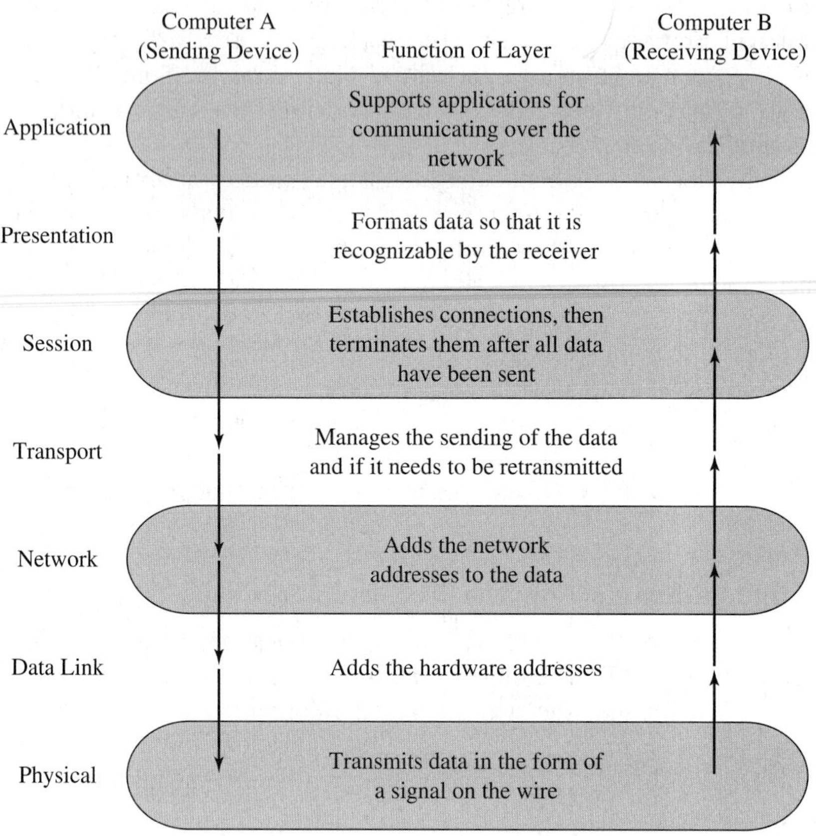

OSI model functional diagram.

When a user wants to access information on another computer, the user's computer must request conversation with the destination computer. As part of its request (and any subsequent messages), it needs to add the information for the recipient computer to understand how to process the information. The process of adding information to data as it passes through the layers is known as **encapsulation**.

The encapsulation process is shown in Figure 2-4. As the data move down through the OSI layers, header and trailer information is added to the packet. The packet **header** describes the packet, including the source and destination computers, and something about what the packet contains. The **trailer** identifies the end of the packet and usually includes data that help identify transmission errors when they occur. The data inside the packet do not change during the encapsulation process. At the destination device, the header and trailer information is put through a process sometimes referred to as **decapsulation**, leaving just the original data.

Figure 2-4

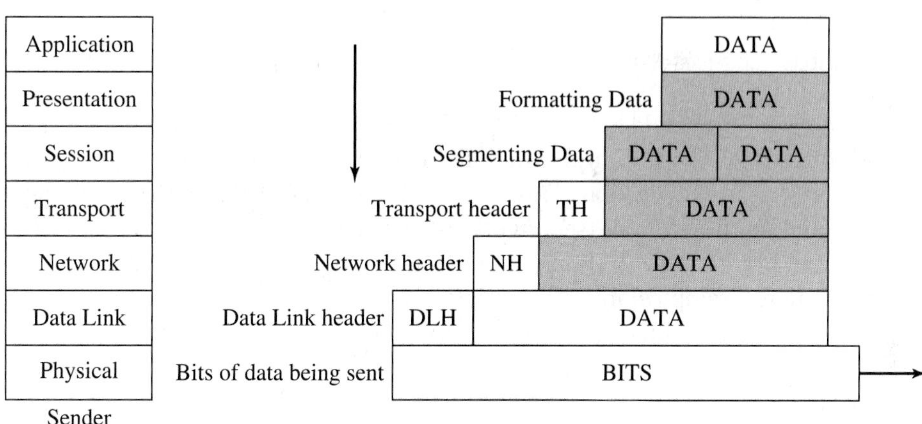

The OSI model encapsulation process.

The encapsulation/decapsulation process is repeated at every computer sending or receiving data and for every packet sent through the network. The process is generally the same for other networking models.

2.2.2 Understanding the OSI Model Layers

Part of each OSI model layer's job is to perform specific functions for processing the data before they are passed on to the layer above or below. For the source, that means each layer processes the data and prepares them for the layer below it, ending with transmission on the network. The process is reversed as the destination prepares the data for application processing or display.

You can think of the services provided by each layer as horizontal and vertical communication relationships. The data transfer between layers in the same device represents a **vertical relationship** between the layers. **Horizontal relationships** exist between the corresponding layers in different devices. This relationship is known as **peer layer communication.**

The Application Layer

The **Application layer** is the end user's access to the network, providing a set of utilities for application programs. Protocols functioning at the Application layer work with the applications you use to communicate over the network.

Although other services exist, five categories of services are very common to most Internet and network users:

- ▲ Files services.
- ▲ Email services.

- Network printing services.
- Application services.
- Database services.

Examples of protocols from the TCP/IP suite that are needed for applications to work on a network are **Simple Mail Transfer Protocol (SMTP)** to send email to another person, **Hypertext Transfer Protocol (HTTP)** to access webpages while surfing on the Internet (see Figure 2-5), and **File Transfer Protocol (FTP)** to download files from an FTP server, a file server that is based on Internet technologies. These examples are only a partial list.

It's a common mistake to equate the purpose of the Application layer with computer applications or programs. Business productivity software, for example, does not inherently run at the Application layer, although the software may make use of network services. For example, a word processing application might use email or network printing services.

The Presentation Layer

The **Presentation layer** formats the data for presentation to the user. Its job is to accommodate different interfaces on different terminals or computers so the application program need not worry about them.

The Presentation layer has three main jobs:

- **Data presentation: Data presentation** ensures that the data being sent to the recipient are in a format that the recipient can process. This function is important because it enables the receiving device to understand the information from the sending device.

Figure 2-5

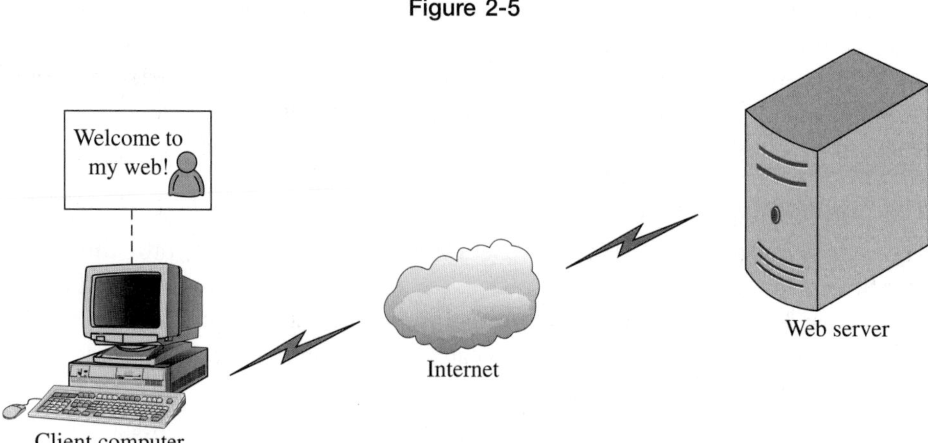

The Application layer (HTTP).

▲ **Data compression: Data compression** shrinks large amounts of data into smaller pieces. This allows data to be transferred more quickly across a network.

▲ **Data encryption: Data encryption** uses algorithms to modify the data based on encryption sequence or key. Encryption is important because it helps hide information from unintended disclosure. It's a common practice to encrypt sensitive data before transmission. Various encryption methods are used, resulting in various levels of protection.

In the Presentation layer example in Figure 2-6, the source computer is sending a text document to the destination computer. At the Application layer, these data look like a normal sentence with formatting intact. When it reaches the Presentation layer, the text data are compressed, transformed, and possibly encrypted, and then they are sent on through the remaining layers.

At the destination computer, when the information reaches the Presentation layer, it is returned to its original format (with spaces and formatting), and then it is sent on to the Application layer.

Figure 2-6

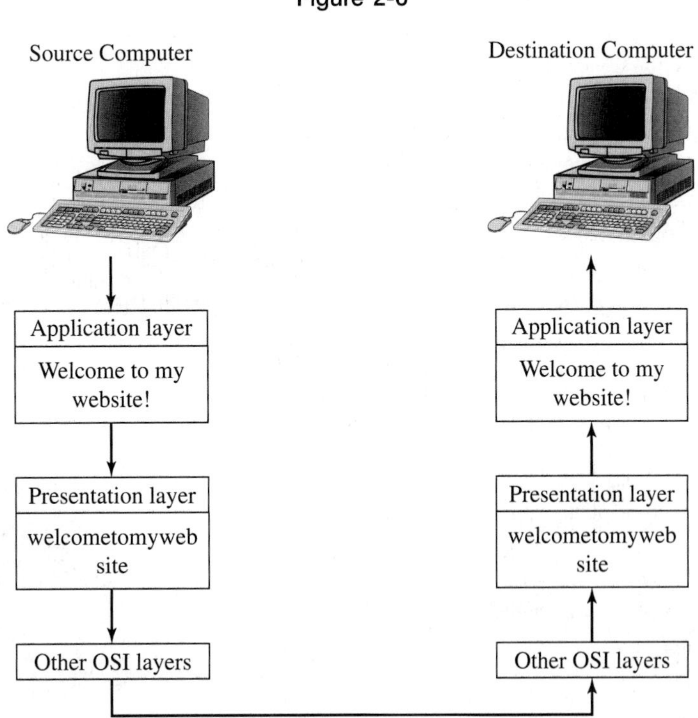

The Presentation layer.

The Session Layer

The **Session layer** is responsible for initiating, maintaining, and terminating each logical session between computers. The Session layer also handles dialog control and dialog separation.

Session initiation arranges for the desired and required services between session participants, such as logging on to circuit equipment, transferring files, and performing security checks. **Session termination** provides an orderly way to end a session, as well as a means to abort a session prematurely. There may be some redundancy built in to recover from an unexpected broken or interrupted transport connection. The Session layer also handles **session accounting** so the correct party receives the bill when billing by session time or data volume, as is done with some WAN connection methods.

To understand the Session layer's basic functions, think of your telephone. When you dial a number and the other person answers, you create a connection. When you start speaking with the person at the other end, you initiate a session. You terminate the session by hanging up. You would be responsible for related charges, though if the person on the other end is on a cell phone, there may be additional charges at that end also.

Dialog control is responsible for determining which device participating in the communication will transmit at any given time and controlling the amount of data that can be sent in a transmission (see Figure 2-7). Transmission types managed through dialog control include simplex, half duplex, and full duplex. In **simplex communication**, the information moves in one direction only, as in a broadcast (e.g., TV, radio). **Half duplex** lets the two ends communicate, but one at a time, as in a polite telephone conversation. **Full duplex** enables the two ends of a conversation to communicate simultaneously, usually through separate send and receive channels.

Data separation is the process of inserting markers into packets to ensure that if there is a loss of packets or other problems during transmission, the conversation can recover and continue. These markers let the Session layer know what data it needs to retransmit.

Figure 2-7

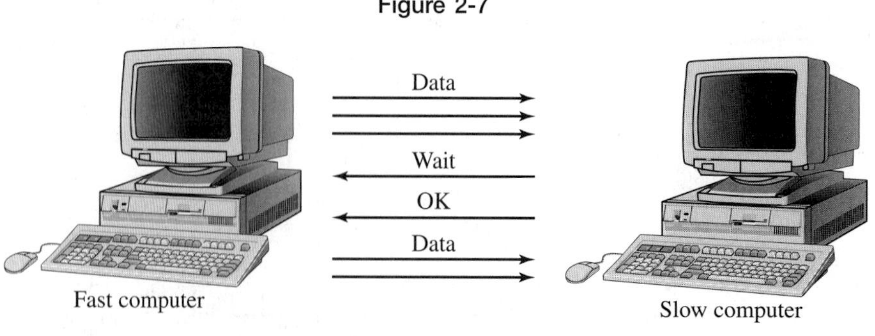

Dialog control.

The Transport Layer

The **Transport layer** deals with end-to-end issues, such as procedures for entering and departing from the network. It establishes, maintains, and terminates logical connections for data transfer between the original sender and the final destination. It is responsible for obtaining the address of the destination computer (if needed), breaking a large data transmission into smaller packets (if needed), ensuring that all the packets have been received, eliminating duplicate packets, and performing **flow control** to ensure that no computer is overwhelmed by the number of messages it receives. Flow control keeps the source from sending data packets faster than the destination can handle. The Transport layer can also perform error checking, but this function is normally performed by the Data Link layer. The Transport layer manages two types of transmissions: connection-oriented and connectionless.

Connection-oriented transmission, as shown in Figure 2-8, has the receiving device send an acknowledgment, or **ACK**, back to the source after a packet or group of packets is received. If no ACK is received, the sending system can assume that the packets were lost and retransmit, or the destination can request a retransmission if it detects that it missed a packet in sequence. This type of transmission is known as a **reliable transport method.** Because connection-oriented transmission requires the additional response traffic, it has often been considered a slower method than connectionless transmission, although this tends to be a moot point in today's fast networks.

Figure 2-8

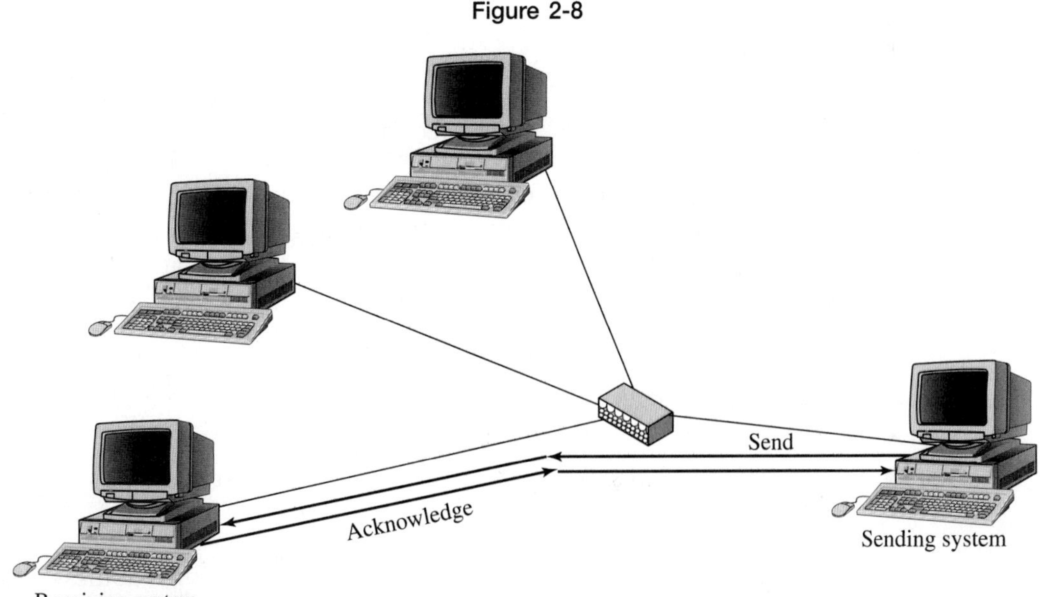

Connection-oriented transmission.

Figure 2-9

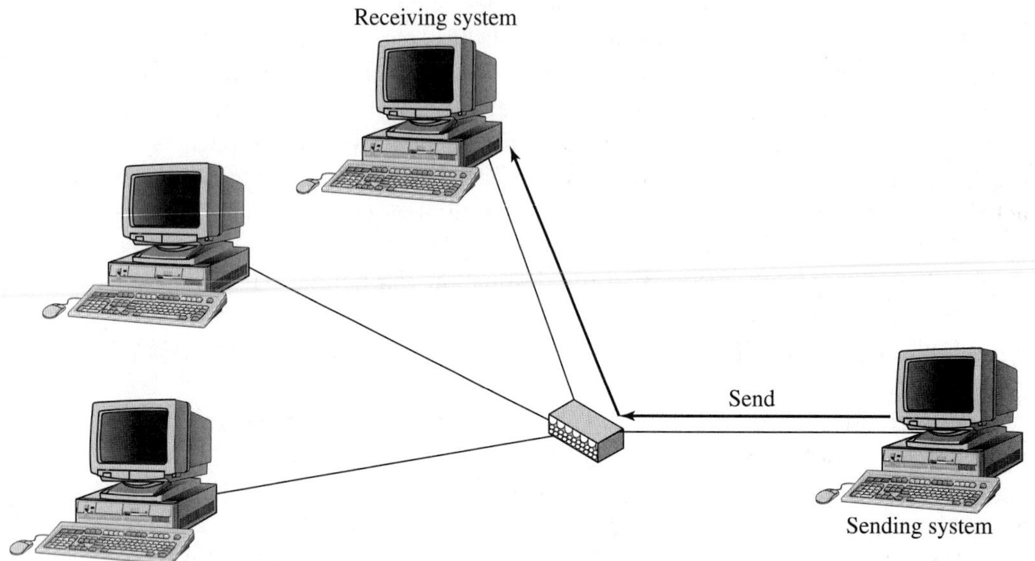

Connectionless transmission.

Connection-oriented transmission features include the following:

- ▲ It is reliable.
- ▲ It allows for relatively slow communication.
- ▲ Packets are re-sent if a packet is unrecognizable or is not received.

Connectionless transmissions (see Figure 2-9) do not have the receiver acknowledge receipt of a packet. Instead, the sending device assumes that the packet arrived. This approach allows for much faster communication but is less reliable than connection-oriented transmission.

Connectionless transmission features include the following:

- ▲ It offers little or no reliability.
- ▲ It provides relatively fast transmission.
- ▲ Packets are not retransmitted (because transmission errors are not detected).

The TCP/IP protocol suite includes examples of both connectionless and connection-oriented protocols. We'll discuss those a little later in the chapter, but a detailed discussion of these protocols is beyond the scope of this chapter.

The Network Layer

The **Network layer** is responsible for the addressing and delivery of packets, also known as **datagrams**, and performing routing. **Routing** is the process of finding a path through the routers connecting networks into an internetwork so that packets (represented by the arrow in Figure 2-10) are delivered to the correct network, and finally to the correct computer. Routing ensures that a packet is delivered to and through the appropriate router. Notice that the path that the packet takes passes through other networks only when they are part of the path to the next router.

Each computer has a **physical address**, which is coded on the network card, and a **logical address** that is assigned through the system networking software. Both are unique addresses. The Network layer relies on the logical address for routing purposes. When a packet arrives at the Network layer, the Network layer adds source and destination addresses through encapsulation. The destination computer can be on either a local network or a remote network, in which case the packet must be routed to arrive at the right destination.

Figure 2-10

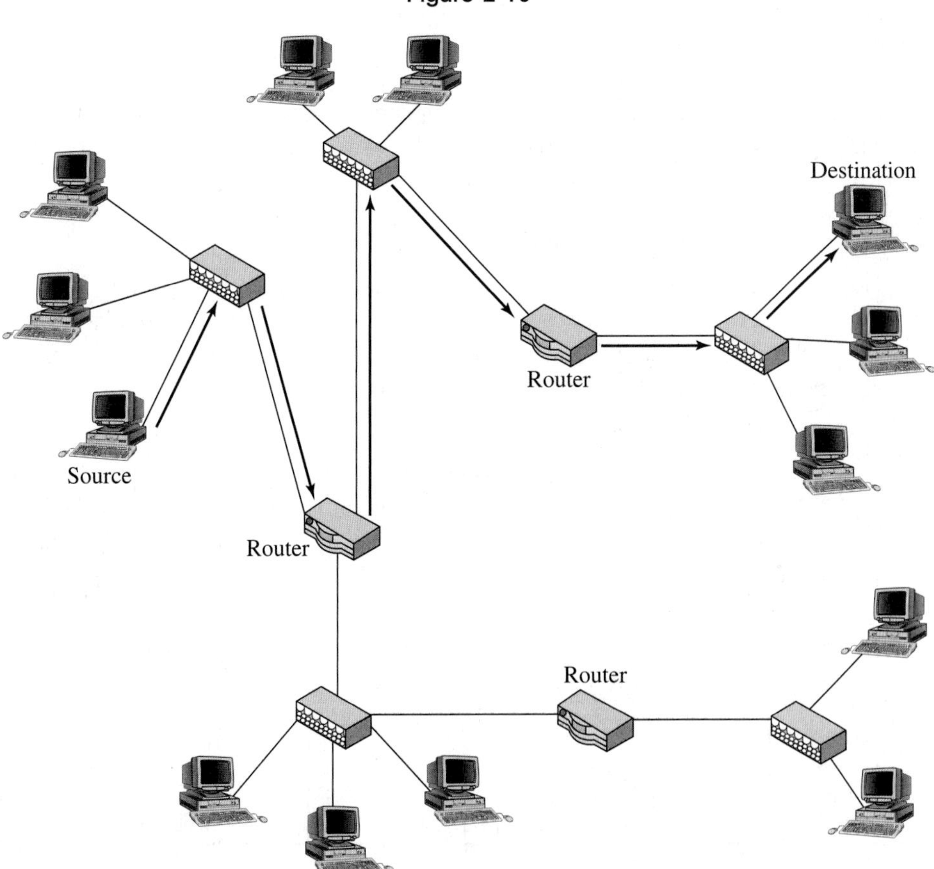

A routed packet.

There are two basic ways that routing can be handled. One is **source routing**, where the addresses of all the routers along the way are embedded in the packet, and the packet follows the specified path. However, the more common method is to have each router along the way direct the packet to the next router, or **hop**, in the path. It does this by checking the destination address and comparing it against an internal table, called the **routing table**, to choose the best path. A counter is decremented each time the packet crosses a router, and when it reaches zero, it's assumed that the packet is lost or stuck in a loop and is discarded.

Routers can use various algorithms to determine the best path. Most often, the decision is made on the shortest path, based on the number of hops (intervening routers) to the destination. However, routers can also take into consideration factors such as the bandwidth and traffic levels on alternate routes and make routing decisions based on current network conditions. The way that routing is managed is determined by the **routing protocol** used by the routers. Alternate routes aren't an issue in Figure 2-10 because there is only one path between the source and destination systems.

A router is the primary piece of hardware working at the Network layer, which is why routers are sometimes called layer 3 devices. Brouters also operate, at least partially, at the Network layer. Some switches, identified as layer 3 switches, also operate at the Network layer. Devices that a packet passes through on its way to the destination device are called *intermediate systems*. Intermediate routers need to deal with the packet only up to the Network layer of the OSI model, as shown in Figure 2-11.

The Network layer also has the job of making sure a data packet is compatible with the network it is entering. For example, if a network's media require shorter packet lengths, then some routers can break up and reformat the packets so that the network they are entering can handle them.

Figure 2-11

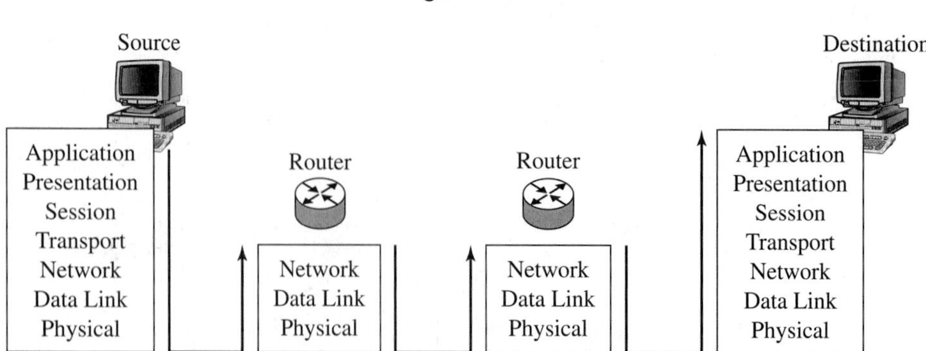

Route operation.

Figure 2-12

Header	Destination MAC	Source MAC	Destination address	Source address	LLC header	Data	CRC	Trailer

A completed frame.

The Data Link Layer

The **Data Link layer** manages the physical **transmission circuit** in the Physical layer and transforms it into a circuit that is free of transmission errors (as far as the upper layers are concerned) by performing error detection, correction, and retransmission. It also converts data packets into frames; a **frame** is the data packet plus the encapsulating information, including layer 2 addresses (see Figure 2-12). The Data Link layer is made up of two sublayers, each providing services. These are the Logical Link Control (LLC) sublayer and the Media Access Control (MAC) sublayer.

The **Logical Link Control (LLC)** sublayer provides the interface between the **media access method** (for physical network traffic control) and Network layer protocols. The **Media Access Control (MAC)** sublayer is responsible for the connection to the physical media and physical address.

The LLC sublayer bridges the MAC sublayer to the upper-layer protocols through connectionless and connection-oriented services. LLC standards are defined through the IEEE 802.2 standards. The LLC sublayer supports a connectionless service (**LLC type 1**), which assumes that data has arrived correctly at the destination. It also supports a connection-oriented service (**LLC type 2**), which checks that a message arrives correctly. Because of the additional overhead for LLC type 2 and the fact that connection-oriented service is already provided at the Transport layer, LLC type 1 is most commonly used.

The MAC sublayer adds the actual physical address of the device, called the **MAC address**, to the packet. The frame then has all the addressing information necessary to travel from the source device to the destination device. Why is the MAC address necessary? Because that is the address used to locate the destination computer when the packet reaches the correct local network.

The MAC address is permanently hard-coded on the NIC by the manufacturer (see Figure 2-13). It is a unique hexadecimal address with six pairs of hexadecimal digits and is not duplicated anywhere in the world. The first six digits are assigned to (and identify) the NIC manufacturer. The last six are a unique value assigned by the manufacturer.

The Physical Layer

The **Physical layer** defines the rules by which data are transmitted, such as voltages of electricity, the number of bits sent per second, and the physical structure of the cables and connectors used. This is the layer for which the most, and clearest, operational standards are defined.

Figure 2-13

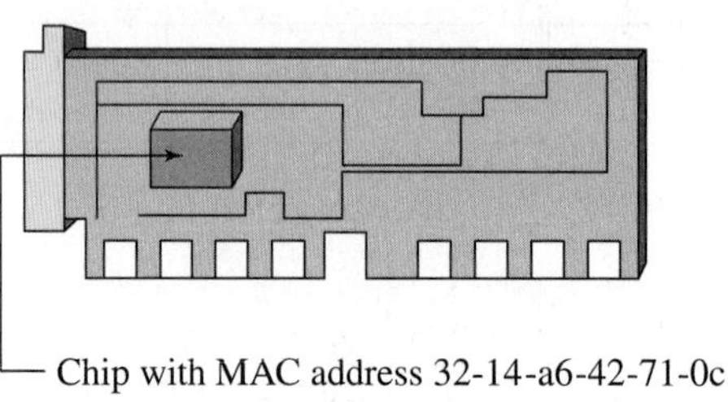

A MAC address.

The NIC operates at this level, converting data into transmission signals. The signals generated depend on the network connection medium. These transmissions can be analog or digital, though both types transmit binary data. The Physical layer defines both the transmissions and the rate at which these transmissions are sent.

The Physical layer also manages the way a device connects to the network medium. For example, if the physical connection from the device to the network uses coaxial cable, the hardware that functions at the Physical layer is designed for that specific type of network. All components, including the connectors (see Figure 2-14), are specified at the Physical layer as well.

Figure 2-14

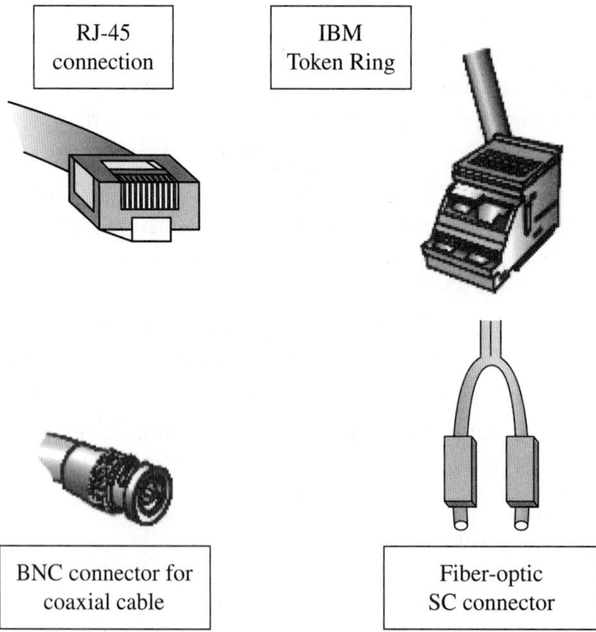

Sample connectors.

FOR EXAMPLE

Practical Consequences

Most network addresses do not implement functionality from all layers of the OSI model. Hubs are dumb connection devices and operate at the Physical layer only. Routers, on the other hand, are more sophisticated and implement functionality through the Network layer. The communication protocols operating at the network clients and servers implement all seven layers. At least, that's how it usually works. For every rule, there's usually at least one exception.

The NetBEUI protocol is an example of a protocol that does not implement all the layers of the OSI model. NetBEUI has no equivalent of the Networking layer. What's the consequence of this? If you don't have the Network layer, you don't have logical network addresses. That also means that you can't support routing. Routers ignore NetBEUI frames because they don't have source or destination network addresses. The routers have no idea what to do with them, so they do nothing. Frames are trapped on the network segment on which they are generated.

What does this mean to network communications? It means that if you need to communicate with a computer located on a different network, you must use a protocol other than NetBEUI, such as IPX/SPX or TCP/IP. Both of these include Network layer functionality and can therefore support routing.

Because of the limitations of NetBEUI, it was common for computers deployed in a routed network and running NetBEUI to also run one or more additional protocols. There were other justifications for multiple protocols, as well. Some applications were written to use functionality specific to a communication protocol. In other words, you might have needed IPX/SPX to run one application but NetBEUI to run another. Internet access and Internet applications required (and still require) TCP/IP. This could get to be a problem, especially on computers with limited resources. Each protocol that you load on the computer adds to the memory overhead. Performance suffers. Background traffic increases because of the "housekeeping" traffic required by the protocols. On some older systems, if you try to run too many simultaneous protocols, your computer won't be able to do much of anything else. This makes it easier to see why the industry has settled on a de facto standard, doesn't it?

Table 2-1: Selected IEEE Standards

Standard	*Name*	*Description*
802.3	Ethernet	The most commonly used networking standard, with support for speeds ranging from 10Mbps to 10Gbps in current implementations.
802.5	Token Ring	Originally developed by IBM and used primarily on IBM networks and mainframe connections. Is not as commonly used today as was in previous years.
802.11	Wi-Fi	Wireless networking standards, including 802.11b and 802.11g, the two standards most commonly used by PC networks and compatible devices.

The most commonly used standards are those defined by the IEEE. The three most well-known IEEE network standards are listed in Table 2-1.

1. List and describe the seven OSI model layers.
2. List and describe common IEEE Physical layer standards.

2.3 Understanding Other Network Models

The OSI model is the model most commonly referenced from a theoretical standpoint or when discussing networks in general, but it is rarely seen in real-world applications. For that, we need to look at two other, nearly identical standard models: the TCP/IP model and the Internet model.

Technically, the four-layer TCP/IP model is known as the **DoD model** because the U.S. Department of Defense (DoD) funded the original project from which TCP/IP was developed. The Internet model evolved from the work of thousands of people who developed pieces of the Internet. The Internet model has never been formally defined, but it is generally accepted as a five-layer model. These two models are nearly identical. This is understandable because the Internet

Figure 2-15

OSI Model	TCP/IP Model
Application layer Presentation layer Session layer	Process layer
Trasnsport layer	Host-to-Host layer
Network layer	Internet layer
Data Link layer	Network Interface layer
Physical layer	

Comparing the OSI and TCP/IP models.

is based on the TCP/IP protocol suite, so it reflects the structure of that suite and its underlying model.

2.3.1 The TCP/IP Model

The **TCP/IP (DoD) model** is considered a working model because it was used as the basis for the development of the TCP/IP protocol suite. For documentation purposes, the TCP/IP suite of protocols is often mapped to the more contemporary OSI model. The TCP/IP model does not have clearly defined layers, but it is possible to compare the functions of the layers of the DoD model to those of the OSI model, as you can see in Figure 2-15. From the comparison, a four-layer DoD model can be derived. Some overviews of the TCP/IP model include a Physical layer as part of the stack that is not defined as a part of the DoD model. TCP/IP leaves the physical connection to manage itself.

The Application or Process Layer

The **Application layer** of the TCP/IP model, also known as the **Process layer**, handles the way applications at both the source and destination devices process information as it is sent and received. The Application layer of the DoD model maps to the Application layer, Presentation layer, and most of the Session layer of the OSI model.

The Host-to-Host or Transport Layer

Like the OSI model's Transport layer, the DoD's **Host-to-Host layer** or **Transport layer** manages the flow of data between devices and the type of transmission as either connection-oriented or connectionless. The name comes from TCP/IP terminology, in which network devices are referred to as **hosts**. TCP/IP uses two protocols to provide this service: Transmission Control Protocol (TCP) provides reliable connection-oriented service, and User Datagram Protocol (UDP) provides the less reliable connectionless service.

The Internet Layer (Network Layer)

You may sometimes hear the **Internet layer** called the *Network layer* or the *Internetwork layer*. No one name is more right or wrong than the others. It is easiest to define the Internet layer by the primary protocol referred to at this layer, Internet Protocol. The Internet Protocol (IP) serves several functions, the foremost of which is to provide a hierarchical addressing scheme used to identify devices on the network, so that every device on the Internet has a unique address. IP addresses also let you configure your own network so that each node is uniquely identified. The Internet layer relies on the hierarchical addressing of IP to route data independently of the type of network media, like the Network layer in the OSI model.

The Network Interface Layer

The **Network Interface layer** manages the transmission of data within a network. After the Internet layer routes packets to the correct network, the Network Interface layer makes sure the data is sent to the correct device, functioning like the OSI Data Link layer.

2.3.2 The Internet Model

Although the OSI model is the most well-known network model, the one that dominates current hardware and software is the simpler five-layer **Internet model**. The two models have very much in common (see Figure 2-16). The Internet model collapses the top three OSI layers into one layer. The biggest difference between the Internet and TCP/IP models is that the Internet model, unlike the TCP/IP model, includes a Physical layer.

Figure 2-16

OSI Model	Internet Model
Application layer Presentation layer Session layer	Process layer
Trasnsport layer	Host-to-Host layer
Network layer	Internet layer
Data Link layer	Network Interface layer
Physical layer	Physical layer

Comparing the OSI and Internet models.

The Application Layer

The Internet model **Application layer** is the application software used by the network user and includes much of what the OSI model contains in the Application, Presentation, and Session layers. It is the user's access to the network. By using the application software, the user defines what messages are sent over the network.

The Transport Layer

The **Transport layer** in the Internet model is very similar to the Transport layer in the OSI model. The Transport layer:

- ▲ Is responsible for linking the Application layer software to the network and establishing end-to-end connections between the sender and receiver when such connections are needed.
- ▲ Provides tools so that addresses used at the Application layer (Internet universal resource locators [URLs]) can be translated into numeric IP addresses.
- ▲ Is responsible for breaking long messages into several smaller messages to make them easier to transmit.

The Network Layer

The **Network layer** of the Internet model is responsible for the end-to-end transfer of messages from the sender to the final destination. The Network layer in the Internet model performs the same functions as the Network layer in the OSI model. It performs routing, in that it selects the next computer to which the message should be sent and can find the address of that computer if it doesn't already know it.

The Data Link Layer

The **Data Link layer** is responsible for moving a message from one computer to the next computer in the network path from the sender to the receiver. The Data Link layer in the Internet model performs the same basic functions as the Data Link layer in the OSI model:

- ▲ It controls the physical layer by deciding when to transmit messages over the media.
- ▲ It formats the messages by indicating where they start and end.
- ▲ It detects and corrects any errors that have occurred during transmission.

The Physical Layer

The **Physical layer** in the Internet model, as in the OSI model, is the physical connection between the sender and receiver. Its role is to transfer a series of electrical, radio, or light signals through the circuit. The Physical layer includes all the hardware devices (e.g., computers, modems, hubs) and physical media (e.g., cables, satellites, radio frequency). The Physical layer specifies the type of connection and the signals that pass through it.

2.3.3 Groups of Layers

The layers in the Internet model are often so closely coupled that decisions in one layer impose certain requirements on other layers. The Data Link layer and the Physical layer are closely tied together because the Data Link layer controls the Physical layer in terms of when the Physical layer can transmit. Decisions

FOR EXAMPLE

Troubleshooting by the Layers

Just why is all this talk about layers important? After all, these are just logical models, right? That's true, but these layers represent divisions used by hardware manufacturers and software vendors when developing new products. Let's consider the Internet model. Someone can develop new software, or enhance existing software that operates at the Application layer knowing that the processes at the underlying layers as well as the interface to those layers are already defined. The role of a router is already clearly established. You know exactly what is expected of a network adapter.

These defined layers, and their relationship to standard hardware and software, can also help you when problems arise. Consider a problem in which a network computer can communicate with other computers on the local network but can't communicate with computers on other network segments. That immediately gives you a starting place for your troubleshooting. You know that this is a routing problem because you can't make the hop from one network to another. Now you can start asking other questions. Can other computers on this network communicate with other networks? If not, the problem is likely related to the router. If they can, then it's something with this computer, maybe an address configuration problem.

Now say that you have a computer that can't communicate with any other computer on the network. This time, you probably want to start your search at the Physical or Data Link layer. It could be that the network adapter is failing or simply that it has become disconnected from the cable.

You may not specifically step through the layers when problems occur, but even so, understanding the layered structure will help you direct your troubleshooting efforts. Not responsible for troubleshooting? Then having an understanding of the Internet model will help you explain your problem in terms that make sense to you and the technician.

Figure 2-17

OSI Model	Internet Model	Groups of layers	Examples
Application layer Presentation layer Session layer	Process layer	Application layer	Internet Explorer Netscape Navigator Web servers and pages TCP/IP suite protocols (HTTP, FTP, etc.)
Trasnsport layer	Host-to-Host layer	Internetwork layer	TCP/IP suite protocols (TCP, UDP, IP)
Network layer	Internet layer		
Data Link layer	Network Interface layer	Hardware layer	NIC Cable plant NIC device drivers
Physical layer	Physical layer		

Grouping layers.

about the Data Link layer often drive the decisions about the Physical layer. For this reason, some people group them together and call them the Hardware layers. You can see this in Figure 2-17.

Similarly, the Transport and Network layers are so closely coupled that sometimes these layers are called the Internetwork layers. When you design a network, you often think about the network design in terms of three groups of layers: the Hardware layers (Physical and Data Link), the Internetwork layers (Network and Transport), and the Application layer. The same groupings of Hardware, Internetwork, and Application can also apply to the OSI model and, to a lesser extent, to the TCP/IP model (because of its lack of a Physical layer).

SELF-CHECK

1. Compare the OSI, TCP/IP (or DoD), and Internet models.
2. How are Internet model layers organized into groups?

SUMMARY

In this chapter, you learned about standards, specifically network standards. First, you learned about the formal standards process and major networking standards bodies, as well as the role of de facto standards. You next learned about the OSI model, which is the model most commonly used to describe network hardware and software. The chapter concluded with a discussion of the differences between the OSI model and two other models also used in the network world: the TCP/IP model (also known as the DoD model) and the Internet model.

KEY TERMS

Acceptance stage
ACK
American National Standards Institute (ANSI)
Application layer (DoD and Internet models)
Application layer (OSI model)
Connectionless transmission
Connection-oriented transmission
Data compression
Data encryption
Data Link layer (Internet model)
Data Link layer (OSI model)
Data presentation
Data separation
Datagram
De facto standard
Decapsulation
Department of Defense (DoD) model
Dialog control
Draft standards
Encapsulation
File Transfer Protocol (FTP)
Flow control
Formal standard
Frame
Full duplex communication
Half duplex communication
Header
Hop
Horizontal relationship
Host
Host-to-Host layer (DoD model)
Hypertext Transfer Protocol (HTTP)
Identification of choices stage
Institute of Electrical and Electronics Engineers (IEEE)
International Organization for Standardization (ISO)
International Telecommunications Union (ITU)
International Telecommunications Union–Telecommunications Group (ITU-T)
Internet Engineering Task Force (IETF)
Internet layer (DoD model)
Internet model
LLC type 1
LLC type 2
Logical address
Logical Link Control (LLC)
MAC address
Media Access Control (MAC)
Media access method
Network Interface layer (DoD model)
Network layer (Internet model)

Network layer (OSI model)
Open Systems Interconnection (OSI) model
Peer layer communication
Physical address
Physical layer (Internet model)
Physical layer (OSI model)
Presentation layer (OSI model)
Process layer (DoD model)
Reliable transport method
Request for Comments (RFC)
Routing
Routing protocol
Routing table
Session accounting
Session initiation
Session layer (OSI model)
Session termination
Simple Mail Transfer Protocol (SMTP)
Simplex communication
Source routing
Specification stage
Standardization process
TCP/IP model
Trailer
Transmission circuit
Transport layer (DoD and Internet models)
Transport layer (OSI model)
Vertical relationship

ASSESS YOUR UNDERSTANDING

Go to www.wiley.com/college/ciccarelli to evaluate your knowledge of network standards and models.
Measure your learning by comparing pre-test and post-test results.

Summary Questions

1. A de facto standard is one that emerges in the marketplace but has no official standing. True or false?
2. What standards body developed the OSI model?
   (a) ISO
   (b) ITU-T
   (c) IEEE
   (d) ANSI
3. Which of the following is used to develop and publish Internet standards?
   (a) DoD
   (b) ITU
   (c) RFC
   (d) IETF
4. ANSI is a U.S. standards-making body. True or false?
5. Which layer of the OSI model is responsible for routing?
   (a) Data Link layer
   (b) Transport layer
   (c) Session layer
   (d) Network layer
6. Which of the following terms is used to describe a connection in which both ends are able to communicate simultaneously?
   (a) full duplex communication
   (b) reliable transport method
   (c) connection-oriented transmission
   (d) half duplex communication
7. The connectors that are used to attach a NIC to a network cable are defined at what layer of the OSI model?
   (a) Data Link layer
   (b) Physical layer
   (c) Transport layer
   (d) Network layer

8. What is a MAC address?
   (a) a logical address defined at the Internet model Network layer
   (b) the address used to determine the route taken through an internetwork
   (c) a value used for data encryption by the Internet Application layer
   (d) the globally unique address hard-coded on a network adapter
9. The Internet networking model consists of how many layers?
   (a) four
   (b) five
   (c) seven
   (d) ten
10. What is the most commonly used network physical standard?
   (a) 802.11
   (b) 802.5
   (c) 802.3
   (d) 802.2
11. Which of the following are associated most closely with the OSI model Application layer?
   (a) email services
   (b) logical addresses
   (c) connection-oriented transmissions
   (d) dialog control
12. Which OSI model layer is *not* represented in the DoD network model?
   (a) Physical layer
   (b) Network layer
   (c) Transport layer
   (d) Presentation layer
13. Which protocol is most closely associated with the Internet model Internet layer?
   (a) TCP
   (b) UDP
   (c) IP
   (d) HTTP
14. Which Host-to-Host layer protocol provides connection-oriented service?
   (a) TCP
   (b) UDP
   (c) IP
   (d) HTTP

Applying This Chapter

1. For each of the following, identify the layer primarily responsible for the requested action in both the OSI model and the Internet model.
   - (a) The source file is encoded in seven-bit ASCII code. The destination system expects the file in EBCDIC.
   - (b) The network is an Internet environment. Clients in Chicago need to access content in New York. The packets need to cross several hops to make it to the server.
   - (c) You need to order the correct cables for connecting client computers to hubs.
   - (d) A word processing application needs to be designed so that users can email documents in progress.
   - (e) A MAC address is hard-coded in removable read-only memory (ROM). You can change the physical address by changing the ROM.
2. For each of the following descriptions, identify the correct standards organization.
   - (a) Accepts standards developed by other organizations and publishes them as U.S. standards.
   - (b) Developed the OSI seven-layer model.
   - (c) Developed standards for Token Ring and Wi-Fi.
   - (d) Publishes Internet standards as RFCs.

YOU TRY IT

Standards Role

You are expected to understand the role of standards in networking design and implementation. Answer each of the following:

1. What is the significance of specifications defined by standards at the Internet model Physical layer?
2. What is the relationship between OSI model standards, network hardware, and network software?
3. How do network hardware and software overlap at the OSI model Network layer?

3 NETWORK ARCHITECTURES

Starting Point

Go to www.wiley.com/college/ciccarelli to assess your knowledge of network architectures.
Determine where you need to concentrate your effort.

What You'll Learn in This Chapter

- ▲ Peer-to-peer network architecture
- ▲ Client/server network architecture
- ▲ Directory services network architecture
- ▲ Hybrid network architecture

After Studying This Chapter, You'll Be Able To

- ▲ Describe advantages and disadvantages of peer-to-peer, client/server, and directory services networks
- ▲ Compare and contrast peer-to-peer, client/server, and directory services networks
- ▲ Describe how security is managed in peer-to-peer, client/server, and directory services networks
- ▲ Explain the relationship between logical and physical network designs
- ▲ Design a network to meet operational requirements

INTRODUCTION

If you want to understand PC networking, you need to understand how the various components of a network interconnect and interact.

As software development has improved over the past several decades, computers have become better at interacting on a network. The way in which computers interact on a network is known as the **network architecture**, which is a way of describing the logical design. The physical design, the nuts and bolts of how network devices connect to one another, is known as the **network topology**. This chapter focuses on network architecture models.

The three types of network architecture models that are the most common in current use and therefore are important for you to understand are peer-to-peer, client/server, and directory services. You sometimes see references to an additional architecture, the hybrid network, which is actually a network that uses a combination of peer-to-peer and client/server networking. The type of architecture that is appropriate for an organization depends on several factors, including geographic location(s), the number of users, special application needs, and the amount of technical and administrative support available.

3.1 Understanding Architecture Basics

A network's design, the computers included in the network, and how those computers interact with each other and with the user are all influenced by the network architecture. If you know the architecture on which a network is based, you have a general idea of how resources are shared on the network and of the network security structure.

Despite the differences between network architectures, they all share some common features. All network architectures come from the same common roots. All involve computers connected so that they can communicate. All are based on the same set of hardware devices and use the same communication protocols.

3.1.1 Architecture Evolution

The very first data communications networks developed in the 1960s were **host-based networks**, with the server (usually a large mainframe computer) performing all processing functions. The clients (usually terminals) enabled users to send and receive messages to and from the host computer. The clients merely captured keystrokes, sent them to the server for processing, and accepted instructions from the server on what to display, usually a simple text stream.

The simple host-based network architecture often worked well. In fact, it is still in use in some applications, and if you've ever used a terminal (or a PC with **Telnet** software), you've used a host-based application. There is one point of control because all messages flow through the one central server. In theory, there are **economies of scale**, because all computer resources are centralized. However, when you consider the high cost of host systems and relatively low cost of microcomputers, microcomputer-based LANs quickly become a more cost-effective option.

Cost isn't the only issue with host-based networks. The server must process all messages. As the demands for more and more network applications grow, many servers become overloaded and unable to quickly process all the users' demands. Prioritizing users' access becomes difficult. Response time becomes slower, and network managers are required to spend increasingly more money to upgrade the server. Unfortunately, upgrades to the mainframes (which are usually the servers in this architecture) are "lumpy"—that is, upgrades come in large increments and are expensive (e.g., $500,000 or more for "minor" upgrades).

PC networks grew out of a desire to bring the shared resources and common applications of a host-based network to desktop computers. Manufacturers based much of the communication infrastructure on that used in host-based networks, but designs varied by manufacturer. Some manufacturers, such as Novell, tried to emulate host-based networks as closely as possible, using a PC as the network's central server. Others, such as 3Com and later Microsoft, opted for a more distributed design with multiple servers. Today's architectural models evolved from these early designs. PC networks continue to be a vibrant, rapidly changing environment.

In the late 1980s, there was an explosion in the use of PCs and PC-based LANs. Today, more than 90 percent of most organizations' total computer processing power now resides on LANs rather than centralized mainframe computers. This shift was fueled in part by low-cost, popular applications such as word processors, spreadsheets, and presentation graphics programs. Added to this have been managers' frustrations with application software on host mainframe computers. Most mainframe software is not as easy to use as PC software and is far more expensive, and it can take years to develop or even to change incrementally. In the late 1980s, organizations still using host-based computing had development backlogs of two to three years for any new application. New York City, for example, had a six-year backlog. In contrast, managers could buy PC packages off the shelf or develop PC-based applications in a few months.

These and other advantages led to ready (if not always appropriate) acceptance of available network architectures. Then, as now, many organizations depended on retailers or consultants to recommend networking solutions. While this remains the case, consumers today are more likely to have some PC network experience. Employees and management staff have both a better understanding and increased expectations. As organizations got a better idea of their needs and made requests and suggestions to LAN software manufacturers, LAN features changed to meet their needs. In the process, network architectures also changed, with specific models developed to meet the needs of different business sizes and segments.

3.1.2 Common Server Types

Network servers are a critical part of any network. How servers are deployed and interact with other computers on a network depends on the network architecture. It's important that you know what types of servers you might find on a network and the role of each.

Servers might be dedicated to specific roles or configured as peer servers, acting as both a client and server. The following are some of the most common types of network servers:

- **File servers: File servers** offer users a central location to save files. The security control access to these files depends on the network architecture and server configuration. In many configurations, files stored on a file server are secure because they require a user to log in with a unique login name and a unique password.
- **Print servers: Print servers** make shared printers available to network users by allowing users to print to the server simultaneously. The print server stores the **print jobs** (i.e., documents waiting to print) in a **print queue** (i.e., a storage location) until the printer is available. The file containing the print queue is often referred to as the **spooler file**, and the process of queuing the print jobs is often referred to as **spooling**.
- **Messaging servers:** Messaging servers answer requests for email by clients or route mail messages to appropriate mail servers. These are most commonly seen on large networks that manage their own mail accounts. Smaller networks more often use mail services provided by ISPs.
- **Application servers:** Application servers provide services to the network clients or support enterprise-based applications. Some application servers keep data and the application on the same computer, but this varies by application. Application servers are specific to the applications they support, such as database servers or business-related applications. For example, a website uses at least one application server: a web server. Depending on the website, additional application servers may also be used in supporting roles (e.g., a database server storing content used by the web server and hosted websites).

The most common server types are file and print servers. These are usually the first server types deployed on a network, with others implemented over time, as needed. Some companies never have a need to go beyond offering just file and print services.

With application servers, you need to understand the specific server types and the services that they provide to the network. Web servers give users access to information over the Internet or through a private intranet. A database server stores information formatted for efficient storage and data access.

In some cases, a computer may be configured to support multiple server types. For example, it's relatively common on small networks to have the same server acting as both a file server and a print server. It is recommended that most server types, such as database servers, not be configured to also host other services.

3.1.3 Evolving Network Connections

Just as it is essential to create a blueprint before constructing a building, it is equally important to decide on a network architecture before setting up a network. The technologies that make up a network are not much good used separately. People who want to use a network to solve a problem or improve a process need the different components to function as one. A network architecture provides the blueprint for designing and implementing a network.

An important part of implementing a network is matching the network size and capabilities to the company's needs. In the early days of PC networks, networking was seen as a solution best suited to large companies, while smaller companies struggled along with stand-alone PCs. With time, the number of networking options increased while costs decreased, making PC networks more readily available to most, if not all, companies.

Networks also tend to evolve over time. As companies grow, so do their networks. Today, companies of all sizes are using networks so employees can communicate and work more efficiently. In some companies, a day's work may involve collaborating with coworkers located in offices around the world. These companies require networks that support thousands of users who need to access information across the company. These large networks, like the one shown in Figure 3-1, are called **enterprise networks**.

Figure 3-1

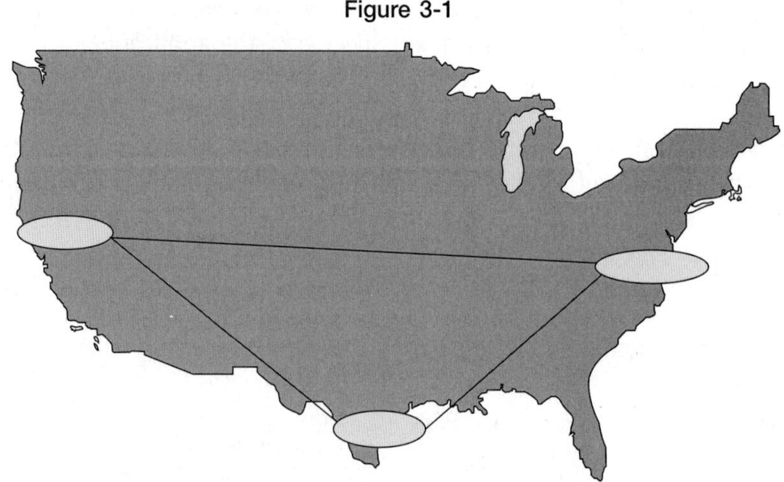

An enterprise network.

FOR EXAMPLE

The Curse of Organic Networking

Quite often, organic terms are used to describe networks. This isn't that inaccurate when you consider that most networks look like something that grew up in place rather than something carefully planned and designed. This is especially true of older networks that have gone through multiple generations of hardware, software, and various network administrators, each with his or her own idea of the "best" network design.

A network grows with the company. Even though the network growth is something that should be carefully planned and implemented, more often than not, it "just happens." Computers are added as new employees are hired. Additional cable is laid, and new hubs are added in as necessary. The cable plant branches and intertwines until it sometimes becomes difficult to figure out just what goes where.

The life cycle often goes something like this: The company starts out with a simple network, maybe no more than one or two file servers and a few clients. Other servers get added: a mail server so the company can handle its own email, a database server to handle a custom database application, maybe even a web server for internal communications. Eventually, these servers get consolidated into a secure server room for their protection.

Software features and available technologies change. The company upgrades the cable plant and pulls new cable throughout. It might upgrade hubs and other hardware at the same time or, if not, save that for later to spread out the costs. The end result, more often than not, is a mess. Crawl spaces are filled with cable going nowhere, and it's likely that no one person knows what is or isn't actually used. Troubleshooting cable problems becomes a nightmare, often making it easier to just run yet another new length of cable than try to locate and fix the correct one. Network communication is routed through different cable and support hardware, often mixing specifications that weren't designed to be mixed, and as a result, intermittent problems become a common feature of the network.

What's the solution? More often than not, the best solution is to start over. Pick an appropriate network architecture, select appropriate hardware, identify the hardware you can reuse, and rewire the network. However, this time, you need to be sure to label the new cable and, once everyone has migrated to the new network, pull out the old cable so that it's no longer a source of confusion. This solution is neither cheap nor easy, but you will probably find that it pays for itself over time in improved reliability and performance.

Enterprise networks can be enormous, with thousands of users and possibly hundreds of servers. Each office location may look like a single-server or multiserver network, except that each location is connected to the rest of the corporate WAN. Wide area networking has become a testing ground for new client/server applications, which are capable of communicating between distant servers. This extends the client/server model across many LANs, involving several servers to fulfill a user request.

SELF-CHECK

1. What is the root of modern PC network architectures?
2. What are the two most common server types?
3. What is the basic purpose of a network architecture?

3.2 Evaluating Peer-to-Peer Networking

A **peer-to-peer network** is a design in which any computer can act as both a server and a client, with no central security control. In peer-to-peer networks, users share their computers' resources with other users. Peer-to-peer networks were available as early as 1984, with Apple's **Macintosh Plus**. Microsoft introduced peer-to-peer networking capabilities in 1992, with **Windows for Workgroups 3.11**. The term most commonly used by Microsoft to describe a peer-to-peer network is a **workgroup**, which is a logical peer-to-peer grouping identified by a workgroup name.

At its most basic, a peer-to-peer network allows people to share resources such as folders, printers, and CD-ROM drives. What does this mean in practical terms? Peer-to-peer networking lets a user access a file or printer across the network, thereby reducing costs associated with a centralized server or multiple printers. The most popular peer-to-peer networks have advanced to the point that peer-to-peer networks are accessible over the Internet for use in online gaming, virtual reality, and peer-to-peer file sharing applications.

3.2.1 Understanding Peer-to-Peer Features

Peer-to-peer networking enables **decentralized resource sharing**. Specific characteristics of peer-to-peer networks include the following:

- Allow users to share many resources from their computers, including files and printers.
- Are best suited to groups of 12 or fewer users, though some manufacturers suggest configurations with up to 20 users.

Figure 3-2

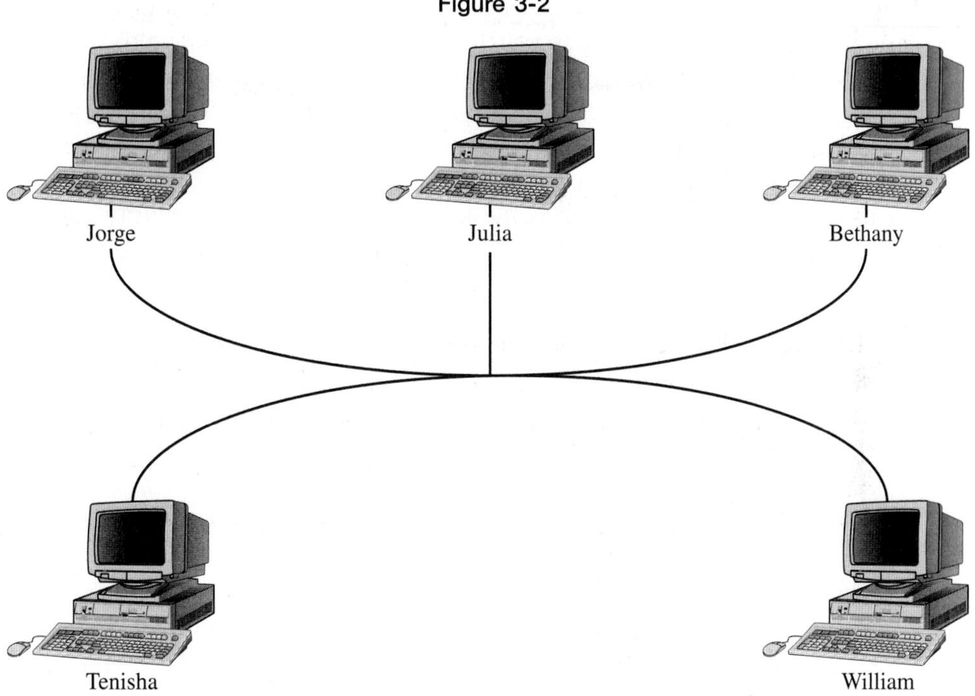

A sample peer-to-peer network.

- Are decentralized so that users' files are not stored in a central location.
- Allow computers (and users) to communicate easily.

Peer-to-peer networking is built into the operating system software on a computer. After the software is configured on each workstation, users are responsible for making their specific information available to others (i.e., sharing it) and managing the access to that information. A sample peer-to-peer network is shown in Figure 3-2.

When users are participating in the same peer network, they belong to a workgroup. The workgroup is assigned a **workgroup name**, which may represent users who work in the marketing department or the group of people who sit in the cubicles in the northeast corner of the building. Because this is a logical group, based on workgroup name, membership isn't necessarily related to the computers' physical locations on the network. The workgroup name makes it easier to remember who is participating in the peer-to-peer network. This is important when you have multiple workgroups on the same network.

3.2.2 Choosing a Peer-to-Peer Network

You must consider user needs when choosing a network architecture. You may have a business that does not have the necessary network hardware and cabling.

You should use a peer-to-peer network only when the needs are significant and budgetary constraints prevent you from using a client/server or directory-based model. Keep in mind, however, that a peer-to-peer network assumes a certain level of computer literacy because users are expected to handle their own resource sharing. If users don't have that level of expertise, then some type of client/server model might be more appropriate. Peer-to-peer networking is still used in some small businesses, but it has become less popular because of security concerns.

The following are some of the basic criteria for selecting a peer-to-peer architecture:

- ▲ Twenty or fewer users will be sharing resources.
- ▲ You don't want to include a server or don't have a server available.
- ▲ Nobody has the time or knowledge to act as a network administrator.
- ▲ There is minimal concern about security.

The following are some of the advantages of using a peer-to-peer architecture:

- ▲ Peer-to-peer networks are easy to configure.
- ▲ Networking software is already integrated in the operating system, so no additional software is required.
- ▲ These networks typically don't require additional server hardware and software.
- ▲ Users can manage their own resources.
- ▲ These networks don't require a network administrator.
- ▲ These networks reduce total cost in comparison to other network architectures.

The problem with having cost listed as a peer-to-peer networking advantage is that this usually doesn't account for **hidden costs**, such as the added cost of supporting users and correcting their mistakes. The total cost of a system can be difficult to calculate. The **total cost of ownership (TCO)** includes the cost of equipment and software as well as the cost for managing the technology. It's important to be aware of these hidden costs, which are often overlooked.

The potential disadvantages of peer-to-peer networks are relatively easy to see by looking at the architecture's features. They include the following:

- ▲ Peer-to-peer networks provide a limited number of connections for shared resources.
- ▲ Computers with shared resources may suffer from sluggish performance.
- ▲ These networks don't allow for central management.
- ▲ These networks don't provide a central location for saving files.

- ▲ Users are responsible for managing resources.
- ▲ These networks offer poor security.

A peer-to-peer network is best suited to a very small business or to a small, autonomous group within a larger company. However, there are migration paths from peer-to-peer networking to other architectures, so a company may start out with a peer-to-peer network and then move to a different network architecture as its needs change.

3.2.3 Securing a Peer-to-Peer Network

Workgroups are anything but secure. Peer-to-peer networks sometimes use **share-level security**, which gives users the authority to assign passwords to the local resources on their computers. Share-level security is a feature of Windows 95 and Windows 98, but it is not available in more recent versions such as Windows XP and Windows Vista.

Share-level security allows a person who is sharing a resource to implement security with a password or, by not assigning a password, the person can let anyone on the network use the resource. In some older operating systems, assigning a password to protect a resource required that the password be given to all the people who needed to be able to access that resource. Passwords that are shared seldom stay secret, or secure, for very long.

The same password could be assigned to every resource, but this would be like a building manager creating the same key for every apartment in the building. Figure 3-3 demonstrates a better security scheme, which is to use a different key for each apartment. In peer-to-peer networking, assigning each resource a unique password minimizes the security risks. The drawback, however, is that managing the

Figure 3-3

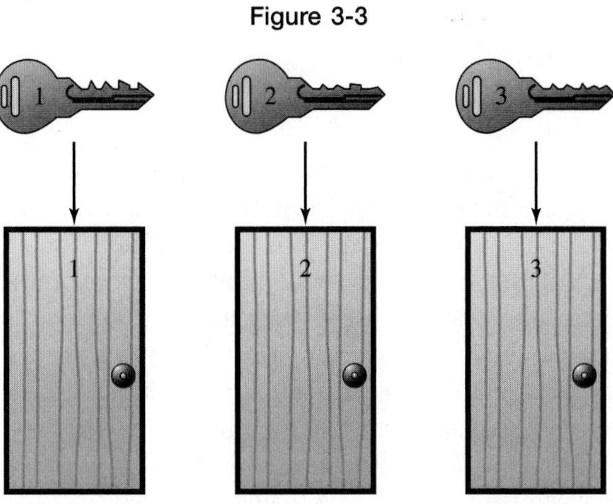

Peer-to-peer security.

passwords can be more difficult. For example, it could mean that users not only have to remember multiple passwords but the resources with which the passwords are associated. This can result in users keeping a password list handy in a desk drawer, taped under the keyboard, or even posted on a display screen for all to see.

Modern operating systems provide better security than peer-to-peer security. Windows 2000, XP Professional, and Vista, Macintosh OS 9 and OS X, and Linux all support a user-management feature that allows you to assign a separate username and password for each individual. But once again, users and their passwords are being created and managed individually on each workstation. You can also manage security through groups of users, but group management is usually more trouble than it's worth at this level. The decentralized model of a peer-to-peer network makes for a cumbersome system because you have to create a user account for each user who needs access on each computer sharing resources. When passwords change, they have to be manually changed on each computer.

In Windows XP, the default file-sharing configuration is known as simple file sharing. With **simple file sharing**, you can share folders and their contents with the members of your workgroup. You can control access to the data, but the same permissions are granted for all workgroup members. If you want to control access permissions by user or group, you need to disable simple file sharing through the computer's folder options. Note that Windows Vista by default does not allow simple file sharing. Access to shared folders requires a user name and password. Members of a workgroup can share files and folders either directly from their computer via share permissions, or from a Public folder.

3.2.4 Implementing a Peer-to-Peer Network

Implementing a peer-to-peer network typically involves three steps:

1. Install network hardware.
2. Configure the peers and workgroup members.
3. Share resources with the network.

The basic hardware requirements are common to most LANs, without regard to the network architecture: You need a network adapter installed in each network member and a communication path. Nearly all computers come with an Ethernet network adapter integrated in the motherboard circuitry, so for a wired network, you just need to lay the cable plant and connect the computers. These requirements are shown in Figure 3-4. Most laptops ship with wireless networking built in, often eliminating the need for a physical cable plant.

To configure network members, you configure the network communication properties, which depend on your communication protocol, and identify the computer as a workgroup member. The dialog box used to configure a Windows XP computer as a workgroup member is shown in Figure 3-5. This is also where

Figure 3-4

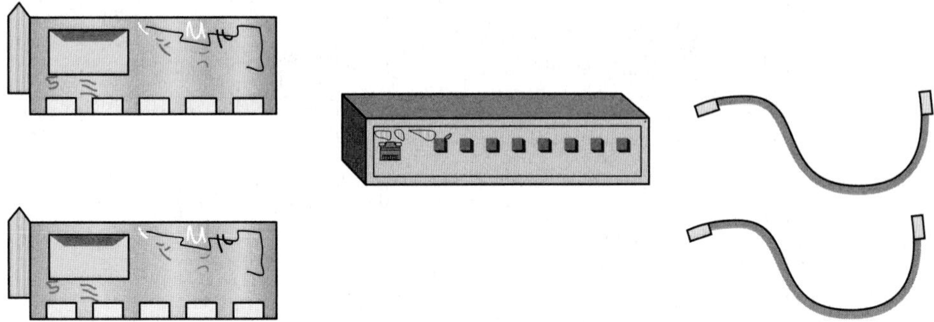

Network hardware requirements.

Figure 3-5

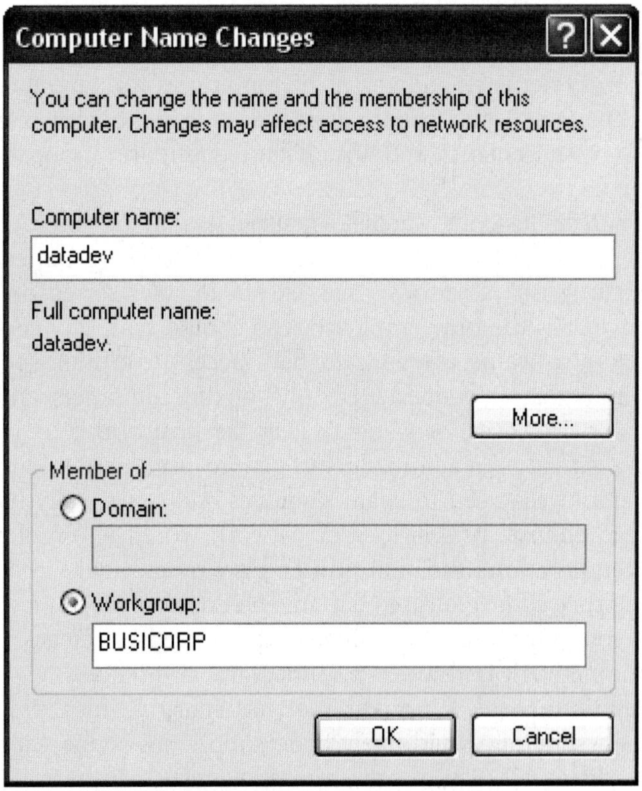

Computer Name Changes

You can change the name and the membership of this computer. Changes may affect access to network resources.

Computer name:

datadev

Full computer name:

datadev.

More...

Member of

Domain:

Workgroup:

BUSICORP

OK Cancel

Configuring a workgroup name.

you configure membership in an Active Directory domain. Active Directory is Microsoft's term for its version of directory services networking. Directory services networking is discussed in Section 3.4.1.

The procedures for sharing resources depend on the operating system and version. You specify share-level security or access permissions when you share a resource, but you can change them later, as necessary.

FOR EXAMPLE

The Birth of a Network

Busicorp started out as a small custom print shop. Over the years, the business has grown to offer not only printing services but reproduction, editing, and graphics services as well. The company has Internet access through a cable modem, and the company's six employees use email addresses provided through the company's ISP. The problem is that each employee has to log in through the same computer, the only one with access to the Internet, to check or send mail.

All of Busicorp's computers run Windows XP Professional and have built-in Ethernet network adapters. The employees all have quite a bit of computer experience, and each can manage his or her own computer's configuration requirements and install and configure applications when needed.

The owner of Busicorp wants to make it easier for employees to collaborate on projects. He wants to make it easier to share project files and graphics. Security isn't a serious issue, except for files stored on one computer. The owner is the only employee who should have any access to that computer. He also wants everyone to have access to a high-speed, multifunction printer that is connected to one of the computers and used for most print jobs. However, he wants to keep the cost of this to a minimum.

This is a situation ready-made for peer-to-peer networking: A small number of employees need to share resources and don't really have a need for centralized control. A peer-to-peer network would let employees share project files and the multifunction printer. Employees would also be able to share the Internet connection so that anyone could manage email from his or her own computer. The only thing Busicorp needs to create this configuration is the network hardware to connect the computers.

What about the one computer that has sensitive files? For the time being, the best solution would likely be to simply not connect it to the network. That's the surest way of protecting it against unauthorized access.

SELF-CHECK

1. What are the basic criteria for selecting peer-to-peer networking?
2. What are the two security methods supported in a peer-to-peer networking environment?
3. What are the basic steps for implementing a peer-to-peer network?

3.3 Evaluating Client/Server Networking

Companies have traditionally chosen the client/server architecture instead of peer-to-peer networking because it better meets their needs. Client/server network architectures yield cost savings because they centralize resources, data, and security. One reason for the added security is that it is easier to secure important information when it is located in one place. Centralization also makes it easier to protect information in the event of a fire or other disaster. Client/server architectures offer a performance improvement over peer-to-peer networks by taking advantage of the processing capabilities of workstations along with the power of servers. In a client/server network, the client and the server can process information simultaneously.

3.3.1 Understanding Client/Server Networks

The **client/server network** architecture is a centralized model for data storage, security, network applications, and network administration. The client/server architectural model, along with its more recent variations, is the most common networking architecture in use today. Many companies that start with peer-to-peer networking quickly outgrow that model and have to find better networking solutions. Most end up installing some kind of client/server network.

Characteristics of client/server networks, also referred to as server-based networks, include the following:

- ▲ They are based on a scalable model that can support small networks of a few (fewer than 10) users up to large networks with thousands of users.
- ▲ They employ specialized servers that provide services to the client workstations.
- ▲ They provide shared services such as print and file services.
- ▲ They allow a high level of security, based on access permissions.
- ▲ They can be centrally managed by a network administrator or a team of network administrators.

Figure 3-6

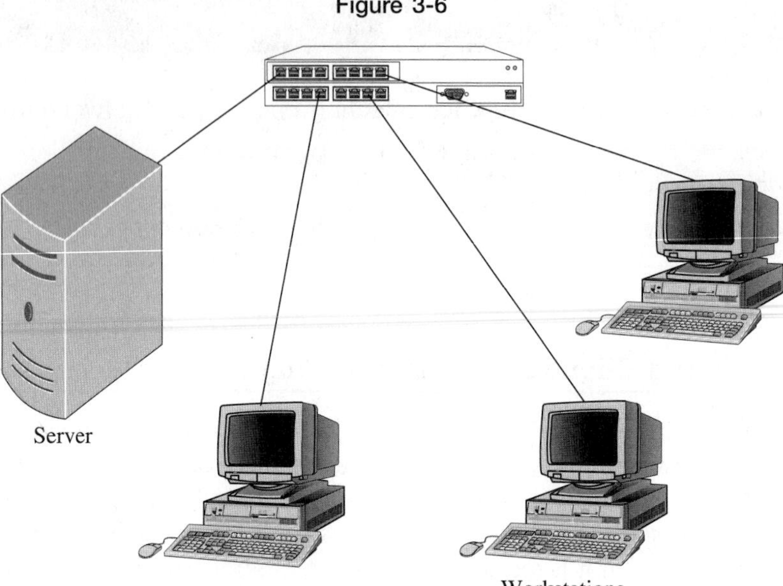

A sample client/server network.

A simple client/server network is shown in Figure 3-6. The client/server model requires network servers to be designed and implemented. The computers used as servers are often (but not always) more powerful than the network's client computers. They also run special software or operating system versions that enable them to act as network servers. In this model, most applications run locally at the client, with data stored on central file servers. In some cases, the network might include **server applications**, which are simply applications designed to run at the server and provide some service to the network (e.g., database servers, web servers).

As a company grows, it is likely that the server it started with will become less capable to meet user demands. When performance begins to degrade, it often becomes necessary to dedicate servers to specific roles, with each running different applications and performing specific tasks. It is not unusual for a large company to have two or more servers dedicated, for example, to responding to users' login requests, other services acting primarily as file servers, and others providing print services to the network.

3.3.2 Choosing a Client/Server Network

Most companies use some type of **server-based network**, either based on the traditional client/server model or on the directory services model discussed in

Section 3.4. Planning and selecting the right client/server technology is not always easy. There are several possible variations on the basic model, and recent enhancements provide even greater control and flexibility.

The following are the basic criteria for selecting a client/server network:

- ▲ Files need to be stored centrally.
- ▲ Security is important to protect sensitive and valuable data.
- ▲ Users need access to the server applications, shared data, and other resources.
- ▲ One or more network administrators will be managing the server(s).
- ▲ There are too many users for a peer-to-peer network.

You need to be sure to consider the advantages and disadvantages before investing in a client/server network. The advantages include the following:

- ▲ Data are stored centrally and can be easily backed up.
- ▲ User accounts and account security are centrally managed.
- ▲ A high level of security can be implemented at the server(s).
- ▲ Expensive resources can be shared with multiple users.
- ▲ Server hardware and software are optimized for performance and reliability.
- ▲ Users are relieved of the burden of managing resources.

The potential disadvantages of client/server networking include the following:

- ▲ Planning, design, and management are more complicated than with typical peer-to-peer networks.
- ▲ Managing servers requires dedicated staff.
- ▲ Server hardware and software can be expensive.

Server hardware expense has become less of an issue as computer costs have dropped, while the processing power and hardware resources in the typical computer have improved. However, the hardware necessary for some specialized servers, such as for a high-volume database application, can still be relatively expensive. However, this is an issue that relates to the specific application, not to the network architecture.

3.3.3 Securing a Client/Server Network

By design, client/server networks are more secure than peer-to-peer networks. First, servers centralize resources on a network, making it easier to manage resource access through user and group accounts. Managing user accounts and the resources the users have access to is the responsibility of the network

Figure 3-7

A revised security example.

administrator or administration staff, not individual users. Finally, servers offer stronger security features, such as sophisticated authentication systems.

Let's revisit the earlier example comparing network security to keys and apartments. In Figure 3-7, the apartment tenants Sue, Julia, and Bethany live in the same apartment building. When they moved in, the apartment manager gave each person a separate key that was unique to her apartment. The apartment manager keeps track of who has what key. If someone loses a key, the apartment manager will reissue a duplicate only to the person who was originally assigned the key.

Now say that Sue, Julia, and Bethany are also coworkers. Each has been assigned a password. The names they use to log on to the network, called usernames or login names, and their passwords differentiate them from each other. When the network administrator grants one of them permission to use a resource, that person has been given a "key" that applies only to that user.

Most server-based networking products also let you define groups of users. When you grant access permissions to groups, the same permissions are granted to the group members (unless explicitly blocked). This makes sense in a network environment because groups of users often do similar tasks and need similar access permissions. When you need to make changes, you can make the changes to the group rather than to each individual user, providing for more efficient use of network administrators' time and effort.

3.3.4 Implementing a Client/Server Network

Except for the additional servers, the network hardware required for a client/server network is generally the same as for a peer-to-peer network. The difference is not so much in the type of hardware required as in the volume of hardware. More computers mean more NICs, more cable, and more hubs. If the network becomes large enough, you might need to use routers to break the network into smaller **segments**, which are individual network sections designed so that most of the traffic generated remains local to that segment. As the network grows, you may also need to include wide area connection hardware in the network design.

In general, implementing server-based networks is not as simple as implementing peer-to-peer networks. There are many ways to design server-based networks. Likewise, there are many ways to configure hardware and software for servers. Selecting the right design depends on the size of the organization, the network requirements, and the cost. The traditional client/server network is less often used as a network architecture and is most often seen in older networks of companies that haven't had the need or the budget to migrate to newer architectural models. Still, even in newer architectures, you might see individual servers that operate on the client/server model. This model is commonly seen, for example, in database servers.

Implementing a Single-Server Network

When a company outgrows its peer-to-peer network, it usually adds a server and converts the network into a client/server network. Many companies, knowing that they are too large for a peer-to-peer architecture, start out with this design. You saw a simple example of a single-server network in Figure 3-6. The network capacity and the number of users that the network can support depend on various factors, such as the network operating system, the software that runs on the network servers, and the server hardware configuration. Network servers are typically designed to support hundreds of users but realistically can provide optimum support for a significantly smaller number.

Server capacity may be further reduced by other requirements placed on the server. When you configure a network with a single server, not only is that server responsible for processing user logins and handling user security, it typically also acts as a file and print server. You also have a potential problem in that the server represents a **single point of failure**—that is, if the server fails, so does the network.

Implementing a Multiserver Network

It's common to see companies, even small businesses, deploy client/server networks based on multiple servers, known as a **multiserver network**. One reason is avoiding the potential problems that could result from a server failure on a single-server network. Also, because servers can provide a variety of functions, you often see multiple servers, with each providing different services. The number of users on this type of network varies widely by company but often reaches hundreds or even thousands of users, though at the higher end of that range, they can become very difficult to manage.

Many companies go to a multiserver design, like the one in Figure 3-8, because it provides improved user support. That is because separating services across multiple servers improves performance and reliability. Each server can be optimized to run a particular service. If one service fails, other servers continue to function normally and, in some cases, can even take over for the malfunctioning server. Notice that the network configuration is more complex than that of a single-server network and can grow to become even more complex with time and added requirements.

Figure 3-8

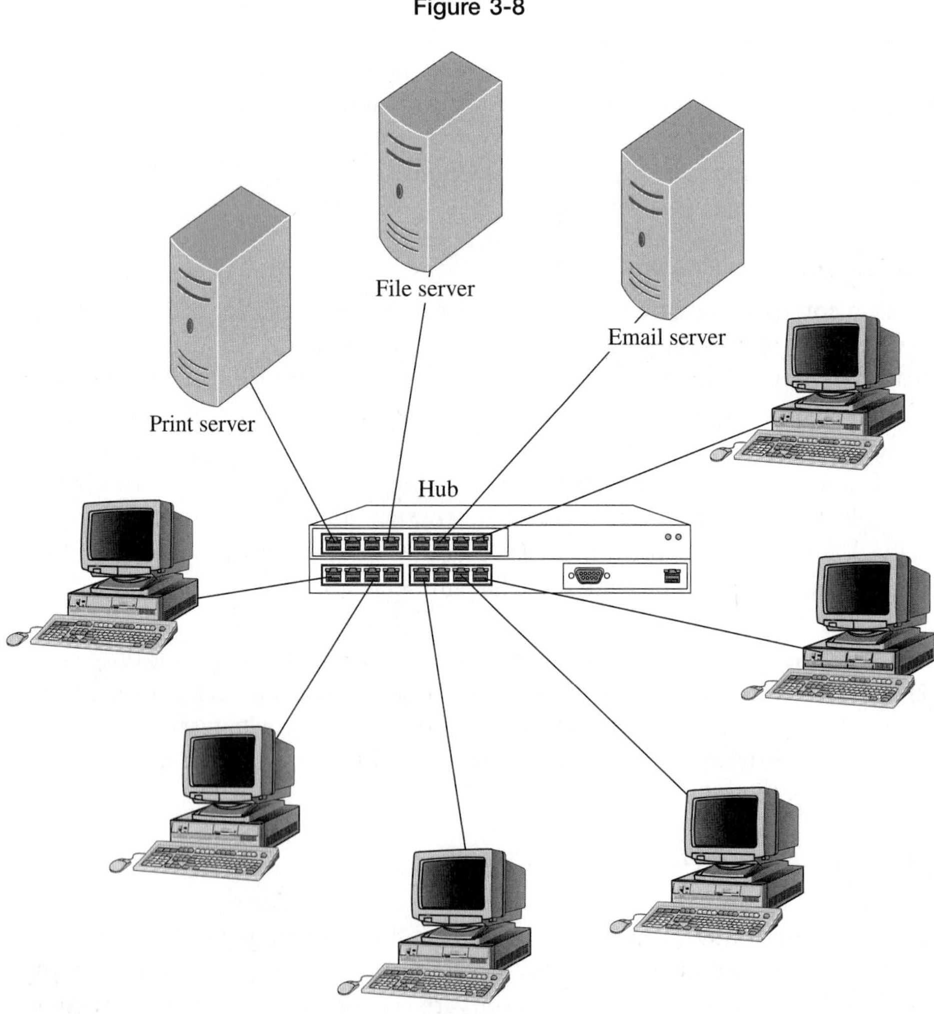

A simple multiserver network.

Figure 3-9

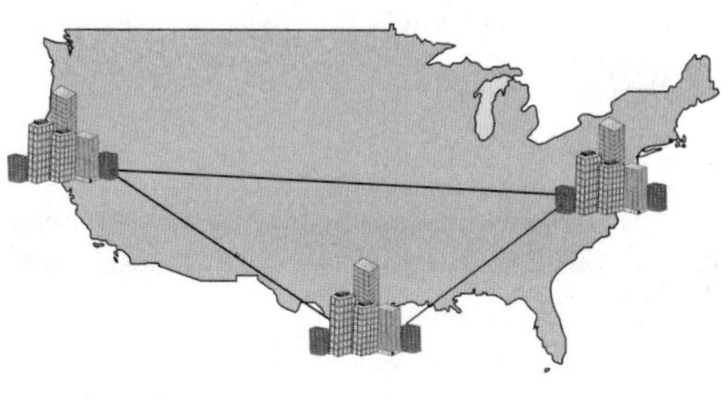

A WAN.

This model can be expanded over a wide area by connecting individual LANs, as shown in Figure 3-9. Users can access not only the servers in their own local networks but also the servers in the remote networks. Typically, you want to keep the resources that a user most often needs local to that user to minimize network traffic and management concerns. Figure 3-9 shows a multiserver network; note that it is more complex than a single-server network.

To get a better idea of what is happening with client/server models over WAN links, let's consider an example based on Figure 3-9: Julia, a user in San Francisco, needs information from Sue, a user in Washington, DC. Julia sends an email message routed through a messaging server on her local network. The message is forwarded through the network in Chicago, finally arriving at the messaging server in Washington and through that server to Sue. In this multiserver example,

FOR EXAMPLE

Growing Your Network

Each server in a multiserver network means more costs (for computer hardware and software) and more management overhead. Not only do you have the cost of the computer, which is often the smallest investment, you have the cost of the operating system and any additional server applications. Why go to the expense? Because you need to if you want to have an efficient and reliable network.

How do you determine the best time to expand your network? A company may avoid that decision as long as possible, sometimes until it is forced to make the decision while the network is down and waiting for the server to be repaired. A better way is to closely monitor network activity to determine the cost of downtime, as a monetary justification, and the perceived server performance, which is key to keeping users satisfied. When any load becomes too much, or too much of a risk, for a single server, it's time to expand.

email servers are deployed in each local network. Typically, the network would also have, at minimum, a server in each location to process users' login requests and evaluate access security.

1. Why is having a single server a potential risk?
2. What are the potential disadvantages of a server-based network?
3. What is an indication that server capacity is approaching its physical limits?

3.4 Evaluating Directory Services Networking

Many see directory services networks as an evolutionary development from the traditional client/server network root. There are some who might argue that directory services doesn't qualify as a separate architecture, but even so, it deserves separate mention because of the significant differences between how it and traditional client/server networks manage security, resource management, and resource access.

Immediately popular after their initial release, directory services networks have quickly replaced many, if not most, traditional client/server networks, especially in large companies and large enterprise networks. However, this is not meant to imply that directory services architecture is limited to large networks. In fact, it scales from the very small to the very large, meeting the networking needs of most organizations. Directory services networks provide great flexibility and enhanced security, and they are, by design, well suited to **heterogeneous networking** environments that have a mix of hardware platforms, operating systems, and server applications.

3.4.1 Understanding Directory Services Networking

Like a client/server network architecture, the **directory services network** (also known as a **directory-based network**) is based on a centralized model for security and resource management. Directory services networks are built around an **object model** where everything in the network is treated as a **directory object** (i.e., an entity that belongs to the directory). This includes the servers that manage login processing and security and **resource servers** that provide resources to the network, users, groups, security definitions, and even directory services–aware applications. The two major networking software manufacturers, Microsoft and Novell, have migrated their server products to a directory services network model.

Figure 3-10

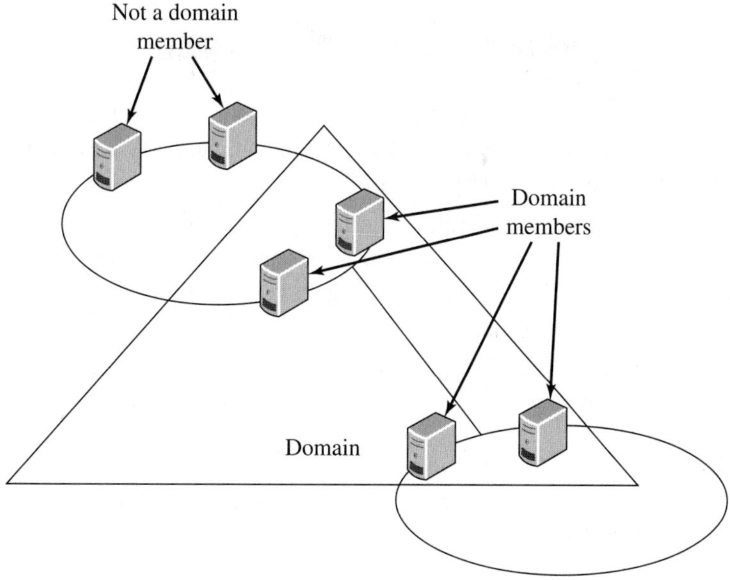

A sample domain.

The easiest way to understand a directory services network is to look at a specific example. Microsoft refers to its implementation of directory services as **Active Directory**. Active Directory uses domains, which are groups of directory services objects, as security boundaries. A simplified example is shown in Figure 3-10. It's important that you understand that this is a logical, not physical, organization.

Domain members—users and computers assigned to a domain—can be physically located anywhere on the organization's network. A domain resource server, for example, is commonly referred to as a **member server**, and it can be any server that is part of the domain except those that manage the directory and security functions, such as user logins. Everything within a domain is managed through a centralized security model, and an object such as a user or computer can belong to one domain only. Access to resources within the domain, as well as the user's rights and privileges within the domain, are based on a single login. Network administrators can also define resource access between domains, which gives you increased flexibility in managing large organizations and providing a way for organizations to work together and share resources.

Characteristics of directory services–based networking include the following:

- Directory services networking is based on a model that scales from very small to very large organizations, including wide area enterprise networks.

- ▲ Specialized servers, sometimes referred to as **domain controllers**, process user authentication and authorization.
- ▲ Directory services networking uses a logical security boundary, called a **domain**, that centralizes security and resource management.
- ▲ Directory services networking provides flexible security for shared resources, including management of server applications designed for use in a directory services environment.
- ▲ Directory services networking provides a high level of security, with detailed control over rights and permissions and the ability to **audit**, which involves tracking and recording user activity on the network.
- ▲ A directory services network is centrally managed, from a logical standpoint, but network administrators can be located anywhere on the network, as long as they have access to domain controllers.

The domain controller (i.e., the network security server) is key to the design of a directory services network. In an Active Directory network, you define a domain by promoting a Windows server to the domain controller role. The directory containing all domain objects, including security definitions, is maintained on the domain controllers. As shown in Figure 3-11, changes made to any domain controller are propagated to other domain controllers automatically, keeping all copies of the directory synchronized. This means that any domain controller can authenticate user logins and authorize user access to domain resources. It also means that keeping at least one domain controller up and running at all times is critical to the network, so it is strongly recommended that you have at least two domain controllers for any domain, no matter how small.

In addition to user authentication and authorization, Windows servers acting as domain controllers can also support other roles, including those of file servers, print servers, or even running server applications. However, this is discouraged in all but the smallest of networks because there is a great deal of overhead involved in supporting user access, and when you force the server to support additional roles, overall domain performance usually suffers.

3.4.2 Choosing a Directory Services Network

Organizations began deploying directory services–based networks even before the software on which they are based was officially released, acting as live test cases for the software manufacturers. Though it is not a strict requirement in every case, as most companies upgrade to the most recent versions of their chosen server operating systems, they also migrate to a directory services networking environment. The greater flexibility, enhanced management capabilities, and enhanced security are primary motivating factors. Another important

Figure 3-11

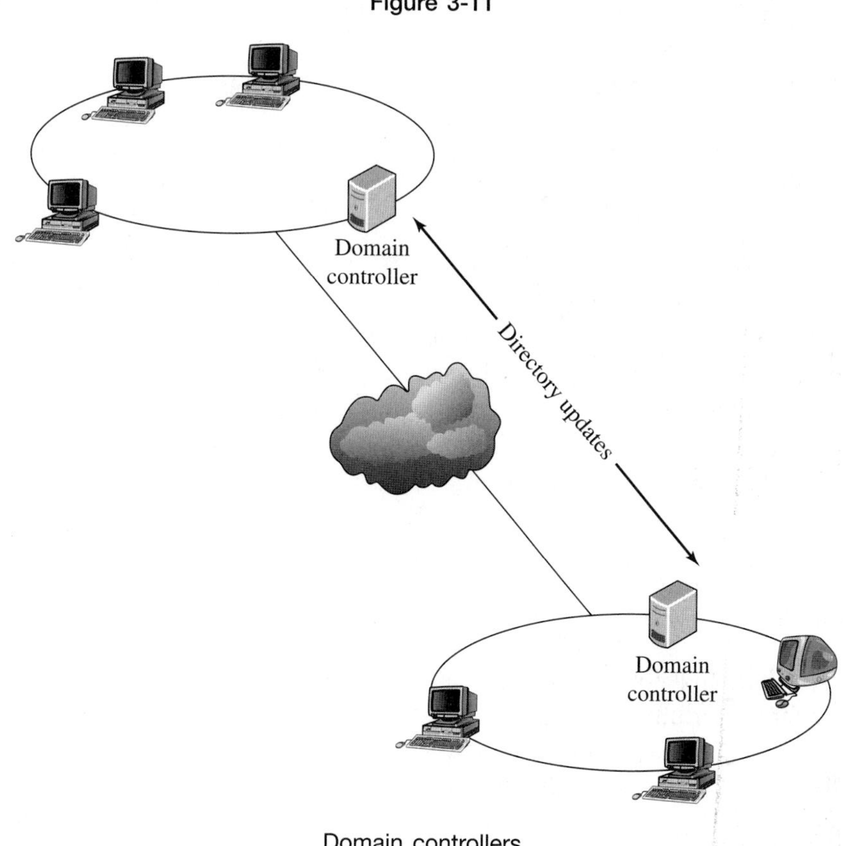

Domain controllers.

factor is that manufacturers are gradually phasing out support for earlier server software versions, and with it, support for more traditional client/server networking models.

The following are the basic criteria for selecting a directory services network:

- ▲ You need to support more users than can easily be supported in a peer-to-peer networking architecture.
- ▲ There is a need for centralized management of network resources.
- ▲ Security is a primary concern, and you need detailed control over security and access management.
- ▲ You need to define multiple logical security boundaries, with different security and management requirements for each.
- ▲ One or more domain administrators will be managing the network domain(s).

We've already touched on several of the advantages of a directory services network:

- ▲ It is a flexible, highly secure environment.
- ▲ Domain objects, including users, computers, and domain resources, are centrally managed.
- ▲ You can group both users and computers for management purposes.
- ▲ Security boundaries are defined through logical domains and not limited by physical locations, as long as communication paths exist.
- ▲ You can define security between domains.
- ▲ A directory services network provides support for heterogeneous networking.
- ▲ Management responsibilities default to domain administrators but can be delegated at a granular level to other administrators, managers, and users.

Before you get the idea that this is a perfect networking environment, you need to realize that there are innate disadvantages, including the following:

- ▲ Network and domain designs can quickly become very complex and potentially difficult to maintain.
- ▲ Domain administrators require specialized training because of the complexity of the environment and management options.
- ▲ At least one domain controller needs to be up and running at all times.
- ▲ Administrators must have access, either directly or across the network via management utilities, to a domain controller when making any change to the domain.

Some changes, such as moving a computer from one domain to another, are relatively easy to make. However, careful planning is required because other changes, such as moving users or changing domain names, can be relatively difficult. A directory services network is an environment where you want to avoid letting administrators just "learn as they go." Mistakes can be disastrous and expensive. Even though small domains can be relatively easy to maintain, the number of management options can quickly become confusing as you move beyond the most basic administrative activities.

3.4.3 Securing a Directory Services Network

As stated earlier, one of the key features of a directory services network is the high level of security. Both network servers and clients are configured as part of the directory of the domain, which makes it possible to organize them into

Figure 3-12

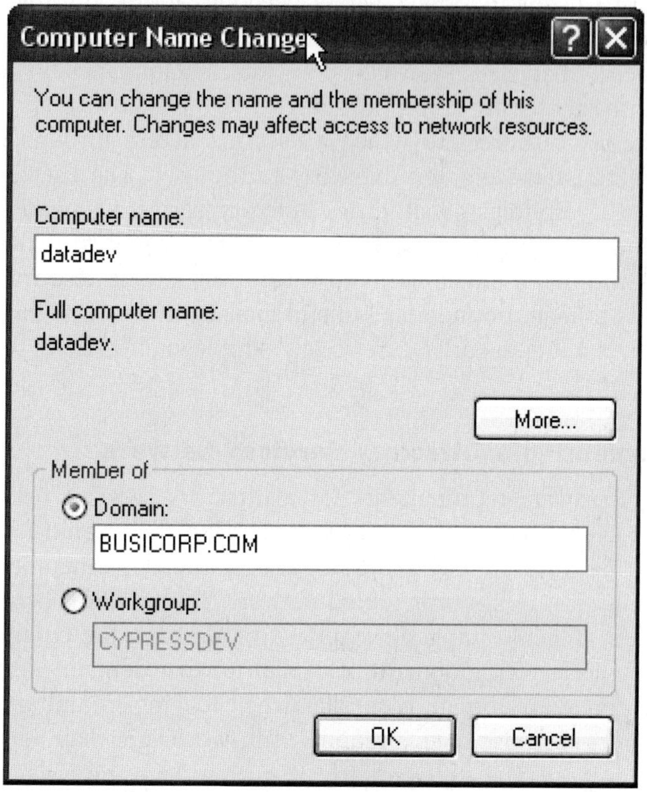

Domain membership.

groups and centrally manage local security and computer properties. You can see this in Figure 3-12, which shows how you would add a Windows XP computer as a member of a domain. When you make this change, you are prompted for the name and password for a user who is authorized to make this change. Whether any user can join computers to a domain depends on the Windows Server version on which the network is based. For security reasons, with Windows 2000 Server, not everyone can join a computer to a domain. With Windows Server 2003, any user can join up to 10 computers to a domain. It is necessary to restart the Windows XP computer before the change takes affect.

You also have various ways of organizing users into the groups available, with the end effect of making it significantly easier to manage resource access because most management requirements can be handled as a group, rather than at the individual user level.

Current Windows operating systems allow you control over user passwords, giving you a way of raising the bar on network security. Not only can you require all users to have passwords, you can also set requirements for password length and complexity. Current Windows Server versions require **complex passwords** by default, which means passwords that include a mix of numbers, letters, and nonalphanumeric characters. You can even check automatically for passwords that appear to be too easily compromised.

You define the resources to which a user has access through group membership and permissions granted explicitly to the user. The user gets access to all the domain's resources—including directory services—aware applications and applications such as database applications, messaging or mail servers, and web servers—through a single login. You can even define resource access permissions across domain boundaries but still manage them through the same single user login, making security a relatively simple matter from the context of the domain user.

3.4.4 Implementing a Directory Services Network

The network hardware requirements for a directory services network are the same as for a client/server network and depend on the size and complexity of the network. Because domains are logical definitions, membership is not restricted by physical location or routed network boundaries. There is, however, a limiting factor: When joining a computer to a domain, the computer must be able to communicate with a domain controller for that domain. Also, users need to be able to contact a domain controller when logging in and when accessing domain resources. Because of this requirement, when a domain is spread across wide area links, you typically want to place a domain controller in each geographic location, as shown in Figure 3-11. Keep in mind that this increases the background traffic across the links because of the need to keep the domain controllers synchronized, but this traffic is usually minimal.

A key part of the design process is designing your domain or domains. Your domain design determines how you manage network security and access. This process can sometimes become very complex. A detailed discussion of domain design is beyond the scope of this book, but a few key points should be mentioned. When you design a multiple-domain environment, each domain must have a unique name, as shown in Figure 3-13. Also, you have a hierarchical domain structure, with parent and child domains. This structure is sometimes referred to as a **domain tree**. The uppermost domain is known as the **root domain**. Domains can also be organized into larger entities that are effectively groups of domains, known as **forests**.

In the domain structure in Figure 3-13, the root domain is Busicorp.com. This name is used as the name suffix for all member computers in that domain. There are also two child domains: Ops.busicorp.com and Product.busicorp.com. You might create such domains, for example, so that you can have different management and security structures for different divisions within an organization,

Figure 3-13

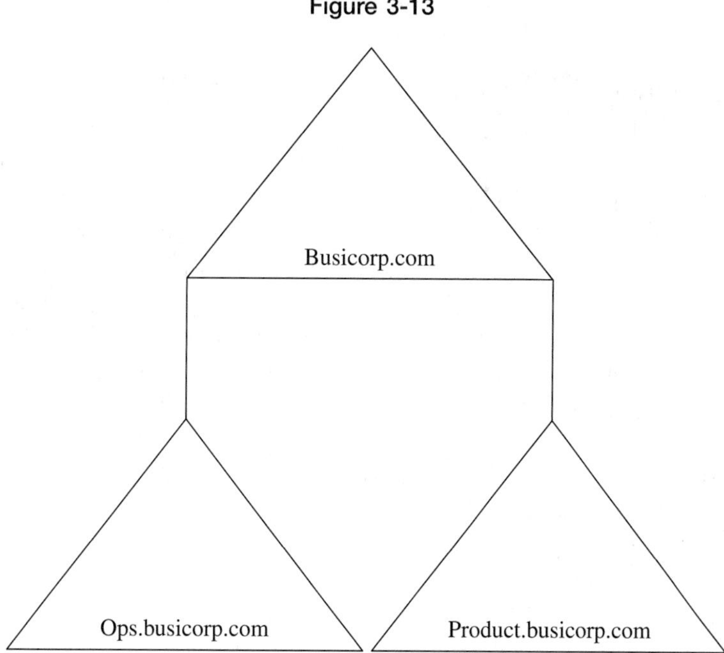

A hierarchical domain structure.

while still letting users in those different divisions share resources and work together in a collaborative environment.

You need to determine how the physical design of your network impacts the logical design. The network's physical design affects factors such as placement of domain controllers and resource servers. In most cases, you want to try to keep resources physically close to the users who most often need access to them to improve performance and to keep network traffic, especially over potentially slower wide area links, to a minimum.

As a final word on domain names, as long as you keep a domain private (i.e., don't expose it directly to the Internet), you don't have to register the domain name. A name used on the Internet, such as Microsoft.com, must be registered and can be used only by the entity (i.e., person or company) to which it is registered. If you want to put a public face on your organization, such as a publicly accessible web server, you need a registered domain name. However, even if you do register the name you use on your network domain, exposing your domain directly to the Internet is strongly discouraged because it opens a vast number of potential security holes. Access to the Internet should always be protected by a **firewall**, which filters all traffic into and out of your network, or a similar security device. Many networks set up multiple layers of security devices between themselves and the Internet.

FOR EXAMPLE

Working within Your Architecture

Directory-based networks such as Microsoft's Active Directory provide different options for grouping users and computers. One of these is through the use of **organizational units (OUs)**, which are like containers that hold other directory objects, such as users and computers. One key point about OUs is that from the standpoints of the administrator and security, they can be somewhat autonomous logical boundaries within the larger boundary of the domain. What this means to you is that you have a way of setting up a structure that is functionally similar to a workgroup environment without leaving the security protections and control of the domain. You can delegate rights and permissions, including administrative-level permission, within an OU so that they apply only to the objects in the OU. You can put your workgroup members and their computers (and no one else) into an OU and set up security to meet their specific requirements. As a protective measure, ultimate control and responsibility can be maintained at the domain administrator level, giving the administrators the ability to override anything done at the OU level, if necessary.

SELF-CHECK

1. What is the role of a domain?
2. Describe the basic security model of a directory services network.
3. What is the relationship between the logical and physical network designs in a directory services network?

3.5 Recognizing Hybrid Architectures

In today's ever-changing network environments, it is possible to see variations and combinations of the basic networking architectures described in this chapter. Organization structures often require flexibility and a certain amount of innovation in designing a network that's a match to operational requirements. For example, in large organizations in which client/server or directory services network architectures are implemented, it may be difficult for small, independent groups of people to work efficiently without getting bogged down in the structural overhead. **Hybrid networks** allow various standard network architectures to coexist on the same network. With such an architecture, small groups of users can easily share files and other resources without requiring the intervention of the network administrator.

3.5.1 Using Hybrid Architectures

Hybrid networks incorporate the best features of workgroups in peer-to-peer networks with the performance, security, and reliability of server- or directory-based networks. In large corporate networks, users often do not have the ability to share files. The information technology department typically provides users with the ability to use their workstations and nothing more. Users can't make changes to their workstations. This tight security is needed to prevent the introduction of illegal applications and viruses and to simplify workstation support.

The specifics of how you can implement a hybrid network vary between manufacturers, but the basic idea is that hybrid networks provide the centralized services of servers, and they also allow users to share and manage their own resources. A sample network is shown in Figure 3-14. After a user in a workgroup logs in to the network, the user doesn't have to have any other interactions with the server while accessing shared files in the workgroup. However, this configuration is

Figure 3-14

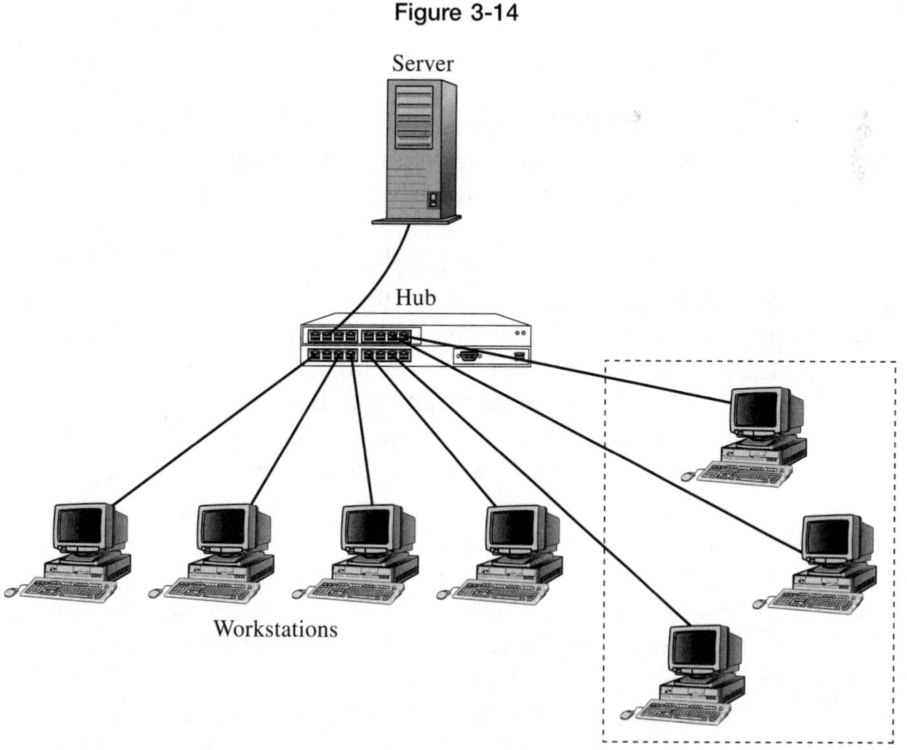

A hybrid network.

supported in limited situations only. Windows Server 2003, for example, does not support a hybrid network based on this configuration.

The advantages of hybrid networks include the following:

- ▲ Server applications are centrally located and managed.
- ▲ Users can assign local access to resources on their computers.
- ▲ Users can manage resources without requiring assistance from the network administrator.

FOR EXAMPLE

Considering Migration to a Different Network Architecture

Busicorp has grown too large to continue working as a peer-to-peer network. You're ready to make the jump into a network architecture designed for larger organizations. What exactly does this mean? It means that you're going to make the jump from peer servers to real network servers, with operating systems such as Windows Server 2003. However, you don't want to jump straight into a new environment without first considering the changes. You need to determine what you need as a domain structure. You'll be able to get by with a single domain. Truthfully, most organizations, even those that have deployed multiple domains, could get by just as well (maybe better) in a single domain.

Migrating to a network architecture designed for larger organizations also means that your security structure—and your network culture—is going to change. You are moving from distributed to centralized security and resource management, which means users will no longer have complete control over their computers or the resources hosted on them. As their computers join the domain, domain administrators are added to the local security structure and have the ability to make changes directly to the client computers. Even though this means less work for your users in the long run, some users might have trouble adjusting to this change and to the idea that someone else has access to their computers and control over their security. On the plus side, it means that newly hired employees don't need to be quite as computer literate because they won't be responsible for things like resource sharing or security management.

Changing network environments is a major shift that affects all network users. Going into the process, you need to expect that it's going to require an adjustment period as employees get used to the new environment and accept that there may be some people who never fully embrace the changes. However, whether users embrace the changes doesn't make much difference in the long run; once administrative functions are centralized, they'll have to learn to live with it, like it or not.

The following are some of the disadvantages of hybrid networks:

- Network access can become burdensome for the users.
- Users may need to remember multiple passwords.
- Files can be duplicated and changes overwritten between the computer with the shared folder and the server.
- Files saved on the workstation are not backed up.

Before deploying a hybrid architecture, you need to carefully consider your requirements and the capabilities of your primary network architecture. You may find that it is just as easy, and definitely more secure, to configure the requirements through features provided in your server- or directory-based network.

3.5.2 Separating Workgroups

One hybrid architecture design you might see is to have a peer-to-peer network that resides on the same physical network as a server- or directory-based network but not taking part in that logical security structure. For example, you could do this with Windows XP or Windows Vista computers by configuring them as workgroup members rather than as domain members. Because the computers are not taking part in the domain, they are neither restricted nor protected by domain security, so workgroups can become a security risk. You might consider using an internal firewall to segregate the workgroup on its own screened subnet as a way of protecting both it and the domain. A **subnet** is a physical network division within a larger physical network, and a **screened subnet** is a subnet that is isolated from the rest of the physical network by a firewall.

Another justification for doing this is that you don't want the rest of the domain to be aware of or have access to whatever the workgroup members are doing. For example, you might use this structure to isolate a product design group. In that case, not only does the firewall protect the domain from the workgroup, it also protects workgroup members and their work from the domain.

SELF-CHECK

1. In general terms, what is a hybrid architecture?
2. When setting up both a directory-based and peer-to-peer network on the same physical network, how can you minimize the potential security risks inherent in the peer-to-peer network?

SUMMARY

This chapter introduced and discussed basic network architecture models, including basic network requirements and the advantages and disadvantages of each. You learned about network architecture evolution and basic server types. You were introduced to the peer-to-peer, client/server (i.e., server-based), and directory services (i.e., directory-based) network architectures. You also learned about hybrid architectures, which are combinations based on standard network architectures.

KEY TERMS

Active Directory
Audit
Client/server network
Complex password
Decentralized resource sharing
Directory object
Directory services network
Directory-based network
Domain
Domain controller
Domain member
Domain tree
Economies of scale
Enterprise network
File server
Firewall
Forest
Heterogeneous networking
Hidden cost
Host-based network
Hybrid network
Macintosh Plus
Member server
Multiserver network
Network architecture
Network topology
Object model
Organizational unit (OU)
Peer-to-peer network
Print job
Print queue
Print server
Resource server
Root domain
Screened subnet
Segment
Server application
Server-based network
Share-level security
Simple file sharing
Single point of failure
Spooler file
Spooling
Subnet
Telnet
Total cost of ownership (TCO)
Windows for Workgroups 3.11
Workgroup
Workgroup name

ASSESS YOUR UNDERSTANDING

Go to www.wiley.com/college/ciccarelli to evaluate your knowledge of network architectures.
Measure your learning by comparing pre-test and post-test results.

Summary Questions

1. In which network type do network users take responsibility for resource sharing and access security?
   (a) peer-to-peer
   (b) client/server
   (c) server-based
   (d) directory-based
2. A disadvantage of host-based computing is that there is no central control. True or false?
3. On what kind of server would you most likely expect to find a spooler file?
   (a) file server
   (b) print server
   (c) messaging server
   (d) application server
4. A network architecture provides the blueprint for designing and implementing a network. True or false?
5. A workgroup is a logical peer-to-peer grouping. True or false?
6. What is the maximum number of users a peer-to-peer network should have?
   (a) 5
   (b) 20
   (c) 100
   (d) 500
7. Which of the following is *not* a feature of a client/server network?
   (a) centralized security management
   (b) centralized resource management
   (c) dedicated administrative personnel
   (d) user control of resources

8. How are computers organized for security management purposes in a directory-based network?
   (a) by physical location in the network
   (b) by domain membership
   (c) by network address
   (d) by workgroup name
9. Which of the following is considered a disadvantage of a client/server network?
   (a) It is difficult to manage data storage and backups.
   (b) It is the least secure network architecture.
   (c) It requires dedicated management staff.
   (d) User accounts are managed locally on each network computer.
10. When designing a traditional client/server network, you must consider the number of users, ______________________, and geographic location.
   (a) resource requirements
   (b) transmission media
   (c) communication protocol
   (d) domain names
11. The topmost domain in a hierarchical domain structure is known as the root domain. True or false?
12. A forest is a group of servers in a server-based network. True or false?
13. In a directory-based network, resource servers are also known as what?
   (a) domain controllers
   (b) member servers
   (c) organizational units
   (d) child domains
14. Domain membership is determined strictly by a computer's location on the physical network. True or false?
15. What is the logical security boundary in a directory services network?
   (a) a domain
   (b) a hybrid network
   (c) a subnet
   (d) a firewall
16. What is a hybrid network?
   (a) a network containing heterogeneous computers
   (b) another name for a peer-to-peer network

(c) a network architecture that combines two or more standard architectures
(d) a security boundary in a directory services network

Applying This Chapter

1. For each of the following, identify the network architecture or architectures (peer-to-peer, client/server, or directory services) that most closely match(es) the specified requirements.
   (a) Users must be able to share resources from their computers and manage resource security.
   (b) You have slightly more than 50 users but want to keep the network design as simple as possible.
   (c) You need central control over network resources.
   (d) You want to be able to use different security boundaries.
   (e) You want to use a distributed security model.
2. You need to implement a network that will have three physical locations connected by wide area links. For security purposes, you want to divide users by the four departments, each of which has very different security and resource requirements. However, there are users from each department in each of the physical locations.
   (a) What type of network architecture should you use?
   (b) How can you organize users for security purposes?
   (c) In general, how will access security be managed?
   (d) How do you identify computers that are part of each department?

YOU TRY IT

Contrasting Directory-Based Networks

1. Research features of directory-based network as implemented by Novell and Microsoft.
2. Compare and contrast the two models, pointing out key similarities and differences.

Migrating to a Directory-Based Network

1. Describe the impact on users of migrating from a server-based to a directory-based network. Assume a multiple-server network in each case.
2. Describe the impact on network designers and administrators.

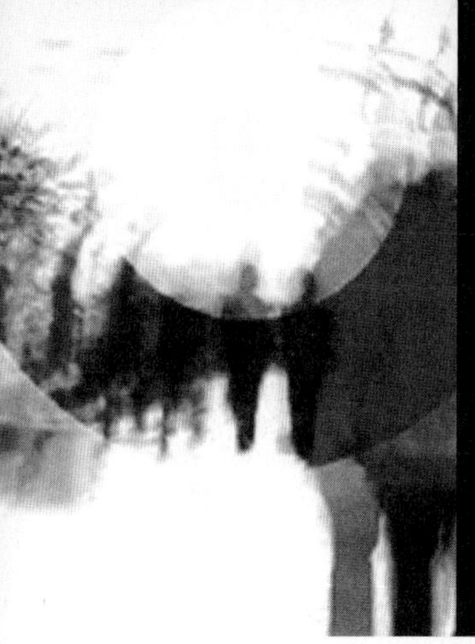

4

NETWORK TOPOLOGIES

Starting Point

Go to www.wiley.com/college/ciccarelli to assess your knowledge of network topologies.
Determine where you need to concentrate your effort.

What You'll Learn in This Chapter

- ▲ Wired physical topologies
- ▲ Wired logical topologies
- ▲ Wireless topologies
- ▲ Hybrid topologies

After Studying This Chapter, You'll Be Able To

- ▲ Identify physical and logical topology structures
- ▲ Given networking requirements, identify the most appropriate topology
- ▲ Explain the access methods used by various topologies
- ▲ Compare and contrast CSMA/CD and Token Ring
- ▲ Identify situations in which it is appropriate to use a hybrid topology

INTRODUCTION

Network **topology** refers to the structure of a network, or how connections are made between network computers. It's important not to confuse the physical topology with the logical network architecture. The same architectural model can be implemented using various physical topologies.

A **physical topology** is a description of the layout of the network media that interconnect the devices on a network. The physical topologies that are implemented today include bus, ring, star, and mesh. A **logical topology** defines the way in which devices communicate and data are transmitted throughout the network. This chapter introduces both wired and wireless topologies.

The type of physical topology you choose for a network is important because it affects how devices communicate. Some of the factors to consider when choosing a topology include the following:

- **Cost:** You need to consider both the initial installation cost and ongoing maintenance cost.
- **Scalability:** Does the topology have the capacity to grow to meet your long-term needs?
- **Bandwidth capacity:** You need to make sure there is an implementation of the topology that can handle your traffic requirements.
- **Ease of installation:** The easier the network is to install, the more likely that it will go right the first time.
- **Ease of troubleshooting:** Downtime is expensive and directly affects the bottom line.

Network topology is a hardware issue. Even though Windows operating systems are sometimes used in examples, especially when discussing setting up and connecting to a network, the information about network topologies applies equally to other operating systems and to non-PC (and even noncomputer) network hardware devices.

4.1 Comparing Physical Network Topologies

When you implement a wired network, your network topology determines how you wire the physical cable plant. One thing to remember is that you are not restricted to a single topology. You can find many examples of networks, especially older networks that have gone through multiple upgrades, which employ a variety of network topologies. You can also find networks that use a mix of wired and wireless topologies.

A good place to start a discussion about network topologies is with the traditional topologies that were originally used in creating host-based networks and carried over as companies moved to PC networks. This chapter discusses four wired topologies: bus, ring, star, and mesh. You may also hear mention of a network having a **hybrid topology**, which simply means that it employs more than one topology in its physical structure.

4.1.1 Bus Topology

A physical **bus topology** utilizes a single main cable that runs throughout the network and to which devices are attached. A physical bus topology looks something like a rail line—a long unbroken path with stations along the way where trains can take on and drop off passengers and cargo. The main **cable segment** must end with a **terminator** that absorbs the signal when it reaches the end of the line, as shown in Figure 4-1. Without a terminator, the electrical signal that represents the data would reach the end of the copper wire and bounce back, causing errors on the network. You would end up with multiple, overlapping signals on the line and have no way to differentiate between them or to isolate and process the correct signal.

A network that has a physical bus topology uses coaxial cable, which has a single conductor surrounded by an insulator, a metal shield, and an insulating cover. Most implementations use thin coaxial cable (often referred to as Thinnet in an Ethernet network) that connects to the NIC using a **BNC connector**, as shown in Figure 4-2. As you can see in Figure 4-1, you can connect two or more computers in a daisy-chain fashion. Terminators are installed on both ends of the cable.

The Institute of Electrical and Electronics Engineers (IEEE) 802.3 standard sets the length of a cable segment and the number of devices on an Ethernet bus network. For a **Thinnet** network, also referred to as **10Base2** or **Thin Ethernet**, the maximum segment length is 185 meters (about 600 feet), with no more than 30 devices per cable segment. You can use up to four repeaters to

Figure 4-1

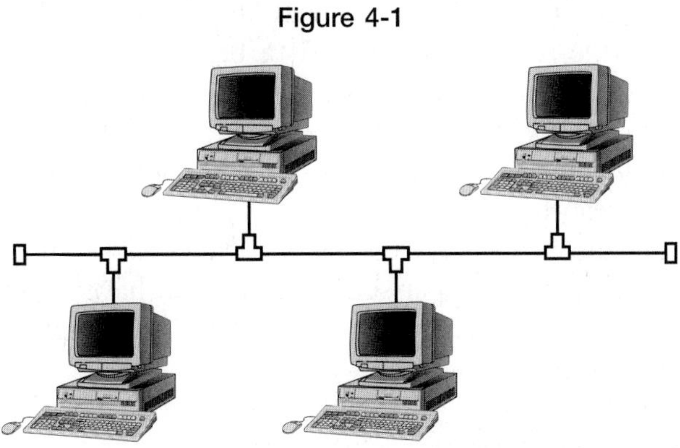

Bus topology example.

Figure 4-2

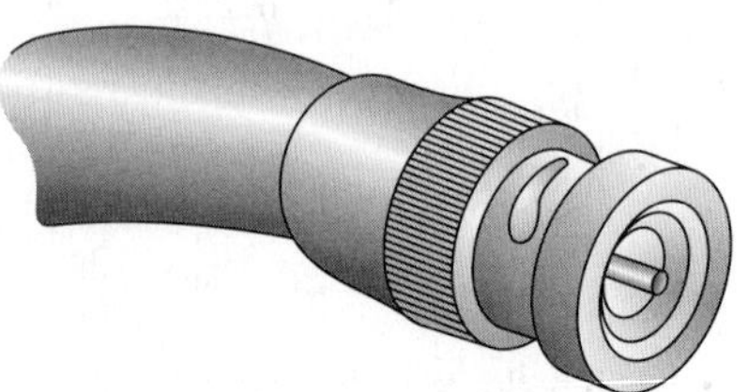

BNC (bayonet connector) plug

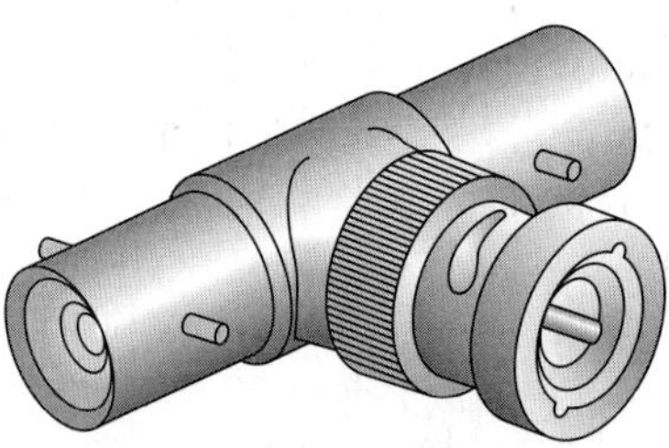

BNC T connector

BNC connectors.

join a maximum of five segments (three of which can be populated with devices), for a total cable length of 925 meters (3,035 feet). The total number of nodes allowed is 150. As you can see in Figure 4-3, you must arrange the segments so that you alternate segments with and without devices.

A **repeater** is, in effect, a simple amplifier. It takes whatever signal is on the cable (including electronic noise, or unwanted background electronic signals) and amplifies it before passing it on to the next segment.

Another, less common, option is **Thicknet**, which is also known as **Thick Ethernet** or **10Base5**. The *10* refers to the 10Mbps bandwidth of the cable, and *Base* indicates that the transmission type is a baseband transmission. Thicknet cable uses a heavier **gauge** (i.e., a measurement of the copper core's diameter) coaxial cable than Thinnet and is sometimes used as a backbone network. Thicknet is extremely difficult to install and work with because of the unusual size and stiffness of the cable.

The maximum cable segment length for Thicknet is 500 meters (1,625 feet), with a maximum of 100 nodes per segment. You can have up to four repeaters joining five segments, for a total cable length of 2500 meters (8,125 feet) and up to 300 nodes.

It's important to understand the difference between a cable segment and a network segment, or subnetwork. Cable segments like those in Figure 4-3 are all part of the same network segment. Hosts on any of the segments have the

Figure 4-3

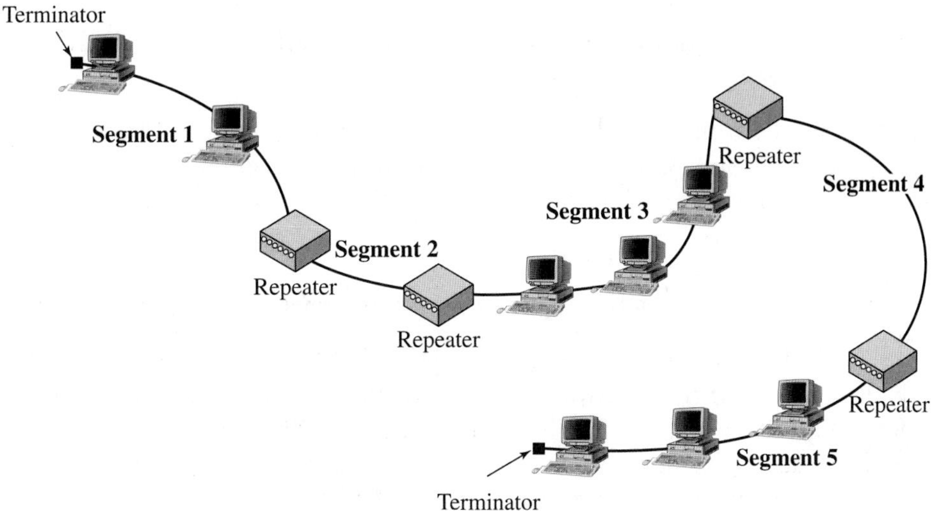

10Base2 cable segments.

same network address. The repeaters are effectively invisible to the network. Network segments are separated by routers and have different network addresses.

Packets on an Ethernet network are received by all devices on the network (i.e., all cable segments) at effectively the same time. Each device must open the packet and check the destination address to determine whether it is the desired recipient. Also, all devices have (in theory) equal access to the network. Any device can transmit at any time, as long as the network is available (i.e., not currently carrying any traffic).

The advantages of a bus topology include the following:

▲ Thinnet networks are relatively inexpensive to install.
▲ You can easily add more workstations.
▲ Bus networks use less cable than other physical topologies. (However, the cable can be more expensive than other cable.)
▲ The bus topology works well with smaller networks.

The disadvantages of a bus topology include the following:

▲ If the cable breaks, the network is down (i.e., all devices lose network access).
▲ Access time and network performance degrade as devices are added to the network.
▲ The maximum bandwidth for Thinnet is no more than 10Mbps.

- ▲ While you're adding devices, all devices are temporarily prevented from using the network.
- ▲ It's difficult to locate problems, such as cable breaks, shorts, or bad terminators.

Thinnet networks were, at one time, the most common type of PC network. Now, nearly all bus networks are **legacy networks**, existing installations that haven't been migrated to different topologies. It's difficult to purchase new NICs

FOR EXAMPLE

Talking on the Bus

Nodes on an Ethernet network use an access method known as **Carrier-Sense Multiple Access/Collision Detect (CSMA/CD)**. CSMA/CD is a multiple-access method that manages conflicts through collision detection. Let's break down what that mouthful means. First, all devices are connected to and monitoring the bus at all times (multiple access). When a node wants to transmit, it waits for the bus to become available (carrier sense). If two nodes try to transmit at the same time, a **collision** occurs, and both transmissions are corrupted so that nothing gets through. The nodes recognize this (collision detection), and both wait a pseudorandom time period before trying to transmit again. After the time-out, a node waits for the bus to become available and tries again.

Imagine a meeting with a heated discussion where everyone wants to talk. The folks around the table are polite enough to wait until the current speaker finishes, but as soon as that happens, they try to come in with their comments. Two, three, maybe more all start talking at the same time. No one can understand what any of the others are saying, so they negotiate who gets to speak, usually through rank in the organization and through the use of body language. As soon as a person finishes, it happens again, and so on.

The biggest problem with this method is relatively easy to see. The more nodes you have on a network, the more devices you having trying to transmit. As the number of collisions goes up, so does the number of retransmissions, which adds to the problem. You eventually reach a point where collisions become so prevalent that performance noticeably suffers. It can get bad enough that users notice and complain about slow access.

Part of the problem is that you can't always accurately determine in advance when you're going to reach the tipping point. It depends on the number of devices on the network and the level of network activity. If a network is running close to its limit, the performance degradation will become noticeable at peak traffic periods, such as when everyone is starting up their computers and trying to log on first thing in the morning.

that include a BNC connector, and when found, they're more expensive than newer, higher-performance NICs. The same is true of cable and connectors. For most network consultants and support technicians, the biggest reason for moving away from bus networks is that they are difficult to troubleshoot. Unless you have specialized test equipment, finding cable or NIC problems is a slow, tedious process.

4.1.2 Ring Topology

As its name implies, a **ring topology** is a topology in which the stations are connected in a ring (i.e., circle) and in which the data flow in a circle, from station to station. It has no beginning or end, so there is no need to terminate the cable. This allows every device to have an equal advantage in accessing the media. There are two kinds of ring topologies: single ring and dual ring.

The original version of ring topology was the single-ring topology, as shown in Figure 4-4. The most common implementation is a **Token Ring** network,

Figure 4-4

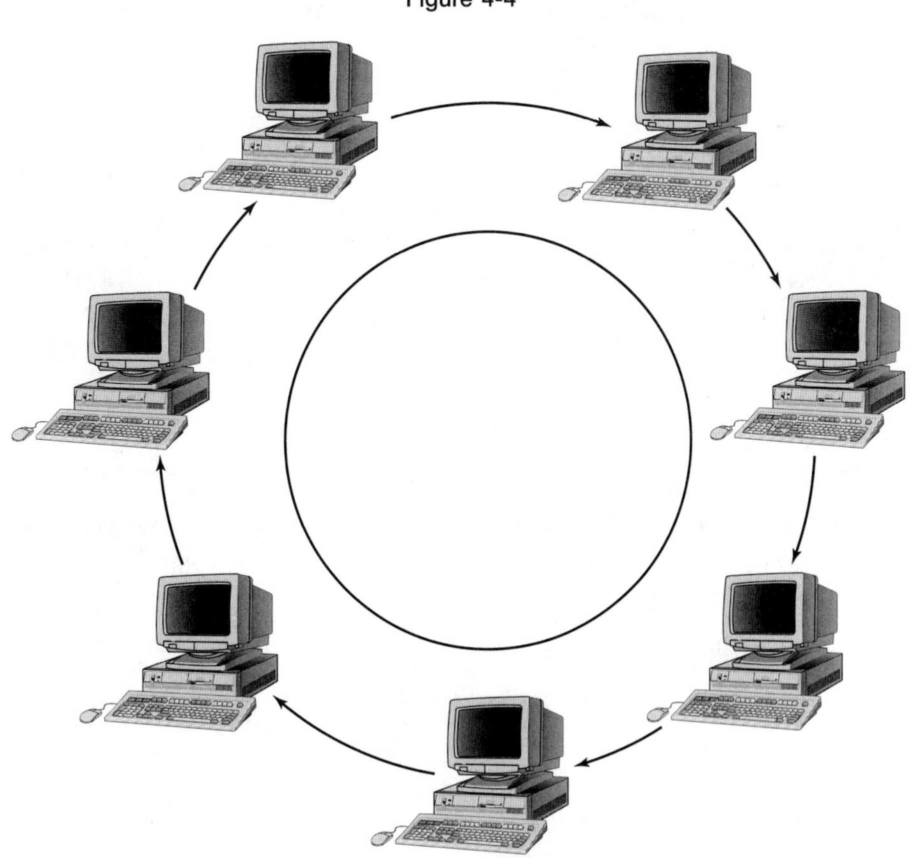

Single-ring topology.

IEEE 802.5. In a single-ring network, all the devices share a single cable, and the data travel in one direction, like a merry-go-round. Each device waits its turn and then transmits. When the data reach their destination, another device can transmit. Each data packet is received and then retransmitted by each device in turn, boosting the signal back to its original level, so repeaters typically aren't needed in this topology.

As technology evolved, a dual-ring topology was developed. This topology uses **counter-rotating rings**; in this topology, two rings send data, each in a different direction (see Figure 4-5), and all the devices connect to both rings. Not only does this let more packets travel over the network, it provides **redundancy** (i.e., duplicate paths), which means the network continues to communicate even if one of the rings fails.

Figure 4-5

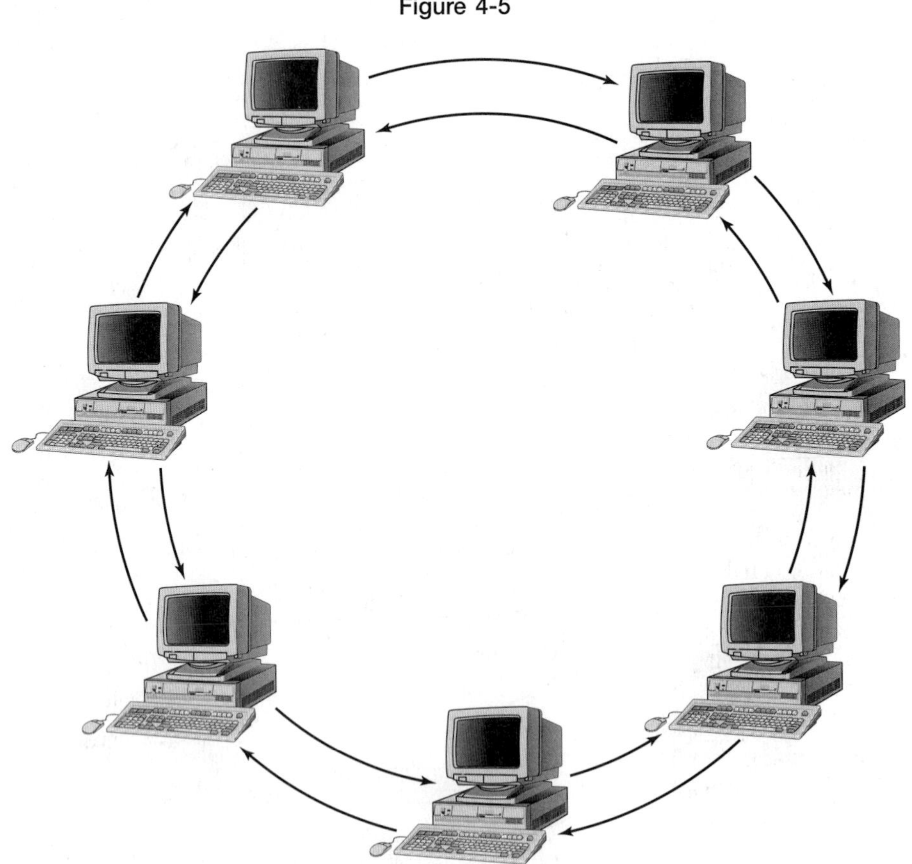

In a dual-ring topology, the data travel in two directions.

Dual-ring topology.

The most common dual-ring implementation is **Fiber Distributed Data Interface (FDDI)**, which is a technology similar to Token Ring. However, whereas Token Ring uses copper wire to carry electronic signals, FDDI uses fiber-optic cable to carry modulated light.

The advantages of a ring topology include the following:

- There are no collisions, which makes communication more reliable.
- It is relatively easy to locate and correct problems with devices and cable.
- In most implementations, failing devices can be automatically detected and isolated from the ring.
- No terminators are needed.

The disadvantages of a ring topology include the following:

- A ring network requires more cable than a bus network.
- In some implementations, a break in the cable brings the entire network down.

FOR EXAMPLE

Around the Ring

Say you have a ring with five devices connected in a single ring, named One, Two, Three, Four, and Five. Communication starts with a single, empty packet called a **token**. (There can be two or more tokens in some implementations, but we're going to keep things simple.) Device One gets the packet first, loads it with data, and addresses it to Three.

Device One can't send the packet directly to Three. Instead, it must go through each device in the ring. Two receives the packet and sees that it's addressed to Three, so it transmits the packet back out. Three receives the packet, sees that it is the destination, and reloads the packet with a response telling One that the packet was received. This packet then goes to Four and Five, and finally back to One. One receives the response.

Everyone gets a chance to load the packet with data, so after One gets the receipt, it has to release the packet. Next, Two gets to load and address the packet, and then Three and so on, with the empty packet eventually making its way back to One.

A dual-ring network has twice the paths and twice the tokens, but the process is the same. Tokens travel clockwise in one ring and counterclockwise in the other. Not only does one ring keep going if the other one fails, depending on exactly where the breaks occur, some implementations can even compensate for breaks in both rings.

- ▲ As you add devices to the ring, all devices are temporarily prevented from using the network.
- ▲ Equipment can be difficult to locate and relatively expensive.

Token Ring was originally developed by IBM and was, for many years, the preferred topology for IBM equipment. This is no longer the case, and many Token Ring networks have been replaced by high-speed Ethernet networks. The hardware needed for Token Ring networks is available, but it is not as common as the hardware for Ethernet networks.

FDDI was designed for use in high-speed networks and was most often used as building or campus backbone networks. It is still used in this implementation and, in rare circumstances, as a MAN backbone. The biggest drawbacks to FDDI are that the cable and network hardware are relatively expensive, easily damaged, and more difficult to install than copper wire cables (or wireless networks). However, this is often outweighed by the facts that it is more difficult to physically tap into a fiber-optic line, making FDDI inherently more secure, and it is immune to electrical interference.

4.1.3 Star Topology

The star topology is, by far, the topology most commonly seen in modern network implementations. As bus and ring networks are phased out or upgraded, they are most often replaced by some kind of star. A physical **star topology** gets its name because it is installed in the shape of a star, like spokes in a bicycle wheel. As you can see in Figure 4-6, a star topology is made up of a central connection point, a hub (or switch), where the cable segments meet. Each device in a star network is connected to the central hub with its own cable. Although this requires more media than a bus or ring topology, the media are relatively inexpensive and very easy to install.

If a star network is expanded to include one or more additional hubs connected to the main hub, as shown in Figure 4-7, it is called an **extended star topology**.

The advantages of a star topology include the following:

- ▲ It's easy to add more devices as the network expands.
- ▲ Hardware is relatively inexpensive and easy to install.
- ▲ The failure of one cable or one cable break does not bring down the entire network.
- ▲ The hub provides centralized management.
- ▲ It's easy to find and fix device and cable problems.
- ▲ A star network can be upgraded to support faster network transmission speeds.

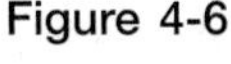

Figure 4-6

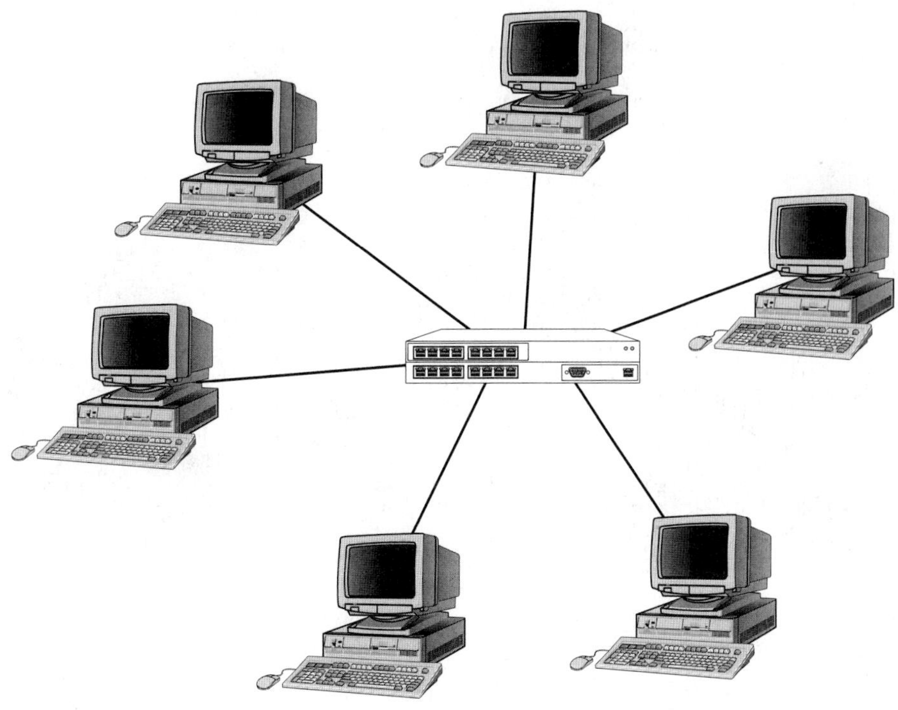

Star topology.

- ▲ It's the most common topology, so numerous equipment options are available.

The disadvantages of a star topology include the following:

- ▲ A star network requires more media than a ring or bus network.
- ▲ The failure of a single central hub can bring down the entire network.
- ▲ The failure of one hub in an extended star affects all devices connected to that hub.

Nearly all new network installations, including home networks, use some form of physical star. Extended stars can be expanded to include hundreds or even thousands of devices and can support speeds exceeding 1Gbps. Most star configurations use copper wire **twisted-pair cable**, a line with multiple conductors that is similar to telephone cable, but some high-speed versions use fiber-optic cable. Some of the earliest star configurations used coaxial cable, but coax-based stars are now almost never seen.

Figure 4-7

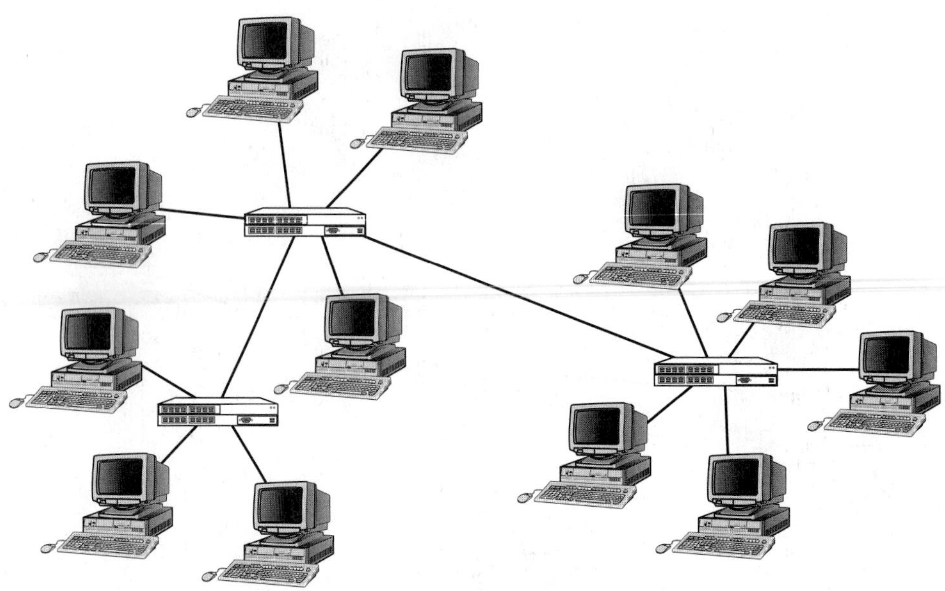

Extended star topology.

FOR EXAMPLE

Don't Forget to Raise Your Hand

Depending on the implementation, various access methods can be used in physical star networks. The most common use either collision detection (e.g., CSMA/CD), token passing (e.g., Token Ring), or polling. We've already talked about the first two, so let's talk a little about polling. In polling, each computer communicates in turn, as in Token Ring, but with central control deciding which device gets to transmit.

Think about a well-behaved classroom. Everyone gets to talk, but first a student has to raise his or her hand to be recognized by the teacher. The teacher makes note of who raised a hand, calls on a student, and then has the students raise their hands again.

Most polling schemes are similar. The central control contacts each device and determines which devices have data they need to transmit. Each of those devices gets a chance to transmit its data, and then all the devices are polled again, over and over. Communication priority is based on various factors, such as how long since a device was last permitted to transmit and how often the device is making transmit requests when polled.

Figure 4-8

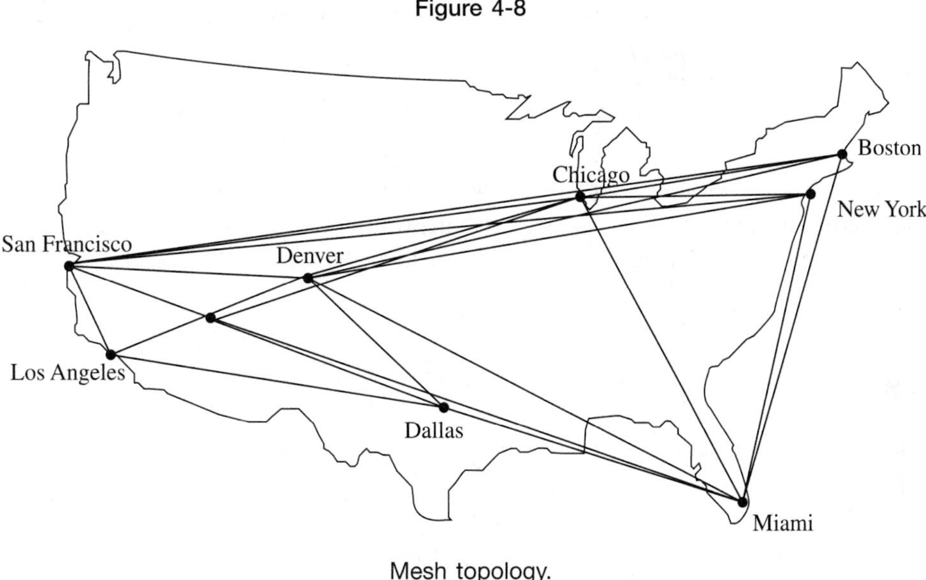

Mesh topology.

4.1.4 Mesh Topology

In a **mesh topology** (see Figure 4-8)—sometimes called a **net topology** because it looks something like a fisherman's net—each device is connected to every other device. This allows all the devices to continue to communicate if one connection goes down. It is the ultimate in network interconnection reliability.

Mesh topology is rarely used as a LAN topology, but it is often used to create reliable WANs. The reliability comes from having multiple communication paths. The network (or internetwork) is able to automatically compensate for line breaks and failing devices. Many implementations can even compensate for changing traffic patterns and reroute packets to optimize communication speeds.

Take another look at Figure 4-8. Based on distance, you would probably say that the shortest path between Boston and New York is the direct link between the two. However, if this link is experiencing especially heavy traffic, the best link between the two might be to route traffic through Chicago, then Miami, and then to New York. This routing process is transparent to the network users.

Different mesh topology implementations vary widely, depending on the underlying communication technology and physical connections. Some use dedicated lines run between the connection points, and others use leased (or even shared) public networks, such as the public telephone system. Connection speeds also vary. The one common factor in all mesh topologies is the fact that each node supports multiple connections and multiple paths.

The advantages of mesh topology include the following:

- ▲ Flexible variations can meet most network communication needs.
- ▲ Multiple communication paths provide fault tolerance and the ability to recover from failures.
- ▲ It is possible to choose routes based on factors such as traffic and congestion.
- ▲ Many implementations use leased hardware and lines, so maintenance and upkeep are handled for you (instead of by you).

The disadvantages of a mesh topology include the following:

- ▲ Designs are often very complex and may require the assistance of an outside consultant.
- ▲ Network hardware can be expensive and difficult to install.
- ▲ If managed internally, a mesh network is difficult to manage and maintain.
- ▲ Some billing methods are based on traffic volume and are potentially expensive.
- ▲ A mesh network can be difficult to troubleshoot.

You might be using a mesh network and not even know it. When using leased communications, you don't always know what happens when the traffic

FOR EXAMPLE

Mesh Topology Access: It Depends!

The only blanket statement you can make about mesh topology access methods is "It depends." It depends on the underlying hardware used to build the mesh infrastructure. It depends on the OSI layer 2 protocol used to manage connections and traffic control. Before you can know how access is managed, you need to know what kind of mesh you have.

The most common access methods involve some version of collision detection, collision avoidance, or polling. We've already discussed collision detection and polling. Collision avoidance involves using careful timing to optimize communications and avoid collisions between network devices rather than reacting after the collisions occur.

The truth is that, in most cases, you don't care what kind of access method is used because you aren't directly responsible for its management or maintenance. Your only concerns are your entry and exit points, the places where you connect to the mesh. Anything beyond that is out of your hands.

leaves your local network. The only things you ever deal with are the entry and exit points.

A well-known mesh network, possibly the best known and most used, is the U.S. **public switched telephone network (PSTN)**. A fast-growing rival is the mobile phone network that has grown up in recent years, but that's primarily a wireless mesh topology. Though it's not a true mesh because it doesn't have full connectivity between all nodes, the Internet has a mesh infrastructure. It has multiple connections between major **nexus points** where several lines of communication come together, traffic routes can be updated automatically, and route determinations are often made on current conditions rather than physical proximity.

SELF-CHECK

1. List and briefly describe the four most common wired topologies.
2. Which topology is most often used in new networks?

4.2 Comparing Wireless Network Topologies

Wireless topologies are relatively new to PC networks, but they are based on established radio-frequency communication technologies. Several IEEE standards have been defined, the most common of which are 802.11b and 802.11g. The **802.11g** standard supports **802.11b** clients. There is also a much lesser-used 802.11a standard that is not compatible with either 802.11b or 802.11g, and there is an emerging 802.11n standard that is being developed to provide compatibility with all the standards currently in use as well as provide better performance for native clients. The 802 standards are discussed in greater depth in Chapter 6.

The two primary topologies, referred to as **modes**, are ad hoc mode and infrastructure mode; the basic difference between them is whether there is a central access point that acts something like the central hub in a star topology. Another wireless topology you might see, though usually on a larger scale, is a wireless mesh.

4.2.1 Ad Hoc Mode

In **ad hoc mode** (also referred to as **peer-to-peer mode**), wireless network devices communicate directly with each other, as shown in Figure 4-9. There is no central access point device involved. There are no physical placement requirements, as long as the devices are in range of each other. Devices can relay messages between each other, extending the range of the network.

Figure 4-9

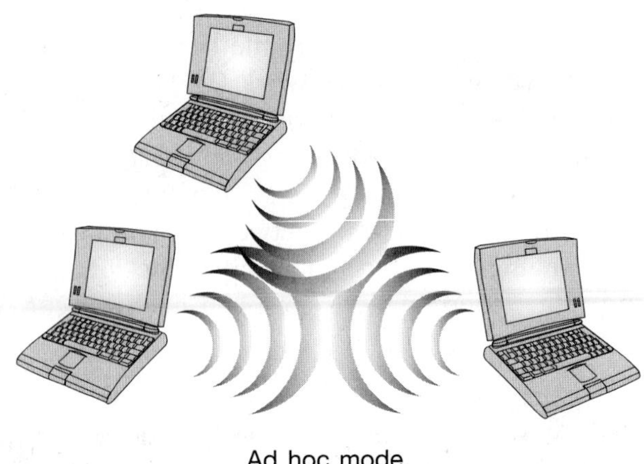

Ad hoc mode.

Ad hoc mode has the following advantages:

- ▲ It is inexpensive, and the hardware is often preinstalled in the computer.
- ▲ It is easy to configure.
- ▲ It is easy to manage and maintain.

The disadvantages of ad hoc mode include the following:

- ▲ It offers little security and is easily accessed by unauthorized computers.
- ▲ It is suitable for very small networks only.

You are more likely to encounter an ad hoc mode network in a home than in an office environment. When used, an ad hoc mode topology is most often implemented using a peer-to-peer architecture.

4.2.2 Infrastructure Mode

Infrastructure mode lets you combine wired and wireless networks through the use of a **wireless access point (WAP)**, as shown in Figure 4-10. The WAP provides a central access point for the wireless computers, and it also passes data to and from the wired network. However, this isn't the only possible configuration. An infrastructure mode network can be completely wireless, consisting of just a WAP and the wireless clients.

Wireless clients must be configured for either ad hoc or infrastructure mode. They can't operate in both at the same time. In infrastructure mode, the wireless computer is either configured to communicate through a specific WAP or will attempt to dynamically detect and then connect to a WAP. The WAP handles the process of moving data on and off the wired network.

Figure 4-10

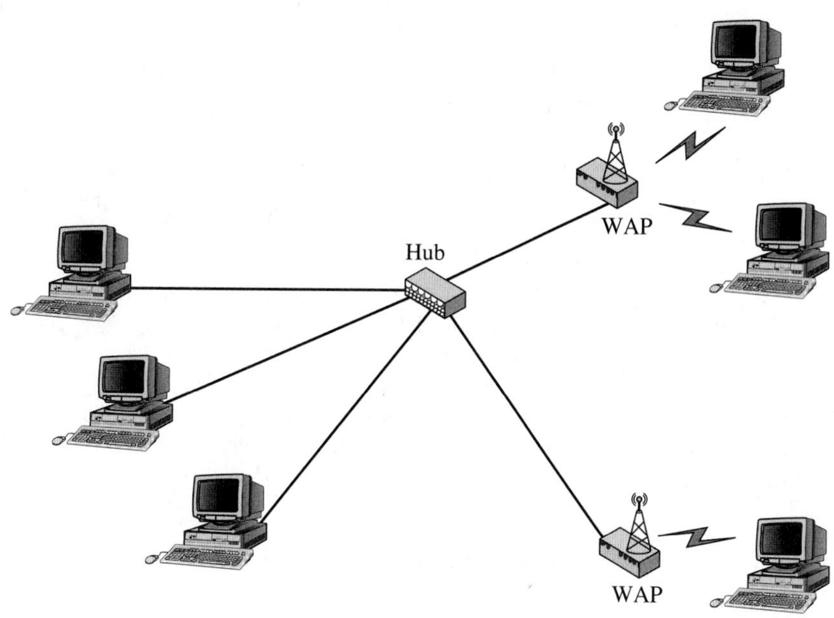

Infrastructure mode.

Infrastructure mode has the following advantages:

- ▲ It is inexpensive and easy to configure.
- ▲ It provides easy access between wired and wireless networks.
- ▲ It is scalable to meet the requirements of large networks.
- ▲ It is easy to manage and maintain.

The disadvantages of infrastructure mode include the following:

- ▲ It is not secured by default.
- ▲ It has limited security options, and it is somewhat difficult to configure a secure network.
- ▲ Unauthorized access to the network might be allowed.

Infrastructure mode is commonly used as an inexpensive way of expanding existing wired networks to include new devices. Wireless-only infrastructure networks are commonly seen in home networks. When used in a home network, the WAP is often a wireless router that is used to connect the computers and to share a single Internet connection between the computers.

Figure 4-11

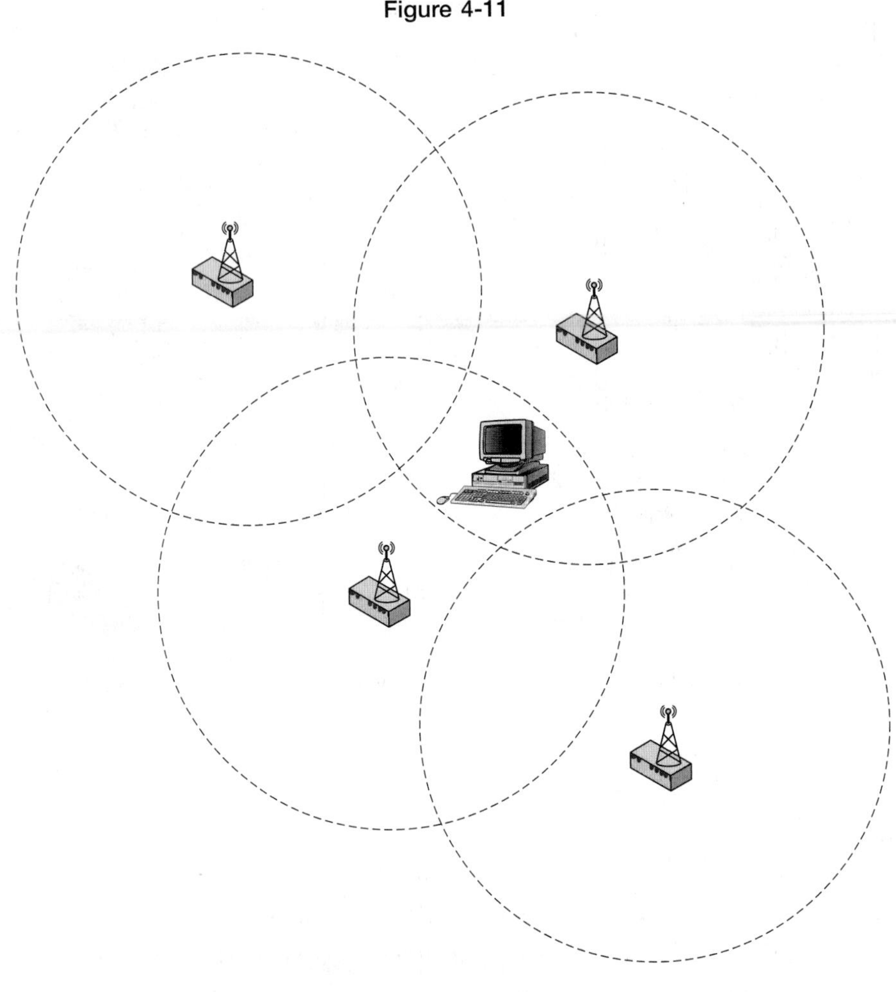

Wireless mesh.

4.2.3 Wireless Mesh

A **wireless mesh**, which is a set of WAPs or other transmission towers with overlapping ranges (see Figure 4-11), can take various forms. The computer shown in Figure 4-11 is in the range of two different WAPs and could potentially connect with either of them.

The network of cell phone towers in most regions of the United States is configured as a wireless mesh. This is done so you don't lose your call as you move out of the range of one cell tower and into the range of another. Wi-Fi hotspots are often set up as wireless meshes (e.g., in a hotel), so you can move around the location without losing your network connectivity.

FOR EXAMPLE

Peek-a-boo!

Many organizations deploy WAPs without realizing the potential security hole that they represent. A WAP, by default, broadcasts its **service set identifier (SSID)**, a text string that identifies the WAP to wireless clients, so that client computers can discover the WAP and connect. Also by default, the WAP accepts connections from any wireless computer and broadcasts all data in clear text.

It's important, when implementing an infrastructure mode network, that you make use of available security features. With most WAPs, you can turn off SSID broadcasts so clients have to know the WAP ID before they can connect. Other features include **MAC address filtering** (so that the connection isn't allowed if the MAC address isn't on the list), encrypted data transmissions, and requirement of user authentication before a connection can be authorized.

A common activity in office buildings and around home networks (especially in apartments) is having someone piggyback on your Internet connection. While you aren't responsible for their actions, having some activities traced back to your network could be embarrassing. You might wonder what the big concern is. After all, a little Internet time isn't that big a deal, even if they don't completely behave, is it? It's not like they're logging on to your secure network. That is exactly the problem: The first step in hacking into your networking is gaining a physical connection to the network. Once someone has a physical connection, he or she can use a variety of attacks to try to gain access to network servers. However, if others are blocked from ever accessing your physical network, they don't get a chance to try.

In a LAN, you typically don't initially design the topology as a wireless mesh, but it becomes one as you add more WAPs. The range of a WAP is typically 30 to 100 meters (100 to 300 feet) or more, depending on the device and manufacturer, so it's easy to end up with overlapping ranges.

SELF-CHECK

1. List the two wireless network modes and describe how devices communicate in each.
2. When does an infrastructure mode network become a wireless mesh?

4.3 Understanding Other Topology Issues

Before leaving the topic of topology, a few additional issues need to be discussed. We need to talk about logical topologies and how they relate to physical topologies. We also need to introduce hybrid topologies, including common examples of wired hybrid topologies. Finally, we need to talk a little more about hybrid topologies that integrate wired and wireless topologies.

4.3.1 Understanding Logical Topology

Whereas the physical topology describes how the network is structured, the logical topology describes how devices on the LAN communicate and transmit data. In current PC network technologies, you see the network using one of two logical topologies: bus or ring.

As illustrated in Figure 4-12, it's easy to figure out the logical topology for a physical bus or ring. When a network is physically cabled in a bus, it is easy to understand that it is sending data in a logical bus topology throughout the network. The data move from device to device, in a linear fashion. Likewise, a physical ring is easily interpreted as a logical ring.

When a network uses a physical star topology, media can be accessed and data sent in either a logical bus or a logical ring. It depends on the network connection devices used and the layer 2 protocol implemented.

Logical Bus

In a **logical bus**, data travel in a linear fashion away from the source to all destinations. This is what you see in recently implemented Ethernet networks.

Figure 4-12

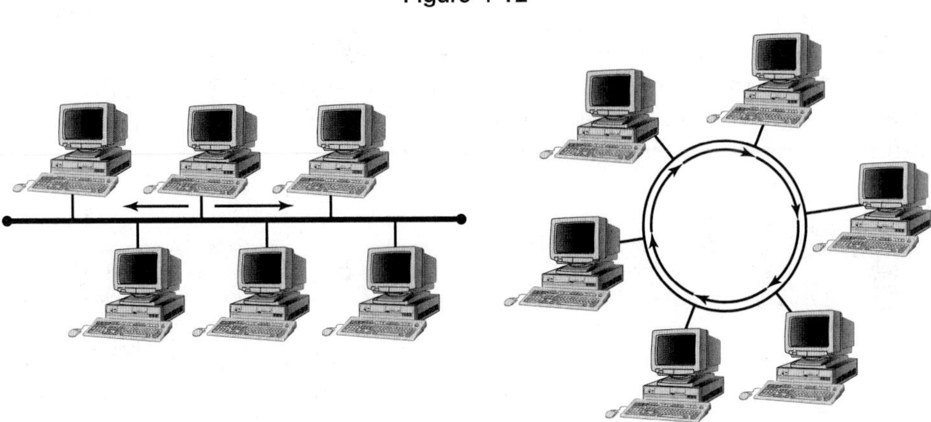

Logical bus vs. ring.

Figure 4-13

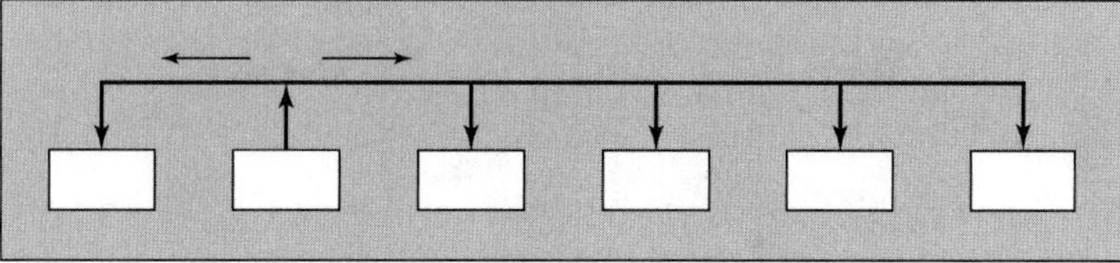

An Ethernet hub.

In modern Ethernet networks, the physical layout is a star topology. At the center of the star is a hub. It is what happens inside that hub that defines the logical topology. As you can see in Figure 4-13, an Ethernet hub uses a logical bus topology inside to transmit data to all the segments of its star.

The advantages of a logical bus topology include the following:

- ▲ If a node is down, this does not bring down the entire network.
- ▲ It's the most widely implemented of the logical topologies.
- ▲ The necessary hardware is readily available and relatively inexpensive.
- ▲ Logical bus topology is easy to troubleshoot and maintain.
- ▲ Additions and changes can be made easily, without affecting other workstations.

The disadvantages of a logical bus topology are similar to those of any other bus network:

- ▲ Collisions can occur easily.
- ▲ Only one device can access the media at a time.
- ▲ Performance degrades as more devices are added.

The original standard for this type of network was the **10BaseT** standard, which defined a 10Mbps star topology network. The most common current configuration is 100Mbps Ethernet, occasionally referred to as **10Base100**. Most hubs can compensate for bandwidth differences, supporting both 10Mbps and 100Mbps devices connected to the same hub. Recent additions to the standards include Ethernet networks that support 1Gbps on twisted-pair cable.

Logical Ring

In a **logical ring**, data travel in a ring from one device to another and back around to the beginning of the circle. In a Token Ring network, the most common implementation of the logical ring, devices are connected to a **multistation access unit (MAU)**, which is the central hub in a Token Ring network that is wired as a physical star.

Figure 4-14

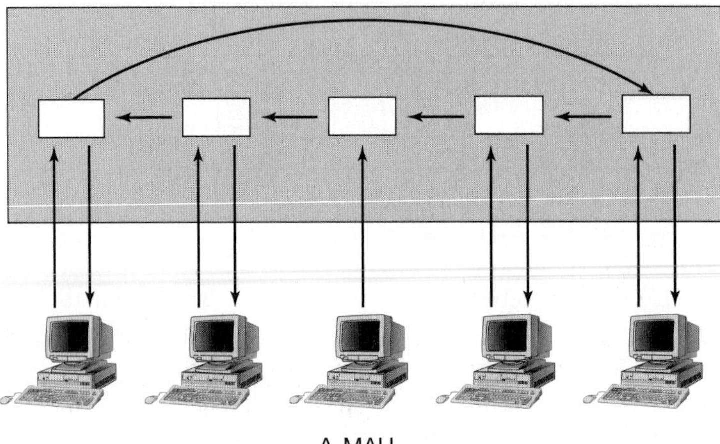

A MAU.

The MAU (pronounced "mauw" as in "mouse") may look just like a regular hub. But as you can see in Figure 4-14, inside the MAU, the data are passed from device to device using a logical ring. The MAU makes it possible for a network with a physical star topology to transmit data in a logical ring. If you connect a second MAU, the ring is extended to include both, and it continually expands as you add more MAUs.

The advantages of a logical ring topology are similar to those you would expect in a ring topology, including the following:

- There are no collisions because a token-passing access method is used.
- It is easy to locate and correct problems with devices and cable.
- You can usually add devices without interrupting the network.
- In most implementations, failing devices can be automatically detected and isolated from the ring.

The disadvantages of a logical ring topology are also common to ring networks:

- A broken ring can stop all transmissions.
- A device must wait for an empty token before it can transmit.
- The necessary hardware is more expensive than that for a logical bus.

Logical rings are most often seen in legacy networks that include (or included, at some time) an IBM host or in companies that were "IBM shops," contracting with IBM to supply their network hardware and maintain their network. Most of these legacy network segments now exist as part of a hybrid topology.

Figure 4-15

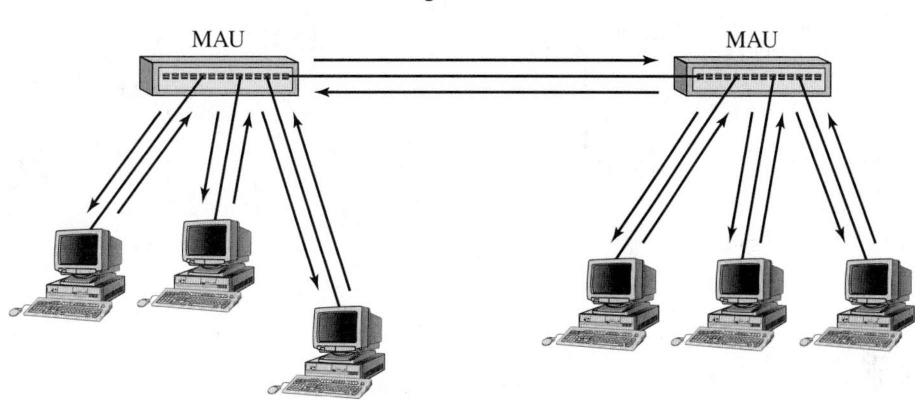

Star-ring topology.

4.3.2 Using Wired Hybrid Topologies

A hybrid topology combines two or more different physical topologies in a single network. This often occurs simply as part of a network's evolutionary cycle. As old networks are updated and replaced, older segments may be left with a legacy topology.

You sometimes see extended star topologies, like the one shown in Figure 4-7, referred to as a hybrid **star-bus topology**. This term refers to the connection between the hubs as a bus, but most networking professionals don't consider that description to be technically accurate. A situation that you often see in Token Ring networks is two or more MAUs connected as shown in Figure 4-15. This is known as a **star-ring topology**. Physically, the network looks just like an extended star.

Most wired hybrids don't have a special name. They're just a combination of two or more bus, star, or ring topologies. There are, however, two relatively common hybrid topologies you might encounter. First, you might use a vertical bus between floors in a building to connect LANs deployed on the different floors. Second, you could connect LANs with a WAN mesh. In either case, the LANs being connected have their own internal bus, ring, star, or hybrid topology.

The advantages of using a hybrid topology include the advantages inherent in the topologies involved, and they also include the following:

- ▲ A hybrid topology allows you to make use of legacy networks and hardware.
- ▲ A hybrid topology lets you scale out of your network without the expense of changing existing network segments.
- ▲ A hybrid topology provides greater flexibility in network design.

Figure 4-16

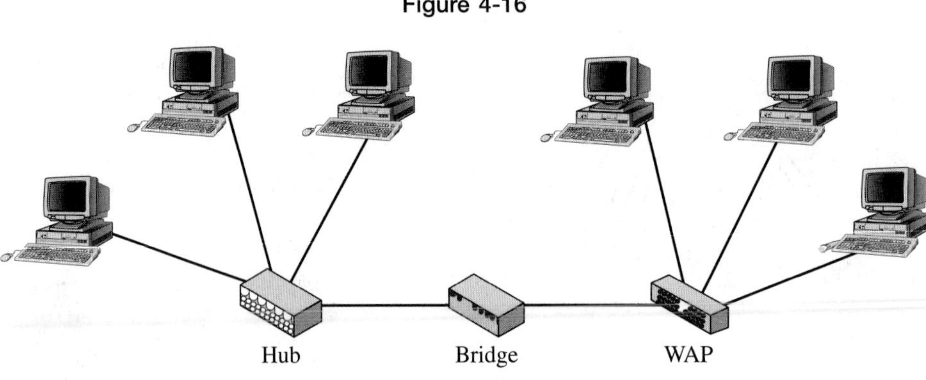

A bridged network.

The disadvantages of using a hybrid topology include the following:

- ▲ The network is more complex and more difficult to maintain.
- ▲ Communication problems can be difficult to isolate without sophisticated monitoring equipment.
- ▲ Specialized equipment is needed to connect the different topologies.

One function of a **bridge** is to convert data packets between different layer 2 protocols. Therefore, a bridge is most often used to connect different topologies into a hybrid network. A bridge operating in this role is invisible to devices operating at higher layers in the OSI model. If you were to connect an Ethernet logical bus and Token Ring logical star, as shown in Figure 4-16, they would be seen as part of the same network segment for routing purposes.

If you wanted to connect the two topologies in Figure 4-16 as separate network segments, you would use a **brouter**, which combines bridge and router functionality. One cost-effective way to do this is to "grow your own" brouter. You could do this, for example, by installing both Ethernet and Token Ring NICs in a Windows Server computer and then configuring the computer as a router.

4.3.3 Combining Wired and Wireless Topologies

Probably the most common hybrids seen at this time are wired/wireless Ethernet hybrids. A WAP is designed with a wired Ethernet port so you can connect it directly to a wired hub. By doing this, you extend the logical bus to your wired computers, as well (refer to Figure 4-10). The primary reasons for doing this are cost and convenience.

The following are some of the advantages of combining wired and wireless networks:

- Doing so allows for cost-effective scaling to meet growth requirements.
- Wireless NICs come preinstalled in most laptop computers.
- Because no cables are needed, you can extend the network into areas that would be difficult to wire.

Some of the disadvantages of combining wired and wireless networks are the same disadvantages you see in any other hybrid topology, including the following:

- The network is more complex than a single topology, and it can be more difficult to isolate problems.
- The default WAP security settings represent a potential security risk.
- The organization could lose site of careful network planning.

Because it is easy to extend a network by using WAPs and wireless computers, some organizations have had a tendency to just let their networks grow without careful planning and evaluation of network changes. Such uncontrolled growth makes for a poorly documented and poorly implemented network and could be a disaster in the making.

FOR EXAMPLE

Growing a Real-World Hybrid Network

In most organizations, it's unrealistic to think that you will have the personnel or budget to tear out all the old network cable each time you expand or upgrade your network. Instead, you often end up with a mix of topologies resulting from whatever was popular when each network segment was deployed. You might see something like the example in Figure 4-17, which shows three floors, connected by a vertical backbone running between them. Routers connect the floor LANs to the backbone. The first floor, the oldest in this example, is wired as a physical bus. The second is a logical bus network wired as a star. The third floor is a logical ring, as shown in the drawing, but is wired using MAUs as a physical star.

Let's fast-forward a few years to the hybrid network shown in Figure 4-18. Problems with the network hardware on the first and third floors led to a physical upgrade. Bus topologies are notoriously hard to troubleshoot. Ring network hardware has become more difficult to purchase and relatively more

(continued)

Figure 4-17

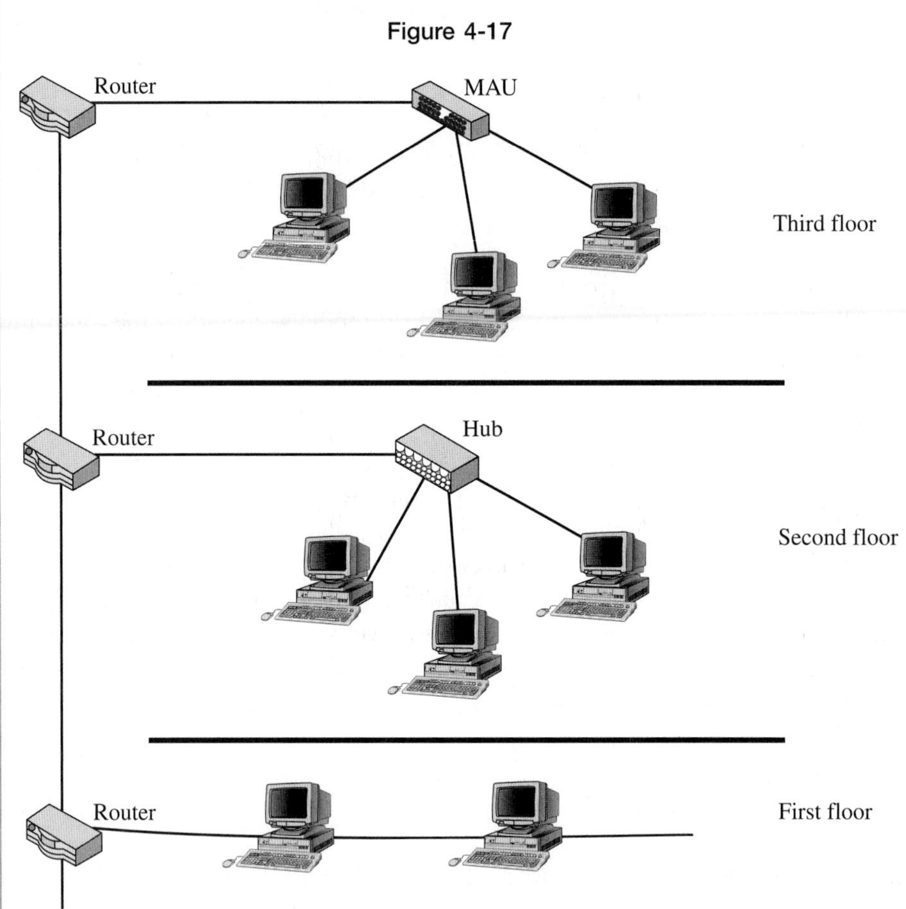

The original network.

expensive than its logical bus counterparts. Both have been replaced by logical bus networks physically wired in a star topology.

Also in Figure 4-18, you can see that WAPs are now in place on each of the floors. On the top two floors, the WAPs make it easier to deploy new computers because you don't have to run additional cable. On the first floor, you also see something else. This time, the WAP is also a wireless router and an Internet proxy server (or, more accurately, a network address translation [NAT] server that enables Internet access for client computers and can issue local IP addresses). It is supporting multiple roles by providing the following:

- Infrastructure mode connections for wireless computers.
- A shared high-speed Internet connection for wired and wireless computers.

Figure 4-18

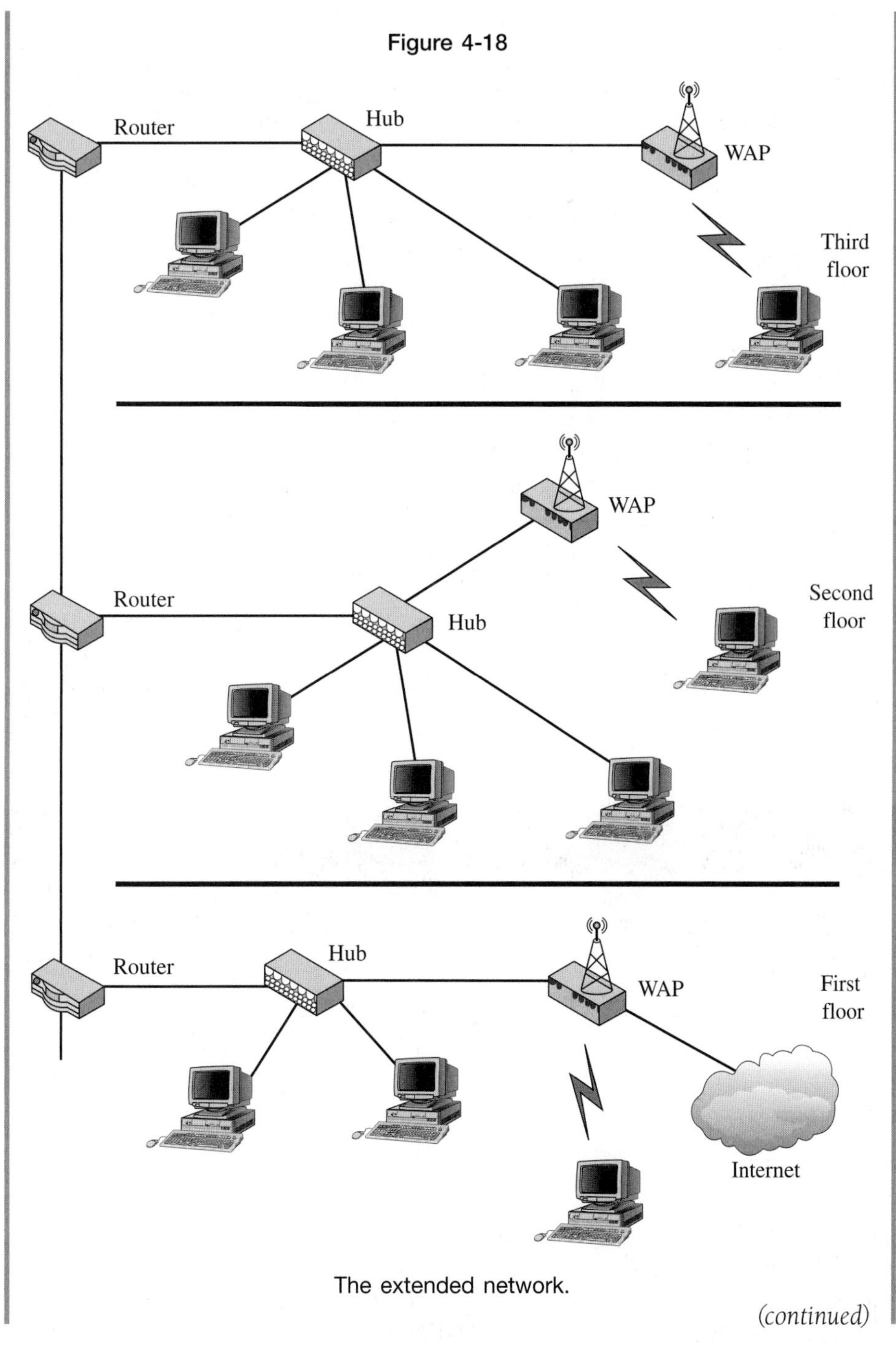

The extended network.

(continued)

- ▲ Leased IP addresses to computers on the local LAN.
- ▲ NAT provided through the proxy to enable Internet access.
- ▲ Basic firewall protection that filters unwanted Internet traffic.

Something else is happening here that might not be immediately apparent. It's very likely—in fact, it's probable—that the ranges of the new WAPs overlap. This means that the WAPs are potentially forming an effective mesh topology. Wireless computers could connect to any one of the WAPs, with the WAPs on the second and third floors offering redundancy for each other.

Are there any potential problems with this configuration? Unfortunately, yes, because the less control you have over the network, the less control you have over security. The network can become unbalanced, with excessive traffic on some segments while there is little traffic on others. When problems arise (and they always do), it can be difficult to isolate and correct the cause. A better design would be to assign each wireless computer a specific WAP as its primary network connection and implement security measures such as authentication and MAC address filtering at the WAPs.

SELF-CHECK

1. **When joining wired and wireless networks, what wireless mode is used and why?**
2. **Describe the physical structure of a logical bus and a logical ring.**

SUMMARY

This chapter introduced network topologies. You learned about the four basic wired network topologies—bus, ring, star, and mesh—and their advantages and disadvantages. You also learned about basic wireless topologies. You saw how a physical star can actually be a logical bus or ring. This chapter also introduced hybrid topologies, with a look at both wired hybrids and wired/wireless hybrids.

KEY TERMS

10Base2
10Base5
10Base100
10BaseT
802.11b
802.11g
Ad hoc mode
BNC connector
Bridge
Brouter
Bus topology
Cable segment
Carrier-Sense Multiple Access/Collision Detect (CSMA/CD)
Collision
Counter-rotating rings
Extended star topology
Fiber Distributed Data Interface (FDDI)
Gauge
Hybrid topology
IEEE 802.5
Infrastructure mode
Legacy network
Logical bus
Logical ring
Logical topology
MAC address filtering
Mesh topology
Mode
Multistation access unit (MAU)
Net topology
Nexus point
Peer-to-peer mode
Physical topology
Public switched telephone network (PSTN)
Redundancy
Repeater
Ring topology
Service set identifier (SSID)
Star topology
Star-bus topology
Star-ring topology
Terminator
Thick Ethernet
Thicknet
Thin Ethernet
Thinnet
Token
Token Ring
Topology
Twisted-pair cable
Wireless access point (WAP)
Wireless mesh

ASSESS YOUR UNDERSTANDING

Go to www.wiley.com/college/ciccarelli to evaluate your knowledge of network topologies.
Measure your learning by comparing pre-test and post-test results.

Summary Questions

1. Infrastructure mode is used in hybrid networks that include wired and wireless clients. True or false?
2. In which physical topology can a single break in the cable bring down the entire network?
   (a) bus
   (b) dual ring
   (c) star
   (d) mesh
3. What kind of device is used to connect bus network segments?
   (a) bridge
   (b) router
   (c) repeater
   (d) brouter
4. FDDI is an example of which physical topology?
   (a) bus
   (b) ring
   (c) star
   (d) mesh
5. Which of the following is a disadvantage of ad hoc mode?
   (a) The hardware required is prohibitively expensive.
   (b) It is difficult to manage and maintain.
   (c) Clients cannot access resources on a wired network.
   (d) Laptop clients are not supported.
6. 10Base2 is an example of which physical topology?
   (a) bus
   (b) ring
   (c) star
   (d) mesh
7. A physical bus topology uses twisted-pair cabling. True or false?

8. Which of the following is a disadvantage of a logical bus?
   (a) Performance degrades as more devices are added.
   (b) If a single node fails, it brings down the entire network.
   (c) The hardware is expensive and hard to come by.
   (d) The network must be brought down in order to add nodes.
9. A MAU is used to wire which of the following?
   (a) physical ring
   (b) logical ring
   (c) physical bus
   (d) logical bus
10. You can use a bridge to connect a physical bus to a physical star. True or false?
11. When wiring multiple IEEE 802.3 coaxial cable segments, each one must have a different network address. True or false?
12. A MAU is wired internally as what?
   (a) a bus
   (b) a star
   (c) a single ring
   (d) a dual ring
13. Which of the following would be considered a legacy network?
   (a) a 10Base2 physical bus
   (b) a 10Base100 logical bus
   (c) an infrastructure mode network
   (d) an ad hoc mode network
14. A token is associated with which of the following?
   (a) a physical bus
   (b) a logical bus
   (c) ad hoc mode
   (d) a logical ring
15. A hub is associated with which of the following?
   (a) a physical bus
   (b) a physical ring
   (c) a physical star
   (d) a physical mesh
16. A net topology is another name for which physical topology?
   (a) bus
   (b) ring
   (c) star
   (d) mesh

Applying This Chapter

1. Your company occupies the first two floors in an office building. Each floor is configured as a 10Base2 LAN. The first floor has 20 nodes. The second floor has 45 nodes. Both are connected to a vertical backbone wired as a physical star.
   (a) What physical topology is used on both LANs?
   (b) What is the minimum number of cable segments on the first floor? What is the minimum number of cable segments on the second floor?
   (c) Taken as a whole, what term best describes the network topology?
   (d) What symptoms would you see if a cable breaks on the second floor?
2. Your network is wired as shown in Figure 4-19.

Figure 4-19

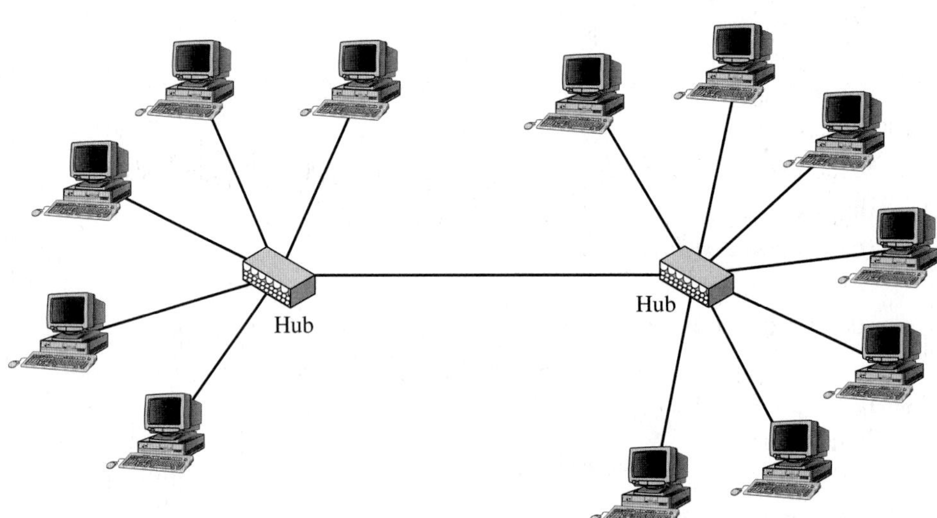

A sample network.

You plan to use the same topology when you expand the network.
   (a) What term most accurately describes this topology?
   (b) How can you determine whether this is a logical ring or logical bus?
   (c) The wire leading to one node is accidentally cut. What should you expect as the effect from this?
   (d) Users on one star can't communicate with users on the other. What would most likely cause this?

3. You support a small ad hoc mode network with five nodes. You are planning to add two additional computers in the near future.

(a) Why is security a potential concern in this configuration?

(b) What other term is used to refer to this topology?

(c) What additional hardware is needed to add two computers?

(d) What hardware would be needed if the network were configured as an infrastructure mode network?

YOU TRY IT

Designing Your Network Topology

Your office network is currently wired in a physical bus topology. Because of the age of the cable, how it is routed, and physical wear and damage over time, cable plant failures are occurring almost daily. You have been authorized to buy the equipment necessary to rewire the office, including new NICs (if necessary) and connection devices.

In two months, the office is expanding into additional adjoining floor space. This is a temporary move until new offices can be made ready for move-in, which is expected to happen in six or seven months. Only a few employees will be moving into the extra space, and you want to minimize the cost and effort needed to give these employees network access.

1. What happens if the cable fails in a physical bus network?
2. What kind of logical topology does the current network use?
3. What type of physical topology should you use when rewiring the current office area?
4. Why would you use that physical topology?
5. What logical topology should you use?
6. What kind of topology should you use to support the additional space you are moving into in two months?
7. Why would you use that topology?
8. Describe the general steps you would need to take in two months to support the employees moving into the additional space.

5 NETWORK MEDIA AND DEVICES

Starting Point

Go to www.wiley.com/college/ciccarelli to assess your knowledge of network media and devices.
Determine where you need to concentrate your effort.

What You'll Learn in This Chapter

- ▲ Coaxial cable type specifications
- ▲ Shielded twisted-pair (STP) cable type specifications
- ▲ Unshielded twisted-pair (UTP) cable category specifications
- ▲ Network devices
- ▲ Internetwork connection devices

After Studying This Chapter, You'll Be Able To

- ▲ Compare and contrast wired network media options
- ▲ Given a network application, identify the correct type of cable
- ▲ Describe appropriate applications for fiber-optic media
- ▲ Identify the devices needed to implement an Ethernet or Token Ring network
- ▲ Given internetwork connectivity and feature requirements, select the appropriate connection device
- ▲ Compare the appropriate use of bridges and routers

INTRODUCTION

This chapter focuses on physical network hardware. Before you can deploy a network, you need to collect the necessary hardware. But before you do that, you need to understand what hardware is required and the various functions that different types of hardware perform. Today's technical marketplace offers a staggering variety of vendor and equipment options.

Your goals when selecting network hardware typically include meeting target goals for the following:

- **Cost:** You want to keep costs to a minimum without sacrificing quality.
- **Scalability:** Your choices need to be able to grow and expand as your organization grows, so interoperability and adherence to standards are important.
- **Reliability:** Downtime is annoying and expensive, so you want to be sure that you can rely on your choices.
- **Management:** Management and maintenance are a significant part of your ongoing costs, so it pays to keep the design as simple as possible.

Everything in a network is interrelated. When installing a new network, most of your hardware selections are driven by your topology choice. When expanding an existing network, you need to understand and consider existing hardware in order to make topology and hardware decisions for new network segments.

5.1 Choosing Network Media

A network's transmission media is a long-term investment. Unlike computer equipment, which is often replaced every 2 to 5 years, a company may use the same networking media for 10 or 15 years. Thus, choosing the correct media is crucial to having a functioning network.

For now, we're going to focus on four basic wired media types:

- Coaxial cable (using copper wire)
- Shielded twisted-pair (using copper wire)
- Unshielded twisted-pair (using copper wire)
- Fiber optic (using glass or plastic)

You need to consider variations within each of these categories when making your media selections. The appropriate media type is determined by your physical topology, logical topology, and bandwidth requirements. Included with your media selection are the physical connectors used to connect to the network.

Copper cable is the oldest form of networking media. In addition, the vast majority of existing networks use some form of copper cable. For higher-speed networks, many organizations are electing to use fiber-optic media, although copper can provide exceptional transmission rates—into the gigabits per second (Gbps) range.

Media are possibly the single most important long-term investment you will make in your network and should be chosen with great consideration. Your choice of media type affects the type of NICs installed, the speed of the network, and the capability of the network to meet the needs of the future.

You also need to consider a number of factors related to cable routing and placement. Let's start there.

5.1.1 Routing Your Cable Plant

Most regions have building codes that include specifications for network cable installation. This includes items such as how or where cable can be routed, the use of **conduit** (i.e., metal or plastic pipe used to contain the cable), and even the type of outer insulation the cable can have. One of the reasons many companies have contractors install network cable for them is to make sure that all code requirements are met.

Even when code requirements are not a factor, there are commonsense guidelines (most of which happen to match up with typical code requirements) for installing network cable. Where you route your cable can be significant and can directly affect reliability and safety. Cable insulation is another safety consideration.

When installing network cable, you want to avoid high-traffic areas. In other words, you shouldn't put your cable where people will be walking. There are two reasons for this: to protect the cable and to protect employees (or others walking through the work area). It's easy to overlook loose cables, and wherever you have loose cables, someone will eventually trip over them. However, it's just as hazardous for the cables. The constant movement and flexing as people walk over the cables eventually causes the internal conductors to break. The most common symptom is intermittent communication problems as the connection is made and lost. Because of this, cables are most often routed through suspended ceilings or through floors with a cable space for that purpose.

When it becomes necessary to cross a traffic lane, cables should be covered and protected. You need to protect network cables even when they are just running down a wall. The best way to do this is to run the cables through conduit that contains network cables only or, at most, network cables and telephone lines. You should not run network cables through the same conduit as electrical lines. The copper wire cables can pick up a voltage through **induction**, the process through which a moving electrical current causes a voltage on a nearby wire. The voltage can reach levels that can damage computer equipment or even cause injury.

You also need to route copper wire network cables to avoid sources of **electromagnetic interference (EMI)** and **radio-frequency interference (RFI)**. Both EMI and RFI are sources of unwanted signals on network cable that degrade signal quality. The interference levels depend on how the cables are routed and the type of cable used. (You'll learn more on cable types in the following sections.)

EMI sources include any strong magnetic field, such as electric motors and fluorescent lights. You should avoid routing cables near sources such as refrigerators or copy machines. When running past fluorescent lights, you should route the cable as far above the lights as possible and across, rather than with, the direction of the bulbs. RFI can be picked up from any radio-frequency sources, including wireless transmitters if located too close to long cable lengths, and microwave sources.

Fiber-optic cable is immune to problems with induction, EMI, and RFI. It is not, however, immune to physical damage. In fact, it is more fragile than copper wire cables, so you need to take extra care to avoid compression or vibration. Also, fiber-optic cable is more expensive and more difficult to work with than copper wire.

Most codes require any cable routed through walls, floors, and ceilings, and some require all cable, to have plenum insulation. **Plenum** is made from Teflon and is fire retardant, so in case of a fire, the cable won't help to spread the fire. The other insulation types you commonly see, such as **polyvinyl chloride (PVC)** plastic, not only burn but also give off toxic vapors while burning.

5.1.2 Using Coax

Coaxial cable (coax) was the first type of networking media used in Ethernet LANs. There are still many networks that use coaxial cable, though most are legacy networks.

Coaxial cable, as you can see in Figure 5-1, is constructed from one central copper wire that is covered with a plastic insulator, called a dielectric, and shielded from interference by a foil wrapping or braid. The outer jacket that protects the cable is either PVC or plenum. The foil or braided shielding in the coaxial cable must be grounded at one end to protect against EMI and RFI.

Figure 5-1

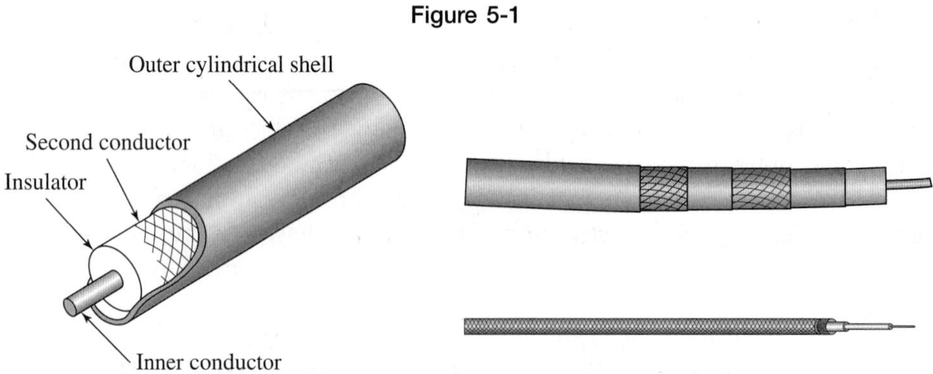

Coaxial cable.

All coax cables share the same basic structure but vary in the size of the central copper core and cable **impedance** (i.e., a measurement of opposition to electrical current or, more accurately, to a varying electrical current), measured in **ohms**. Higher impedance means higher resistance to a changing current, which is what you have in a data signal. Higher resistance means greater signal loss over a distance.

Recognizing Types of Coax

There are many types of coaxial cable, used in various applications, including networking and cable television, which is currently the most common implementation of coax. Each type of coax has specific characteristics that meet the needs of the type of transmission being carried. Table 5-1 shows the most common types of coax, comparing their impedance in ohms, common uses, and some of their basic characteristics. Many types of coax use the **radio grade (RG)**

Table 5-1: Coaxial Cable Types

Classification	*Impedance*	*Implementation*	*Description*
RG-6	93 ohms	Cable TV	Like RG-59 but larger in diameter to accommodate higher bandwidth for cable TV transmissions
RG-8	50 ohms	Thick Ethernet (Thicknet)	Solid copper core approximately 0.4 inches in diameter; must use a drop cable to attach to a device's NIC
RG-11	75 ohms	Cable TV	Often has four layers of shielding
RG-58/U	50 ohms	Thin Ethernet (Thinnet)	Solid copper core less than 0.2 inches in diameter
RG-58 A/U	50 ohms	Thinnet	Like RG-58/U but with a stranded copper core
RG-58 C/U	50 ohms	Thinnet	Same as RG A/U but used in military applications
RG-59	75 ohms	ARCNET* and Cable TV	Thick copper core with a large outer housing
RG-62	93 ohms	ARCNET and IBM mainframes	Used in IBM 3270 systems to connect terminals to the mainframe

*ARCNET was an early OSI layer 2 networking protocol that you are unlikely to ever see.

classification, which defines the size of the copper center and the diameter of the outer jacket. The coax types most commonly used in networks are Thinnet (still used, but very rarely) and Thicknet (found only in legacy networks but not used in new deployments).

Comparing Ethernet Coaxial Cables

Thicknet (10Base5) was the original cable used in Ethernet networks. It was typically used as a backbone, and it typically used a connection device known as a **vampire tap** (because it pierced the dielectric to connect to the inner core) to connect devices to the main cable through the use of a **drop cable**, or **DIX cable**, a device cable specific to this network implementation. The name comes from the way that the cable usually dropped from a Thicknet cable running through the ceiling to the device. Figure 5-2 shows a common Thicknet cable with vampire taps and drop cables.

Thinnet (10Base2) was developed after Thicknet. Compared to Thicknet, Thinnet is smaller in diameter and much easier to work with. The connectors used with Thinnet, known as BNC connectors, can be either barrel connectors that attach one cable to another or T connectors that attach devices to one cable. These connectors simply have to be connected and twisted into place to ensure their connection.

The advantages of Thinnet coaxial cable include the following:

- ▲ It's easy to install (especially compared to Thicknet).
- ▲ It's small in diameter.
- ▲ Its shielding, when grounded, reduces EMI and RFI.

The disadvantages of using Thinnet include the following:

- ▲ If a cable breaks, the entire network goes down.
- ▲ The cable must be grounded to prevent interference.

Figure 5-2

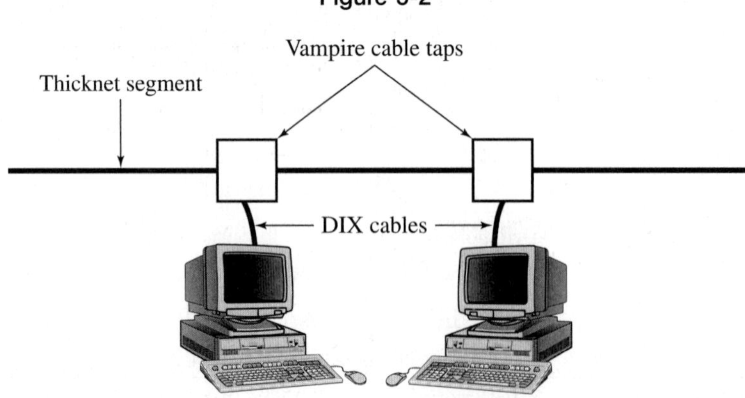

Thicknet client connections.

- ▲ It's more expensive than twisted-pair cable.
- ▲ The connectors and compatible NICs can be expensive.
- ▲ It does not support high-speed transmissions.

The shielding of Thinnet must be grounded on one end (and only one end) to be effective. Many implementations are not grounded, giving a false sense of security and protection. The cable must also be terminated at both ends.

Thinnet is considered antiquated by most network implementers, but its relative ease of use is appealing to some. A few manufacturers produced NICs that have both a coaxial cable connector and an unshielded twisted-pair (UTP) connector, allowing you to change media as the network develops and the coaxial cable is phased out. NICs of this type have become uncommon and difficult to find, however, but are sometimes purchased as used equipment.

5.1.3 Using STP

Shielded twisted-pair (STP) is made up of pairs of copper wires that are twisted together (see Figure 5-3). The pairs are covered in a foil or braided shielding, as well as an outer PVC jacket. As with coaxial cable, the shielding must be grounded to prevent the foil or braided shielding from becoming a magnet for electricity.

STP is subject to near-end crosstalk and EMI. **Crosstalk** is the electromagnetic interference that occurs when the electrical signal on one wire changes the electrical properties of a signal on an adjacent wire. The twists in the pair provide

Figure 5-3

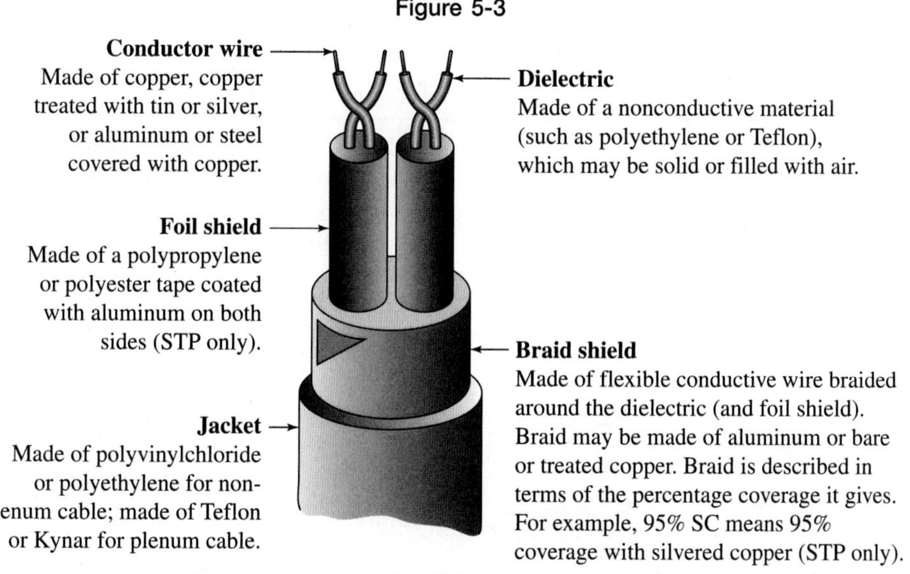
Conductor wire
Made of copper, copper treated with tin or silver, or aluminum or steel covered with copper.
Foil shield
Made of a polypropylene or polyester tape coated with aluminum on both sides (STP only).
Jacket
Made of polyvinylchloride or polyethylene for non-plenum cable; made of Teflon or Kynar for plenum cable.
Dielectric
Made of a nonconductive material (such as polyethylene or Teflon), which may be solid or filled with air.
Braid shield
Made of flexible conductive wire braided around the dielectric (and foil shield). Braid may be made of aluminum or bare or treated copper. Braid is described in terms of the percentage coverage it gives. For example, 95% SC means 95% coverage with silvered copper (STP only).

STP cable.

cancellation, which is a process in which two wires are twisted together to prevent outside interference or crosstalk.

The pairs in STP are color-coded to make installation easier. For example, the color codes for 150-ohm STP-A cable are red and green wires for pair 1 and orange and black wires for pair 2.

Comparing STP Types

Five types of STP are used in LAN implementations; STP is commonly used in Token Ring networks, occasionally in legacy ARCNET networks, and rarely in Ethernet networks. STP is most commonly referred to by IBM categories (i.e., **Type numbers**).

Ethernet implementations usually use UTP cable. The structure of UTP is similar to that of STP: two or more pairs of twisted wires covered in a plastic jacket, but without the shield.

Table 5-2 compares the types of STP cable, the number of pairs within each cable, the gauge of copper used, and the implementation of each. Cables used for voice-only and other non-networking applications are not included in the table.

Table 5-2: STP Cable Types

Type	*Number of Pairs*	*Gauge of Copper Conductor*	*Implementation*
Type 1	2	22	Used in IBM's Token Ring networks for the main ring or to connect nodes to the MAU
Type 2	4	22	Used as a hybrid cable, one designed for multiple concurrent applications, for voice and data
Type 6	2	26	Used as an adapter cable to connect a node to a MAU in Token Ring environments; can be used as a patch cable
Type 8	2	26	Data cable that uses flat wire and is designed to run under carpets; is prone to signal loss but is adequate for short distances
Type 9	2	26	Used between floors of a building; typically used in backbone implementations; has a solid or stranded core and a plenum jacket

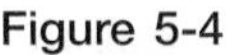

Figure 5-4

An IBM data connector.

The connectors developed for use with IBM cable are known as **IBM data connectors**. They are square, hermaphroditic connectors that are designed to interconnect with one another. Figure 5-4 shows a data connector.

The IBM data connector is designed specifically for use in a ring topology. If you connect the cable to a port in a MAU but not to a computer, the cable completes the circuit. When not connected, the cable internally connects transmit to receive and receive to transmit, completing the circuit (and the ring). The most common cable configurations are to have IBM data connectors at both ends of the cable or an IBM data connector on one end and an **RJ-45** modular jack at the other. An RJ-45 modular jack looks a lot like a phone plug (i.e., an R-11 jack), although RJ-45 jacks are slightly larger.

Choosing STP Cable

At one time, STP was the nearly exclusive choice for wiring a Token Ring network. This is no longer the case, since the introduction of MAUs and NICs designed to use UTP cable with modular connectors for RJ-45 jacks at each end.

The advantages of STP cable include the following:

- Shielding, if it is terminated, reduces EMI and RFI.
- STP can be used with RJ connectors, which are common and inexpensive, instead of the IBM hermaphroditic connectors.

The disadvantages of STP cable include the following:

- ▲ It must be properly grounded.
- ▲ It's more expensive than UTP.
- ▲ It's difficult to terminate.

Though not necessarily an advantage or a disadvantage, STP is specifically designed for use with Token Ring, so it is best matched to that use. However, terminating STP for IBM Token Ring networks takes time, due primarily to the fact that the cable is bulky and awkward, and the cable has to be grounded.

5.1.4 Using UTP

Unshielded twisted-pair (UTP), shown in Figure 5-5, is the most common implementation of copper media today. It is made from twisted pairs of color-coded copper wires, but without insulation to protect against interference. Instead, the wire pairs within each cable have varied numbers of twists per foot to provide cancellation to help prevent interference.

The most common use of UTP that is not related to PC LANs is as telephone cable. As a network media selection, there are variations of UTP that support Token Ring and Ethernet star topology networks.

Comparing UTP Types

Table 5-3 shows the UTP categories, the number of pairs in each, the grade of cable each uses, and how the different types are implemented. Standards defining UTP categories include **Electronic Industries Alliance/Telecommunications Industry Association (EIA/TIA)** 568-A and 568-B2. Backbone UTP versions, not listed in Table 5-3, have more than two pairs of wires, usually in multiples of 25 pairs.

Figure 5-5

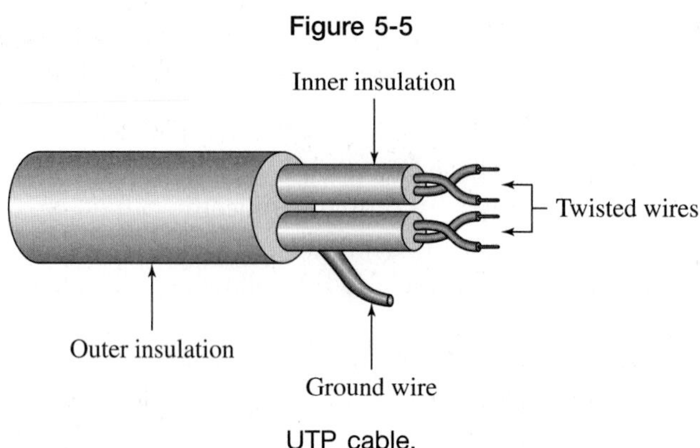

UTP cable.

Table 5-3: UTP Cable Categories

Type	*Number of Pairs*	*Transmission Rate*	*Implementation*
Category 1	2	Voice grade	Used in the telephone industry but not suitable for data transmissions (though it has been used for short distances)
Category 2	2	4Mbps	Can be used in data communications (e.g., Token Ring) but is rarely installed; no longer recognized under the 568-A standard
Category 3	4	10Mbps	Used for 10BaseT networks and for voice communication
Category 4	4	16Mbps	Used in IBM Token Ring networks
Category 5	4	100Mbps and higher	Used in Ethernet and 100BaseX networks; certified to 100Mbps
Category 5e	4	100Mbps and shigher	Used in Ethernet and 100BaseX–1000BaseX networks; certified to 1000Mbps
Category 6	4	100Mbps and higher or 400MHz transmissions	Used in Ethernet and 100BaseX networks; certified to up 10Gbps
Category 6e	4	10Gbps or 625MHz transmissions	Standard cable for 10 Gigabit Ethernet **(10GBaseT)**
Category 7	4	700MHz or up to 1.2GHz in special applications	Full-motion video and special government and manufacturing applications; not currently used for LAN applications

The UTP category number should be marked on the plastic jacket, as required by Underwriters Laboratories (UL), the organization responsible for testing the safety of electrical wires, including the types of cable used in networks. Figure 5-6 shows the category marking on UTP cable.

In July 2002, EIA/TIA approved the Category 6 (Cat 6) standard, called 568-B2.1, designed to support applications running at 1Gbps or better. Cat 6

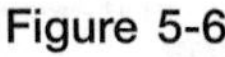

Figure 5-6

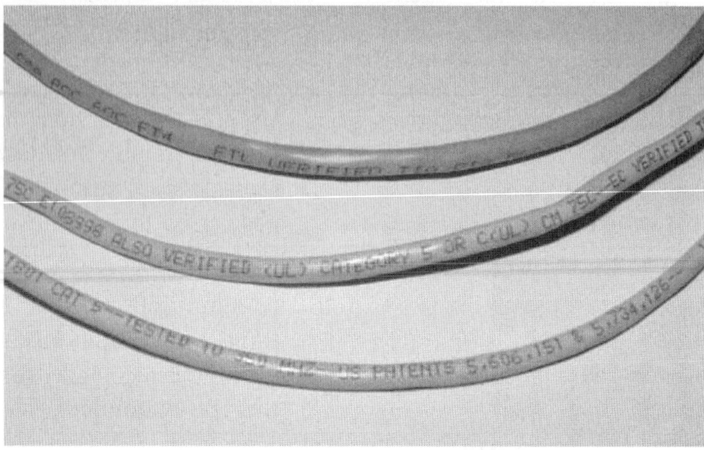

UTP cables showing labeling.

installations are generally considered more cost-effective than Cat 5 due to the greater variety of supported applications, higher potential bandwidth, and longer life span without need for cable upgrade (because it should meet future needs).

Choosing UTP Cable

When using UTP cable, you need to consider the type of cable and connectors to use. Solid UTP, which consists of solid wires of copper twisted together, is used for permanent installations, such as within walls or **raceways**. These permanent cable runs, referred to as **horizontal cross-connects**, are terminated at one end at a patch panel in the wiring closet and at the other end with, typically, an RJ-45 jack and wall plate. A patch panel is a wiring panel that simplifies wiring connections to multipair cables. Figure 5-7 shows a variety of RJ-45 jacks from different vendors. Jacks can be purchased for either the 568-A or 568-B standard, though some provide the color order for both standards within one plug.

UTP stranded cable consists of thin strands of copper within each individual wire. This type of UTP is more flexible than solid UTP and is used for patch cords that connect devices to the RJ-45 jacks in the wall. Within the wiring closet, a patch cord is used between the patch panel and a hub or switch to connect the devices.

The advantages of UTP include the following:

- ▲ It's inexpensive and easy to install.
- ▲ It's easy to terminate.
- ▲ It's widely used and tested.

Figure 5-7

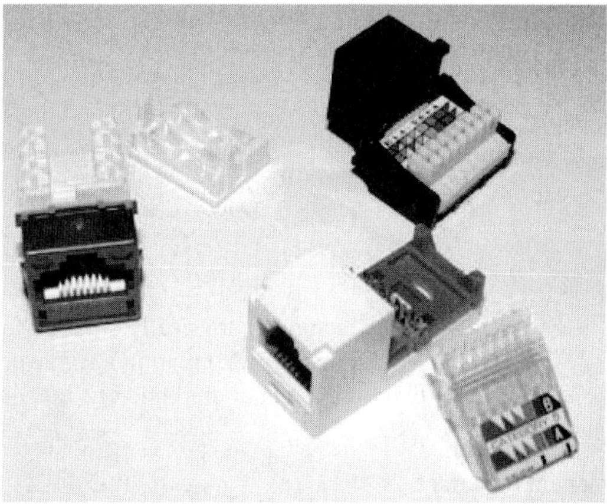

UTP connectors.

- ▲ It's easy to maintain and troubleshoot.
- ▲ Patch cables come precut in most popular lengths.
- ▲ It supports many network types.

The disadvantages of UTP include the following:

- ▲ It's susceptible to interference.
- ▲ It's prone to damage during installation if mishandled.
- ▲ It's prone to physical damage if routed through traffic areas and not protected.
- ▲ Distance limits are often misunderstood or not followed.

UTP cable is being installed in the vast majority of today's LANs, with Cat 6 cable the most popular choice for new installations. Most existing installations are wired with either Cat 3 or Cat 5 cable. Although fiber-optic cable might be used as the backbone cable between network segments, UTP is installed as the media to support connections to desktop computers and other devices.

5.1.5 Using Fiber-Optic Cable

Compared to copper media, fiber-optic media offer several advantages and only a few disadvantages. **Fiber-optic cable** is constructed of a center core of silica, extruded glass, or plastic. It is designed to pass specific types of light waves over long distances with very little **attenuation** (i.e., signal loss over distance). The center core of a multimode fiber-optic cable has a diameter of 125 microns

Figure 5-8

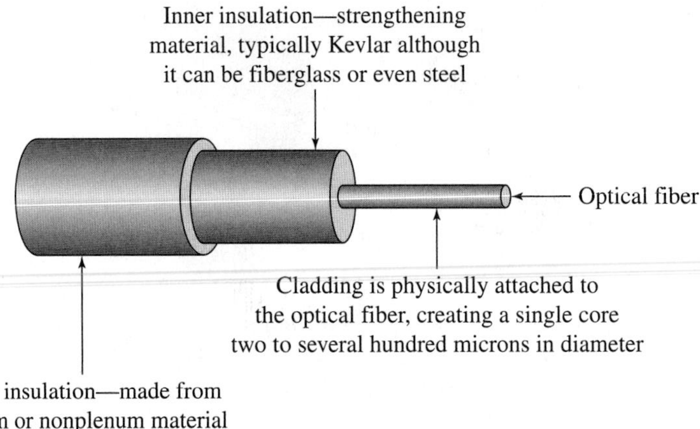

Fiber-optic cable.

(125μ), approximately the size of two human hairs. Fiber-optic cables can be purchased as single fibers or as pairs of up to 36 fiber strands. Pairs of fiber are needed to complete a full-duplex circuit.

Figure 5-8 is a cross-section of a typical fiber-optic cable. Outside the center core is **cladding**, which is reflective material that helps bend the light waves as they travel down the cable. **Kevlar**, the material used in bulletproof vests, is typically used to strengthen the cable and protect the glass fibers. Kevlar is extremely strong and resistant to damage.

Fiber-optic cable is immune to EMI and RFI and typically not affected by lightning and electrical surges, which can travel through copper media. In addition, compared to copper cable, fiber-optic cable can support a higher bandwidth for longer distances without the use of a repeater. Fiber-optic media transmit data using light, using either a laser light or a **light-emitting diode (LED)** as its light source. Laser is the preferred source for very long distance requirements (over several kilometers) because it typically emits a brighter light, but LED sources are preferred in most general LAN applications because they are more common, less expensive, more reliable, and have a longer projected life span.

Although many existing networks only utilize a fiber-optic cable as the backbone media, some companies are installing fiber-optic cable to the desktop. Plastic fiber is not currently accepted by the EIA/TIA 568-A standard, but despite this, it is widely used because the cables are usually less expensive and are less likely to be damaged during installation.

Recognizing Cables and Connectors

Fiber-optic cables come in various sizes that are identified by the size of the center core. The most common size for **multimode fiber**, which supports multiple

Figure 5-9

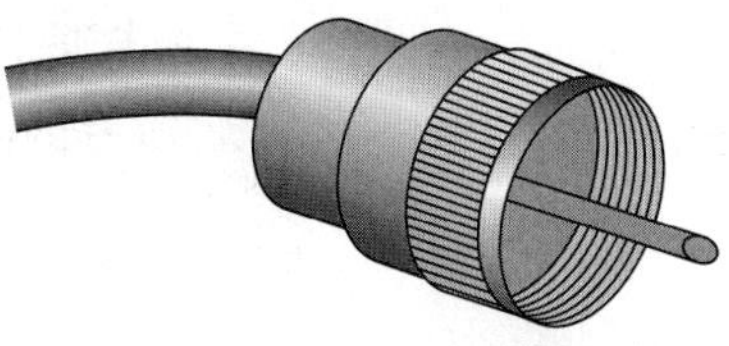

An SMA connector.

transmission signals, is 62.5/125 microns. **Single-mode fiber**, which carries a single transmission signal, is more commonly used in long-distance applications and has a core of 8/125 microns. Single-mode fiber can be implemented over 3 kilometers without needing a repeater. Several types of fiber-optic connectors are used, including SMA, ST, and SC connectors.

There are two variations of the **SMA connector** screw-on connection shown in Figure 5-9. The 905 type has a straight connector. The 906 type has a connector that is smaller at the end so that two connectors can be joined with the use of a coupler. The difficulty in pairing two connectors to meet the needs of the dual-fiber interface has limited the use of the SMA connector in many new installations.

A **straight tip (ST) connector** uses a connection similar to that of a BNC connector. After you insert the connector, you twist and lock it into place. An ST connector is quick and simple to install, but it is difficult to pair in dual-fiber installations. Figure 5-10 shows two ST connector variations.

A **subscriber connector (SC)**, shown in Figure 5-11, is currently the most popular and is easy to recognize, with its square tip. An SC connector is easy to

Figure 5-10

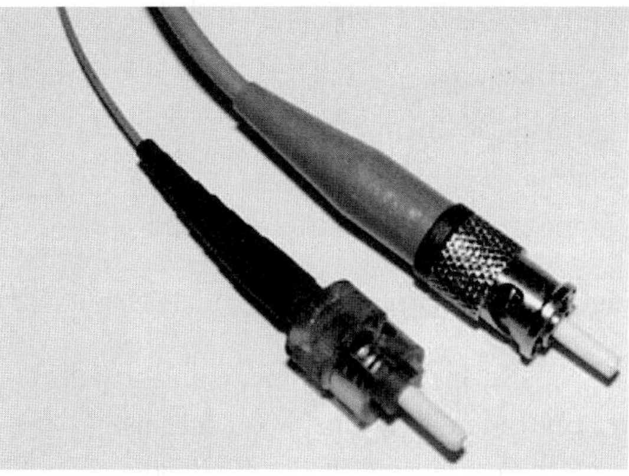

ST connectors.

Figure 5-11

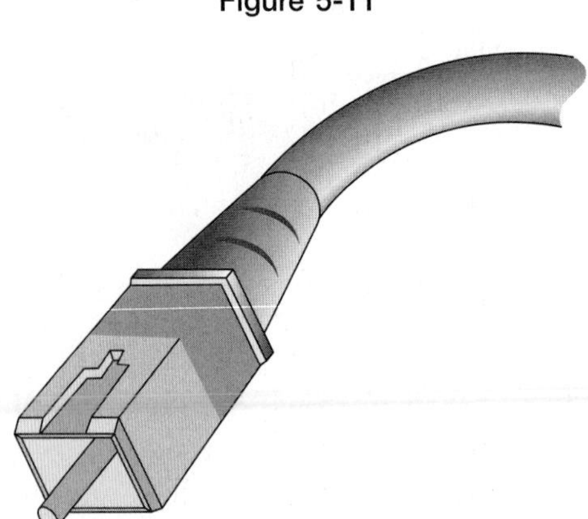

A keyed SC connector.

install and is often coupled into duplex cables that form sets. A paired set may include keying, which prevents it from being installed incorrectly. In a **keyed set**, one connector is shaped slightly differently from its mate on the other end. This prevents the fibers from being crossed at installation.

The keyed SC connector, shown in Figure 5-11, has been adopted under EIA/TIA 568-A as the recommended fiber connector, referenced as 568-SC.

Justifying the Use of Fiber-Optic Cable

Fiber-optic cable can be used in many LAN architectures and applications, including Ethernet, 10BaseF, FDDI, Optical Token Ring (i.e., Token Ring using fiber-optic cable), and some **Asynchronous Transfer Mode (ATM)** architectures. ATM is a dedicated connection-switching technology often used for WAN connections.

The advantages of fiber-optic cable include the following:

- ▲ It can be installed over long distances.
- ▲ It provides a great deal of bandwidth.
- ▲ It is not susceptible to EMI or RFI.
- ▲ It cannot be tapped easily, so security is better.

The disadvantages of fiber-optic cable include the following:

- ▲ It's the most expensive media to purchase and install.
- ▲ It requires an appropriate conduit for outside use.
- ▲ You must match the cable type to the application.
- ▲ Strict installation guidelines must be met for the cable to be certified.

Terminating fiber-optic cable used to require extensive training, but today new techniques allow novices to learn how to terminate fiber in a matter of minutes. These new kits and fiber tips use specialized cutters and epoxy to ensure success. This has helped drive greater use of fiber-optic cable in LAN applications.

FOR EXAMPLE

A Cable Runs Through It

Wiring a home network is usually a simple matter involving just a hub and a few device cables. Most office environments are much more challenging and complex. Typically, you can't have hubs spread around with cables running every which way. Such a configuration would lead to an unreliable network and a potential safety hazard.

When wiring an office, you usually have one central connection point, often the same room where you keep all your network servers. That's where you have all your hubs. The hubs then go not directly to the network devices but to a patch panel like the type of panel used to wire a telephone system. Networking patch panels are typically designed with a set of jacks, often 100 or more, that are wired to connectors designed to let you attach your multipair cable used to wire the building.

How the multipair cable is routed depends on the building design. If raceways are available, they are used. Otherwise, the cable is run through the suspended ceiling. Either way, the cables eventually terminate with wall jacks. Prewired cables with RJ-45 connectors are then used to connect the devices to the jacks.

You might think this setup would make for a troubleshooting nightmare, but in fact, it's designed to make troubleshooting as easy as possible. Indicator lights at the hub and patch panel give you the status of connections at that end. At the device end, indicator lights on the NIC give you the status there. For the run from the patch panel to the device jack, you can use an inexpensive continuity checker to test the line for breaks or shorts.

SELF-CHECK

1. List the UTP categories and the typical application of each.

2. Contrast the structure of STP, UTP, and fiber-optic cable.

5.2 Implementing Network Devices

The transmission media carry the signal, but devices need a way of connecting to the media to transmit and receive. Most networks also have a selection of other devices, as needed, to perform various functions on the network.

In this section, we focus primarily on wired networks and wired network devices. These include the network adapter (or NIC), central hub devices, and repeaters.

5.2.1 Using NICs

A NIC provides a device with a physical connection to the network. NICs can provide connections for any type of networking media, including wireless media. Not only do servers and workstations have NICs, so do network printers and all other network devices. Sample NICs are shown in Figure 5-12.

Specialized software known as a **device driver** lets the computer's operating system communicate with and control the NIC. Ethernet and Token Ring NICs have the MAC address hard-coded into the NIC by the manufacturer. The MAC address is unique so that data packets can be addressed appropriately to reach

Figure 5-12

NICs.

specific devices. If the NIC or the ROM chip containing the MAC address is replaced, the device's MAC address changes.

When selecting a NIC, it's important to check the following:

- The NIC must support the type of network you wish to connect to (Ethernet, Token Ring, etc.).
- The NIC must offer the right type of connector for the network media you're using (BNC, RJ-45, etc.).
- The NIC must support the available expansion slots (e.g., PCI for desktop, mini-PCI or PCMCIA for laptops).

To understand where a NIC fits in the process, think about the layers in the OSI networking model. When acting as a communication source device, the NIC does the following:

- Receives the data packet from the Network layer.
- Attaches its MAC address to the data packet.
- Attaches the MAC address of the destination device to the data packet.
- Converts data into packets (technically frames, but packets are also acceptable) appropriate to the network access method (e.g., Ethernet, Token Ring, FDDI).
- Converts packets into electrical, light, or radio signals to transmit over the network.
- Provides the physical connection to the media.

As a destination device, the NIC does the following:

- Provides the physical connection to the media.
- Translates the electrical, light, or radio signals into data.
- Reads the destination MAC address to see whether it matches the device's own address.
- Passes the packet to the Network layer if the destination MAC address matches its own.

The NIC's role is the same, no matter what type of device it is installed in or the type of media for which it is designed. If you are changing network type or architecture, you typically have to replace the computer's NIC as part of the process.

5.2.2 Using Hubs

A hub is the central point of connection for cable segments in a physical star topology. Technically, a hub is a multiport repeater for use with twisted-pair cable. Some hubs can also provide different services, depending on the sophistication of the hub. These specialty hubs include:

- **Managed hubs: Managed hubs** support remote management and monitoring, such as remotely disabling a hub port.
- **Switched hubs: Switched hubs** integrate functionality from switches (discussed later in this chapter) into the hub.
- **Intelligent hubs: Intelligent hubs** have on-board processors that can perform various functions, such as automatic error reporting, monitoring and reporting of network traffic statistics, traffic buffering and collision avoidance, and so forth.

You need to know what services you want so that you can select your hub accordingly.

You use a hub to create a logical bus wired as a physical star. A hub passes along all data that it receives, no matter which device it is addressed to, which can add to congestion on the network. Figure 5-13 shows a simple four-port hub connected to networking devices and creating a physical star topology. With simple hubs, collisions can occur at the hub, the same as on the cable in a physical bus.

The advantages of hubs include the following:

- They are inexpensive and readily available.
- They are easy to deploy and maintain.
- They can connect media operating at different speeds.

Figure 5-13

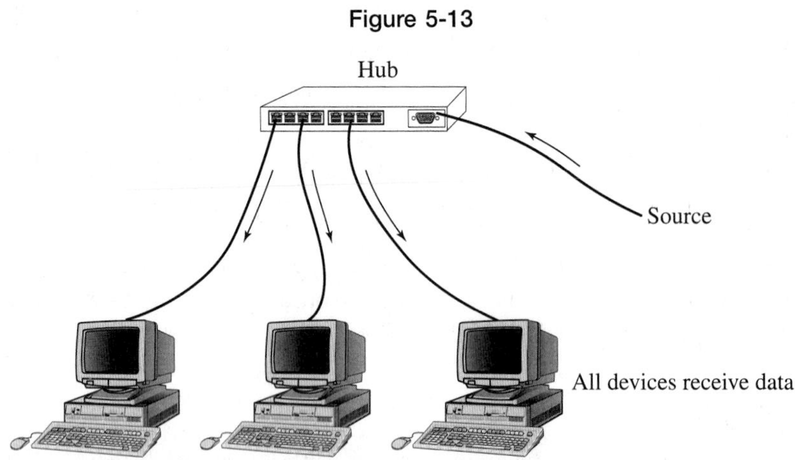

A hub and a physical star.

The disadvantages of hubs include the following:

- Simple hubs extend the **collision domain**—that is, the segment in which collisions can occur—so collisions can still occur.
- Hubs can't filter the information passing through them, so all packets transmit to all segments (i.e., all connected devices).

When choosing a hub for an Ethernet network, you need to consider the following:

- **The type of media connection you'll need:** Typically, hubs provide one type of network connection, although some do provide another port of a different type. Some older 10BaseT hubs include one BNC port with their RJ-45 ports.
- **The number of ports you'll need:** Hubs are typically available in 4- to 48-port configurations. It's also possible, with most hubs, to link them together to create a single logical bus.
- **Speed:** A hub's speed depends on the type of network it is designed for use with, typically supporting both 10Mbps and 100Mbps, but 1Gbps and faster hubs are available. Some hubs let you mix speeds, detecting the device speed and converting the signal as necessary, so that slower devices don't slow down the network as a whole.
- **Whether it's managed or unmanaged:** Managed hubs allow a network administrator to use software to view how the device is functioning from a remote workstation.
- **Whether there's an uplink port:** An **uplink port** lets you interconnect two hubs using a standard connection cable. The uplink port can be a separate port and identified as such or one that can be used as either a standard or uplink port, controlled by a switch.

It is possible to connect hubs without an uplink port by running a crossover cable between the hubs. A **crossover cable** is wired so that the transmit and receive pairs are reversed on one end. In other words, data transmitted at one end come in as received data on the other. When using an uplink port, however, you use a standard cable, not a crossover cable.

5.2.3 Using Switches

Current switches often look and are commonly used exactly like hubs, but they are in fact much more sophisticated devices. Switches are specific to the access method they are designed to support, so that an Ethernet switch is used in Ethernet networks only, a Token Ring switch in Token Ring networks, and so forth.

Figure 5-14

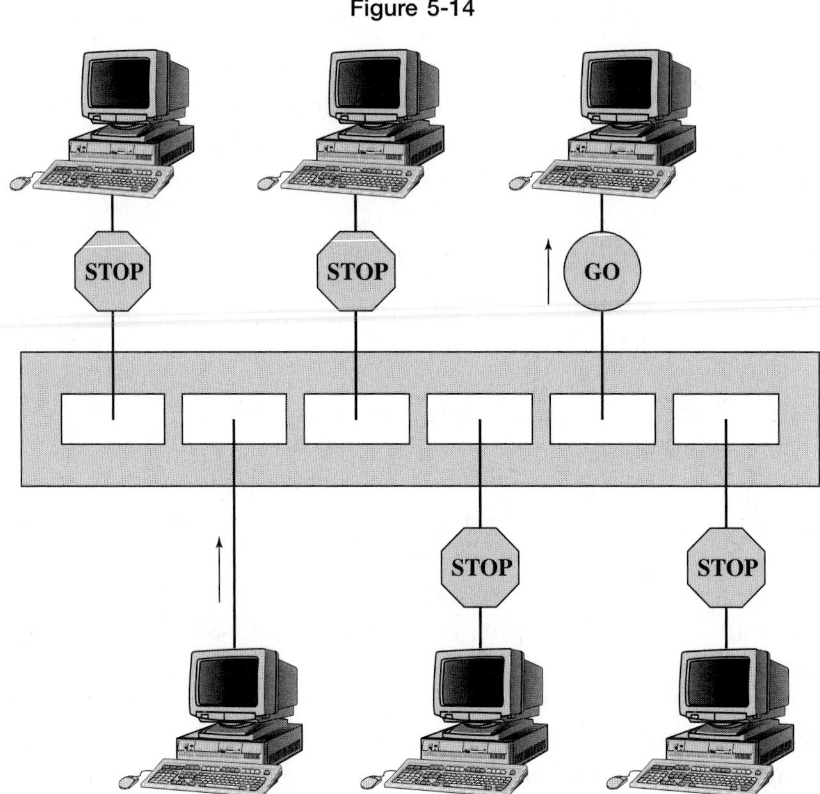

A switch and MAC address filtering.

Switches are actually multiport bridges that function at the Data Link layer of the OSI model. As shown in Figure 5-14, each port of a switch makes a decision about whether to forward data packets to the attached network. The switch keeps track of the MAC addresses of all attached node addresses and the port to which each node is connected. With some switches, this can be a MAC address list, if a hub is connected to the switch port instead of a single device. This information can help filter traffic and eliminate unwanted congestion.

Switches have become increasingly popular with network administrators and designers. Prices have become competitive with those of hubs, though switches are still more expensive than hubs, and many of today's networks have switches installed in their wiring closets. Switches cut down on network traffic and keep the transmission of bandwidth-intensive data from affecting the entire network because each port on a switch is a separate collision domain.

The advantages of switches include the following:

- ▲ They limit the collision domain.
- ▲ They can segment the network into multiple segments with separate collision domains.
- ▲ They support intelligent management capabilities, including, in many servers, a built-in Web server for remote management over the Internet.
- ▲ They can limit broadcast traffic propagated between segments. A **broadcast** goes out to every device on the network segment. If a response is required, every device can potentially respond, greatly increasing the amount of traffic generated.

The disadvantages of switches include the following:

- ▲ They are typically more expensive than a hub of the same size.
- ▲ Some switches are typically complex and difficult to configure.
- ▲ Additional, optional, functionality can add to the potential complexity.

The most important advancement in switching to date is the capability to create **virtual LANs (VLANs)**. A VLAN is a LAN in which devices are logically configured to communicate as if they were attached to the same network, without regard to their physical locations.

A VLAN is used to create a **broadcast domain**, which is a set of nodes that receive broadcasts in a group, as if they were all on (and the only nodes on) the same physical segment. In a VLAN, ports are grouped into a single broadcast domain. Figure 5-15 shows how a VLAN allows devices to function as part of the same network segment, despite their physical location and connection. This type of VLAN can be created at layer 2, using MAC addresses, or at layer 3 using network addresses.

VLANs are defined by the **802.1p** and **802.1Q** standards, which specify the use of a router to pass packets between VLANs and to other networks. Routers typically do not pass broadcast packets.

5.2.4 Using MAUs

A MAU provides the function on a Token Ring network that a hub or switch provides on an Ethernet network. It provides the central connection that lets you wire a logical ring as a physical star, as shown in Figure 5-16.

The ring is created inside the MAU. When you connect additional MAUs, as shown in Figure 5-16, the ring is extended to the other MAUs. The ports used to connect the MAUs are typically labeled **Ring In** and **Ring Out.** With some older MAUs, you must physically complete the ring by connecting Ring Out on the last MAU back to Ring In on the first. With current MAUs, if the cable connecting the MAU were disconnected, the network would become two separate logical rings.

Figure 5-15

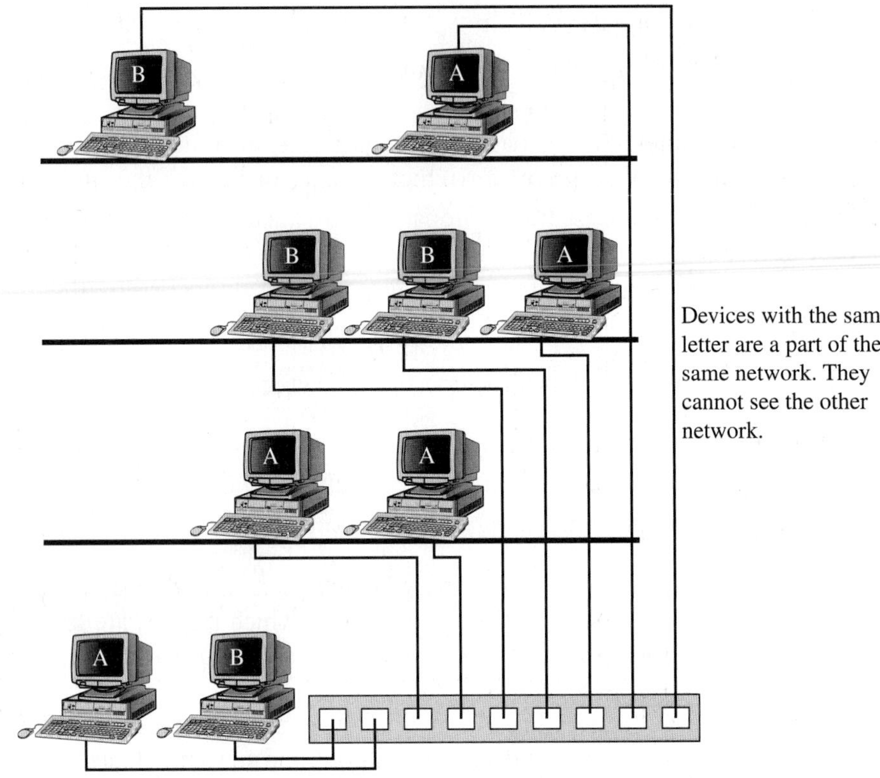
B
A
B
B
A
Devices with the same letter are a part of the same network. They cannot see the other network.
A
A
A
B

A VLAN configuration.

Figure 5-16

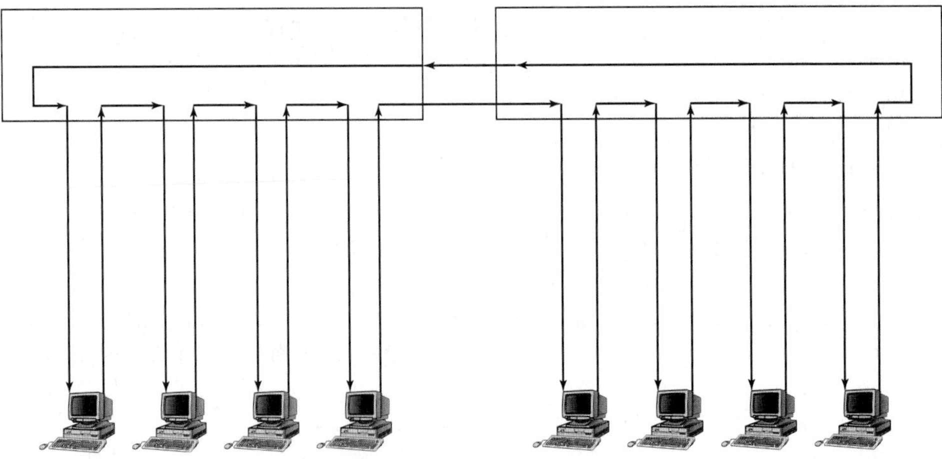

A MAU star.

When no device is connected to a MAU device port, the signal passes on to the next port. When a device is connected, the ring includes the device. Each token (i.e., data packet) is received by every node in the path in order. If the device isn't the destination, it retransmits the token so that the signal is constantly being boosted. This means that each device also acts as a repeater.

The advantages of MAUs include the following:

- ▲ They are easy to install and configure.
- ▲ They have a long, reliable track record, often remaining in use for several years.
- ▲ MAUs are easy to troubleshoot and, in some instances, are self-healing.

The disadvantages of MAUs include the following:

- ▲ MAUs are more expensive than Ethernet hubs or switches.
- ▲ Compatible hardware, cables, and NICs are relatively expensive and sometimes difficult to locate.
- ▲ MAUs are designed specifically for either 4Mbps or 16Mbps Token Ring, so the two cannot be mixed.
- ▲ MAUs are based on older technology and support a maximum bandwidth of 16Mbps.

You cannot directly connect 4Mbps and 16Mbps MAUs. You cannot use a 4Mbps NIC with a 16Mbps MAU or vice versa. You can have both on the same network, but they must be on different cable segments connected by a bridge that manages the conversion between the two.

In most MAUs, a physical relay is used to open or close the connection to the device. You therefore often hear a series of "clicks" whenever the MAU is powered up or reset. Many MAUs support intelligent control that lets you remotely reset the MAU, view the status of the ports, and even enable or disable individual ports. Often, they can detect common communication problems, such as a device that fails to responds to a token, and automatically remove the device from the ring.

5.2.5 Using Repeaters

Repeaters are networking devices that allow you to connect segments, thus extending a network beyond the maximum length of the cable segment. A repeater functions at the Physical layer of the OSI model and connects two segments of the same network. There are repeaters that can connect segments of the same network that use different media types, such as an Ethernet segment using coaxial cable and another using Cat 5. A hub that includes a BNC

Figure 5-17

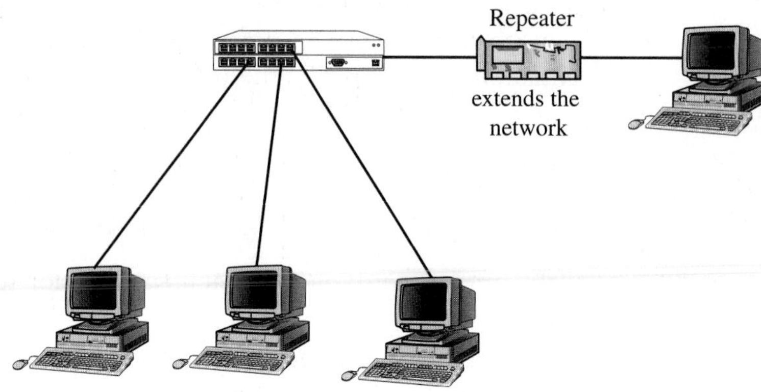

Using a repeater.

connector is effectively a repeater of this type. Figure 5-17 shows a router used to extend a network segment.

Simple repeaters are nothing more than amplifiers. They take the signal they receive, no matter how clean or dirty, and amplify it. Any unwanted noise is amplified along with the signal. More advanced repeaters have the ability to clean up the signal somewhat before retransmitting. Intelligent hubs acting also as repeaters can help to minimize collisions.

The advantages of repeaters include the following:

- ▲ A repeater can connect different types of media (such as coax to twisted-pair).
- ▲ Repeaters extend the distance a network can reach.
- ▲ Repeaters do not increase network traffic.

The disadvantages of repeaters include the following:

- ▲ A repeater extends the collision domain.
- ▲ Repeaters cannot filter information, so the same information goes to all nodes.
- ▲ Repeaters cannot connect different logical network architectures.
- ▲ A network can include only a limited number of repeaters.

It's difficult to use advantages and disadvantages of repeaters to compare them to other devices (except possibly hubs or switches). With repeaters and the applications where they are used, you either need a repeater or you don't. It's rare that you could use a different device in place of a repeater, though a bridge might be substituted in some situations.

FOR EXAMPLE

Making the Connection

Say that you're wiring an Ethernet network. Central connections are being made in a wiring closet. You want to try to keep down your costs and the network complexity, but you're concerned about collisions becoming a problem as the network grows. You also don't want to have to run to the wiring closet every time a user complains about a network problem. What are you going to do? You actually have a number of solutions available, given these network requirements, and some of your decisions will be based on personal preference, but let's look at one possible solution.

One way to wire this network is to use managed hubs and intelligent switches. Each switch port connects to a hub with a crossover cable. That hub represents a collision domain, meaning that collisions can occur at the hub but not between hubs. Traffic buffering at the switch prevents collisions between hubs.

How many switches do you need? You need enough to provide a separate port for each hub and, possibly, a port for each network server. Because of the amount of traffic likely at some servers, they might each justify being connected as their own collision domain.

What about the hubs? How many ports do you need on each hub? For that, you need to consider your network traffic requirements. You want to use as few hubs as possible to keep the network easy to manage, but the fewer hubs you have, the more ports per hub you have and the larger the collision domain. Most users often have limited network access requirements, so you might be able to use hubs somewhere in the 32-port or higher range. For more active clients, you can drop that number down to 16 ports or even fewer.

When installing a repeater, you should split the difference between network segments whenever possible. Consider the situation in Figure 5-18, in which a few devices are at either end, with 700 feet of 10Base2 Thinnet cable in between. The further the signal goes on the cable before reaching a repeater, the more the signal drops and the more noise can be introduced with the signal. One possibility is shown on top: You could run a 300-foot length, a repeater, another 300-foot length, another repeater, and finally 100 feet. The bottom of the figure shows a different solution: You would get a better network with a cleaner signal and better performance if you ran it as three lengths of 233 feet each, with a repeater between each.

Though typically thought of as being used with Ethernet networks, most often with physical bus networks, the situation depicted in Figure 5-18 is the

Figure 5-18

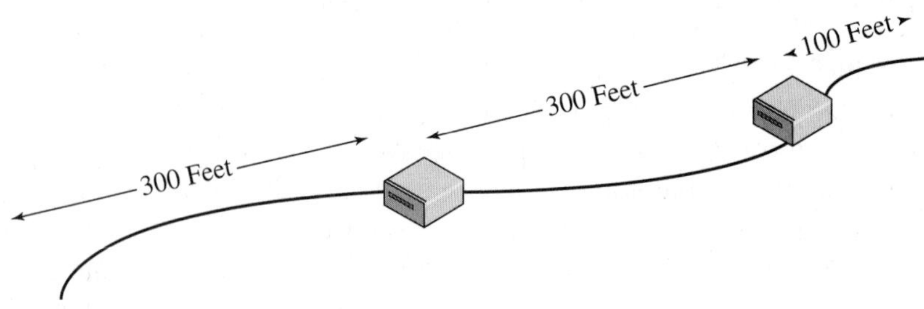

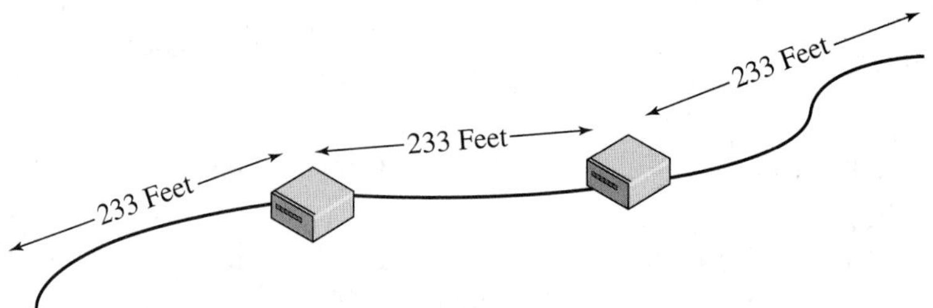

Repeater configurations.

only application of repeaters that you are likely to see. For example, a fiber-optic MAN backbone cable might include a repeater if a required segment run is longer than specified by the applicable fiber-optic standard. Even though supported, repeaters are rarely seen in Token Ring networks.

SELF-CHECK

1. What are the functional differences between a hub, a switch, and a MAU?
2. What is a VLAN?

5.3 Implementing Internetwork Devices

You can build a simple network with just NICs, hubs (or switches), and (if needed) repeaters. As networks grow and become more complex, additional devices are needed. What devices you need depend on the functionality you require. Commonly used devices include bridges, routers, brouters, and gateways. (Remember that you need to be sure of your context when discussing gateways. In a TCP/IP network, the term *gateway* is used to refer to a router. In its classic definition, a gateway can be a much more sophisticated device.)

5.3.1 Using Bridges

Bridges, like hubs, connect LAN segments, but they work at the Data Link layer of the OSI model. Because bridges work at the Data Link layer, they can use MAC addresses to make decisions about the data packets they receive. A bridge provides four key functions:

- It builds a bridging table to keep track of devices on each segment.
- It filters packets that do not need to be forwarded to other segments based on their MAC addresses.
- It forwards any packet whose destination MAC address is on a different network segment from the source.
- It divides one network into multiple collision domains, thereby reducing the number of collisions on any network segment.

Figure 5-19 illustrates how a bridge filters data. Bridges use the **Spanning Tree Protocol (STP)** to decide whether to forward a packet through the

Figure 5-19

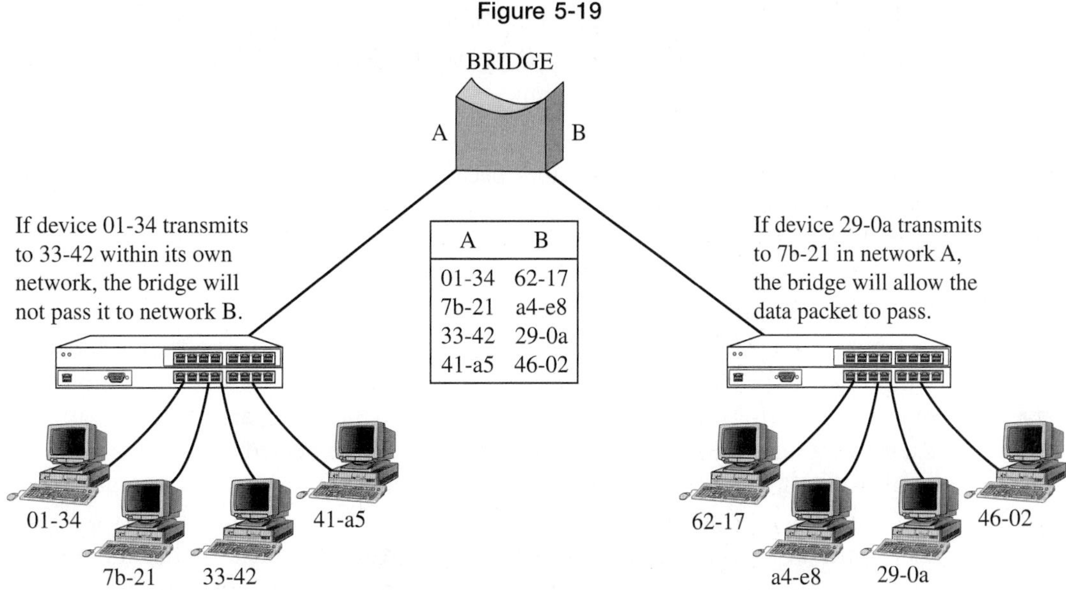

Bridge filtering.

bridge and on to a different network segment. STP serves two functions: First, it determines a main bridge, called a **root**, when there is more than one bridge present. The root makes all the bridging decisions and deals with all bridging problems. Second, it prevents **bridging loops**, which occur when traffic gets stuck traveling between bridges and never reaches the destination computer.

In some situations, you could use either a bridge or repeater to extend a network segment. The choice often comes down to determining which is more appropriate.

The advantages of bridges include the following:

- They limit the collision domain.
- They can extend network distances by boosting the signal.
- They can filter packets based on MAC addresses.
- They can connect different types of media.
- Some can connect different types of network architectures.
- Packets are processed by the bridge and retransmitted—not just amplified—providing a cleaner signal.

The potential disadvantages of bridges include the following:

- Broadcast packets cannot be filtered, so their impact on traffic is not changed.
- They are more expensive than repeaters.
- Compared to repeaters, they are more difficult to configure and create more complex network designs.
- They can make troubleshooting communication failures more difficult.
- They are slower than repeaters because they must process addresses and filter packets.

Many bridges have the ability to convert between architectures or encapsulate data for passing through a foreign network type. Encapsulation is the process of wrapping a network packet inside another network packet, such as wrapping an Ethernet packet inside an FDDI packet. Figure 5-20 shows an example of using a bridge to convert between network architectures; in this example, a Token Ring network (logical ring) is connected to an Ethernet network (logical bus). One thing you need to understand in this example is that both the Token Ring and Ethernet networks are part of the same network segment and would have the same network address. This means that for routing purposes, the two connected cable segments look to the router as if they were a single network segment.

Figure 5-20

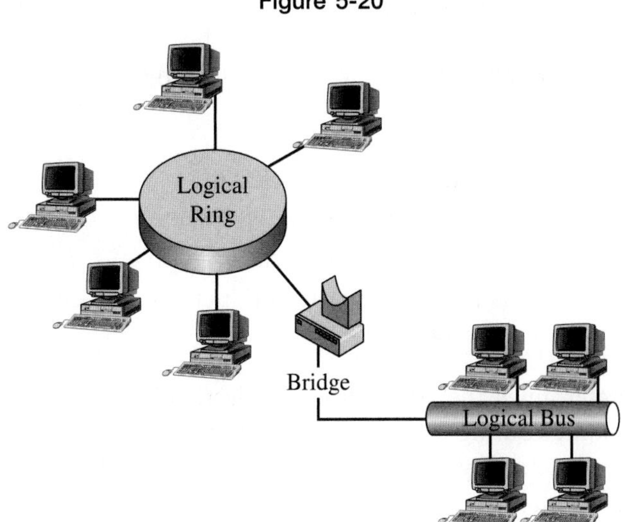

Connecting different architectures.

5.3.2 Using Routers

Routers connect different network segments that may be located in the same building or thousands of miles apart. They can connect different types of networks, such as Token Ring and Ethernet networks, or using different routed protocols including IP, IPX, DECnet, and AppleTalk. The router changes the packet's size, format, and addressing to fit the type of destination network on which the packet is being sent. Routers use the network address—the IP address in the TCP/IP environment, for example—to determine the best path for the packet to take to reach the destination quickly.

A router (or possibly a brouter) is usually not considered optional hardware. A network either does or doesn't have routing requirements. One situation in which a router might be considered optional is when it is used to segment a network as a way of reducing overall traffic requirements to improve network performance. Routers reduce broadcast traffic, for example. Except in a few examples, such as when supporting a broadcast domain or passing packets used to request automatic address assignments, routers block broadcast packets.

The advantages of routers include the following:

- ▲ They limit the collision domain.
- ▲ They can connect networks using different media and architectures.
- ▲ They determine the best path for a packet to reach another network.
- ▲ They can filter or block broadcasts.

When a router is used primarily to limit the collision domain or segregate traffic, you might consider using a bridge instead.

The disadvantages of routers include the following:

- ▲ They are more expensive than bridges.
- ▲ They must be used with routable protocols.
- ▲ They can be difficult to configure and maintain.
- ▲ They make troubleshooting communication problems more complex.
- ▲ They are slower than bridges due to the increased processing and routing updates sent between routers.

A router determines the best path to a destination based on either static routing or dynamic routing and shares path information (i.e., the **route**) with other network routers. Figure 5-21 shows several networks connected with routers. Even though there are several paths that the data could take to travel from network 1 to network 6, the router determines the best path based on the cost associated with getting there. The **cost** is based on an algorithm determined by the routing protocol being used, or it is set manually by the network administrator.

Figure 5-21

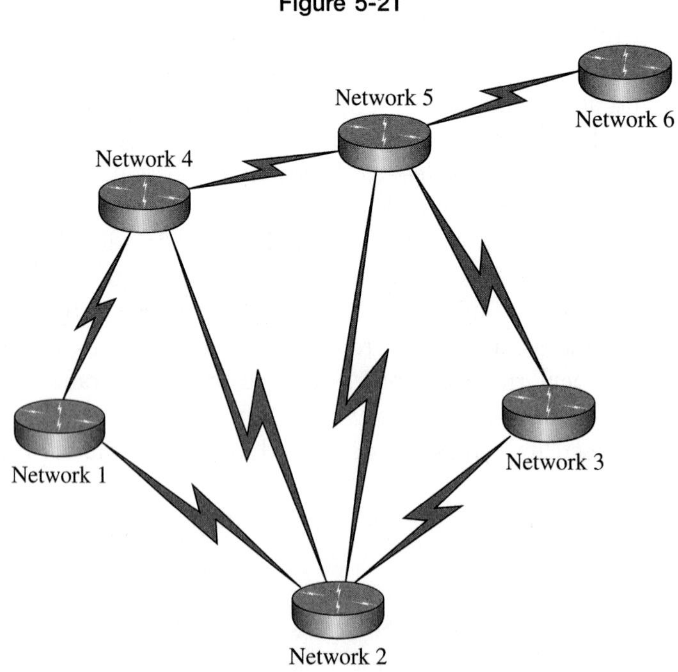

Determining the best path.

With **static routing**, a network administrator manually configures a route into the router's routing table. **Dynamic routing** adjusts automatically to network topology or traffic changes, based on information it receives from other routers. Whichever type of routing is used, the router determines the path for a packet by looking at the routing table, in which information about other networks is stored by the router. The **routing table** keeps track of known networks, the port on the router that should be used to send data to a particular network, and the cost for a data packet to get to that network.

5.3.3 Using Brouters

A brouter is a hybrid device that functions as both a bridge and a router. Brouters can work on networks using many different protocols. Any networking requirement that calls for a bridge or router can be filled by a brouter. Figure 5-22 shows a brouter acting as both a bridge and router.

A brouter can be programmed to function in a specific way. If a brouter is forwarding data packets for a nonroutable protocol, such as NetBEUI, the brouter is functioning as a bridge. NetBEUI is a nonroutable layer 2 protocol. If a brouter is set to route data packets to the appropriate network for a routed protocol such as IP, it is functioning as a router.

Advantages of using a brouter include those of both bridges and routers. However, a brouter is not without inherent disadvantages. The two primary disadvantages are cost and complexity, both exceeding those of either routers or bridges.

Figure 5-22

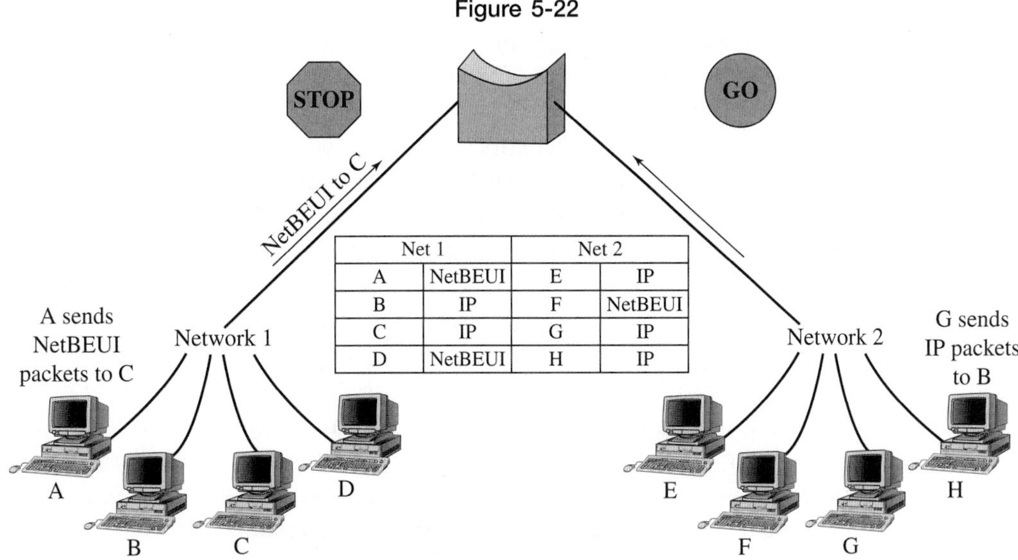

Net 1		Net 2	
A	NetBEUI	E	IP
B	IP	F	NetBEUI
C	IP	G	IP
D	NetBEUI	H	IP

A brouter.

5.3.4 Using Gateways

Gateways, by classic definition, are devices that allow different types of network systems to communicate with one another. The term *gateway* is used in a very general way in networking and can mean a variety of things. If the term is used in reference to a device on a network, it means the device is providing some type of translation services to systems that could otherwise not communicate. Translation services can include address, protocol, and data translations. A router that also provides protocol translation can be considered to be acting as a gateway. Common gateway applications include:

- **Mail gateway:** Transfers mail between different types of email services.
- **Host gateway:** Enables PCs to communicate natively with host computers.

FOR EXAMPLE

Software Routers

In this chapter we've talked about bridges, routers, and brouters as if they are separate, dedicated devices. In many applications, they are. Companies such as Cisco Systems have made their mark in the technology world by providing network devices dedicated to performing specific functions on a network and doing so well. Actually, however, the devices are a combination of dedicated hardware and software designed specifically for that purpose.

When you have critical, high-volume requirements, a dedicated device is the way to go. However, that isn't your only option. Most network operating systems, including Windows Server versions, let you create a router that is configured through the operating system. Need to connect to network segments? All you need to do is install network adapters in your server and enable routing. Need to bridge between Token Ring and Ethernet at the same time? No problem, as long as you have the right kind of NICs. Your software router is actually a brouter and can handle that for you, too. The necessary software ships with the operating system, so there's no additional software requirement.

If it's so easy and inexpensive to set up a router through software, why spend the money for a separate device? There are two primary reasons: performance and features. Because Windows Server is a general-purpose operating system, it does a wide range of things relatively well, but it doesn't do anything quite as well as dedicated software designed specifically for that purpose. Also, in order to be competitive and easier to cost-justify, dedicated routers include advanced management and maintenance features, making them more flexible that software routers.

Gateways tend to be expensive, difficult to configure, and, because of the processing overhead required, often relatively slow devices. However, in some situations, they are the best solution. For example, say that you have a network that includes a legacy Novell NetWare server that supports a proprietary server application. You have two options for accessing that server with Microsoft network clients. One is to install a NetWare client running in parallel with the built-in Microsoft client. If the client computers are running with minimal resources, however, installing an additional client could severely degrade performance. There are also licensing concerns because each client would require a separate license. The other option is to set up a Microsoft server configured as a NetWare gateway. The server could access the server resources and then share those resources with the Microsoft clients on the network. Also, because technically only one computer is accessing the NetWare server, only one client license is required.

SELF-CHECK

1. From the standpoint of collision zones and network segmentation, how do bridges and routers compare?
2. Contrast how bridges and routers filter traffic.

SUMMARY

This chapter focused on network hardware. You learned about four types of network media: coax, STP, UTP, and fiber-optic cable. You were introduced to different media types (categories) and their applications. You also learned about the devices needed to connect to the network, specifically NICS, hubs, switches, and MAUs. You also saw how a repeater can be used to extend a network. Finally, you learned about using bridges, routers, brouters, and gateways for internetwork connections.

KEY TERMS

10GBaseT

802.1p

802.1Q

Asynchronous Transfer Mode (ATM)

Attenuation

Bridging loop

Broadcast

Broadcast domain

Cladding

Coaxial cable (coax)
Collision domain
Conduit
Cost
Crossover cable
Crosstalk
Device driver
DIX cable
Drop cable
Dynamic routing
Electromagnetic interference (EMI)
Electronics Industries Alliance/ Telecommunications Industry Association (EIA/TIA)
Fiber-optic cable
Horizontal cross-connect
IBM data connector
Impedance
Induction
Intelligent hub
Kevlar
Keyed set
Light-emitting diode (LED)
Managed hub
Multimode fiber
Ohm
Plenum
Polyvinyl chloride (PVC)
Raceway
Radio grade (RG)
Radio-frequency interference (RFI)
Repeater
Ring In
Ring Out
RJ-45
Root
Route
Routing table
Shielded twisted-pair (STP) cable
Single-mode fiber
SMA connector
Spanning Tree Protocol (STP)
Static routing
Straight tip (ST) connector
Subscriber connector (SC)
Switch
Switched hub
Type number
Unshielded twisted-pair (UTP) cable
Uplink port
Vampire tap
Virtual LAN (VLAN)

ASSESS YOUR UNDERSTANDING

Go to www.wiley.com/college/ciccarelli to evaluate your knowledge of network media and devices.
Measure your learning by comparing pre-test and post-test results.

Summary Questions

1. A switch is effectively a multiport repeater. True or false?
2. What type of device do you use to configure a VLAN?
   (a) hub
   (b) switch
   (c) bridge
   (d) router
3. You need to connect two network cable segments: one that is Token Ring and one that is Ethernet 10BaseT. Both need to be part of the same network segment. Which device should you use?
   (a) hub
   (b) switch
   (c) bridge
   (d) router
4. How does a router filter traffic?
   (a) by network address
   (b) by MAC address
   (c) by host name
   (d) by network architecture
5. A hub operates at the same OSI layer as what other device?
   (a) repeater
   (b) switch
   (c) bridge
   (d) router
6. What kind of media has a central copper core, dielectric, shield, and insulation?
   (a) STP
   (b) UTP
   (c) fiber-optic cable
   (d) coaxial cable
7. Extruded glass is the only material used for fiber-optic cores. True or false?

8. By specification, a 10BaseT network is wired with what kind of cable?
   (a) STP
   (b) UTP
   (c) fiber optic
   (d) coaxial
9. Which STP cable type uses a flat-wire, 26-gauge conductor?
   (a) type 2
   (b) type 6
   (c) type 8
   (d) type 9
10. Cat 6 UTP is certified up to what bandwidth?
    (a) 4Mbps
    (b) 16Mbps
    (c) 100Mbps
    (d) 10Gbps
11. You can use either an uplink port or a crossover cable to connect two hubs. True or false?
12. A bridge extends the collision domain. True or false?
13. How does a bridge filter traffic?
    (a) by network address
    (b) by MAC address
    (c) by host name
    (d) by network architecture
14. What connector type is most commonly used with fiber-optic network applications?
    (a) SMA
    (b) ST
    (c) SC
    (d) BNC

Applying This Chapter

1. Your network is wired as shown in Figure 5-23. A fiber-optic cable is used as the vertical backbone. Each floor should be configured as a separate network segment.
   (a) What kind of device should you use to connect each floor to the backbone? Why?

Figure 5-23

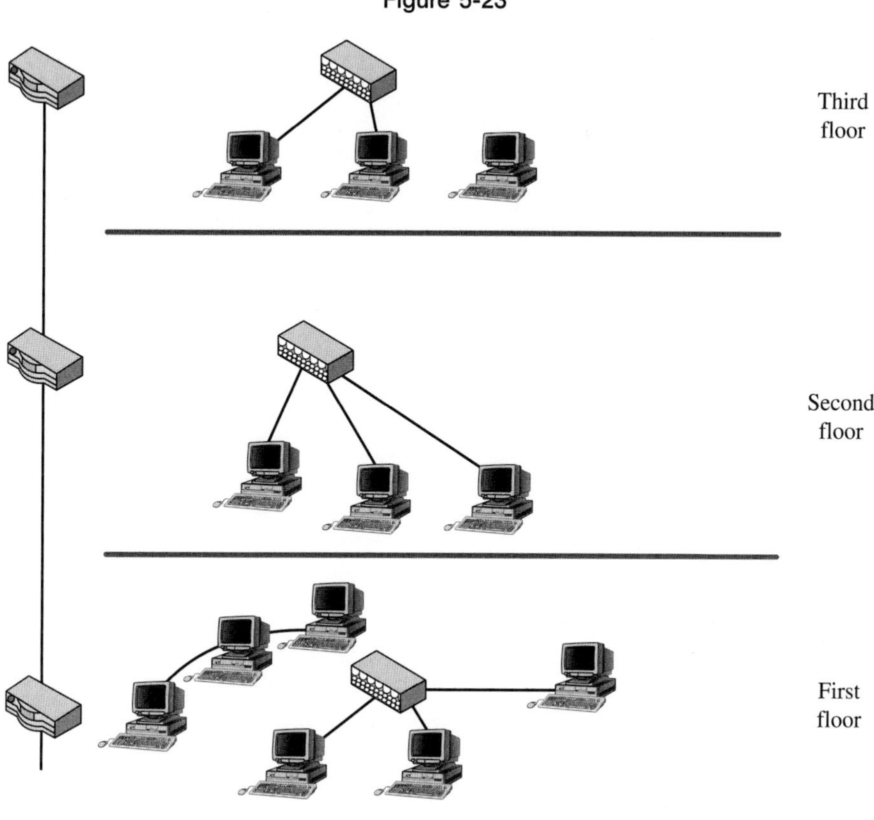

A sample network.

(b) How many network segments (total) will you have when you're finished?

(c) What should you use at the central connection point on each floor if each floor will be a single collision domain?

(d) What should you use at the central connection point on each floor if each floor will have multiple collision domains?

(e) What should you use at the central connection point on each floor if you want to configure broadcast domains that include devices on different floors?

(f) The first floor currently has two separate physical networks: a physical bus Ethernet network and a physical star Token Ring network. What are your options for connecting the networks?

(g) What must you consider when selecting your connection device?

2. You are wiring a new Ethernet network. The network must route through several rooms, all on the same floor. Cable will route through

raceways to a central patch panel in the server room. All PCs have 100Mbps NICs installed.

(a) What are your available copper wire cable options, and what is the maximum bandwidth for each?

(b) If cost is not a consideration, which cable option should you use and why?

(c) What would be possible justifications for using fiber-optic instead of copper wire cable?

(d) What kind of connectors would you most likely use to connect the devices to a fiber-optic network?

YOU TRY IT

Designing a Physical Network

You are brought in to design a company's physical network. The company is preparing to move into new office space. The company leases offices on the first and third floors. It does not currently have a network in place.

Each floor of the building has a wiring closet that can be used by anyone leasing office space on that floor. You will design the network, but the building management company requires that you hire a bonded contractor to physically run the cables. You cannot install any additional hardware in the wiring closet. There are two patch panels on each floor: one for the vertical backbone and one for wiring the horizontal raceways for that floor.

You have a secure server room already wired on the third floor. Currently, the only thing in the server room is a patch panel and 200-pair cable that is already run from the server room patch panel to the third-floor cable closet patch panel. You do not have a securable server room on the first floor.

There is a vertical backbone in place. A 200-pair cable runs through all the floors and is connected to a patch panel on each floor. Building management will make 16 pairs on the vertical backbone available to you to use however you wish.

The network design must support up to 150 nodes, more or less evenly divided between the two floors. The network will include six secure servers that will be installed in the server room. The entire network should be treated as a single network segment, but with three collision domains, each with clients on both floors. You want to keep as much of the network support hardware on the third floor as possible.

1. Where should you install network connection devices for the third floor? Why?
2. Describe how you would wire device support for the third floor.
3. Explain how you would wire for first-floor devices, keeping the number of vertical backbone pairs used to a minimum. Trace the wiring back to the third floor.
4. The company's IT department authorizes the contractor to use Cat 5e cable only for horizontal runs. What are the potential adverse effects of this decision, if any?

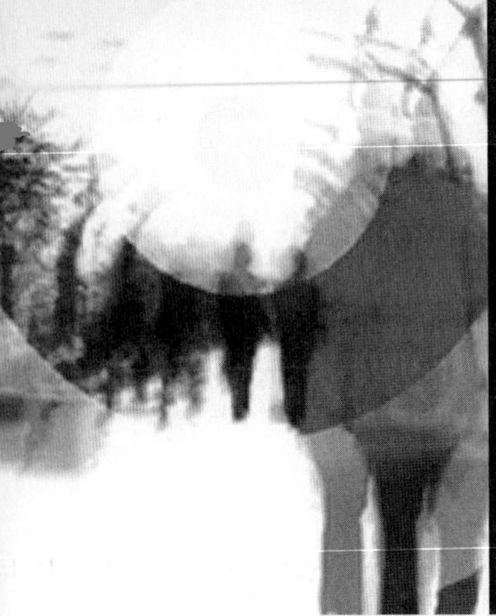

6 NETWORK PROTOCOLS

Starting Point

Go to www.wiley.com/college/ciccarelli to assess your knowledge of network protocols.
Determine where you need to concentrate your effort.

What You'll Learn in This Chapter

- ▲ The role of protocols
- ▲ IEEE 802 access standards
- ▲ Common network protocol suites

After Studying This Chapter, You'll Be Able To

- ▲ Compare and contrast the roles of Data Link layer and Network layer protocols
- ▲ Describe how data are digitally transmitted
- ▲ List and describe the various IEEE 802 access standards
- ▲ Compare the use of Ethernet and Token Ring
- ▲ Explain the significance of using a protocol suite for network communication
- ▲ Compare and contrast TCP/IP, IPX/SPX, and AppleTalk features and benefits
- ▲ List and describe the protocols included in the TCP/IP, IPX/SPX, and AppleTalk protocol suites

INTRODUCTION

Most networks have several different protocols in use: protocols that manage access to the network, protocols that manage traffic between computers, protocols that manage and update routers, and maybe even protocols that manage special applications such as VLANs. The OSI model is handy when you're working with multiple protocols because the most commonly used protocols can be defined in terms of OSI model layers. This chapter looks at the two critical types of protocols that are present in every network: Data Link layer protocols, known as **access protocols** or **access methods**, and Network layer protocols, known as **network protocols** or **communication protocols**. This chapter also looks at protocols from the context of defined standards because each protocol is defined through one or more published standards.

In order to understand how a network works, which is a prerequisite for efficient and effective troubleshooting, you need to be familiar with the protocols used on the network. Access and network protocols are two of the pillars on which a network is constructed. Also, you have to consider both the capabilities and limitations of available protocols when designing a new network or expanding an existing network so you can make choices that meet both the organization's guidelines (if any) and the users' requirements.

6.1 Understanding the Role of Protocols

Before we begin taking protocols apart and discussing what they do, it will help to have a common understanding of what they are, at least in the context of this chapter. A protocol, in simple terms, can be thought of as a language that a computer or another network device speaks. It defines methods and rules for communication.

6.1.1 Understanding Communication Requirements

Consider the two people in Figure 6-1. They have a basic, but common, problem: They simply can't understand each other. What do they need in order to be able to communicate? They either need a language in common—one that they both speak and understand—and to agree to speak that language or they need a translator who understands and speaks both of their native languages.

The preferred solution, if possible, is for both to speak a common language because that way, communication goes faster, and there's less opportunity for confusion. With a translator, communication goes more slowly (talking at least twice as long) because of the time needed to translate the content. There's also a chance of something being lost or confused in the translation.

Figure 6-1

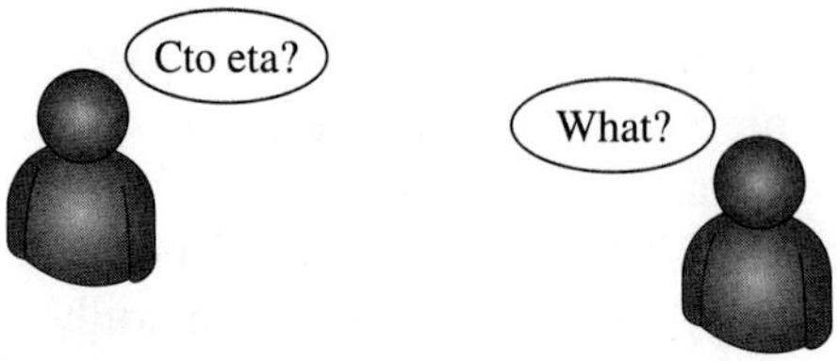

Confused speakers.

Similarly, for two computers to communicate, they must either have at least one language (i.e., a protocol) in common or a translator (i.e., a bridge). If a translator is required, performance suffers because of the processing overhead needed to convert data from one protocol to another.

6.1.2 Identifying Protocols by Role

Every network device must support at least two protocols: a Data Link layer protocol used for network access and a Network layer protocol used to manage higher-level communication requirements. To understand why two protocols are needed, it's important to understand their roles in network communication. To do this, we're going to take a typical network computer and break it out using the OSI model.

Despite the wide range of variations you might see, you can describe a typical computer based on the technologies currently in use. For example, it may be running the current, or a recent, version of the Windows operating system. And it may be connected to an Ethernet network wired as a physical star and configured to use TCP/IP. Take a look at Figure 6-2.

Moving down through the OSI model, you can see that a data packet is wrapped up in layers like an onion. Layers are added as the data move down through the **protocol stack**, the protocol software components running on the computer. The protocol stack is made up of different protocols in the **protocol suite**, a group of network protocols used as a group (e.g., TCP/IP). Each layer performs various functions, wrapping the message content with control information on its way down through the stack. In this example, at the Data Link layer, our message is encapsulated in an Ethernet frame and sent out on the network cable (represented by the Physical layer). The process is reversed at the receiver end, unwrapping the layers down to the original message.

In an Ethernet network, all the computers on the network segment receive the message, except possibly for areas where the message was blocked by MAC

Figure 6-2

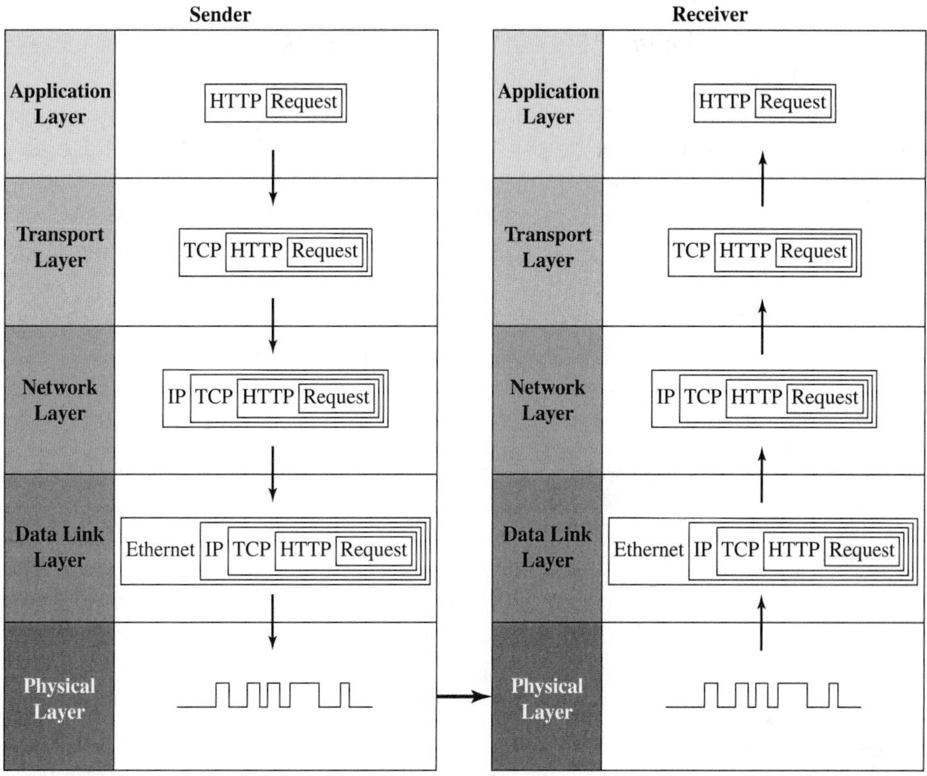

TCP/IP protocol stack use.

address filtering. For the computers that are not the addressed recipient, the packet never makes it past the Data Link layer. The destination address, which is a MAC address, is checked at the Data Link layer, and if the address on the packet doesn't match the address on the computer, it's ignored.

There may also be decisions to be made at higher layers of the OSI model. You can configure a computer to concurrently run multiple protocol suites, such as TCP/IP, IPX/SPX, and AppleTalk. Each protocol encodes data that uniquely identify a packet as having been generated by that protocol. As the packet moves up through the OSI model, it is checked first against the protocol configured as the computer's default protocol. If there's no match, the packet is checked against all other protocols running on the computer until a match is found; at that point, the packet is processed, based on that protocol's requirements. If no match is found, an error is noted, and the packet contents are ignored.

6.1.3 Transmitting Digital Data (Digitally)

This chapter focuses on LAN access and data transmission, so you might find it interesting to know something about how digital data are transmitted, a process known as **digital transmission**.

Digital transmission is the transmission of binary electrical or light signals, and it has only two possible states, a 1 or a 0. The most common voltage levels range from a low of +3/−3 to a high of +24/−24 volts. Digital signals are usually sent over wire no longer than a few thousand feet. To successfully send and receive a message, both the sender and receiver have to agree on the following:

▲ **Voltage levels:** The voltage ranges used represent 1s and 0s.

FOR EXAMPLE

Decisions, Decisions

How do you decide what protocols to use? Let's take them one at a time.

All the computers on a network segment use the same Data Link layer access protocol. If you have an Ethernet network, all computers use Ethernet. For a Token Ring network, they all use Token Ring.

What about the Network layer and above? First, you need to understand that you aren't limited by your access protocol. All current communication protocols support all current access methods (i.e., either Ethernet, Token Ring, or wireless networking). The requirement is that all the computers that need to communicate must have at least one protocol in common. For most networking requirements, that protocol is TCP/IP, which is the current de facto standard for PC LANs. However, it's not the only protocol in use.

Let's say your network includes a legacy NetWare server that uses IPX/SPX as its only communication protocol suite. That means that any and all clients that need to access the server directly must also have the IPX/SPX protocol suite or its equivalent. Realistically, that means clients with both TCP/IP and IPX/SPX. This isn't a problem for newer computers and more recent Windows versions, but the added memory overhead can be a problem on older computers with limited random-access memory (RAM).

There are other options, of course, depending on the exact network needs and service resources. For example, you can configure most Windows Server versions as NetWare gateways, giving Windows clients indirect access to NetWare resources through that gateway.

▲ **Encoding method:** The **encoding method** (also called the **digital signaling technique**) indicates how information is represented as voltage levels or electrical current changes.

▲ **Data rate:** The **data rate** indicates how fast the sender can transmit data.

Figure 6-3 shows four types of digital signaling techniques. With **unipolar signaling**, the voltage is always positive or negative. The unipolar technique, at the top of Figure 6-3, uses a signal of 0 volts (no current) to transmit a 0 and a signal of +5 volts to transmit a 1.

In **bipolar signaling**, the 1s and 0s vary from a plus voltage to a minus voltage. The first bipolar technique shown in Figure 6-3 is called **nonreturn to zero (NRZ)** because the voltage alternates between +5 volts (indicating a 1) and −5 volts (indicating a 0), without resting at 0 volts. The second bipolar technique is called **return to zero (RZ)** because it always returns to 0 volts after each bit

Figure 6-3

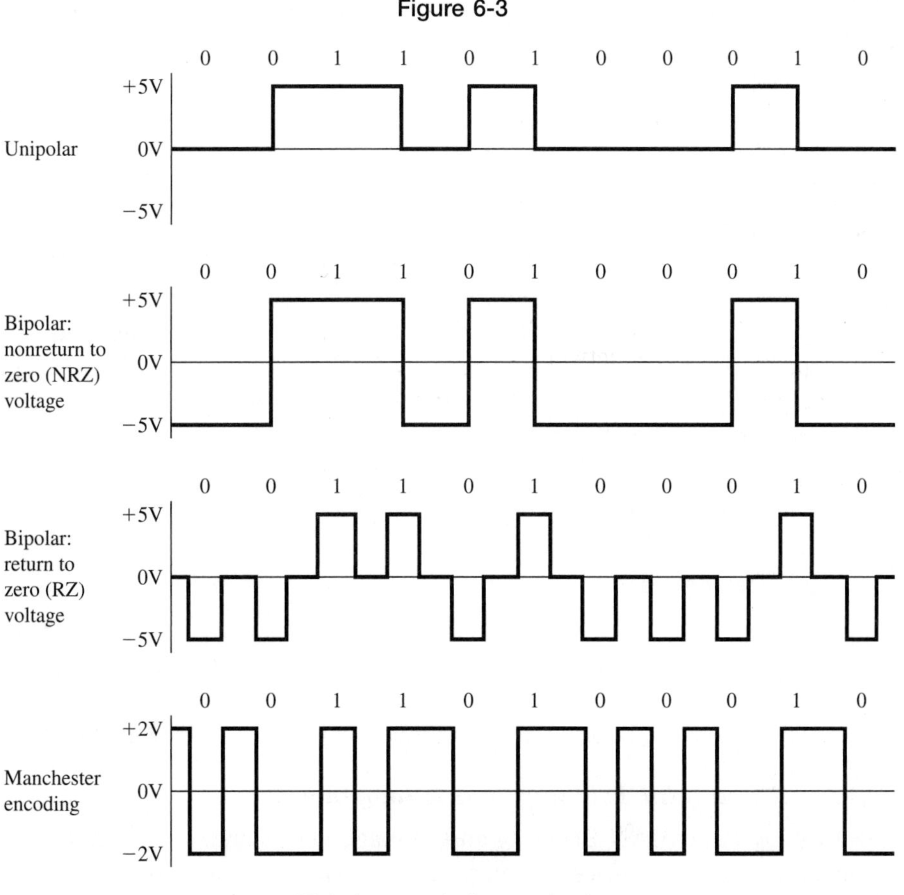

Digital transmission methods.

before going to +5 volts (for a 1) or −5 volts (for a 0) for the next volt. In Europe, bipolar signaling is sometimes called **double current signaling** because it involves moving between a positive and negative voltage potential.

Ethernet uses **Manchester encoding**, which is a special type of unipolar signaling in which the signal is changed from high to low or from low to high in the middle of the signal. A change from high to low is used to represent a 0, whereas a change from low to high is used to represent a 1. Manchester encoding is less susceptible than other techniques to having errors go undetected because if there is no transition in midsignal, the receiver knows that an error must have occurred.

SELF-CHECK

1. In general terms, what is the purpose of access and network protocols?
2. What is Manchester encoding?

6.2 Comparing Access Methods

Network access methods used in PC networks are defined by the IEEE 802 standards. The 802 standards include not only access methods used in PC networks but also low-level protocols used for other types of data communications. In fact, the 802 standards are an overview of the standards that define the Physical layer and MAC sublayer connections of LAN and MAN devices. All the 802 standards are compatible and work together at the Data Link layer—that is, moving above the MAC sublayer into the Logical Link Control layer, which in itself is defined through an 802 standard.

6.2.1 802 Standards

The goal of this section is to give you an idea of the scope of the types of protocols defined by the 802 standards. This section doesn't discuss the protocols in detail; it simply provides a brief overview. There is no 802.13 standard in this list because there is no 802.13 standard; the numbering jumps from 802.12 to 802.14.

802.1: LAN and MAN Bridging and Management

The **802.1 LAN and MAN Bridging and Management** standard defines the way in which a networking device, such as a bridge, selects a path to connect LANs and MANs.

802.2: Logical Link Control

The **802.2 Logical Link Control** standard defines the upper portion of the Data Link layer, known as the LLC sublayer, which uses the LLC protocol. The LLC protocol is responsible for providing connection-oriented service. The LLC protocol uses an extended 2-byte address. The first byte indicates a destination service access point (DSAP), and the second indicates a source service access point (SSAP). The DSAP indicates whether the destination address is the address of a single computer or a group of computers. The SSAP, in current applications, always indicates the address of a single computer.

802.3: CSMA/CD

The **802.3 Carrier-Sense Multiple Access/Collision Detection (CSMA/CD)** standard specifies the access method that is the basis for Ethernet. CSMA/CD and Ethernet are commonly used interchangeably, but Ethernet technically defines the cable, and CSMA/CD defines the way the cable is accessed. CSMA/CD requires that all devices on the network listen to the cable before it can transmit (carrier sense). Only one device on the network can transmit at a time. So if a device senses a transmission already on the wire, it must wait. Once the line is clear, any device can send its message (multiple access). If two computers transmit at the same time, a collision occurs, and both must retransmit (collision detection).

802.4: Token Bus

The **802.4 Token Bus** standard was developed to provide the benefits of Token Ring without the physical requirements of a ring. Physically, an 802.4 network is installed in a line or tree-shaped cable. Logically, the data travel through the wires in the form of a ring. 802.4 is not used in LANs or PC networking. It is used, however, in some specialized manufacturing control systems.

802.5: Token Ring

Token Ring was originally developed and trademarked by IBM. The **802.5 Token Ring** standard was developed to describe Token Ring. Although Token Ring can use a physical ring cabling, the most commonly used topology is a physical star, a logical ring.

Under the 802.5 standard, devices take turns transmitting data. They are able to transmit if they receive an empty token. The data they have to transmit is placed in the token and passed on to the next device in the network. The token travels around the entire network, looking for the device it is addressed to, until the destination device receives the token. The destination device takes its message out and replaces it with a response to the source device. Once the source device gets the token back and takes out its own message, the next computer in the ring gets a chance to use the token to transmit.

802.6: DQDB

The **802.6 Distributed Queue Dual Bus (DQDB)** standard was developed for MANs. This standard uses two parallel cables in a bus network topology. Each of the two cables in the bus transmits in a different direction, so devices can send messages in either direction for bidirectional communication. The bus has a **head** (i.e., a terminating device) that generates **cells** (i.e., fixed-size data packets) that travel throughout the network until they reach the end of the cable.

802.7: Broadband LANs

The **802.7 Broadband LANs** standard specifies the design, installation, and testing necessary for broadband transmissions, which allow for multiple transmissions using different channels at the same time. The broadband bus topology creates a full-duplex medium that supports **multiplexing**, which is a communication method that allows multiple signals to transmit simultaneously across a single physical channel by varying length of transmission, frequency used, or both.

802.8: Fiber-Optic LANs and MANs

The **802.8 Fiber-Optic LANs and MANs** standard states the recommendations for configuring and testing fiber-optic LANs and MANs. The testing specified under this standard ensures the integrity of the fiber-optic cable.

802.9: Integrated Services

The **802.9 Integrated Services** standard defines a unified access method that offers integrated services for both public and private backbone networks, such as FDDI. It also defines the MAC sublayer and Physical layer interfaces. The 802.9 standard allows for internetworking between different subnetworks (i.e., networks that are a part of a larger network and are connected with bridges, routers, and gateways).

802.10: LAN/MAN Security

The **802.10 LAN/MAN Security** standard defines the assignment of unique **security association identifiers (SAIDs)** for the purpose of security within and between LANs and MANs.

802.11: Wireless LANs

The **802.11 Wireless** standard identifies a group of standards developed for wireless LAN technology. It defines communication between two wireless clients or a wireless client and an access point. It uses the 2.4GHz frequency band to transmit at up to 2Mbps. The 802.11 standard uses various specific transmission methods, depending on the particular substandard. 802.11b and 802.11g use the same transmission method. An emerging standard that is still under development at the time this text was written is 802.11n. The 802.11n standard is designed to provide higher-speed wireless networking and backward compatibility with 802.11a, 802.11b, and 802.11g clients.

The **802.11a** standard was the first high-speed wireless standard, and it extends 802.11. 802.11a defines transmissions that utilize the 5GHz frequency band with 54Mbps of wireless throughput. The standard was not commonly used.

The **802.11b** standard was the basis for most of the early wireless devices. 802.11b uses the 2.4GHz frequency band for communication and allows for up to 11Mbps of throughput to be transmitted. Upon the release of 802.11b devices, wireless networking became popular both at home and in the workplace.

In July 2003, the IEEE adopted the **802.11g** standard, which uses the 2.4GHz frequency bank, like 802.11b, although transmitting at up to 54Mbps. Most 802.11g devices support and provide connectivity to 802.11b devices on the network because they are communicating within the same frequency band.

802.12: High-Speed LANs

The **802.12 High-Speed LAN** standards define how the Physical layer and MAC sublayer support 100Mbps signal transmission using the **demand priority access method**, which puts the responsibility for transmissions on the hub. Devices request permission to transmit, and the hub determines the order of the transmissions and provides access to the network. Demand priority also allows for devices to be assigned a priority status so that their transmissions take precedence over other transmissions. This method allows for higher-bandwidth transmissions between devices.

802.14: Cable TV

The **802.14 Cable TV** standard provides a reference for digital communications services over cable television networks using a branching bus system. The MAC and physical characteristics follow the 802 standards, including connectionless and connection-oriented communications.

802.15: WPANs

The **802.15 WPANs** standard is under development by the IEEE and focuses on short-distance wireless networks called **wireless personal area networks (WPANs).** A WPAN can include mobile devices such as laptops, personal digital assistants (PDAs), cell phones, pagers, and much more. The 802.15 standard that was adopted in 2002 utilized a portion of the Bluetooth specifications. **Bluetooth** was developed independently by a group of manufacturers as a peripheral connection standard so that those companies' devices could interoperate. Bluetooth and 802.15 are fully compatible. Today, Bluetooth is gaining popularity and can be found in devices such as PDAs, cell phones, headsets, and standard computer peripherals such as printers.

6.2.2 Focusing on LAN Access

It's likely that, at most, you will encounter only Ethernet and Token Ring used as access methods on PC LANs. That said, this chapter takes time to put special emphasis on IEEE 802.3, IEEE 802.5, and IEEE 802.11b and 802.11g. You're also likely to see Bluetooth in use, but you'll see it for peripheral connections, not for PC networking.

Connecting with Token Ring

Token Ring standards have remained relatively unchanged for well over a decade. During the same period, Token Ring has become a less popular choice in PC LANs, many existing implementations having been replaced by higher-speed Ethernet networks. This doesn't mean that you won't see Token Ring installations, but those that you do see will most likely be part of a legacy network or a link to an IBM mainframe or minicomputer.

Figure 6-4 is an example of a hybrid network that includes Token Ring. When you find a network like this, rather than spending too much time trying to decide how the network might develop, you need to focus on what you have and how you need to support it. In this case, you need to support both logical bus and logical ring networks configured as a single network segment and connected by a bridge.

Figure 6-4

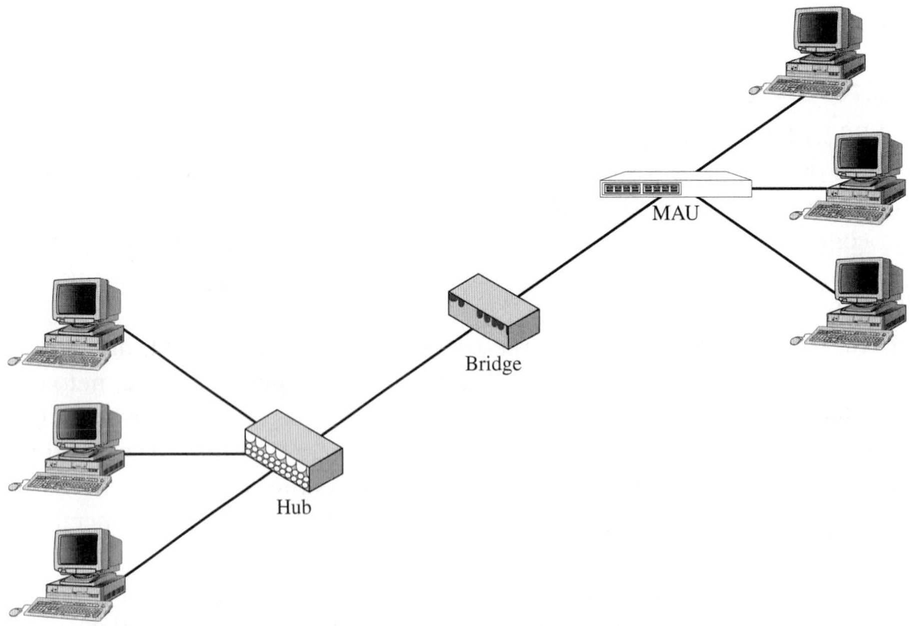

MAU

Bridge

Hub

A hybrid network.

Figure 6-5

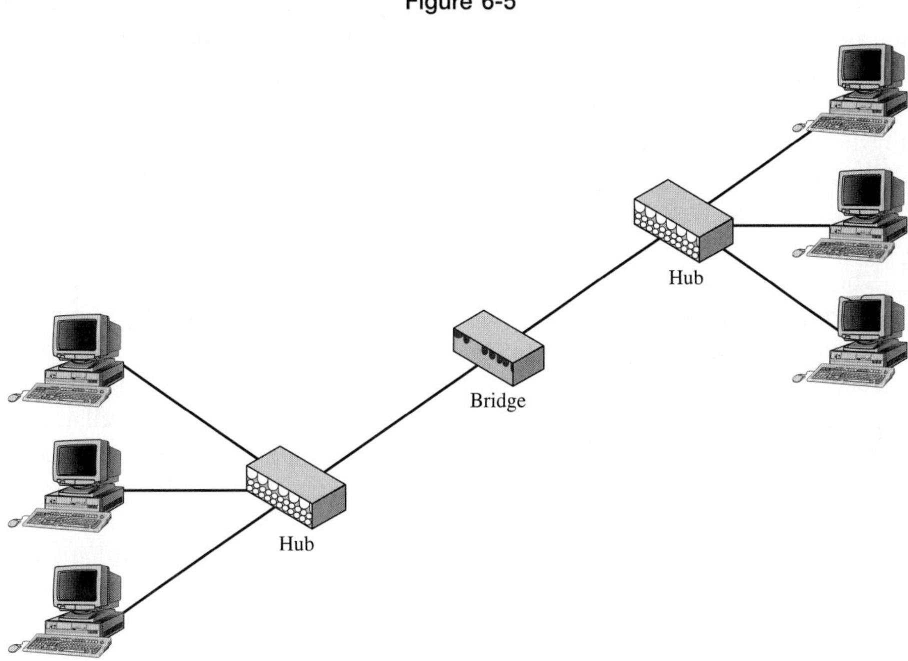

A simple Ethernet network.

One of the advantages of a Token Ring network is that is it a **determinant access method**, which means that you can trace the token's path through the network. It is possible to determine where a packet is and, given its current location, know where it will be going next because the token always follows the same path in the same order. Token Ring is also somewhat self-healing in the event of errors. Most MAUs are able to block out a computer that is not responding or is corrupting packets. Also, if a computer becomes temporarily disconnected from the ring, in most cases, when reconnected, it will pick up where it left off.

The disadvantages of Token Ring are its cost and performance. As Token Ring has fallen out of favor, the necessary hardware has gotten more difficult to buy and more expensive. Most hardware purchases are made to replace failing hardware, not to deploy new networks. Token Ring performance is severely limited compared to that of recent Ethernet versions. Token Ring networks operate at either 4Mbps or 16Mbps, with no revisions to these standards under consideration.

Connecting with Ethernet

Various Ethernet versions are, by far, the most commonly used in current networking configurations. Figure 6-5 shows a typical simple Ethernet network. At a quick glance, it looks identical to the hybrid network in Figure 6-4.

Why is Ethernet so popular? The most common implementation is 100Mbps Ethernet, but 1Gbps and faster versions are gaining in popularity as hardware prices continue to drop and equipment becomes more readily available. Most hubs and switches are designed to compensate for different versions automatically. For example, the most common hubs provide concurrent support for both 10Mbps and 100Mbps Ethernet. The hub detects the speed when the computer is connected and makes the necessary conversions so that the computers can communicate.

The biggest advantages of Ethernet are related to cost, availability, and performance. The hardware needed is relatively inexpensive, and most computers come with 100Mbps Ethernet integrated into the motherboard or already installed as a network adapter. Hubs and switches can be purchased from nearly any store that sells consumer electronics. Standards are already available for 1Gbps and faster Ethernet. The **802.3x** standard defines 100Mbps Ethernet, commonly called Fast Ethernet, and the **802.3z** standard defines 1Gbps Ethernet, or Gigabit Ethernet.

The biggest disadvantage with Ethernet is that performance can suffer as the network size increases. The more computers on a cable segment, the more likely collisions will occur. The problem can be lessened somewhat by setting up collision zones through the use of switches, bridges, and routers.

Anytime you have two or more computers on the same cable segment, collisions can occur. If more than one device sends a message at the same time, a collision occurs. This collision spreads throughout the segment in which it occurred. Thus, all the devices learn about the collision and must back off from transmitting. The devices wait a pseudorandom amount of time and retransmit. This time is knows as the **backoff**.

The backoff period is based on a binary algorithm. After a device has waited its allotted time, it then listens to the line again before it sends a message. This is often referred to as the **listen before transmit method**. The delays resulting from collisions and backoff times can have a noticeable impact on network performance as the number of collisions increases.

Connecting with Wireless LANs

Wireless LAN standards, specifically the current 802.11g standard, are quickly becoming the rule in some networking applications. You'll find wireless LANs in company networks when it is difficult to install a wired network or where there is a need to provide easy access for portable computers. Even more common are wireless LANs used for home networks, both because they are easy to implement and because they provide an easy way to share an Internet connection between multiple computers.

Obviously, ease of implementation is one of the primary benefits of wireless LANs. Another benefit is cost, especially in most new computers. Wireless

FOR EXAMPLE

Can You Hear Me Now?

Why can't you use different access methods on the same cable segment? It's not because of differences in packet structures. That's a factor of the higher-level protocols. If a computer receives a packet with a structure it doesn't recognize, it simply records an error and discards the packet. The problem is that the different access methods, even when they use the same (or very similar) media, use different signaling methods. That means that not only do they use different encoding methods (bipolar methods vs. unipolar methods), they also use different voltage levels.

A network adapter designed for one access method cannot understand the encoded data sent by another access method. Not only that, if there is enough difference between the voltage levels used, you can even physically damage a network adapter by connecting it to the wrong type of network (or damage the other network adapters on the network) in some situations. With Ethernet and Token Ring adapters, the most likely result is that you will simply bring down the network so that none of the computers can communicate, though some MAUs and even some intelligent hubs can detect that you've connected the wrong type of adapter and lock out the computer.

In the early days of PC networking, this aspect of network adapters wasn't a problem because the standards for each access method required a different connector type that was incompatible with every other access method. The problem is that several access methods now use RJ-45 modular adapters either as their primary connection method or a supported option. That means that it is, in some cases, physically possible to connect to the wrong type of network. Some network adapters now include current-limiting circuitry to help prevent physical damage.

networking support is a hidden cost because most laptops and many desktop computers come with wireless network adapters already installed.

There are drawbacks to wireless LANs, but how serious they are depends on how the network is used and how much effort you plan on investing in setting up the network. Security is the biggest problem because wireless LANs are, by default, almost completely unsecured. That means, depending on the network's range (with ranges steadily increasing), someone outside your company (or home) might be able to connect into the network. It could be that they're just piggybacking on your Internet connection, which is bad enough, but if you are using less-than-secure resource sharing methods, they could have access to sensitive information.

SELF-CHECK

1. Which 802 standard access methods are currently used in PC networking applications?
2. What is backoff?

6.3 Comparing Network Protocols

Network protocols define how devices and even applications communicate. Prior to the development of protocols, there was no intercommunication between devices. The protocols used on a network have an impact on both how the network functions and its ability to communicate with other networks. For example, a protocol that is available for all Windows machines is NetBEUI. It is very fast, but it is seldom used because it is not routable. Another common protocol suite, IPX/SPX, is a part of Novell's system of communication within a NetWare client/server environment. It can be routed but only to communicate with other NetWare networks and not on the Internet.

Part of the problem is that a single protocol can't provide complete intercommunication independently. It must work with other protocols, operating at different layers of the OSI model, to provide complete end-to-end communication. When a set of protocols works together, it is called a protocol suite, or stack, because it includes individual protocols that work together at different layers of the OSI model.

The three most important protocol suites used in internetworking are:

- **Transmission Control Protocol/Internet Protocol (TCP/IP):** This is the most common of all network protocol suites, the standard in today's networks, and the protocol suite used for communication on the Internet.
- **Internetwork Packet Exchange/Sequenced Packet Exchange (IPX/SPX):** IPX/SPX, which was developed by Novell, uses its own methods to ensure communication between devices using the NetWare operating system; each of the individual protocols is proprietary to Novell.
- **AppleTalk:** AppleTalk was designed for communication between devices using the Mac OS and is often found within the educational arena.

In recent years, TCP/IP has become the protocol of choice even in NetWare networks and for computers using various versions of the Mac OS. Each of these protocol suites implements a set of rules that provides a unique method for intercommunication between devices. The protocols within each suite function at layers within the OSI model from layer 2 (the Data Link layer) through layer 7 (the Application layer). Because the TCP/IP and IPX/SPX protocol suites were developed before the adoption of the OSI model, they do not map perfectly to its layers.

When deciding what protocol or protocols to use, keep in mind that you should minimize the number of protocol stacks running on any one client and that computers must share a common protocol in order to communicate. This means that IPX/SPX will be required if clients need to directly access a legacy NetWare server. TCP/IP will be required if the clients need to support Internet access. Also, any protocol-dependent applications—that is, applications that rely on a specific protocol being present in order to work—will fail if that protocol is not available. For example, some older multiplayer PC games relied on SPX for the clients playing the game to communicate. If you remove IPX/SPX (or NWLink, as the case may be), you eliminate the possibility of multiuser play.

6.3.1 Using the TCP/IP Suite

The TCP/IP suite was developed for use on the Internet. Its origins lie in the first RFC, which was discussed in Chapter 3. It is also known as the DoD or ARPANET protocol suite. Its name comes from two of the main protocols within the stack: Transmission Control Protocol and Internet Protocol. TCP is responsible for connection-oriented communications using error checking, and IP is implemented in the addressing system used to identify devices.

Although it was developed for use on the Internet, you can use TCP/IP to build LANs, MANs, and WANs. TCP/IP is the most widely implemented protocol suite and is used with a variety of platforms, including Unix, Windows, and Macintosh. Even though it doesn't map directly to the OSI model, Figure 6-6 shows how protocols in the TCP/IP protocol suite relate to that model.

TCP/IP is designed to work with a wide range of physical access methods. In fact, the TCP/IP standards provide the links for physical access but don't define physical access methods.

Understanding TCP/IP Features

The TCP/IP suite offers a number of features and benefits, including interoperability, flexibility, and multivendor support.

Let's look at interoperability first. TCP/IP has become the standard protocol suite because of its capability to connect LANs, WANs, and the Internet. As more LANs connect to the Internet, TCP/IP is quickly becoming the most universally available protocol today.

TCP/IP's flexibility comes from the wide variety of protocols built into the protocol suite. These range from protocols that manage the mechanics of connection-oriented and connectionless communications up through protocols that

Figure 6-6

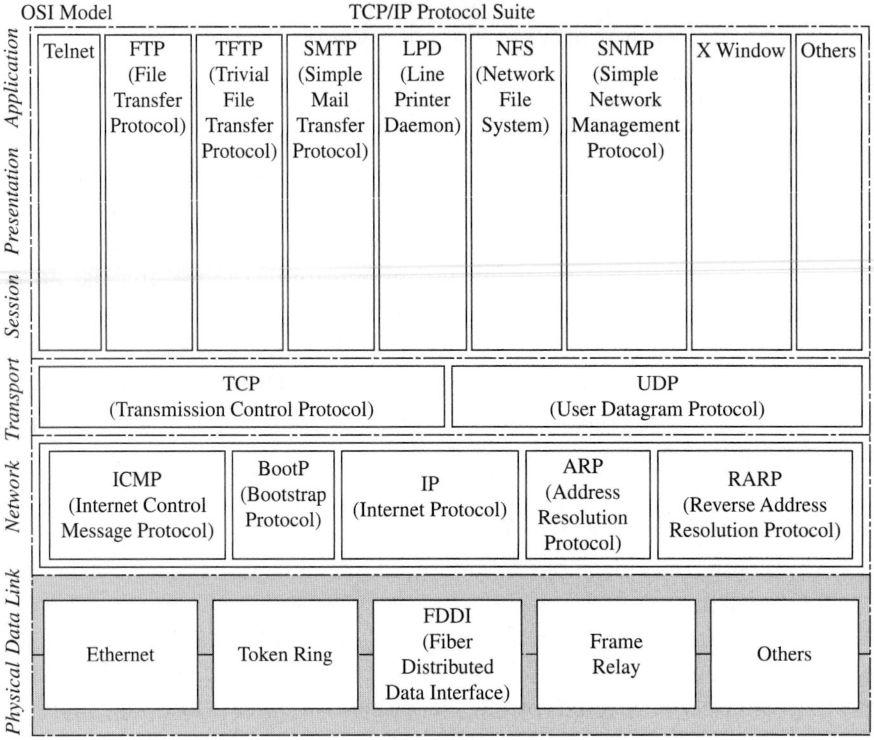

OSI Model	TCP/IP Protocol Suite								
Application / Presentation / Session	Telnet	FTP (File Transfer Protocol)	TFTP (Trivial File Transfer Protocol)	SMTP (Simple Mail Transfer Protocol)	LPD (Line Printer Daemon)	NFS (Network File System)	SNMP (Simple Network Management Protocol)	X Window	Others
Transport	TCP (Transmission Control Protocol)				UDP (User Datagram Protocol)				
Network	ICMP (Internet Control Message Protocol)	BootP (Bootstrap Protocol)	IP (Internet Protocol)	ARP (Address Resolution Protocol)	RARP (Reverse Address Resolution Protocol)				
Physical Data Link	Ethernet	Token Ring	FDDI (Fiber Distributed Data Interface)	Frame Relay	Others				

The TCP/IP suite and the OSI model.

support specialized applications such as file transfer and delivery of webpage content.

Another big benefit of the TCP/IP suite is the fact that almost all network software vendors support its use. Apple, DEC, IBM, Novell, Microsoft, and Sun are just a few of the many companies that support the suite. In fact, it is much more difficult to find a manufacturer that does not support TCP/IP than one that does.

Both a benefit and a drawback of TCP/IP is its addressing scheme. The IP addresses used by TCP/IP identify a two-part address: a **network address** and a **host address**. The network address identifies the network to which the host belongs and is used for routing purposes. The host portion of the address uniquely identifies the computer or other device on that network segment. A second value, known as the **subnet mask**, identifies which portion of the address is used as the network address and which is used as the host address. Figure 6-7 shows an IP address being manually configured on a Windows XP computer.

As you might imagine, manually configuring addresses for a LAN with hundreds, not to mention thousands, of hosts would be a daunting task. TCP/IP

Figure 6-7

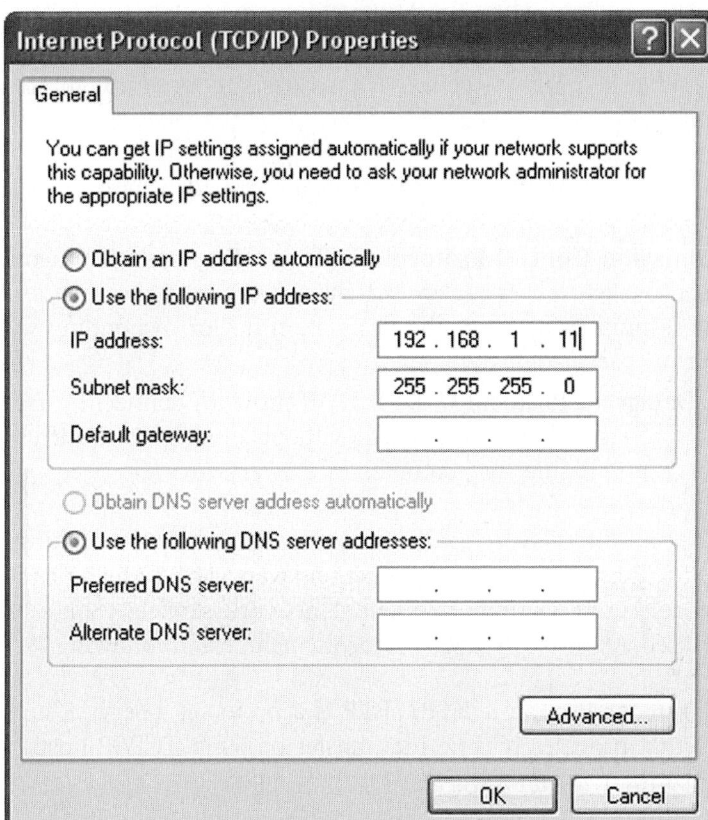

A manually assigned IP address.

therefore supports automated address assignment through the **Dynamic Host Configuration Protocol (DHCP)** service.

Identifying the TCP/IP Protocols

The easiest way to break down the many protocols of the TCP/IP suite is according to where they operate within the OSI model. Each protocol in this stack operates at one of three layers: the Network layer (also known as the Internet layer in the TCP/IP model), the Transport layer, or the Application layer.

The following Network layer protocols are provided with TCP/IP:

- **Internet Protocol (IP): IP** provides for network identification through addressing and connectionless delivery of packets.
- **Address Resolution Protocol (ARP): ARP** provides a device's MAC address from its IP address.

- ▲ **Reverse Address Resolution Protocol (RARP): RARP** provides a device's IP address when the MAC address is known.
- ▲ **Internet Control Message Protocol (ICMP): ICMP** is a management and troubleshooting protocol that provides support through error and control messages.

The following Transport layer protocols are provided with TCP/IP:

- ▲ **Transmission Control Protocol (TCP): TCP** provides connection-oriented packet delivery services that include error checking and sequence numbering, with the destination device responding with a receipt on packet delivery.
- ▲ **User Datagram Protocol (UDP): UDP** provides connectionless packet delivery services that send packets without any type of error checking, sequence numbering, or guarantee of delivery.

TCP/IP Application layer protocols include the protocols operating at the OSI model Session, Presentation, and Application layers. TCP/IP includes a wide variety of protocols used to support different network services. Some of the most commonly used Application layer protocols include the following:

- ▲ **File Transfer Protocol (FTP): FTP** is a protocol, a service, and an application that provides reliable file transfer between TCP/IP hosts.
- ▲ **Trivial File Transfer Protocol (TFTP): TFTP** is used for file transfer over the Internet using UDP, but requiring acknowledgement (through TFTP) for each packet before the next packet is sent.
- ▲ **Simple Mail Transfer Protocol (SMTP): SMTP** is used to transfer email messages between computers, using TCP as its delivery protocol.
- ▲ **Hypertext Transfer Protocol (HTTP): HTTP** is used to access Hypertext Markup Language (HTML) files (i.e., webpages) over the Internet or through an intranet, allowing for rapid, reliable data exchange.
- ▲ **Domain Name System (DNS): DNS** is a protocol and service used for host name–to–IP address resolution.
- ▲ **Telnet: Telnet** is a protocol and application that provides remote terminal emulation services in clear text.
- ▲ **Dynamic Host Configuration Protocol (DHCP):** DHCP is a protocol and service used to automatically provide IP address and other TCP/IP configuration settings for host computers.
- ▲ **Simple Network Management Protocol (SNMP): SNMP** is a protocol that enables remote configuration, monitoring, and management of network devices, services, and resources.

Some operating systems' implementations of the TCP/IP protocol suite support only a portion of the full protocol stack. Several protocols and services are considered optional, which means you can enable or disable them as necessary. You should disable any protocols that are not needed or used on your network. For example, if it is not needed, you should disable FTP to avoid allowing unauthorized access to your network's computers.

6.3.2 Using IPX/SPX

The IPX/SPX protocol suite was developed for use with Novell NetWare networks. Its name comes from the two most important protocols of the suite: Internetwork Packet Exchange (IPX) and Sequenced Packet Exchange (SPX). While IPX and SPX have been widely implemented in Novell NetWare networks, the latest versions of NetWare offer TCP and IP and a full suite of TCP/IP applications, thus providing the Internet capabilities lacking in IPX and SPX.

IPX/SPX networks communicate using a proprietary protocol suite based on a modification of the **Xerox Network System (XNS)**, one of the first protocols used with Ethernet. Actually, XNS became the model used by many vendors for developing protocols. Even though IPX/SPX does not map directly to the OSI model, Figure 6-8 shows how the most commonly used protocols in the suite relate to the model.

The Link Support Layer (LSL) is not a protocol but provides support for IEEE 802 physical address protocols. The Multiple Link Interface Driver (MLID) links the protocol suite to the network adapter driver. Most legacy NetWare (before version 4.0) client interface versions required you to generate and install a new version of the client software whenever you changed the network adapter (manufacturer or model) installed in a computer.

Understanding IPX/SPX Features

Features and benefits of IPX/SPX include ease of addressing and the use of **dynamic service discovery**, a way of recognizing resources made available to the network by network servers.

The IPX/SPX logical addressing system is much more user friendly than the IP addressing system. IPX uses a **network number** that is chosen by the network administrator when the network is installed and the Data Link (MAC) address of the device, which is used as the unique computer address. These two numbers make up the entire IPX address. Many people feel that the IPX addressing system is much easier to implement than the IP addressing system, in which addresses must be requested from an ISP. On a small LAN, IPX addressing is almost completely automatic.

One of the key features of the IPX/SPX protocol suite is the use of service advertisements for dynamic service discovery. **Service Advertisement Protocol (SAP)**

Figure 6-8

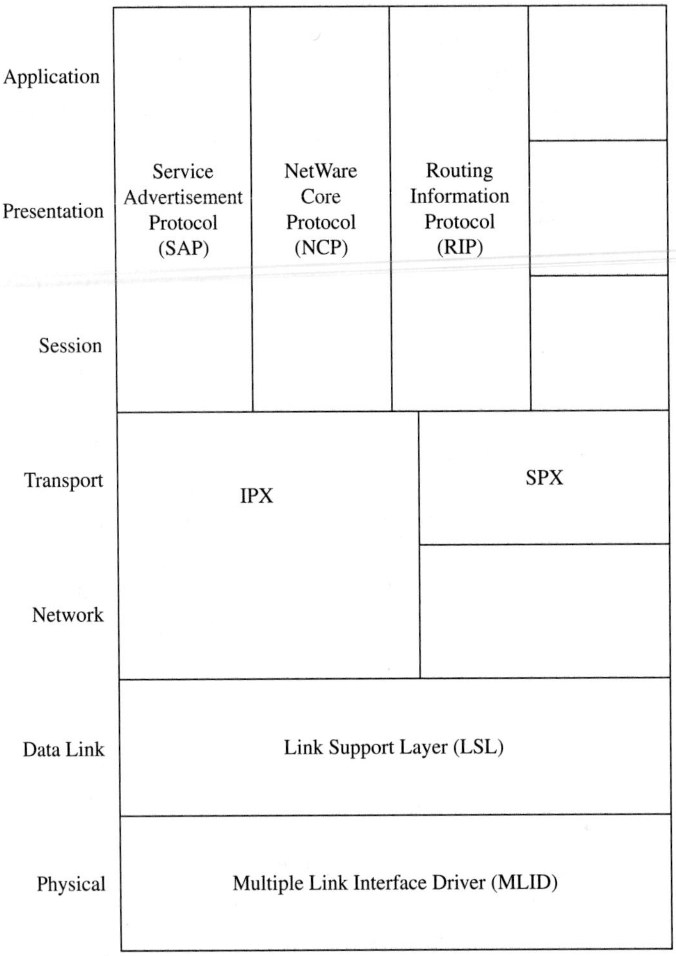

Application	Service Advertisement Protocol (SAP)	NetWare Core Protocol (NCP)	Routing Information Protocol (RIP)	
Presentation				
Session				
Transport	IPX		SPX	
Network				
Data Link	Link Support Layer (LSL)			
Physical	Multiple Link Interface Driver (MLID)			

The IPX/SPX protocol stack.

allows servers to advertise the services they can provide with broadcasts. These advertisements occur every 60 seconds by default, which adds traffic to the network. This system of advertisements allows for nodes to discover which servers they need to communicate with for specific services. Through a process called **Get Nearest Server (GNS)**, clients send out broadcast messages on the network in an attempt to locate the nearest server. Servers respond to the request with a **GNS response**. This way, servers that are nearest to the client and that have the needed services can be used. SAP broadcasts are not routable, but a router that receives a SAP broadcast records it in a SAP table and shares these SAP tables with other routers. That way, a device making a service request may receive a reply from a router that knows how to find the requested services.

Identifying IPX/SPX Protocols

As with TCP/IP, it's fairly easy to understand the relationship between the various protocols of the IPX/SPX suite and the OSI layers. IPX/SPX has one Network layer protocol, one Transport layer protocol, and a few Application layer protocols, three of which we focus on here.

The IPX/SPX Network layer protocol is **Internetwork Packet Exchange (IPX)**. IPX was used with NetWare versions 2 through 4.3, and TCP/IP (specifically IP) was available as an option starting with version 5. Like IP, IPX is responsible for addressing and routing.

The IPX/SPX Transport layer protocol is **Sequenced Packet Exchange (SPX)**. SPX performs the same function in IPX/SPX as TCP performs in TCP/IP: It provides connection-oriented delivery services, packet sequencing to ensure proper delivery order, and flow control.

IPX/SPX supports the following common Application layer protocols:

- ▲ **Service Advertisement Protocol (SAP):** This protocol lets NetWare servers send broadcasts that advertise the services provided by the servers.
- ▲ **NetWare Core Protocol (NCP): NCP** provides services spanning the Session, Presentation, and Application OSI layers that support client connections to NetWare servers. NCP establishes the connection between the client and server and supports file, printing, and security services.
- ▲ **Routing Information Protocol (RIP):** This protocol is used by IPX/SPX routers to share routing tables and route information, including information about networks to which the router is directly connected. There is also a version of the protocol that is used with TCP/IP.

Microsoft provides an equivalent protocol stack to IPX/SPX called NWLink. **NWLink** enables Windows computers to act as NetWare clients for NetWare versions 4.3 and earlier.

6.3.3 Using AppleTalk

AppleTalk is the proprietary protocol suite developed in the mid-1980s for use with Apple Macintosh networks. It is a multilayer architecture that is built into the Macintosh operating system, which means all Macintosh computers are capable of networking right out of the box. Windows server computers also support AppleTalk as a way of providing resources to Apple Macintosh clients. Recently, changes have been made to the suite to improve its communication capabilities. Unlike the TCP/IP and IPX/SPX protocol suites, the AppleTalk protocol suite was developed with the OSI model in mind and maps directly to the OSI model.

Features and benefits of AppleTalk include ease of addressing and built-in mechanisms for limiting network traffic.

The network portion of an AppleTalk address is manually configured by the network administrator, although **device numbers** are dynamically assigned, using 8 bits or the numbers 1–253. The numbers 0, 254, and 255 are reserved. This dynamic addressing happens when a device is turned on. A device chooses a random number from the range available and sends out a message, asking if it is being used. If a device replies that it is using that address, another address is tried. If no one responds to the advertisement of that number, the device maintains it as its address. It then saves the address in RAM.

Devices located within an AppleTalk network are assembled into logical zones. These **zones** block the broadcasts that are sent within the network. Each zone can then be connected to an interface on a router. The router can block the broadcasts but can provide information about all the connected zones to the user. In this way, traffic is limited while access is provided to all devices throughout the network.

One reason this is important is because AppleTalk is the "chattiest" of all protocols. Devices using AppleTalk send broadcast messages every 10 seconds. These constant broadcasts, which can be limited only by layer 3 devices such as routers, dramatically affect network performance. If you implement an AppleTalk network, you need to be sure to limit the number of devices within the broadcast domain by using a router.

Identifying AppleTalk Protocols

AppleTalk protocols were designed as a client-distributed network system to provide sharing of resources within the Macintosh environment. As with SAP in the IPX suite, AppleTalk clients use broadcasts to find out what services are available to them.

There are currently two versions of AppleTalk: Phase 1 and Phase 2. **Phase 1** AppleTalk supports one physical network with one logical network or zone. **Phase 2** supports one physical network with more than one logical network and multiple zones. The zone provides the boundary for automatic device number assignments, so you can have up to 253 devices per zone.

AppleTalk protocols are described as Data Link layer protocols, midlayer protocols, and upper-layer protocols. The following protocols operate at the Data Link layer:

- ▲ **EtherTalk Link Access Protocol (ELAP): ELAP** provides physical access to an 802.3 (Ethernet) network.
- ▲ **AppleTalk Address Resolution Protocol (AARP): AARP** is used to retrieve a computer's physical address for packet delivery.

- **LocalTalk Link Access Protocol (LLAP): LLAP** is Apple's combined Physical and Data Link layer protocol, which supports multipoint connectivity in a bus topology wired as a daisy chain. It supports dynamically addressed workgroups with up to 32 computers per workgroup.
- **TokenTalk Link Access Protocol (TLAP): TLAP** provides physical access to an 802.5 (Token Ring) network.

LLAP was originally based on the LocalTalk protocol suite, which was used with Apple brand computers before the development of AppleTalk. Four mid-layer protocols operate at the Network and Transport layers of the OSI model:

- **Datagram Delivery Protocol (DDP): DDP** provides what is described as best-effort, but not guaranteed, delivery. **Short DDP** is used to send packets to computers on the same network. **Long DDP** is used to send packets between different networks when routing services are required.
- **Routing Table Maintenance Protocol (RTMP): RTMP** is used to manage and maintain AppleTalk routers and pass routing table information between the routers.
- **Name Binding Protocol (NBP): NBP** matches device names to network addresses, similarly to DNS on a TCP/IP network, allowing for user-defined logical naming conventions.
- **AppleTalk Transaction Protocol (ATP): ATP** provides reliable transport services between computers or applications, including keeping track of application transactions.

Upper-layer protocols are implemented at the Session, Presentation, and Application layers of the OSI model. AppleTalk supports five upper-layer protocols:

- **AppleTalk Data Stream Protocol (ADSP): ADSP** is the protocol responsible for establishing connections, sequencing, and packet flow control and can be used as an alternative to ATP, but without transaction tracking.
- **AppleTalk Session Protocol (ASP): ASP**, which is implemented specifically at the OSI Session layer, provides Session layer services.
- **Printer Access Protocol (PAP): PAP** is the protocol used to support shared and network printers and print job management.
- **Zone Information Protocol (ZIP): ZIP** is the protocol responsible for keeping track of network numbers and zones as well as matching network numbers to AppleTalk network zones.
- **AppleTalk Filing Protocol (AFP): AFP** supports file sharing, file transfer, and end-user printer sharing to Macintosh and non-Macintosh clients.

FOR EXAMPLE

The Growth of TCP/IP

It's been said (and repeated several times) that TCP/IP is the protocol of choice for most current PC LANs. One of the driving factors for this has been the explosive growth of the Internet, especially the World Wide Web. In the early days of the Internet, only a few hard-core technophiles knew of the existence of TCP/IP, let alone tried to access it. Now, Internet access is one of the primary motivations for first-time computer buyers. However, that's not the only reason. Internet access alone can't account for all of the growth of TCP/IP.

The other primary motivation for switching networks over to TCP/IP is interoperability. TCP/IP has been the default protocol for Unix computers for years. Its introduction into Windows, NetWare, and Apple Macintosh networks has made it easier for these different platforms to share files and other resources. Heterogeneous networks, once a network administrator's worst nightmare, have become relatively easy to set up and maintain.

That doesn't mean that the Internet hasn't also been an important factor for company and other organizational LANs. A website has become a matter of necessity for credibility in today's increasingly web-driven marketplace. Email sent and received through the Internet has become a key tool for both professional and personal communication. Think about it. When was the last time you saw a business card that didn't include an email address? Not only that, more and more companies are using the Internet for their communication backbone for wide area networking.

Windows servers support the AppleTalk protocol suite as a way of providing services and resources to Macintosh clients in a Windows network. More recent versions of the Mac OS use TCP/IP instead of AppleTalk as their primary protocol suite.

SELF-CHECK

1. How do the IPX and SPX protocols relate to protocols in the TCP/IP protocol suite?
2. How are unique computer addresses assigned in TCP/IP, IPX/SPX, and AppleTalk?

SUMMARY

In this chapter, you learned about access and network protocols. Access protocols operate at the Data Link and Physical layers of the OSI model. Network protocols, even when they don't specifically map to the OSI model, are considered to act at the Network layer and higher.

You learned about the IEEE 802 standards that define access methods, with a special look at 802.3, 802.5, and 802.11, the three standards most commonly used in PC LAN applications. You also learned about the three most common network protocol suites, TCP/IP, IPX/SPX, and AppleTalk.

KEY TERMS

802.1 LAN and MAN Bridging and Management

802.2 Logical Link Control

802.3 CSMA/CD

802.3x Fast Ethernet

802.3z Gigabit Ethernet

802.4 Token Bus

802.5 Token Ring

802.6 Distributed Queue Dual Bus (DQDB)

802.7 Broadband LANs

802.8 Fiber-Optic LANs and MANs

802.9 Integrated Services

802.10 LAN/MAN Security

802.11 Wireless LANs

802.11a

802.11b

802.11g

802.12 High-Speed LANs

802.14 Cable TV

802.15 WPANs

Access method

Access protocol

Address Resolution Protocol (ARP)

AppleTalk Address Resolution Protocol (AARP)

AppleTalk Data Stream Protocol (ADSP)

AppleTalk Filing Protocol (AFP)

AppleTalk Session Protocol (ASP)

AppleTalk Transaction Protocol (ATP)

Backoff

Bipolar signaling

Bluetooth

Cell

Communication protocol

Data rate

Datagram Delivery Protocol (DDP)

Demand priority access method

Determinant access method

Device number

Digital signaling technique

Digital transmission

Domain Name System (DNS)

Double current signaling

Dynamic Host Configuration Protocol (DHCP)
Dynamic service discovery
Encoding method
EtherTalk Link Access Protocol (ELAP)
File Transfer Protocol (FTP)
Get Nearest Server (GNS)
GNS response
Head
Host address
Hypertext Transfer Protocol (HTTP)
Internet Control Message Protocol (ICMP)
Internet Protocol (IP)
Internetwork Packet Exchange (IPX)
Listen before transmit method
LocalTalk Link Access Protocol (LLAP)
Long DDP
Manchester encoding
Multiplexing
Name Binding Protocol (NBP)
NetWare Core Protocol (NCP)
Network address
Network number
Network protocol
Nonreturn to zero (NRZ)
NWLink
Phase 1
Phase 2
Printer Access Protocol (PAP)
Protocol stack
Protocol suite
Return to zero (RZ)
Reverse Address Resolution Protocol (RARP)
Routing Information Protocol (RIP)
Routing Table Maintenance Protocol (RTMP)
Security association identifier (SAID)
Sequenced Packet Exchange (SPX)
Service Advertisement Protocol (SAP)
Short DDP
Simple Mail Transfer Protocol (SMTP)
Simple Network Management Protocol (SNMP)
Subnet mask
Telnet
TokenTalk Link Access Protocol (TLAP)
Transmission Control Protocol (TCP)
Trivial File Transfer Protocol (TFTP)
Unipolar signaling
User Datagram Protocol (UDP)
Wireless personal area network (WPAN)
Xerox Network System (XNS)
Zone
Zone Information Protocol (ZIP)

ASSESS YOUR UNDERSTANDING

Go to www.wiley.com/college/ciccarelli to evaluate your knowledge of network protocols.
Measure your learning by comparing pre-test and post-test results.

Summary Questions

1. AppleTalk is a single, monolithic protocol that handles all network communication requirements for computers running a Mac OS. True or false?
2. Which IPX/SPX protocol is responsible for providing connection-oriented transport?
   (a) SPX
   (b) IPX
   (c) SAP
   (d) UDP
3. Which TCP/IP protocol is responsible for providing connection-oriented transport?
   (a) ARP
   (b) FTP
   (c) TCP
   (d) UDP
4. Which IEEE standard was created to document IBM Token Ring?
   (a) 802.3
   (b) 802.5
   (c) 802.11
   (d) 802.14
5. Which of the following is an example of a PC LAN access protocol?
   (a) TCP/IP
   (b) NetBEUI
   (c) Ethernet
   (d) Token Bus
6. Manchester encoding is the digital transmission method used by Ethernet. True or false?
7. Two or more access methods can share the same physical media segment. True or false?
8. The LLC standard is defined by which IEEE standard?
   (a) 802.1
   (b) 802.2

(c) 802.11
(d) 802.15

9. Bluetooth is compatible with which IEEE standard?
(a) 802.5
(b) 802.11
(c) 802.13
(d) 802.15

10. What does RARP do?
(a) Maps a known IP address to a MAC address.
(b) Maps a known MAC address to an IP address.
(c) Maps a known IP address to a host name.
(d) Maps a known host name to an IP address.

11. IPX/SPX is the only protocol supported by NetWare versions 2 through 5. True or false?

12. Which TCP/IP protocol provides clients with access to HTML files?
(a) HTTP
(b) FTP
(c) SNMP
(d) DHCP

13. Which of the following AppleTalk protocols is not used to provide clients with physical access to network media?
(a) ELAP
(b) LLAP
(c) AARP
(d) TLAP

14. What is the maximum number of computers that can be dynamically addressed as part of an AppleTalk zone?
(a) 16
(b) 32
(c) 128
(d) 253

15. Which TCP/IP network provides terminal emulation?
(a) DNS
(b) Telnet
(c) TFTP
(d) SNMP

Applying This Chapter

1. You are hired as a network administrator. During your initial network inventory, you determine that all computers on the network are configured for either 10Mbps or 100Mbps Ethernet. Also, all computers have both the IPX/SPX (or NWLink) and TCP/IP protocol stacks installed and enabled. All network servers are running either Windows NT Server or Windows 2000 Server.
   - (a) At the Network layer and above, from a protocol standpoint, what is necessary for a client and server to communicate?
   - (b) When is it required that you have clients running the IPX/SPX protocol stack?
   - (c) The network is wired as a physical star, with computers running 10Mbps and 100Mbps Ethernet mixed throughout the building. What is necessary when selecting a new hub to replace one that has failed?
   - (d) What is a potential drawback of having computers run more than one protocol stack?
   - (e) What happens if a computer configured to use TCP/IP as its primary protocol and IPX/SPX as its secondary protocol receives an IPX/SPX packet?
2. Your network is currently wired as a 16Mbps Token Ring network. You are preparing to expand the network. The new network is being installed as 100Mbps Ethernet. You will not be upgrading the Token Ring network at this time.
   - (a) What must you do for the old and new segments to communicate?
   - (b) Both the Ethernet and Token Ring network adapters are designed to use RJ-45 adapters. What would you expect to happen if you connected a computer to the wrong type of network?
   - (c) What is a potential disadvantage of the Ethernet network that is not a problem on the Token Ring network?

YOU TRY IT

Optimizing Your Network

Your company network includes 16Mbps Token Ring, 10Mbps Ethernet, and 100Mbps Ethernet clients. Each client type is currently connected to its own isolated cable segment. Client computers are configured to use both TCP/IP and IPX/SPX. Most client computers need to support Internet access.

1. How can you optimize the network's available bandwidth, based on the technologies currently in use?
2. What is the potential performance bottleneck in the upgraded network configuration?
3. How can you reduce the possibility of bottlenecks happening?
4. What determines whether a network protocol is needed on a client computer?
5. In the current environment, which protocol would you most likely configure as the default (or primary) protocol? Why?
6. What change could you make to the network protocols to improve client performance?
7. Using other research references, if necessary, describe the steps you would take, in terms of both hardware and software, to optimize the network. Choose the best available access method and network protocol from those currently in use on the network. Include any potential pitfalls that you need to watch out for when removing or disabling support for any protocols currently in use.

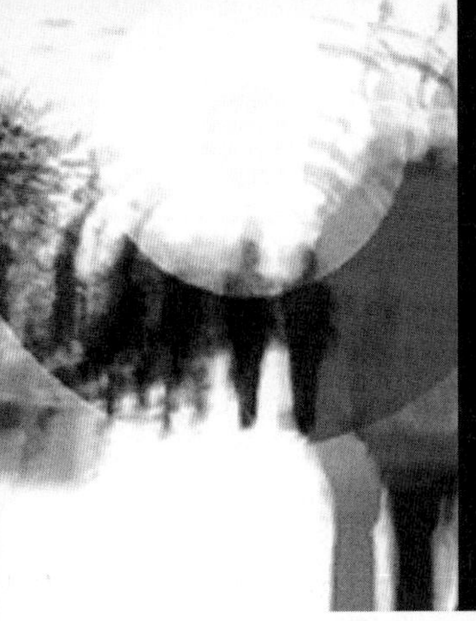

7

TRANSMISSION CONTROL PROTOCOL/INTERNET PROTOCOL (TCP/IP)

Starting Point

Go to www.wiley.com/college/ciccarelli to assess your knowledge of TCP/IP protocol fundamentals.
Determine where you need to concentrate your effort.

What You'll Learn in This Chapter

▲ TCP/IP design fundamentals
▲ IP addresses
▲ TCP/IP name resolution
▲ TCP/IP configuration

After Studying This Chapter, You'll Be Able To

▲ Describe TCP/IP features and benefits
▲ Describe TCP and IP header information
▲ Identify IPv4 and IPv6 addressing requirements
▲ Explain host name resolution methods and their use
▲ Configure TCP/IP properties
▲ Use TCP/IP utilities

INTRODUCTION

Transmission Control Protocol/Internet Protocol (TCP/IP) is the most common connectivity protocol suite currently in use. It is the protocol on which the Internet is based, the protocol found on nearly all PC networks, and the default protocol used by all current PC operating systems. Because of its widespread acceptance and use, it is essential that you know how to configure TCP/IP hosts (i.e., devices on a TCP/IP network).

This chapter starts with a look at TCP/IP fundamentals and the two basic protocols from which it takes its name: Transmission Control Protocol (TCP) and Internet Protocol (IP). From there, we'll look at TCP/IP addressing. Address assignment is a critical part of network design and deployment, so you need to know something about how IP addresses are structured. We'll also spend some time on name resolution and how human-recognizable names (e.g., www.busicorp.com) are resolved to numeric addresses. Finally, we'll look at configurable properties and some basic TCP/IP utilities.

7.1 Understanding TCP/IP Fundamentals

To understand TCP/IP, it helps if you understand a bit about some of the goals in its development. The history of TCP/IP and the Internet are so closely tied together that they cannot be separated. Both were developed as part of the electronic battleground of the Cold War between the United States and Soviet Union. From its origins as a way to facilitate communication between a few university campuses, the Internet has grown into a worldwide phenomenon, helping drive the growth of the PC industry in the process and changing the way people communicate, collaborate, and do business.

TCP/IP is a suite of protocols, with TCP and IP at its fundamental base. We're going to take a look at each of these two protocols, including a quick breakdown of how the packets sent out on the network are structured. While you might never need to know this information as a requirement for your job, it does help you understand keys points, such as how IP addresses are used to ensure packet delivery.

7.1.1 TCP/IP Design Goals

TCP/IP was first proposed in 1973 and was split into separate protocols, TCP and IP, in 1978. When the U.S. Department of Defense (DoD) began to define the TCP/IP network protocols, its design goals included the following:

- TCP/IP had to be independent of all hardware and software manufacturers. Even today, this is fundamentally why TCP/IP makes such good

- It had to have good built-in failure recovery. Because TCP/IP was originally a military proposal, the protocol had to be able to continue operating even if large parts of the network suddenly disappeared from view (e.g., after an enemy attack).
- It had to handle high error rates and still provide completely reliable end-to-end service.
- It had to be efficient and have low data overhead. The majority of IP packets have a simple, 20-byte header, which means better performance in comparison with other network protocols. A simple protocol translates directly into faster transmissions, giving more efficient service.
- It had to allow the addition of new networks without any service disruptions. This has helped fuel the growth and expansion of the Internet and PC networks.

TCP/IP was therefore developed with each component performing unique and vital functions that allowed all the problems involved in moving data between machines over networks to be solved in an elegant and efficient way.

The popularity that the TCP/IP family of protocols enjoys today did not arise just because the protocols were there, or even because the U.S. government mandated their use. They are popular because they are robust, solid protocols that solve many of the most difficult networking problems and do so elegantly and efficiently.

The result of meeting the DoD design goals was a protocol that had, and continues to have, several inherent benefits over other networking protocols. These include:

- TCP/IP is a widely published open standard and is completely independent of any hardware or software manufacturer.
- TCP/IP can send data between different computer systems running completely different operating systems, from small PCs all the way to mainframes and everything in between.
- TCP/IP is separated from the underlying hardware and can run over Ethernet, Token Ring, and other networks.
- TCP/IP is a routable protocol, which means it can send **datagrams** (i.e., TCP/IP network packets, also known as **segments**) over a specific route, thus reducing traffic on other parts of the network.
- TCP/IP has reliable and efficient data-delivery mechanisms.
- TCP/IP uses a common addressing scheme. Therefore, any system can address any other system, even in a network as large as the Internet.

The TCP/IP family continued to evolve and add new members. One of the most important aspects of this growth was the continuing development of the certification and testing program carried out by the U.S. government to ensure that the published standards, which were free, were met. Publication ensured that the developers did not change anything or add any features specific to their own needs. This open approach has continued to the present day; use of the TCP/IP family of protocols virtually guarantees a trouble-free connection between many hardware and software platforms.

7.1.2 Internet Protocol (IP) and Transmission Control Protocol (TCP)

Internet Protocol (IP) operates at the Network layer of the OSI model, or more accurately, at the Internetwork layer of the DoD network model (remember that the two are effectively equivalent). In fact, IP is the main protocol at the Internetwork layer. IP is what actually moves the data from point A to point B. IP is considered connectionless and does not exchange information in order to establish an end-to-end connection before starting a transmission. This type of communication is known as **best-effort transmission**. By itself, it can't recover lost packets or even tell if a packet is lost in transmission. That's one of the reasons other protocols are needed in the TCP/IP suite. IP's only job is to route data to its destination.

During transmission, IP receives a datagram from a higher-level protocol such as TCP (for connection-oriented transmissions) or User Datagram Protocol (UDP; for connectionless transmissions). IP adds to the datagram its header, consisting of information such as the **source address**, the **destination address**, the **protocol number** (identifying the higher-level protocol in use), a **checksum** (to check for errors at the destination), and a code representing the enclosed higher-layer protocol. The information in the header provides the information needed for routing and delivery, including the **Time to Live (TTL)** field.

The TTL field contains the **hop count** (i.e., the maximum number of routers the packet can cross, usually set to the default value of 32 hops), which is used to determine when to discard a packet as lost or undeliverable. The number is decremented by each router through which the packet passes. When it reaches 0, the current router (known as the **executioner**) sends an Internet Control Message Protocol time exceeded message back to the original source.

Figure 7-1 is a simplified representation of how the IP header, upper-layer header, and data fit together.

The data in the packet immediately follow this header information, which may correspond to a complete TCP segment, UDP datagram, or other IP-supported protocol data.

Transmission Control Protocol (TCP) serves to ensure a reliable, verifiable data exchange between hosts on a network. TCP breaks data into datagrams, wraps them with the information needed to identify the pieces of the original message, and allows the pieces to be reassembled at the receiving end of the communications link. The most important information in the header includes

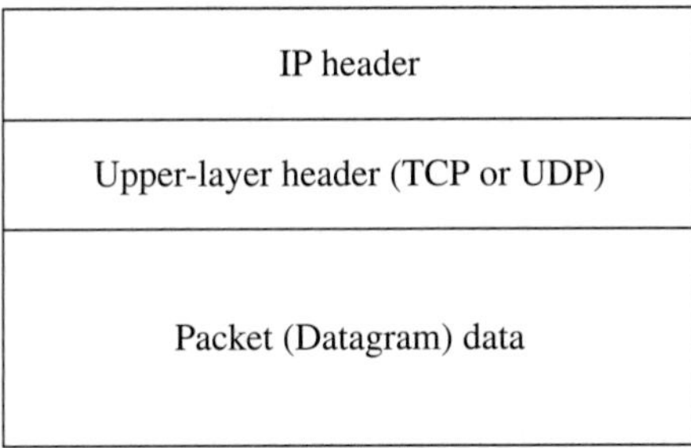

A datagram with headers.

the source and destination port numbers, a sequence number for the datagram, and a checksum.

To understand the role of the header, it might help to take a brief look at the TCP communication process. Key features of TCP communication include the following:

- Flow control, which allows two systems to cooperate in datagram transmission to prevent **overflows** (which occur when more data are sent than the destination can receive) and lost segments.
- **Acknowledgment**, which lets the sender know that the recipient has received the information.
- Sequencing, which is used to ensure that segments arrive in the proper order.
- Checksums, which allow easy detection of corrupted segments.
- Retransmission of lost or corrupted segments that are managed in a timely manner.

TCP adds a certain amount of overhead compared to connectionless communication. However, where reliable delivery is a must, the overhead is an acceptable expense.

Fields in the TCP header support connection-oriented transmission. The source port number and the destination port number ensure that the data are sent back and forth to the correct application process running on each computer. Port numbers and their use are discussed in more detail later in this chapter.

The header is also designed to enable **fragmented datagrams** (i.e., datagrams broken into smaller pieces) and their reassembly. A sequence number and fragmentation offset value showing where the fragment fits as part of the complete datagram allow the datagrams to be rebuilt in the correct order in the receiving device.

A checksum value enables the protocol to check whether the data sent are the same as the data received.

The **Window field** determines the number of segments transmitted before the sender expects an acknowledgment. Increasing this value helps improve efficiency in data transfers on a reliable network. The value is decreased when there are network problems that endanger the integrity of the data so more segments need to be acknowledged until conditions improve.

The **Urgent Pointer field** gives the location in the segment where the urgent data end, assuming that the urgent data begin at the beginning of the segment. This allows out-of-band transmission of special data, which signifies to the receiving device that these data should be pushed ahead of any other that it has received but has not yet processed. Special data could be, for example, a keyboard break sequence in a Telnet (terminal emulation) session, which should immediately be processed by the receiving device.

Once the header is on the datagram, TCP passes the datagram to IP to be routed to its destination. The receiving device performs a checksum calculation, and if the values do not match, an error has occurred somewhere along the line, so the datagram is silently discarded by the destination device. The source resends any packet that is not acknowledged after a set time-out period.

FOR EXAMPLE

Routers and Routing

The IP portion of the TCP/IP protocol inserts its header in the datagram. It is then sent to the first router on the way to the destination or, if the source doesn't know the best route to take, to the host's default gateway. Each host on a TCP/IP network can have a default gateway. Its job is to forward datagrams toward their destination (if known) or to its default router, and so forth, until the destination is reached. Because routers don't know the location of every IP address, they have their own default gateways that act just like any TCP/IP host. Each router has a defined set of routing tables that help track routes to specific destinations.

Datagrams intended for the same destination may actually take different routes to get there. Many variables determine the route, and most modern routers are designed to compensate automatically for changing conditions, such as excessive congestion or detection of a failed route. Key to this process is the destination address, which includes both the address of the destination network and host.

The destination network is the network on which the final destination is located. The host address uniquely identifies the host device on that network. It is therefore critical that each host (and network location) is uniquely identifiable within the network's scope. Part of the design process when deploying a TCP/IP network is determining what addresses will be used and how they will be assigned to the hosts.

1. Describe the relationship between datagrams, IP header information, and TCP header information.

7.2 Managing IP Addresses

Each IP datagram destination includes an IP address and a destination port or socket number. These allow for successful delivery to any host on a LAN or, if connected to the Internet, potentially to any location in the world.

Each Ethernet network card (and any other NIC, for that matter) has its own unique hardware address, known as the Media Access Control (MAC) address. This hardware address is predefined and preprogrammed on the NIC by the manufacturer of the board as a unique 48-bit number. Don't confuse this address, which is implemented as part of the Data Link layer of the OSI model, with the IP address, which is implemented at the Network layer (or the Internet layer of the DoD networking model). The IP address is assigned, rather than hard-coded, and can be changed as necessary.

Our primary focus is on the current TCP/IP standard, known as **IP version 4 (IPv4)**. Also in (currently limited) use is a new standard, **IP version 6 (IPv6)**, developed to solve the looming problem that the Internet is rapidly running out of available addresses. We'll take a brief look at IPv6, but only for comparison purposes and to let you know what's eventually coming your way.

7.2.1 Breaking Down IP Addresses

An IPv4 address is a 32-bit number, usually represented as a four-part decimal number, with each of the four parts separated by a period, or decimal point (e.g., 192.168.10.1). This method of representation is often called **dotted-decimal** notation. In an IPv4 address, each individual byte, or **octet** as it is sometimes called, can have a decimal value of 0 through 255. The way these addresses are used varies according to the **class** of the network, which is how the addresses are organized, so all you can say with certainty is that a 32-bit IPv4 address is divided to create an identifier for the network, which all hosts on that network share, and for each host, which is unique among all hosts on that network. In addition, the address can be divided further to allow for a **subnetwork address**, which is a way of dividing an assigned network address among smaller networks for organizational and management purposes.

Some host addresses are reserved for special use. For example, in all network addresses, host numbers of all 0s and all 1s are reserved. An IPv4 host address with all host bits set to 0 in binary identifies the network itself, so 10.0.0.0 refers to network 10. An IP address with all host bits set to 1 in binary is known as a broadcast address. The broadcast address for network 172.16 is 172.16.255.255. A datagram sent to this address is automatically sent to every individual host on the 172.16 network.

The **Internet Corporation for Assigned Names and Numbers (ICANN)** is responsible for registering and maintaining IP address and Internet domain name registrations. In theory, you could get an IP address from ICANN. In real-world applications, you are most likely to have to ask your ISP to secure an IP address on your behalf. However, registered addresses are required only if you are connecting to the Internet and you need an address that is recognized by the Internet. For your local network, you have the option of using addresses that have been set aside as **private addresses**.

Private addresses are not recognized by Internet routers, so a computer with a private address cannot directly access the Internet. This is where services such as Network Address Translation (NAT) and Internet proxy servers come into play. As shown in Figure 7-2, they replace the computer's private address with a valid Internet address on outgoing packets. As packets come in destined for a local host, the Internet address is replaced with the host's private address.

Managing Address Classes

In an IPv4 address, the default number of bits used to identify the network and the host vary according to the network class of the address. The classes of IP addresses offer a default set of boundaries for varying sizes of address.

IPv4 address classes are shown in Figure 7-3. Address **Classes A**, **B**, and **C** are used for IP host addressing. **Class D** is a special-use address class, used for **multicast**, which is a way of sending to defined groups of computers.

Figure 7-2

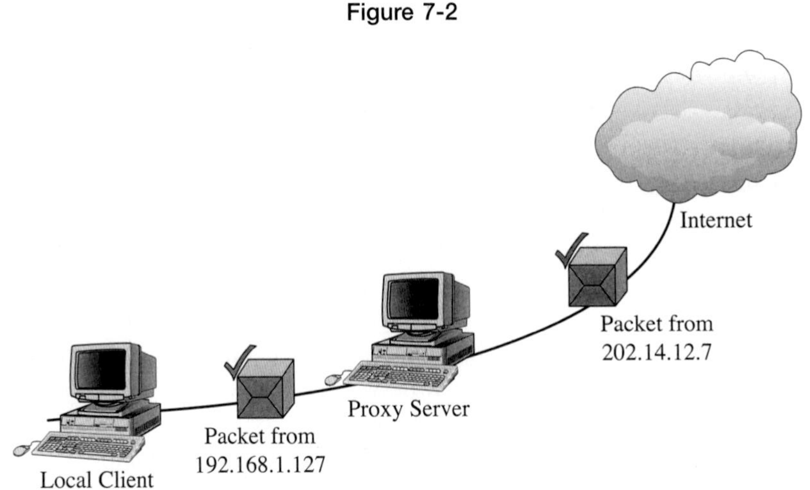

Address translation.

Figure 7-3

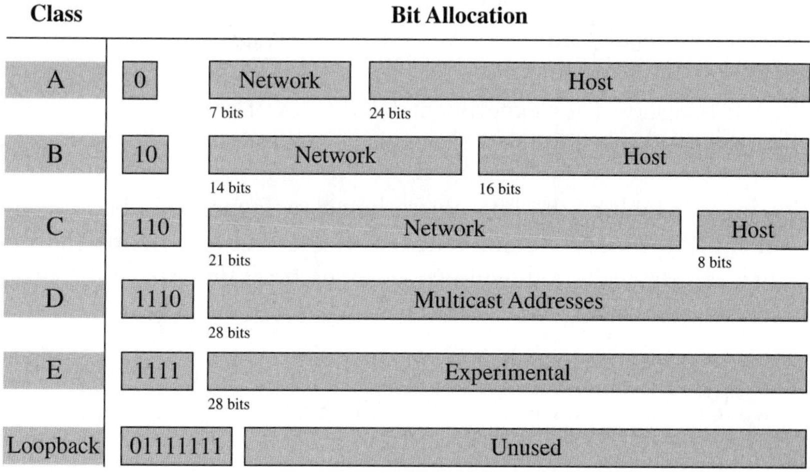

IPv4 address classes.

Let's take a closer look at each of these classes and their use:

- Class A was designed for very large networks only. The default network portion for Class A networks is the first 8 bits, leaving 24 bits for host identification. The high-order bit is always binary 0, which leaves 7 bits defining 127 networks. The remaining 24 bits of the address allow each Class A network to hold as many as 16,777,214 hosts. All possible Class A networks are in use; no more are available.
- Class B was designed for medium-sized networks. The default network portion for Class B networks is the first 16 bits, leaving 16 bits for host identification. The 2 high-order bits are always binary 10, and the remaining 14 bits define 16,384 networks, each with as many as 65,534 hosts attached. Class B networks are generally regarded as unavailable, but address conservation techniques have allowed some of these addresses to become available from time to time over the years.
- Class C was designed for smaller networks. The default network portion for Class C networks is the first 24 bits, leaving 8 bits for host identification. The 3 high-order bits are always binary 110, and the remaining 21 bits define 2,097,152 networks, but each network can have a maximum of only 254 hosts.
- Class D is the multicast address range and cannot be used for networks. There is no network/host structure to these addresses. They are taken as a complete address and used as destination addresses only, just like broadcast addresses. The 4 high-order bits are always 1110, and the

remaining 28 bits allow access to more than 268 million possible addresses. Multicast addresses are used for managing broadcasts to defined groups of computers, such as streaming video out to specific computers on a network.

- ▲ Class E is reserved for experimental purposes. The first 4 bits in the address are always 1111.

Take another look at the bit values shown in Figure 7-3. Because the bits used to identify the class are combined with the bits that define the network address, we can draw the following conclusions from the size of the first octet, or byte, of the address:

- ▲ A value of 126 or less indicates a Class A address. The first octet is the network number; the next three are the host ID.
- ▲ A value of exactly 127, while technically in the Class A range, is reserved as a software **loopback** test address. If you send an **echo request** to 127.0.0.1, it doesn't actually generate any network traffic. It does, however, test that TCP/IP is installed correctly. Using this number as a special test address has the unfortunate effect of wasting almost 17 million possible IP addresses, a case of early 1970s shortsightedness.
- ▲ A value of 128 through 191 is a Class B address. The first two octets are the network number, and the last two are the host address.
- ▲ A value of 192 through 223 is a Class C address. The first three octets are the network address, and the last octet is the host address.
- ▲ A value of 224 through 239 is a Class D multicast address. Again, there are no network or host portions to multicast addresses.
- ▲ A value greater than 239 indicates a reserved Class E address.

7.2.2 Using Subnets

The IP addressing scheme provides a flexible solution to the task of addressing thousands of networks, but it is not without problems. The original designers did not envision the Internet growing as large as it has; at that time, a 32-bit address seemed so large that the designers quickly divided it into different classes of networks to facilitate routing rather than reserving more bits to manage the growth in network addresses. To solve this problem, and to create a large number of new network addresses, another way of dividing the 32-bit address was developed, called **subnetting**.

When faced with the choice of whether to subnet a network, you must remember several of the advantages of subnetting. The following list summarizes the advantages of the subnetting solution:

- ▲ It minimizes network traffic, decreasing congestion because routers filter traffic by network address, keeping local traffic on the local network.
- ▲ It isolates networks from others, requiring routers to provide connectivity between the subnets.
- ▲ It can improve performance by reducing the traffic in a network segment, especially in Ethernet networks, where collisions have become a problem.
- ▲ It defines the limits of a broadcast domain because routers do not forward broadcast packets.
- ▲ It optimizes use of IP address space by letting you specify the number of hosts per network.
- ▲ It enhances the ability to secure a network through careful segmentation and the use, where needed, of firewalls between subnetworks.

An IP subnet modifies the IP address by using host ID bits as additional network address bits. In other words, the dividing line between the network address and the host ID is moved to the right, thus creating additional networks but reducing the number of hosts that can belong to each network.

When IP networks are subnetted, they can be routed independently, which allows a much better use of address space and available bandwidth. To subnet an IP network, you define a bit mask, known as a subnet mask, in which a bit pattern of consecutive 1s followed by consecutive 0s is logically ANDed with the IP address to produce a network address with all 0s in the host ID.

Working out subnet masks can be one of the most complex tasks in network administration and is not for the faint of heart. However, if you have two or more segments (or subnets), you need to make some sort of provision for distributing IP addresses appropriately. One way is to assign different network class addresses (such as using multiple Class C addresses), but subnetting makes more efficient use of available addresses.

If you are using private addresses, which are discussed in some detail later in this section, you might well be able to use multiple network addresses, but this is not the case in all networks. There is also the possibility that you might encounter a routed network that someone else has set up, so you need to understand at least the basics involved. The goal of this chapter is to introduce you to subnetting but not to try to make you an expert in the process.

A subnet mask is similar in structure to an IP address, but it works a bit like a template that, when superimposed on top of the IP address, indicates which bits in the IP address identify the network and which bits identify the host. In binary, if a bit is on (i.e., set to 1) in the mask, the corresponding bit in the address is interpreted as a network bit. If a bit is off (i.e., reset to 0) in the mask, the corresponding bit in the address is part of the host ID. Often, you use only one subnet mask throughout to subnet your network, as in Figure 7-4.

Figure 7-4

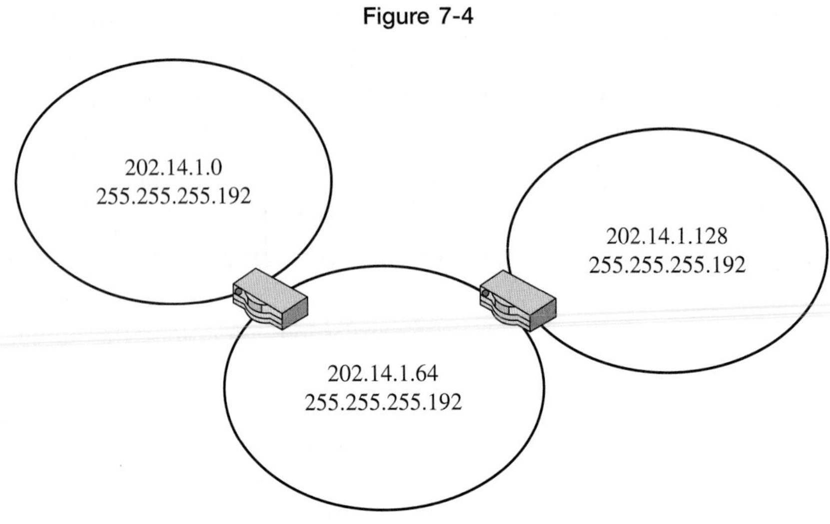

A sample internetwork.

Variable-length subnet masking (VLSM), another subnetting option, is the practice of using more appropriate varied subnet masks with the same classful network for the different subnet sizes. A **classful network** is a network that is subnetted to the default boundaries of network and host bits, based on the class of IP address.

A subnet is known and understood only locally; to the rest of the Internet, the address is still interpreted as a classful IP address (and maybe even as a group of classful addresses) if an entity has administrative control over a contiguous block of such addresses. Table 7-1 shows how this works for the standard IP address classes.

Routers use the subnet mask to extract the network portion of the address so that they can compare the computed network address with the routing table entry corresponding to the mask used and send the data packets along the proper route on the network.

Table 7-1: Default Subnet Masks

Class	*Subnet Mask Bit Pattern*	*Subnet Mask*
A	11111111 00000000 00000000 00000000	255.0.0.0
B	11111111 11111111 00000000 00000000	255.255.0.0
C	11111111 11111111 11111111 00000000	255.255.255.0

Table 7-2: CIDR vs. Subnet Mask Representations

InterNIC Network Type	*Subnet Mask*	*Number of Usable IP Addresses*
/8	255.0.0.0	16,777,214
/12	255.240.0.0	1,048,574
/16	255.255.0.0	65,534
/20	255.255.240.0	4,094
/21	255.255.248.0	2,046
/22	255.255.252.0	1,022
/23	255.255.254.0	510
/24	255.255.255.0	254
/25	255.255.255.128	126
/26	255.255.255.128	126
/27	255.255.255.192	62
/28	255.255.255.224	30
/29	255.255.255.248	6
/30	255.255.255.252	2

Classless Interdomain Routing (CIDR)

The traditional way of representing addresses is with an IP address and subnet mask value. It has become common, however, to use the **classless interdomain routing** (**CIDR**; usually pronounced "cider") standard representation. CIDR networks are described as "slash x" (/x) networks, where the x represents the number of bits in the IP address range used as the network address. The idea is that this is more easily seen as the number of bits in the subnet mask set to 1 than the decimal values, though network administrators used to the original method often disagree. You can see an example of this in Table 7-2.

In CIDR terms, a network classified as a Class C network under the old scheme becomes a /24. The real purpose of CIDR is that you can use it to define networks that fall between the old classifications, as shown in Table 7-2.

Subnetting a Class C Network

How do you find out the values that you can use for a Class C network subnet mask? The leftmost three octets in a Class C address are defined for you, leaving you with the rightmost octet for your own host and subnetting use. If your network consists of a single segment, you have the following subnet mask:

11111111 11111111 11111111 00000000

When expressed as a decimal number, this is 255.255.255.0.

Because all your addresses must match the leftmost 24 bits, you can do what you'd like with the last 8 bits, given a couple of exceptions that we'll look at in a moment.

You might decide to divide your network into two equally sized segments, with, for example, the numbers 0 through 127 as the first subnet (00000000 through 01111111 in binary) and the numbers 128 through 255 as the second subnet (10000000 through 11111111 in binary). Notice how the numbers within each subnet can vary only in the last seven places. So, placing 1s in the mask where the bits should be identical for all hosts in a subnet, the subnet mask becomes 255.255.255.128. In binary this is

11111111.11111111.11111111.10000000

As a quick tip, you can use the Windows Calculator in scientific mode (by selecting View and then Scientific) to look at binary-to-decimal and decimal-to-binary conversions. You click the Bin button and then type the bit pattern that you want to convert. Then you click Dec to display its decimal value. You can also go the other way and display a decimal number in binary form. This works great for hexadecimal and octal numbering systems, as well.

Now let's get back to the exceptions mentioned earlier. The network number is the first number in each range, so the first subnet's network number is X.Y.Z.0, and the second is X.Y.Z.128 (the host address set to all 0s). The default router address is commonly the second number in each range—X.Y.Z.1 and X.Y.Z.129; this is not required, but a lot of network administrators like to set them up this way. The broadcast address is the last address (with the host address portion set to all 1s), or X.Y.Z.127 and X.Y.Z.255 in this case. The broadcast address is set by definition, so you can't play around with it. You can use all the other addresses within the range as you see fit on your network. Table 7-3 shows

Table 7-3: Class C Network as Four Subnetworks

Network Number	*First Address*	*Broadcast Address*
X.Y.Z.0	X.Y.Z.1	X.Y.Z.63
X.Y.Z.64	X.Y.Z.65	X.Y.Z.127
X.Y.Z.128	X.Y.Z.129	X.Y.Z.191
X.Y.Z.1292	X.Y.Z.193	X.Y.Z.225

Figure 7-5

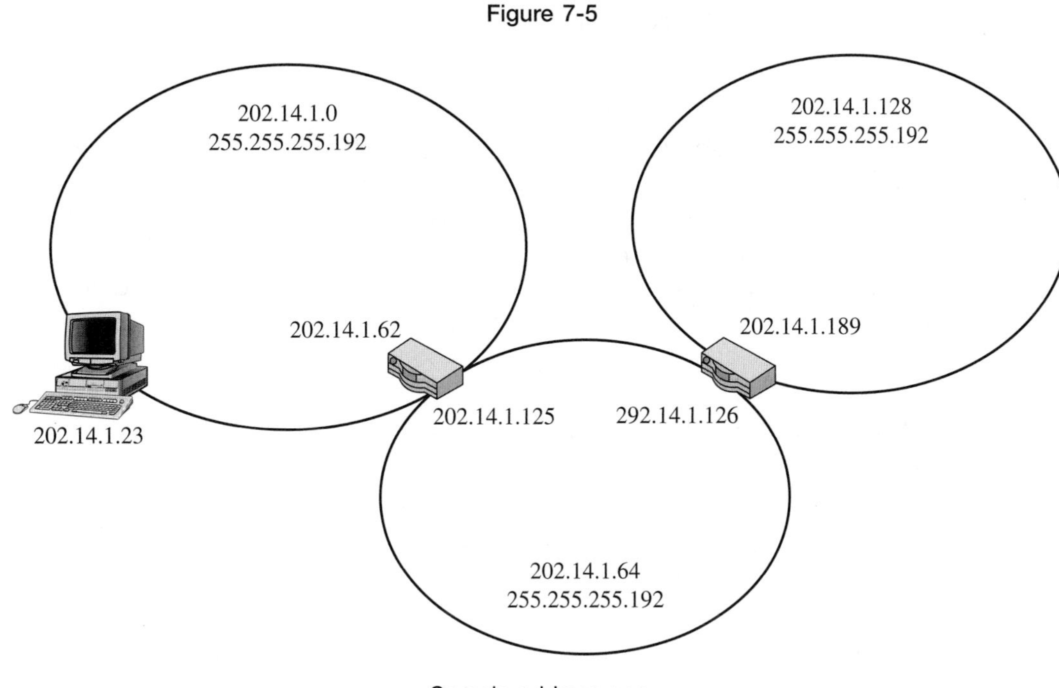

Sample address use.

how you can divide a Class C network into four equally sized subnets with a subnet mask of 255.255.255.192. This gives you 62 IP addresses on each subnet after you have accounted for the network and broadcast addresses.

In Figure 7-5, we've put in some real numbers (using addresses out of the private address range) to let you see how the addresses might be used in your network.

Keep in mind that except for the network address and broadcast address, there are no firm and fast rules as to how you use the other available addresses. However, you might find it worth your while to set up internal addressing standards.

Assigning Private Addresses

You will often use a private address when setting up a network and use public addresses only at those points where you are directly exposed to the Internet. There are several benefits to this method. The most obvious one is that you don't need a registered address to set up the network. Also, these addresses are isolated from the Internet, so devices must access the Internet through a NAT server, a proxy server, or another device to facilitate communication. This provides a boundary between the network and the Internet and prevents hosts on the Internet from knowing the internal addressing scheme of your network.

These are the private address ranges:

10.0.0.0–10.255.255.255 (10 /8)
172.16.0.0–172.31.255.255 (172.16 /16)
192.168.0.0–192.168.255.255 (192.168 /24)

The private address spaces listed with each class description are specified in Request for Comment 1918 as being available to anyone who wants to use IP addressing on a private network but does not want to connect these networks directly to the Internet. Private addresses are those addresses that are not permitted to be routed by Internet routers. In fact, ISPs can be fined for passing traffic with these addresses as source or destination.

7.2.3 Using Ports and Sockets

In addition to an IP address, a packet also has port addresses, or **port numbers**. Data travel from a port on the sending computer to a port on the receiving computer. A port is a numeric value that identifies applications associated with the data, a source port for the source application, and a destination port for the destination application. TCP/IP supports two types of ports, UDP and TCP ports, and within these, each port is assigned a unique 16-bit number in the range of 0 through 65,535, through a separately maintained list.

The very existence of ports and their numbers is more or less transparent to the users of a network because many server-side ports are standardized. Thus, a client application protocol knows which remote port it should connect to for a specific service. For example, all servers that offer Telnet services usually do so on TCP port 23 by default, and web servers normally run on TCP port 80. This means that when you connect to the Internet to browse to a web server, you automatically connect to port 80, and when you use Telnet, you automatically connect to port 23. The TCP/IP protocol suite uses a modifiable lookup table to determine the correct port for the data type. Table 7-4 lists some of the well-known port numbers for common protocols.

Applications can also define their own port numbers with values of 1024 through 49151. TCP and UDP temporarily assign these port numbers to client application protocols when communicating with a remote device and its server application protocol. Ports from 49152 to 65535 are set aside for special use.

You may hear or see the terms *socket* and *port* used as if they were interchangeable terms, but they are not. The combination of an IP address and a port number is known as a **socket**. A socket identifies a single network process in terms of the entire Internet or other end-to-end IP-based internetwork. Two sockets—one on the sending system and one on the receiving host—are needed to define a connection for connection-oriented protocols, such as TCP.

Table 7-4: Well-Known Port Numbers

Port	*Protocol*
UDP port 15	Netstat
TCP port 20	FTP data
TCP port 21	FTP control
TCP port 22	SSH
TCP port 23	Telnet
TCP port 25	SMTP
TCP port 53	DNS zone transfers
UDP port 53	DNS queries
UDP port 69	TFTP
TCP port 70	Gopher
TCP port 79	Finger
TCP port 80	HTTP
TCP port 110	POP3
UDP port 111	RPC
TCP port 119	NNTP
TCP port 123	NTP
UDP port 137	NetBIOS name service
TCP port 143	IMAP4
UDP port 161	SNMP
TCP port 443	HTTPS
UDP port 520	RIP
UDP port 2049	NFS

7.2.4 Looking Ahead to IPv6

A detailed discussion of IPv6 is beyond the scope of this chapter, but we can't leave the subject of addressing without at least a mention. Careful management of existing addresses and extensive use of private addressing on LANs have kept the Internet from running out of address space, but these solutions won't work forever. At some point, the address space has to be extended. That process, at least the beginning of it, is going on now.

IPv6 uses a 128-bit addressing scheme, so it has more than 79 octillion (that's 79,000,000,000,000,000,000,000,000,000 to you and me) times as many available addresses as IPv4. Also, instead of representing the binary digits as decimal digits, IPv6 uses eight sets of four hexadecimal digits, like so:

3FFE:0B00:0800:0002:0000:0000:0000:000C

When writing IPv6 addresses, you can abbreviate these very long addresses by dropping leading 0s like the 0 before the B in "0B00" in the previous example. You can also drop any single grouping of complete zero octets (i.e., those having all zeros) between numbers as long as you replace them with a double colon (::) and they are complete octets. If you apply this rule (known as the zero compression rule) to the above address, the would address look like this:

3FFE:0B00:0800:0002::000C

As with IPv4, there are several addresses that are reserved for special uses. For example, the IPv6 address ::/0 is the default address for a host that has yet to be assigned an address. The address ::1/128 is reserved for the local loopback (e.g., 127.0.0.1 in IPv4). IPv6 also includes provisions for the old IPv4 hosts so they can be migrated to the new addressing scheme. This is accomplished by using the address ::xxx. . ., where the last four sets of digits refer to the old IPv4 address.

The details of how IPv6 addresses are implemented is beyond the scope of the chapter, but suffice to say that addressing is significantly more complicated with IPv6 than with IPv4. Every host has three different addresses, used to uniquely identify it on the network, the network to which it belongs, and routing information. There are also several concepts and enhancements that are unique to IPv6.

Most current operating systems include support for IPv6. This is provided at varying levels between the operating systems and primarily for the purpose of testing IPv6 implementation in preparation for an eventual changeover from IPv4. When this finally occurs, it is expected to be a gradual migration that will take place over several years, with some industry pundits saying it is unlikely that IPv4 addresses will never be fully retired.

FOR EXAMPLE

Further Subnetting

Say that you have a single Class C network address at your disposal. You need to create eight more-or-less equal-sized subnetworks. The maximum number of hosts in any one subnetwork is 30. What can you do?

Table 7-5: A Class C Network as Eight Subnetworks

Network Number	*First Address*	*Broadcast Address*
192.168.10.0	192.168.10.1	192.168.10.31
192.168.10.32	192.168.10.33	192.168.10.63
192.168.10.64	192.168.10.65	192.168.10.95
192.168.10.96	192.168.10.97	192.168.10.127
192.168.10.128	192.168.10.129	192.168.10.159
192.168.10.160	192.168.10.161	192.168.10.191
192.168.10.192	192.168.10.193	192.168.10.223
192.168.10.224	192.168.10.225	192.168.10.255

Table 7-5 describes how you can divide a Class C network into eight equally sized subnets with a subnet mask of 255.255.255.224. This gives you 30 IP addresses on each subnet, once you have accounted for the network and broadcast addresses. You can continue this trend for subnet masks with fourth-octet values of 240, 248, and 252. A fourth-octet value of 254 is widely regarded as unusable because the only possible values in each subnet have only 0s or 1s in the host portion, which are illegal for assignment to hosts.

See anything funny about these network numbers? Did you catch it? You weren't necessarily required to subnet the network. You probably could have just as easily used 192.168.10 through 192.168.17 (or a similar range) with the default Class C subnet mask (255.255.255.0). Your Class C network address is a private address.

SELF-CHECK

1. List the network address ranges and default subnet masks for the classes assigned as network addresses.
2. List the supported private address ranges by class.

7.3 Implementing Name Resolution

Not only do you need to concern yourself with IP addresses, you also have to worry about host names. Why? Most people find it easier to remember a textual name than a string of numbers. When they need to find a file server, it's easier to remember to look for file1.busicorp.local than for 192.168.11.152. To make this easier, TCP/IP provides different mechanisms for resolving host names to IP addresses and, conversely, IP addresses to host names.

A host name is typically the name of a device that has a specific IP address and on the Internet is part of what is known as a **fully qualified domain name (FQDN)**. An FQDN consists of a host name and a domain name, which is how names are organized on the Internet and in a large number of TCP/IP LANs. An example of an FQDN is hostname.company.com.

Let's take a quick overview of host names and how they are organized. The process of finding the IP address for any given host name is known as **name resolution**, and it can be performed in several ways: via a **HOSTS** file, a request broadcast on the local network, the Domain Name System (DNS), or **Windows Internet Naming Service (WINS)** for **NetBIOS** names.

7.3.1 Organizing TCP/IP Host Names

On the Internet, domains are arranged in a hierarchical tree structure. The following list includes some of the top-level domains currently in use, with several more not listed that have been added in recent years:

- **.com:** A commercial organization. Most companies are part of this domain.
- **.edu:** An educational establishment, such as a university.
- **.gov:** A branch of the U.S. government.
- **.int:** An international organization, such as NATO or the United Nations.
- **.mil:** A branch of the U.S. military.
- **.net:** A network organization.
- **.org:** A nonprofit organization.

For example, your local ISP is probably a member of the .net domain, and your company is probably part of the .com domain. The .gov and .mil domains are reserved strictly for use by the government and the military within the United States. In other parts of the world, the final part of a domain name represents the country in which the server is located, such as .ca for Canada, .jp for Japan, .uk for the United Kingdom, and .ru for Russia. The .com domain is the largest, followed by the .edu domain.

ICANN assigns all Internet domain names and makes sure that a name is not duplicated. Names are assigned on a first-come, first-served basis, but if you try to register a name that infringes on someone else's registered trademark, your use of that name will be rescinded if the trademark holder objects. Several companies can handle the details for registering your domain name for you, at a price.

The unique host name, the part before the domain name, is under your control. Some names have become standard host names through their use, such as using www for a web server. You should develop internal naming standards to make machines on your local network easier to recognize, such as using ftp for FTP servers, fs (or something similar) for file servers, or possibly user names for end-user computers. Be careful, though, because too descriptive a name on a sensitive server could lead an attacker directly to it.

7.3.2 Resolving with HOSTS

Several automatic conversion systems are available to translate an IP address into a host name, and HOSTS is one of the simplest. You create a file called HOSTS, located in a folder or directory based on the requirements of your operating system, and enter a line in the file for each system, as in the following example:

198.34.56.25 myserver.com #My server's information
198.34.57.03 yourserver.com

The problem, from an administrative standpoint, is that you must store this ASCII file on every single workstation on your network. When you make a change, you must change the contents of the HOSTS file on every single workstation on your network. This is a simple but painful process inside a network. But what happens if you want to go outside the network to other networks or to the Internet? The file would be too large and too complicated to manage. The HOSTS file method is used only when just a few host devices need to be managed.

7.3.3 Resolving with Domain Name System (DNS)

Compared to using a HOSTS file, the Domain Name System (DNS) is a more automated method for managing DNS names. You use DNS to translate host names and domain names to IP addresses, and vice versa, by means of a standardized lookup table. The system works like a giant telephone directory. With some DNS systems, network administrators must maintain the table manually. Other systems, known as **dynamic DNSs**, support automatic updates.

DNS is an essential part of large TCP/IP networks because it simplifies the task of remembering addresses; all you have to do is simply remember the hos name and domain name. You enter the URL http://www.microsoft.com in you web browser to go to the Microsoft homepage. Your web browser has TCP/I query a DNS server for the IP address www.microsoft.com. If necessary, th

Figure 7-6

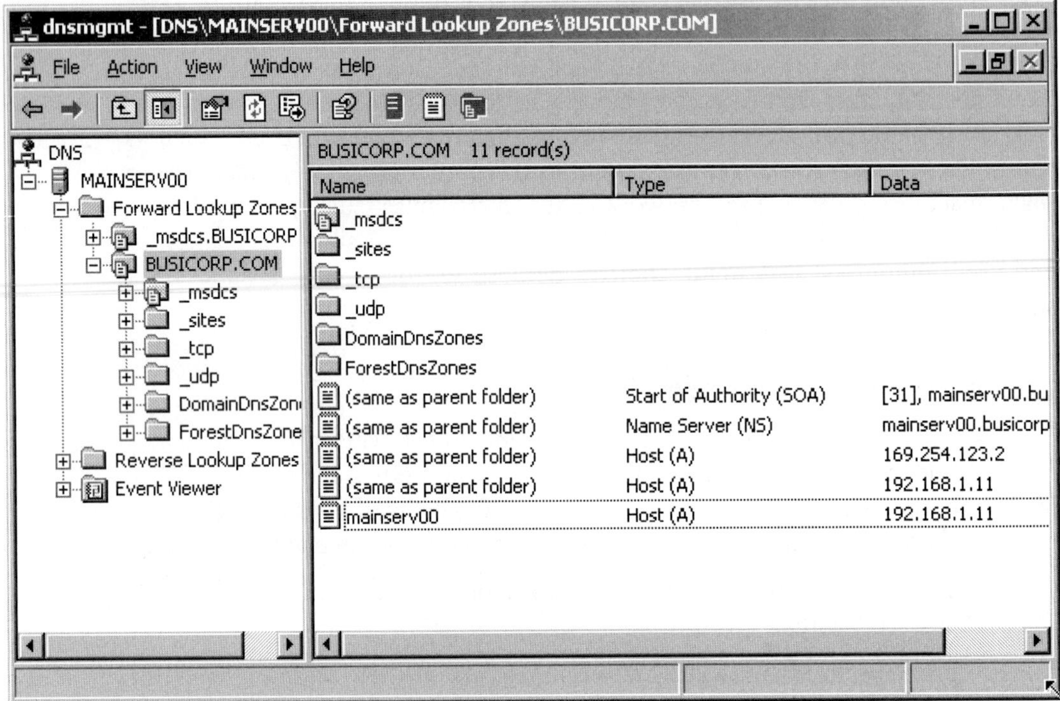

Sample DNS records.

request is forwarded to another DNS server until an entry for the host name is found and returned. Your web browser connects to the Microsoft web server and downloads the homepage.

A **DNS zone** is an administrative area or name space within a DNS domain. The DNS server with primary responsibility over that zone is said to be the **authoritative server** over the zone. You can configure additional, hierarchical zones to make the system easier to maintain. The DNS servers contain the **zone file**, or **DNS table**, which contains the DNS records for that zone. Most records include a host name, a record type, and an IP address. Figure 7-6 shows entries from a DNS table taken from a small Windows Active Directory domain.

A **primary DNS server** is authoritative for the zone for which it carries the zone file, and a **secondary DNS server** has a nonauthoritative copy of the zone file updated from the primary server. Changes are made at the primary server that is authoritative for that zone.

The most common record type is the **address record**, also known as a **host record** or an **A record**, which maps a host name to an IP address. Each zone can have a single **start of authority (SOA) record**, which describes the zone and authoritative server. Mail servers are mapped as **mail exchange (MX) records**. DNS servers are mapped as **name server (NS) records**. The **canonical name (CNAME) record**, or **alias record**, lets you map additional names to the same IP address. You might want to do this, for example, if your web server has the host name www, and you want that machine to also have the name ftp so that users can use FTP to access a different portion of the file system as an FTP root.

7.3.4 Resolving with Windows Internet Naming Service (WINS)

Windows Internet Naming Service (WINS) provides name resolution where NetBIOS is still in use. NetBIOS (pronounced "net-bye-ose") is an acronym formed from network basic input/output system, and NetBIOS is used to manage data exchange and network access. NetBIOS provides an application programming interface with a consistent set of commands for requesting lower-level network services to transmit information from node to node. With NetBIOS, devices are recognized and accessed by their NetBIOS names.

NetBIOS support is needed with legacy Windows systems, NetBIOS applications, and when the NetBEUI protocol is in use. If a network doesn't have any of these requirements, then it doesn't have any need for NetBIOS or NetBIOS name resolution support.

WINS maps NetBIOS names to IP addresses. Routers don't forward NetBIOS name resolution broadcasts, so broadcasting can't be used to resolve names for

FOR EXAMPLE

Active Directory and DNS

Having a DNS server is not a requirement for all TCP/IP networks. Smaller networks can often get away without having DNS servers, with one major exception. A DNS server is a required part of a Windows Active Directory network. When you promote a Windows server to the role of Active Directory domain controller, you must either identify a DNS server that will be authoritative for the domain or let the Domain Controller Wizard configure the computer as a DNS server.

Domain names, which are structured like Internet domain names, are used to define security boundaries in an Active Directory network. Host names are used to identify client computers in most of the Active Directory management utilities. Because of this, support for host name resolution is a key component.

One of the most common configurations is to either use an existing Windows DNS server or configure the domain controller as a DNS server. Often, network administrators configure all the domain controllers as DNS servers to provide fault tolerance.

devices on a different network segment. WINS lets you continue using the NetBIOS names that you have previously used to access the resources because WINS provides the cross-reference from NetBIOS name to IP address. When you install and configure TCP/IP on a Windows system, you can specify one or more WINS server addresses. The computer sends its NetBIOS name and IP address to the WINS server, and the WINS server uses this information to automatically update its mapping table.

As an additional note, if you have only limited NetBIOS name resolution requirements, you can use **LMHOSTS** files. *LMHOSTS* files are name resolution mapping files, similar to HOSTS files, but used for NetBIOS names.

SELF-CHECK

1. At minimum, what kind of records do you have in the DNS table for a host that is known by multiple names?
2. When do you need a WINS server on a TCP/IP network?

7.4 Supporting TCP/IP

Before leaving our discussion of TCP/IP, we need to talk a little about TCP/IP configuration and some of the most commonly used TCP/IP tools and utilities. There are several available parameters when configuring a TCP/IP host. IP address information is required. Other parameters you can configure include the default gateway, the DNS server, and the WINS server. You can also configure the host to receive configuration information automatically.

TCP/IP includes a wide array of tools and utilities. Most run as command-line interface (text-based) commands, but graphical user interface (GUI) utilities are being developed for use in environments such as Microsoft Windows and graphical Linux and Unix desktop environments. One advantage of TCP/IP is that many of the commands have the same command name and options when run from different operating systems. One thing that Windows administrators need to watch, however, is that unlike Windows and MS-DOS commands, TCP/IP optional parameters are sometimes case-sensitive.

7.4.1 Configuring TCP/IP Parameters

When using Windows, you configure TCP/IP through the Network Connection Properties dialog box. Figure 7-7 shows the properties you might see for a typical wired LAN connection.

Figure 7-7

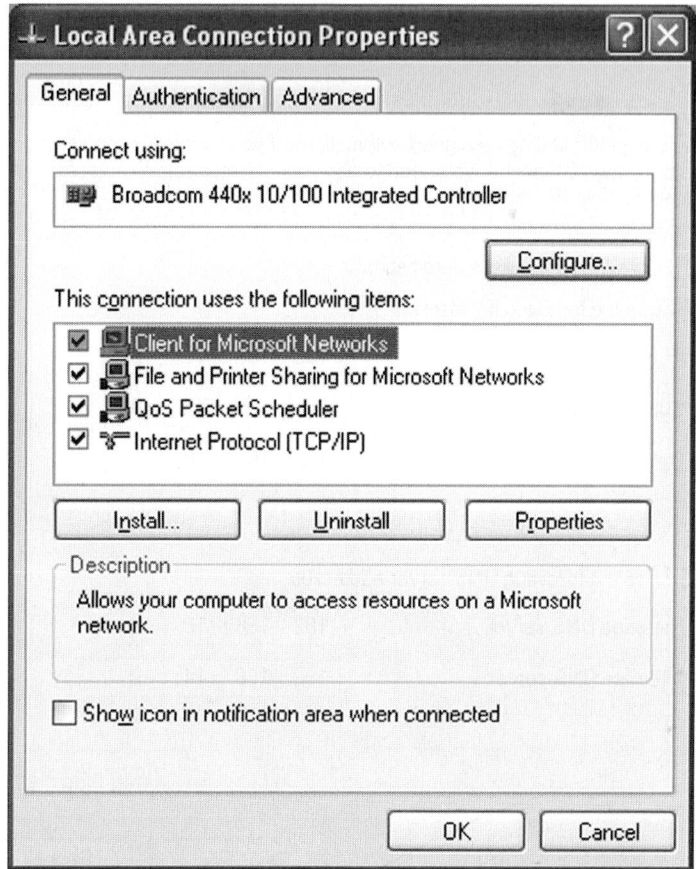

The Local Area Connection Properties dialog box.

You select Internet Protocol (TCP/IP) and click Properties to view and configure TCP/IP properties. Figure 7-8 shows the general properties for a computer configured with a static IP address (i.e., one that has been entered manually for the computer). Other parameters include the subnet mask, default gateway, and DNS server addresses.

You click Advanced to configure additional TCP/IP parameters. The IP settings properties, shown in Figure 7-9, let you configure additional IP addresses, configuring the computer as a **multihomed** host. You can also configure additional default gateways and router metric information, which is interface speed information used in best route calculations.

Figure 7-8

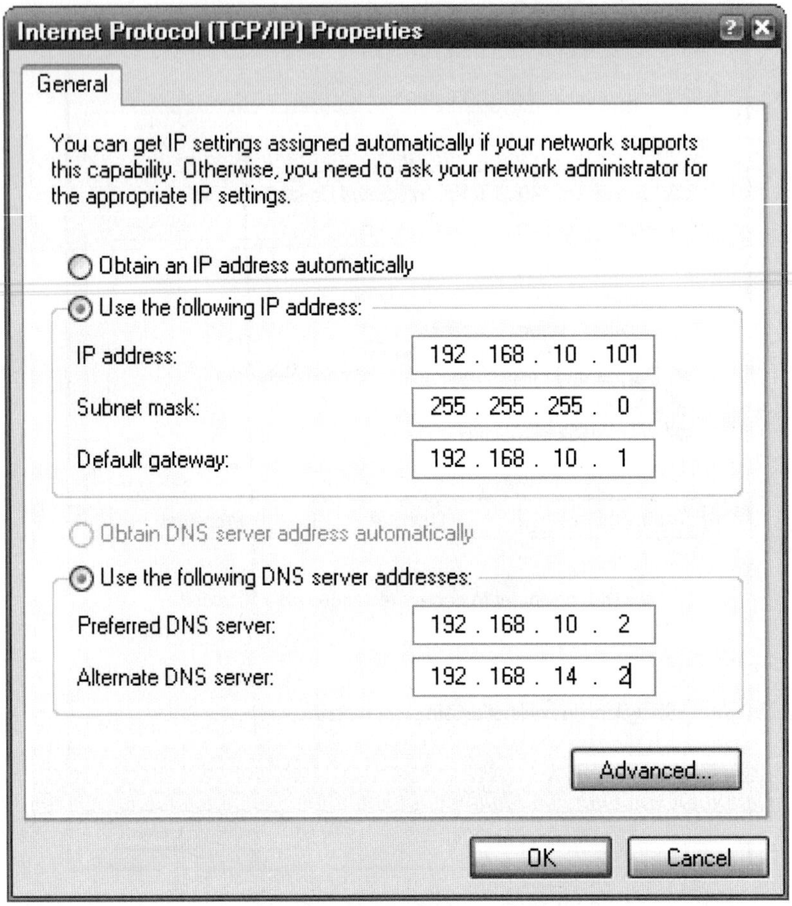

Internet Protocol (TCP/IP) Properties

General

You can get IP settings assigned automatically if your network supports this capability. Otherwise, you need to ask your network administrator for the appropriate IP settings.

Obtain an IP address automatically

Use the following IP address:

IP address: 192 . 168 . 10 . 101

Subnet mask: 255 . 255 . 255 . 0

Default gateway: 192 . 168 . 10 . 1

Obtain DNS server address automatically

Use the following DNS server addresses:

Preferred DNS server: 192 . 168 . 10 . 2

Alternate DNS server: 192 . 168 . 14 . 2

Advanced...

OK Cancel

The General tab of the Internet Protocol (TCP/IP) Properties dialog box.

Figure 7-10 shows the DNS tab. Here, you can enter additional DNS server address information as well as domain name suffix information for host name resolution. The Register This Connection's Addresses in DNS check box is used to enable dynamic DNS support, so the computer can register itself with the primary DNS server.

The properties on the WINS tab shown in Figure 7-11 are necessary only if you have NetBIOS name resolution requirements on a routed network. You can list the WINS servers and NetBIOS support. If your network doesn't have any NetBIOS support requirements, you can select Disable NetBIOS over TCP/IP to disable NetBIOS support.

Figure 7-9

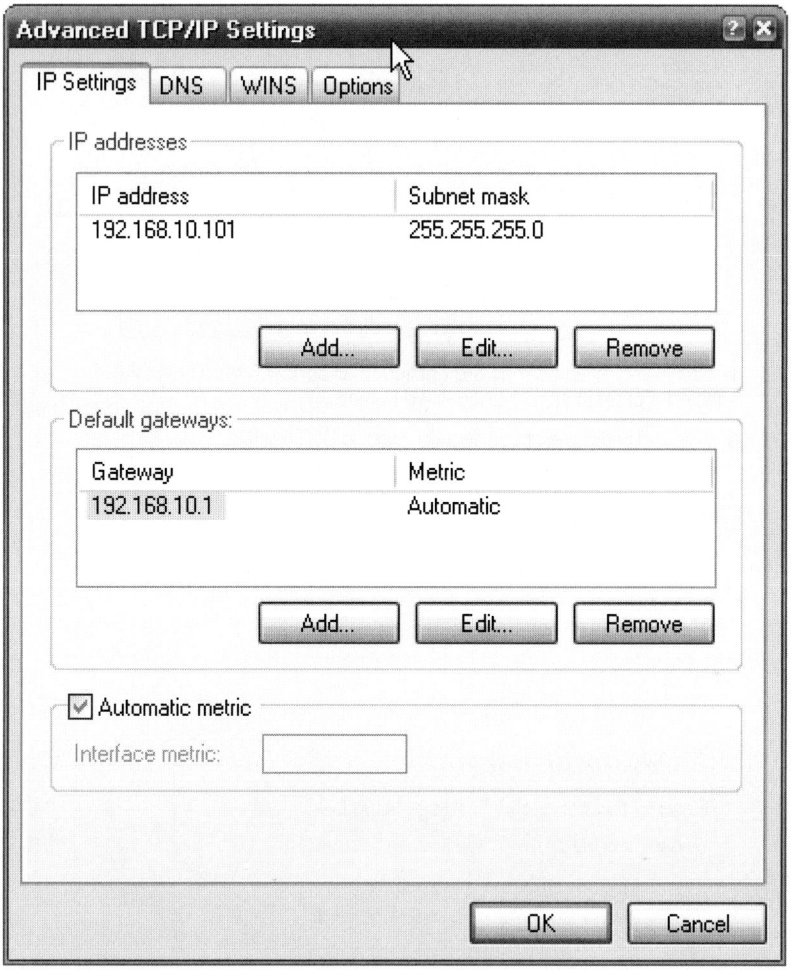

Advanced TCP/IP Settings

IP address	Subnet mask
192.168.10.101	255.255.255.0

Gateway	Metric
192.168.10.1	Automatic

The IP Settings tab.

The properties on the Options tab, shown in Figure 7-12, let you control TCP/IP filtering. You can choose to pass or block selected TCP ports, UDP ports, and IP protocols.

7.4.2 Automating IP Configuration

Although it is not especially complicated, TCP/IP configuration can be a daunting task with a very large TCP/IP network. In that case, it is often better to configure hosts to receive TCP/IP address and configuration information automatically, as shown in Figure 7-13.

Figure 7-10

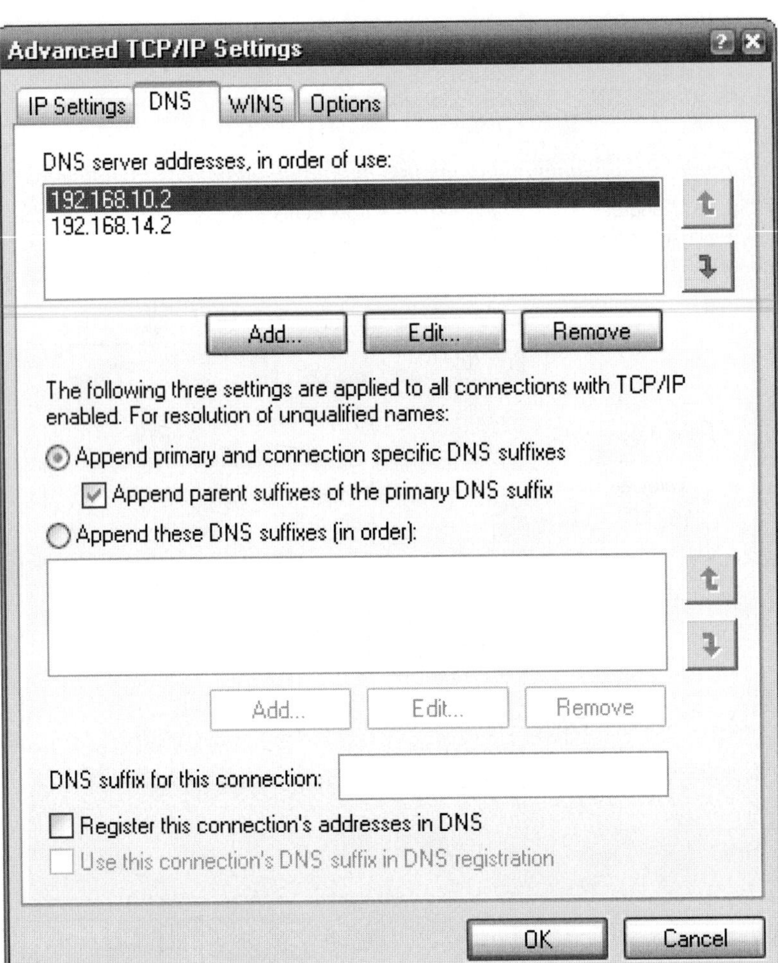

The DNS tab.

As you learned in Chapter 6, IP address and configuration information is provided by a **Dynamic Host Configuration Protocol (DHCP)** server. The properties on the Alternate Configuration tab, shown in Figure 7-14, determine what the host does if it is unable to receive an address from the DHCP server. By default, it uses **Automatic Private IP Addressing (APIPA)** to assign itself an IP address in the 169.254.0.0/16 address range. APIPA is a feature of Windows operating systems and provides a failover method to ensure that the host has an IP address. The other option is to choose User Configured and specify alternate

Figure 7-11

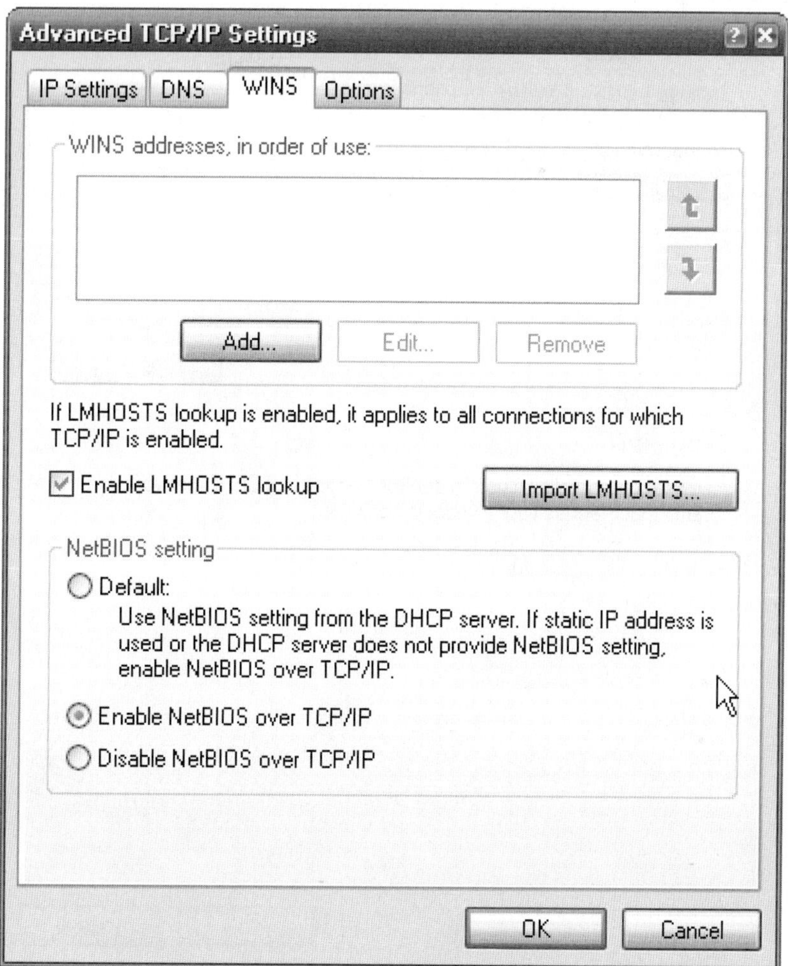

The WINS tab.

IP address information to use if the host cannot get IP addressing information automatically.

The primary reason for using DHCP is to centralize the management of IP addresses. DHCP can also assign DNS servers, WINS servers, default gateway addresses, subnet masks, and many other options.

When the DHCP service is used, DHCP scopes include pools of IP addresses that are assigned for automatic distribution to client computers on an as-needed basis, in the form of leases, which are periods of time for which the DHCP client may keep the configuration assignment. The process is managed through

Figure 7-12

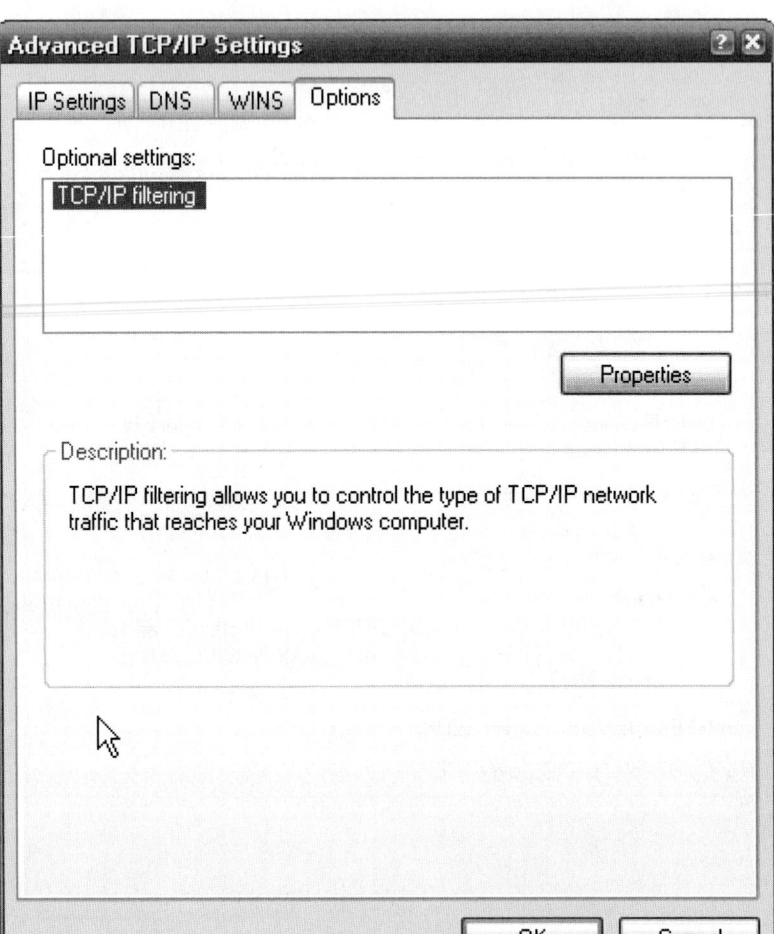

The Options tab.

a series of four messages between the host requesting the address and the DHCP server:

- ▲ **DHCPDISCOVER:** The client sends a DHCPDISCOVER message to try to locate a DHCP server. The message requests the server location (i.e., its IP address) and includes the requesting host's MAC address and host name.
- ▲ **DHCPOFFER:** Any available DHCP server with a valid IP address available for lease responds with a DHCPOFFER message. Message contents

Figure 7-13

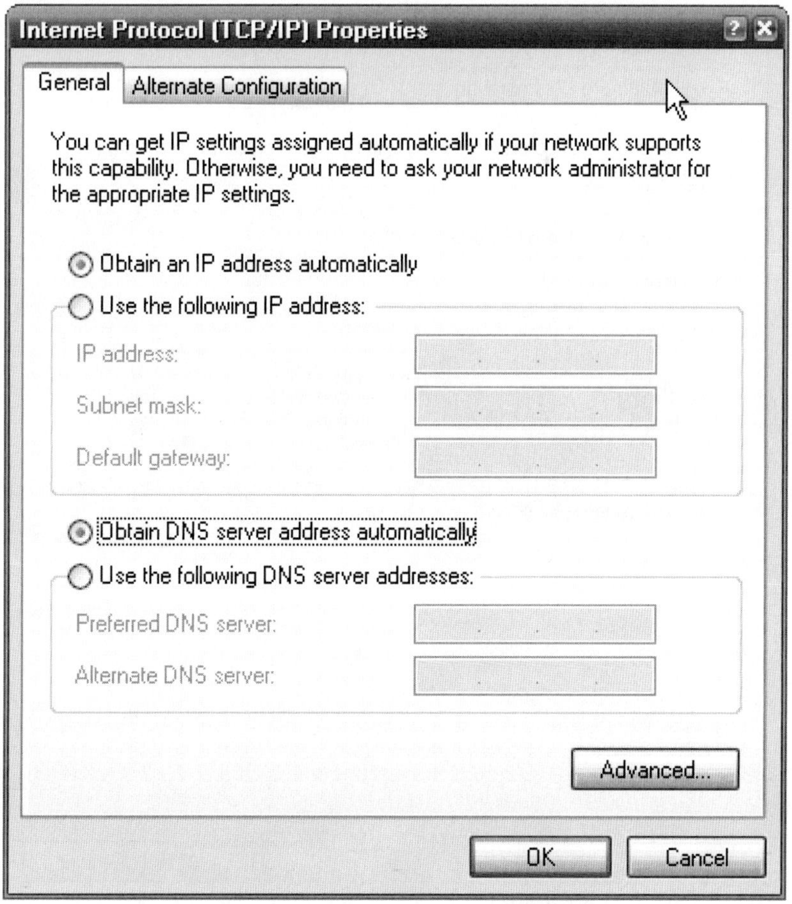

Automatic IP configuration enabled.

include the requesting host's MAC address, an available IP address and subnet mask, the lease period (i.e., how long the address is valid before is must be renewed), and the DHCP server's IP address.

- **DHCPREQUEST:** The client accepts an IP address offered by sending a DHCPREQUEST that includes the IP address of the server that offered the address. If the client receives multiple offers, it accepts the first address offered.
- **DHCPACK:** The server whose offer was accepted sends a DHCPACK message, acknowledging the client. The message includes a valid lease for the address and can include optional TCP/IP configuration settings.

Figure 7-14

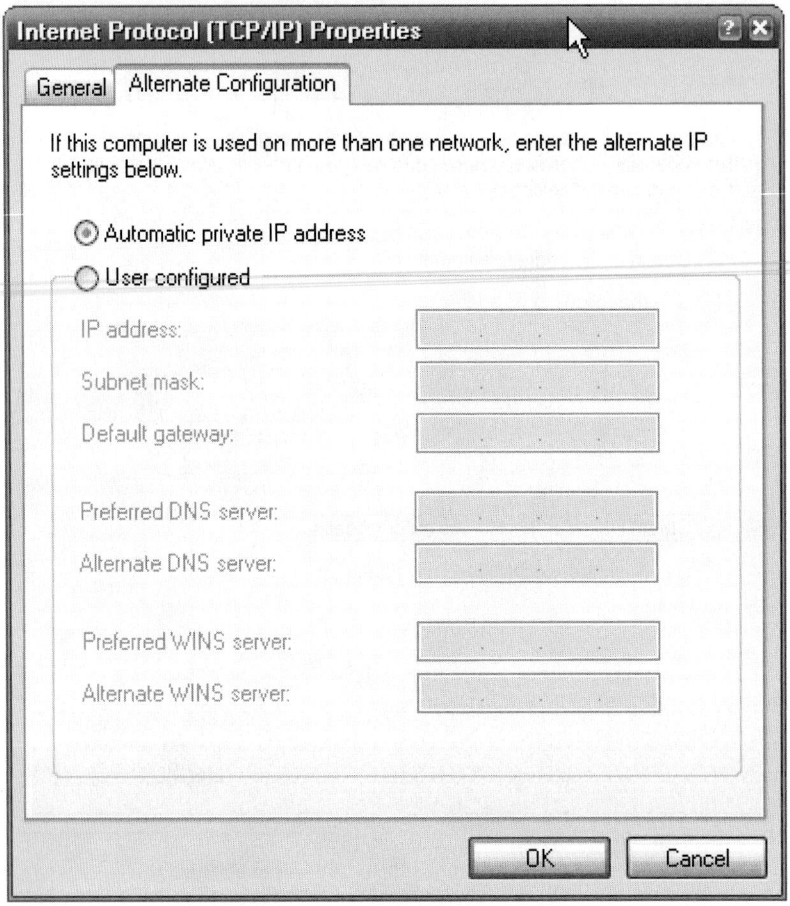

The Alternate Configuration tab.

Because broadcast messages are used, if a router separates the DHCP server from any clients, the router must be configured to pass the DHCP broadcast. This configuration is referred to as being **BOOTP enabled**. In a Windows network, you can also configure one or more computers as **DHCP proxies** to forward requests. If a server's offer is not accepted or some other problem occurs during the lease process, the DHCP server broadcasts a **DHCPNACK** message, canceling the lease offer.

As long as the lease period is valid, the client continues to use the IP address unless the address is released or the client renews the lease and receives a different address in the process. Clients attempt to renew their lease at 50 percent of the lease period. The address pools are centralized on the DHCP server, allowing all IP addresses on the network to be administered from a single server. It should be apparent that this saves a lot of time when changing the IP addresses on a network. Instead of running around to every workstation and server and resetting the IP address to a new address, you simply reset the IP address pool on the DHCP server. The next time the client computers are rebooted, they are assigned new addresses. If the client workstation cannot locate the DHCP server on the network automatically, APIPA is used, unless it is disabled. If APIPA is disabled and no alternate address is specified, the computer has an address of 0.0.0.0.

7.4.3 Recognizing Common Utilities

TCP/IP utilities include a wide variety of management and troubleshooting tools. They include tools that let you trace the process of a packet through the network and test communication between TCP/IP hosts. They also let you force a host to release a leased IP address or request configuration information from a DHCP server. The following are some of the most commonly used utilities:

- **ping**
- **pathping**
- **tracert (traceroute)**
- **ipconfig (ifconfig/winipcfg)**
- **nslookup (dig)**

We'll take a brief look at each of these utilities. A more advanced discussion of these utilities and command options is beyond the scope of this chapter. Additional information about TCP/IP utilities is available through the Windows Help system, the Unix and Linux Help systems, and several online reference sources.

Using ping, pathping, tracert, and traceroute

The ping, pathping, tracert, and traceroute commands are all used for testing TCP/IP communications. The simplest of these, the *ping* command, is used to test communication between two host computers. In its simplest form, you run it as follows:

ping *destination_host*

You can specify the destination host by host name or by IP address. The command reports whether the destination host responds and the round trip time. If you specify the destination host name, you can test both communications and DNS host name resolution.

The *pathping* command returns not only the destination host but also information about each of the routers encountered along the way.

You can also get route information from the tracert or traceroute commands. The *tracert* command is the Windows and MS-DOS version of the command. The same command is run as *traceroute* on Linux and Unix computers.

Using ipconfig, ifconfig, and winipcfg

The *ipconfig* command reports IP configuration information and lets you manage automatic IP address configuration. Run without any additional parameters, the command returns basic configuration information for the local host, including the host's DNS suffix, primary IP address, subnet mask, and default gateway. To get more detailed information, you can run the following:

```
ipconfig /all
```

This returns more detailed information, including multihomed addresses (if any); DHCP, DNS, and WINS server information; and the host's MAC address (or addresses, if it has multiple network adapters installed).

You can also use the ipconfig command to manage automatic IP address assignment. To have a host release a leased address, you can run the following:

```
ipconfig /release
```

After this command runs, the host has an IP address of 0.0.0.0. To force the host to broadcast a DHCPREQUEST and lease a new IP address, you run the following:

```
ipconfig /renew
```

Legacy Windows versions include a GUI version of the ipconfig command, *winipcfg*. Current Windows versions no longer support this command. For Linux and Unix systems, you use *ifconfig* instead of ipconfig. Except for the command name, the command function and supported options are the same.

Using nslookup and dig

The most common use of the *nslookup* and *dig* commands is troubleshooting DNS servers on a network. The nslookup command is supported on Windows NT and later, Unix, and Linux systems. The dig command is available on Unix and Linux systems, but not with the Windows version of the TCP/IP protocol suite.

When you run nslookup without any additional parameters, it returns the host name and IP address of the default DNS server. It also returns an nslookup prompt (>), from which you can run additional nslookup commands that let you test DNS server operations, such as requesting the IP address for specified host names. You can also view and set DNS server options.

The dig and nslookup command syntax and command options are different, but they have the same function.

FOR EXAMPLE

Using Multiple DHCP Servers

For most networks, one DHCP server is physically able to meet the operational requirements of issuing IP address leases and configuration settings to clients. In fact, under normal operating conditions, the load can be relatively light after the initial address assignments are made. In addition, one DHCP server can be configured with multiple scopes and support multiple subnetworks from one central location, and the log and the routers can be configured to forward DHCP broadcasts.

So, why should you configure multiple servers? Fault tolerance. A network depends on DHCP to provide IP addresses and configuration parameters. If you have only one DHCP server and it goes down, you might not notice right away. In fact, you might not even notice until leases start expiring, clients are unable to renew their address leases, and users start complaining that they can't access anything on the network.

If you set up multiple DHCP servers, they can cover for each other. The typical configuration is to put about 80 percent of a subnet's addresses on one server and 20 percent on the other. If either one fails, the other should be able to handle IP addressing requirements at least long enough for you to fix the failing server. When you set up the servers, however, you need to be careful not to overlap the **address scopes** (i.e., the addresses available for assignment) configured on the DHCP servers. If you do, you could end up with duplicate address assignments and a whole other set of problems.

SELF-CHECK

1. What messages are passed, and in what direction, when a client successfully leases an IP address from a DHCP server?
2. How could you quickly determine whether a Windows computer that is configured for automatic IP address assignment received a valid address?

SUMMARY

This chapter took at look at some of the features and support requirements for the TCP/IP protocol suite. It began with a few fundamentals, including TCP/IP benefits and the structure of IP and TCP packet headers. Then it looked at IP addressing requirements in some detail, including the role of port addresses. You were also introduced to IPv6, which is destined to gradually replace the IPv4 addressing standard as a way of making more IP addresses available. You also learned about name resolution methods for both host names and NetBIOS names, including when NetBIOS name support is actually required. Finally, you looked at the configuration requirements when setting up TCP/IP on a Windows family computer and a few of the most commonly used TCP/IP utilities.

KEY TERMS

A record
Acknowledgement
Address record
Address scope
Alias record
Authoritative server
Automatic Private IP Addressing (APIPA)
Best-effort transmission
BOOTP enabled
Canonical name (CNAME) record
Checksum
Class
Class A
Class B
Class C
Class D
Class E
Classful network
Classless interdomain routing (CIDR)
Datagram
Destination address
DHCP proxy
DHCPACK
DHCPDISCOVER
DHCPNACK
DHCPOFFER
DHCPREQUEST
dig
DNS table
DNS zone
Dotted-decimal
Dynamic DNS
Dynamic Host Configuration Protocol (DHCP)
Echo request
Executioner
Fragmented datagram
Fully qualified domain name (FQDN)
Hop count
Host record

HOSTS
ifconfig
Internet Corporation for Assigned Names and Numbers (ICANN)
IP version 4 (IPv4)
IP version 6 (IPv6)
ipconfig
LMHOSTS
Loopback
Mail exchange (MX) record
Multicast
Multihomed
Name resolution
Name server (NS) record
NetBIOS
nslookup
Octet
Overflow
pathping
ping
Port number
Primary DNS server
Private address
Protocol number (IP header)
Secondary DNS server
Segment
Socket
Source address
Start of authority (SOA) record
Subnetting
Subnetwork address
Time to Live (TTL)
traceroute
tracert
Urgent Pointer field
Variable-length subnet masking (VLSM)
Window field
Windows Internet Naming Service (WINS)
winipcfg
Zone file

ASSESS YOUR UNDERSTANDING

Go to www.wiley.com/college/ciccarelli to evaluate your knowledge of TCP/IP protocol fundamentals.
Measure your learning by comparing pre-test and post-test results.

Summary Questions

1. You want to force a Windows XP client on a TCP/IP network to release a leased address. What utility should you use?
   (a) ping
   (b) ifconfig
   (c) ipconfig
   (d) dig
2. What is a socket?
   (a) another term for a port
   (b) the combination of an IP address and port number
   (c) a link used for updating dynamic DNS
   (d) another term for a router
3. In what order are messages sent during a successful DHCP lease?
   (a) DHCPREQUEST, DHCPOFFER, DHCPACK, DHCPDISCOVER
   (b) DHCPDISCOVER, DHCPREQUEST, DHCPOFFER, DHCPACK
   (c) DHCPREQUEST, DHCPDISCOVER, DHCPOFFER, DHCPACK
   (d) DHCPDISCOVER, DHCPOFFER, DHCPREQUEST, DHCPACK
4. A multihomed host must have two or more network adapters installed. True or false?
5. What does the TCP header Window field specify?
   (a) the number of segments that can be transmitted before an acknowledgement is required
   (b) that the host is running some version of Microsoft Windows
   (c) the maximum allowable datagram size
   (d) reassembly information for reassembling fragmented datagrams
6. What is the primary name resolution method used on the Internet?
   (a) WINS
   (b) DNS

(c) HOSTS
(d) LMHOSTS

7. NetBIOS name resolution is required at all times on Windows PC networks. True or false?
8. The IP address 201.220.102.14 is an example of an address from what address class?
   (a) Class A
   (b) Class B
   (c) Class C
   (d) Class D
9. A private address can be used on a local intranet but not on the Internet. True or false?
10. The process of subdividing a standard class address into smaller network segments is known as what?
    (a) segmenting
    (b) subnetting
    (c) fragmenting
    (d) routing
11. What is the significance of the IP address 127.0.0.1?
    (a) It's a private Class B host address.
    (b) It's a Class E address.
    (c) It's used for loopback testing.
    (d) It's assigned by default if a host cannot lease an address.
12. Which of the following cannot be specified on the General tab when configuring TCP/IP configuration properties on a Windows XP computer?
    (a) primary DNS server
    (b) primary WINS server
    (c) default gateway
    (d) subnet mask
13. How would you use the CIDR specification format to specify the network address 192.168.10.0?
    (a) 192.168.10 /24
    (b) 192.168.10 /16
    (c) 192.168 /32
    (d) 192.168 /24
14. IPv6 supports a larger address pool than IPv4. True or false?

Applying This Chapter

1. You are identifying TCP/IP configuration requirements for the network shown in Figure 7-15. You are to use the network address 192.168.12.0 for the entire network. Each subnet must support up to 55 hosts. All the clients will share the proxy server for Internet access.

Figure 7-15

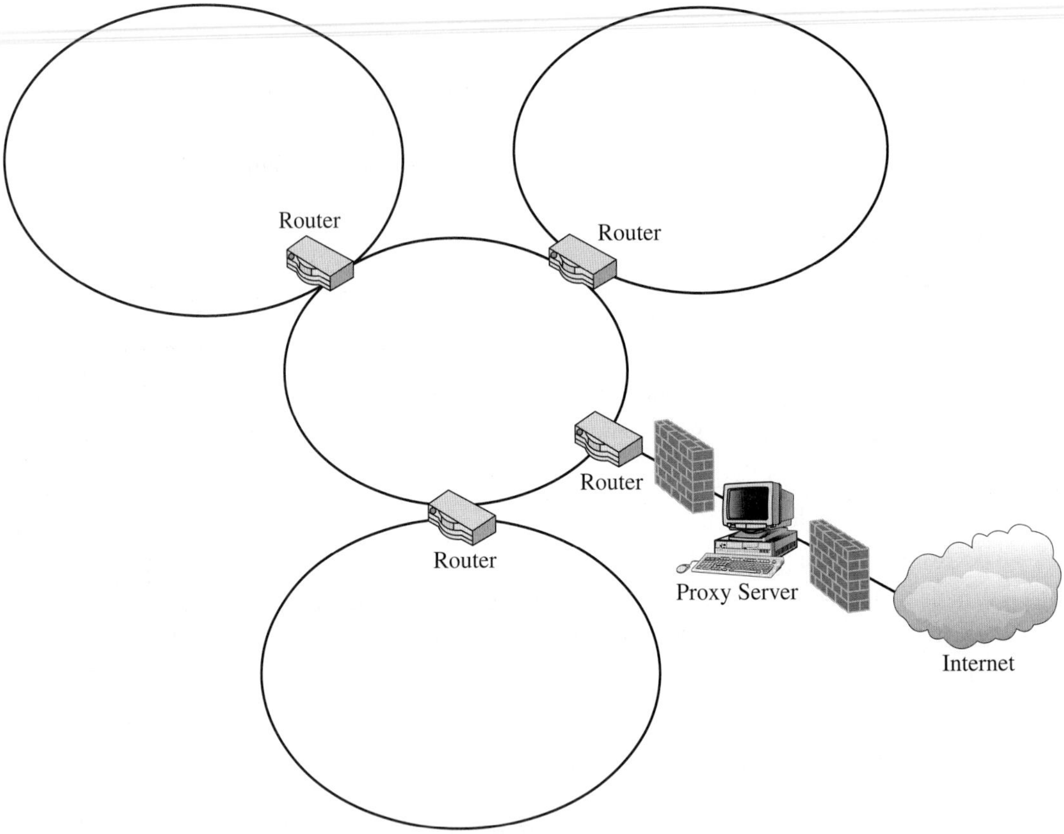

A sample network for configuration.

(a) What network addresses will you use?
(b) Why must you use a different network address for each segment?
(c) What is the subnet mask?
(d) At minimum, how many public IP addresses will be required?
(e) Why?

(f) How can you keep to a minimum the administrative overhead required to manage host IP addresses?

(g) What are the configuration requirements for this to work?

2. You are configuring the network shown in Figure 7-16. The network addresses of selected static host addresses are shown. All hosts are running either Windows XP or Windows Server 2003. TCP/IP is the only protocol in use on the network.

Figure 7-16

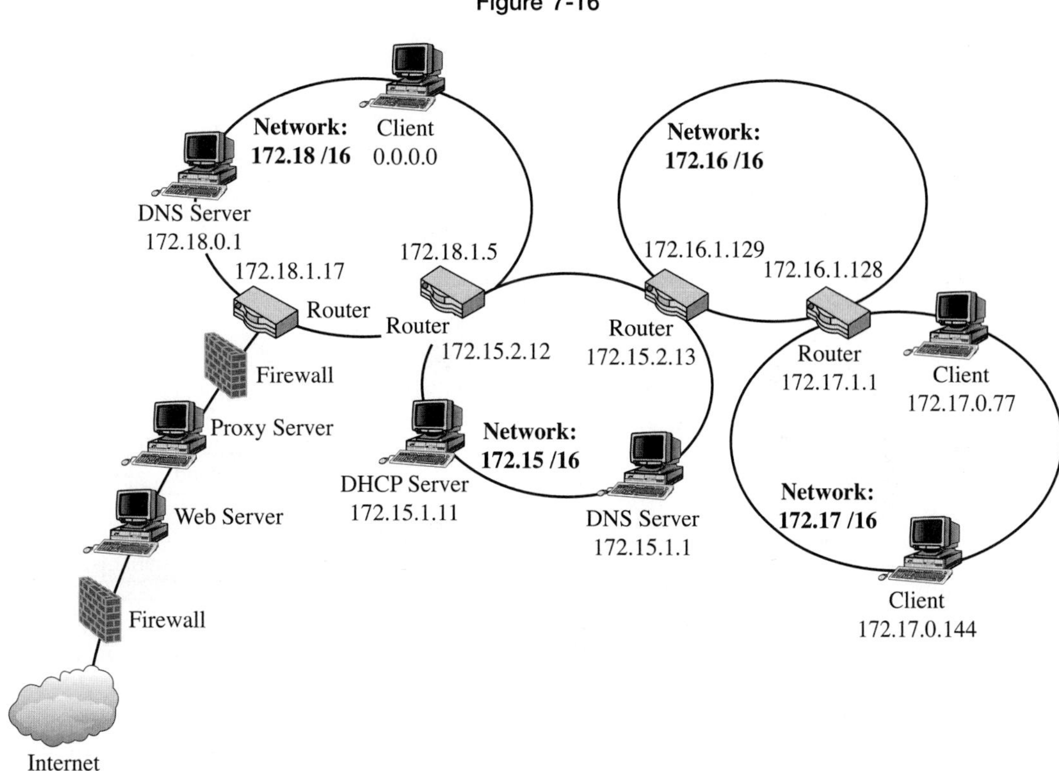

A routed LAN.

The standard configuration for end-user host computers is shown in Figure 7-17.

(a) After deploying the network, all end users in 172.18 /16 cannot communicate with any other hosts. What are the possible causes of this problem?

(b) Each host has the IP address 0.0.0.0. What does this tell you?

Figure 7-17

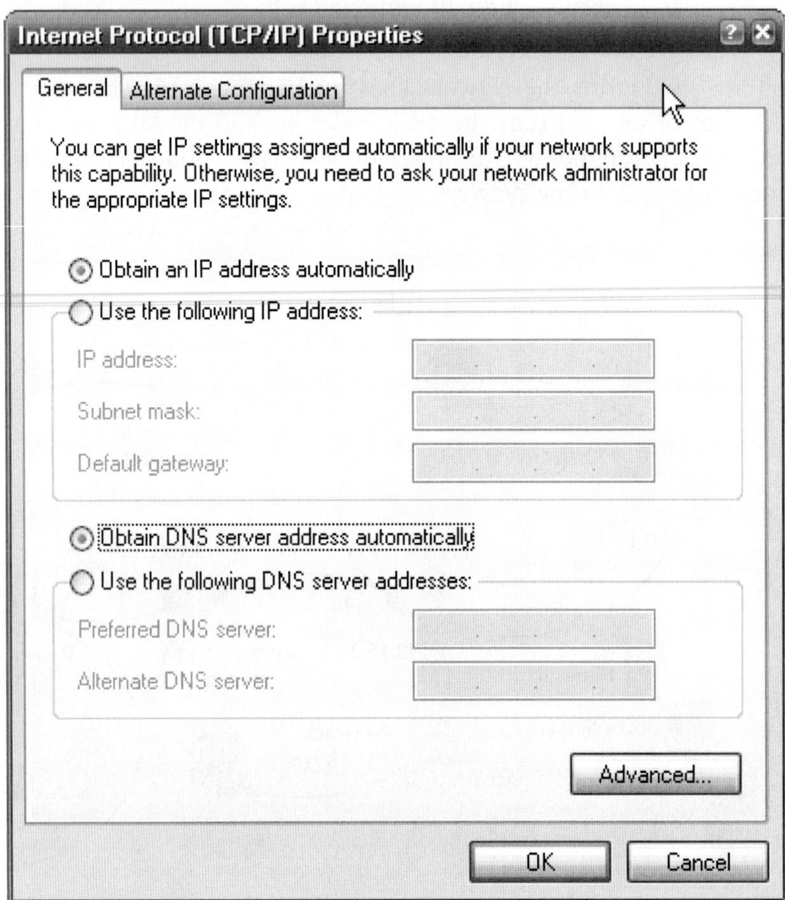

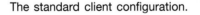

The standard client configuration.

(c) What could you run to force a computer to try again to lease an address?
(d) Why might you add a second DHCP server?
(e) If given multiple offers, how does a client determine which offer to accept?
(f) For what purpose are the DNS servers used?
(g) Under what circumstances would WINS servers also be required?
(h) What role would port numbers play in network operations?
(i) Port 21 is associated with what kind of activity?
(j) Port 80 is associated with what kind of activity?

(k) Why is each router configured with two IP addresses?

(l) Figure 7-18 is from a host configured with a static IP address. What additional information is required?

(m) Why is the additional information necessary?

Figure 7-18

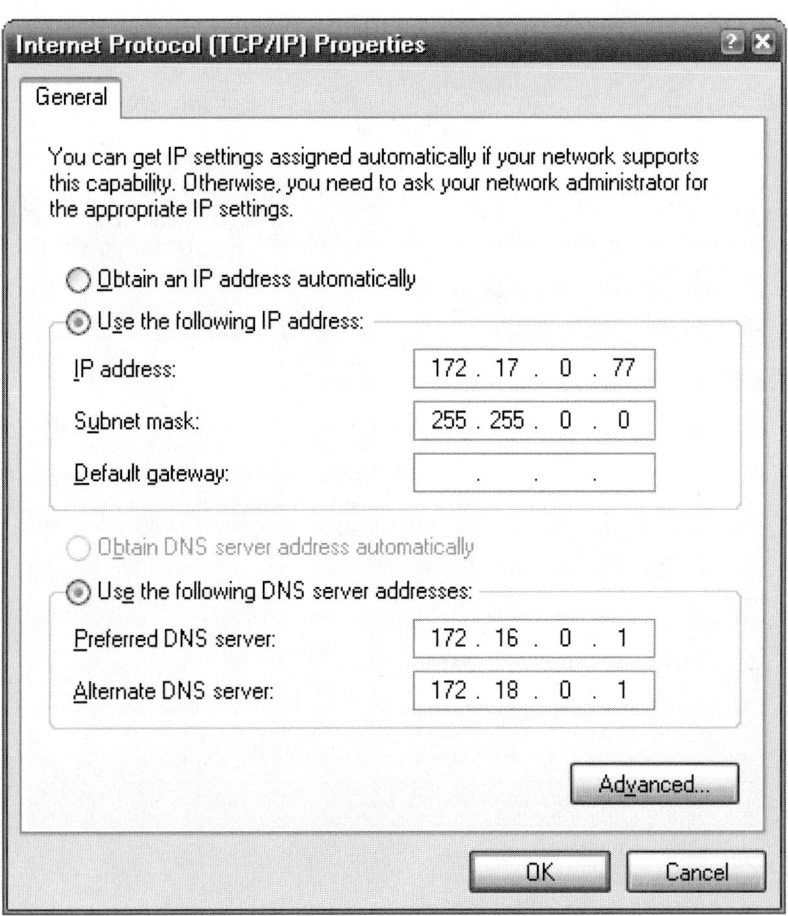

A custom client configuration.

YOU TRY IT

Building a TCP/IP Network

You are designing a network that will eventually support up to 1,000 hosts. The network will be wired as a physical star, using hubs as the central connection points. TCP/IP is the only protocol that will be used on the network. The network will be configured as a Windows Active Directory domain with a domain controller in each subnetwork. Network hosts will not have direct access to the Internet but will be able to access Internet resources through four shared proxy servers. The network will also include two public web servers that will connect to the Internet through a firewall.

1. What guidelines should you use to configure subnetworks?
2. What type of network addresses should you use for configuring the subnetworks to support all the hosts but also minimize the complexity of the network?
3. What public IP address requirements are there on the network, if any?
4. Describe how you would manage IP address and TCP/IP property configuration for the majority of the hosts.
5. Describe how you would handle host name resolution requirements, assuming that there are no NetBIOS name requirements.
6. What is the role of routers, if any, in the network, and what special configuration issues might you have?
7. What is the role of bridges, if any, in the network, and what specific configuration issues might you have?

8

WIRELESS, REMOTE, AND WIDE AREA NETWORKING

Starting Point

Go to www.wiley.com/college/ciccarelli to assess your knowledge of wireless, remote, and wide area networking.
Determine where you need to concentrate your effort.

What You'll Learn in This Chapter

▲ Wireless networking requirements
▲ Wireless networking standards
▲ Remote access requirements
▲ Remote access configurations
▲ WAN connection options

After Studying This Chapter, You'll Be Able To

▲ Compare and contrast Wi-Fi standards
▲ Explain Wi-Fi networking requirements
▲ List justifications for enabling remote access
▲ Compare dial-in and VPN remote access
▲ List and describe access and authentication protocols
▲ Describe basic WAN connection requirements
▲ Compare and contrast WAN connectivity methods

INTRODUCTION

Traditional wired LANs meet the networking requirements of many, if not most, organizations. Some organizations, however, have networking requirements that require the introduction of additional networking technologies. Wireless networking solutions are becoming increasing popular, especially with the rapid drop in associated costs. Remote access has long been a key part of many companies' networking requirements. WAN solutions, used to create internetworks ranging from two connected LANs and up, are another important part of the networking mix for larger companies.

This chapter takes a look at these different network technologies, with an eye on justifying their place in network design. It also looks at some of the special deployment and configuration requirements.

8.1 Deploying Wireless Networking

There are several reasons behind the rapid growth of **wireless LANs (WLANs)**. Physically, wireless is often the easiest type of networking to deploy and maintain. In environments where you can't run the cable for a wired network, wireless might be your only available solution. In addition, nearly all laptop computers sold in the United States come preconfigured to support wireless networking.

We focus our discussion in this chapter on Wi-Fi, which is the commercial name for a set of standards developed by the IEEE **802.11** standards group. A group of vendors selling 802.11 equipment trademarked the name Wi-Fi to refer to 802.11 because they believed that consumers were more likely to buy equipment with a catchier name than 802.11. Wi-Fi is intended to evoke memories of Hi-Fi, the name for the original stereo music systems.

8.1.1 Understanding Wireless Fundamentals

The 802.11 family of technologies is much like the Ethernet family. The 802.11 standards reuse many of the Ethernet 802.3 components and are designed to connect easily into Ethernet LANs. For these reasons, IEEE 802.11 is often called **wireless Ethernet**.

Identifying Basic Components

There are three basic component requirements for WLAN or Wi-Fi deployment—two that you need to buy (or that come already installed) and one that is a built-in part of both of those:

- Each network device must have a compatible network adapter.

- If you are deploying an infrastructure-mode WLAN (the most common type), you need one or more wireless access points (WAPs).
- You also need what is taking the place of the wired media, an assigned **frequency range**—the radio frequencies that the wireless devices can use.

Most countries permit WLANs to operate in two frequency ranges that have been reserved for unlicensed transmissions: the 2.4GHz and 5GHz ranges. These are the frequency ranges allowed by the North American standard. There is a potential problem that a variety of consumer electronics items, such as radio-controlled toys, baby monitors, telephones, and even microwave ovens, use these same frequency ranges and can all interfere with wireless networking devices.

The frequency range directly affects data rates. The larger the **bandwidth** (i.e., the frequency range available), the greater the capacity of the wireless circuit and the faster data can be sent. You can think of the frequency range by picturing the width of a pipe carrying water. The wider the pipe, the more water it carries. Similarly, the wider the frequency range, the more data it carries. The 2.4GHz range has a smaller bandwidth than the 5GHz range, so the 5GHz range (potentially) transmits data faster than the 2.4GHz range.

Data transmission is also affected by attenuation, the weakening of a signal the farther it is from its source. Higher frequencies suffer attenuation more quickly than lower frequencies. Because of this, transmissions in the 2.4GHz range can travel farther and through more walls and other sources of interference than can transmissions in the 5GHz range. As interference increases and the signal strength weakens, the effective bandwidth that can be used decreases, and the capacity and the data rate decrease. This means that wireless technologies that use the 5GHz range have a shorter effective range than those that use the 2.4GHz range.

One potential problem with WLANs is security. Because anyone within range of a WAP can receive transmissions, eavesdropping is a serious threat. Well-designed WLANs encrypt transmissions so that only authorized computers can decode and read the messages.

Understanding Topology and Access Control

The Wi-Fi logical and physical topologies are the same as those used by Ethernet, using a physical star and logical bus when configured for infrastructure mode. There is a central WAP to which all devices direct their transmissions (star), but the radio frequencies are shared (bus) so that all computers must take turns transmitting.

Wi-Fi media access uses **Carrier-Sense Multiple Access/Collision Avoidance (CSMA/CA)**, which is similar to the CSMA/CD used by Ethernet. With CSMA/CA, computers listen before they transmit, and if no one else is transmitting, they proceed with transmission. Detecting collisions is more difficult in radio transmission than in transmission over wired media, so Wi-Fi attempts to avoid collisions to a greater degree than does traditional Ethernet. CSMA/CA simultaneously uses two media access control approaches.

The first media access control method used is the **distributed coordination function (DCF)**, which is also called the **physical carrier-sense method (PCSM)** because it relies on the ability of computers to physically listen before they transmit. With DCF, each packet is sent using stop-and-wait **automatic repeat request (ARQ)**. After the sender transmits one packet, it immediately stops and waits for an acknowledgement (ACK) from the receiver before attempting to send another packet. When the receiver of a packet detects the end of the packet in a transmission, it waits a fraction of a second to make sure the sender has really stopped transmitting, and then it immediately transmits an ACK (or a negative acknowledgement [NAK]). The original sender can then send another packet, stop and wait for an ACK, and so on.

While the sender and receiver are exchanging packets and ACKs, other computers may also want to transmit. So when the sender ends its transmission, why doesn't some other computer begin transmitting before the receiver can transmit an ACK? The answer is that the PCSM is designed so that the time the receiver waits after the transmission ends before sending an ACK is significantly less time than the time a computer must listen to determine that no one else is transmitting before initiating a new transmission. Thus, the time interval between a transmission and the matching ACK is so short that no other computer has the opportunity to begin transmitting.

The other technique used is the **point coordination function (PCF)**, also called the **virtual carrier-sense method (VCSM)**. DCF works well in traditional Ethernet because every computer on the shared circuit receives every transmission on the shared circuit. However, in a wireless environment, this is not always true. A computer at the extreme edge of the range limit from the WAP on one side may not receive transmissions from a computer on the extreme opposite edge of the WAP's range limit. In the example shown in Figure 8-1, all the computers are in range of the WAP but may not be within range of each other. In this case, if one computer transmits, another computer on the opposite edge may not sense the other transmission and may transmit at the same time, causing a collision at the WAP. This is called the **hidden node problem** because the computers at the opposite edges of the WLAN are hidden from each other.

When the hidden node problem exists, the WAP is the only device guaranteed to be able to communicate with all computers on the WLAN. Therefore, the WAP must manage the shared circuit using a controlled-access technique, not the contention-based approach of traditional Ethernet. With this approach, any computer wishing to transmit first sends a **request to send (RTS)** to the WAP, which may or may not be heard by all computers. The RTS requests permission to transmit and to reserve the circuit for the sole use of the requesting computer for a specified time period. If no other computer is transmitting, the

Figure 8-1

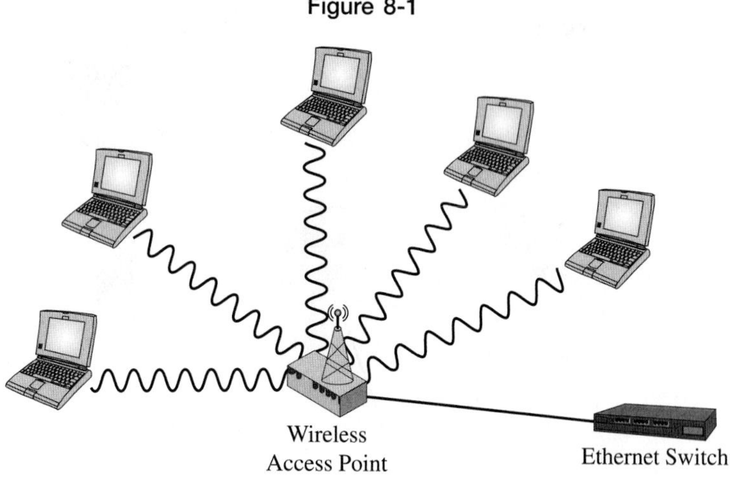

A sample infrastructure network.

WAP responds with a **clear to send** (CTS), specifying the amount of time for which the circuit is reserved for the requesting computer.

8.1.2 Comparing Wi-Fi 802.11 Standards

Wi-Fi is the fastest-growing and most rapidly changing area in networking technologies today, so you can expect Wi-Fi applications to continue to change. There are three 802.11 Wi-Fi transmission standards currently in use and one that is under development that is designed to provide higher-speed WLAN networks:

- ▲ **802.11a:** This is rarely used in PC networking applications.
- ▲ **802.11b:** This is the original Wi-Fi standard.
- ▲ **802.11g:** This is the standard currently used for Wi-Fi.
- ▲ **802.11n:** This is a high-speed standard currently under development.

Supported channels given for each of the standards are based on U.S. usage standards. Other countries may allow more or fewer channels, depending on frequency spectrum regulations. With each of these standards, the typical configuration is an infrastructure-mode WLAN connected to an Ethernet wired network, as shown in Figure 8-2. In this configuration, the WLAN is being used as an **overlay network**, one that provides support for mobile computers in the same areas and the wired network. In this example, the network is configured with two WAPs to provide a wider range.

With a Wi-Fi network, bandwidth use is a potential concern, just as it is with Ethernet networks. PCF initially imposes more fixed-cost delays than wired Ethernet

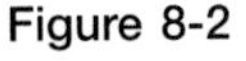

Figure 8-2

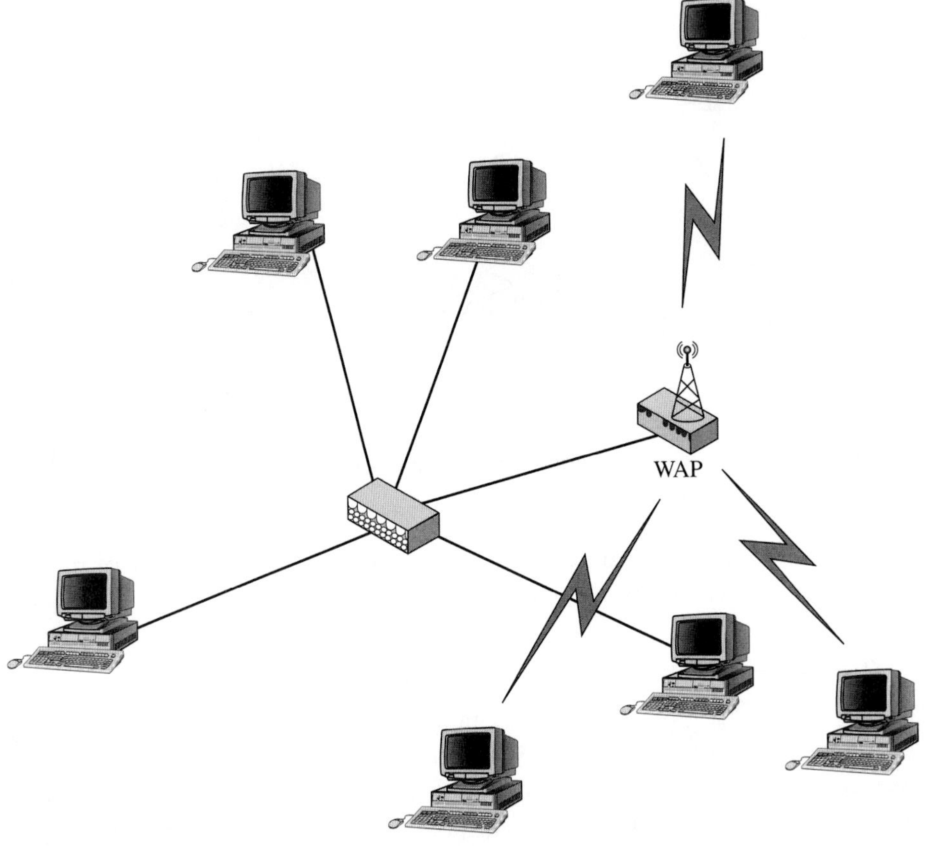

A sample overlay network.

when traffic is low because computers must request permission before they can transmit. Typically, Wi-Fi users experience few response-time delays as long as the total network traffic remains below 85 to 90 percent of the total available bandwidth. Still, it is important to monitor traffic patterns. The response time delays increase slowly up to the 85 to 90 percent threshold. Once this level is reached, the number of noticeable delays increases rapidly until the network is 100 percent saturated.

There is an additional set of commercial wireless standards, known as the **802.16 WiMAX** (or just **WiMAX**) standards. WiMAX standards are not currently used in LAN configurations. The **802.16d Fixed WiMAX** standard is used in some areas for wireless MAN connections or for connecting Wi-Fi public access points to a central, shared connection to the Internet. The **802.16e Mobile WiMAX** standard is designed to provide an alternative to current mobile Wi-Fi and cellular telephone standards. Theoretical ranges are up to 30 miles, with real-world effective ranges between 2.5 and 5.0 miles.

802.11a

The IEEE 802.11a standard provides high-speed wireless networking in the 5GHz range. It provides eight channels for indoor use in the United States and one channel for outdoor use. The indoor channels are identified as 36, 40, 44, 48, 52, 56, 60, and 64; 149 is the outdoor channel.

Each channel provides speeds of up to 54Mbps under perfect conditions. The range, under perfect conditions, is rated at about 150 feet (about 50 meters). In practice, it is usually less. The farther you are from the WAP, the lower the supported data rate. Typically, 54Mbps is supported at no more than about 50 feet (about 15 meters) between the WAP and networked devices. Under normal operating conditions, speeds of 26Mbps to 34Mbps are common, and the speed may even drop to 6Mbps if interference is present.

802.11b

The IEEE 802.11b standard provides moderate-speed wireless networking in the 2.4GHz range. It provides three channels for indoor use in the United States: channels 1, 6, and 11.

Each channel provides a maximum data rate of 11Mbps. Only where there is significant interference or the signal begins to weaken because the user is moving far from the WLAN does the data rate change in an attempt to improve signal quality. Thus, for users close to the center of the WLAN, 6Mbps to 11Mbps is common. The range under ideal conditions is about 450 feet (about 140 meters), although the actual range in practice is typically much less. The speed may drop to 1Mbps in the presence of heavy interference.

The advantage over 802.11a is that 802.11b suffers less attenuation. The signal has a greater range with less decrease in speed as distance from the WAP increases. However, under optimal conditions, 802.11b supports lower speeds than 802.11a.

802.11g

The 802.11g standard supports high-speed wireless networking in the 2.4GHz range. It provides three channels for indoor use in the United States, using the same channel numbers as 802.11b: 1, 6, and 11.

Each channel provides a maximum data rate of 54Mbps. The range under ideal conditions is about 450 feet (about 140 meters). The actual range under normal conditions is less. The data rate can drop as low as 6Mbps when significant interference is present.

802.11g is backward compatible with 802.11b, so 802.11b devices can communicate with an 802.11g WAP. In fact, you can deploy a WLAN that has 802.11g WAPs and any mix of 802.11b and 802.11g client devices. This means that it supports existing laptops that have built-in 802.11b NICs.

However, this mixed configuration is not without potential problems. 802.11b devices are still limited to the 802.11b transmission maximum of 11Mbps. In

addition, 802.11b devices become confused when 802.11g devices operate at high speed near them. Because of this, when an 802.11g device detects an 802.11b device nearby, the 802.11g device drops into a lower-bandwidth operational mode.

802.11n

The IEEE 802.11n standard is currently under development. Its goal is to provide very high-speed wireless networking, using both the 2.4GHz and 5GHz frequency ranges simultaneously, by using multiple sets of antennas optimized to the different frequencies. This will increase the data speeds that it can attain. The standard has not been finalized, but current drafts propose speeds in the 100Mbps to 240Mbps range. It is also designed to be backward compatible with 802.11a, 802.11b, and 802.11g. The idea is to provide continued support for all these standards while gradually replacing them.

8.1.3 Configuring Wi-Fi

There are two parts to configuring a WLAN using Wi-Fi: You need to configure the access point and also each of the wireless devices. WAP configuration procedures and options can vary widely between manufacturers and different WAP applications. All WAPs can act as bridges when connected to a wired Ethernet network. Most also act as broadband routers and network access servers, supporting shared high-speed Internet access.

Consider the configuration shown in Figure 8-3. The WAP provides shared Internet access and IP address and configuration information for all the wireless computers. By default, it also provides addresses for any wired computer in the connected network segment that is configured to receive an IP address automatically.

The design and implementation process begins with a site survey that determines the feasibility of the desired coverage, the potential sources of interference, the current locations of the wired network into which the WLAN will connect, and an estimate of the number of WAPs needed. Sources of interference include radio-frequency interference sources (e.g., microwave ovens, cordless telephones, industrial equipment) and walls. WLANs work best when there is a clear line of sight between the WAP and networked devices. The heavier the wall, or the more walls the signal must pass through, the greater the interference.

Configuring a WAP

The specific procedures for configuring a WAP are manufacturer, and sometimes model, specific. While most work "out of the box" without any special configuration, this is not recommended because the WAP will broadcast its default service set identifier (SSID) and not use any type of security. This makes it easy for unauthorized users to connect to the network.

Most manufacturers let you connect to a USB port, through the local intranet, and sometimes through the public Internet to configure a WAP. Remote

Figure 8-3

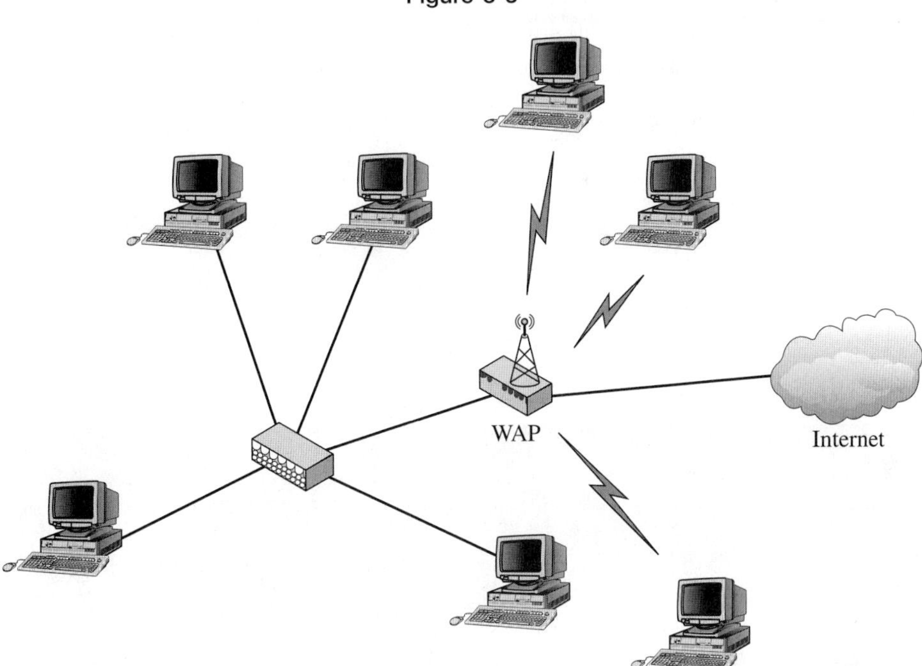

A sample network configuration.

management is typically disabled by default and typically should not be enabled. Configuration options usually include the following:

- **Internet connection information:** This includes IP address configuration, router name, and similar information.
- **Local network information:** This includes DHCP configuration, including address scope available for assignment, routing configuration, and possibly simple dynamic DNS support.
- **Wireless configuration:** This includes mode (as 802.11b, 802.11g, or both, in **mixed mode**), SSID, channel used, and whether the SSID is broadcast.
- **Wireless security:** This includes wireless security mode and configuration, authentication requirements (if any), MAC filtering information, and, in some cases, more advanced or custom security settings.
- **Network security:** This can include a built-in firewall and the ability to pass or block VPN traffic.

Other options can include setting different types of Internet access restrictions by URL, address, domain, service, or TCP or UDP port information. Some WAPs have settings related to application support, including Internet gaming support. Most let you set an administrator password to control access to WAP configuration settings.

Figure 8-4 shows a typical configuration screen. Notice from the menu across the top that this specific WAP supports a variety of configuration screens and a large number of configurable parameters.

Figure 8-4

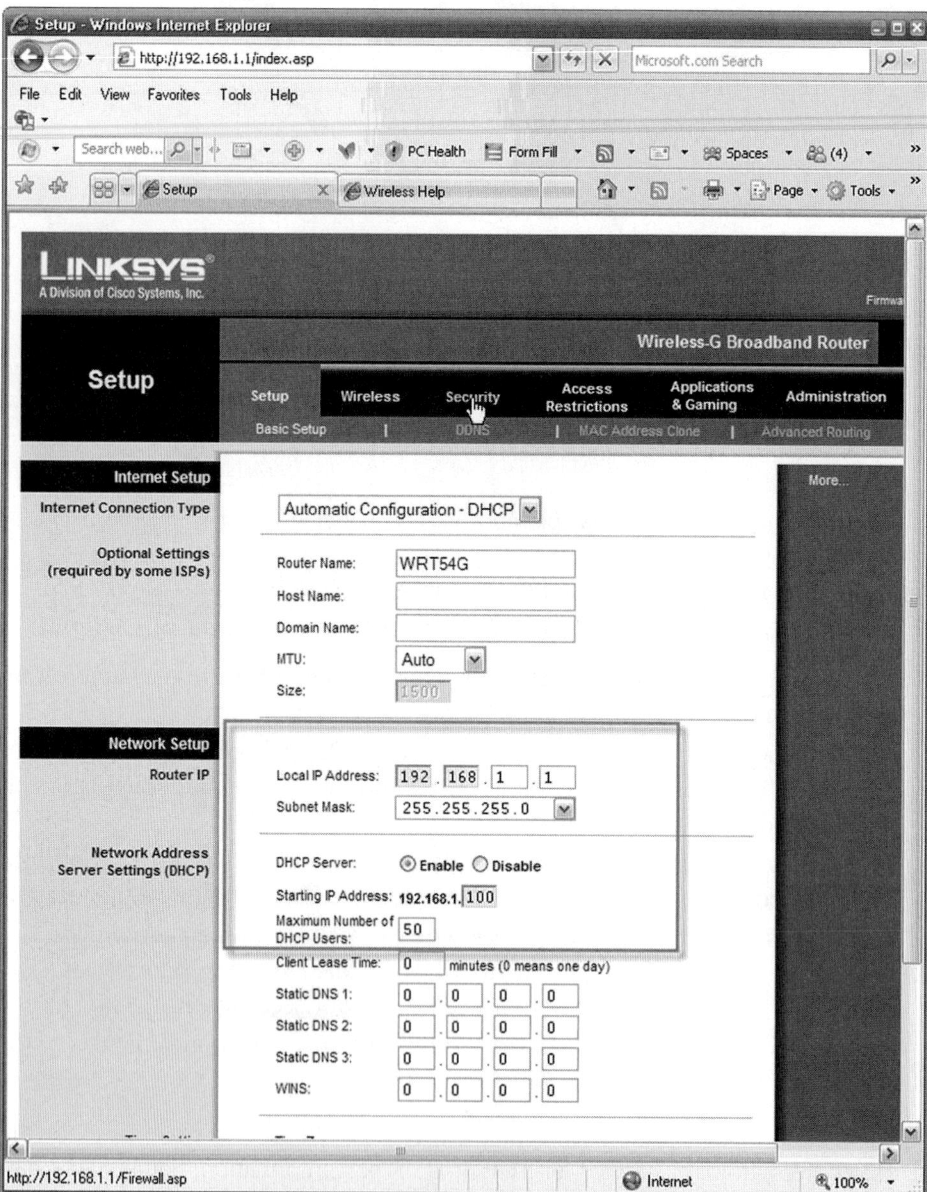

Setup parameters.

Notice that in this case, the WAP is configured to provide DHCP support. The settings shown here are defaults for this model, and as you can see, 192.168.1.1 through 192.168.1.99 are unused by the scope and available for assigning through other means, such as static addresses. Also, this configuration will support no more than 50 clients, so addresses above 192.168.1.150 will typically be available for other uses.

Figure 8-5 shows typical wireless configuration parameters. This WAP has obviously not been secured. It is supporting to both 802.11b and 802.11g clients, is using its default SSID, and is broadcasting the SSID, making it easy for anyone in range to see and connect to the WAP. The WAP is using channel 6, which means any clients connecting to this WAP also have to use channel 6.

Wireless security settings are beyond the scope of this chapter, but you should be aware that available options vary by manufacturer. Security configuration options should be one of your primary considerations when selecting a WAP.

Figure 8-5

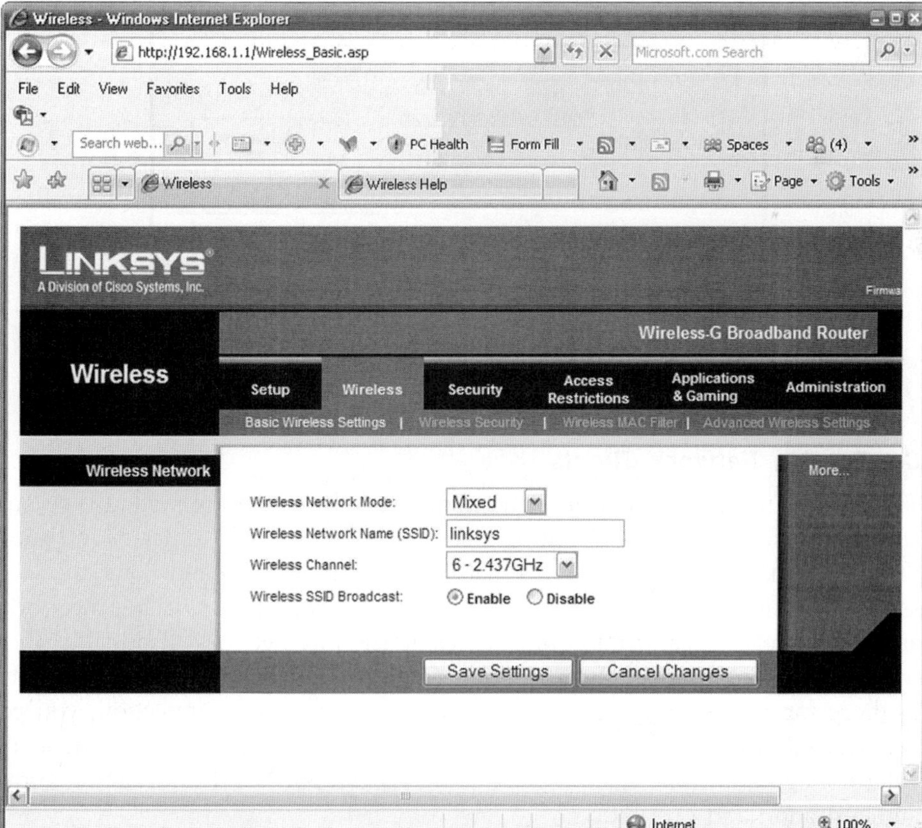

Wireless parameters.

Figure 8-6

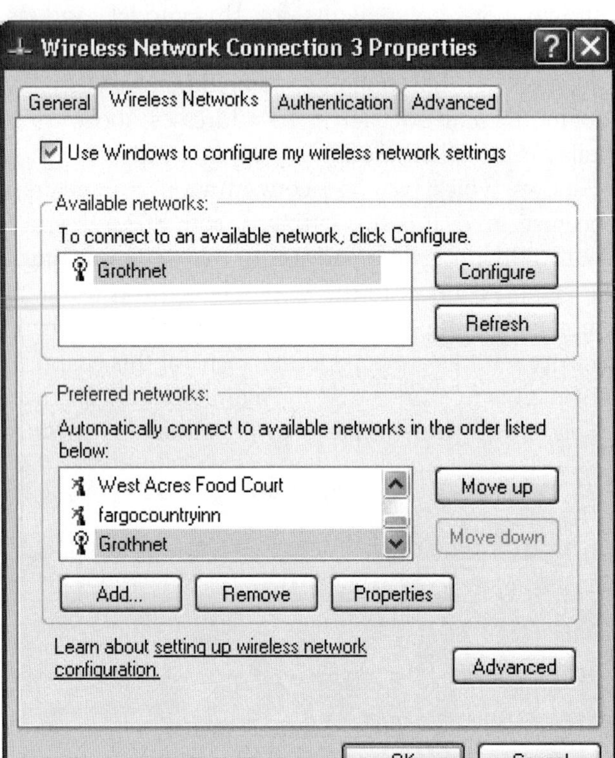

The Wireless Networks tab.

Configuring Network Clients

The options for configuring network clients vary by operating system type and version. Current Windows operating system versions are able to detect and automatically configure access to WAPs that broadcast their SSID and don't have any security configuration requirements. You can view a list of available networks and set the relative connection priority, using the first network, if possible, then the next, and so on. The properties for a wireless connection are much the same as those for a wired connection, except that for a wireless connection, you get a Wireless Networks tab, as shown in Figure 8-6. From here, you can manually enter configuration information such as the WAP's SSID and information about authentication and encryption.

Some information, such as the signal strength, can be helpful when troubleshooting wireless connections.

FOR EXAMPLE

Wireless Interference

The following is a true story that illustrates the potential effect of wireless interference.

"Most of the buildings at Indiana University have both wired and wireless network access. The Kelly School of Business at Indiana University has two major buildings: a modern building built in 2002 and an older building built in 1968. The new building was designed with wireless networks in mind; the old building was not. My office is in the old building.

"There is one Wi-Fi access point on the floor, which should provide sufficient coverage. However, the walls are made of concrete, which is hard for wireless signals to penetrate. Figure 8-7 shows the floor plan, the position

Figure 8-7

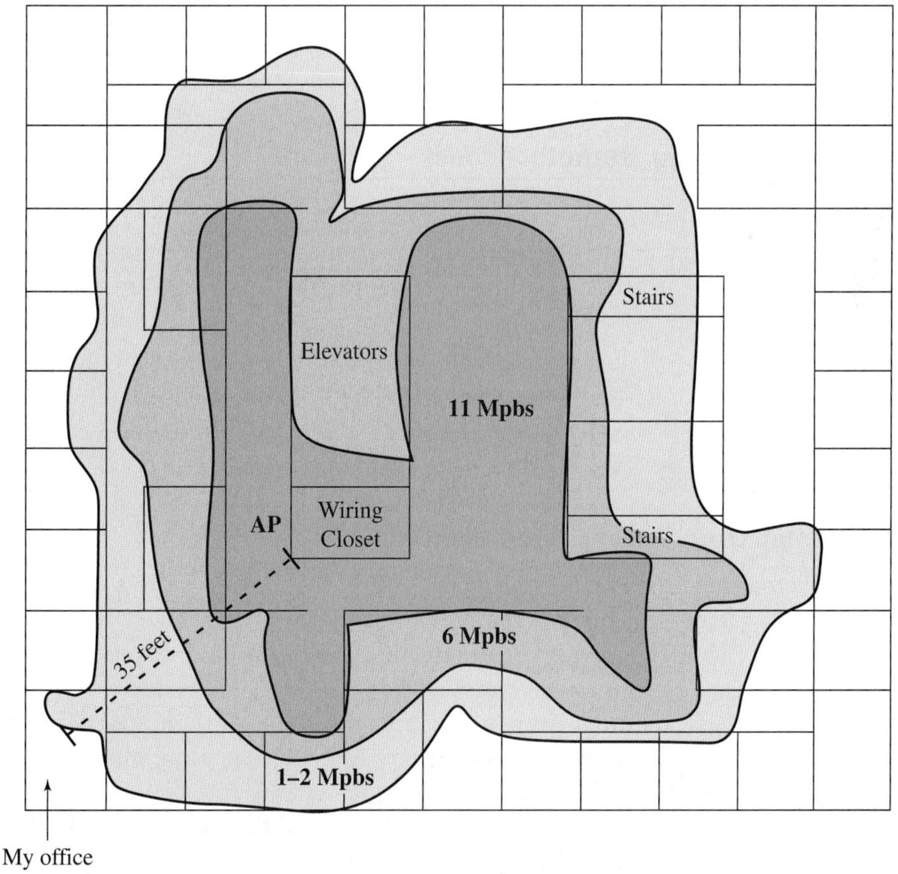

WLAN design.

of the access point, and the data rates that are available at different locations on the floor.

"My office is located about 35 feet from the access point (less than 12 meters), which is well within the normal range for high-speed access. However, because of the concrete walls, I am unable to receive a signal in most of my office."

SELF-CHECK

1. How does the access method used by Wi-Fi differ from that used by Ethernet?
2. What happens if an 802.11g device detects an 802.11b device nearby?

8.2 Implementing Remote Access

Nearly all network operating systems (NOSs) support some option for remote client access. The details vary by NOS, but you typically have the option of either connecting through a dial-up connection or via the Internet through a VPN connection.

In this section, we're going to take a look at remote access fundamentals, including an overview of remote access protocols, and a sample of how you might configure remote access. Note that a detailed discussion of security issues relating to remote access is beyond the scope of this chapter.

8.2.1 Comparing Access Fundamentals

Several factors must be considered when configuring remote access connection options. How many concurrent remote connections do you need to support? What are the clients' bandwidth requirements? Do client computers have Internet access available? Do they have modems?

Remote access requires one or more computers configured to provide access, usually called **remote access servers**, and one or more clients requiring access. The traditional access method is for clients to call in through the dial-up telephone network, formally called the **public switched telephone network (PSTN)** or **plain old telephone service (POTS)**. This is shown in Figure 8-8.

Figure 8-8

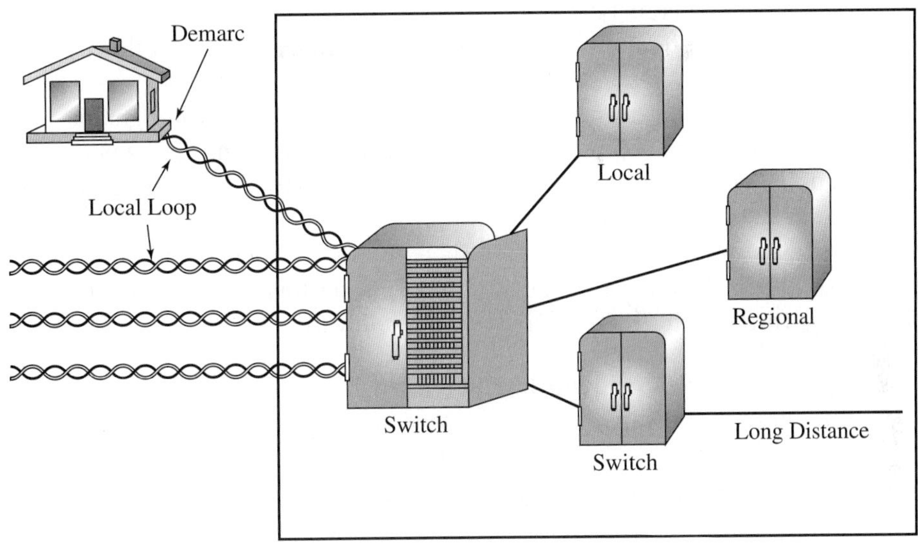

A local connection to the PSTN.

The advantages of dial-up access include the following:

- **Ready availability:** You can usually find a telephone line available in nearly any population center in the world.
- **Low initial cost:** Modems are inexpensive, and many computers come with modems already installed.
- **No LAN hardware requirements for the client:** Because you're connecting through a modem, you don't need a NIC or any network cabling.

You must also consider the following disadvantages:

- **Variable incremental costs:** Your incremental costs (i.e., cost per connection) depend on your long-distance charges (if any) and how long you stay connected.
- **Low bandwidth:** For example, dial-up bandwidth in the United States is limited to no more than 56Kbps and can be lower, depending on line conditions.
- **Little communication security:** It's relatively easy to tap telephone conversations, even between computers, and if the data are not encrypted, it is easy to intercept and steal sensitive data.

Access security can also be a concern. How (or even if) user authentication is managed varies by NOS type and version. Some administrators go with default, minimal security configurations, making it relatively easy for unauthorized personnel to access the network.

In recent years, access methods that rely on connecting through the Internet have become more popular. In that case, both the user and the remote access server must obviously have Internet access. A VPN connection is used, as in the example shown in Figure 8-9.

Other methods have been used at different times, but nearly all of them have been phased out in favor of connecting through the Internet. The advantages of connecting through the Internet include the following:

- **Higher available bandwidth:** High-speed Internet connections ranging from around 300Kbps up through several megabits per second are readily available in most regions of the United States.
- **Minimal incremental changes:** Most ISPs charge a flat monthly fee for unlimited access, and even most hotels provide access for free or at reasonable rates (typically $10 per day or less).
- **Flexible security configurations:** VPN connection methods provide for a wide variety of authentication options and secure encryption methods.

Figure 8-9

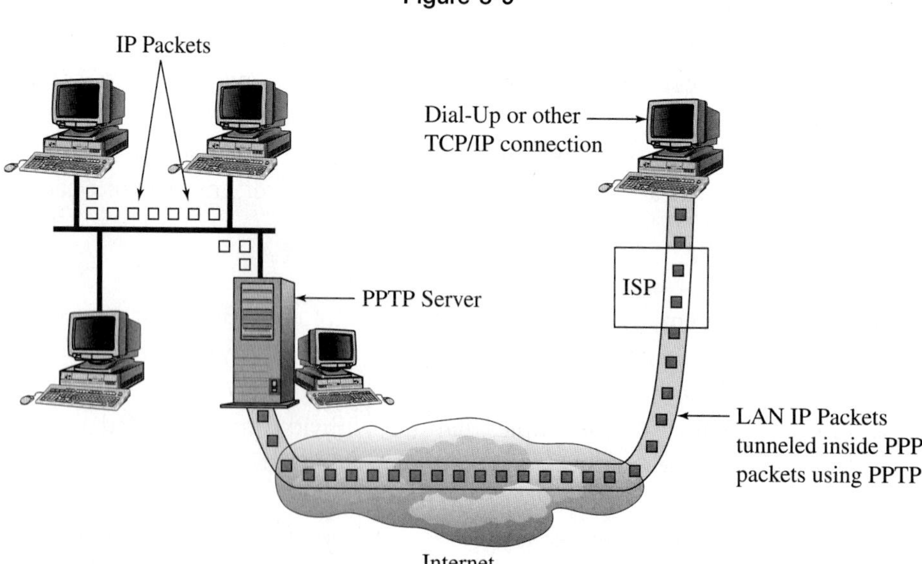

A remote access VPN connection.

Of course, there are disadvantages, such as the following:

- **Internet access requirement:** Mobile users don't always have convenient Internet access available and might find themselves working, for example, from a public Wi-Fi hotspot.
- **More complex configuration requirements:** Internet access is more complex and there is a possibility that administrators and users might try to save time by cutting corners and skimping on security.
- **Lack of support by some NOSs:** Some older NOSs provide native support for dial-in access only, and although there are work-arounds for configuring VPN access, they often aren't worth the time or expense involved.

In most configurations, from the user's standpoint, there is very little difference between connecting locally or through a remote access connection. Users must be authenticated before they are allowed access to the network, and their resource access is determined by the rights and permissions they've been granted. There are, however, a couple significant potential differences. In some remote access configurations, users can access resources physically hosted on the remote access server only. The other difference is that if the user is connecting through a low-bandwidth method (e.g., through a dial-up modem), the delays when copying or opening files from the network can be noticeable.

8.2.2 Comparing Access and Authentication

A remote access protocol manages the connection between a remote computer and a remote access server. These are the primary remote access protocols in use today:

- **Serial Line Internet Protocol (SLIP)**.
- **Point-to-Point Protocol (PPP)** and **Point-to-Point Protocol over Ethernet (PPPoE)**.
- **Point-to-Point Tunneling Protocol (PPTP)**.
- **Layer 2 Tunneling Protocol (L2TP)**.

SLIP, PPP, and PPPoE are used to create dial-up remote access connections. PPTP and L2TP are VPN protocols and are used not only with client remote access but also when connecting LANs to create WANs.

Another consideration when configuring remote access is the authentication protocol used. Authentication protocol options vary by client and server. Authentication methods also vary by NOS and remote access server type. Authentication can be handled by an individual server using network authentication methods or with a remote access server handling authentication itself, or authentication can be centralized using **Remote Authentication Dial-in User Service (RADIUS)** or other centralized authentication methods. Microsoft has its own implementation of RADIUS technology, which it refers to as **Internet Authentication Service (IAS)**.

Comparing SLIP and PPP

Serial Line Internet Protocol (*SLIP*) was originally developed for use with Unix as a way for terminals to connect to Unix servers. It is still sometimes used for that purpose with both Unix and Linux servers. In general, however, SLIP is used less frequently today because it lacks features compared with other protocols. Although low overhead is associated with using SLIP, and you can use it to transport TCP/IP over serial connections, it does no error checking or packet addressing, and it can be used only on serial connections. SLIP does not support encrypted passwords and therefore transmits passwords in clear text, which is inherently not secure.

Setting up SLIP for a remote connection requires a SLIP account on the host machine and usually a batch file or a script on the workstation. When SLIP is used to log in to a remote computer, a terminal mode must be configured after login to the remote site so that the script can enter each parameter. If you don't use a script, you have to establish the connection and then open a terminal window to log in to the remote access server manually. Many modern operating systems, such as Windows 2000 Server (and later), don't support inbound SLIP connections. Windows still supports outbound SLIP to allow connections to Unix computers.

Point-to-Point Protocol (*PPP*) is used to implement TCP/IP connections over point-to-point links (e.g., dial-up lines, dedicated leased lines), but it also supports other network protocols, such as IPX. PPP encapsulates the packets of protocols being carried by PPP. Because it features error checking and can run over many types of physical media, PPP has almost completely replaced SLIP. It is most commonly used for remote connections to ISPs and LANs. PPP uses the **Link Control Protocol (LCP)** to communicate between the PPP client and host. LCP tests the link between client and PPP host and specifies PPP client configuration. Through LCP, PPP also supports authentication negotiation, as well as negotiation of encryption and compression between client and server, using **Compression Control Protocol (CCP)**, which handles data compression, and **Encryption Control Protocol (ECP)**, which is responsible for data encryption.

PPP can support several network protocols through the use of protocol-specific **network control protocols (NCPs)**. PPP can automatically configure TCP/IP and other protocol parameters through the use of the **IP Control Protocol (IPCP)**, an NCP. On the downside, high overhead is associated with using PPP, and it is not compatible with some older configurations.

From a technician's standpoint, PPP is easy to configure. Once you connect to a router using PPP, the router assigns all other TCP/IP parameters. This is typically done with DHCP. IP configuration information can be assigned over a LAN connection or a dial-up connection. When you connect to an ISP, you are most likely getting your IP address from a DHCP server.

Point-to-Point Protocol over Ethernet (*PPPoE*) is a protocol for encapsulating PPP frames over an Ethernet network. Although it is mentioned here for your reference, it is not used for configuring remote access clients. Instead, it is most often used to let network users share an always-on high-speed Internet connection, such as a DSL line or cable modem.

Comparing PPTP and L2TP

Point-to-Point Tunneling Protocol (*PPTP*) and *Layer 2 Tunneling Protocol* (*L2TP*) are both VPN protocols. They can be used to configure VPN connections through the Internet or configure secure communications over a LAN connection. PPTP is a Microsoft-created protocol based on PPP that is used to create virtual connections across the Internet using TCP/IP and PPP. It is supported by Windows NT 4.0 and later servers and Windows 95 and later clients. L2TP, which was designed by the Internet Engineering Task Force, supports both TCP/IP and non-TCP/IP protocols on VPNs by encapsulating them in IP frames as wrappers.

To use PPTP, you set up a PPP session between the client and server, typically over the Internet. Once the session is established, you create a session that connects through the existing PPP session using PPTP. The PPTP session tunnels through the existing PPP connection, creating a secure session. PPP packets are encapsulated inside IP packets for transmission. In this way, you can use the Internet to create a secure session between the client and the server. In most situations, it is likely that you will want to encrypt the communications between the server and the remote client. Microsoft supports encryption through the **Microsoft Point-to-Point Encryption (MPPE)** protocol.

The advantages of using PPTP include the following:

- ▲ Native support on Windows NT 4.0 or later and Windows 95 or later.
- ▲ Compatible with NAT devices.

As with any network technology, there can be disadvantages to using PPTP:

- ▲ PPTP is not available on all types of servers.
- ▲ PPTP is not a fully accepted standard.
- ▲ PPTP supports user authentication only (no machine authentication support).
- ▲ Tunneling can reduce throughput.

L2TP is a combination of Microsoft PPTP and Cisco's **Layer 2 Forwarding (L2F)** technology. It supports a variety of protocols, including IPX and AppleTalk. This gives it the advantage that it lets you connect non-TCP/IP clients to networks running protocols other than TCP/IP. It is supported on Windows 2000 Server and later servers and Windows Me, Windows 98, and later clients. Other advantages include the following:

- ▲ L2TP is an industry-standard protocol, which means it has broad-based support.
- ▲ L2TP can authenticate both the user and client computer by using certificates (a method of defining shared security) or a preshared key (a value known to the server and client).
- ▲ L2TP supports stronger authentication methods than PPTP.

However, L2TP has some disadvantages:

- ▲ L2TP does not support Windows 95 and earlier Windows client versions.
- ▲ L2TP is not compatible with some NAT devices (but Windows Server 2003 NAT is supported).
- ▲ Tunneling can reduce throughput.

Security for L2TP is provided through **Internet Protocol Security (IPsec)**, which is another industry standard. IPsec is a set of open standards designed to secure IP networks. It provides support for peer computer authentication and data authentication and data encryption. It supports two modes of operation. When operating in **transport mode**, only the message portion of the IP packet is encrypted. It is used for host-to-host communications. Remote access connections always use transport mode. It also supports **tunnel mode**, in which the entire packet is encrypted and then encapsulated inside another IP packet. Tunnel mode enables IPsec support for non-IPsec-aware client operating systems. Tunnel mode can be used with host-to-host communications but is also used with host-to-network and network-to-network communications. On a Windows network, IPsec is supported by Windows 2000 and later servers and Windows XP and later clients unless used for VPN access with L2TP client software installed.

VPN connections using PPTP or L2TP can be used to configure a single remote workstation to connect to a corporate network over the Internet. The workstation is configured to connect to the Internet via an ISP, and the VPN client is configured with the address of the VPN remote access server, as shown in Figure 8-9. A VPN connection is often used to connect remote workstations to corporate LANs when a workstation must communicate with a corporate network. PPTP is typically used when communicating over a dial-up or broadband PPP link through an ISP and the link must be secure.

Understanding Authentication Protocols

Several authentication protocols can be used with PPP and PPTP. If configured with support for multiple protocols, the server and client negotiate the authentication protocol used while negotiating other communication parameters. Supported protocols include the following:

- ▲ PAP: **Password Authentication Protocol (PAP)** is based on a user name and password passed as clear text and authenticated against information stored on the server.
- ▲ SPAP: **Shiva Password Authentication Protocol (SPAP)** passes the password in a relatively easy-to-break encryption method.
- ▲ CHAP: **Challenge Handshake Authentication Protocol (CHAP)** is the industry standard, using a challenge-and-response format, where the server sends a challenge to the client, and the client returns a 128-bit response that is based on the original challenge and the user's password.
- ▲ MS-CHAP: **Microsoft Challenge Handshake Authentication Protocol (MS-CHAP)** was developed by Microsoft (originally supporting Windows 3.1) as its own CHAP version that sends two parallel hashes (i.e., values derived from the challenge, response, and a key value) during authentication, a LAN Manager hash, and an NT LAN Manager hash.
- ▲ MS-CHAPv2: **Microsoft Challenge Handshake Authentication Protocol version 2 (MS-CHAPv2)** is an enhanced CHAP version with security improvements that include not using the LAN Manager hash, making it more secure than MS-CHAP.
- ▲ EAP: **Extensible Authentication Protocol (EAP)** is the industry standard for adding additional authentication protocols, such as support for smart cards, which are specialized access and authentication security devices.

Windows Server 2003's implementation of EAP includes support for **EAP–Transport Layer Security (EAP-TLS)**, designed for use with smart cards. It also includes the **MD5–Challenge Handshake Authentication Protocol (MD5-CHAP)**, which is a protocol designed for testing and troubleshooting EAP connections and should not be used when configuring network security.

Because of security concerns, use of PAP and SPAP should be limited to clients or servers that don't support more secure authentication methods. It is usually recommended that you avoid MS-CHAP as well, for security reasons. MS-CHAP does not authenticate the server, and the LAN Manager hash is not very secure and is easily broken. EAP and MS-CHAPv2 are preferred options, depending on the capabilities of the remote access server and the client operating systems supported. MS-CHAPv2 cannot be used with Windows 95 and older Windows clients because it doesn't send the LAN Manager hash needed by those clients. CHAP is required when using non-Microsoft clients that don't support EAP. CHAP and EAP, because they are both industry-standard protocols, support a wide variety of client types. One potential disadvantage of CHAP is that passwords must be stored using reversible encryption.

You can implement additional, centralized support for authentication, especially when you have multiple remote access servers, by including a RADIUS server in the networking mix. The RADIUS server can use passwords provided by the NOS or can maintain its own password database. RADIUS is a de facto standard supported by several manufacturers, including Microsoft, to support authentication and authorization and even provide logging for remote connections. One of the advantages of using RADIUS is that it supports several connection methods, including dial-up connections, VPN, and even computers connecting through WAPs on a wireless network.

8.2.3 Configuring Remote Access

The specific requirements for configuring remote access vary by NOS, but the necessary parameters are all very similar. In this section, we will look at the requirements for Windows, which are fairly typical.

Figure 8-10

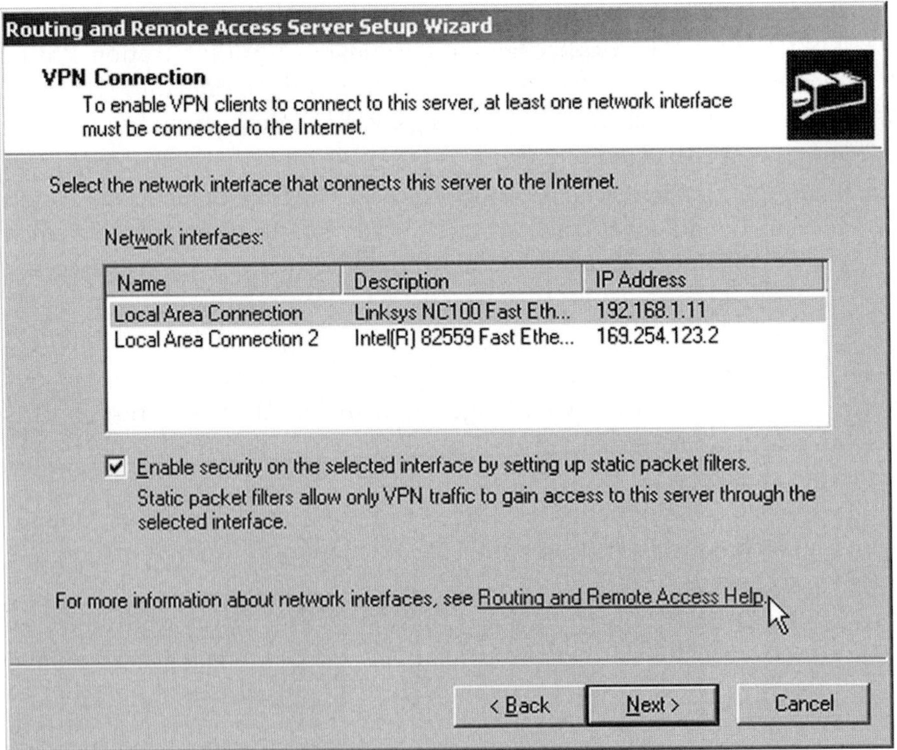

Available network interfaces.

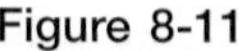

Figure 8-11

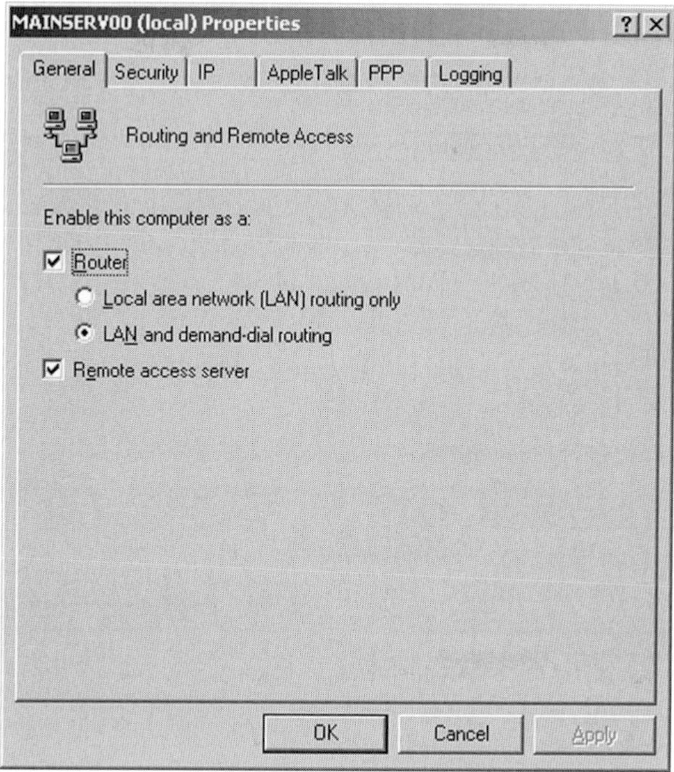

The RRAS server Properties dialog box.

With Windows Server 2003, you set up remote access through **Routing and Remote Access Service (RRAS)**. You can configure a server to support dial-up connections, VPN connections, or both. Dial-up connection support requires one or more modems. Some companies install modem banks, several dial-up modems built onto a device or an interface card, so that one server can support several dial-up users. A separate phone is also needed. The number of modem ports and phone lines physically limits the number of concurrent users.

When configuring VPN connection support, you must identify the network interfaces that can be used. You also need to identify how clients are issued IP addresses—either from an existing DHCP server or from a specified range of addresses issued directly by the RRAS server. By default, a server is configured to support MS-CHAP, MS-CHAPv2, and EAP. Figure 8-10 shows the wizard where you configure these settings.

To manage the authentication methods supported, you open the Properties dialog box (see Figure 8-11) to the Security tab and then click Authentication Methods.

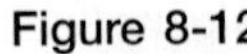

Figure 8-12

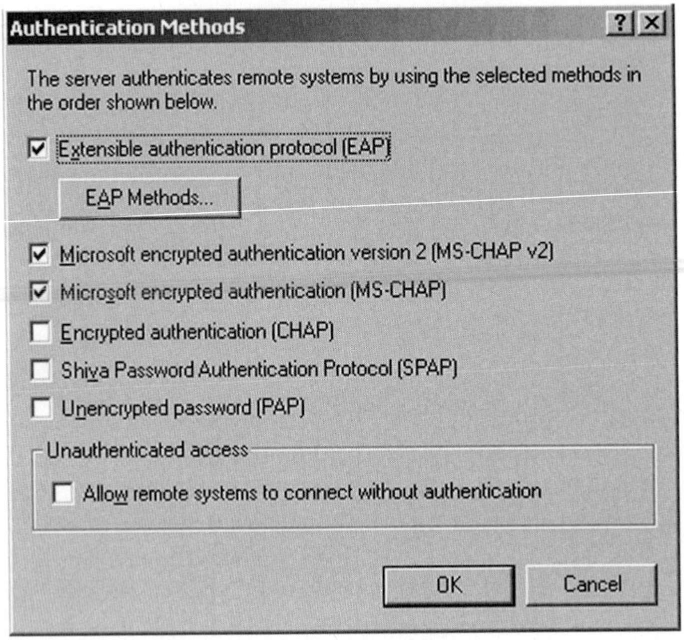

Authentication options.

Authentication options are shown in Figure 8-12. Checked authentication methods are supported. To remove support for an authentication method, you remove the check.

When configuring clients, you typically configure a client as either a dial-up or VPN client, but you may have situations in which you might configure a client to support both. On Windows computers, you configure client connections through Network Connections. When configuring a dial-up connection, you specify the company name, phone number, and who can use the connection. Client-side security is configured through the connection properties. The client connection's advanced security settings, shown in Figure 8-13, let you choose the authentication protocols supported by the client.

Configuring a VPN connection over the Internet is just as easy as configuring a dial-up connection. You need to tell the computer whether it needs to dial the initial connection (e.g., if it needs to dial in to an ISP before establishing the connection) and the name of the server to which it will connect. You also configure who can use the connection.

One difference with a VPN connection is the security configuration settings. A detailed discussion of these settings is beyond the scope of this

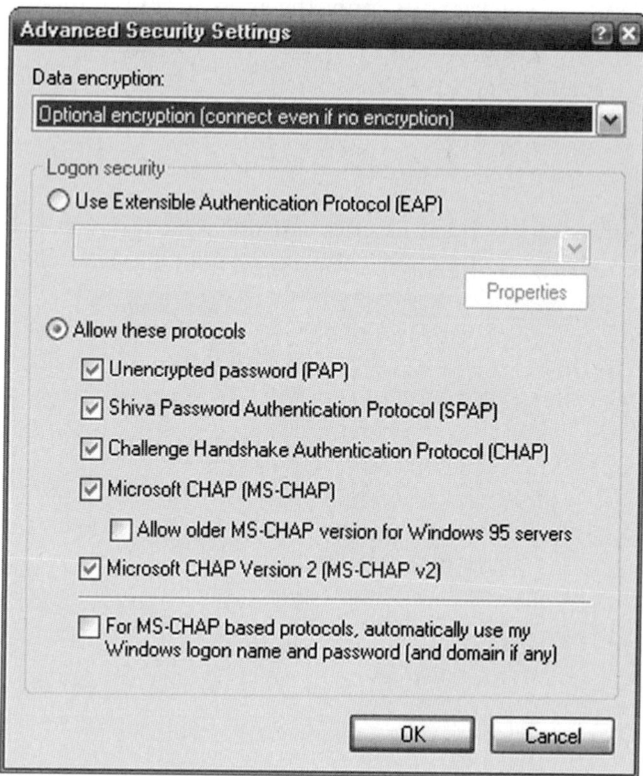

Dial-up client advanced security settings.

FOR EXAMPLE

Cutting Costs with the Internet

Some companies have found it cost-effective to get rid of dial-in remote access services and switch to Internet VPN connections, paying for some employees' Internet connections as part of the deal. Many companies that allow (or even encourage) some employees to telecommute have traditionally covered the associated costs. If that connection involves a long-distance call and long connection times to the company network, the connection charges can be quite expensive.

Companies have found that it is usually cheaper to pay a flat fee to cover an employee's Internet connection instead of paying for dial-up connection charges. Often, there is an added benefit because the employees are able to get high-speed Internet connections, making them more efficient. Another added benefit is employee satisfaction. When an employee has a high-speed Internet connection coming into the house, it's an easy matter to share it for the rest of the family's use.

chapter, but Figure 8-14 gives a quick look at the default authentication protocols. By default, as you can see, only the most secure authentication protocols are supported.

Figure 8-14

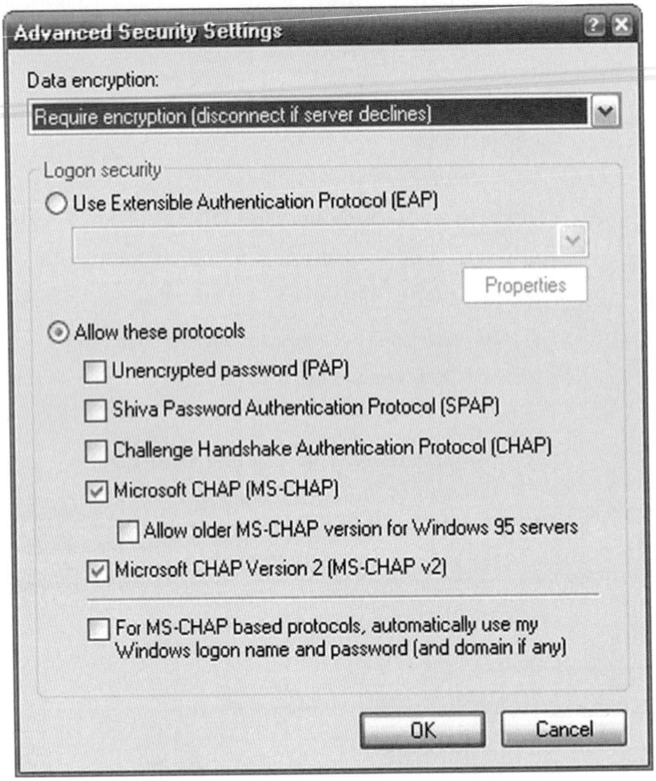

Advanced Security Settings

Data encryption:

Require encryption (disconnect if server declines)

Logon security

Use Extensible Authentication Protocol (EAP)

Properties

Allow these protocols

Unencrypted password (PAP)

Shiva Password Authentication Protocol (SPAP)

Challenge Handshake Authentication Protocol (CHAP)

Microsoft CHAP (MS-CHAP)

Allow older MS-CHAP version for Windows 95 servers

Microsoft CHAP Version 2 (MS-CHAP v2)

For MS-CHAP based protocols, automatically use my Windows logon name and password (and domain if any)

OK Cancel

VPN client advanced security settings.

SELF-CHECK

1. What are the two protocols that support VPN connections over the Internet?
2. What authentication protocols are supported for PPP connections?

8.3 Joining LANs into WANs

By classic definition, a LAN becomes a WAN when traffic between the networks crosses through a public carrier. When using a VPN over a network to make a WAN connection, it works much the same as a VPN remote client, except that you are connecting a network instead of a single server, as in Figure 8-15. This method of connecting LANs has gained popularity of late, but several other connection methods are supported and still in common use.

No matter how the connection is made, the basic idea is the same: You need a router at each end, with some kind of connection between them. Although this is simple in theory, the configuration details can vary widely, depending on how the connection is made between the routers. Each carrier option and connection type has its own configuration requirements and special considerations.

8.3.1 Considering WAN Options

You need to consider a number of different variables when planning a WAN. You need to consider items such as the following:

- ▲ Number of LANs you need to connect.
- ▲ Geographic location of the LANs.

Figure 8-15

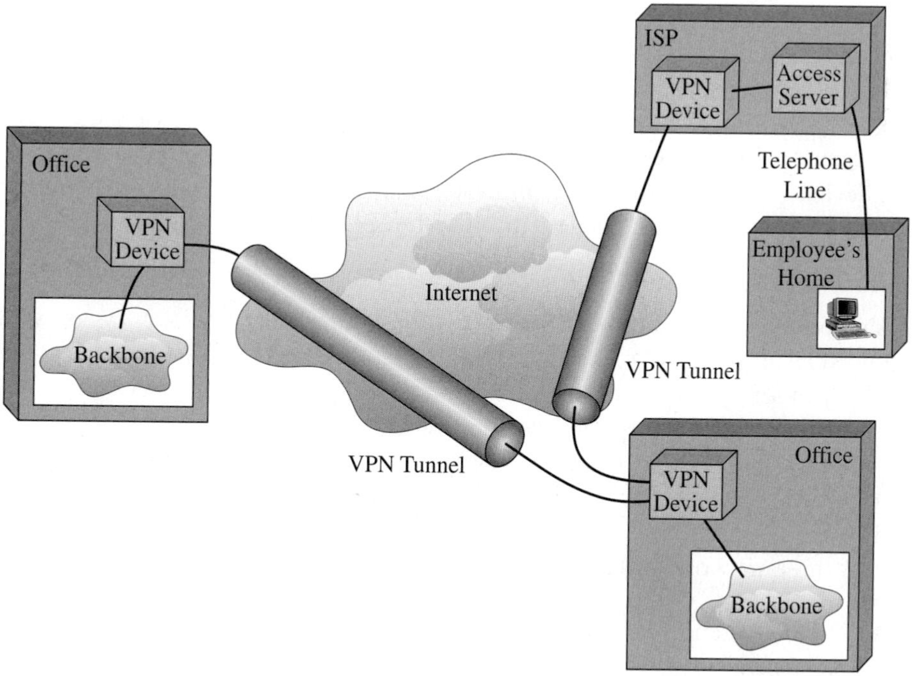

An Internet VPN.

- ▲ Number of computers in each LAN.
- ▲ Implementation budget.
- ▲ Network operating system(s).
- ▲ Network servers and services.
- ▲ Bandwidth requirements.

Many WAN configurations are heterogeneous networks, requiring you to support a mix of network operating systems, server types, and client types. A WAN might even include one or more mainframe computers.

Planning LAN Configurations

Deciding on computer placement can be a complicated issue. Client computers are the easiest part; you need enough client computers to support your network users at each location. Servers are a different issue.

You need to consider the types of servers that you need and which users need access to those servers. Many NOSs recommend that you place critical servers, such as Windows Active Directory domain controllers, local on each LAN. For other types of servers, as much as possible, you want to place servers so that they are local to the majority of the clients that need to access them. Why? Bandwidth between LANs is often a limited resource on a WAN, and you want to try to keep traffic between LANs to a minimum. However, this isn't a strict rule. Availability is another consideration. Do you need a full-time connection to the servers? Or do you need periodic connections only?

Server placement can be something of a balancing act. You need to balance the cost and other requirements of placing multiple servers against the support requirements for accessing a server through a wide area link. There is at least one device—a router—that you will have in every location. A router is a required device, managing the connection to other LANs.

Planning WAN Connections

WAN connections are supported over a wide variety of connection types. With many NOSs, the easiest to configure is a VPN connection over the Internet. Technically, you set up both a VPN connection and NAT to enable the network clients to share the single connection over the Internet.

Other connection methods are very similar, at least at the most basic level. A router connects to a circuit that carries the traffic. Another router at the other end of the connection completes the circuit. The connection can be made over one of three network types:

- ▲ Circuit-switched networks.
- ▲ Dedicated circuit networks.
- ▲ Packet-switched networks.

One thing you need to understand is that these network connections can be used to connect network routers or, in many cases, to connect the network to the Internet to support a VPN connection.

8.3.2 Connecting with Circuit-Switched Networks

Using **circuit-switched** networks is the oldest and simplest approach to MAN and WAN circuits. These services operate over the PSTN (i.e., the telephone networks operated by the common carriers such as Verizon, BellSouth, Ameritech).

Circuit-switched services use a **cloud architecture**. The users lease connection points (e.g., telephone lines) into the common carrier's network, which is called the cloud, as shown in Figure 8-16. A person (or computer) dials the telephone number of the destination computer and establishes a temporary circuit between the two computers. The computers exchange data, and when the task is complete, the circuit is disconnected (e.g., by hanging up the phone).

Cloud-based designs are simple for an organization because they move the burden of network design and management inside the cloud from the organization to the common carrier. Network managers do not need to worry about the amount of traffic sent between each computer; they just need to specify the amount of traffic entering and leaving each computer and buy the appropriate size and

Figure 8-16

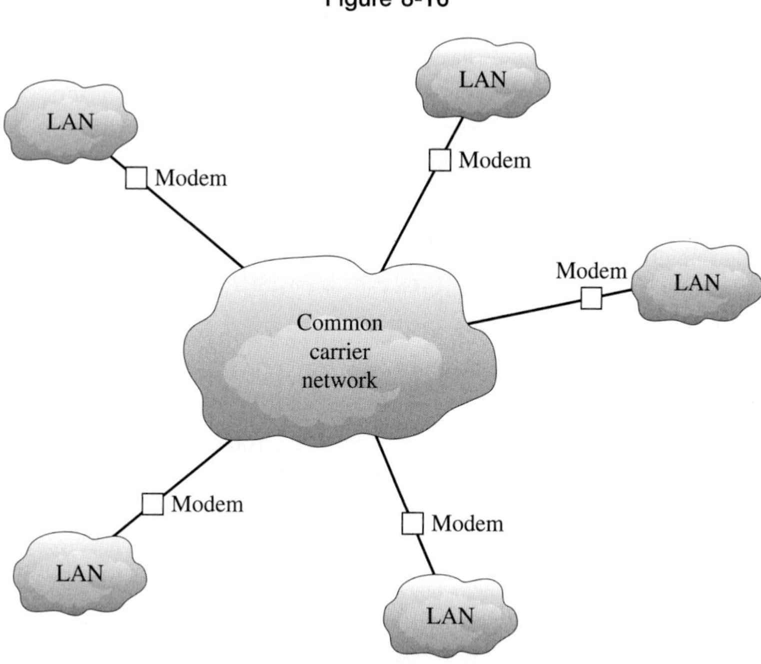

Dialed circuit services.

number of connections into the PSTN. However, this comes at a price. Cloud-based designs can be expensive because users must pay for each connection into the network and pay on the basis of the amount of time each circuit is used.

To use POTS, the standard dial-up system, you need to lease a circuit into the network (i.e., a telephone line) and install special equipment (i.e., a modem) to enable a computer to talk to the PSTN. To transfer data to and from another computer on the network, you instruct your modem to dial the other computer's telephone.

A higher-bandwidth option is to use **Integrated Services Digital Network (ISDN)**, which combines voice, video, and data over the same digital circuit. The original version is occasionally called **narrowband ISDN (N-ISDN)**, and the most current is referred to as **broadband ISDN (B-ISDN)**. ISDN is widely available from a number of common carriers in North America.

To use ISDN, you must lease connection points in the PSTN, which are telephone lines just like POTS. Next, special equipment is needed to connect the computers (or networks) into the PSTN. Users need an ISDN **network terminator (NT-1 or NT-2)** that functions much like a hub, and a NIC (called a **terminal adapter** [TA] or an **ISDN modem**) in every computer attached to the NT-1/NT-2. In most cases, the ISDN service appears identical to the regular dialed telephone service, with the exception that usually (but not always) each device attached to the NT-1/NT-2 needs a unique **service profile identifier (SPID)** to identify it. To connect to another computer (e.g., a remote router) using ISDN, you dial that computer's telephone number using the ISDN NIC in much the same way as you would with a modem on a regular telephone line.

There are various ISDN configurations, each supporting different capacities. The configurations shown here are those supported in the United States; Europe and other regions can vary in the number of channels supported:

- **BRI: Basic rate interface (BRI)** supports two 64Kbps digital channels (called **B channels**) and one 16Kbps control signaling channel (called a **D channel**).
- **PRI: Primary rate interface (PRI)** is offered to commercial customers and supports 23 64Kbps B channels and 1 64Kbps D channel.
- **B-ISDN**: This is a circuit-switched service that uses **Asynchronous Transfer Mode (ATM)** circuits, discussed later in this chapter, to carry data at 622.08Mbps and 155.52Mbps. B-ISDN is backward compatible and can accept transmissions from BRI and PRI circuits.

There are three main problems with POTS and ISDN circuit-switched networks:

- Each connection goes through the regular telephone network on a different circuit. These circuits may vary in quality, so although one connection may be fairly clear, the next call may be noisy.

- ▲ The data transmission rates on these circuits are usually low. Generally speaking, transmission rates range from 28.8Kbps to 56Kbps for dialed POTS circuits to 128Kbps to 1.5Mbps for ISDN circuits.
- ▲ You usually pay per use for circuit-switched services, which can get very expensive over time.

PSTN connection methods, especially POTS, are most commonly used for Internet connections and for remote access connections when the bandwidth requirements are minimal.

8.3.3 Connecting with Dedicated Circuit Networks

With a **dedicated circuit network**, you lease circuits from common carriers. All connections are point to point, from one building in one city to another building in the same city or a different city. The carrier installs the circuit connections at the two end points of the circuit and makes the connection between them. The circuits still run through the common carrier's cloud, but the network behaves as if you have your own physical circuits running from one point to another, as in Figure 8-17.

Figure 8-17

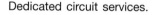

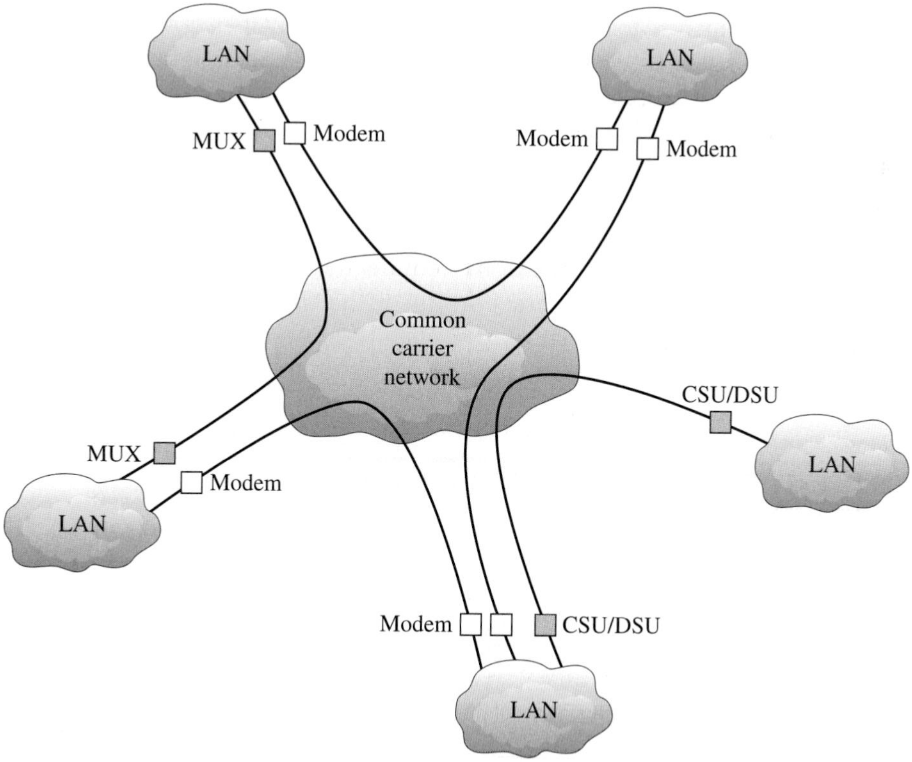

Dedicated circuit services.

Once again, the user leases the desired circuit from the common carrier (specifying the physical end points of the circuit) and installs the equipment needed to connect computers and devices (e.g., routers, switches) to the circuit. This equipment may include **multiplexers** or a **channel service unit (CSU)** and/or a **data service unit (DSU)**; a CSU/DSU is the WAN equivalent of a NIC in a LAN.

Unlike circuit-switched services that typically use a pay-per-use model, dedicated circuits are billed at a flat fee per month, and the user has unlimited use of the circuit. Once you sign a contract, making changes can be expensive because it means rewiring the buildings and signing a new contract with the carrier. Therefore, dedicated circuits require more care in network design than do switched circuits, both in terms of location and the amount of capacity purchased.

Three basic architectures are used in dedicated circuit networks: ring, star, and mesh. These are effectively the same as the network topologies of the same names. In practice, most networks use a combination of architectures. For example, a distributed star architecture has a series of star networks that are connected by a mesh or ring architecture.

T-carrier circuits are the most commonly used form of dedicated circuit services in North America today. Costs are a fixed amount per month, regardless of how much or how little traffic flows through the circuit. There are several types of T-carrier circuits, as shown in Table 8-1.

T1 lines are commonly used to carry data and voice transmissions. T2, T3, and T4 lines are made by bundling multiple T1 lines. T3 or T4 are sometimes used by large corporations with high bandwidth requirements.

Fractional T1 (FT1) service is provided for companies that need high-bandwidth communications but don't require the bandwidth provided by a full T1 circuit. Companies lease a portion of the T1 line, usually in 65Kbps multiples. Many companies that used to use FT1 lines have switched to high-speed Internet instead.

Table 8-1: T-Carrier Service Characteristics

T-carrier Designation	*DS Designation*	*Speed*
FT1	DS0	64Kbps
T1	DS1	1.544Mbps
T2	DS2	6.312Mbps
T3	DS3	44.376Mbps
T4	DS3	274.176Mbps

Table 8-2: SONET/SDH Services

SONET Designation	*SDH Designation*	*Speed*
OC-1	—	51.84Mbps
OC-3	STM-1	155.52Mbps
OC-9	STM-3	466.56Mbps
OC-12	STM-4	622.08Mbps
OC-18	STM-6	933.12Mbps
OC-24	STM-8	1.244Gbps
OC-36	STM-12	1.866Gbps
OC-48	STM-16	2.488Gbps
OC-192	STM-24	9.953Gbps

Synchronous Optical Network (SONET) is the American standard (from ANSI) for high-speed dedicated circuit services. A recently standardized and almost identical service that easily interconnects with SONET is marketed under the name **Synchronous Digital Hierarchy (SDH)**.

SONET transmission speeds begin at **optical carrier (OC) level** 1 (OC-1), which is 51.84Mbps. Each succeeding rate in the SONET fiber hierarchy is defined as a multiple of OC-1, with SONET data rates defined as high as OC-192, or about 10Gbps. Table 8-2 presents the other major SONET and SDH services. Notice that the slowest SONET transmission rate (OC-1) of 51.84Mbps is slightly faster than the T3 rate of 44.376Mbps.

SONET and SDH are available in limited areas only, with most availability restricted to major metropolitan areas.

8.3.4 Connecting with Packet-Switched Networks

With **packet-switched networks**, as with circuit-switched networks, you buy a connection into the common carrier cloud, as shown in Figure 8-18. The user pays a fixed fee for the connection into the network (depending on the type and capacity of the service) and is charged for the number of packets transmitted.

The user's connection into the network is a **packet assembly/disassembly device (PAD)**, which can be owned and operated by the customer or by the common carrier. The PAD converts the sender's data into the Network layer and Data Link layer packets used by the packet-switched network and then sends

Figure 8-18

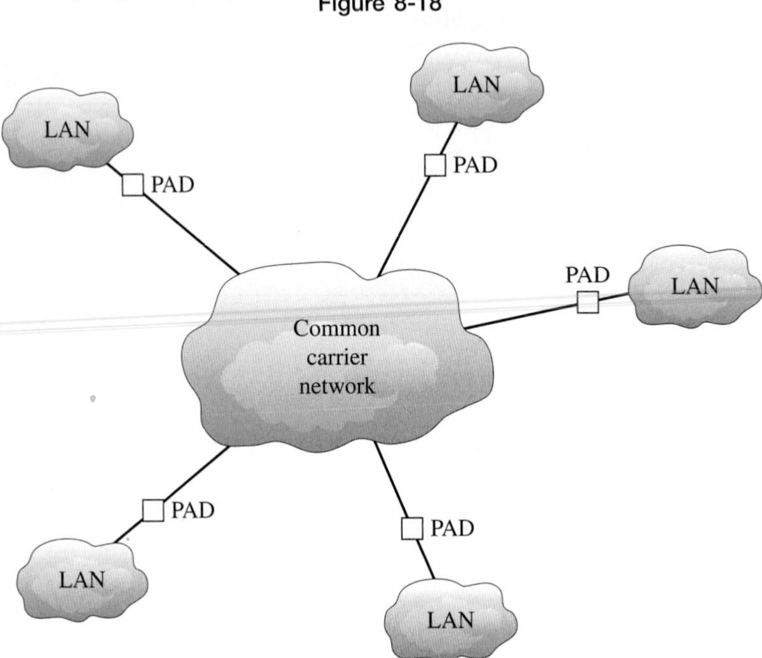

Packet-switched services.

them through the network. At the other end, another PAD reassembles the packets back into the Network layer and Data Link layer protocols expected by the destination and delivers them to the appropriate computer. The PAD also compensates for differences in transmission speed between sender and receiver; for example, the circuit at the sender might be 1.5Mbps, whereas the receiver may have only a 64Kbps circuit.

The oldest packet-switched service is **X.25**. X.25 offers various services, including datagram services for network communication. When packets arrive at the PAD, connecting the user's network to the packet-switched network, their Data Link (e.g., Ethernet) and Network layer (e.g., IP) packets are removed, and X.25-specific packets are substituted. Packets are moved through the X.25 network in much the same way as in TCP/IP networks. When they arrive at the edge of the X.25 network, new destination protocols (e.g., Ethernet, IP) are created, and the message is sent on its way. X.25 is sometimes called a reliable packet service because it provides complete error checking and guaranteed delivery on all packets transmitted.

Although common in Europe, X.25 is not widespread in North America. The primary reason is its transmission speed. For many years, the maximum speed into North American X.25 networks was 64Kbps, but this has increased to

2.048Mbps, which is the European standard for ISDN. However, for many users, 2.048Mbps is still not fast enough.

Asynchronous Transfer Mode (*ATM*), also standardized, is a newer technology than X.25. ATM is similar to X.25 in that it provides packet-switched services, but it has four distinct operating characteristics that differ from X.25. First, ATM performs encapsulation of packets, so packets are delivered unchanged through the network. Second, ATM provides no error control in the network; error control is the responsibility of the source and destination. ATM is considered an unreliable packet service. Because the user's data link packet remains intact, it is simple for the devices at the edge of the ATM network to check the error-control information in the packet to ensure that no errors have occurred and to request transmission of damaged or lost packets. Figure 8-19 illustrates the difference in error control between X.25 networks and ATM networks.

The left side of Figure 8-19 shows that when an X.25 packet leaves its Source A and moves through Node B, to Node C, to Node D, and finally to Destination E, each intermediate node acknowledges the packet as it passes. The right side of the figure shows how an ATM packet moves through Node B, Node C, and Node D and on to Destination E. When Destination E receives the packet correctly, a single acknowledgment is sent back through the nodes to Source A, as shown by the numbers 5, 6, 7, and 8. Some common carriers have started using the term fast packet services instead to refer to these services that do not provide error control (because it sounds better for marketing).

Third, ATM provides extensive information that enables the setting of very precise priorities among different types of transmissions (e.g., high priority for voice and video, lower priority for email).

Figure 8-19

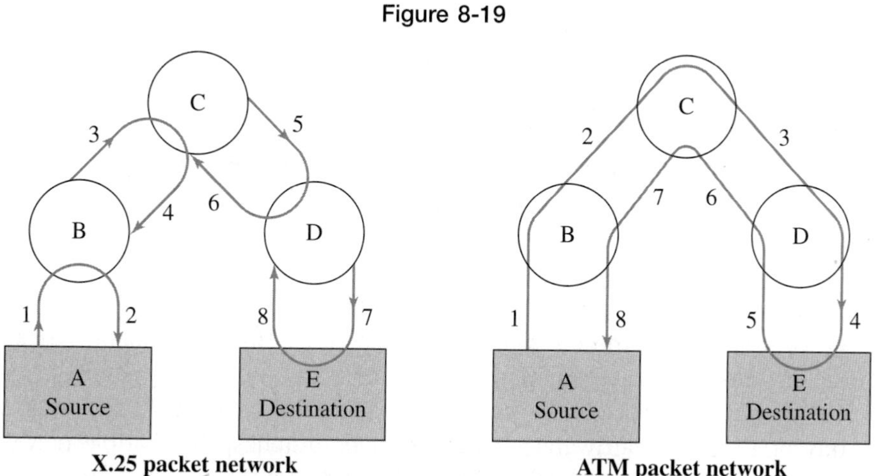

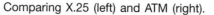

Comparing X.25 (left) and ATM (right).

Finally, ATM is scalable; it is easy to combine basic ATM circuits into much faster ATM circuits. Most common carriers offer ATM circuits that provide the same data transmission rates as SONET: 51.84Mbps, 466.56Mbps, 622.08Mbps, and so on up to 39Gbps (equivalent to OC-768). New versions called T1 ATM (1.544Mbps) and T3 ATM (45Mbps) are also available.

Frame Relay is an even newer packet-switching technology that transmits data faster than X.25 but more slowly than ATM. It has sometimes been called poor-man's ATM. Like ATM, Frame Relay performs encapsulation of packets, so packets are delivered, unchanged, through the network. Like ATM, it is an unreliable packet service because it does not perform error control. It is up to the software at the source and destination to perform error correction and to control for lost messages.

Frame Relay does not yet provide **quality of service (QoS)** capabilities, such as priority scheduling and other quality controls, but this is under development. Different common carriers offer Frame Relay networks with different transmission speeds. Most offer a range of committed information rate speeds that include 56Kbps, 128Kbps, 256Kbps, 384Kbps, 1.544Mbps, 2.048Mbps, and 45Mbps.

Switched Multimegabit Data Service (SMDS) is an unreliable packet service like ATM and Frame Relay. And like ATM and Frame Relay, SMDS does not perform error checking; the user is responsible for error checking. As with ATM and Frame Relay, SMDS encapsulates incoming packets. SMDS is not yet standardized. At present, most (but not all) common carriers offer it. SMDS was originally aimed at MANs, particularly the interconnection of LANs. Recently, it has also made its way into the WAN environment. Regional telephone companies offer SMDS at a variety of transmission rates, ranging from 56Kbps up to 44.376Mbps. There are no widely accepted standards, so transmission rates vary by carrier. The future of SMDS is uncertain because it is not standardized and offers no clear advantages over Frame Relay.

8.3.5 Choosing a Connection Type

The connection type you use depends on your connection requirements. You need to consider the data rates supported and also the costs involved. Table 8-3 provides an overview of the currently supported connection methods.

Table 8-4 outlines some generally accepted guidelines for choosing a connection type based on bandwidth requirements.

When considering the costs involved, remember that you not only need to include the cost of the circuit (and incremental costs, if appropriate), you also need to consider the cost of the connection hardware. With most methods, you can buy or lease the hardware from a carrier or purchase compatible hardware from a third-party vendor. Keep in mind, however, that if you buy your hardware from a third party, you need to make sure that it has a service department that

Table 8-3: Comparing Wide Area Connection Services

Type of Service	*Nominal Data Rates*	*Effective Data Rates*	*Relative Cost*	*Reliability*	*Network Integration*
Circuit-Switched Services					
POTS	33.6Kbps to 56Kbps	33Kbps to 300Kbps[1]	Low	High	Difficult
ISDN	128Kbps to 1.5Mbps	122Kbps to 1.3Mbps	Moderate	Moderate	Difficult
B-ISDN	155Mbps to 622Mbps	300Mbps to 1200Mbps[2]	High	Low	Difficult
Dedicated Circuit Services					
T-carrier	64Kbps to 274Mbps	53Kbps to 218Mbps	Moderate	High	Moderate
SONET	50Mbps to 10Gbps	48Mbps to 9.1Gbps	High	High	Moderate
Packet-Switched Services					
X.25	56Kbps to 2Mbps	50Kbps to 1.5Mbps	Moderate	High	Difficult
ATM	52Mbps to 10Gbps	84Mbps to 16Gbps[3]	High	Moderate	Moderate
Frame Relay	56Kbps to 45Mbps	56Kbps to 44Mbps	Moderate	Moderate	Moderate
SMDS	56Kbps to 45Mbps	45Kbps to 36Mbps	Moderate	Low	Difficult
Ethernet	1Mbps to 40Gbps	900Kbps to 36Gbps	Low	High	Simple
VPN Services					
VPN	56Kbps to 2Mbps	50Kbps to 1.5Mbps	Very low	Low	Moderate

[1] Assuming data compression and no noise.
[2] B-ISDN is full duplex.
[3] ATM is full duplex.

Table 8-4: WAN Connection Recommendations

Network Needs	*Recommendations*
Low traffic needs (64Kbps or less)	Use POTS if dial-up is acceptable, VPN if reliability is less important, and Frame Relay otherwise.
Moderate traffic needs (64Kbps to 2Mbps)	Use VPN if reliability is less important, T1 if network volume is stable and predictable, and Frame Relay otherwise.
High traffic needs (2Mbps to 45Mbps)	Use Ethernet if available, T3 if network volume is stable and predictable, and Frame Relay otherwise.
Very high traffic needs (45Mbps to 10Gbps)	Use Ethernet if available, SONET if network volume is stable and predictable, and ATM otherwise.

will stand behind the equipment; if you run into problems in the future and have third-party hardware, you can expect the local carrier to blame any and all problems on the hardware.

Another consideration is the maturity of the technology. While newer connection options might offer higher-speed connectivity, and maybe even at a lower cost, you need to consider what kind of a track record a new option has. Is information available about reliability or, if problems do occur, the average time before they are repaired? The newest and fastest is not always the best, especially when you figure in the costs that come with downtime.

FOR EXAMPLE

Growing a Network

WAN connection methods often evolve over time. A company might initially use a circuit-switched network method before it has an accurate idea of the bandwidth and connectivity requirements. It usually isn't long before the company upgrades to a faster connection method, either deciding that the initial choice isn't fast enough or that the remote office's needs have outgrown the connection's capabilities.

Why not go with a faster connection from the beginning? Traditionally, the main reason has been cost. Not only are the lease costs relatively expensive for most dedicated circuit and packet-switched networks, the necessary hardware can be as or even more expensive. Add in the per-packet cost for packet-switched networks, and the costs continue to climb. Still, companies that need the bandwidth are often willing to pay the price. Companies that want the added security of an effectively private line are even willing to pay the added costs related to secure connections. At least, that's the way it's always worked in the past. But this is quickly changing, especially with smaller businesses, which are diving straight in with connectivity in the moderate to the low end of the high-speed range. How? With high-speed Internet connections, most often DSL lines or cable Internet connections. Connectivity in the 3Mbps to 5Mbps (and even higher) range is both readily available and relatively inexpensive. Not only that, current Windows versions make it relatively easy for network administrators to configure and maintain their own VPN connections.

SELF-CHECK

1. What are the connection methods supported for circuit-switched, dedicated circuit, and packet-switched networks?
2. What are the architectures supported by circuit-switched, dedicated circuit, and packet-switched networks?

SUMMARY

This chapter looked at three subjects relating to network connectivity: wireless networking, remote access, and WANs. You learned that wireless networking is growing rapidly, driven in part by rapidly dropping costs and ease of configuration. Remote access has been part of the network mix since the early days of PC LANs, driven by business access needs. You saw that remote access can be configured as dial-up or Internet VPN connections. WAN connectivity is similar to remote access, with the difference being one of scale. Rather than connecting individual remote clients, you connect remote networks over public carriers. You learned about WAN connection options, including a variety of carrier options.

KEY TERMS

802.11
802.11a
802.11b
802.11g
802.11n
802.16 WiMAX
802.16d Fixed WiMAX
802.16e Mobile WiMAX
Asynchronous Transfer Mode (ATM)
Automatic repeat request (ARQ)
B channel
Bandwidth
Basic rate interface (BRI)
Broadband ISDN (B-ISDN)
Carrier-Sense Multiple Access/Collision Avoidance (CSMA/CA)
Challenge Handshake Authentication Protocol (CHAP)
Channel service unit (CSU)
Circuit-switch network
Clear to send (CTS)
Cloud architecture
Compression Control Protocol (CCP)
D channel
Data service unit (DSU)
Dedicated circuit network
Distributed coordination function (DCF)
EAP–Transport Layer Security (EAP-TLS)
Encryption Control Protocol (ECP)
Extensible Authentication Protocol (EAP)
Frame Relay
Frequency range
Hidden node problem
Integrated Services Digital Network (ISDN)
Internet Authentication Service (IAS)
Internet Protocol Security (IPsec)
IP Control Protocol (IPCP)
ISDN modem
Layer 2 Forwarding (L2F)
Layer 2 Tunneling Protocol (L2TP)
Link Control Protocol (LCP)
MD5–Challenge Handshake Authentication Protocol (MD5-CHAP)
Microsoft Challenge Handshake Authentication Protocol (MS-CHAP)
Microsoft Challenge Handshake Authentication Protocol version 2 (MS-CHAPv2)
Microsoft Point-to-Point Encryption (MPPE)
Mixed mode
Multiplexer
Narrowband ISDN (N-ISDN)
Network control protocol (NCP)
Network terminator (NT-1 or NT-2)
Optical carrier (OC) level
Overlay network

Packet assembly/disassembly device (PAD)

Packet-switched network

Password Authentication Protocol (PAP)

Physical carrier-sense method (PSCM)

Plain old telephone service (POTS)

Point coordination function (PCF)

Point-to-Point Protocol (PPP)

Point-to-Point Protocol over Ethernet (PPPoE)

Point-to-Point Tunneling Protocol (PPTP)

Primary rate interface (PRI)

Public switched telephone network (PSTN)

Quality of service (QoS)

Remote access server (RAS)

Remote Authentication Dial-in User Service (RADIUS)

Request to send (RTS)

Routing and Remote Access Service (RRAS)

Serial Line Internet Protocol (SLIP)

Service profile identifier (SPID)

Shiva Password Authentication Protocol (SPAP)

Switched Multimegabit Data Service (SMDS)

Synchronous Digital Hierarchy (SDH)

Synchronous Optical Network (SONET)

T-carrier circuit

T1

Terminal adapter (TA)

Transport mode

Tunnel mode

Virtual carrier-sense method (VCSM)

WiMAX

Wireless Ethernet

Wireless LAN (WLAN)

X.25

ASSESS YOUR UNDERSTANDING

Go to www.wiley.com/college/ciccarelli to evaluate your knowledge of wireless, remote, and wide area networking.
Measure your learning by comparing pre-test and post-test results.

Summary Questions

1. Which packet-switched connection method supports the highest-bandwidth connections?
   (a) X.25
   (b) Frame Relay
   (c) ATM
   (d) T-carrier service
2. SONET optical carrier levels are measured in multiples of what speed?
   (a) 16Kbps
   (b) 51.84Mbps
   (c) 45Mbps
   (d) 622.08Mbps
3. Standard dial-up remote access connections use which of the following?
   (a) POTS
   (b) X.25
   (c) ISDN
   (d) T1
4. MS-CHAP is the most secure authentication protocol supported for Windows PPP clients. True or false?
5. What is the Wi-Fi standard currently in widest use?
   (a) 802.16e
   (b) 802.11a
   (c) 802.11b
   (d) 802.11g
6. Secure remote access connections can be established over the Internet by using a VPN. True or false?
7. Which protocol is used for Windows client dial-in remote access to a Windows server?
   (a) PPP
   (b) SLIP
   (c) PPTP

(d) L2TP

8. Which PPP subprotocol includes network protocol–specific support protocols that support network protocol configuration?
   (a) LCP
   (b) EAP
   (c) NCP
   (d) CCP
9. By classic definition, a LAN becomes a WAN when connections cross a public carrier. True or false?
10. What is the industry-standard protocol for configuring VPN connections?
   (a) PPTP
   (b) L2TP
   (c) SLIP
   (d) MPPE

Applying This Chapter

1. You are designing a remote access solution for a company. There are three sets of requirements:

▲ Field service personnel need as flexible a connection method as possible that will work from nearly any location; there are five users total.

▲ Telecommuters need a full-time connection to the company network that supports at least 1Mbps; there are three users total.

▲ Researchers need to have high-speed access (at least 2Mbps) when possible but sometimes need to connect from remote locations; there are two users total.

In addition, you need to keep hardware purchases to a minimum. User counts represent current requirements. Field engineers seldom need to be online for more than a few minutes at a time. Telecommuters need nearly full-time access during working hours. Researcher time requirements vary, depending on whether they are gathering information or processing the data.

   (a) For which type of user is dial-up access most appropriate?
   (b) For which type of user is dial-up access least appropriate?
   (c) For which type of user is a VPN over the Internet most appropriate?
   (d) For which type of user is a VPN over the Internet least appropriate?
   (e) When configuring support for field service personnel, what is needed at the client end?

(f) When configuring support for field service personnel, what is needed at the network end?

(g) When configuring support for telecommuters, what is needed at the client end?

(h) When configuring support for telecommuters, what is needed at the network end?

(i) How can you determine the number of modems that will be required at the network end, if any?

2. A company is putting in a second office at a remote location. The office will be set up as part of the same Windows Active Directory domain as the main office. The initial office configuration will include client computers, a domain controller, a DNS server, and file and print servers. A DHCP server in the main office will provide IP configuration information for client computers in the remote office.

   (a) What are the major factors affecting the connection bandwidth requirements?

   (b) What are the requirements to configure a connection between the offices?

   (c) From the standpoint of IP address assignment at the remote office, how would you be able to tell if the link fails?

   (d) How could link failure be avoided?

   (e) You configure the network with a single connection. What are your options for correcting the problem if the connection becomes saturated as the remote office grows?

YOU TRY IT

Building a WAN

You are designing a WAN solution that will connect five offices at various locations in the United States. Reliability and access to data in any location are critical concerns, and a failure at any one location should not prevent other locations from communicating. You want to be able to specify the exact topology used to connect with remote offices, with a determinate path between the offices. The offices need full-time connections.

You estimate the current peak bandwidth requirements as 1Mbps between each office and the other four offices. Requirements can vary from month to month and are the highest at end of quarter and end of year. You want to be able to predict connectivity costs in advance.

1. How well does a circuit-switched solution meet your requirements? (Explain your answer.)
2. How well does a direct circuit solution meet your requirements? (Explain your answer.)
3. How well does a packet-switched solution meet your requirements? (Explain your answer.)
4. What kind of topology would you use? Describe the connection and hardware requirements at each location.
5. The link between two offices fails. Based on your answer to Question 4, how does this affect the network?

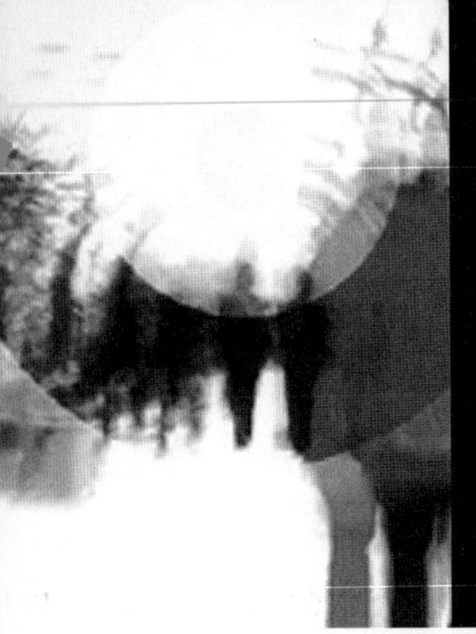

9

NETWORK SERVERS AND SERVICES FUNDAMENTALS

Starting Point

Go to www.wiley.com/college/ciccarelli to assess your knowledge of network servers and services fundamentals.
Determine where you need to concentrate your effort.

What You'll Learn in This Chapter

- ▲ Basic network services
- ▲ Novell NetWare and Open Enterprise
- ▲ Windows Server versions
- ▲ Unix and Linux networks
- ▲ Mac OS X networking
- ▲ Server placement

After Studying This Chapter, You'll Be Able To

- ▲ Identify the role of common network services
- ▲ Compare and contrast Novell networking servers, Windows servers, Unix, Linux, and Mac OS X
- ▲ Describe interoperability issues and how they are resolved by various network operating systems
- ▲ Address issues related to traffic flow and server placement

INTRODUCTION

Network servers are a vital part of any network. A network administrator's primary tasks are network server maintenance and upkeep, and these tasks require an understanding of the role of basic network services. This includes understanding the network operating system (NOS). This chapter will give you an overview of some of the most popular NOS options and compare and contrast their features and functionality. It will also look at some basic design issues and server placement considerations.

9.1 Considering Basic Service Requirements

The primary functionality of a LAN is to enable shared services of different types. Service requirements vary by organization, but we can divide them into some general categories:

- **File and print services:** File and print services, which enable the sharing of files, programs, and printers, are among the most fundamental of services and are found on nearly every network, from the smallest peer-to-peer home network to the largest enterprise.
- **Server applications:** These are specialized applications that are typically present only when there is a specific need.
- **Network support services:** Most of the services included in this category are the background "nuts and bolts" that keep a network running smoothly.

Keep in mind that the details of what services are provided (or even needed) and how they are implemented can vary widely between different NOSs. In this chapter, we're looking at services from a more general standpoint and keeping vendor-specific considerations to a minimum.

Servers are often deployed throughout a network, as shown in Figure 9-1. However, their placement should not be random. You need to consider requirements such as user access, traffic flow patterns, and so forth when deciding on server placement. All network configurations have a maximum bandwidth, and with Ethernet networks, performance degrades and traffic levels (and collisions) increase as more computers are placed on a network.

Another issue that may arise when discussing network servers is their ability to scale. **Scaling** is the process of increasing the resources available to a NOS, a server application, or another resource until it meets your needs. By saying that a product is scalable, manufacturers usually imply two things:

- You don't have to initially buy more than you really need.
- The product can grow as you grow.

Figure 9-1

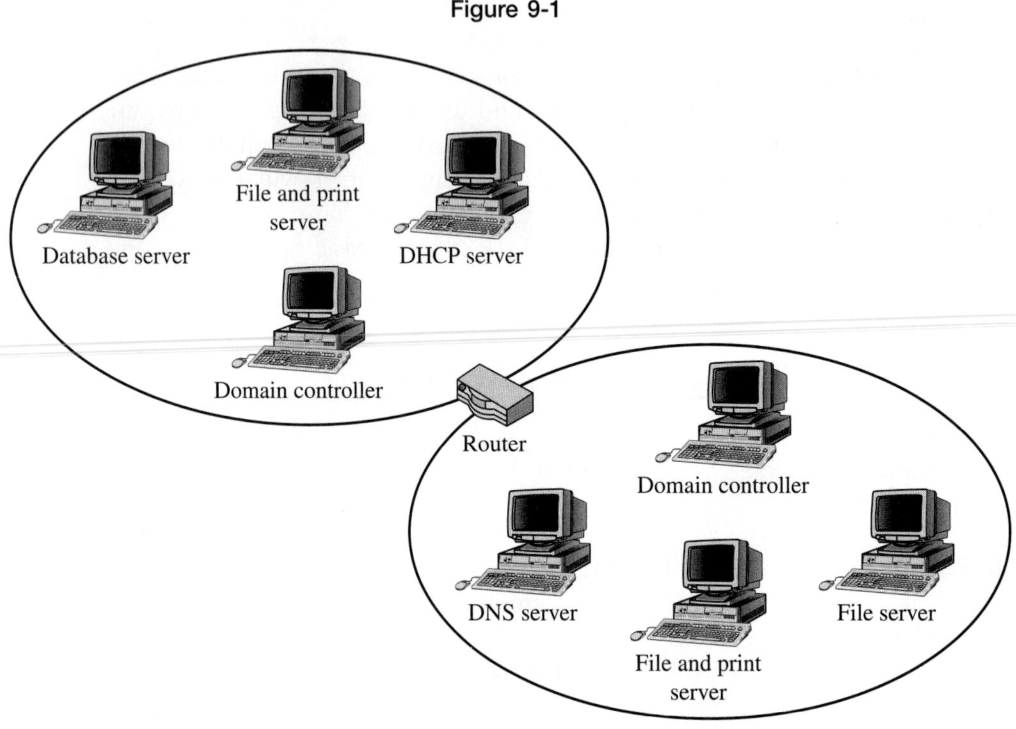

Network servers.

When talking about servers and server applications, you can scale up, out, or both. When you **scale up**, you increase a server's hardware resources. This means adding more disk space, more memory, or maybe a faster (or an additional) processor. When you **scale out**, you add more servers of the same type.

9.1.1 Using File and Print Services

For most organizations, especially in the early days of PC LANs, file and print services were the driving force in justifying a network. Users need to share information for an organization to thrive, so the most common types of network servers are file servers and print servers.

File servers make files and directories (i.e., file folders) available to network users. You can use file servers to share programs and files that users need to access, such as templates and reference files. You can use them to store files for a project or design team. One of the primary reasons for having file servers is to give the users a central location for storing their files and to ensure that the files are backed up regularly. The unfortunate truth is that files stored on a user's own local computers are seldom, if ever, backed up.

Print servers give users access to shared printers. They also let you manage user access so that you can limit access to specialty printers, large-format printers, or other print devices. You can also specify user priorities for printer use (i.e., whose print jobs—documents waiting to print—print first) and which users have permission to manage printers and print jobs. Typically, any user who can print to a printer can manage his or her own print jobs, but only those users given special permissions can manage other users' print jobs. Print job management tasks include suspending or canceling (i.e., deleting) print jobs, changing the order of print jobs in the queue, and so forth. Print devices controlled by a print server can be directly connected to the server or, in some cases, connected directly to the network and managed remotely by the print server.

It is common, especially on small networks, to see a server supporting both file server and print server responsibilities. If this is the case on your network, you need to carefully monitor hard disk use and available disk space. Some print jobs, especially those that include large, complex graphics, can require very large files. These files are temporarily stored in a print spooler or print queue (temporary storage area) on the hard disk and can affect available disk space.

9.1.2 Introducing Server Applications

Server applications are usually deployed on an as-needed basis. The most common server applications are relational database applications and web servers. Web servers can host websites (for public access or for internal use) and **web services**, which are applications that are accessible from the Internet or a local intranet. Web services accept parameters and return values formatted using **Extensible Markup Language (XML)**, a format used for formatting data for transfer. XML has become a standard for data transfers across the Internet. There are also other server applications you might see, such as email servers, servers designed to support group projects and other shared documents, and even team development servers that facilitate team-based software development.

Servers that support public access are sometimes deployed outside a LAN on an isolated perimeter network, as shown in Figure 9-2. A firewall, a network security device that filters network traffic, isolates the perimeter network from the rest of the LAN, acting like a gatekeeper that keeps the outside world out but allows limited interaction with servers deployed on the network. Often, you will have two firewalls, as in Figure 9-2, with one between the perimeter network and the internal LAN and another between the perimeter network and the Internet, so that you can control the traffic between the web server and Internet users.

Most server applications are resource intensive. Often, they have special security and access requirements, and direct access to the servers is often strictly limited. Because of this, the documentation for a server application is likely to recommend that it be configured as the only application running on the server. However, even when this is recommended by the application's manufacturer,

Figure 9-2

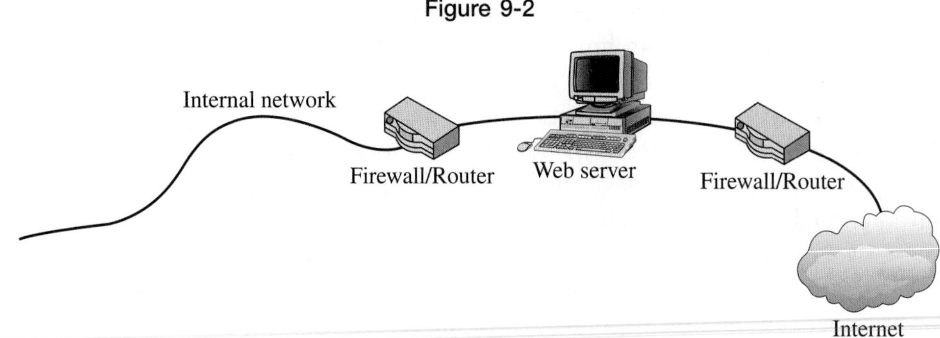

A network with a perimeter network.

network administrators do not always follow these guidelines and may try to run multiple applications on the same server.

Because of the expense involved in both the server hardware and application software, it's common to have only one instance of a particular type of application server that is shared throughout a network. One exception to this is web servers. It's relatively common for companies to deploy multiple public web servers, often all hosting the same content, to improve user access performance and to provide fault tolerance in case one server fails. Other server applications also usually support fault-tolerant configurations, but whether they are deployed depends on how critical the application is to business operations.

9.1.3 Network Support Services

Some network support services are required. Others are optional, depending on the network configuration. This is an area where servers might be called on to perform multiple duties, depending on the specific services they are hosting.

Servers that support network services include as the following:

- Network control and management servers, which run the NOS, handle the control functions for the network, authenticate users, and take care of network background management tasks.
- Specialty authentication and authorization servers, such as RADIUS servers.
- Remote access servers, VPN end points, and software-configured routers.
- Network protocol support servers, such as DNS and DHCP servers.
- Servers that provide shared or public resources.
- NAT and Internet connection sharing servers.
- Specialized gateway devices, such as mainframe computer gateways for mainframe access.

This is by no means a complete list of the types of servers you might see. As with application servers, the types of servers you have depends on your network's specific requirements. For example, if you don't have any remote access requirements, you won't have a remote access server.

FOR EXAMPLE

The Lure of False Economy

Computers have become relatively inexpensive in recent years, at least for typical end-user and home-use systems. High-end computers built to support resource-intensive server applications can still be relatively expensive, depending on the application's specific requirements. Because of this, network designers and administrators are sometimes tempted to deploy application servers as multiuse servers. While this may save some money up front, it's usually not a good idea in the long run.

To begin with, multiuse servers can be difficult to set up and maintain. Most server applications are written with expectations that the application will be the only one running on the server. Such an application assumes that it has unlimited access to all of the server's resources. Convincing the application to share hardware resources usually requires custom configuration at both the operating system and server levels. Typically, none of the applications run at truly optimum capacity.

There may also be other issues that you have to deal with. The applications can have different security requirements or support different levels of access. User access permissions granted to users of one application could allow them to accidentally (or maliciously) delete files for the other application. Recovery can be difficult, if not impossible.

As application requirements evolve over time, upgrading the server to meet the new requirements can be a daunting task. Performance of one or more of the applications might suffer, and you may eventually have to move it to a separate server and migrate any related data and configuration settings. Migration procedures are often complicated and riddled with pitfalls.

SELF-CHECK

1. What types of servers are most commonly found on PC LANs?
2. What is the role of application servers?

9.2 Considering Novell NetWare and Open Enterprise

In this and the following three sections, we'll give you an overview of some of the most popular NOS options, beginning with Novell NetWare, various versions of Windows, **Unix/Linux**, and the Apple Macintosh operating system.

Novell **NetWare**, the first NOS we'll examine, is a powerful, flexible, and full-featured NOS. It is highly scalable, meaning you can grow its capabilities to meet your requirements, and has support for multiple client platforms. It's found on networks ranging from small LANs to large enterprises.

The most recent version of the NetWare product is version 6.5, and it includes workstation management support, Internet connectivity, web proxy, native TCP/IP support, and continued support for its directory service, **Novell Directory Services (NDS)**. Novell has recently migrated its server product to a Linux-based platform that supports the same functionality as NetWare, called **Open Enterprise**, that runs on SUSE Linux. Novell also offers server and desktop Linux products. Open Enterprise is designed to support medium to large business and data centers, which are in effect massive data repositories. It also markets a product called GroupWise that is targeted at the small business market.

9.2.1 Exploring NetWare Features

NetWare was one of the first PC networking products on the market. It was originally modeled on a paradigm based on mainframe computing environments, with a focus on resource access and security. NetWare remains popular, especially in large networks (i.e., those with more than 20 servers) because of features such as centralized administration of all users and their properties. The most important features of current NetWare versions include the following:

- NDS.
- Easy-to-use interface.
- Relatively minimal hardware requirements.
- Scalable hardware support.
- Third-party support.
- Interoperability with many types of computer systems.

NetWare has a strong history as a directory, file, and print server solution, but with its acquisition of many Java technologies (including the Java GUI on the server introduced with NetWare 5), it is starting to encroach on the application server market.

NetWare servers have traditionally run as **dedicated servers**, which means that a computer running the NOS acts only as a network server; it does not provide a "generic" client interface and cannot be used as both a server and a client. Some network administrators prefer this design. Because the server doesn't include an interface for running client applications, there's no temptation to use it in that role, which ultimately makes it more secure.

9.2.2 NetWare Interoperability Support

NetWare is one of the most flexible NOSs and supports a wide range of clients through its client software. Even though some client operating systems include built-in NetWare client support, Novell strongly suggests that you use its client software on the client operating systems you are running to get the most functionality out of NetWare. The NetWare client written by Novell for a particular operating system provides full NDS. Table 9-1 lists the Novell clients that are available for Windows.

Table 9-1: NetWare Client Support

Operating System	*Client*	*Features*
Windows 95/98	Novell Client for Windows 95/98	Fully integrated with Windows 95/98 Explorer. Included with NetWare versions after 4.11.
Windows NT/2000	Novell Client for Windows NT/2000	Replaced graphical login screen with an interface that allows you to simultaneously log in to both NetWare and Windows NT/2000.
Windows XP/2003	Novell Client 4.91 for Windows XP	Enables access to NetWare services from either Windows XP or Windows Server 2003 workstations.
Windows Vista	Novell Client for Windows Vista	Supports both 32- and 64-bit versions of Windows Vista, with many of same features as Novell Client 4.91.

In addition to Windows clients, NetWare supports access for Linux, Unix, Apple Macintosh, and IBM's **OS/400** and **OS/2** operating systems. NetWare servers have the capability to provide client support in some environments by emulating a native server (i.e., a server designed for that environment). For example, on a Mac OS network, a NetWare server can appear to be just another Macintosh server, but in reality it may be a Pentium-class box running NetWare. Some people feel that a NetWare server makes a better server for Macs than Apple's own servers running the AppleShare NOS. NetWare can also emulate **Network File Services (NFS)**, the most commonly used Unix and Linux file service, through its **NFS Gateway** product.

9.2.3 NetWare Service Support

Service support includes support for authentication, file and print services, applications, and security. Many of the features built into NetWare—because of its place as the first NOS designed for business environment requirements—have been used as a model for other NOS products.

Authentication is the process by which users prove they are who they say they are to the NOS. All NetWare versions since version 4.0, including Open Enterprise, use Novell Directory Services (NDS) for resource access control and authentication. Three main types of authentication services are supported:

- **Bindery:** The **bindery** (pronounced with a long *i*) is a simple, flat database of users, groups, and security information that resides on a server. It was used in versions of NetWare prior to version 4, with later versions providing support for backward compatibility.
- **Novell Directory Services (NDS):** A **directory service** is a feature of a NOS that enables users to find network resources. NDS provides access to a global, hierarchical database of network entities (called **objects**). It is available in NetWare version 4 and later. Based on the X.500 Internet directory standard (a standard way of naming network entities), this database (called the Directory with a capital *D*, not to be confused with a DOS directory) is distributed and replicated to all NetWare servers on the network. Each server contains a part of the directory database. In addition, all servers know about one another and the directory information that each contains. The current version of NDS, **eDirectory**, is an extension of the original NDS version. It allows NDS trees to be connected over the Internet, essentially creating a **meta directory**, or a directory of directories.

The bindery contains user information for only the server on which it resides; it is considered to have a **server-centric** design. A user must log in separately to each server to which he or she wants access.

Figure 9-3

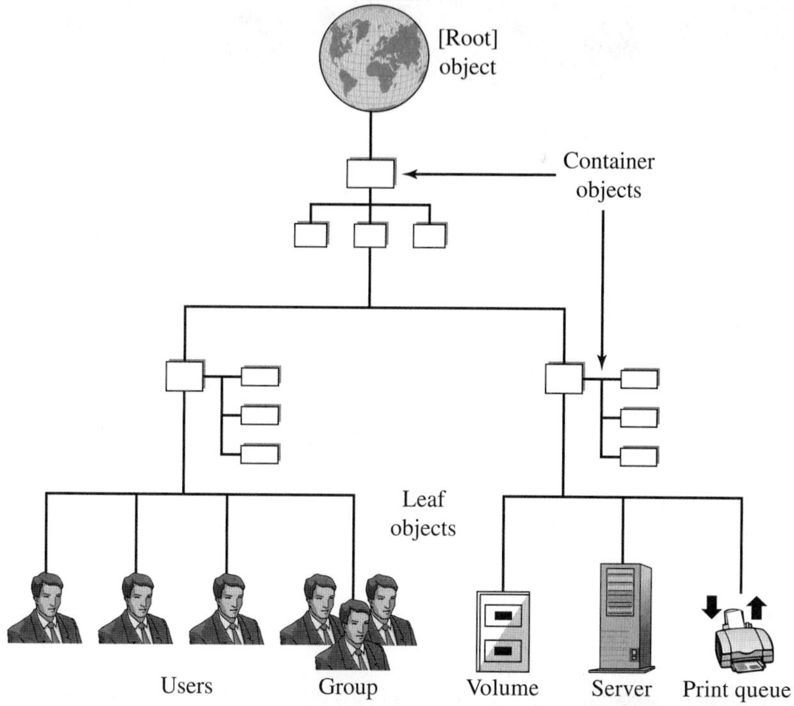

[Root] object

Container objects

Leaf objects

Users Group Volume Server Print queue

A sample NDS tree.

A major advantage of NDS over the bindery is that the entire network is organized into a hierarchical structure, called an **NDS tree**. This tree is a logical representation of a network and includes objects that represent the network's users, servers, printers, and other resources (see Figure 9-3). Because of this structure, NDS is described as a **network-centric** directory service. The user logs in with a single user object and can access resources throughout the directory. This is sometimes referred to as **single sign-in**. Microsoft Windows Server 2000 and later Active Directory networks use a similar directory structure. Unix and Linux servers can also be deployed in a directory structure environment.

A NetWare network administrator uses a program called NetWare Administrator to manage the Directory, and this is the only administrative utility needed to modify NDS objects and their properties. In addition, NetWare includes other specialized utilities for special functions, duplicating part of the NetWare Administrator functionality. Figure 9-4 shows a sample NetWare Administrator screen.

NetWare was the first NOS to provide file and print services for PCs, and some network administrators believe it is still the best. However, application support is one possibly weak area for NetWare, although application support broadened

Figure 9-4

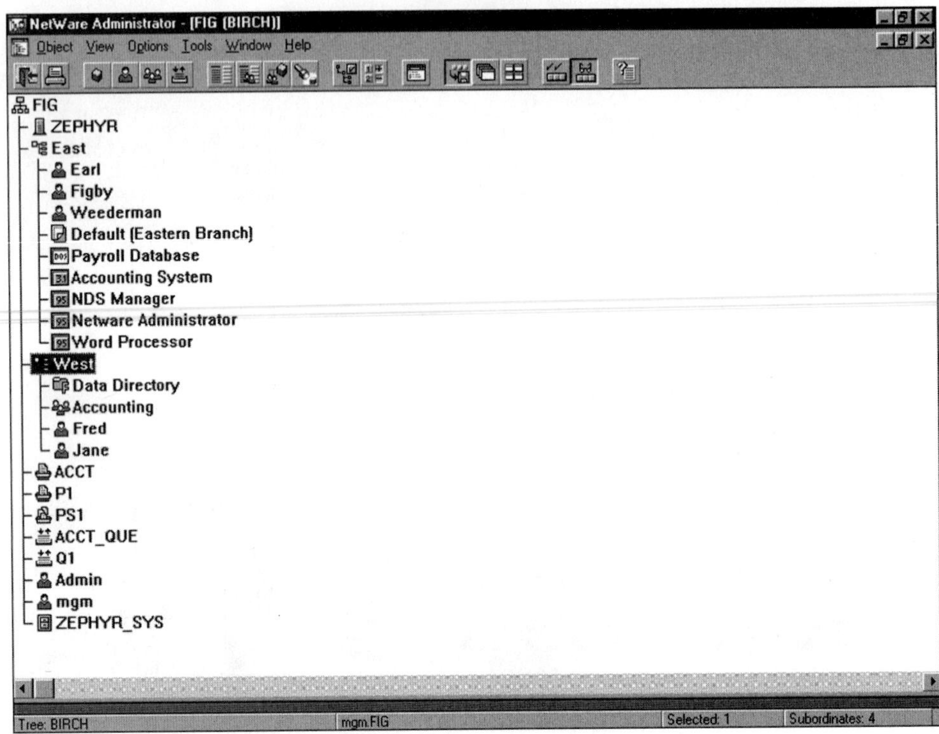

NetWare Administrator.

with the move to a Linux base. With its NetWare, Novell's view is that a server should run only services, not desktop-type applications. To that end, NetWare servers run services very well. A server application designed to run on a NetWare server must run as a service.

Novell has developed and markets some server-level applications, including products designed to simplify network management, messaging and collaboration products, and security management, and it offers sales and support for the MySQL relational database management product. Over the past few years, Novell has increased the suite of third-party applications that work with Novell networking products through a partner program.

NetWare and Open Enterprise are secure NOS products. They use NDS for **back-end authentication**. Clients send authentication requests to NDS, and NDS looks up the user in the Directory and verifies that the attempted login is an appropriate request and that the user information is valid. NDS uses an encryption system during the login process so that passwords are never sent in clear text between client and server. You cannot get access to the files on any file server unless you are logged in with a proper client. NetWare has been certified by the

National Security Agency as C2 Red Book secure, which means it is secure enough for U.S. government use.

When accessing a particular object, you must understand the idea of context. An object's **context** is its exact location within the tree, taking into account all of the containers that it is in. For example, say that a user, Connie, is in the sales organizational unit (OU). An OU is a container object that can hold other

FOR EXAMPLE

Understanding NDS

In order to understand Novell's security model, as well as similar security structures used in other NOSs, you need to know something about NDS and directory-based network structures in general. Because this information generally applies to Windows Active Directory and Unix networking, as well as NetWare, here is a good place to talk about it.

Directories such as Novell's that use the X.500 standard are hierarchical in nature and use a structure called a **directory information tree (DIT)**. In a DIT, the top level of the structure is called the **root**, which leads to the fact that the DIT is commonly referred to as an inverted tree. Making up the structure below the root are intermediate objects and leaf objects.

The Directory is organized through the use of **intermediate objects**. They can be likened to alphabetized subsections of a telephone book (e.g., A, B, C). **Leaf objects** represent resources in the organization (e.g., people, devices, applications, services) and can be likened to names in a telephone book (e.g., Smith, Chang, Moreau).

Each leaf object in the tree has **attributes**, which are properties that define the object. Information stored in an attribute is called a **value**. An example of an attribute in a telephone book is phone number, and the value is the number itself. Objects can have many different attributes.

Each object (depending on its type) can be located only in certain places within the DIT. **Labels** are used to identify object types and thus their possible locations in the tree. Each label is a one- or two-character abbreviation of the object type or of an object attribute. Each object is also graphically represented in the tree. A leaf object's graphical representation varies depending on the type of leaf object (e.g., user, printer, application). Object types, where in the tree an object is allowed to reside, and object attributes follow rules called the **schema**. Table 9-2 describes each of the possible object labels in an NDS tree, the associated object type, and the possible location of the object in the tree.

Table 9-2: Labels, Object Types, and Object Locations

Label	*Object Type*	*Location in the Tree*
C	Country	Below [Root]
O	Organization	Below [Root] or below country objects
OU	Organizational unit	Below organization or organizational unit objects (intermediate grouping object)
CN	Leaf (CN is an abbreviation for Common Name, a leaf object attribute)	Below organization or organizational unit objects

objects, including other OUs. The sales OU is in the Acme organization. The user object Connie would have the following context:

OU=SALES.O=ACME.

Because it has the OU= and O= labels, this name is known as a **typeful context**. This type of name is used when there must be no doubt about the type of container that exists at a particular level. In addition, Connie's **typeful distinguished name** (i.e., the **common name** of an object plus its context) would be as follows:

CN=CONNIE.OU=SALES.O=ACME.

Contexts and names can also be used without their container labels, like so:

SALES.ACME (for a context)
CONNIE.SALES.ACME (for an object's distinguished name)

This is known as a **typeless context** and is used most often because it's easier to type and, for some users, easier to remember.

SELF-CHECK

1. What is a typeful distinguished name?
2. From the standpoint of authentication, what is the difference between a server-centric network and a network-centric network?

9.3 Considering Microsoft Windows

Windows Server 2003, the latest version of Microsoft's NOS, is possibly the most popular NOS in use today. Microsoft introduced its first true NOS, Windows NT, in 1993. Around the same time, Microsoft released a version of its Windows client operating system with built-in peer-to-peer networking, called Windows for Workgroups (WFW). Windows NT went pretty much unnoticed until Windows NT 3.51 was introduced about a year later. Windows NT 3.51 was relatively stable, and by that time, hardware vendors had released computers using 486 and Pentium processors, which significantly improved the operating system's performance.

Because of its similarity to Windows 3.1 and its powerful networking features, Windows NT gained popularity. Microsoft began to put significant marketing muscle behind it, and Windows NT became a viable alternative in the NOS market previously dominated by Novell NetWare and the various flavors of Unix. Windows NT was succeeded by Windows 2000 Server, then Windows Server 2003.

The Windows server platform is the first choice of many developers because of the similarity in programming for all Windows platforms. Microsoft provides several tools and references to support developers for download and as free online references. In addition, all current Windows products have built-in client software and the built-in capacity to operate in a peer-to-peer networking environment. That means you can build a simple network to share files, printers, and other resources without having to deploy Microsoft's Active Directory. The major drawbacks of this, however, are that peer-to-peer networks work well only with a small number of computers involved, and the security management is very limited.

9.3.1 Exploring Windows Features

Although there are subtle differences between the desktop operating systems and their server counterparts, the basic look and feel is the same (see Figure 9-5). Because of this, a novice administrator can easily learn the fundamentals of working with a Windows NOS. Analysts refer to this as a **shallow learning curve**.

Windows as a server platform is designed to work seamlessly with current Windows clients and, with additional client software, most down-level versions. However, it also has integrated support for Macintosh and Unix clients, although some client features are limited.

A feature that is important to network designers and administrators is the level of scalability built into the Windows 2000 Server and Windows Server 2003 product families, which Microsoft refers to as different **editions**. These include one designed specifically for use as a web platform, the Standard Edition

Figure 9-5

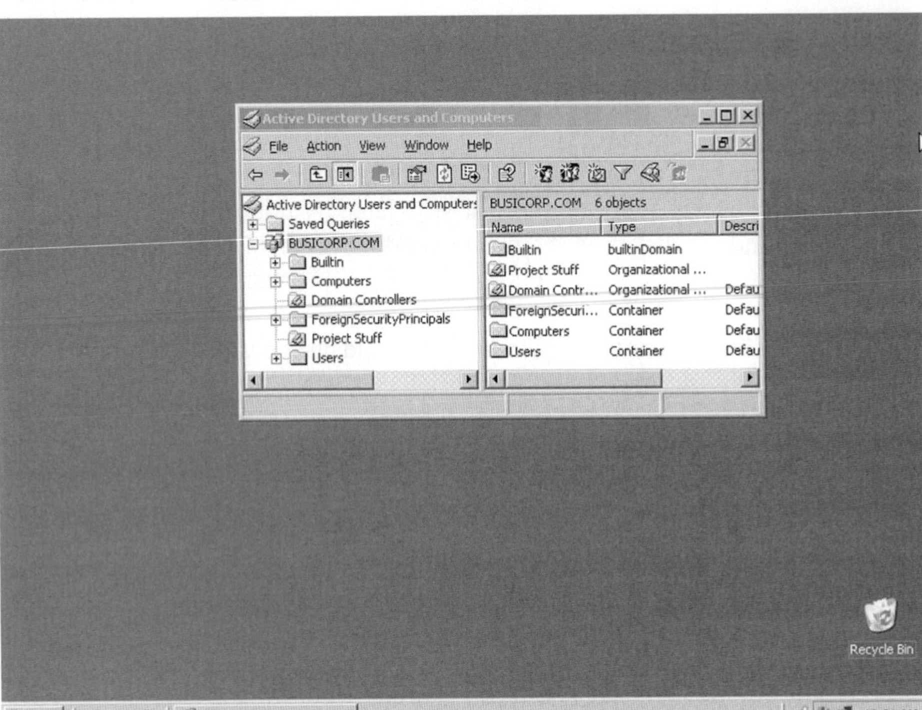

The Windows Server 2003 desktop.

designed for small to medium (and some large) businesses, and the two most scalable editions, Enterprise and Datacenter. The idea is that you need to buy only as much server functionality as you actually need, and you can mix multiple editions on your network as appropriate.

9.3.2 Windows Interoperability Support

Windows Server has many tools for platform interoperability. One is **Windows Services for Unix (SFU)**, which provides a framework for Unix scripts as well as Unix services such as NFS to run on Windows. With SFU, an administrator can port network services and scripts to a Windows Server machine and run them on the Interix subsystem (i.e., a sort of "mini-Unix" part of Windows that comes with SFU).

Windows can interoperate with NetWare. When Windows NT Server was first introduced in 1993, NetWare was the primary NOS available. Three main programs facilitate the integration of Windows and NetWare:

Figure 9-6

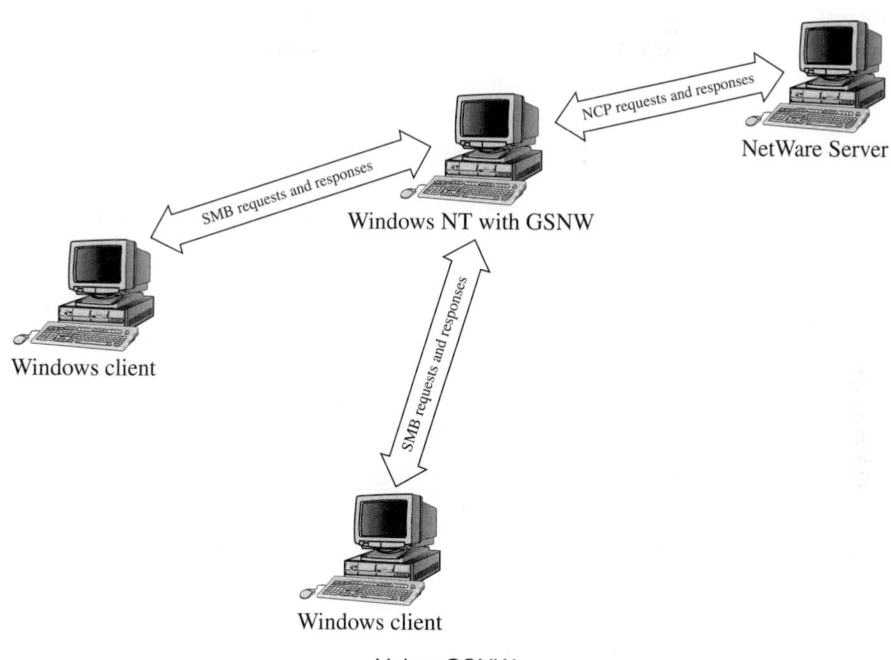

Using GSNW.

- ▲ Gateway Services for NetWare (GSNW).
- ▲ Client Services for NetWare (CSNW).
- ▲ File and Print Services for NetWare (FPNW).

These products are supported on Windows Server 2000 and earlier and are compatible with NetWare version 4 and earlier. They can be used with IPX/SPX (Microsoft NWLink) only, with no support for TCP/IP.

Gateway Services for NetWare (GSNW) installs as a service on a Windows Server machine and translates requests for Windows resources into NetWare requests. At a lower level, GSNW is translating **Server Message Block (SMB)** protocol requests, which support access requests placed for Windows resources, into NetWare Core Protocol (NCP) requests, used to request NetWare resources. GSNW allows multiple Windows NT and Windows 2000 clients to connect through a Windows NT server to NetWare servers using only Windows client software and protocols. Figure 9-6 illustrates this arrangement. Any number of Windows clients can connect to NetWare resources through GSNW and use only one license on the NetWare server being accessed.

Clients Services for NetWare (CSNW) allows clients to directly access NetWare servers, but it must be installed on every Windows workstation computer that needs access to NetWare resources. In addition, all users who want to access NetWare resources need user accounts and rights on the NetWare servers they access.

File and Print Services for NetWare (FPNW) is a service for providing to Novell clients files and printers hosted by Windows Server. When installed and configured on a Windows server, this service makes a Windows server look to Novell clients like a NetWare server.

9.3.3 Windows Service Support

Windows Server 2003 supports a full range of network services. We're going to look at a few key areas for comparison, including authentication, file and print services, application support, and security.

Since Windows 2000 Server and Windows XP, all Windows products have been able to use **Kerberos** for authentication. Kerberos support is also built into clients (and network servers) running Unix and Linux. Authentication also works in conjunction with Microsoft's Active Directory when authenticating Kerberos clients. With Kerberos authentication, a unique identifier known as a **ticket** is given to every user that successfully authenticates to the Active Directory authentication service. From then on, that ticket is sent along with all transmissions to indicate exactly who sent the information.

Because not all Windows clients and legacy servers, specifically Windows 98 and earlier and Windows NT, support Kerberos for authentication, Windows 2000 Server and later also include support for **NT LAN Manager (NTLM)** authentication, a legacy authentication mechanism. If you don't need to support any legacy servers or clients, you can require NTLM version 2 (NTLMv2) instead of NTLM support to improve network security. You cannot completely disable NTLM (or NTLMv2), however, because Kerberos can be used only when authenticating to the **domain controller**. Windows also maintains peer-to-peer support, which requires a version of NTLM.

The directory-based model used by Windows Server versions means that users log in one time to get access to all of a domain's resources. Access security is built around domains, which define the boundaries for security management and are based around a directory structure containing objects that represent network entities and containers used to organize them. You can also define and control security between domains, which means you can build enterprise and extranet security models to meet your specific needs.

Windows Server's file and print services are designed to meet resource-sharing requirements for nearly any network. The major advantage of Windows Server over other server platforms is that it uses the familiar Windows interface and terminology. Windows even supports **caching**, keeping copies of files on the local computer that are updated whenever the client connects to the network. This is especially useful with remote access clients and telecommuters.

Windows Server uses the concept of folders (representing directories) and shares for its file sharing. To make files accessible to network users, the folders in which they are stored are shared to the network, so that they are available to network users. Once a folder is shared, a client can access all the files within it (depending on the security settings, of course) and any folders within it as well. In addition, Windows Server supports the **sharing** of printers in the same manner. When configured correctly, the driver for a printer shared under Windows NT, 2000, XP, or 2003 Server can be automatically installed by the client connecting to the printer.

Windows is arguably the platform with the most developer support. Third-party vendors write thousands of software titles for Windows. Developers can create these programs using the same development tools they use to write Windows client programs. Microsoft makes programming references readily available at no charge. Finally, a program that is certified as Windows Compatible must work on a range of Windows platforms, with various application certification levels supported. Many server applications run as services, giving them more direct access to the operating system and hardware resources, as a way to provide optimum performance.

It's important to note that Microsoft doesn't look at Windows Server 2003 as a stand-alone product but as part of a suite of server products, including database, business productivity, IT management, program development, and security products. They are sold as server applications designed specifically to run on Microsoft's server operating systems and optimized for that environment. They are also designed to interact relatively seamlessly with each other to provide a coherent application environment. Microsoft carries its model of offering different product editions to meet different business needs to its server application products.

Most of the patches Microsoft releases for Windows Server are security patches. Some of the same features that make Windows Server easy to use also make it vulnerable to hacker attacks. However, the most likely reason that Windows has been the target of many attacks (especially Internet attacks) is simply because it is there. Despite its flaws, Windows Server has a full-featured security system. Where the security works, it works relatively well. You have detailed control over security configuration settings and can even configure different security schemes for different groups of users or computers. In an Active Directory network environment, you can use security definition policies, known as **group policy objects (GPOs)**, which are distributed and applied to client computers (and to user accounts) automatically. The current Windows Server version is designed to be secure by default, with unused services disable by default.

FOR EXAMPLE

What About Viruses?

Why do so many hackers spend time developing malicious attacks against Windows? Probably because it's such a big target.

The vast majority of desktop and laptop computers worldwide run some version of Windows, which means attackers can strike a massive number of potential victims at once, with self-propagating attacks more likely to flourish than on other platforms. Unix and Linux are, in many ways, more vulnerable than Windows. However, because of their relatively small population, they haven't been targets in recent years. Similarly, Apple Macintosh OS versions have seen very few attacks. The primary reason for this is the relatively small population, which means an attack would be much less effective and less likely to spread. This situation might change if the number of Linux and Macintosh systems in use continues to grow.

SELF-CHECK

1. What are the roles of the different Windows editions?
2. What kinds of authentication are supported by Windows Server 2003?
3. What is the difference between scaling up and scaling out?

9.4 Considering Unix and Linux

Of the other NOSs available, the various forms of Unix (including Linux) probably have some of the most loyal supporters. *Unix* is the oldest of the NOSs. Early Unix networks had a single Unix server accessed by dumb terminals, not a network made up of intelligent devices.

Bell Labs developed Unix, in part, in 1969. We say "in part" because there are now so many iterations, commonly called flavors, of Unix that it is almost a completely different operating system than it once was. Although the basic architecture of all flavors is the same (32-bit kernel, command-line based, capable of having a graphical interface, as in **X Window** system), the subtle details of each may make one flavor better in a particular situation than another.

Linux, although also sometimes described as a flavor or version of Unix, is actually something different. It is a separate operating system that was written to look and act exactly like Unix, but with a license structure to help it more quickly grow and evolve. Linux versions and variations, commonly referred to as Linux distributions, include the source code so that you can create your own flavor. Throughout this section, statements made about Unix features and functionality also apply to Linux, unless explicitly stated otherwise.

9.4.1 Exploring Unix/Linux Features

Unix flavors incorporate a **kernel**, which constitutes the core of the operating system and can access hardware and communicate with user interfaces. Unix versions are most often identified by their kernel version. The Unix kernel is like the core operating system components of Windows Server and NetWare; it is sometimes also referred to as the operating system kernel.

Unix supports two types of user interfaces: several versions of the command-line interface (know as **shells**) and the graphical interfaces (with *X Window* probably the best-known version).

Linux, whose popularity has grown rapidly in the past several years, was originally developed by Linus Torvalds at the University of Helsinki, Finland. Torvalds started his work in 1991 and released version 1 of the Linux kernel in 1994. Linux is now available in literally hundreds of different downloadable versions, known as **distributions**, all with one common feature: They are licensed using an **open source license**, specifically called the **GNU public license**, which means you can modify a distribution, as long as you include the source code when you redistribute it. The different distributions support different features sets, have different embedded applications, and have different hardware requirements. It's important to check the requirements before starting installation; it is sometimes difficult to recover a computer from a failed installation attempt.

There are Linux distributions that run on a wide variety of platforms, including Reduced (or Rapid) Instruction Set Computing (RISC) processors such as MIPS and Alpha, and the Motorola processor traditionally used in Apple Macintosh. The vast majority of Linux distributions run on Intel processors, simply because that is the most common type of processor in computers worldwide.

Like Unix, Linux comes with network support for TCP/IP. Some distributions also support other protocols. There are hundreds of different distributions that can be downloaded at no charge, but most businesses use one of the commercial versions, such as Caldera's OpenLinux, **SUSE**, or **Red Hat**. Red Hat Linux is one of the most portable versions of Linux, with code that runs natively on Intel, Alpha, and SPARC processors. SUSE was acquired by and is now sold by Novell, and a number of server and office productivity programs have been written specifically for use with SUSE.

Also common are distributions available for free download. There are literally hundreds of distributions available, such as Debian GNU Linux, Fedora (a free distribution based on Red Hat), Gentoo, Mandrake, and Ubuntu. One unique example is KNOPPIX, which runs completely from a CD or DVD, without the need to install it on the system's hard disk. Linux Online (www.linux.org) provides an extensive list of Linux distributions, including sites from which they can be downloaded, as well as sources for Linux applications, custom server appliances, and Linux support.

9.4.2 Unix/Linux Interoperability Support

With Unix, when discussing interoperability, it's important to talk about client support. Unix was originally designed for dumb terminal access and therefore still supports access by any operating system that supports terminal emulation. This includes Windows, which supports terminal emulation through Telnet, included with the TCP/IP suite.

Unix servers use primarily Internet standard protocols, such as TCP/IP, FTP, HTTP, and so on. Therefore, just about any client that can be configured with TCP/IP and a web browser is also a potential client. In addition, major PC operating systems have taken responsibility from their end for ensuring interoperability.

9.4.3 Unix/Linux Service Support

Unix can use multiple methods of authentication, but Unix generally uses Internet standard protocols. Most often, Unix uses **Lightweight Directory Access Protocol (LDAP)** or Kerberos for authentication. There are client versions designed for use with NDS and Active Directory networks as well. Flexibility is one of the reasons for its continued popularity.

Unix file and print services are TCP/IP based. Therefore, protocols such as FTP, NFS, and HTTP are used with standard file sharing. Unix printing uses the **LPD/LPR** protocols to handle the print process and printer management. There is also Unix software available, called **Samba**, that makes Unix appear as a Windows server for file sharing. It uses the standard SMB protocol—the same protocol that Windows networking uses. Samba is freely available on the Internet.

Unix has plenty of application support, mainly because it has been around so long. However, it is important to note that applications are usually made to run on the specific version and flavor of Unix, or at the very least, a specific kernel version, and are not always forward or cross-platform compatible. For example, an application written for Sun Solaris may not run on SCO Unix, even though they are both Unix. However, Unix applications that comply with the **POSIX** standard should run on most Unix and Linux versions with little or no modification.

A large amount of Unix software, most of it identified as Linux software now, is available for free on the Internet. It can be downloaded and installed, but there may not be any technical support available. Also, quality and reliability vary, and authors typically offer no guarantees.

Most Linux distributions include a full suite of productivity applications, such as a word processor, the X Window graphical interface, and source code compilers. Entertainment software, such as media players, video editors, and even games, are also typically included in the mix. In addition, nearly all distributions include a web server and an assortment of web development tools. Most Linux setup programs let you choose which optional applications, if any, to install.

Unix has existed for quite some time, and therefore many of its security issues have been discovered and their causes fixed. Even though new security issues are always popping up, fixes are usually easy to come by. Many users can come up with fixes themselves because the average Unix administrator is extremely well versed in fixing problems.

FOR EXAMPLE

Computing on the Cheap

Psssst. Wanna free computer? Yeah, free. What's the catch? Well...

Computer hardware is cheap. Used computer hardware is dirt cheap. In fact, ask around, and you probably won't have too much trouble finding companies or individuals disposing of old computers when they upgrade—computers you might even get for free. However, without an operating system, a computer is little more than a large, heavy doorstop.

Have you priced operating systems lately? You can pay as much for a full copy of the latest Windows version as you might pay for a low-end computer with Windows already installed. And don't even think about going with a bootleg version. Microsoft has all sorts of protections to turn Windows off if you try to bootleg it, or track the copy back to you—and they do prosecute. Once you have an operating system, you still need applications. There's not much reason to have a computer without applications.

The answer to outfitting a free computer inexpensively is Linux. You can download it free, most distributions come with a full suite of varied applications, and it runs on pretty much any computer you find that can physically run. Laptop, desktop, wired network, or wireless—it doesn't matter. Unless you have some kind of brand-new, super-hot hardware accessories, device drivers are probably also available. Remember, we're talking about free, so you won't have the latest and greatest. If you're just running simple applications, maybe some email and web browsing, an old Pentium II with 64MB RAM would probably meet your needs without too noticeable of a performance lag. Besides, all the cool geeks use Linux. Well, they have it on at least one computer.

SELF-CHECK

1. How is Linux related to Unix?
2. What is a Linux distribution?
3. What is the significance of Linux being distributed under an open source license?

9.5 Considering Apple Macintosh

The Apple Macintosh's biggest problem for the past several years has been one of perception rather than performance. Macintosh (Mac) opponents (read: competitors) relied on embedded prejudices, wondering aloud how any system that easy and fun to use could be taken seriously for business. They also pointed to the larger catalog of business applications available for Windows PCs. They usually did this, of course, without mentioning that many of those applications were developed either by Microsoft or by application programmers working closely with Microsoft.

Some computer professionals who started out with command-line interfaces such as Unix shells were often frightened off by the Mac's graphical user interface (GUI) and the fact that there was no command-line interface available. If you couldn't click it, you couldn't run it. They preferred an operating system where you could dig down and "get your hands dirty" in the system internals. Never mind that these explorations into the operating system often resulted in failure, with the problem worse when they finished than when they started.

The Macintosh interface is considered to be the easiest to use of all GUIs. It was the first computer system to offer a reliable GUI desktop, shown in Figure 9-7. Developed in 1983 by Apple, the Macintosh Operating System (or Mac OS) is seeing a resurgence of popularity with the introduction of several new models and aggressive advertising campaigns with head-to-head comparisons between Macs and PCs.

The Mac has always had a very loyal following, and with good reason. The Mac OS (combined with the Macintosh hardware platform) is a very user-friendly computer, maybe the most user-friendly interface available. Many people who have never used computers before, after comparing Macs with PCs, buy Macs. The Macintosh is especially well suited to multimedia applications and holds its own on office productivity applications.

Perhaps the most revolutionary change in Macs has been Apple's switch from the Motorola processors it had used since the first days of the Mac to an Intel

Figure 9-7

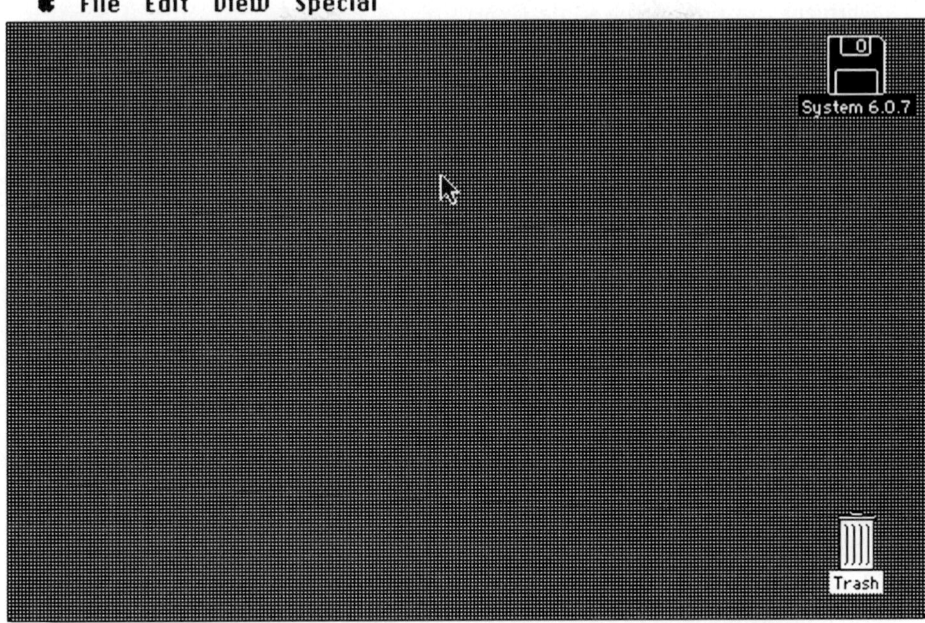

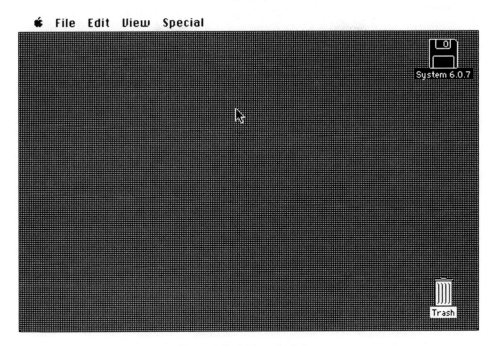

The original Mac desktop.

processor architecture, the one used by Windows PCs. What this means is that you can install both the Mac OS and Windows on the same computer in a **dual boot** configuration, and you can decide at startup whether you want to run Windows or the Mac OS.

9.5.1 Exploring Mac Features

The Mac OS has gone through several major revisions, with each version having many more features than the one before it. Perhaps the best way to understand the Mac is to understand its operating system and the changes it has gone through over the years. The major Mac OS releases include the following:

- **System 1:** When the original Macintosh was released in 1984, the Mac OS interface was pretty bare. **System 1** contained the basic elements of the current Mac OS. It had no support for color, but it had a very powerful GUI that made many people go out and buy it.
- **System 6: System 6** was introduced around 1986 and introduced color to the operating system, displaying thousands or even millions of colors. This was when the PC was still struggling to show 256 colors. System 6

could switch between programs using a product known as Multifinder, but didn't support true **multitasking** (i.e., concurrent applications actively running at the same time).

- **System 7:** Macintosh **System 7** added true multitasking support. In addition, it added support for **TrueType fonts**, which are automatically scalable fonts (and an important part of the current Windows interface), added the ability to share out a disk onto the network, and gave users the ability to use virtual memory, another feature key to the Windows family.
- **System 7 Pro: System 7 Pro**, an improvement on System 7 that included digital signature technology, integrated email, and speech recognition. Apple introduced the keychain, which stored the various online passwords for a user so that only one password was required when a user went online. System 7 Pro was not considered a major release because it couldn't be **happy macked** (i.e., the operating system could not fit on a single floppy disk).
- **Mac OS 8:** 1997 brought a name change to actively promote the Macintosh. System software was now to be known as Mac OS, and this version was called **Mac OS 8.** Also, due to a partnership with Microsoft (and an infusion of capital from the same), Internet Explorer was installed as the default browser. Mac also increased its cross-platform connectivity with the introduction of an updated version of its PC Exchange product, which now had support for Windows 9x long filenames. Finally, Mac OS contained its own **Java Virtual Machine** for running Java applications.
- **Mac OS 9:** With **Mac OS 9**, Apple brought the Mac OS up to speed with Microsoft's multiuser offerings. It was now possible to specify different settings and environments for multiple users of the same Macintosh.
- **Mac OS X (OS 10):** Amid much hoopla, in 2001 Apple introduced **Mac OS X**, the current version and first major rewrite of the Mac OS in years. The basic interface still looks the same; but the use of color, graphics, and moving graphics is much improved over previous versions. Also, Mac OS X is based on a Unix kernel, which makes it more stable, more scalable, and generally more powerful than previous versions. Also, for the first time, you can save directly to **Portable Document Format (PDF)**, a common document format that was developed by Adobe and has since become a de facto standard.

The Mac OS X desktop is shown in Figure 9-8. It is considered a flexible, user-friendly, and Internet-friendly interface. It is also supports a credible NOS version, Mac OS X Server.

As you would expect, Mac OS X Server supports Mac clients, but, with its latest versions, it includes Samba so that Windows clients can authenticate to a

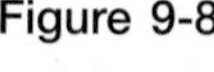

Figure 9-8

The OS X desktop.

Mac OS X Server machine and access server resources. The Samba support isn't immediately apparent because it is implemented at the lower levels of the operating system. Samba support is a function of the Unix kernel on which Mac OS X is based. Windows client support, like other configuration options, is managed through GUI configuration menus. Also, a Mac OS X Server machine can function beautifully as an Internet server due to its Unix-based core kernel and the kernel's close ties with TCP/IP.

9.5.2 Mac Interoperability Support

As a server platform, Mac OS is reliable and fairly scalable. It really can't compete with the largest Unix or high-end Open Enterprise or Windows Server 2003 platforms in the enterprise, but it makes for a good workgroup and web server platform. In that respect, Mac OS is compatible with many different clients.

Mac OS X, like all other current operating systems, supports TCP/IP for network and Internet connectivity. Still, the Mac isn't quite as flexible as a client, requiring the network server to provide a compatible computing environment.

One aid to interoperability is that Microsoft provides a Mac version of its popular Office productivity suite.

9.5.3 Mac Service Support

Authentication for Mac OS X is handled through the Kerberos authentication mechanism, which makes Mac OS X compatible with other popular networking environments. In addition, Mac OS X includes a feature known as the **keychain**, mentioned earlier, which is a storage location for all the passwords you might use on the Internet (e.g., website passwords, FTP passwords) or anywhere else. When a user authenticates to the system, that procedure unlocks the keychain. From then on, any time the user revisits a location that has credentials stored in the keychain, the keychain automatically provides them on behalf of the user.

In addition to Kerberos and the keychain, Mac OS X and newer versions include support for Apple's **Open Directory**. Open Directory is a directory much like Microsoft's Active Directory and Novell's eDirectory. It allows all users to authenticate to a central database of users so a user has to authenticate only once to the directory. From then on, the security settings stored in the directory for that user dictate what parts of the network can be accessed and under what conditions.

In addition to being a client, a Macintosh can be a file and print server, using AppleShare (Apple's proprietary networking software), as well as an Internet server, using various Apple and third-party software. The advantage of having a Macintosh as a server is that it is extremely easy to administer. It is so easy, in fact, that many first-time users have no problems networking Macs and turning them into file (or other) servers. In small companies where there isn't a budget for an IT staff or money for outsourced support, a Mac OS server can be managed by existing staff.

Mac OS X has a unique position as far as application support is concerned. It can run older Mac OS applications as well as those written specifically for Mac OS X. Plus, it can run some Unix and X Window applications, provided that they support the Mac OS kernel.

Many application developers are creating small business suite packages for Mac OS X Server. Mac OS X Server comes with the **Apache web server**, the most popular Unix-based (and possibly most popular overall) web server, and MySQL 4, making for a very powerful open source web platform for developing database-driven websites.

The Mac OS offers reliable security. Mac OS X has local user account security built in as part of the OS. Network security has also been taken into account. Many services that would be susceptible to hacking are turned off by default, making the Mac secure by default right out of the box. In addition, there are many third-party security products (including some that implement Kerberos security) that can make the Mac OS extremely secure over the network.

FOR EXAMPLE

Has the Mac's Time Finally Come?

The Mac has carved out a niche in some business areas. Since its original release, it has been the computer of choice for graphic applications, commercial artists, and publishing firms. Many multimedia developers consider it the only choice for music and video editing because of its inherent strengths and the power multimedia applications available for the Mac.

However, something else has also been going on—a bit of a quiet revolution. Through marketing arrangements and special discounts, Macs have found a place as the recommended (and preferred) computer on many college and university campuses. Why does this make a difference? As these new graduates make their way into the job market with diploma in hand and Mac nestled in briefcase, if they are called on to make any recommendations about computer hardware or software, they're going to recommend the Macintosh. That way, they can integrate a familiar environment into a primarily PC world. The ability of Macs to now run both the Mac OS and Windows via dual booting is likely to accelerate this trend.

SELF-CHECK

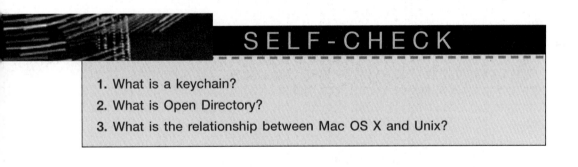

1. What is a keychain?
2. What is Open Directory?
3. What is the relationship between Mac OS X and Unix?

9.6 Implementing Basic Network Services

Okay, you have the pieces and parts, you understand the basic network services available, but how do you put them together? How do you decide which NOS to use? What about client operating systems?

As networks continue to grow larger and more complex, network design and determining server placement can become almost as much an art as a science. A detailed look at network design issues is beyond the scope of this chapter, but while on the subject of NOSs and network services, we'll take the time to discuss a few fundamentals.

9.6.1 Deciding on Network Basics

You've decided that you need a LAN. Maybe you already have a LAN, but you need a better one. Where do you go from here? For our discussion, we're going to work from a few basic assumptions that apply to most networking environments:

- You have a (predominately) wired network.
- Your network is based on a physical star/logical bus topology.
- You have one or more WAPs to support wireless clients.
- You use Ethernet for network access and run TCP/IP as your network protocol.
- You need to access the Internet.
- The majority of your network clients run some version of Windows (though not necessarily the most recent).
- You have, or are considering using, one or more non-Windows computers.

Does this describe all LANs? Of course not, but it does cover the majority. Each LAN is uniquely matched to an organization's specific requirements.

During this discussion about implementing network servers, keep in mind that we are limiting our discussion to LANs only, including routed LANs made up of multiple subnetworks. WANs have additional considerations beyond those discussed here and require you to address issues that are beyond the scope of this chapter.

9.6.2 Thinking About Heterogeneous Networks

A heterogeneous network is one that has a mix of different hardware platforms, client types, and operating systems. In the early days of PC networking, heterogeneous network support could be a nightmare. Nonstandard equipment was common, and different operating systems were not designed to work with each other.

Hardware and system software manufacturers have worked hard in recent years to try to reduce interoperability problems, primarily because it's good for business. Industry standards have been developed that define networking requirements and common network interfaces. Software manufacturers have integrated interoperability into their designs.

Keep in mind what is necessary for computers to communicate with each other. At the most basic level, the requirements include the following:

- A physical connection to the network.
- A common access method.
- A common network protocol.

The unprecedented growth of Ethernet (and Wi-Fi wireless) networks covers the first two requirements. TCP/IP meets the third. However, these only give you a packet-level compatibility. They don't mean that a computer can understand the data inside the packet.

Data compatibility is a software issue. Sometimes, this means services and service clients that are standardized across multiple platforms, such as downloading files from an FTP server. Compatibility is provided across platforms by TCP/IP. Sometimes, it means having the appropriate client software, such as a NetWare client so that you can access files on a NetWare file server or a SQL Server client that lets you access a Microsoft SQL Server database.

9.6.3 Thinking About Traffic Flow

Two of the biggest concerns about a network, and areas about which users are most likely to complain, are performance and reliability. People want a network to work, to be available when they need it, and to get them what they want when they want it. One of the major issues affecting both of these is traffic flow.

With Ethernet networks especially, it keeps coming back to bandwidth, but available bandwidth is an issue in any networking environment. It's more noticeable with Ethernet because you reach a threshold point where collisions become a critical concern and so much time is spent trying to recover that the network grinds to a halt. Token Ring performance also suffers as the number of computers increases, but the change is more gradual; it doesn't become completely overwhelming, and there is a physical limit on how many computers you can put in a ring.

How do you keep collisions at a manageable level? You do it by creating collision zones, network segments where traffic is somewhat isolated to each segment and a limited number of devices are competing for time on the media. You can use routers, bridges, or switches to define collision zones. You can see a simple example of how this works in Figure 9-9, which shows a network that includes two routers and a bridge.

The bridge filters traffic by MAC address. The routers filter traffic by network address. With either, traffic local to the segment attached to the device remains on that segment, and only traffic bound for a different segment is passed. Collisions impact each segment separately, so their impact isn't passed through the device to other network segments.

There is one area where routers provide additional traffic management over that provided by bridges. Bridges propagate broadcasts, packets addressed to all computers, to connected segments. Except for special cases, such as DHCP traffic, routers block broadcasts, which helps minimize overall traffic volume.

Even though these devices help manage traffic, this management comes with a cost. Bridge and router operations come with a certain amount of overhead. Depending on the device capacity and the amount of traffic it has to carry, a bridge or router can become a problem in itself. One way to avoid this problem is careful server placement.

Figure 9-9

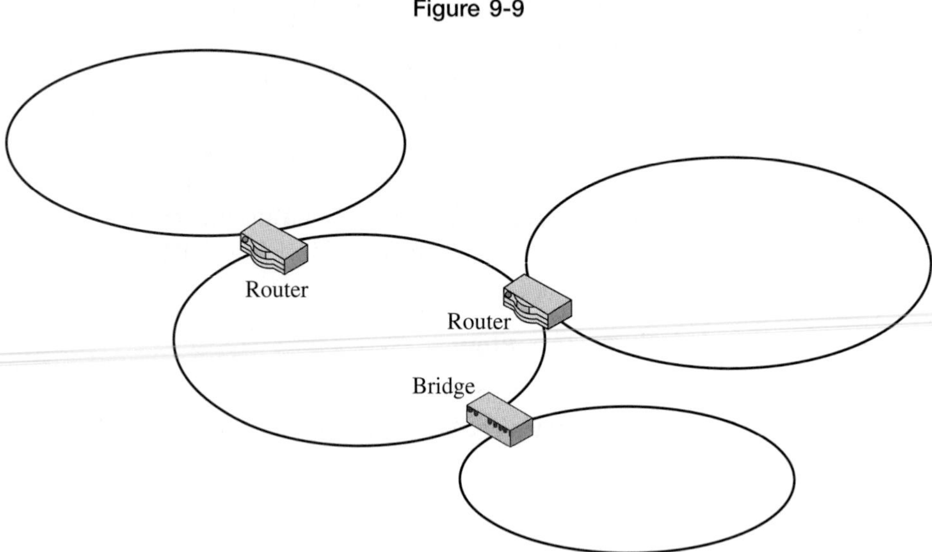

A sample routed/bridged network.

9.6.4 Thinking About Server Placement

One of the determining factors when placing servers in a routed (or bridged) network is how server placement is going to affect network traffic. The general rule of thumb is to place servers so that they are local to the devices that most often need access to them.

Placing File and Print Servers

Guidelines for placing file and print servers can be used as good general guidelines for most other types of servers. We'll look at file servers first. Consider the sample network in Figure 9-10. Accounting sits in one area in the office; sales, marketing, and operations in another; manufacturing and the warehouse in a third; and support and IT in a fourth. You could create subnetworks based on these physical divisions and put all the file servers back physically with support and IT.

The problem with this design is that when any users (other than support and IT) need to access a server, the traffic has to cross at least one router. With accounting, it has to cross two routers, going through either operations or manufacturing. That traffic also increases the amount of traffic through those subnetworks and increases the likelihood that collisions could become a problem.

Figure 9-11 shows a more efficient network design. Departmental file servers are physically placed with the departments that need access to them. By doing this, we're able to keep more of the traffic local to the network, reducing the load on the routers and dropping the bandwidth use on the networks along the way.

Figure 9-10

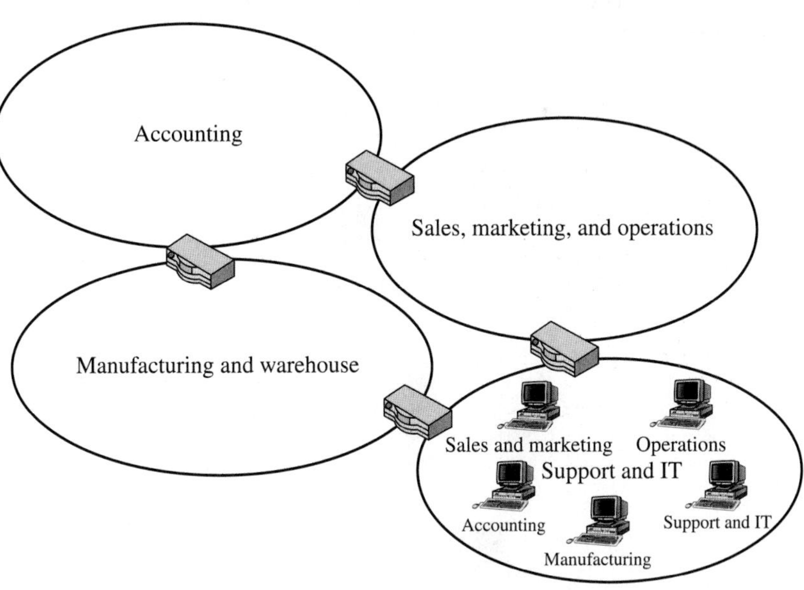

A network with centralized servers.

Figure 9-11

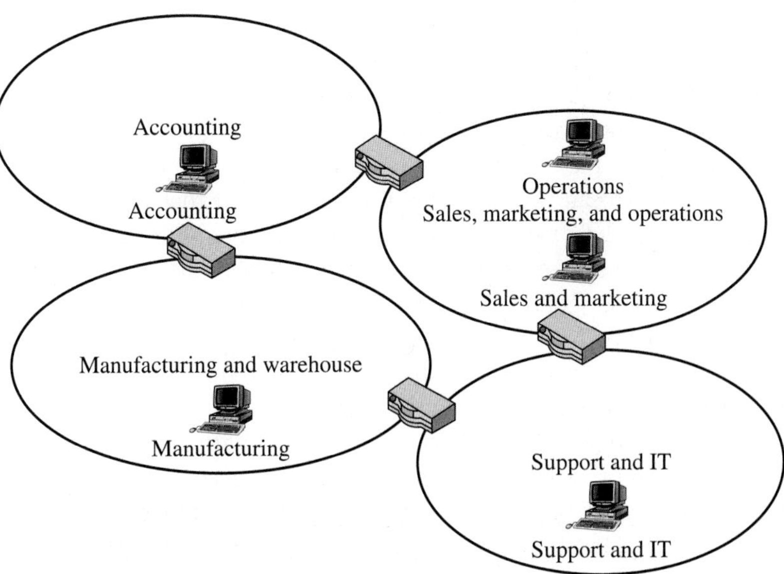

A network with distributed servers.

Figure 9-12

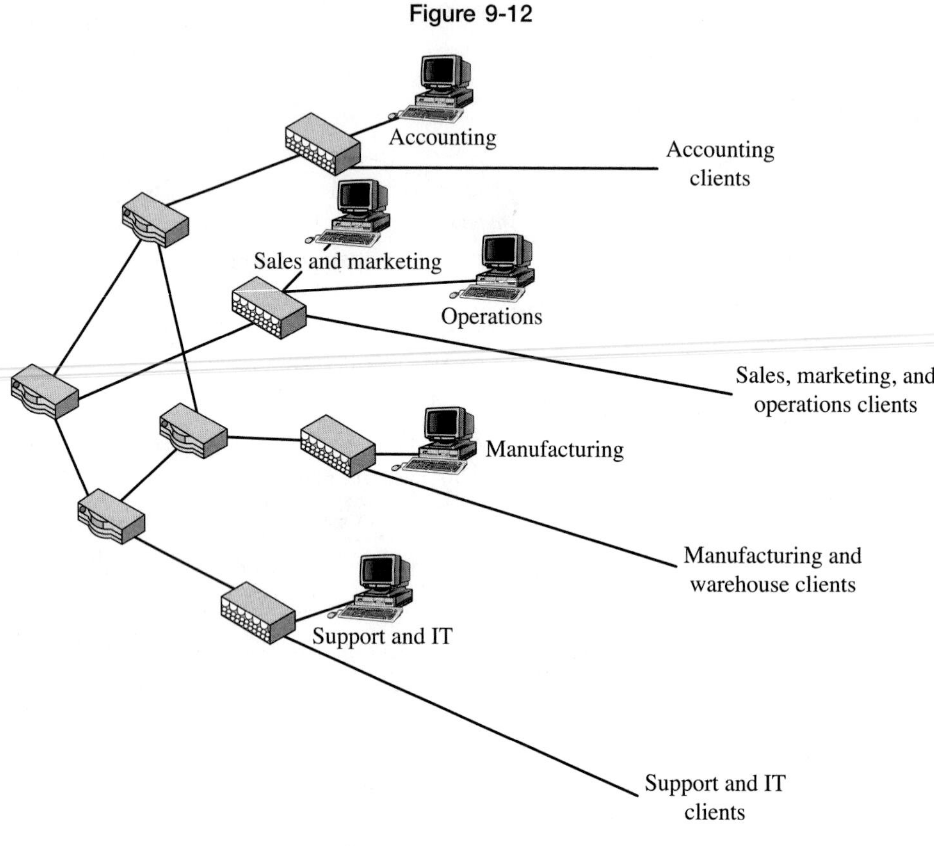

Physical network layout.

Figure 9-12 shows the same network from a logical design standpoint. Just because, for example, the accounting file server is physically part of the accounting subnetwork doesn't mean that it is physically located in that part of the building. What you are more likely to see is a situation like the one in Figure 9-12. Here, the file servers are in a secure server room. The network hubs are physically located the same room. Servers are connected to the appropriate hubs, with lines running out to the network clients. Network routers are also located in the same secure server room, making it easier to wire the network. This also simplifies things should you want to reconfigure your network in the future.

The concerns are similar with print servers as with file servers: It's a good idea to place them local to the users who need to access them. Print jobs can be very large, especially those that include complex graphics.

Along with server placement, you have to consider the placement of network-connected printers that use separate printer servers (some act as their own print servers). With that configuration, you have the traffic from the client to the print server as it queues the print job, then across the network from the print server to the printer when it actually prints.

Placing Domain Controllers/Network Servers

NOS manufacturers generally provide guidelines for how many network servers you need and how they should be placed in common network scenarios. Network servers handle critical tasks such as user authentication and authorization control. It is therefore usually recommended that any network, no matter how small, have two network servers. This provides fault tolerance in case one of the servers fails.

In a routed network, manufacturers typically recommend that you place at least one network server (e.g., an Active Directory domain controller) in each subnetwork. That keeps traffic associated with user login local. Login generates a significant amount of traffic for most NOSs, and when you consider that most users typically log in about the same time each morning, the traffic that generates through the routers could be significant. If the local server gets overwhelmed, login requests could be handled by a server on a different subnetwork, but these would be the exception. This configuration provides fault tolerance, although a failed server will result in an increase in traffic between subnetworks. It also helps ensure that users will be able to log in even if a router is temporarily out of service. Without a local network server, a failed router could prevent users on that network segment from logging in. They might still be able to log in locally to their computers, but they wouldn't have access to network resources, including those on the local network, because there would be no server available to authenticate the access requests.

Placing Support Servers (DHCP, DNS, WINS, etc.)

The number and placement of support servers, such as DHCP servers, name resolution servers, and the like, depend on factors related to the number of clients on each subnetwork, client configurations, and security concerns. DHCP servers and DNS servers are a fact of life on most networks. With WINS servers, it depends on whether you have NetBIOS requirements.

With both DHCP servers and name resolution servers, you typically want to have at least two to provide fault tolerance. A DHCP server can be configured with multiple address scopes and thereby support multiple subnetworks. The routers need to be configured to support **BOOTP forwarding** to ensure that they pass DHCP packets.

As long as the name resolution requirements aren't excessive, the network might be able to get by with one DNS server and one WINS server. One important point is that on networks that connect to the Internet, you want to isolate the DHCP and internal DNS servers from Internet hosts because the more information you expose about your network, the more you invite a potentially successful attack.

Placing Specialty Servers

Specialty servers include shared servers such as email servers and application servers such as database servers. Because of the expenses involved, most small- to medium-sized networks make do with one of each of these server types. On very large LANs, or when supporting a broad base of resource-intensive applications, you may need multiple servers, though not necessarily on different network segments. Take database servers, for example. Some networks have two database servers that host duplicate databases so that, if one of the servers fails, the other one can take over automatically, without users ever realizing that a problem occurred. That said, this is the hardest group for which to apply any general guidelines. Application servers, their capabilities, and their deployment requirements vary widely by their very natures. When provided, you should use any manufacturer guidelines in determining best placement.

9.6.5 Documenting Your Success

Say that you are successful in placing your network servers. What then? You need to recognize that networks are not static environments. The numbers, types, and placement of users changes with time. Network and client operating systems capabilities and requirements change as manufacturers release new versions. Business support needs evolve over time. Network server placement is not a situation in which you can just consider the job done and not worry about it anymore.

When you have your network set up as you want it, you should collect network performance statistics. You should save information such as typical and peak bandwidth usage, including when peaks occur during the day. If you suspect network problems in the future, these **baseline values** give you something against which you can compare current network conditions. It may be necessary to relocate some of your servers or even deploy additional servers. However, after you make any major changes to the network, you need to collect and save another set of baseline statistics.

FOR EXAMPLE

Heterogeneous Application Compatibility

You've configured your Linux server to support Windows clients. Does this guarantee full file compatibility? Not necessarily. We've focused on network compatibility issues so far, but you also have to worry about file formats supported on the local computer.

Let's take a closer look at your Linux server. You deployed it for use as an internal web server to handle intra-office communication needs. The

(continued)

computer has a large hard disk, so you install and configure Samba so you can share directories to the network and use the Linux server as an additional file server. So far, so good.

You deploy the Linux server at your desk. You plan to use it as an additional network client, but you also want have it handy in case there are any problems. A user uploads a Microsoft Word file to the server that contains information you need. Will you be able to read the file?

The correct answer is a strong "it depends." Applications use their own, typically proprietary, internal file formats. That way, in order to read or modify the file, you need the same application or one that supports that file format. In the case of Linux, if you install the right distribution, you're in luck. One of the software packages often included with Linux distributions is an office productivity package (word processor, spreadsheet, etc.) that supports the same file formats as Microsoft Office suite applications. If you have it installed on your computer, you can probably read the file.

SELF-CHECK

1. What is the rule of thumb for server placement in a routed LAN?
2. How do bridges and routers filter traffic?

SUMMARY

This chapter looked at issues related to network servers. It started with an introduction to basic server types and their use. You were then introduced to the NOSs in most common use at this time, including Novell offerings, Windows server versions and editions, Unix, Linux, and Apple Macintosh. You compared them by looking at key features and functionality supported by each. The chapter also discussed basic issues related to the role of server placement in LAN design.

KEY TERMS

Apache web server
Attribute
Authentication
Back-end authentication
Baseline values
Bindery
BOOTP forwarding
Caching
Client Services for NetWare (CSNW)

Common name
Context
Dedicated server
Directory information tree (DIT)
Directory service
Distribution
Domain controller
Dual boot
eDirectory
Edition
Extensible Markup Language (XML)
File and Print Services for NetWare (FPNW)
Gateway Services for NetWare (GSNW)
GNU public license
Group policy object (GPO)
Happy macked
Intermediate object
Java Virtual Machine
Kerberos
Kernel
Keychain
Label
Leaf object
Lightweight Directory Access Protocol (LDAP)
Linux
LPD/LPR
Mac OS 8
Mac OS 9
Mac OS X
Meta directory
Multitasking
NDS tree
NetWare
Network-centric
Network File Services (NFS)
NFS Gateway
Novell Directory Services (NDS)
NT LAN Manager (NTLM)
Object
Open Directory
Open Enterprise
Open source license
OS/2
OS/400
Portable Document Format (PDF)
POSIX
Red Hat
Root
Samba
Scale out
Scale up
Scaling
Schema
Server application
Server-centric
Server Message Block (SMB)
Shallow learning curve
Sharing
Shell
Single sign-in
SUSE
System 1
System 6
System 7
System 7 Pro

Ticket
TrueType fonts
Typeful context
Typeful distinguished name
Typeless context
Unix
Value
Web services
Windows Services for Unix (SFU)
X Window

ASSESS YOUR UNDERSTANDING

Go to www.wiley.com/college/ciccarelli to evaluate your knowledge of network servers and services fundamentals.
Measure your learning by comparing pre-test and post-test results.

Summary Questions

1. Tickets are used with which authentication method?
   (a) Kerberos
   (b) LDAP
   (c) NTLM
   (d) DHCP
2. Which of the following runs as a dedicated server only?
   (a) Unix
   (b) Windows 2000 Server
   (c) Windows Server 2003
   (d) NetWare 6.5
3. The core components of the Unix operating system are referred to as what?
   (a) Samba
   (b) kernel
   (c) Directory
   (d) source
4. Which of the following is an example of an application that could be deployed as a server application?
   (a) a word processor
   (b) a spreadsheet
   (c) a relational database management system
   (d) a media player
5. With which operating system version did the Macintosh OS move to a Unix kernel base?
   (a) System 6
   (b) System 7
   (c) Mac OS 8
   (d) Mac OS X
6. Macs that are built on an Intel processor architecture can run both Mac OS and Windows. True or false?

7. In most cases, an application server should be configured as the only application running on a server. True or false?
8. Which Windows server application gives Windows clients access to NetWare 4 server resources?
   (a) SFU
   (b) GSNW
   (c) CSNW
   (d) FPNW
9. OPERATIONS.BUSICORP is an example of what?
   (a) a typeless context
   (b) a common object name
   (c) a typeful context
   (d) a typeful distinguished name
10. Which statement is true of Linux but not Unix?
    (a) It supports both command-line and GUI interfaces.
    (b) It is distributed under an open source license.
    (c) It can use POSIX-compliant applications.
    (d) It supports LDAP and Kerberos for authentication.
11. Which of the following provides the functionality that lets a Mac OS X server provide shared file resources to Windows clients?
    (a) NFS
    (b) SFU
    (c) Samba
    (d) LDAP
12. Which server type would you most likely allow direct access to the Internet?
    (a) DHCP server
    (b) WINS server
    (c) Active Directory domain controller
    (d) web server

Applying This Chapter

1. You are updating a LAN and need to identify NOS requirements. The network currently has three Novell NetWare 3.2 servers. You have Windows clients that access the NetWare servers through a Windows 2000 Server running GSNW. You plan to replace the NetWare servers with new servers, eventually removing the NetWare servers from the network.

(a) What type of authentication is used between the Windows 2000 Server and the NetWare servers?

(b) What network-centric directory structure, if any, is currently being used?

(c) If you replace the NetWare servers with NetWare 6.5 servers, how would this impact the configuration for client access? Explain your answer.

2. You have a Windows Server 2003 Active Directory network. You are planning to make some changes to the network and the services it offers. The network is currently configured as a single LAN with two domain controllers, one DHCP server, three files servers, and a Microsoft SQL Server database server. You also have two web servers running Windows 2000 Server on a perimeter network that is separated from the main network by a Linux server configured as a router and firewall (see Figure 9-13). Most network clients are running Windows XP Professional, but some are running Mac OS X. You plan to deploy a Mac OS X server that will be used to store digital video development projects and commercial artwork. Collisions are becoming a problem, and you plan to divide the LAN into two subnetworks connected by a router. You are configuring a Linux computer to act as the router for the networks.

(a) What can you do to give PC users access to files on the Mac OS X server?

(b) What network protocol changes will you have to make to current network systems?

(c) After you subdivide the network, how many additional domain controllers will you be required to deploy, if any?

Figure 9-13

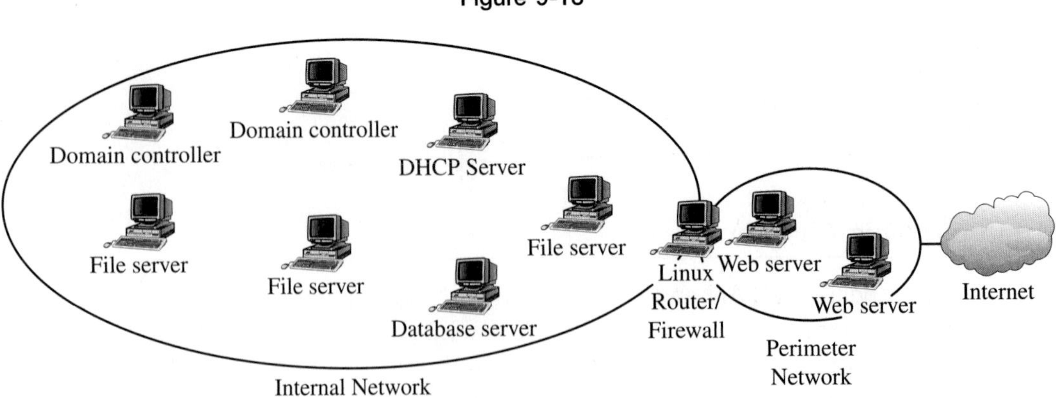

A sample network.

(d) Where should you place the domain controllers?

(e) How will the placement of the domain controllers affect traffic through the router?

(f) What is the minimum number of DHCP servers needed in the new configuration?

(g) How will DHCP server configurations change after you deploy the router, assuming that there are DHCP clients on both subnetworks?

(h) What special router configuration will be needed?

(i) The Linux server includes the software needed to configure it as an IP router. What additional special software would be required to support Windows and Mac OS X clients?

(j) What configuration changes would be needed on the clients?

(k) File sizes on the Mac OS X server will be very large. You want to minimize their impact on traffic through the router. How should you do this?

(l) What effect would the configuration changes have on the web servers?

YOU TRY IT

Network Design

You are designing a routed LAN that will have four subnetworks. The network will be configured as a Windows Active Directory domain. Most clients will receive their IP configuration information from DHCP servers. Clients will include a mix of computers running Windows XP, Windows 95, Mac OS X, and various Linux distributions.

One of your design goals is to keep the traffic through the routers to a minimum. Also, the network should be configured so that the clients will be able to reach any subnetwork, even if one of the routers fails. Your current plans do not include any wireless client support requirements. You are expected to minimize unnecessary costs.

Because of file and security requirements, you estimate that you will need at least three file servers. You plan to configure Windows XP clients as print servers, as needed. You will have an internal web server and a MySQL database server, both running on Linux computers.

1. Describe how you will configure network protocols up through the Network layer of the OSI model. Justify your choices.
2. In general, how will you determine the best placement for the file servers?
3. Describe how you will configure and deploy domain controllers and support for automatic IP address configuration, keeping the design requirements in mind.
4. The MySQL database server's primary role is providing content for the internal web server. How will you determine the best place to deploy these servers?
5. Your purchasing department got a great deal on 20 low-end desktop computers. The computers will come without an operating system. The users who will get these computers need basic office productivity applications and access to the internal web server. What is the least expensive way to meet these requirements?
6. Describe your network, including router placement and domain controller placement. Explain how the design meets configuration requirements.

10

WIDE AREA AND ENTERPRISE NETWORKING SERVICES

Starting Point

Go to www.wiley.com/college/ciccarelli to assess your knowledge of wide area and enterprise networking services.
Determine where you need to concentrate your effort.

What You'll Learn in This Chapter

- ▲ Internet architecture
- ▲ Internet technologies
- ▲ Needs analysis
- ▲ Technical design
- ▲ Cost assessment
- ▲ Network deployment

After Studying This Chapter, You'll Be Able To

- ▲ Explain the Internet's hierarchical architecture
- ▲ Identify Internet technologies commonly found on PC networks
- ▲ Compare and contrast traditional and building-block network design processes
- ▲ Identify critical tasks performed during needs analysis
- ▲ Explain the purpose and expected result of technical design
- ▲ Compare options for implementing a network design

INTRODUCTION

The larger and more complex a network, the more important it is that you spend the necessary time and effort in developing a network design before implementing the network. With small LANs, you can sometimes get away with just letting the network grow and evolve as your requirements change. With a large enterprise, you need to carefully consider all aspects of the network.

This chapter looks at WAN servers and services, as well as other WAN components, from the context of network design. Having a thorough understanding of the network design process will help you understand how to address issues such as service requirements and server placement.

The chapter starts with a discussion of the largest WAN in current use, the Internet, including a look at the Internet's hierarchical architecture and Internet technologies commonly found on PC networks. From there, the discussion moves on to the design process, including expected deliverables at the end of each phase. The chapter ends by talking a little about network implementation issues.

In general, for the purpose of this chapter, any discussions about LAN technologies and requirements include the backbone network (BN), if any. Also, any discussions of MAN connectivity are lumped together with WAN connectivity; for the purposes of this chapter, the two are effectively the same.

10.1 Looking to the Internet

Why start a discussion about enterprise wide area networking with a look at the Internet? The Internet is the world's largest, most complex WAN. Any WAN you design and deploy will have some features in common with the Internet. Also, almost any WAN you might see includes Internet technologies.

The Internet is a network of networks—a set of separate and distinct networks operated by various agencies and organizations. The Internet exists only to the extent that these thousands of separate networks agree to use Internet protocols and to exchange data packets with one another.

10.1.1 Introducing Internet Architecture

Why do you care about the Internet's architecture or about its capacity? In the past few years, the Internet has rapidly replaced traditional WAN infrastructure designs, becoming the backbone of choice. If you're using, or even considering, the Internet as your corporate backbone, you need to know how it works.

The Internet is hierarchical in structure. At the top are the very large national ISPs, such as AT&T and Sprint, which are responsible for large Internet networks. These **national ISPs** connect together and exchange data at **network access points (NAPs)**, as shown in Figure 10-1.

Figure 10-1

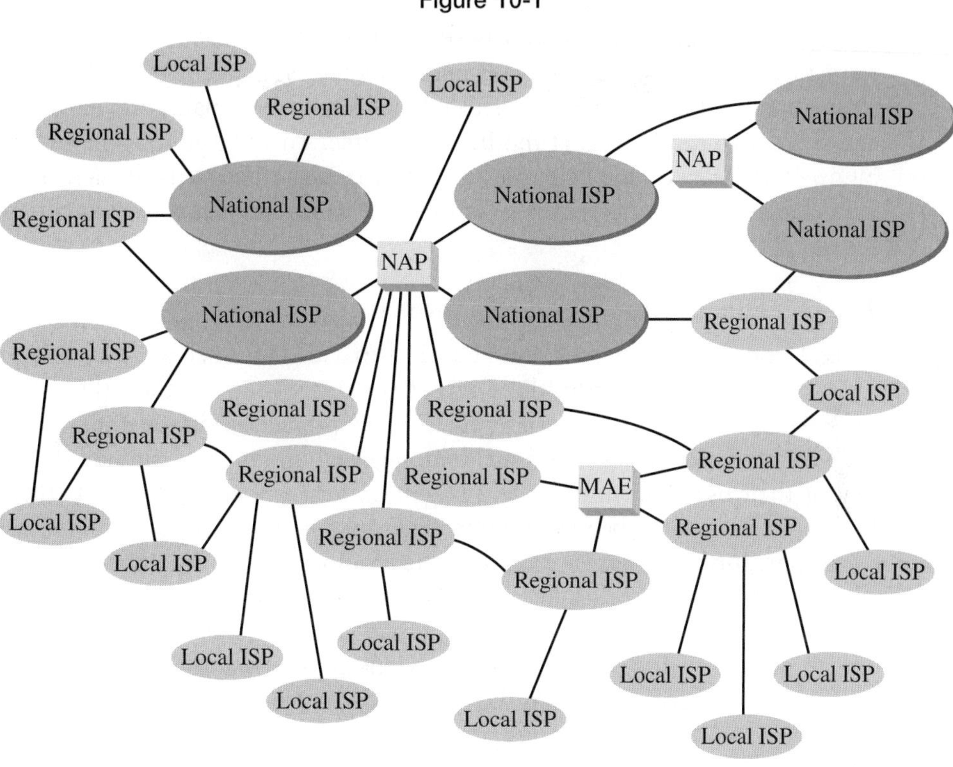

Internet hierarchy.

In the early 1990s, when the Internet was still primarily run by the **National Science Foundation (NSF)**, the NSF established four main NAPs in the United States to connect the major national ISPs. This has since grown to about a dozen NAPs in the United States, with many more spread elsewhere around the world. When the NSF stopped funding the Internet, the companies running these NAPs began charging the national ISPs for connections, so today the NAPs in the United States are all commercial enterprises run by various common carriers, such as Ameritech and Sprint.

National ISPs provide services for their customers and to **regional ISPs**, such as BellSouth and EarthLink. These regional ISPs rely on the national ISPs to transmit their messages to national ISPs in other countries. Regional ISPs provide services to their customers and to local ISPs, which sell Internet access to individuals. As the number of ISPs grew, a new form of NAP, called a **metropolitan area exchange (MAE)**, emerged. MAEs are smaller versions of NAPs and typically link a set of regional ISPs whose networks come together in major cities. Today there are about 50 MAEs in the United States.

In general, ISPs at the same level do not charge one another for transferring messages they exchange across a NAP or MAE. That is, a national ISP does not charge another national ISP to transmit its messages, and a regional ISP does not charge another regional ISP. This is called **peering**, which makes the Internet work and has led to the belief that the Internet is free. This is true to some extent, but higher-level ISPs normally charge lower-level ISPs to transmit their data, and local ISPs charge individuals for access. Also, most NAPs now charge national ISPs for access.

10.1.2 Understanding Today's Internet

Several years ago, there was great concern that the Internet would reach capacity. The growth of traffic on the Internet was increasing significantly faster than the construction of new Internet circuits. This prediction didn't come true, however, because companies could make money by building new circuits and charging for their use. Today, there are a large number of fiber-optic circuits that have been built but not yet been turned on; they are being held in reserve until needed to support further Internet expansion. Technological advances have also helped, such as new optical technologies that mean 10 to 20 times more data can now be transmitted through fiber-optic cable than before. Many countries, companies, and universities are now building the **Next-Generation Internet (NGI)**, using even newer, experimental, very high-speed technologies.

Today, the backbone circuits of the major U.S. national ISPs operate at ATM OC-48, or 4 gigabits per second (4Gbps), and OC-192 (10Gbps). A few are experimenting with OC-768 (80Gbps), and several are in the planning stages with OC-3072 (160Gbps). This is important because Internet traffic in the United States is expected to grow to a peak of 40Tbps (40 trillion bits per second) by sometime in 2007.

As traffic increases, ISPs can add more and faster circuits relatively easily, but where these circuits come together at NAPs and MAEs, bottlenecks are becoming increasingly common. Network vendors such as Cisco and Juniper are making larger and larger switches capable of handling these high-capacity circuits, but it is a daunting task. When circuit capacities increase by 100 percent, switch manufacturers also must increase their capacities by 100 percent.

10.1.3 Connecting WANs Through the Internet

If your Internet experience were limited to dial-up home connections, you would be justified in wondering why, or even how, companies would want to connect to each other through the Internet. At the most basic level, companies connect their networks to the Internet the same way you do, through an ISP. Larger companies might connect through a regional or even national ISP so that they can connect directly into a high-speed backbone circuit, but some larger local ISPs can also provide this service. Small- to medium-sized companies are probably using the same local ISPs that you use.

Figure 10-2

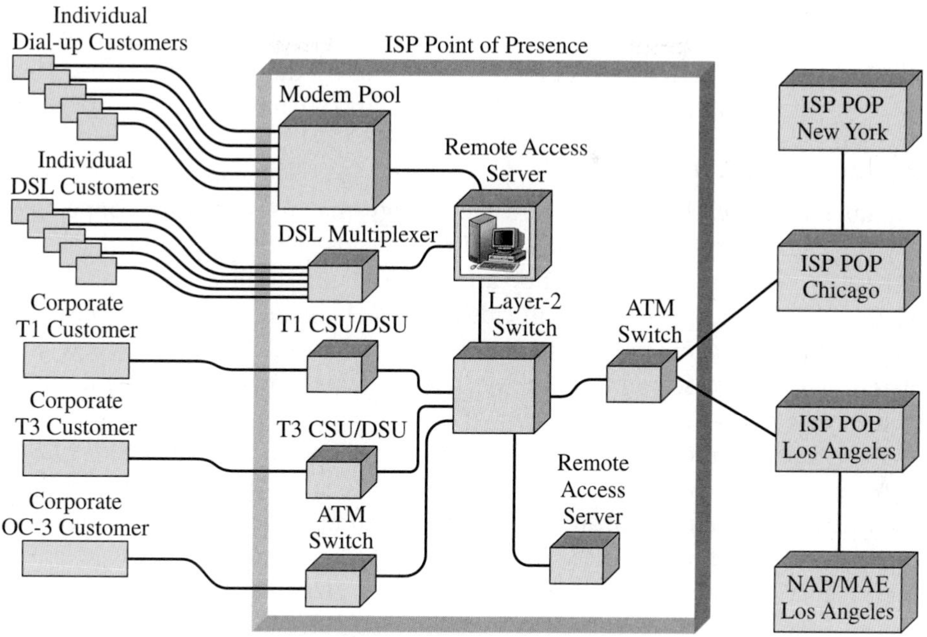

ISP POPs. Inside an Internet service provider (ISP) point of presence (POP). ATM = asynchronous transfer mode; CSU = channel service unit; DSU = data service unit; MAE = metropolitan area exhange; NAP = netweork access point.

Multiple connections can be made because each ISP has one or more **points of presence (POP)**. A POP (not to be confused with POP3, which is a TCP/IP email protocol) is simply the place at which an ISP provides services to its customers. To connect to the Internet, a customer must establish a circuit from his or her location (e.g., home, business) to the ISP POP. For individuals, the connection is through a remote access server, which checks the user ID and password to make sure the user is a valid customer. Once logged in, the user can begin sending TCP/IP packets from his or her computer to the POP. Figure 10-2 shows a POP using a collapsed backbone network (BN) with a layer 2 switch.

So, how do businesses connect? In the early days of using the Internet as a backbone, companies' options were somewhat limited and often prohibitively expensive. One of the most common options was leasing T1 or T3 circuits into the ISP. This has changed as communication technologies have improved and additional options have become available. Some of the most commonly used connection options now include the following:

- Digital subscriber line (DSL).
- Cable modem.
- Fixed wireless.

Some of these technologies should sound familiar. They're the same technologies used to provide high-speed home Internet access. Keep in mind that many companies continue to use traditional WAN link technologies, such as point-to-point T1, ATM, and X.25 circuits, but using the Internet as a backbone is, at least for now, the preferred technology.

Digital Subscriber Line (DSL)

Digital subscriber line (DSL) is a technology that uses existing copper telephone lines to carry digital signals at higher speeds. The biggest drawback with respect to DSL services is that they are not available in all locations and, even where available, connection bandwidth varies. In general, DSL services have advanced more quickly in Canada, Europe, Australia, and Asia than in the United States, owing to those countries' newer telephone networks from the end offices to the customer.

The most common type of DSL in use today is **asymmetrical DSL (ADSL)**. ADSL creates three separate channels over one **local loop circuit**, the connection between the customer and the telephone company's switching center. One channel is the traditional voice telephone circuit. A second channel is a relatively high-speed simplex data channel **downstream circuit** from the carrier's end office to the customer. The third channel is a slightly slower duplex data channel primarily used as an **upstream circuit** from the customer to the carrier's end office. ADSL is called *asymmetrical* because its two data channels have different speeds.

The size of the two digital channels depends on the distance from the **customer premises equipment (CPE)**—the term used to refer to the customer's physical geographic location—to the end office. The shorter the distance, the higher the speed because with a shorter distance, the circuit suffers less attenuation, and higher-frequency signals can be used, providing greater bandwidth. Table 10-1 lists the common types of ADSL.

Table 10-1: ADSL Bandwidths

Type	*Maximum Length of Local Loop*	*Maximum Downstream Rate*	*Maximum Upstream Rate*
ADSL T1 (G.Lite)	18,000 feet	1.5Mbps	384Kbps
ADSL E1*	16,000 feet	2.0Mbps	384Kbps
ADSL T2	12,000 feet	6.0Mbps	640Kbps
SDSL	18,000 feet	1.5Mbps	1.5Mbps

*E1 is the European standard service, similar to T1 services in North America.

Table 10-2: VDSL Types

Type	*Maximum Length of Local Loop*	*Maximum Downstream Rate*	*Maximum Upstream Rate*
1/4 OC-1	4,500 feet	13Mbps	1.6Mbps
1/2 OC-1	4,000 feet	26Mbps	2.3Mbps
OC-1	4,000 feet	52Mbps	16Mbps

A second common type of DSL is **very-high-data-rate DSL (VDSL)**. VDSL is an ADSL service designed for use over very short local loops of at most 4,500 feet, with 1,000 feet being more typical. It also provides three channels: the normal analog voice channel, an upstream digital channel, and a downstream digital channel. Table 10-2 lists the types of VDSL many industry experts anticipate will become common.

One problem is that VDSL has not yet been standardized, and five separate standards groups are working on different VDSL standards. Therefore, the exact data speeds and channels are likely to change as manufacturers, telephone companies, and the industry in general gain more experience and as the standards groups attempt to merge competing standards. Several companies are also developing symmetrical versions of VDSL in which the upstream and downstream channels have the same capacity.

Cable Modem

One alternative to DSL is cable modem access, a digital service offered by cable television companies. There are several competing standards for cable modems; the **Data over Cable Service Interface Specification (DOCSIS)** standard is the dominant one. DOCSIS is not a formal standard but is the one used by most vendors of **hybrid fiber coax (HFC)** networks (i.e., cable networks that use both fiber-optic and coaxial cable). As with DSL, these technologies are changing rapidly.

Cable modem architecture is very similar to DSL—with one very important difference. Whereas DSL is a point-to-point technology, cable modems use **shared multipoint circuits**, as shown in Figure 10-3. With cable modems, each user must compete with other users for the available capacity. Furthermore, because the cable circuit is a multipoint circuit, all messages on the circuit go to all computers on the circuit. If your neighbors were hackers, they could modify their software to read all messages that travel over the cable, including yours. When using a cable modem, the connection to the ISP POP is made by the cable company for you.

There are few widely used standards in the cable modem industry because, unlike the telephone system, each cable TV company was able to build very

Figure 10-3

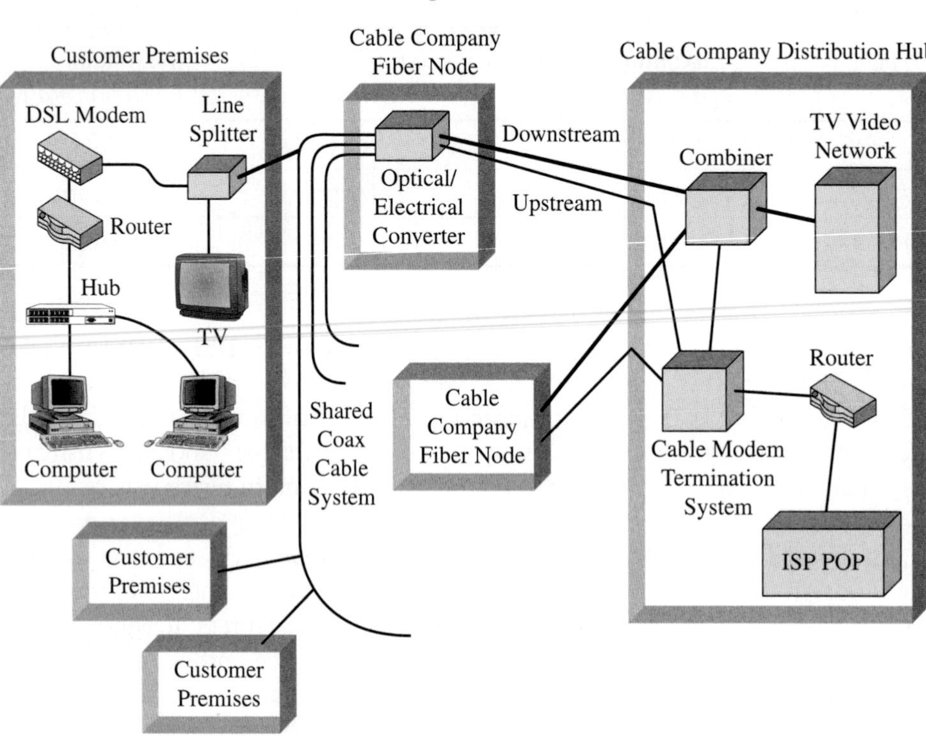

Multipoint circuit connections. Cable modem architecture. ISP = Internet service provider; POP = point of presence.

different HFC cable plants because each cable company was a separate entity, with no need to connect to other cable TV networks. In theory, cable modems can provide downstream speeds of 27Mbps to 55Mbps and upstream speeds of 2Mbps to 10Mbps, depending on the exact nature and quality of the HFC cable plant. In practice, the speeds offered vary widely, depending on the cable provider and factors such as when the current infrastructure was deployed. Service levels can therefore vary a lot, even within a neighborhood. As minimum expected rates, typical downstream speeds range between 1.5Mbps and 2Mbps and typical upstream speeds range between 200Kbps and 2Mbps, with higher rates available in most urban areas or where the infrastructure has been recently upgraded.

Fixed Wireless

The most popular type of **fixed wireless** is **wireless DSL**, which requires a line of sight between the communicating transmitters. For this reason, wireless DSL has limited application because it is not effective without tall buildings or towers. The most common use for wireless DSL today is to provide Internet access to

Figure 10-4

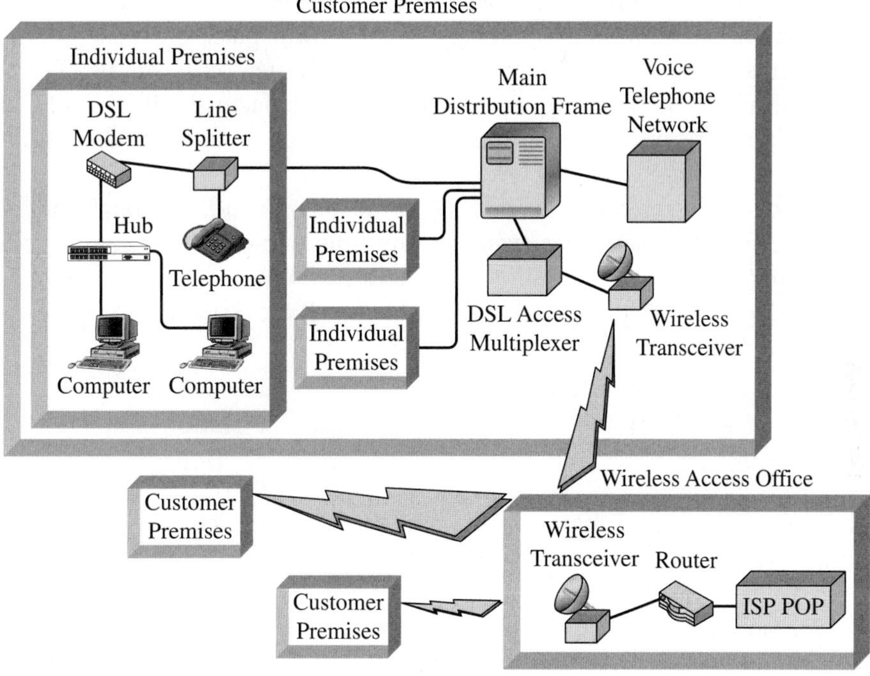

Wired and wireless connection technologies. Fixed wireless achitecture. DSL = digital subscriber line; ISP = Internet service provider; POP = point of presence.

multi-tenant buildings such as remote office buildings, apartment buildings, and hotels. Transmitters are used to connect a building to an ISP, and DSL is used inside the building to connect to the wireless transceiver (see Figure 10-4).

Fixed wireless comes in both point-to-point and multipoint versions. The **point-to-point version** is designed to connect only two locations and is often used as backbone between buildings owned by the same organization. The **multipoint version** is sometimes called **point-to-multipoint** because there is one central receiver and all other locations communicate only with it. The multipoint version is designed as an alternative to DSL and cable modems and is intended for use by an ISP supporting a small number of customers.

As with cable modems, the circuit is a shared circuit, so users must compete for the shared capacity, but most installations are limited to a few dozen users. Data transmission for both point-to-point and multipoint fixed wireless ranges from 1.5Mbps to 11Mbps, depending on the vendor.

Other fixed wireless technologies, such as satellite, are also available. Most satellite technologies use the satellite for downstream and upstream transmissions, but a small number use traditional dial-up modems for upstream transmissions.

10.1.4 Including Internet Technologies in an Enterprise Network

The relationship between enterprise networks and the Internet doesn't end with connectivity issues. Internet technologies have a firm place on most networks, from the smallest LAN to the largest enterprise. The reason is simple: The protocol designed for the Internet, TCP/IP, is also the de facto standard for PC networking. Internet services built in the TCP/IP protocol suite are also available for use on a network.

Many of these services do their work in the background. You might not even realize that they are there. For example, any time one computer communicates with another, it needs to know its MAC address, which is hard-coded on the network adapter. TCP/IP uses Address Resolution Protocol (ARP) to find a com-

> **FOR EXAMPLE**
>
> **Private Websites**
>
> There are probably as many different uses of private websites as there are companies deploying them on their networks. In many ways, websites are limited only by the designers' imaginations.
>
> Probably the most common use of internal websites is as an informational tool. Any kind of information that is of general interest to employees, such as company news, can be posted to the website, making it immediately available to employees. Some companies have found that this is a way of cutting down the seemingly endless stream of company memos. The content presented to employees can be tailored to individuals or by other means, such as by department, so that people see only what they need to see.
>
> Some companies have set up websites as reference libraries. Consider a situation in which a company provides its own customer support on its products. As a general rule, the more information support people have available, the better able they are to do their jobs. That means more efficiency, less time spent on each customer call, and, in many cases, a higher level of customer satisfaction.
>
> Another way that websites are being used to improve communication while cutting down on paperwork is to have employees fill out forms online instead of on paper. For example, some companies require weekly time sheets. When these are done on paper, not only does the employee enter the information, someone else probably needs to copy the same information into a database somewhere. By using a standard form the employee can call up from the corporate website, the information can be filled out online and entered directly into the tracking database without involving another set of hands.

puter's MAC address when its IP address is known. The flip-side is also supported: Reverse Address Resolution Protocol (RARP) finds the IP address when the MAC address is known.

Some services are support services, where inclusion might be considered to be optional, but only in the broadest definition of the term. You want to support automatic IP address assignments to network clients? You need one or more DHCP servers (or other devices that provide IP address information based on DHCP services). Are you using domain names to name your clients (e.g., mycomp.busicorp.com)? You are if you have a directory-based network such as Microsoft's Active Directory, and that means that you probably want to include DNS servers for name resolution.

What about technologies that are truly optional? For most people, the Internet means one thing: the **World Wide Web**, the vast collection of web servers strung around the world that provide access to nearly every type of information and service you can imagine. Many companies have brought that technology down to the local scale, setting up websites on their private intranets and communication tools. Other technologies are also finding their place on private networks; for example, streaming media delivers access to things like company informational meetings to employees' desktops.

SELF-CHECK

1. **Describe the hierarchical structure of Internet ISPs, starting at the highest level.**
2. **Compare the connection technologies used by ADSL and cable modems.**

10.2 Creating a Wide Area Network (WAN)

A WAN is a set of interconnected LANs. Therefore, all the factors that must be considered in LAN design must also be considered in WAN design. However, with an enterprise WAN, you must also consider device placement and traffic flows across wide area links.

A building's architect must accept that a building is no more stable or secure than its foundation. The same is true of a WAN, where the foundation is the individual LANs. The better designed and more reliable the LANs, the more reliable the WAN. Of course, the best-designed LANs can't compensate for poorly selected links, inefficient bandwidth use, or inappropriate server placement.

10.2.1 Identifying Your Goals

It is important to identify your goals for your network. First, what is it you want to do? At one level, this is fairly easy: You want an efficient, reliable network. What does that mean? It means that the network and necessary network resources are available to the users. It also means that sufficient bandwidth is provided to ensure efficient access to those resources.

When designing a network, you should use well-defined design processes to identify your network goals. This provides you with a framework for identifying network needs and developing your network design. This is true whether you are designing a new network or upgrading an existing network.

10.2.2 Using the Traditional Design Process

The **traditional network design process** follows a very structured systems analysis and design process similar to that used to build application systems:

1. The network analyst meets with users to identify user needs and the application systems planned for the network.
2. The analyst develops a precise estimate of the amount of data that each user will send and receive and uses this to estimate the total amount of traffic on each part of the network.
3. The analyst designs the circuits needed to support this traffic plus a modest increase in traffic and obtains cost estimates from vendors.

Finally, a year or two after design begins, the network is ready to be built and implemented. This traditional process, although expensive and time-consuming, works well for static or slowly evolving networks. In the real world, design and deployment have to occur on a faster scale because of the rate at which network technologies and user expectations change. Traffic has also become a more complicated issue. Not only do you need to consider traffic requirements, you need to consider the rate of growth of these requirements. Flexibility in terms of being able to rapidly scale your network to meet changing needs is critical. This rapid rate of deployment and change is sometimes referred to as operating on **Internet time**.

10.2.3 Using the Building-Block Design Process

Many organizations now use a simpler approach to network design than the traditional approach; this simpler approach is called the **building-block process**. The key concept is that networks that use a few standard components throughout the network are less expensive in the long run than networks that use a variety of different components on different parts of the network.

Rather than attempt to accurately predict user traffic on the network and build networks to meet those demands, the building-block process instead starts with a few standard components and uses them over and over. The goal is simplicity of design. This strategy is sometimes called **narrow and deep** because a very narrow range of technologies and devices is used over and over, and it is used very deeply throughout the organization. In theory, this is a simpler design process that yields a more easily managed network built with a smaller range of components.

To understand the narrow and deep concept, think of the requirements when setting up a routed LAN. Let's say that you need to support up to 200 hosts in each subnetwork. You use the same basic configuration for each LAN: a 16-port switch with a 16-port hub connected to each switch port except one, which is reserved for connecting to the router. This configuration supports up to 240 hosts. In the event that problems arise, you know going in how the subnetwork is configured.

The basic design process involves three steps, shown in Figure 10-5, that are performed repeatedly. This process begins with **needs analysis**, during which the designer attempts to understand the fundamental current and future network needs of the various users, departments, and applications. This is likely to be an

Figure 10-5

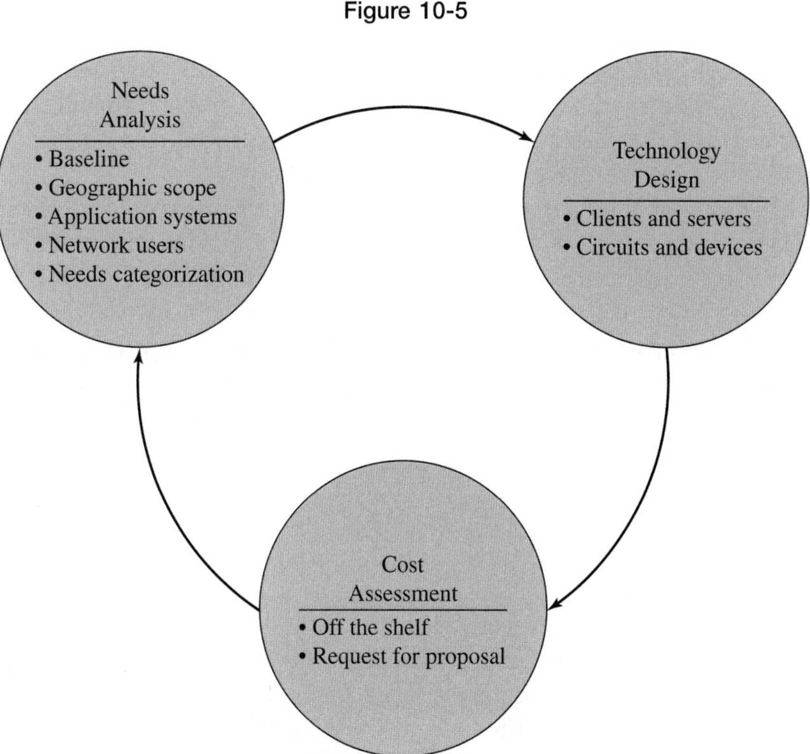

Building-block design process steps.

educated guess, at best. Users and applications are classified as typical or high volume. Technology needs, but not specific technology products, are identified.

The next step, **technology design**, examines the available technologies and assesses which options will meet users' needs. The designer makes some estimates about the network needs of each category of user and circuit in terms of current technology (e.g., 10BaseT, 100BaseT, 1000BaseT, DSL, cable modem) and matches needs to technologies. Because the basic network design is general, it can easily be changed as needs and technologies change. The difficulty lies in predicting user demand in order to define the technologies needed. Most organizations solve this on the LAN level by building more capacity than they expect to need. At the WAN level, organizations try to match solutions closer to the

FOR EXAMPLE

Let's Build a Network!

The decision to design and deploy a WAN is, in almost every case, driven by specific business requirements. Once you leave the comfortable confines of your LAN, the world becomes much more complicated. A well-thought-out network design is therefore a critical issue.

When designing a WAN, you must look at the network as a whole, but to do this, you must look at each of the individual LANs in detail. As you identify LAN requirements, you can also identify the relationships between those LANs and wide area connectivity requirements.

One thing that you must realize and accept is that network requirements change quickly. When you design your network, you need to consider both current needs and future use requirements. That often means building a network that more than meets your current requirements so that you aren't constantly revising and upgrading the network when it is in place. As with nearly any other type of project, the earlier in the process you make changes, the easier they are to implement and the less they cost.

For example, say that Busicorp's long-range business plan calls for growth through acquisition. As another company is acquired, its offices are integrated into the existing Busicorp WAN and Active Directory domain. If there's a network at the acquired company, the plan calls for adding it with minimal interruption. If there isn't a LAN, it's your job to build one. From a design standpoint, this means that you have to go through the network design process each time Busicorp makes a new acquisition. Because each newly acquired company is going to be different, it means going through the complete process from the context of that company's resources, requirements, and relationship to the rest of the network.

needs because of the outside costs involved. By designing networks that can easily grow and then closely monitoring growth, they can expand the network ahead of the growth pattern.

In the third step, **cost assessment**, the relative costs of the technologies are considered, and an attempt is made to get management to buy into the plan. The process then cycles back to the needs analysis, which is refined using the technology and cost information to produce a new assessment of users' needs. This in turn triggers changes in the technology design, cost assessment, and so on, until the design process is finished and the network is ready to deploy.

SELF-CHECK

1. Compare the traditional and building-block design processes.
2. What are the three process steps in the building-block design process?

10.3 Performing Needs Analysis

The goal of needs analysis is to understand why a network is being built and what users and applications it will support. In many cases, the network is being designed to improve poor performance or enable new applications to be used. In other cases, the network is upgraded to replace unreliable or aging equipment or to standardize equipment and technologies.

Often, the goals in network design are slightly different for LANs (including BNs) than for WANs. In the case of a LAN, the organization owns and operates the equipment and the circuits. If major changes are needed, the organization bears the cost. Most network designers tend to err on the side of building LANs that are too big—that is, building in more capacity than they expect to need. In contrast, in most WANs, the organization leases circuits from a common carrier and pays for them on a periodic or per-use basis. Most network designers tend to err on the side of building WANs that are too small because they can lease additional capacity incrementally, but it is difficult to cancel a long-term contract for unused capacity.

The goal of the needs analysis step is to produce a **logical network design**, which is a statement of the network elements needed to meet the needs of the organization. It focuses on the fundamental functionality needed instead of specific technologies or products. Those decisions are the responsibility of the technology design.

10.3.1 Analyzing Geographic Scope

The first step in needs analysis is to break the network into three conceptual parts, based on their geographic and logical scope: the access layer, the distribution layer, and the core layer. The **access layer** is the technology that is closest to the user—the user's first contact with the network—and is often a LAN or a remote access connection. The **distribution layer** is the next part of the network that connects the access layer to the rest of the network, such as the BN(s) in a specific building. The **core layer** is the innermost part of the network, and it connects the different distribution layer networks to each other (e.g., WAN circuits connecting different offices together). The core layer is usually the busiest and most important part of the network. Not all layers are present in all networks; small networks, for example, may not have a distribution layer because the parts of the access layer connect directly together.

When designing a network, it is easiest to start with the highest level, so most designers begin by drawing a network diagram for international or countrywide WAN locations that must be connected. Details such as the type of circuit and other considerations will be added later. Next, the individual locations (i.e., LANs) connected to the WAN are drawn, usually in a series of separate diagrams. The designers gather general information and characteristics of the environment in which the network operates. For example, they must determine whether there are any legal requirements, such as local, state/provincial, federal, or international laws, regulations, or building codes, that might affect the network.

Figure 10-6 shows the initial drawing of a network design for an organization with offices in four areas connected to the core WAN. The Toronto location, for example, has a distribution layer (implemented as a BN) connecting three distinct access layer LANs (for this example, three distinct LANs in the same office building). Chicago has a similar structure, with the addition of a fourth access part that connects to the Internet. Note that the organization has only one Internet connection, so all Internet traffic must route through the core network to the Chicago location.

The Atlantic Canada network section has two distinct access layers; one is a LAN and one is dial-up remote access. The New York network section is more complex, having its own core network component, with a BN connected into the core WAN, which in turn supports three distribution layer BNs. Each of these supports several access layer LANs.

10.3.2 Analyzing Servers and Application Systems

Traditionally, the primary reason for deploying a LAN was to share resources. As LAN technologies matured, another justification was to reduce total cost of ownership (TCO) by centralizing management as support requirements and efforts compared to the distributed management required by individual LANs. The basic reasons are the same with a WAN, but on a broader scale.

Figure 10-6

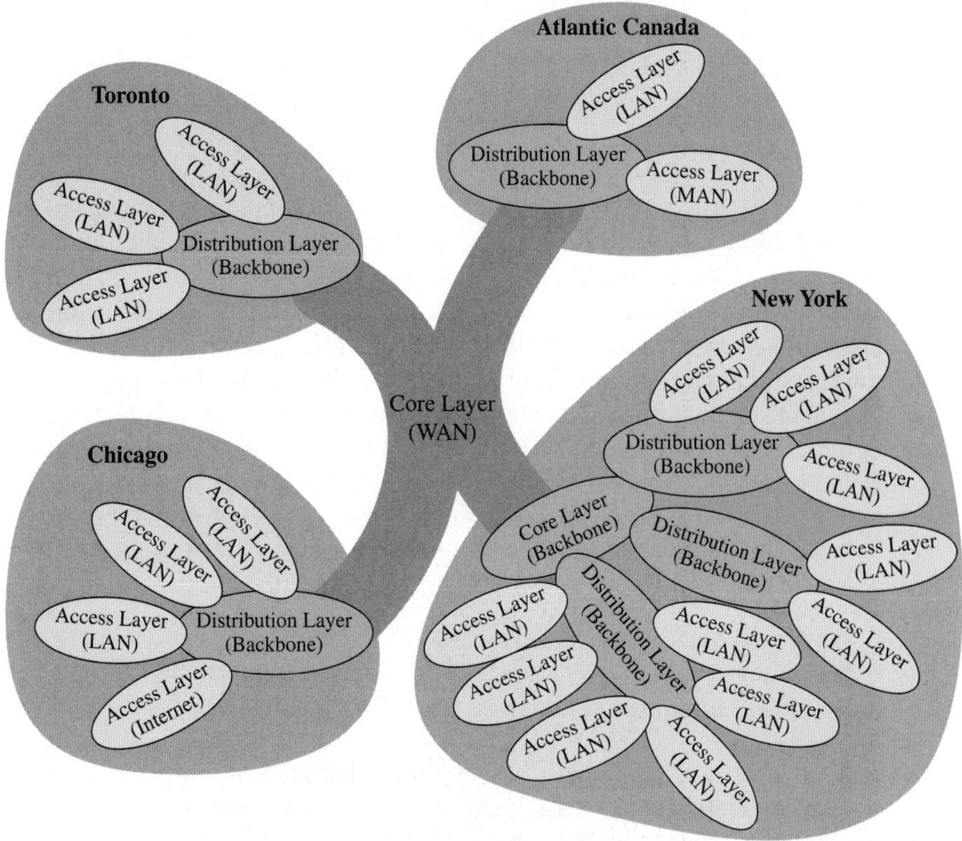

An initial network drawing. Geographic scope. LAN = local area network; MAN = metropolitan area network; WAN = wide area network.

The basic servers on an enterprise WAN are the same as you see on any LAN, including the following:

- ▲ File and print servers.
- ▲ Network support servers.
- ▲ Application servers.

File servers provide centralized file storage and access control. Print servers share printer resources to network users. Network support services include the NOS servers, such as Active Directory domain controllers, remote access servers, DHCP servers, DNS servers, network address translation (NAT) and other Internet access servers, specialized gateways, and other servers of this type. The difference is that with an enterprise WAN, you need more servers, and it's probably going to be more difficult to project traffic patterns and bandwidth requirements. With some server types, such as domain controllers, the best solution is often to have at least one of that type of server in each physical location. For others, such as remote access servers, you may need only one or two servers placed in strategic locations.

When designing an enterprise network, you will start to see differences between it and a LAN when you add application server requirements into the mix. Because it is usually much more expensive to deploy and maintain application servers, it is less likely that you will have one of each application server on every LAN. To start, you should review the list of applications that will be used on the network and identify the location of each. Next, you add to the list the applications expected to be deployed on the network in the future. In most cases, the applications will be relatively well defined. Specific internal applications (e.g., payroll and accounting) and external applications (e.g., web servers) may already be part of the existing network. As part of this process, you review the organization's long- and short-range plans concerning changes in the following:

- ▲ Company goals and strategic plans.
- ▲ Development plans for new products or services.
- ▲ Sales projections and research and development projects.
- ▲ New offices that must be served by the communications network.
- ▲ Future commitments to technology.

This list is just a guideline to the types of changes you need to consider. The network is closely tied to the business and its requirements, so any change to the business means a change to the network. For example, a major expansion in the number of offices or a major electronic commerce initiative will have a significant impact on network requirements.

You should also identify the hardware and software requirements of each application that will use the network. If possible, you need to identify the protocol each application uses. In today's network environment, for most applications, that means either a protocol from the TCP/IP protocol suite or, in some cases, application-specific custom protocols. This knowledge will be particularly useful later, when designers develop technological solutions. For example, if the main financial application Payroll runs is on an IBM mainframe, the network may need to support **Systems Network Architecture (SNA)** traffic (a proprietary IBM architecture used by IBM mainframes) and provide a gateway to translate it into more standard TCP/IP protocols. Another example you might see is a gateway to provide a Windows client access to a legacy NetWare server, which also introduces IPX/SPX protocol requirements.

You also need to look back at geographic scope requirements. You need to consider where the servers are currently located, which users need to access those servers, and the traffic associated with that access. You might find that it is more efficient, from the standpoint of user access and traffic control, to physically relocate one or more of the servers or to deploy additional servers. A good example of this is database servers. It's common to have a database server that acts as the back-end data source for one or more applications. Some of the records on the database server will apply to the business as a whole, while others, such as inventory levels or customer records, will apply specifically to one geographic location.

A possible solution is shown in Figure 10-7, which is based on the network design shown in Figure 10-6. Let's assume that, because the only Internet connection (other than connections possibly used for VPN links) is in Chicago, so that is where you plan to deploy all of the company's web servers. You keep a database server with a master copy of all the data in Chicago. You place the database server on one of the access layer LANs.

Figure 10-7

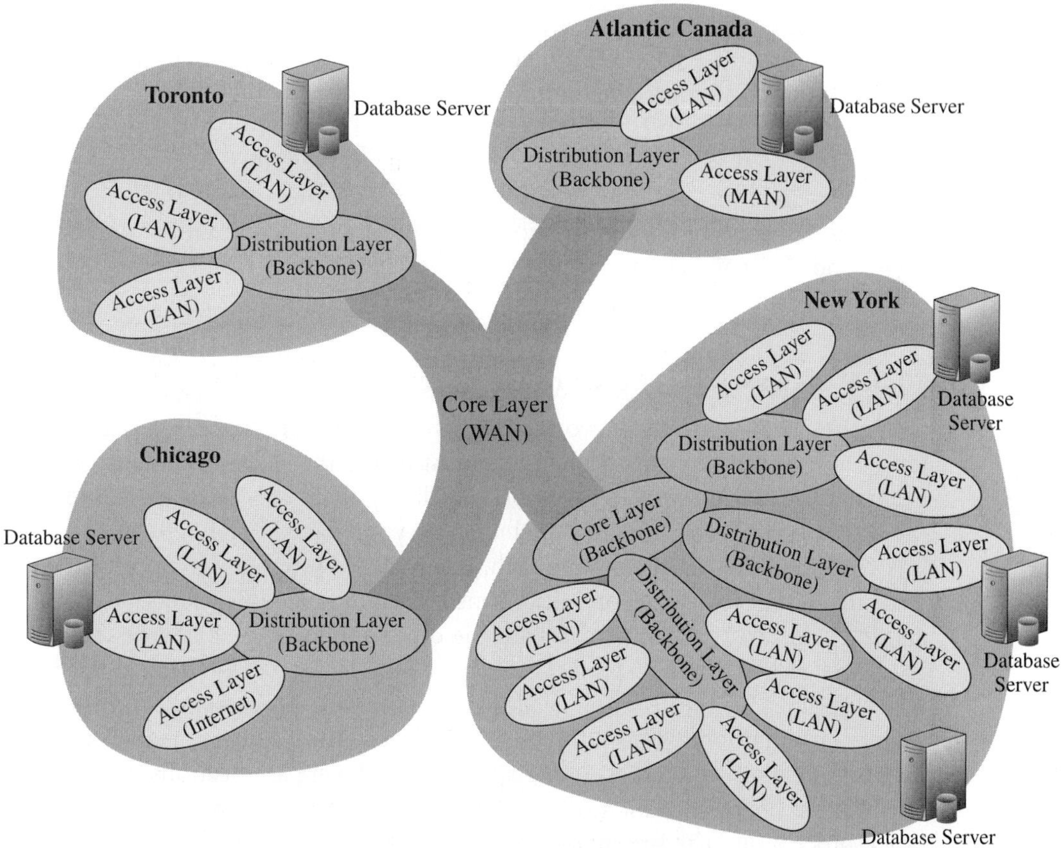

Geographic scope: LAN = local area network; MAN = metropolitan area network; WAN = wide area network.

Database server deployment.

Each of the other locations also has database access requirements, mostly having to do with data related to each region, so you deploy a database server with **partitioned data** only (i.e., a subset of the data that apply to that region). This reduces the traffic generated by user access. There will be some added traffic generated by this configuration because of the need to keep the data updated on each of the servers. For Toronto and Atlantic Canada, for example, you place a database server on one of the access layer LANs. However, in New York, in order to minimize traffic on the core layer, you might choose an access layer LAN from each of the distribution layer backbones. If you look closely, you'll notice that traffic between LANs connected to any of the New York backbones must cross the core layer.

10.3.3 Analyzing User Requirements

In the past, application systems and shared servers accounted for the majority of network traffic. These are still a significant part of the traffic requirements, but they are not the only concern. Today, much network traffic is produced by the discretionary use of the Internet, which also impacts application server traffic. Applications such as email and web servers generate significant traffic, so a network manager is no longer in total control of the network traffic generated on his or her networks. This is likely to continue in the future as network-hungry applications such as desktop videoconferencing become more common. In addition to understanding the applications, you must assess the number and type of users who will generate and receive network traffic and identify their locations on the emerging network diagram.

10.3.4 Categorizing Network Requirements

So far, you've designed a network in terms of geographic scope, application systems, and users. Along with this, you must assess the relative amount of traffic generated in each part of the network. It's likely that you've already started this process at some level, but now it should be your focus.

With the building-block approach, the goal is a rough assessment of the relative magnitude of each application's network traffic requirements, both today and in the future, in comparison with the other applications. Likewise, each user is categorized as either a typical user or a high-traffic user. These assessments will be refined in the technology design stage of the process. Applications that require large amounts of multimedia data or those that load executables over the network are likely to be high-traffic applications. So are applications that are time sensitive or need constant updates, such as financial information systems and order processing. The amount of traffic generated to support word processing applications or a web server's network access requirements is likely to be relatively minimal.

Once the network requirements have been identified, you need to organize them into **mandatory requirements** (i.e., things you must include), **desirable requirements** (i.e., things you should include), and **wish-list requirements** (i.e., things users want you to include). This information enables the development of a minimum level of mandatory requirements and a negotiable list of desirable requirements that are dependent on cost and availability. For example, desktop videoconferencing may be a wish-list item; it will be omitted if it increases the cost of the network beyond what is desired. Look at the list at the bottom of Figure 10-8. This figure focuses on one geographic location, with file server, mail

Figure 10-8

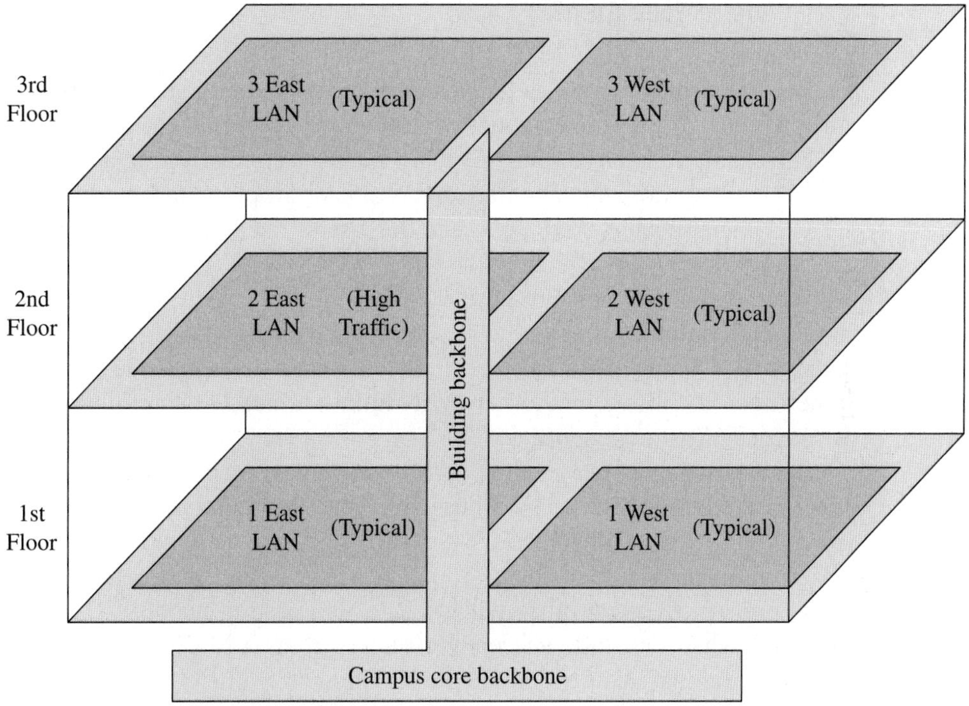

3rd Floor
3 East LAN (Typical)
3 West LAN (Typical)
2nd Floor
2 East LAN (High Traffic)
2 West LAN (Typical)
1st Floor
1 East LAN (Typical)
1 West LAN (Typical)
Building backbone
Campus core backbone

Mandatory Applications
File server
–File sharing
Mail server
–E-mail
Web server
–Web applications for internal and external use

Wish-List Applications
–Desktop videoconferencing (2 East and 2 West)

Network requirements.

server, and web server identified as mandatory applications. There is also one wish-list item identified: videoconferencing.

At this point, the local facility network diagrams need to be prepared. For a really large network, there may be several levels. For example, the designer of the network in Figure 10-8 might choose to draw separate diagrams for Toronto, Chicago, Atlantic Canada, and New York. Conversely, the designer might just add more detail to develop separate, more detailed diagrams for New York. The choice is up to the designer, provided that the diagrams and supporting text clearly explain the network's needs.

FOR EXAMPLE

How Wide Is Your Area?

Needs analysis, like network design in general, is not a one-time activity. A number of business activities and changes in company goals and strategies can force you to rethink your network.

For example, say that Busicorp has a WAN configured as a Windows Active Directory domain. The network is already in place and working well. It has sufficient bandwidth to meet the users' needs, with a little room remaining for growth.

What happens when Busicorp acquires another company, one with its own LAN, in another geographic location? The company's long-range expansion plans call for you to integrate that LAN into the corporate enterprise. Rather than just throw in another WAN link, you need to carefully consider the impact on your network.

Needs analysis issues include considering the connectivity requirements between the existing and new offices. You have to identify what servers are present in the new office, how they're being used, and whether existing offices will need access to them. You also need to determine what kinds of access users in the new office will need to the existing network.

Here's what you find: The network is set up as a NetWare 3.2 network with an additional Windows 2000 Server file server. The clients are running various Windows versions, from Windows 95 up. You need to keep the existing file server in place and bring clients up to current levels, so you will need to add an Active Directory domain controller, allow for client access to the NetWare 3.2 server, and upgrade the clients. Also, because this is a stand-alone LAN, you need some kind of WAN link to the rest of the enterprise. Initially, other than keeping the domain controller up-to-date and possibly email messages, there will probably be little need for communication between this LAN and the rest of the network, although you can expect that to change as users settle in to their new situation.

10.3.5 Compiling Your Deliverables

The key deliverable for the needs assessments stage is a set of logical network diagrams (e.g., Figure 10-8), showing the applications, circuits, clients, and servers in the proposed network, each categorized as either typical or high traffic. You might also need an additional diagram showing the relationship and relative traffic requirements between the LANs. The logical diagram is the conceptual plan for the network and does not consider the specific physical elements that will be used to implement the network.

SELF-CHECK

1. What are the three conceptual layers in a network communication model?
2. How does analysis of network servers relate to geographic analysis?
3. What categories should you use to organize network requirements, from most to least critical?

10.4 Developing a Technology Design

Once the needs have been defined in the logical network design, the next step is to develop a **physical network design** (or set of possible designs). The physical network design starts with the client and server computers needed to support the users and applications. If the network is a new network, new computers will need to be purchased. If the network is an existing network, the servers may need to be upgraded to the newest technology. After the clients and servers are designed, then the circuits and devices connecting them (at the LAN and WAN levels) are designed.

10.4.1 Designing Clients and Servers

The building-block approach specifies needs in terms of some standard units. Typical users are allocated the base-level client computers, as are servers that support typical applications. Users and servers for applications that need more powerful computers are assigned more advanced computers.

Applications (both client and server) typically specify their minimum hardware requirements. When designing computer hardware, keep in mind that real-world requirements often exceed those minimums. With many server applications, it may be necessary to calculate actual hardware requirements on a case-by-case basis. The good news is that hardware costs continue to drop, and you are likely to find that when you get ready to buy the hardware, you can afford more advanced servers for the same price you originally planned to spend for less advanced servers, building in support for growth.

10.4.2 Designing Circuits and Pathways

At least for LAN hardware, the same built-in cost reductions apply for network circuits and devices as for servers. For a WAN, available technologies and associated costs tend to change a little more slowly. With both, there are two interrelated decisions in designing network circuits and devices: the fundamental technology and protocols (e.g., Ethernet, ATM, TCP/IP) and the capacity of each circuit (e.g., 10Mbps, 100Mbps, 1,000Mbps). These are interrelated because each technology offers different circuit capacities.

Designing the circuit capacity means **capacity planning**—estimating the size and type of the standard and advanced network circuits for each type of network (LAN, BN, WAN). For example, should the standard LAN circuit be 10BaseT, 100BaseT, or 10/100 switched Ethernet? Likewise, should the standard BN circuit be 100BaseT, 1000BaseT, or ATM OC-3?

Capacity planning requires assessment of the current and future **circuit loading** (i.e., the amount of data transmitted on a circuit). This analysis can focus on either the **average circuit traffic** (i.e., the usual traffic requirements) or the **peak circuit traffic** (i.e., the maximum traffic requirements). For example, in an online banking network, traffic volume peaks usually occur in the midmorning (at bank opening) and just prior to closing. Telephone companies normally have their highest peak volumes on Mother's Day. Designing for peak circuit traffic is the ideal, but it is not always possible because of the related costs.

Forecasts and estimates are inherently less precise than current network traffic information. One consideration is the **turnpike effect**, which results when the network is used to a greater extent than was anticipated because it is available, is very efficient, and provides new services. The annual growth factor for network use may vary from 5 to 50 percent and, in some cases, may exceed 100 percent for high-growth organizations. You often don't know the actual growth rate until the network is in place and you have real-world numbers to apply.

Although no organization wants to pay for more capacity than it needs, the usual working estimate is that upgrading a network costs 50 to 80 percent more than building it right the first time. Few organizations complain about having too much network capacity, but being under capacity can cause significant problems. Given the rapid growth in network demand and the difficulty in accurately predicting it, most organizations intentionally overbuild (i.e., build more capacity into their network than they plan to use) and then end up using this supposedly unneeded capacity (often within three years or less).

10.4.3 Selecting Design Tools

Network modeling and design tools can perform a number of functions to help in the technology design process. With most tools, the first step is to create a diagram or model of the existing network or proposed network design. Some modeling tools require the user to create the network diagram from scratch. That is, the user must enter all the network components by hand, placing each server, client computer, and circuit on the diagram and defining what each is.

Some tools support **network discovery**; once installed on a network, these tools will explore the network to draw a network diagram. In this case, the user provides some starting point, and the modeling software explores the network and automatically draws the diagram itself. When the diagram is complete, the user can change it to reflect the new network design. Obviously, a network discovery tool helps only if you already have a network. Also, these tools tend to be most helpful with very complex networks.

When the network diagram is complete, the next step is to add information about the expected network traffic and see if the network can support the level of traffic that is expected. **Simulation**, a mathematical technique in which a network comes to life and behaves as it would under real conditions, is used to model the behavior of a communication network. Applications and users generate and respond to messages, and the simulator tracks the number of packets in the network and the delays encountered at each point in the network. Simulation models can be tailored to the users' needs by entering parameter values specific to the network at hand. However, a simulation is no better than the data provided. If the initial parameters aren't accurate, the simulation will be invalid.

An accurate simulation can give you estimated response times throughout the network and, with good modeling tools, highlight potential trouble areas. The very best tools offer suggestions on how to overcome the problems that the simulation identified (e.g., subnetting a LAN, increasing a WAN link from T1 to T3).

10.4.4 Compiling Your Deliverables (Again)

The key deliverable is a set of one or more physical network designs. Most designers like to prepare several physical designs so they can trade off technical benefits against cost. In most cases, the critical part is the design of the network circuits and devices. In the case of a new network designed from scratch, it is

Figure 10-9

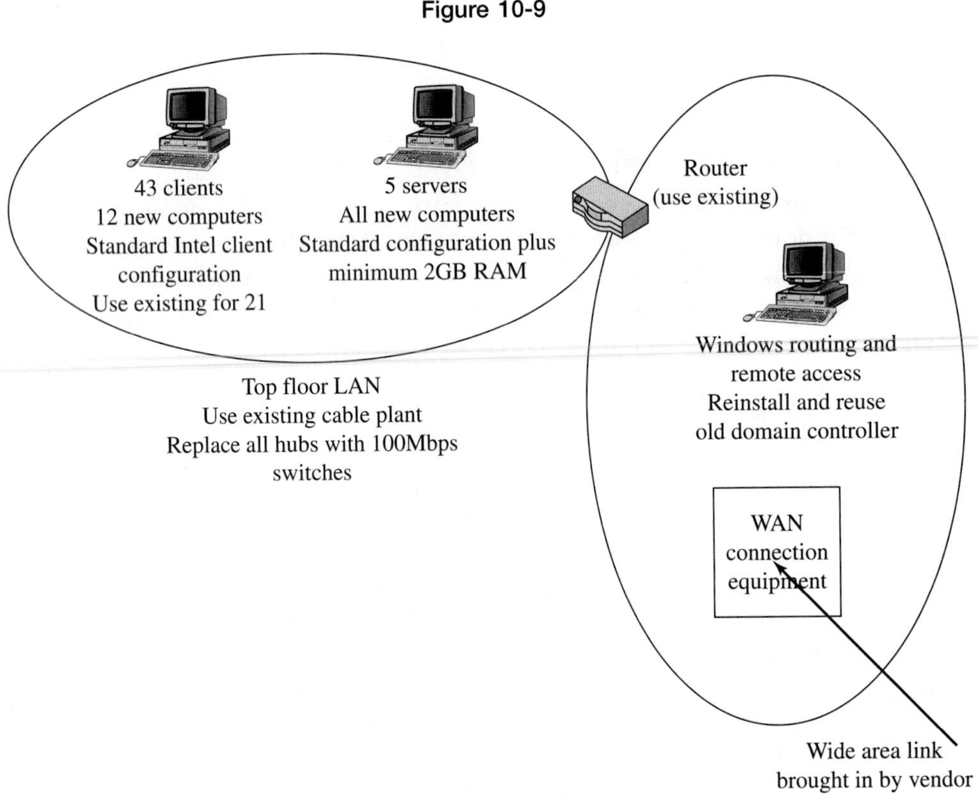

LAN/WAN design.

also important to define the client computers with care because they will form a large portion of the total cost of the network.

You need to diagram the access level LANs and the connections that form your WAN. This time, you need to provide details such as the type of protocols used, connection devices, and number of client computers. Figure 10-9 is a more detailed diagram for one of the LANs and for the network in Toronto. Notice that it lists the number and types of devices but doesn't include information such as vendors. That comes later in the process.

Notice that Figure 10-9 indicates that some of the existing equipment will be reused. Even though it doesn't specifically call it out here, the existence of a backbone implies at least one additional router used to connect the LANs to that backbone. As you get more details about the remote link requirements for the backbone, such as the specific connection type, you would add those to the drawing.

This is another place where a good design tool can make your life easier. Most design tools will let you print your design diagrams, including the equipment list. That way, you can avoid duplicating your effort.

FOR EXAMPLE

Getting Physical

You are designing an extension to the Busicorp WAN. The company is growing through acquisition. The most recent acquisition has a NetWare 3.2 server, a Windows file server running Windows 2000 Server, and an assortment of Windows clients running various versions of Windows client operating systems.

The general guidelines for the extension specify that the LAN should be made part of the Windows Active Directory domain. It will be necessary to leave the NetWare server in place initially, but it will be phased out eventually. Any clients running Windows Me or earlier should be brought up to current operating system levels. The LAN will link through a VPN over the Internet through an ADSL link.

What does the physical design look like? Let's start with the LAN. There's nothing in the design that requires you to upgrade the cable plant or local LAN connection hardware, so there's no need to include it in the design. The design lists three Windows servers, an Active Directory domain controller, a Routing and Remote Access Services (RRAS) server and VPN endpoint, and, to provide access to the NetWare 3.2 server, a server running Gateway Service for NetWare (GSNW). You decide to install GSNW on the file server running Windows 2000 Server and deploy new computers running Windows Server 2003 as the domain controller and RRAS server.

What about the WAN requirements? One component overlaps with the LAN requirements: the RRAS server. You'll also need to identify a local ISP to provide the connection to the Internet. You'll need an ADSL line, provided either directly by the local telephone carrier or indirectly through the ISP, and ADSL connection hardware, either from the telephone carrier, from the ISP, or purchased separately. Because the clients haven't had any contact with the rest of the network in the past, you determine that, at least initially, communications over the WAN link are minimal.

SELF-CHECK

1. What are your design requirements during capacity planning?
2. What is the ideal circuit design in relationship to estimated circuit loading?
3. What is network discovery?

10.5 Selling Your Plan

Before you can begin network implementation, someone has to authorize the plan and the budget. You have to convince the decision makers that your plan is the best (i.e., most cost-effective) design. That means performing a cost assessment to justify your design.

The purpose of this step is to assess the costs of various physical network design alternatives produced in the previous step. The main items are the costs of software, hardware, circuits, and personnel. All these factors are interrelated with regard to cost.

10.5.1 Estimating Costs

Estimating the cost of a network is quite complex because many factors are not immediately obvious. The following are some of the costs that must be considered:

- ▲ Circuit costs, including costs of circuits provided by common carriers or the cost of purchasing and installing your own cable.
- ▲ Costs of internetworking devices and WAN connection devices.
- ▲ Hardware costs, including those for computers, hubs, switches, printers, and uninterruptible power supplies.
- ▲ Software costs for the NOS, application software, middleware, and client applications.
- ▲ Network management costs, including those for special hardware, software, management personnel and training.
- ▲ Test and maintenance costs, including those for diagnostic software and onsite spares.
- ▲ Costs to operate the network.

Some estimates will be closer to actual costs than others. Hardware costs, for example, are relatively easy to estimate. Others, such as personnel costs and training costs, are more difficult. In some organizations, you might be expected to break down the costs by department, based on projected network use. This makes the process even more complicated and, for a new network, could be little better than a rough guess.

10.5.2 Developing a Request for Proposal (RFP)

Even though most LAN components can be purchased off the shelf, organizations often develop a **request for proposal (RFP)** before making large network purchases. Different terms might be used in different organizations, but the concept is common throughout the corporate (and not-for-profit, and government, and any other organization type) world: An RFP is a thumbnail sketch of what

Figure 10-10

Information in a Typical Request for Proposal

- Background information
    - Organizational profile
    - Overview of current network
    - Overview of new network
    - Goals of new network
- Network requirements
    - Choice sets of possible network designs (hardware, software, circuits)
    - Mandatory, desirable, and wish-list items
    - Security and control requirements
    - Response-time requirements
    - Guidelines for proposing new network designs
- Service requirements
    - Implementation time plan
    - Training courses and materials
    - Support services (e.g., spare parts on site)
    - Reliability and performance guarantees
- Bidding process
    - Time schedule for the bidding process
    - Ground rules
    - Bid evaluation criteria
    - Availability of additional information
- Information required from vendor
    - Vendor corporate profile
    - Experience with similar networks
    - Hardware and software benchmarks
    - Reference list

A sample RFP.

you need that specifies what equipment, software, and services are desired. You can use it to ask your vendors to give you their best prices. Some RFPs are very specific about items and time frame. In other cases, items are defined as mandatory, important, or desirable, or several scenarios are provided, and the vendor is asked to propose the best solution. Figure 10-10 is a summary of the key parts of an RFP.

Once the vendors have submitted their proposals, the organization evaluates them against specified criteria and makes its choices. Depending on the scope and complexity of the network, it is sometimes necessary to redesign the network on the basis of the information in the vendors' proposals.

One of the key decisions in the RFP process is the scope of the RFP. Will you use one vendor or several vendors for all hardware, software, and services?

Multivendor environments tend to provide better performance and best prices because it is unlikely that one vendor makes the best (or least expensive) hardware, software, and services in all categories. The problem is that multivendor environments can be more difficult to manage. When failures occur (and they will), each vendor can blame the others.

10.5.3 Selling It to Management

One of the main problems in network design is obtaining the support of senior management. Management often sees a network as little more than a cost center, something on which the organization is spending a lot of money with little apparent change. The network keeps on running just as it did the year before.

One key to gaining the acceptance of senior management lies in speaking management's language. It is pointless to talk about switching from Frame Relay to ADSL because this terminology is meaningless to most members of management. A more compelling argument is to discuss the growth in network use. For example, a simple graph that shows network usage growing at 25 percent per year,

FOR EXAMPLE

Signoff

Busicorp is expanding its WAN by connecting a newly acquired company's LAN. You've identified the physical requirements, which include two servers, a few new client computers to replace those that can't upgrade to the current Windows versions, a wide area link, and wide area connection hardware. On the software side, you need two licensed copies of Windows Server 2003 and client operating system licenses for each of the client computers you need to upgrade. This is the basis of your RFP.

You put together a formal list and send copies to Busicorp's list of approved vendors (whom you refer to as the usual suspects). Because you've never had an office in this geographic location before, and because none of your current ISPs service that location, you also have to locate and contact new vendors for the wide area link. You want it done fast, and you want it done right the first time, so you call a few friends and locate a network consultant in the area to help you with the wide area requirements.

When the bids come back, you hand your selection off through your manager for approval. This is one situation where approval is relatively easy because it falls under the company's public long-range expansion goals. Despite this, you still have to justify your design decisions to show that your choices are the most cost effective.

compared with network budget growing at 10 percent per year, presents a powerful illustration that the network costs are well managed, not out of control. Likewise, a focus on network reliability is an easily understandable issue. Depending on the applications that rely on the network, such as financial processing or customer sales, network downtime can cost hundreds or even thousands of dollars per hour.

10.5.4 Compiling Your Deliverables (One More Time)

You need to bring together three key deliverables at this point. You'll have an RFP that goes to potential vendors. After the vendor has been selected, you need to revise the physical network diagram with the technology design complete and actual hardware filled in. Finally, you need to deliver the business case that provides support for the network design, expressed in business objectives.

SELF-CHECK

1. Which network costs are usually the most difficult to estimate?
2. What should you include in an RFP?

10.6 Deploying Your WAN

After the design process is complete, you can finally order the pieces and parts and start deploying your new network (or network upgrades). Unfortunately, it's seldom a matter of just hooking up everything as it comes in. There's hardware to test to make sure it's working properly, software to install, and a number of other details to manage. One of the first things you should do, whether installing a new network or upgrading, is go back to your design documents and prepare an installation checklist. That way, you can make sure that everything gets done in the right order and nothing gets missed.

You can look at the process as having two broadly defined steps: deploying the LANs and connecting them together. Even if these steps are happening at the same time, it's easier to keep your thought processes (and implementation procedures) organized if you think of them as separate activities. If your LANs are not working properly, you might not be able to tell whether your remote links are working at optimum levels—or at all, in some cases.

10.6.1 Deploying Your LANs

There are two basic LAN scenarios. One is installing a new network, in which case you don't have to worry about existing network users. The other is upgrading an existing LAN, in which case you have to keep everything working while you bring in the new network.

Installing a New Network

When installing a new network, you need to be sure to take care of all the preliminaries that might require outside help. This includes things like registering your domain name, having the network cable run, and so forth. If you expect the users to walk into a turnkey operation where everything is ready to go, you need to have all the software, including client applications, already installed and tested. To help with this task, there are different software packages available that let you install one client computer as the model and duplicate that installation on the other clients. Currently, the most popular product of this type is Norton Ghost.

Upgrading an Existing Network

Things can get difficult when you're upgrading an existing network. Not only do you have the issue of trying to deploy all your new hardware and software, you have to do it with minimal interference to the network users and current network operations. Some companies make the change as an all-at-once switch, but it is more common to use a gradual, phased approach.

Changing all at once requires careful timing and coordination. The switch is usually planned for a period when the network will be unused, or minimally used, and that allows for sufficient time to complete the process. One way companies have done this is to schedule the upgrade over a long holiday weekend. This can be difficult for multinational organizations because many holidays are at least somewhat regional. It may be necessary to schedule upgrades in different locales at different times.

With a phased approach, you upgrade the network a little a time. Maybe you start with the infrastructure, swapping out hubs for higher-speed switches, for example. Then you move on to the next phase, maybe replacing selected servers or exchanging client computers.

10.6.2 Connecting Your LANs

At this point, you need to connect your disconnected LANs into a WAN. A key part of any successful WAN deployment is testing—before you link, during the linkup, and after the LANs are connected.

The exact process involved, and the testing required, depends on how the LANs are connected. There is, however, one common factor: Any time you

Figure 10-11

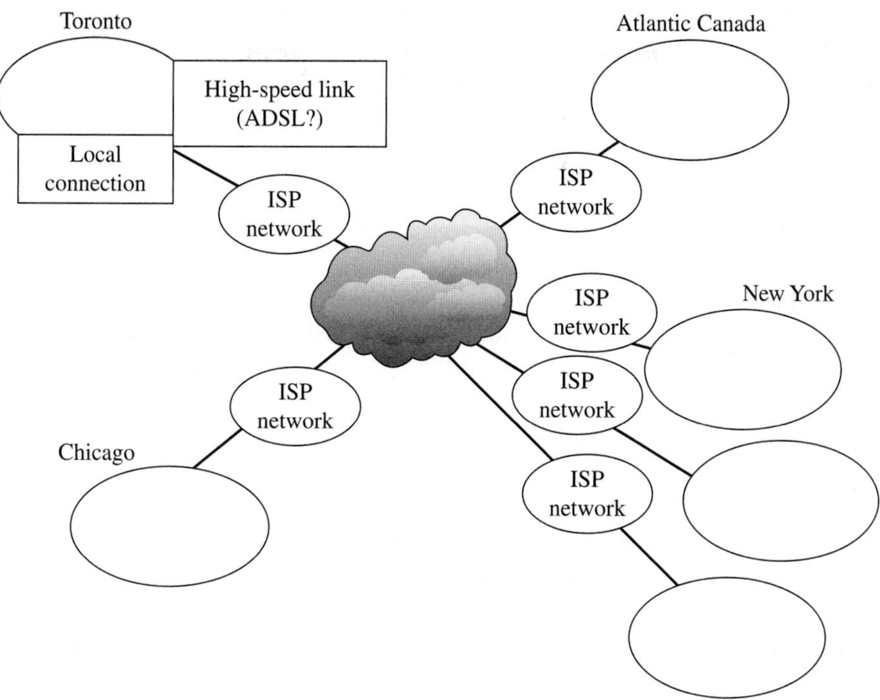

LAN connections.

have wide area links, at least one third party is involved. That means that you aren't completely in control of the process. For example, Figure 10-11 shows a network that makes connections by way of high-speed links through the Internet. The figure shows local distribution layers and the POP location for the ISP.

From this drawing, because each distribution layer's separate connection goes through an ISP in New York, you can tell there are special connection requirements. One possibility is that you have three offices, all in the same city but far enough apart that you can't use local LAN technology for a backbone to link them. The other possibility is that the circuit load on each distribution layer BN is sufficient to justify a separate VPN link.

Key components in connecting LANs might include a local connection device to the high-speed link, a high-speed carrier, and an ISP. It's not uncommon for the point of contact for each of these to be a separate entity. Also, you have the same requirements at the other end, and you usually have different carrier providers and different ISPs at each end of the link. In most cases, it's your responsibility to coordinate with each of these parties to get them together at the same time.

The real potential for nightmare is when you have problems. First, some vendors are more able to provide troubleshooting and problem resolution services than others. Second, isolating the cause of a problem so that it can be resolved can take diplomatic skills as well as technical skills. The only thing that the vendors are likely to agree on is that your LAN is probably somehow at fault. Once that is exhausted, the usual track is for each vendor to spend time blaming the others.

10.6.3 Remaining (Ongoing) Tasks

After a network is deployed and running, your first reaction is that you want to take a long break and get away from it for a while. Unfortunately, if it's your network (i.e., you didn't come in as a temporary resource to set up the network and leave), your job is just starting.

There are some things you'll want to do in the first few days after you get the network operational. You need to validate your design to make sure the network you designed and deployed is really the network you want. You start by updating your final network design documents to include any changes made during the final implementation. You should include detailed information about the equipment you install, such as model numbers, serial numbers, the vendor, and, if available, a contact name and number in case of trouble.

You should collect baseline performance statistics at various times and at various locations on the WAN. You need to collect traffic statistics for each LAN (and each subnet in a routed LAN) and for the WAN links. You should compare these to the projected estimates you developed during the design process. If you find significant variance—for example, places in the network where traffic levels are much higher than expected—you need to come up with a quick resolution. Two of the most likely solutions are increasing the available bandwidth and moving some of the users or network servers to change traffic flow patterns.

One of your goals is ensuring that the network operates at acceptable levels. Network users are sure to give you feedback if the network is running at less than top form. Some users will never be happy, no matter how well the network is performing, but the feedback you get from your users will often help you identify and correct bottlenecks and other performance problems.

From here on, the job comes down to regular upkeep and maintenance. Some periodic maintenance activities, such as regular backups, can be at least partially automated. Others, such as creating and deleting user accounts or managing access permissions, require your direct intervention. Details about regular maintenance procedures and available maintenance tools are beyond the scope of this chapter.

FOR EXAMPLE

D (Deployment)-Day(s)

Let's think again about the Busicorp example. Once you have everything in place, you want to get the new company joined into the enterprise as quickly as possible. After weighing your options, you decide to do this as an all-at-once change over a holiday weekend (after bribing your coworkers with overtime and free food); you want to leave the office with a turnkey network.

Setup includes hardware installation, software installation, and management-related configuration tasks. Management tasks are beyond the scope of this book, so we'll leave those tasks alone except to say that they have to be done.

There are some things you can do in advance without seriously impacting the current network. You can go ahead and install the operating system on the Windows Server 2003 computers. You can also install and test the wide area link. When you set up a domain controller, you need access to the domain, so you need to have the link and RRAS server in place before you finish setting up the domain controller.

You can set up the clients you need to upgrade, and the new clients you need to set up, to run the Windows client installations and upgrades as unattended installations. That means that they run automatically without any human interaction, or with only minimal interaction. You still want to check each installation to make sure the client is running properly. You need to install and configure the GSNW server, configure the client computers, and set up network users and their access permissions for all the local users. You should test everything, as much as possible, to make sure it all works.

When you feel relatively sure that everything's done, you leave behind printed instructions that tell the users how to log on to the new network and (very important) change their passwords the first time they log on. You need to provide them with instructions about how to use the network and differences that they're going to see from what they're used to. It would also be worth your while to leave at least one person on site to provide support, answer users' questions, and fix or replace anything that breaks. On a project like this, something always breaks.

SELF-CHECK

1. What is a *turnkey network*?
2. When upgrading an existing network, what is the advantage of scheduling the changes over a long holiday weekend?

SUMMARY

In this chapter, you were introduced to enterprise network issues. These were presented in the context of network design and deployment, which allowed you to see how they apply to creating new networks and to upgrading existing networks. You learned a few fundamentals about the Internet's hierarchical structure and the types of Internet technologies you might find deployed on a PC network. You learned about the building-block design process and how to use needs analysis, physical design, and cost assessment to design a network and get it approved for implementation. This included a look at network service and server-related issues and how they apply in a WAN enterprise networking environment. Finally, you learned a little about deployment options and how to deploy changes to a network with minimal interruption to network users.

KEY TERMS

Access layer
Asymmetrical DSL (ADSL)
Average circuit traffic
Building-block process
Capacity planning
Circuit loading
Core layer
Cost assessment
Customer premises equipment (CPE)
Data over Cable Service Interface Specification (DOCSIS)
Desirable requirements
Digital subscriber line (DSL)
Distribution layer
Downstream circuit
Fixed wireless
Hybrid fiber coax (HFC)
Internet time
Local loop circuit
Logical network design
Mandatory requirements
Metropolitan area exchange (MAE)
Multipoint version
Multivendor environment
Narrow and deep
National ISP
National Science Foundation (NSF)
Needs analysis
Network access point (NAP)
Network discovery
Next-Generation Internet (NGI)
Partitioned data
Peak circuit traffic
Peering
Physical network design
Point of presence (POP)
Point-to-multipoint version
Point-to-point version
Regional ISP
Request for proposal (RFP)
Shared multipoint circuit

Simulation
Systems Network Architecture (SNA)
Technology design
Traditional network design process
Turnpike effect
Upstream circuit
Very-high-data-rate DSL (VDSL)
Wireless DSL
Wish-list requirements
World Wide Web

ASSESS YOUR UNDERSTANDING

Go to www.wiley.com/college/ciccarelli to evaluate your knowledge of wide area and enterprise networking services.
Measure your learning by comparing pre-test and post-test results.

Summary Questions

1. When upgrading a network, you must make all of the technology changes at the same time. True or false?
2. How is an RFP used?
   (a) to organize network requirements by priority
   (b) to illustrate the complete physical network design
   (c) to track items discovered during needs analysis
   (d) to submit to vendors for bid and recommendations
3. ____________________ requirements are the lowest-priority network requirements.
   (a) Mandatory
   (b) Desirable
   (c) Wish-list
   (d) Management-specified
4. What is the role of core layer network technology?
   (a) It provides the wide area links connecting distribution layer networks.
   (b) It acts as the backbone in a routed LAN.
   (c) It is a technology that directly provides users with access to LAN resources.
   (d) It is the software and services that operate on servers running the NOS.
5. What is circuit loading?
   (a) the process of testing a circuit to determine its maximum capacity
   (b) the process of estimating network circuit requirements
   (c) a reference to the amount of data carried on a circuit
   (d) a reference to buying and installing more capacity than is actually needed
6. Typically, you are more likely to overbuild when designing LAN technology requirements than when designing WAN technology requirements. True or false?

7. Identifying and locating application servers is part of which phase of the design process?
   (a) needs analysis
   (b) physical design
   (c) cost assessment
   (d) It is not a formal part of the design process.
8. What are the connection points at the topmost level of the Internet's hierarchical structure?
   (a) MAEs
   (b) NAPs
   (c) POPs
   (d) regional ISPs
9. When connecting to your local ISP, you connect through which of the following?
   (a) MAE
   (b) NAP
   (c) POP
   (d) NSF
10. Which term best describes cable modem connection architecture?
   (a) point-to-point
   (b) point of presence
   (c) single point circuit
   (d) shared multipoint circuit
11. The narrow and deep design strategy refers to the expected outcome of the traditional network design process. True or false?
12. Which server type would you most likely need to deploy at each physical location in a WAN?
   (a) logon and authentication server
   (b) mail service server
   (c) web server
   (d) mainframe gateway server

Applying This Chapter

1. The following questions refer to the network graphic in Figure 10-12. The connections shown between the LANs are ATM links. Even though single links are shown from each LAN, the WAN is configured as a mesh, with each LAN connecting by ATM to every other LAN.

Figure 10-12

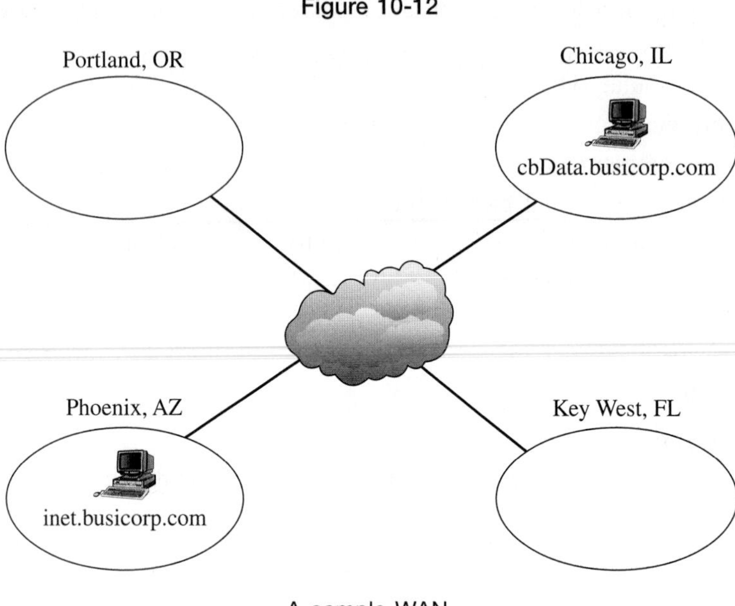

A sample WAN.

The network shown in Figure 10-12 is configured as a single Windows Active Directory domain with a single domain controller in each physical location. The database server on the Chicago LAN is accessed by users and applications from all locations.

The company websites and the NAT server (inet.busicorp.com) that provides users with Internet access are located in the Phoenix office. Web server content is stored on the database server. Most of the content is relatively static. Updates are made weekly.

(a) How does NAT server location affect network traffic?

(b) What are the potential benefits of deploying additional NAT servers?

(c) What are the potential drawbacks of deploying additional NAT servers?

(d) How can you determine whether the change is cost-effective?

(e) Regular business hours are 8:00 a.m. to 5:00 p.m. local time at each location. Between 7:45 a.m. and 8:15 a.m., local to Key West, traffic levels on the links between Key West and the other offices increase significantly and then drop back down to average levels. There is no significant difference in traffic levels between the other offices. To what is the traffic most likely related (justify your answer)?

(f) What is the probable cause?

(g) How should you resolve the problem?

(h) You need to reduce the circuit load into and out of the Phoenix location. You need to keep changes to the web servers to a minimum. The database server deployed in Chicago must host an accurate, up-to-date set of all corporate data. Based on what you know about the network, what should you do?

(i) How does this resolve the problem?

(j) What additional traffic will this solution generate?

2. The following questions refer to the network in Figure 10-13. Linux file servers are responsible for login and authentication. Clients are a mix of various Windows versions and Linux distributions. The network includes a small number of Windows-based application servers, identified in the figure.

- The application servers are as follows:
- **bdata.busicorp.com:** Database server
- **busiweb1.busicorp.com:** Internal web server
- **busiweb2.busicorp.com:** Internal web server
- **ms.busicorp.com:** Internal mail server
- **vs.busicorp.com:** Streaming video server

Figure 10-13

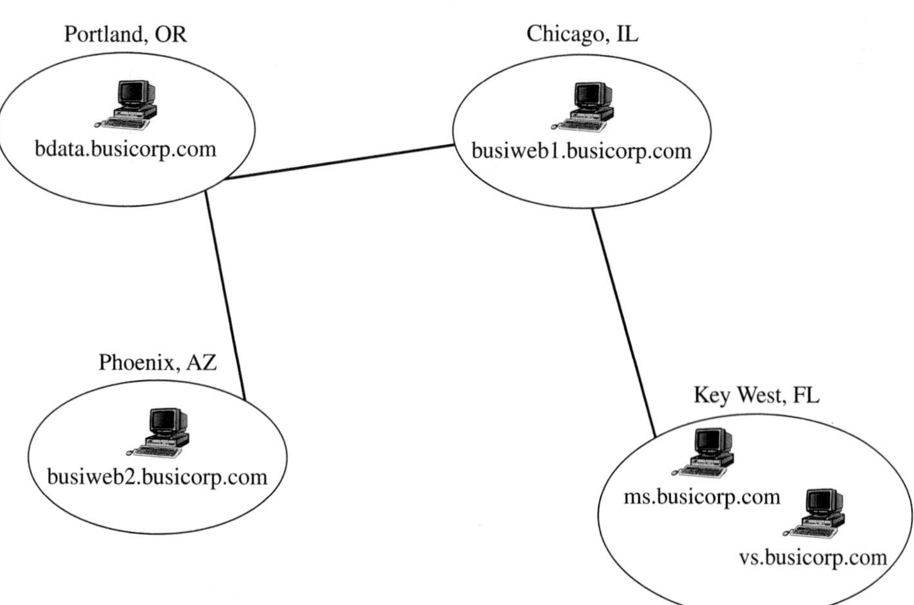

A sample heterogeneous network.

You are redesigning the network to provide optimal performance. This includes determining what changes, if any, need to be made to the wide area links. Currently, the offices are linked by point-to-point T1 carrier circuits.

(a) From the standpoint of reliability and accessibility, what are the potential concerns about the current WAN configuration?
(b) What is the minimal change you can make to the network to minimize the potential impact of this shortcoming?
(c) How does this minimize the potential impact? Give a specific example.
(d) What kinds of information do you need to collect about the application servers?
(e) What type of tools would enable you to predict the estimated circuit load changes if you relocate any of the application servers?
(f) Login and authentication are handled by Linux servers in Key West and Portland. How does this impact network traffic?
(g) How can you minimize average circuit traffic resulting from authentication requests?

3. The following questions refer to the network in Figure 10-14. The WAN links are VPN connections through the Internet. Even though only one connection is shown from each location, the WAN is configured as a mesh.

Figure 10-14

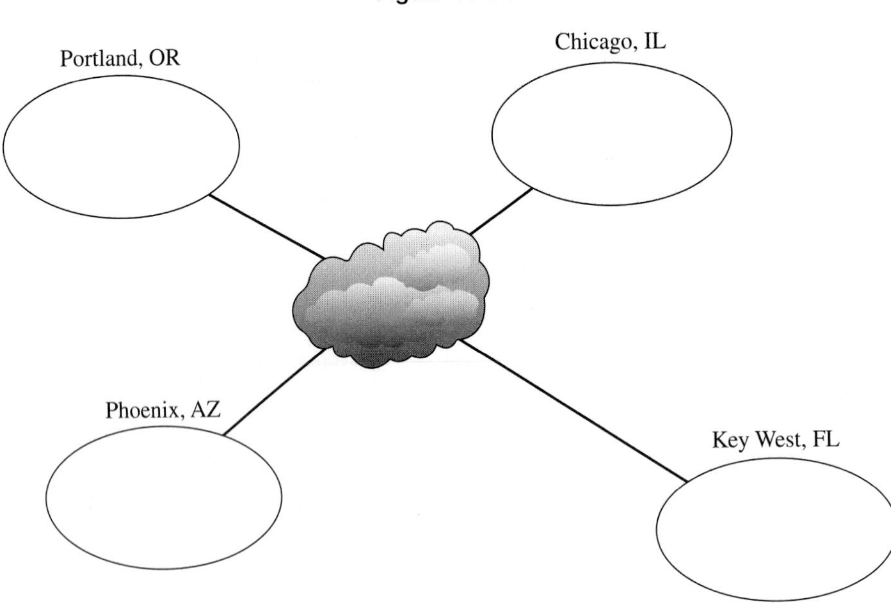

A VPN WAN.

The network is configured as a Windows Active Directory domain. All the clients run Windows 2000 Professional, Windows XP, or Windows Vista. Each location has a Linux computer configured as an internal website.

(a) You want to minimize connection costs. Connections in Portland and Chicago are made using ADSL. How does this affect the types of connections you must use in Phoenix and Key West?

(b) Why?

(c) What are potential concerns when using a cable modem to connect a LAN to the local ISP?

(d) What changes would be required if switching from a cable modem to an ADSL connection?

(e) If the new connection has similar available bandwidth, how would changing the connection type affect local LAN users?

(f) How can you avoid this?

YOU TRY IT

Network Migration

Your company's network is currently configured as a set of stand-alone LANs. Some of the LANs are subnetworked. All the LANs are configured with private IP addresses. Each is configured with the same Class C address range.

Each LAN is configured as a Windows Active Directory domain. After connecting the LANs, you plan to reconfigure the network using a hierarchical structure, with a root domain at the main office and child domains (subdomains) that are dependent on the root domain at the main office and each of the local offices. You plan to deploy new domain controllers at each location and repurpose the current domain controllers as file servers.

Network servers and application servers are duplicated at each location. This includes DHCP, DNS, mail, print, file, web, NAT, and database servers. You plan to use VPN connections over the Internet to connect the LANs. The final architecture will be a mesh configuration.

1. You want to use ADSL connections to the ISPs. What is required at each location?
2. What would prevent you from using the same vendors for each location?
3. You generate a combined list of all the hardware required for the new network configuration. This includes replacing any client computers that cannot be upgraded to current Windows versions. During which building-block network design phase would you identify these requirements?
4. Your company has a list of possible hardware and software vendors. How could you generate bids to find the best prices?
5. What changes, if any, will you need to make to the TCP/IP configuration for each LAN?
6. Why?
7. Based on what you know about the LAN configurations, what is the easiest way to make this change?
8. What cost reduction, if any, might be possible in the new network configuration?
9. In order to ensure that the network is reliable, how many domain controllers will you need?

11

NETWORK MANAGEMENT

Starting Point

Go to www.wiley.com/college/ciccarelli to assess your knowledge of network management.
Determine where you need to concentrate your effort.

What You'll Learn in This Chapter

- ▲ Network management roles
- ▲ Managing reliability
- ▲ Configuration management
- ▲ Network and server monitoring
- ▲ Management systems
- ▲ Management utilities

After Studying This Chapter, You'll Be Able To

- ▲ Justify the network management function in an organization
- ▲ Use backups, fault-tolerant disk systems, and redundancy to help ensure reliability
- ▲ Given a data scenario, design appropriate backup and restore routines
- ▲ Identify requirements for managing users
- ▲ Describe how to implement automated software distribution and updates
- ▲ Identify tools and procedures to improve network and server performance
- ▲ Explain the functions and features of Simple Network Management Protocol (SNMP) network management systems (NMSs)
- ▲ Describe the proper use of server management tools

INTRODUCTION

Network management is the process of operating, monitoring, and controlling a network to ensure that it works as intended and provides value to its users. When discussing network management, you need to consider some general management areas:

- Managing the network as a whole.
- Managing individual servers.
- Managing client computers.
- Managing users.

Obviously, network management is an extremely broad subject area. There's no way we can address all aspects of network management in a single chapter. Even if you limit yourself to a homogeneous network with a single NOS, the subject can fill several volumes.

Our goal in this chapter is to focus on some key management areas and relate them to the types of tasks you might be called upon to perform in a network support role. We start by looking at network management requirements and ways they might be met. From there, we move on to two fundamental management activities: managing backups and managing redundancy. We then look at configuration management and automating software distribution, as well as network and server monitoring. You will also be introduced to tools that are specific to TCP/IP-based networks. Finally, you will get a brief introduction to server and server application management tools.

11.1 Recognizing Network Management Requirements

Effective network management starts with a good network design. Without a well-planned, well-designed network and without well-organized network management staff, operating a network is extremely difficult. Unfortunately, many network managers spend most of their time **firefighting**—dealing with breakdowns and immediate problems. If managers do not spend enough time on planning and organizing their networks and networking staff, they are destined to be reactive rather than proactive in solving problems.

11.1.1 Identifying Management Requirements

Network management requirements have changed dramatically since the late 1980s. There has been an explosion in the use of microcomputer-based networks, with more than 90 percent of most organizations' total computer pro-the number of computers attached to LANs has grown by almost 40 percent per year. In addition, the number of Internet-based servers (e.g., web servers, email servers, FTP servers) has grown dramatically.

Where mainframes are still part of the network mix, mainframe networks remain important, but the real future of network management lies in the successful management of multiple clients and servers communicating over LANs, WANs, and the Internet. Part of the underlying management headache is that LANs, WANs, and web servers have often been initially deployed by individual departments as separate networks and applications. Their initial goals were to meet the needs of their individual owners. Integration and integrated management came later.

Modern network management encompasses management requirements at every level of the network. It means understanding the needs of heterogeneous hardware and software systems as well as the wants and needs of a diverse network user population. The bottom line, in every case, is working to keep the network working—and working well.

11.1.2 Justifying Network Administration

As a **network administrator**, the professional responsible for managing the network, you have the responsibility of ensuring uninterrupted network service to users. Having well-honed troubleshooting skills may be a great asset for a desktop support person, but it is not enough for a network administrator. You need to know about problems before they exist. How is this possible? Solid planning, the right monitoring tools, and detailed documentation will help you stay a step ahead.

Network management is important because it represents the culmination of the past, current, and future work on a network. In essence, network management is the glue that ensures that legacy systems continue to operate with existing and new systems. And in the end, this glue should be transparent to users in your organization.

Even the simplest of today's networks are complex entities that change minute by minute. The challenge for a network administrator or an information technology (IT) team is to have all the tools necessary to identify those changes and determine whether a change warrants an intervention. That means considering everything in the proper context. For example, you might find that a network server is operating near full capacity. However, if the server is under heavy load only in the morning when everyone is logging in, you might determine that you don't need to take any kind of immediate action. But if the server is under heavy load most of the time, you may need to take a closer look.

Well-planned and -executed network management procedures and policies can help reduce the total costs of operating a business. Networks perform several roles, one of which is the automation of processes that were once done by hand. For example, organizing addresses and addressing envelopes for a mass mailing is a task that once would have taken several days. Now it takes only a few minutes if you have a database of addresses and a functioning network. If the network is down, it could take hours or days to retrain staff or reorganize a department to use a manual system. The problem can probably be fixed before the alternative method can be in place, but that time (and money) is still lost. Network **downtime**—unplanned loss of network resources—can have a serious adverse effect on a company's finances, but solid network management can help prevent downtime. Network reliability is important enough that network hardware and software often include an **uptime** rating—that is, a reliability rating based on the percentage of the time the resources will be available.

It's important that you understand your role in network administration, especially as your networks grow and evolve. You have to check your ego at the door, especially when networks are organized around smaller entities. For example, when management is organized around departments, or WAN management is primarily delegated at the LAN level, administrators must work together and keep each other informed about their activities.

A key to integrating LANs, WANs, and the Internet into one overall organization network is for LAN, WAN, and web managers—if the roles are filled by different individuals or teams—to recognize that they cannot make independent decisions without considering their impacts on other parts of the organization's network. There must be a single overall communications and networking goal that best meets the needs of the entire organization. This may require some network managers to compromise on policies that are not in the best interests of their own departments or networks.

11.1.3 Considering Network Management Strategies

For a network management strategy to be well planned and implemented, it is critical that information about the network be readily available and regularly reviewed and analyzed. **Latency** (i.e., network performance delays) and **bottlenecks** (i.e., areas with less-than-optimal performance) can be identified as they occur. The less acceptable, but more common, alternative is that users report performance delays that might have already grown into much bigger problems.

As a network administrator, you must also stay abreast of changes on the network. This includes keeping users informed about their responsibilities in maintaining a healthy network. Users often don't understand everything that goes into building and maintaining a network. Although they typically don't need to know the gory details, it's helpful to explain to users networking basics such as how to access the server, how to deal with software errors, and how the backup process works.

You must also consider how network support is organized. Although technical support is only part of the administration and management team, it is critical

Figure 11-1

End-User Support Resources
Level 1: Desktop Support
Level 2: Diagnostic and Network Support
Level 3: Vendor or Software Engineering Support

Support levels.

that it be responsive, reliable, and predictable. You need to set guidelines for response times based on priority and impact on overall network performance. One approach adopted by some IT departments is to provide support in levels, depending on the problem, as shown in Figure 11-1. This helps ensure that support professionals understand what is expected of them and that problems are directed to the appropriate personnel.

The first level of support, **end-user support resources**, involves creating documentation for your users. This can include resources from vendors, how-to articles, and a list of remedies for common problems called a **FAQ (frequently asked questions)**. Key concerns include making sure the documentation is written at a level the users can understand and that it is readily available and easy to use.

If users are unable to resolve a problem on their own, they will request the frontline services of the Level 1 support team. **Level 1 support staff** are responsible for resolving desktop application issues, assisting with software installation or configuration, and troubleshooting basic network connectivity. Typically, Level 1 support utilizes email or the phone whenever possible to provide a cost-effective support model. Remote desktop control applications allow Level 1 support to view the steps performed by the user or take control of the user's computer when necessary. If all else fails, Level 1 support staff may be called on to provide on-site support, although this is provided as a last resort.

Level 2 support staff (and **Level 3 support staff**, at some companies) are more skilled and experienced in troubleshooting than the Level 1 support team. They have more in-depth knowledge of desktops, networks, and specialized network devices, such as firewalls and routers. These levels of support staff have to know how to deal with dozens of software applications and hardware because a technical problem can have a number of very different causes, depending on the network scenario.

Although some network administrators might also have a technical support role, this isn't true in all organizations. In some organizations, network administrators aren't so much the next step up in support as a separate support path.

Larger networks have more than enough going on to keep a network administrator or network support team busy full time. It's not unusual for technical support personnel to work in parallel with network support personnel and put their heads together on particularly difficult problems. Often, the difference is that technical support personnel are more generalists, needing to know a little about a lot of different subject areas. Network support personnel have in-depth, special knowledge about the NOSs used, network technologies, and applications and services provided on the network.

When all internal support resources are exhausted, the IT staff might turn to outside resources for help. Vendors may be contacted for specific troubleshooting support or to report an undocumented software problem. Or, in the case of customized applications, the software engineering group may need to get involved to

Figure 11-2

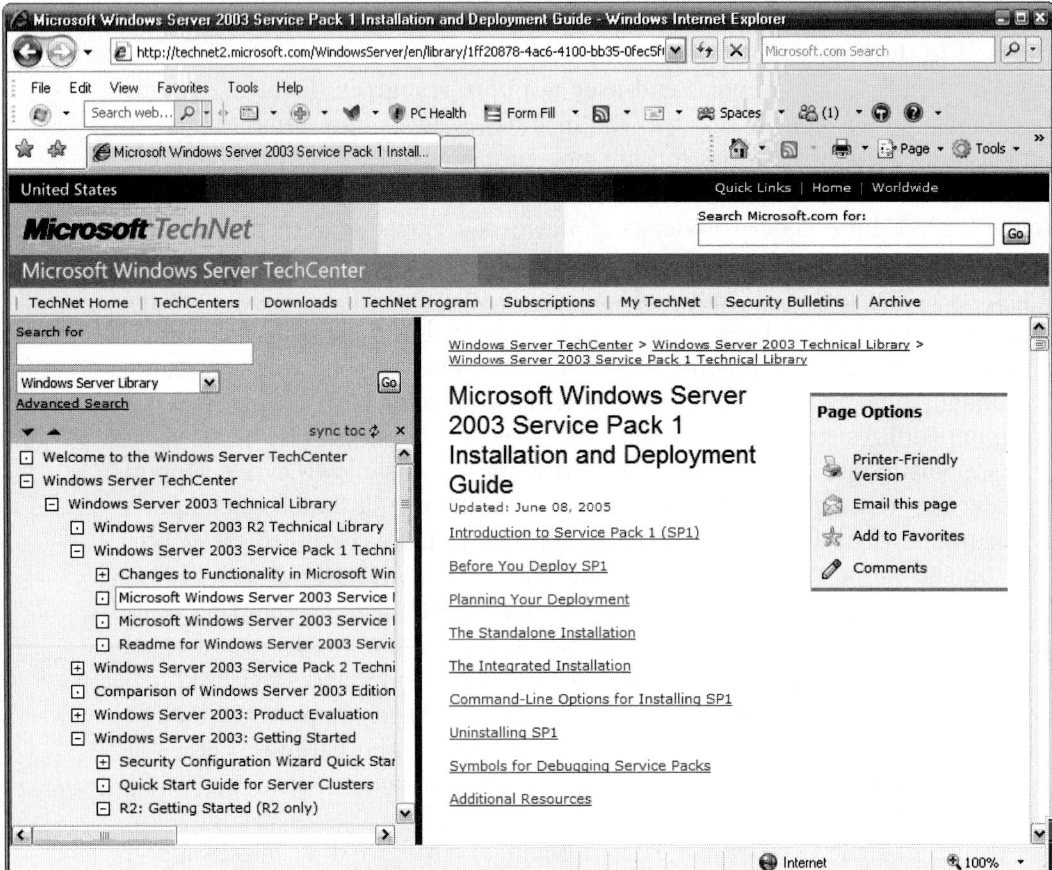

Microsoft TechNet documentation.

determine whether changes need to be made directly to the software. If the latter occurs, you need to have an alternative solution ready for your users because it may take months before the software engineers or vendors are able to provide a fix.

Why the delay before going for outside help? The trend in recent years, after an initial period, is to provide support on a fee-based, per-incident system. These charges can be significant, in part to ensure that you call only when you have a serious problem. However, most manufacturers often also have extensive online, automated support resources. These are designed to not only answer most of your questions but provide access to downloaded resources such as device drivers, program fixes, updates, and the like. One example is Microsoft's TechNet, which includes a massive, searchable documentation database. As shown in Figure 11-2 TechNet includes items such as detailed installation and configuration instructions.

FOR EXAMPLE

Instant Credibility

How does a company know in advance whether a job candidate really knows anything about network administration? Consider this situation: A smaller-sized company has just lost its network administrator to a higher bidder. The administrator has left suddenly, choosing to use up accrued vacation time as his last two weeks on the job. You need a new administrator who can come in ready to dig into the task. The problem is, you don't really have anyone who is really qualified to even ask the right questions.

One thing you can use to evaluate potential candidates is professional certifications. While it is true that some certifications are probably as much a test about how well you can cram for exams and take tests, it's become more common for the exams to force you to apply knowledge rather than just parrot back information. Nearly all the major manufacturers have certifications based on the networking products and server applications.

You have a few Cisco brand routers on your network? Maybe you want to require an entry-level Cisco certification. Your network is based on Windows Active Directory? Microsoft has various levels of Windows certifications that relate to networking applications. Interested in seeing if candidates know anything at all? CompTIA has a general networking certification and another set of certifications targeted at client and end-user support.

As a computer professional, what does this mean to you? Despite the bad press that some certifications have gotten over the past several years, they are still seen as one of the best tools for evaluating whether a job candidate has any credibility. They can help you land that first, important job in your professional career path. Once you get there, it is up to you to prove that you do know what you're talking about.

Finally, network management would not be complete without up-to-date, accurate, and complete network documentation. This begins with your network design or, when building a support organization for an existing network, a complete network inventory. Documentation also includes reports on network performance and security, log files, user problem reports, configuration documentation, and even administrator journal entries.

SELF-CHECK

1. In general terms, what is a network administrator's role?
2. Why is it critical to avoid unplanned downtime?

11.2 Managing Reliability

Whether you are currently managing a network or are taking over a network from another administrator, it is very important that the basic components for protecting and managing the network are in place. Initially, you will need to evaluate some basic systems to ensure that there will be no loss of data in the event of a hardware failure or catastrophe such as a fire or natural disaster. Although you have the goal of providing continuous, uninterrupted service to users, reaching that goal won't mean much if some or all of the user data are lost.

Two key concepts define the first objectives a network administrator should achieve: fault tolerance and redundancy. **Fault tolerance** is found in networks that are able to withstand a partial failure and continue to operate, albeit with some impact on performance. Ensuring the highest levels of fault tolerance requires redundancy. **Redundancy** is a system of duplicating a service or function that already exists on a network.

Redundant systems either perform the same function as primary systems or are available as quick replacements. Redundant systems might provide an exact duplicate of the primary system's hardware, software, and data. In other cases, they might be configured to perform the same function but not require duplicate hardware. For example, Microsoft recommends deploying multiple domain controllers that maintain duplicates of the Active Directory database in case of a failure. However, the domain controllers can (and often do) have different hardware and even different software configurations. How you implement these depends on your network's specific requirements. You should consider backup systems to be a requirement in any network environment. You should consider redundant systems on a case-by-case basis, depending on how critical server resources are to network operations.

11.2.1 Managing Backups

Making a backup is the process of copying data stored on a computer and saving an exact duplicate of it on another storage device. Backups of data can include operating systems, user files, applications, and anything that is stored on a hard disk. Making a backup can be as simple as copying a document onto a removable disk or CD for storage, or it can involve special backup software, hardware, and storage media.

Typically, backups of servers and other computers that maintain important data are performed on dedicated hardware, using special software. Most operating systems, and even some applications, include integrated backup software. This can be a part of the operating system, as is the case with the **Windows Backup** utility, or a separate product that ships with the operating system, as is the case with most Linux distributions.

Backups are a critical part of network management. They are the best protection against hardware failure and data loss. Regardless of the size of the company, whether it is a one-person home office or a multiserver network, backups can become the lifeblood in the event of a disaster. Backups have the following characteristics:

- They provide an inexpensive storage option.
- Removable media (tapes) allow for off-site storage.
- Large amounts of data can be backed up at once.
- Entire data sets can be recovered in case of serious failure.
- Files that are accidentally erased can be restored individually.

You have various options for storage media as your **backup destination**. Two of the most common are backing up to a network share and backing up to magnetic tape.

The following are some of the advantages of backing up to a network share:

- Storage is readily available.
- Backups are easy to configure.
- It is simple to set up fully automated backups.

Tape drives are used to store large amounts of information at a relatively low cost. Most drives use Small Computer System Interface (SCSI) communications, although high-end systems use fiber-optic connections for the best performance when transferring data. They also have the advantage of being removable media, making it possible to keep a recent backup copy off-site in case of catastrophic failure or natural disaster.

Although the whole purpose of a backup is to be able to restore the data when necessary, you may find yourself in a situation in which a restore does not work. You need to understand, when using tapes as your backup media, that they have a limited lifespan and must be replaced periodically. Tape drives also need regular maintenance. You need to clean a tape drive regularly and should make sure you have access to another tape drive that is the same model as your backup drive in case your tape drive fails.

Understanding Backup Types

There are different types of backups, and they vary in the amount of time required and the amount of data backed up. The **archive bit**, which depends on the type of backup you are running, helps determine the files you need to back up. When a file's archive bit is set on, it indicates that the file has changed and needs to be backed up. Most backup systems support the following types of backups:

- **Normal: Normal backups**, also referred to as **full backups**, are used to back up all data, whether or not all the files have changed since the last backup. This type of backup is used the first time a backup is performed on a server and then periodically to back up all data.
- **Differential: Differential backups** use the archive bit to determine whether a file has changed since the last normal backup. The backup does not reset the archive bit when it runs. Differential backups take longer than incremental backups on subsequent runs because all changed data are backed up each time. They require less time to restore data because you restore the full backup and the most recent differential backup only.
- **Incremental: Incremental backups** use the archive bit to determine whether a file has changed since the last full or incremental backup. The archive bit is reset as each file is backed up. Incremental backups take less time than differential backups on subsequent backups. However, data restoration takes more time because the normal backup tape and all incremental tapes made since the last normal backup are needed.

Some backup systems support other backup types, such as daily backups, which back up the files that have changed on a specific day, based on the file's Date modified property, whether or not the archive bit is set.

Planning Backup and Recovery

When planning your backup strategy, keep in mind that a normal backup usually takes place at an off-peak time, such as over the weekend. You can configure the backup to run after everyone has left for the weekend. Because normal backups back up all data, the backup can take a long time to complete. In companies that require support over the weekend, the backup strategy needs to be

Figure 11-3

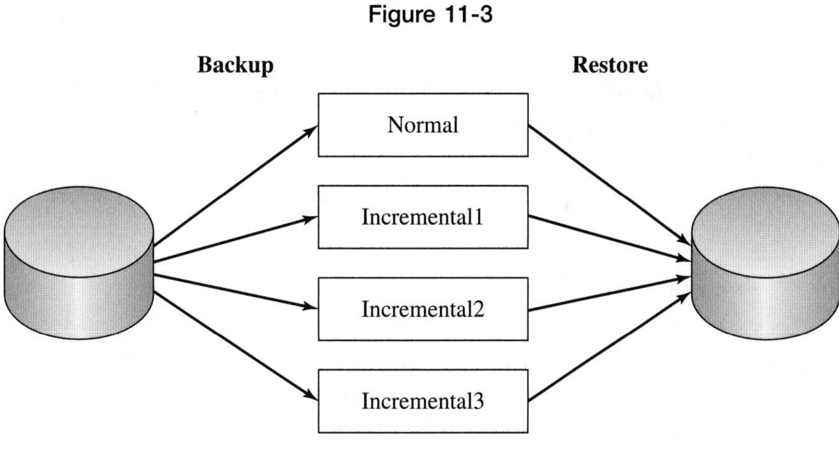

Incremental backups.

carefully planned to back up all data without interfering with the normal functions of the company.

Between normal backups, you can use either incremental or differential backups to minimize data loss in case of a failure. The type of backup you run and the frequency depends on factors such as how long you can allow for backups to run and how quickly you need to recover the data in the event of a failure.

Consider the situation shown in Figure 11-3. You run a normal backup over the weekend and incremental backups nightly. If a failure occurred on Wednesday afternoon, you would have to restore from the normal backup and the two incremental backups made since that normal backup (in order).

Compare this to Figure 11-4. In this scenario, you run a normal backup over the weekend and differential backups nightly. Recovery from the same failure

Figure 11-4

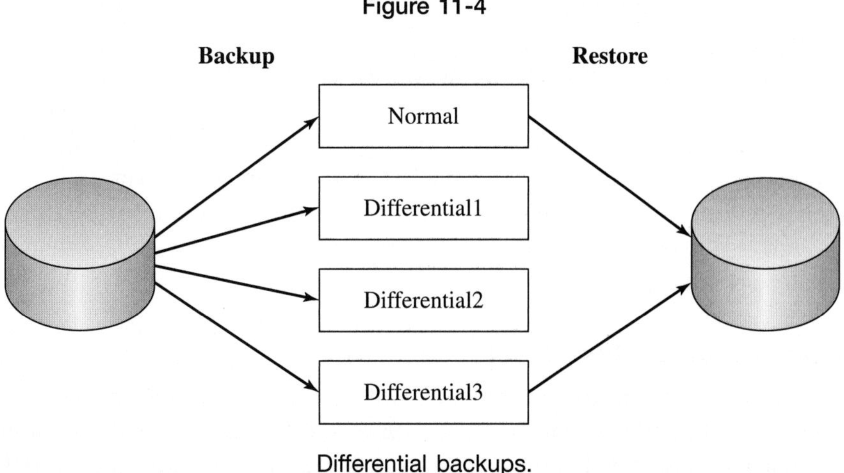

Differential backups.

means restoring from the normal backup and one differential backup—the one made Tuesday.

As a general rule, if your priority is getting backups to run as quickly as possible, you should use incremental backups. If your emphasis is on restoring data with minimal time or effort, you should use differential backups. Keep in mind that any data that are not backed up will have to be re-created or reposted.

11.2.2 Managing Redundancy

Redundancy can be applied almost anywhere in a network, from hard disks to network cables. For instance, the dependence on Internet access for business transactions and communication has prompted many companies to add redundant Internet connections. Most of these companies use two separate providers for more reliable service.

The following are some situations in which you might use redundancy:

- ▲ You should add redundancy to critical servers in the form of a **redundant array of independent (or inexpensive) disks (RAID)** solution.
- ▲ You should add redundant features to any component that must always be running.
- ▲ You should use redundancy for business-critical functions such as a database server or Internet access that clients depend on.
- ▲ If you would lose your job if the network goes down, you need to add redundancy wherever possible.

There are two general redundancy categories: disk-level redundancy and server-level redundancy. Disk-level redundancy is designed to protect a computer against data loss if one hard disk fails (or two or more hard disks, in some configurations). Server-level redundancy protects you in case any critical component, or the entire computer, fails.

If money weren't a problem, networks would be designed with full redundancy. In the real world, cost is a major factor in deciding what services, functions, and equipment need (or at least get) redundancy. The centralized services found on client/server and directory-based networks make a server an ideal candidate for redundancy because it is the most cost-effective way of protecting data. It is much less expensive to add redundancy to one or a few servers than to an office of workstations.

Redundancy at the Disk Level

The most common way of providing disk-level redundancy is through implementation of some type of fault-tolerant RAID solution. A fault-tolerant solution is one that protects your data in case of a disk failure. There are several defined

Figure 11-5

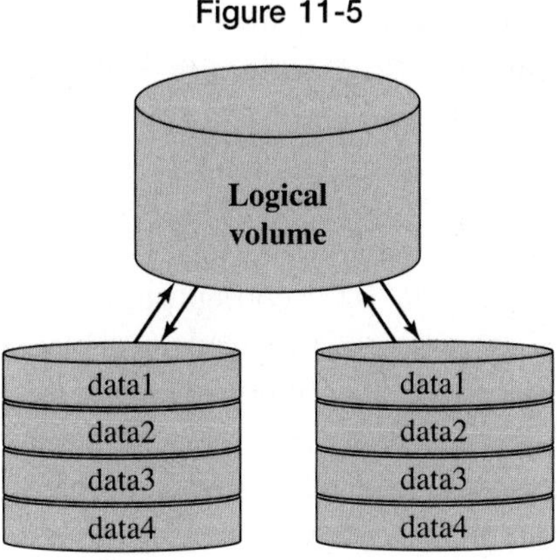

A RAID 1 configuration.

RAID configurations, but the two most commonly used in PC networks are **RAID 1**, which defines disk duplexing and disk mirroring, and **RAID 5**, which defines disk striping with parity.

With *RAID 1,* you have two hard disks, both with identical data, as in Figure 11-5. This means that 50 percent of the storage capacity is lost to providing fault tolerance. If either drive fails, the computer will continue to operate, using data from the other disk drive. With **disk mirroring**, both hard disks are connected to the same disk controller, making it a possible point of failure. With **disk duplexing**, the hard disks are connected to separate disk controllers.

RAID 5, shown in Figure 11-6, requires at least three hard disks. This is also known as **disk striping with parity**. The equivalent of one disk's storage

Figure 11-6

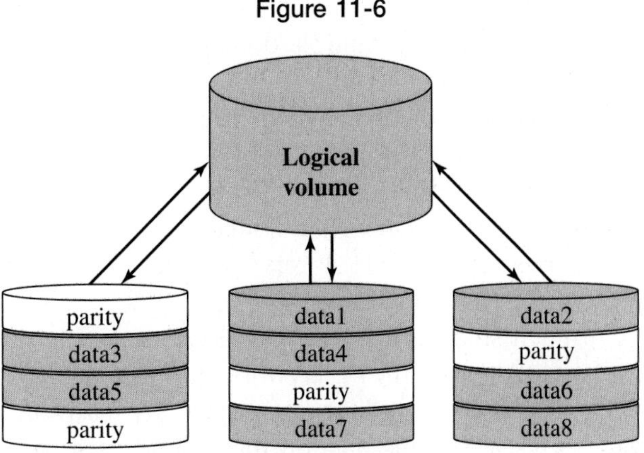

A RAID 5 configuration.

capacity is lost to fault tolerance, so this method becomes more efficient the more disks you use. Data are written in blocks striped across the hard disks. Each set of data will also include parity data, which are used to detect and correct from data errors, including the loss of one hard disk. In fact, the only noticeable difference when a hard disk is lost is a possible loss of performance during reads because of the need to regenerate the missing data.

If one hard disk fails in a RAID 5 configuration, the data are still available. To recover from the failure, you would need to replace the failing disk. Some configurations are **hot-swappable**, meaning that you can replace the disk without shutting down the disk subsystem or interrupting access to the data. After the failed disk is replaced, its data are regenerated.

The other configurations are essentially variations on or combinations of RAID 1 and RAID 5, with some offering better performance, better protection, or both. RAID disk subsystems implement the RAID configuration through hardware. Many operating systems, including Windows Server versions, also support RAID configurations implemented through software. These solutions are typically less expensive than RAID disk subsystems, but they also usually deliver poorer performance. If performance and fault tolerance are critical issues for your organization, you should consider a hardware-based RAID solution.

Redundancy at the Server Level

There are several options for implementing server-level redundancy. Your available options will depend somewhat on your NOS, your server operating systems, and, in some cases, the server applications you are running. However, even with the different available variations, we can look at server redundancy by focusing on a few key features.

There are also redundancy options that fall more into the realm of fault tolerance, where all the servers of a particular type are active on the network. When one server fails, the others take up the additional load. Examples of this include an Active Directory network with multiple domain controllers or deployment of multiple DNS servers on your network. The servers can cover for each other because they all contain the same data. You use a similar configuration when providing fault tolerance for DHCP servers. However, you cannot configure duplicate scopes on DHCP servers. Instead, one server needs to have primary responsibility for a subnet. You configure a small percentage of those addresses as an address scope on a separate DHCP server to keep things running smoothly if the primary DHCP server fails. However, because a second server contains what is typically a much smaller address pool, this is only a temporary solution.

Typically, configurations used in PC networks use either warm redundancy or hot redundancy. With **warm redundancy**, you have the hardware, operating system, and software in place, but the data on the redundant server aren't synchronized with the main server. With **hot redundancy**, you have identical hardware, software, and data. The difference between the two is that hot redundancy allows for immediate or near-immediate switchover between the servers. With warm redundancy, you must first synchronize the data on the redundant server, and then you switch over through a process known as **failover**.

There are two types of failover: automatic and manual. **Automatic failover** is required when you must minimize the downtime while switching between servers. The primary server's failure is detected automatically, and the switch is made to the redundant (also called the secondary or alternate) server automatically, without any type of administrator intervention. With **manual failover**, administrator intervention is required to switch between the primary and redundant servers. Manual failover is typically required when you must perform other actions, such as synchronizing the redundant server, as part of the process.

Many NOSs, such as Windows Server 2003, support multiple options for implementing server redundancy. There are also some third-party solutions that

FOR EXAMPLE

Setting Backup Schedules

Nearly anyone who has used computers for any length of time has a horror story to tell about data loss. This is even true of home users, who may suddenly lose their financial records, family photos, and other difficult-to-replace items. (Now, scale that out to a business.)

One of the primary motivations for bringing in a network is to make it easier for users to share data. Users are told to keep their files on network file servers instead of on their local computers. Database servers hold all of an organization's critical data about inventory, sales and payment records, customer information, and financial accounting. Sudden loss of these data could be devastating. How often you need to back up data depends on how critical and volatile your data are.

Frequent backups can be critical. Say that Busicorp has a website that supports Internet-based customers and sales. Customer orders, credit card payments, and electronic payments post directly to a database server that provides the data back end for the web applications. How often do you need to back up the database? A near-constant running backup—maybe even ongoing updates keeping a redundant server synchronized—could be the appropriate answer. Why put in the effort? If that database fails, that information is lost, and not only are you likely to lose those sales, you're likely to lose those customers, who are going to find a different source for what they need in the future. What about the website? It is only hosting programs, not changing data, so you may only need to back up the website once a week or less.

work with nearly any NOS or server application. However, from a cost standpoint, you should first use any options included with your NOS whenever possible.

As a general rule, the more automated the process and the faster the failover, the more expensive. When choosing your configuration option, before you can determine whether a solution is worth the expense, you must consider the cost of downtime and how long it is likely to take you to finish failover.

SELF-CHECK

1. Describe the three types of backups that are most commonly used in backup plans.
2. Describe RAID 1 and RAID 5 disk subsystems.
3. When would you need to implement automatic failover?

11.3 Controlling Configuration Management

Configuration management means managing the network's hardware and software configuration, documenting it, and ensuring that it is updated as the configuration changes. This includes both server and client configurations, including variations to support different roles and requirements.

Several things can fall under the general category of configuration management. We're going to focus on two: managing user configurations and managing client software. Device configuration management, ways of centralizing device monitoring and control, is discussed separately, later in this chapter.

11.3.1 Understanding User Management

One of the most common configuration activities is adding and deleting user accounts. When new users are added to a network, they are usually categorized as being members of some group of users, such as faculty or students, as in Figure 11-7. Each user group can have its own access privileges, which define what file servers, directories, and files those groups can access. Rights and permissions assigned to groups are also applied to group members unless explicitly blocked.

You can also provide users and groups with their own **login scripts**, which specify commands to run each time the user logs in. Some network operating systems, including recent Windows Server versions, also support separate scripts

Figure 11-7

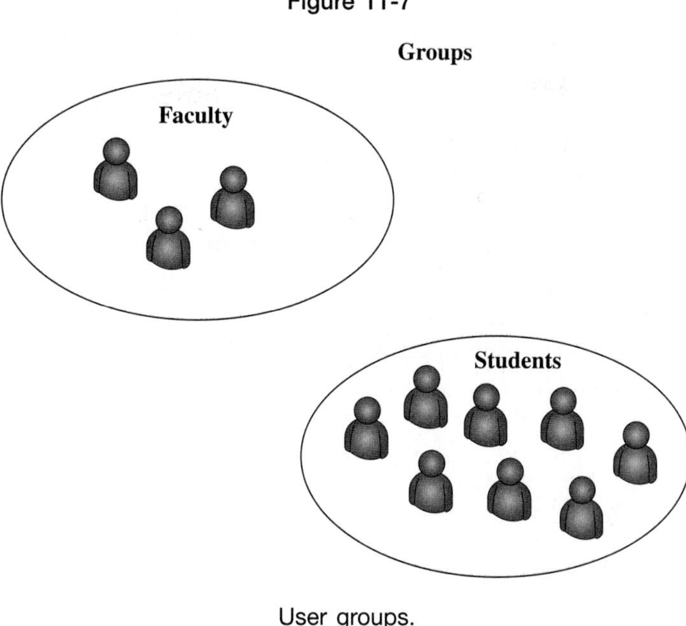

User groups.

associated with the client computer instead of the user. These scripts execute on computer startup.

In a network that uses a peer-to-peer or workgroup configuration, you must manage users separately on each computer. One of the reasons that client/server and directory-based networks are preferred is that they support centralized user management. User account information, including assigned rights and access permissions, are centrally stored on network servers.

The goal is to manage, whenever possible, at the group level, and make changes at the individual user level only when absolutely necessary. That lets you make better use of available time and effort: You can make a change once and have it apply to a group of related users.

11.3.2 Understanding Software Management

A common configuration activity is automatically installing or updating the software on the client computers attached to the network. Every time a new application system is developed or updated (or when a new version is released), each client computer in the organization must be updated. Traditionally, this meant that someone from the networking staff had to go to each client computer and manually install the software. For a small organization, this is time-consuming but not a major problem. For a large organization with hundreds or thousands of clients, it can be a nightmare.

Electronic software distribution (ESD), sometimes called **desktop management** or **automated software delivery**, is one solution to the software management configuration problem. ESD enables network managers to install software on client computers over the network without physically touching each client computer. **Desktop Management Interface (DMI)** is the emerging standard in ESD software.

Some ESD packages provide application software for the network server and all client computers. The server software communicates directly with the ESD application software on the clients and can be instructed to download and install certain application packages on each client at some predefined time. Most can even test for and install application prerequisites, if necessary.

FOR EXAMPLE

Automatic Updates

If you have a small network, you may think you don't need ESD. After all, you don't spend that much time doing software installs or upgrades, and you might even be able to let the users do it themselves. You don't need it, right? It's just not worth the effort. Not so fast . . .

Your network could be using ESD, and you might not even realize it. Do you have any computers running Windows? Do you enable automatic updates? If so, you are using ESD. Windows Update streams software patches, security fixes, and other necessary changes to your operating system gradually as they become available. The only real requirements are that you have a genuine (valid) copy of Windows (yes, Microsoft does check) and an Internet connection. The typical configuration is to have your computer contact the Microsoft Update site and download the updates automatically.

Microsoft isn't the only company updating its software automatically. Do you use Adobe's Reader to view PDF files? Current Reader versions default to checking with Adobe's website for updates and letting you know if anything is available. So do Corel's graphics programs.

Still consider ESD optional? What about antivirus software? Antivirus software has become a fact of life. Connecting to the Internet, even just to receive email, without protection, is a risk. You would have a difficult time finding a new computer that ships without antivirus software already installed. However, the software is no better than its threat database. The risks keep changing, which means the software needs constant updates to remain a viable protection. That means ESD.

With some NOSs, this functionality is built into the operating system, so a separate ESD application is not required. You can, for example, configure software distribution over a Microsoft Active Directory network. You even have the option of associating the application with either the user or the client computer.

ESD software greatly reduces the cost of configuration management over the long term because it eliminates the need to update each and every client computer manually. There is the additional overhead required for configuring software distribution, but it is usually minimal in comparison to the effort required to manually update every network client. Most versions also produce and maintain accurate documentation of all software installed on each client computer, supported at various levels of automation. This makes it easier for network administrators to track software use and to avoid accidentally violating software licenses by installing an application on too many client computers.

SELF-CHECK

1. What is the primary advantage of organizing users into groups?
2. For what purpose is ESD used?

11.4 Monitoring Your Network

After the basic components of a network are installed and running, it is time to get into the next phase of network management. **Performance monitoring** involves several tasks, each of which is intended to be completed with the same goal in mind: to stay informed about the health of the network. This includes evaluating the performance of the network, servers, and workstations. Performance monitoring is also a critical procedure for identifying and correcting network problems. The faster the problems can be identified, the sooner a solution can be decided on and appropriate action taken.

Performance monitoring involves several tasks:

- Setting baselines for network performance.
- Analyzing network traffic performance.
- Assessing server hardware and software performance.

Notice that there are, once again, two levels of activity referenced here. There are network monitoring activities that include the network as a whole and activities associated with individual computers, typically key network servers and application servers.

11.4.1 Establishing a Baseline

If you don't know how a network performs under normal conditions, it is difficult to determine whether it is performing poorly. **Baselining**, or establishing a **performance baseline**, is a way to set a starting point for evaluating performance. Baselines vary on different networks because of the number of variables involved. Performance can be affected by the network protocol, the speed of the workstations and servers, and the speed (i.e., bandwidth) of the network infrastructure. The baseline for a network can be an average of performance measures or can be based on separate values collected to represent typical and peak usage requirements.

When you have this information, you can compare network performance to expected norms. If the comparison indicates a significant decrease in the efficiency of the network, the network administrator knows there might be a problem. Without baseline information for this type of analysis, the network administrator might not know when the network is performing poorly until the network comes to a screeching halt.

11.4.2 Analyzing Network Performance

Network communication is a very complicated process. Nowhere is this more evident than when collecting data on network traffic. Analyzing network performance is a two-part process. The first step is to collect data as it is transmitted on the network. You do this by running a network analysis program that will intercept all information transmitted on the network, whether or not it is intended for you.

The second part of the process involves you, the network administrator. Your responsibility is to evaluate the information for any interesting information. This may include but is not be limited to the following:

- ▲ **The types of traffic on the network:** Some network management protocols and network activities can create a lot of additional, possibly irrelevant, traffic. One thing that might help is disabling unneeded services and, if it is not required, NetBIOS support.
- ▲ **Frequently used protocols:** Some protocols are less efficient than others. Typically, a network is designed to have one primary protocol, usually TCP/IP. If your analysis of protocols in use reveals an excessive amount of another type of traffic, such as AppleTalk traffic, you may want to determine the source of the traffic and determine whether the traffic can be controlled, replaced with a more efficient protocol, or completely eliminated.
- ▲ **Frequency of collisions:** Collisions, which occur on Ethernet networks, are indicative of a network that is saturated with too many devices competing for access. Installing a switch might be a solution to the problem of excessive collisions. Each port on a switch can segment the network into separate collision domains. Another solution might be to subnet your LAN.

▲ **The percentage of frames with errors:** As frames are received on a device, they are checked for errors. Ethernet frames may have errors because of garbled data or because of fragmentation. Packet errors often indicate that a NIC is malfunctioning. The solution is to identify and replace the failing NIC.

▲ **The devices transmitting the most packets:** Workstations or other devices transmitting an unusually high number of frames in comparison to other computers may need attention. This could be due to valid requirements, or it might be an indication of a hardware problem or even of a virus (or other malicious code) infection.

Several tools are available for collecting data on network performance. One is **WildPacket's EtherPeek** software, a performance monitoring program. In Figure 11-8, EtherPeek displays details about several packets it has captured from an Ethernet network. Of special importance are the type of packets and the source of the packets. Alone, the type of packet and who sent it might not be of much interest during the analysis, but when calculating thousands of packets, this information can be critical. From just these two characteristics, you can determine the most heavily used protocol and the source address that is sending out the most packets. The results may be helpful in identifying a protocol problem or a network device that is transmitting a large number of packets for no apparent reason.

You can use a Protocol Summary report, as shown in Figure 11-9, to determine which protocol causes the majority of the traffic on the network.

Figure 11-8

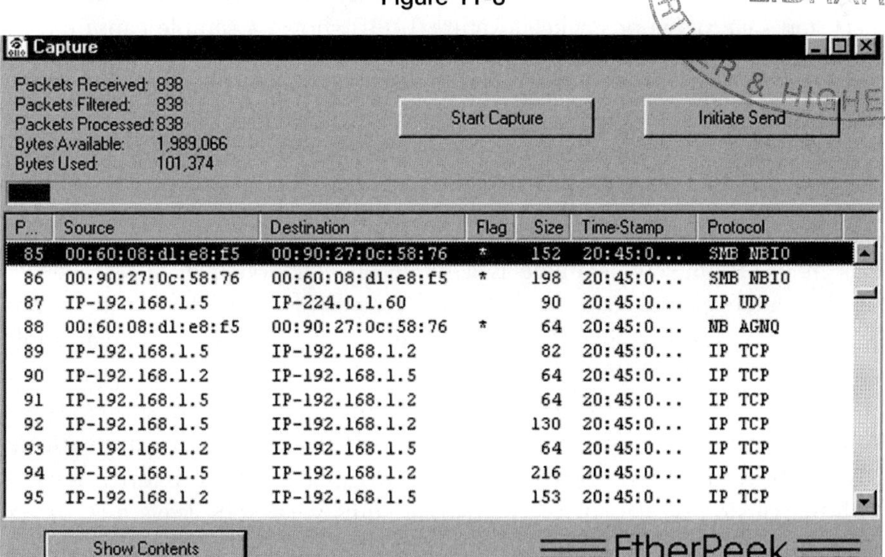

EtherPeek.

Figure 11-9

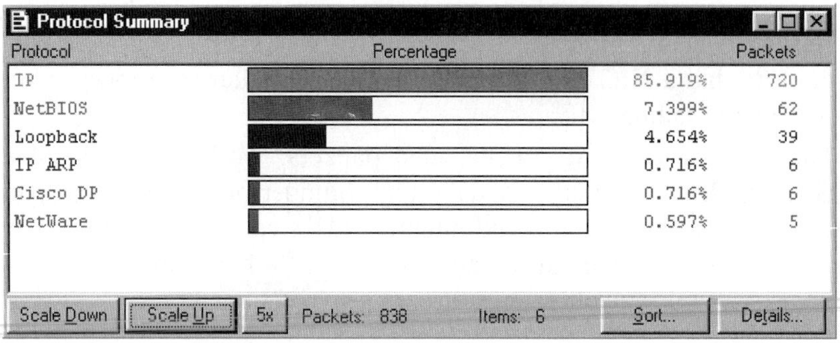

Protocol Summary

Protocol	Percentage	Packets
IP	85.919%	720
NetBIOS	7.399%	62
Loopback	4.654%	39
IP ARP	0.716%	6
Cisco DP	0.716%	6
NetWare	0.597%	5

Scale Down | Scale Up | 5x | Packets: 838 | Items: 6 | Sort... | Details...

A Protocol Summary report.

You can save the data collected from your capture of packets to use later to compare to other reports. You can also perform the capture several times during the day to determine peak usage on the network.

EtherPeek is just one of several applications available. More advanced monitoring devices, known as **network sniffers**, use a combination of hardware and software to monitor network activity and can provide even more detailed information. These devices are also known as **protocol analyzers** or **packet sniffers**. No matter what they're called, they perform pretty much the same function.

It isn't always necessary to buy a separate monitoring application or tool. Microsoft supports the program **Network Monitor** with the Windows Server family of products. Network Monitor can collect network traffic statistics and collect and save network packets. Figure 11-10 shows a sample capture.

The version of Network Monitor that ships with Windows is limited to capturing traffic originating from or destined for computer on which Network Monitor is running. A more advanced version of the application ships with Microsoft's **Systems Management Server (SMS)** product. That version of Network Monitor can capture and store any network traffic, no matter the source or destination, as long the computer on which it is running has a network adapter that supports promiscuous mode. **Promiscuous mode** is a mode of operation that allows a network adapter to intercept and read the complete contents of any packet on the network.

It is important to realize that network monitoring tools and similar applications are also potential security hazards. Unauthorized capture of network traffic could enable a person to collect valid computer names and IP addresses, some user information, and, for applications that require clear text authentication, authentication credentials. A user interested in gathering such information could install the version of Network Monitor that ships with SMS, leave a laptop running and collecting data all day, and review the information later, possibly selling it to the highest bidder.

Figure 11-10

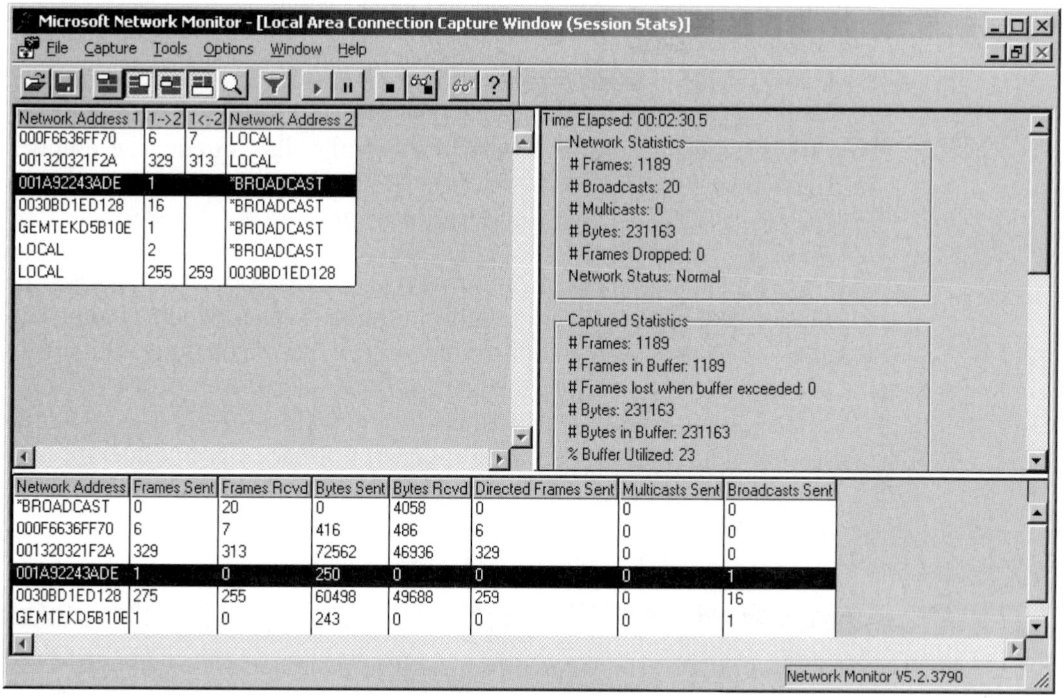

Network Monitor.

11.4.3 Monitoring Network Computers

Network administrators often view servers as the nerve center of a network. When performance lags or a problem occurs, it usually involves the server, and not the network protocol or cables. On the server, particular areas should be monitored regularly, including the following:

- ▲ **CPU usage:** You need to monitor CPU usage closely. If CPU usage frequently holds at over 90 percent, the CPU is a potential performance bottleneck.
- ▲ **Memory usage:** System memory usage is also a critical performance factor. This includes both RAM memory and virtual memory provided through a **swap file**, which is drive space for temporary storage of data that would typically be saved in memory. Excessive **paging**, the processes of moving data between the swap file and RAM, can adversely affect system performance. You also need to watch for **faults** that can occur when the computer can't find the data it is looking for in the swap file; they could indicate that you need a larger swap file.

- **Network traffic:** The demand on the server can be measured by the amount of traffic it is sending and receiving. A high volume of traffic can affect CPU usage as well.
- **Disk read/write:** Excessive reads and writes to the hard disk can indicate that you need a faster hard disk or may need to spread the load between multiple hard disks. You also need to watch the **disk queue**, the number of disk accesses waiting to be serviced. Disk performance problems could be due to excessive paging, indicating that more RAM is needed.

Many products are available for monitoring server performance. Besides the built-in utilities that come with most server products, other products are available to monitor servers. Hewlett-Packard OpenView, IBM Tivoli, and Micromuses NetCool are all very powerful products.

Windows **System Monitor** (called **Performance Monitor** in older Windows versions) is shown in Figure 11-11. Performance information is collected through

Figure 11-11

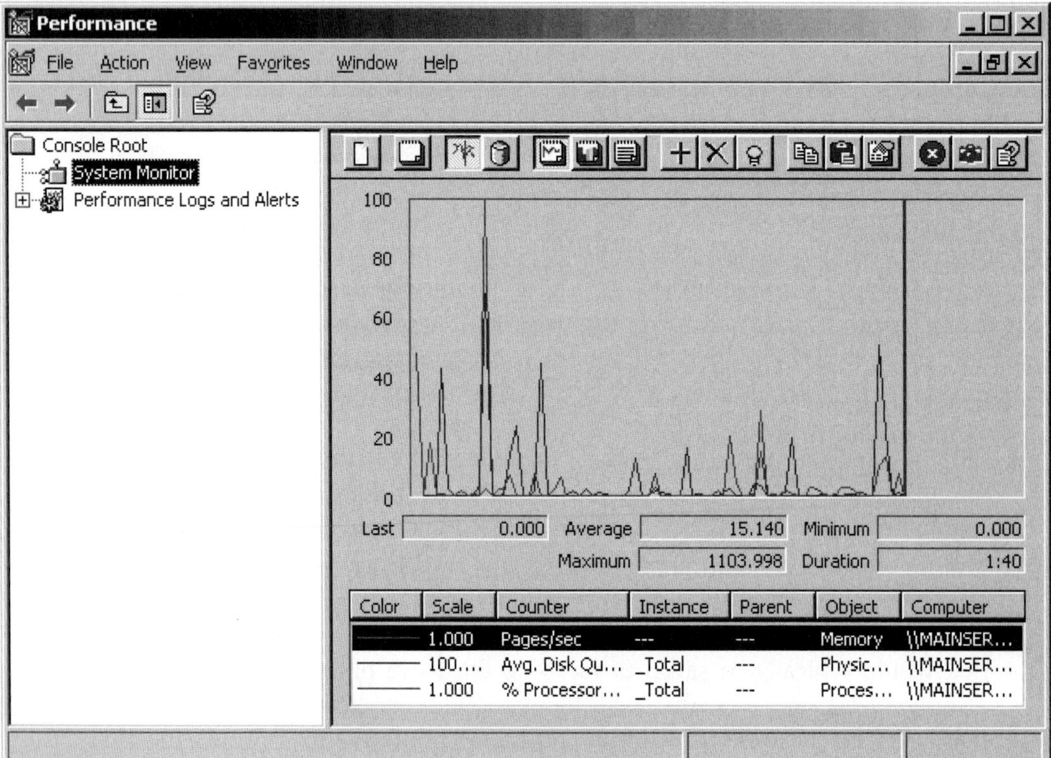

System Monitor.

performance counters, which are grouped into performance objects. For example, the processor's Performance object contains all the performance counters associated directly with the system processor. Some server applications also add their own unique performance counters during installation.

You can monitor real-time activity, as shown in Figure 11-11, or log data for later analysis. You can also log performance data to gather baseline data for individual servers. As with network baseline data, you can use the data later for comparison if you suspect a performance (or other) problem.

System Monitor defaults to the local computer, the computer on which it is running, but you can also collect performance counter information from other

FOR EXAMPLE

Using Alerts

Say that you're the network administrator for Busicorp. You came into the job with the network already in place, and it was a mess. You and your staff spend nearly all your time putting out fires, with very little time for monitoring or advance planning. You know there are some risk areas on the network, not to mention the intermittent problems that you can't quite get a handle on. What can you do?

If you have some idea of the potential problem areas or types of problems you might need to watch for, you can use alerts to help you bring things under control.

Suppose you have an application server that barely meets operational requirements. You suspect that requirements exceed resources during peak use, but you're not even sure when that is. You set up an alert that monitors processor activity. You set the threshold at 90 percent. When it fires, you have the alert write an entry to the application log and send a network message to your computer. After you configure the alert, you can go ahead with your normal day.

When the alert fires, you can do a quick check to see what else is happening on the network, who's attached to the application server, and other related activity. In case you're away from your desk, you can review the event logs to see when the alert fired to help figure out what else was going on at the time. This way, you're able to document the problem and have a better chance of resolving it. You might even use the information as part of your justification for upgrading the server.

One last thing: You shouldn't forget to disable or delete the alert when it's no longer needed. Otherwise, the alert will continue to fire every time the threshold is exceeded.

computers on the network. One way you can use these data is to compare computers side-by-side at the same time. When comparing two (or more) computers, you use an instance of System Monitor running on a completely separate computer. The utility does not put a significant load on a computer's resources, but if you're doing a comparison, it could skew the results.

Another feature of System Monitor is the ability to define **alerts**. You can do this by setting a threshold value based on a performance counter. When the threshold is exceeded by going either too high or too low (depending on how it is defined), the alert is triggered (i.e., fires). When this happens, you can have the computer do one of the following:

- ▲ Log an entry in the application event log so that you have a record of the alert and when it occurred.
- ▲ Send a network message to a specific computer.
- ▲ Start a performance log that you've already defined so that it can collect and record detailed statistics.
- ▲ Run a program, such as a utility designed to clear up the problem that caused the alert to fire.

Alerts are closely related to the Windows log files that record various entries related to warnings, errors, and other activities. By default, a log entry is written when any alert fires. If the logs fill up and can't accept any more entries, alerts stop firing.

SELF-CHECK

1. **Compare the roles of Microsoft's Network Monitor and System Monitor.**
2. **What is the justification for baselining?**

11.5 Using Management Systems

A **network management system (NMS)** uses a combination of hardware and software to monitor and manage devices on a network. Network administrators rely on an NMS for up-to-date information on the health of the network. Whether you're talking about performance, inventory, configuration changes, or notification of network failures, a complete NMS can reduce the time involved in managing the network. More advanced NMS products can include additional functionality, such as a built-in ESD component. Unlike a monitoring program that runs on a server, NMS software will monitor network devices from one workstation, regardless of the vendor of the network device.

A network management model includes objects that represent elements of a network device, such as a port on a hub or system information. These objects and the corresponding attributes that provide details about them can all be monitored and changed remotely. Hubs that have been designed to participate in an NMS have several objects. An object such as an Ethernet interface can be asked to provide detailed information about its configuration and performance. NMS products take configuration management to a level undreamed of in earlier management products.

In order for an NMS to gather information about a device, it has to know about the device's attributes. Attributes can include make, model, software versions, performance information, configuration settings, and technical support contact information. Many of the performance attributes can be recorded temporarily by the device for use by the NMS. If the value for the attribute exceeds a certain percentage, or **threshold**, the NMS can alert the network administrator of a possible problem. This is like the Windows Performance Monitor alerts discussed earlier in this chapter.

Keep in mind the wide variety of standard tools and utilities that can be used in network management in addition to specialized management systems. TCP/IP utilities such as ping, tracert (or traceroute for Linux systems, ipconfig (ifconfig), and nslookup (dig) are all important parts of your management toolkit.

11.5.1 Managing TCP/IP Networks

Managing TCP/IP networks was once an easy task, for which network administrators could use simple tools to test network devices. As TCP/IP networks have grown into complex networks, simple utilities such as ping have become inadequate for managing the network or can't be used due to security restrictions enforced by firewalls.

In 1990, RFC 1157 defined **Simple Network Management Protocol (SNMP)**, which was created to help network administrators manage their growing networks. Network administrators can use SNMP to manage all kinds of network devices from many different vendors, as long as each vendor creates software that is compliant with SNMP. SNMP provides network administrators with a level of control that was previously unavailable.

SNMP is now included as a standard part of the TCP/IP protocol suite. When implemented on a network, it can record specific details about hardware and configurations and IP protocol information. In the event of a failure or performance problem, the information can be used to alert the network administrator.

The SNMP protocol is only one component of the SNMP management model. The model also includes the following:

- ▲ Manageable devices.
- ▲ A network management console.
- ▲ Management information base (MIB) agents.

The SNMP protocol gathers management information from the manageable network devices. Each manageable device, such as a switch, router, or computer, has information on certain variables that are stored in a database. The variables, called **objects**, include history, hardware, configuration, and status. The objects are all defined in RFC 1155 (on management information). All the management information objects that exist on the network are collectively known as the **management information base (MIB)**. Each SNMP-compatible device created by a vendor must have a corresponding **MIB file** that details how to access the object information for that device. Due to the demand for centralized network management, most companies include SNMP functionality on their equipment. Hubs, routers, switches, workstations, and servers that are manageable can respond to SNMP commands. Without the MIB file, the **management console**, the SNMP management software's user interface, and the SNMP software will not be able to recognize the device's objects.

Object information, device status, and other variables stored in the database must be collected and transferred to the management console when requested. When a request for information is made or a configuration change is sent to a device, the agent software running on the device, as shown in Figure 11-12, uses the MIB to collect object information from the database. The **agent** collects MIB information about a managed device and provides the information to the management console. The agent can respond to a request or update the database with information received from the management console.

Unlike other network management protocols, SNMP is relatively simple and reliable because it uses only three basic commands. Administrators use the **get command** to request information from the agent on a manageable device. When network administrators want to change a configuration setting on a device, they use the **set command**. The set command changes the value of a configuration setting rather than initiating the command on the device.

Here's how an administrator would use the get command to get information about a device:

1. From the network management console, the administrator sends a GetRequest, as shown in Figure 11-13, for system information from a device.
2. The device receives the IP packet and passes the SNMP data to the agent.

Figure 11-12

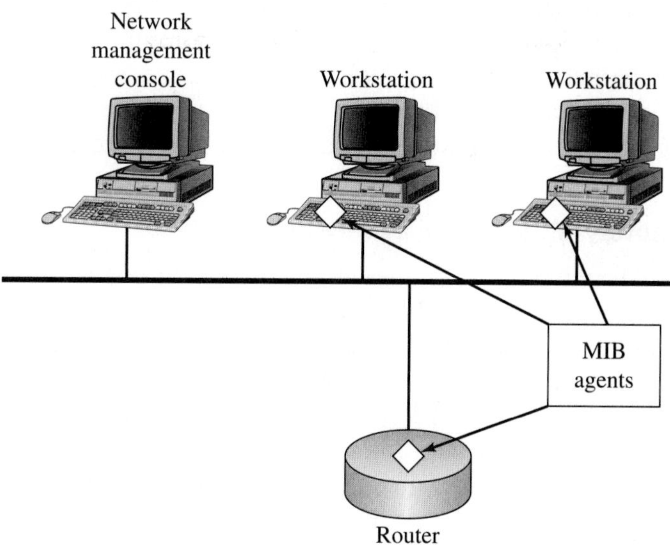

Agent software.

3. The SNMP agent collects the system information and puts it in the right format.
4. The SNMP agent sends back a GetResponse with the system information.
5. The management console receives the GetResponse, with the device's system information enclosed, and updates the device information in the management console software.

The third SNMP command, the **trap command**, is used to set a manageable device to automatically notify the management console of a system failure or

Figure 11-13

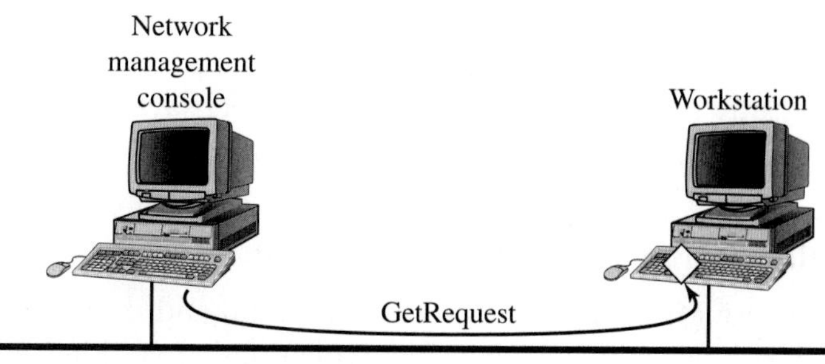

GetRequest.

performance problem. It is common for an attention-getting alarm or alert to be triggered on the network management console when information from a trap command is received. However, because SNMP uses an unreliable protocol, it is possible that the management console may not receive a trap. As a precautionary measure, polling was added to the function of the management console. At regular intervals, the console will poll manageable devices for problems.

11.5.2 Remotely Monitoring a Network

Network administrators who rely heavily on SNMP for critical system information run the risk of burdening the network with SNMP traffic. On large enterprise networks that have thousands of manageable devices, network performance can be seriously affected by the SNMP commands transmitted between the network management console and the manageable devices as part of the **polling process**, the process of gathering information about managed devices and their current status. The problem is further compounded on enterprise networks when the SNMP traffic has to travel over WAN connections.

RMON, a remote monitoring function that is supported by some devices, can help ease this problem. RMON is part of the MIB and it has its own objects. Each object has detailed summary information about the network and devices on the network. Network devices capable of running the RMON functions are called RMON probes. RMON probes do not communicate with the managed devices directly. Instead, an RMON probe collects data from the network in promiscuous mode. As data are transmitted on the network, an RMON probe collects the information on what is being transmitted and by whom. The management information collected by the RMON probe can then be sent to the network management console. Traffic is reduced because the RMON information from that network segment of the internetwork is communicated directly between the RMON device and the network management console.

11.5.3 Using Common Management Information Protocol

The **Common Management Information Protocol (CMIP)** was developed by the ISO in response to the limitations of SNMP. CMIP provides more detailed information about a device and is, in general, a more complex protocol than SNMP. Because it is a fairly new protocol, CMIP is not as widely available as SNMP. Cisco is one vendor that supports SNMP and CMIP in most of its products.

11.5.4 Implementing Network Management Systems

Implementing an NMS on a network requires careful and thorough planning. It is also important that you document your plan and everything you do while implementing the NMS.

As part of implementing an NMS, the management console station should be selected by following certain criteria. First, you need to determine the management software you will use. If you will primarily be supporting Cisco products, you may decide to use CiscoWorks management software. In a primarily Windows networking environment, you might choose SMS, mentioned earlier in this chapter. In addition, many other products are available, including Castle Rock's SNMPc, Hewlett-Packard's OpenView, and Computer Associates' NetworkIT. These programs offer, at a minimum, these basic functions:

- ▲ They allow discovery of nodes.
- ▲ They provide support for both IP and IPX.
- ▲ They offer a graphical view of managed devices (which can be useful in network planning).
- ▲ They enable you to generate reports.
- ▲ They send alerts in the form of audible alarms, email messages, or contact via a pager.

When determining the hardware requirements for your management console, In addition to deciding on hardware and software for your management

FOR EXAMPLE

Taming the Beast

Busicorp's expansion plan has, for years, relied on growth through acquisition of other related businesses. While Busicorp has been acquiring businesses, it has also been acquiring their networks. As Busicorp's network administrator, you therefore have to find a way to integrate these diverse networks with your existing corporate WAN with as little adverse impact as possible.

This is a situation where knowledge is power. The more you know, the better your design decisions as you prepare to integrate the LAN. The problem is that gathering a network inventory is a long, complex, and boring process. Even with checklists to guide your research, it's easy to overlook items that could make a difference. Depending on the size of the LAN, it's probably not possible to go through every configuration parameter on every networked computer.

In a situation like this, a quality NMS can be your best friend. An NMS is specifically designed to analyze the network and dig out the detailed information for you, and it then lets you generate custom reports that lay out that information in a easy-to-understand and easy-to-use format. You can even make changes to configuration parameters remotely, if necessary, to help the network merge more easily into your WAN.

console, you must determine what kind of security will be used on the console. The management console is often capable of collecting configuration information from network devices, including login names and passwords. Also, the network management console gives whoever uses it the ability to view, change, and delete configuration settings on devices. Because of this, the management console should be in a physically secure location such as the **network operations center** (NOC).

SELF-CHECK

1. What is an NMS?
2. What is the possible risk of an unauthorized NMS on a network?
3. What is required for a computer to collect data using RMON?

11.6 Managing Individual Servers

Just as there are a wide variety of network management tools, there are also a variety of server and server application management tools. The primary difference is that these tools are specific to the NOS or server application. Each networking product includes it own suite of management tools, which can even vary widely between different versions of the same product.

11.6.1 Understanding Local Management

Let's start by discussing management from the standpoint of local management. Each commonly used NOS provides either a management console interface or a set of management tools. In the case of Microsoft Windows Server, the majority of these are grouped together under Administrative Tools.

Even though the exact tools vary, we can use Windows as a general example. The concepts discussed here, if not the specific tools, apply to other NOSs and to most server applications.

The management tools fall into two general categories: tools used to manage a server and tools used to manage a network. The tools used to manage a server, in the case of Windows, are generally the same as those used to manage Windows client computers. They include tools such as **Computer Management**, shown in Figure 11-14, which lets you view and manage computer devices and storage media. On member servers (not domain controllers), you can also manage user and group accounts local to that computer. The example in Figure 11-14 is from

Figure 11-14

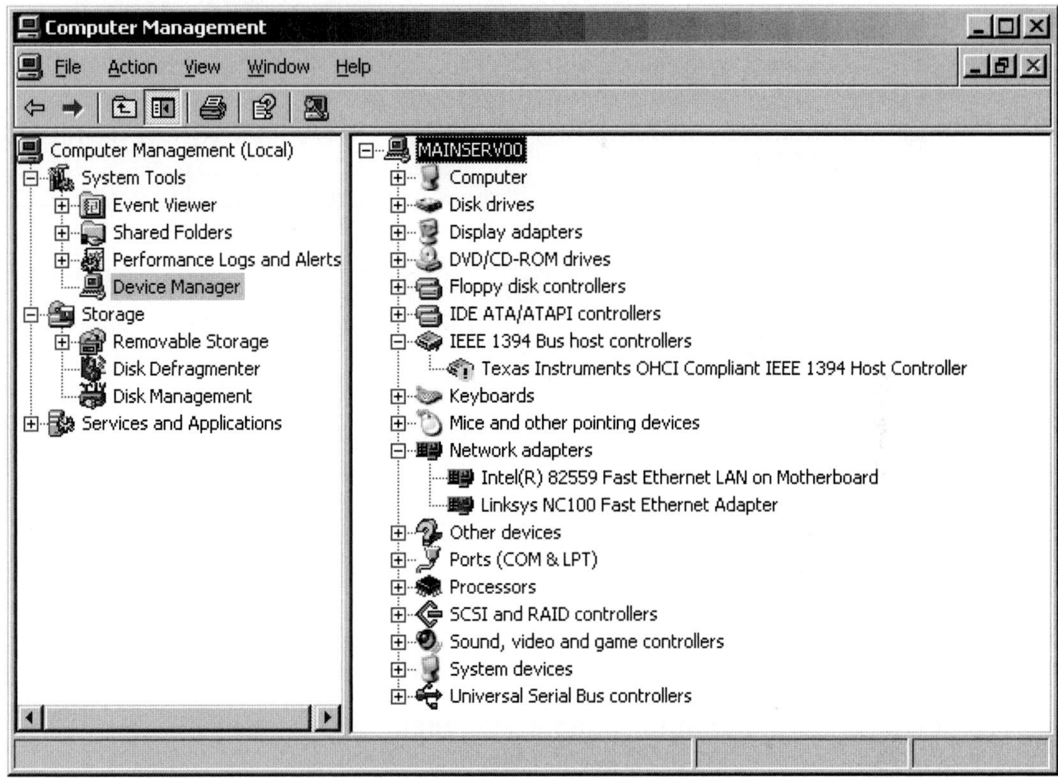

The Computer Management utility.

an Active Directory domain controller, so in that case, local accounts are not supported. Domain controllers support domain user and group accounts only. When you promote a computer to the domain controller role, any local accounts are deleted.

Network management tools are tools that let you view and manage network resources. One of the tools that gets the most use in an Active Directory domain is **Active Directory Users and Computers**, shown in Figure 11-15. This is the primary tool for managing domain users and groups, member computers, domain controllers, and other domain resources.

Other NOSs, such as Novell Network or Linux and Unix, have their own equivalents to these management utilities. The same is true of many server applications. For example, most database management systems include some kind of utility that lets you manage not only the database and its contents but database users, as well.

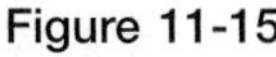

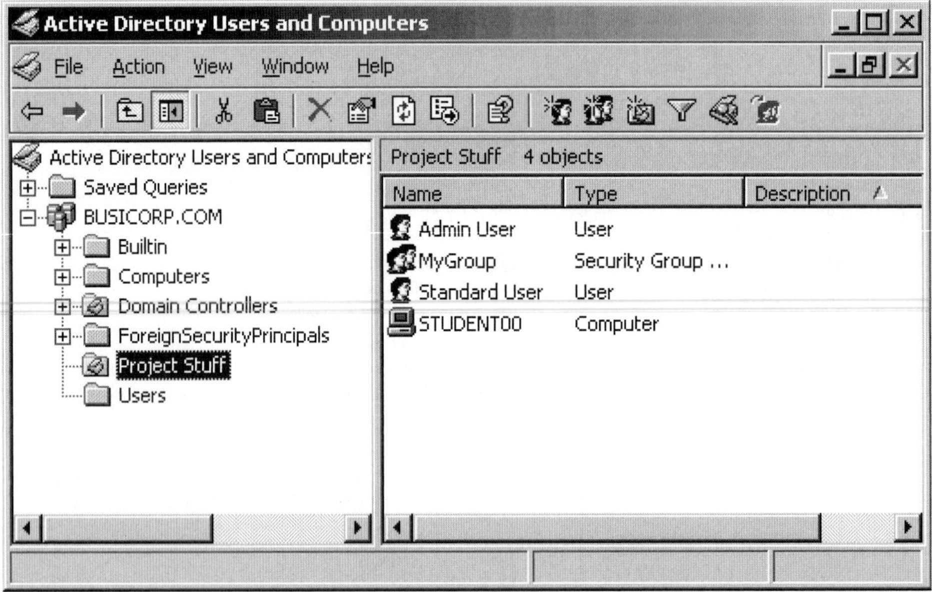

Active Directory Users and Computers.

11.6.2 Understanding Remote Management

Remote management is another area that varies widely, with many features and available tools specific to different NOSs and server applications. Rather than discuss specific remote management tools and utilities, we're going to look at the various ways they can be implemented.

Probably the most common way of supporting remote management is through management tools that can be installed on a client computer. These are usually available for most network servers and server applications. They let you manage the network, and use the same, or very similar utilities, as if you were sitting at the network server. Information is retrieved from the network server and displayed at the client. Changes made at the client are then sent back over the network and written to the servers. These can even, in most cases, be used over remote links. This means that a network administrator might be able to fix problems at odd hours from home with a laptop that has the management utilities installed.

Perhaps the biggest drawback of remote network management tools is that they are a potential security risk. Even though they usually require you to log on as an administrative user (or superuser, in the case of Unix and Linux), there is a risk in installing these on a client computer that is too openly accessible. Some network administrators are more careful about protecting their authentication

FOR EXAMPLE

The Lure of Remote Management

Again say that you're a network administrator for Busicorp. Not only that, you're the person in charge, and you supervise the other administrators and computer technicians throughout the company and across the country. You're also the person who has to cover if any of the other administrators are unavailable. Because the company supports web-based retailing and 24/7 operations, critical support requests can sometimes come in at odd hours.

Your company invested in a support application that helps streamline the process. Users can report problems through an intranet website. Automated monitoring programs watch critical applications to make sure they are performing at optimum levels. When problems are detected, depending on the time and location, a network administrator is paged automatically. As time passes without the problem getting resolved, it gets escalated up the line, also automatically, until it finally reaches you—at 3 o'clock in the morning in the middle of a snowstorm.

The good news is that the problem is at the local office, so you can actually do something about it yourself. The bad news is that the problem is at the local office, so you're expected to do something about it yourself. This is where remote management tools become an important part of your support mix.

Let's assume that you've done everything right and you've got it all set up. You've installed every possible management utility you can on your laptop. The network is set up with a remote access server that lets you connect through a secure VPN over the Internet. You even have a high-bandwidth Internet connection into your home. That means that, instead of getting dressed and slogging your way into the office, you can attach from your home and have a chance of resolving the problem without ever changing out of your pajamas. Just be careful that you don't lose that laptop.

criteria than others; you should never assume that there are not any compromised administrator accounts on your network. You should do your best to restrict access to client computers that have management tools installed.

Another method you are likely to see is to open a remote command prompt, such as through TCP/IP Telnet terminal emulation, and run command-line management utilities. Because of the inherent risk involved, it is usually recommended that you disable support for remote command prompts unless there is a specific requirement for it.

A third way is to use tools that were primarily designed for user support and troubleshooting. These remote control utilities, of which there are both versions that ship with various operating systems and a wide variety of third-party products, let you take over a system as if you were sitting at its keyboard. Actual screen information is sent to your computer, and your keystrokes are applied at the remote computer.

The ability to remotely control a network server or server application is considered a significant security risk and should be avoided if at all possible. If your server's operating system supports a remote control functionality, it should be deleted or disabled. You should also monitor critical network resources for the possible introduction of third-party remote control applications.

The capability for remote control as a support (or management) tool is built into many operating systems. There are also several third-party products, often sold as giving you an easy way to access your office computer from home. One problem with most of these is that no permanent record is made of the remote control session. Until a problem is detected, you may have no way of knowing who has been breaking into a computer through remote control—or even if anyone has been doing so.

Servers aren't the only computers at risk. If individuals can get access to a user's computer through a remote control program, not only do they have access to that computer, they probably have access to your network as a whole. Anything done on the network is done in the context of the local computer, usually without any indication that an outside individual was involved.

SELF-CHECK

1. What is the potential risk of installing management utilities on a client computer?
2. What kinds of support utilities can be used through a Telnet connection?
3. Why shouldn't you enable remote control applications on network servers?

SUMMARY

In this chapter, you learned about selected aspects of network management. You started with a brief look at management requirements. You then learned about some key reliability management tasks: backups and redundancy. You were introduced to configuration management, including software distribution management.

You also learned about various monitoring options, for monitoring both a network and individual computers. You were also introduced to SNMP and the potential role of NMSs. The chapter concluded with a brief look at various network management utilities.

KEY TERMS

Active Directory Users and Computers
Agent
Alert
Archive bit
Automated software delivery
Automatic failover
Backup destination
Baselining
Bottlenecks
Common Management Information Protocol (CMIP)
Computer Management
Configuration management
Desktop management
Desktop Management Interface (DMI)
Differential backup
Disk duplexing
Disk mirroring
Disk queue
Disk striping with parity
Downtime
Electronic software distribution (ESD)
End-user support resources
Failover
Fault
Fault tolerance
Firefighting
Frequently asked questions (FAQs)
Full backup
get command
Hot redundancy
Hot-swappable
Incremental backup
Latency
Level 1 support staff
Level 2 support staff
Level 3 support staff
Login script
Management console
Management information base (MIB)
Manual failover
MIB file
Network administrator
Network management
Network management system (NMS)
Network Monitor
Network operations center (NOC)
Network sniffer
Normal backup
Object
Packet sniffer
Paging
Performance baseline

Performance Monitor
Performance monitoring
Polling process
Promiscuous mode
Protocol analyzer
RAID 1
RAID 5
Redundancy
Redundant array of independent (or inexpensive) disks (RAID)
Redundant system
RMON
set command
Simple Network Management Protocol (SNMP)
Swap file
System Monitor
Systems Management Server (SMS)
Threshold
trap command
Uptime
Warm redundancy
WildPacket's EtherPeek
Windows Backup

ASSESS YOUR UNDERSTANDING

Go to www.wiley.com/college/ciccarelli to evaluate your knowledge of network management.
Measure your learning by comparing pre-test and post-test results.

Summary Questions

1. Windows XP automatic updates are an example of which of the following?
   (a) ESD
   (b) NMS
   (c) SNMP
   (d) NOC
2. For what purpose is an SNMP trap command used?
   (a) to detect unauthorized agents
   (b) to remotely disable a managed device
   (c) to set device configuration parameters
   (d) to have a device send a notification in case of a failure
3. RAID 5 is an example of which of the following?
   (a) an automatic failover remote system
   (b) a fault-tolerant disk subsystem
   (c) a network monitoring device
   (d) a software distribution method
4. A company's LANs, WANs, and Internet websites can be managed separately, without consideration for each other. True or false?
5. Which type of backup is used to back up changed data only, with the archive bit being reset during the backup?
   (a) daily
   (b) normal
   (c) incremental
   (d) differential
6. Redundant systems with automatic failover are designed to enable the network to continue to provide a service without interruption and without direct human intervention. True or false?
7. For most day-to-day management tasks, it is more efficient to manage groups than to manage individual users. True or false?

8. Which of the following statements best describes a performance baseline?
   (a) A performance baseline provides a starting point for evaluation.
   (b) A performance baseline should be collected any time a problem is suspected.
   (c) A performance baseline must be taken when the network is inactive, with no users connected.
   (d) A performance baseline should be taken only during peak use periods.
9. Which of the following could you use to capture network traffic for later analysis?
   (a) an SNMP management console
   (b) a network sniffer
   (c) Windows System Monitor
   (d) a remote control utility
10. A high percentage of frames detected with garbled data and other errors is usually an indication of what?
    (a) an active Ethernet network
    (b) an inefficient network protocol
    (c) a failing network adapter
    (d) unauthorized network access

Applying This Chapter

1. You are a network administrator. You've been hired to take over the network of a midsized company that includes four locations connected by WAN links. Each local network is a routed LAN. Various network and client operating systems are currently in use on the network.

   You have almost no documentation for the network. You cannot find any kind of network inventory. Network failures are common.
   (a) Why is it important to document the network?
   (b) You do not have personnel available to perform a physical inventory. You decide to use an NMS that is based on SNMP. What is required for the management console to be able to recognize a network device?
   (c) Who is responsible for providing this information to the company that developed the NMS?
   (d) From the context of SNMP management, what is an object?
   (e) During device polling, what is the role of an agent?

(f) What types of information can be collected about a managed device?

(g) What commands are supported by SNMP, and how do you use them?

2. You are tasked with minimizing network downtime and the time required to recover after a failure. You have reviewed the current network management procedures and are developing guidelines to improve management.

   (a) You run a full backup on Saturday night and an incremental backup each weekday evening. The network fails during the day Wednesday. Which backups will be necessary to recover the computer, and in what order should they be applied?

   (b) You run a full backup on Saturday night and a differential backup each weekday evening. The network fails during the day Wednesday. Which backups will be necessary to recover the computer, and in what order should they be applied?

   (c) What type of backup minimizes the time required to run backups?

   (d) Why?

   (e) Your network includes a database server. You have a redundant server configured with warm redundancy. If the primary server fails, what must you do before you can fail over to the redundant server?

   (f) You have a file server that stores critical company files, including product design documents, build lists, and manufacturing inventory requirements. The server has a RAID 5 disk subsystem with four hard disks. What would happen if one hard disk failed, and how would you recover from this?

   (g) What would happen if two disks failed, and how would you recover from this?

YOU TRY IT

Network Management

You are looking to improve management of the network shown in Figure 11-16. The wide area links are VPN links over the Internet. Although not shown to that detail in the figure, each location is configured as a routed LAN.

The network is configured as a Windows Server 2003 Active Directory network. Each remote location is configured as a separate domain. All servers run Windows 2000 Server or Windows Server 2003. Client computers include a mix of various Windows versions, Mac OS X,

Figure 11-16

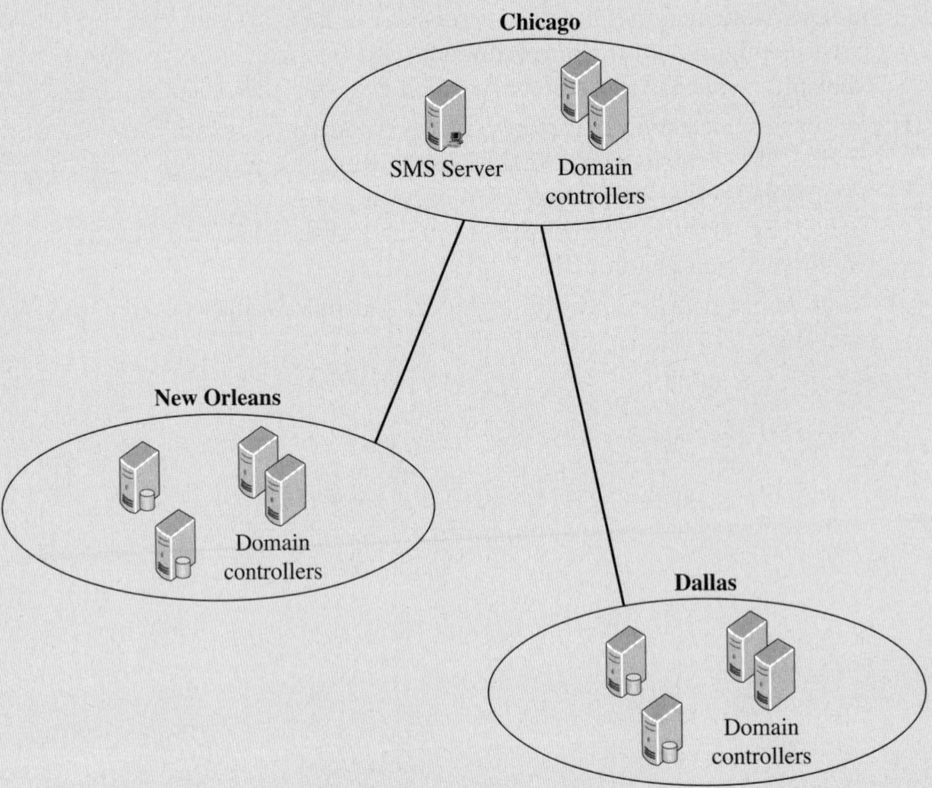

A sample network.

and different Linux distributions. All network devices are designed for use with SNMP management consoles.

1. What kinds of baseline traffic should you collect on the network as a whole?

2. You initially decide to set up Microsoft SMS on the Chicago network. If you do this, what is the possible impact on traffic across the wide area links?

3. Why should you collect performance baseline information for individual application servers?

4. You want to keep your investment in third-party management tools to a minimum. What can you use to collect baseline data for application servers?

5. You are concerned about disk space on network file servers. You want to find out as soon as possible if free space falls below a threshold level, and you want to create a record of the occurrence. You also want to run a custom application that will clear unnecessary temporary files from the servers. What should you do?

6. Currently, server backups use network shares as their destination. The shares are physically located on file servers in Chicago. What is the potential risk in case of catastrophic failure?

7. How could you avoid this?

8. You discover that a user was able to install Network Monitor from the SMS server to his laptop. What is the potential risk of this?

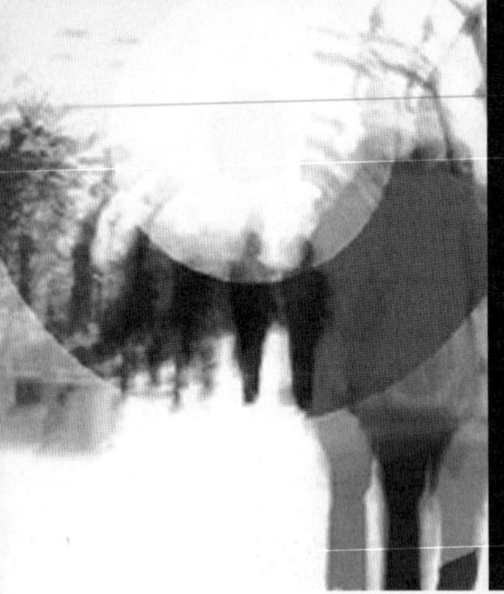

12 NETWORK SECURITY

Starting Point

Go to www.wiley.com/college/ciccarelli to assess your knowledge of network security fundamentals.
Determine where you need to concentrate your effort.

What You'll Learn in This Chapter

- ▲ Security goals
- ▲ Risk assessment
- ▲ User account management
- ▲ Resource access management
- ▲ Network attacks and defenses
- ▲ Wireless security configuration
- ▲ Data encryption
- ▲ Malicious software types and defenses

After Studying This Chapter, You'll Be Able To

- ▲ Justify the need for security management
- ▲ Identify common threats and their potential impact
- ▲ Manage user and group accounts
- ▲ Configure access permissions and user rights
- ▲ Identify common network attacks
- ▲ Explain how to protect a network by using firewalls
- ▲ Compare wireless security configuration options
- ▲ Describe data encryption options and how they are used
- ▲ Identify the most common types of malicious software
- ▲ Explain the role of antivirus and other security suite software

INTRODUCTION

Network security is a broad subject and growing more expansive with nearly every passing day. There's an ongoing race between the people trying to attack your computers and the people trying to protect them. Our discussion in this chapter is limited to an overview of the subject of network security, focusing on a few key topics.

Not only could the subject of security more than fill a book, in most cases, each of the topics introduced in this chapter could easily justify a book in itself. Our discussion of security starts by explaining why security is important and by taking a look at risk analysis. Next, we move on to practical subjects that apply directly to security: management activities such as managing user accounts, resource access permissions, and user rights. This includes a look at guidelines for managing passwords. The chapter also looks at network threats, with an emphasis on threats originating from the Internet and how firewalls can be used to protect a network. The chapter introduces the subject of data encryption and encryption options. It discusses wireless networking and wireless configuration options. It also looks at auditing and why logs can be important. Finally, it talks about malicious software and ways to protect a computer from its effects.

Most of the examples in this chapter focus on the Windows family of operating systems and Windows networks. Despite anecdotal evidence to the contrary, there is a debate as to whether Windows is inherently any less secure than any other operating system (OS). Each OS, many services, and most server applications have their own unique flaws. Windows and Windows applications are often the target of choice because there are so many more Windows PCs out there as potential targets than there are PCs running any other OS.

Although they are less common than Windows attacks, there are attacks specific to other OSs as well, including Linux, Apple Macintosh, and Novell networking products. Each of the major manufacturers keeps a searchable database of known risks and resolutions that is accessible through the Internet. Some free Linux distributions have similar online documentation, but the similarity between different distributions means that the information available on "generic" Linux sites usually applies.

12.1 Understanding the Need for Security

If you're connected to the Internet, your computer is likely under attack. There are probably ongoing attempts to identify and exploit your computer's weaknesses. Even if your network doesn't have Internet access, you might have someone trying to break into secure (or insecure) systems. Why? For some, it's the "thrill of the chase," the excitement they get slipping through security protections. For others, it is money. Not only is corporate espionage rampant, information such as valid names, email addresses, and credit card numbers is worth a great deal when passed into the wrong hands. You'll even find people who attempt to justify their actions for personal reasons, such as revenge against a company or person who wronged them in some way, either real or imagined.

You have two very broad security goals as a network professional. One is to prevent attacks and unauthorized access to data. The other is to detect these occurrences when they happen and take whatever steps are necessary to recover, minimize the damage, and prevent the same thing from happening again in the future.

12.1.1 Understanding the Problem

Computer security has become increasingly important over the past several years. Security incidents have increased, especially when the Internet is involved. The number of Internet security incidents reported to the **Computer Emergency Response Team (CERT)** doubled nearly every year between 1997 and 2003, as shown in Figure 12-1. The most recent CERT summary, covering 2006, shows the number of incidents declining slightly, but it shows the financial impact of each incidence increasing. CERT was established by the U.S. Department of Defense at Carnegie Mellon University, with a mission to work with the Internet community to respond to computer security problems, raise awareness of computer security issues, and prevent security breaches.

Approximately 95 percent of the respondents to a 2005 Computer Security Institute (CSI)/FBI Computer Crime and Security Survey reported that they had detected **security breaches** in the preceding 12 months. About 90 percent reported that they had suffered a measurable financial loss due to a security

Figure 12-1

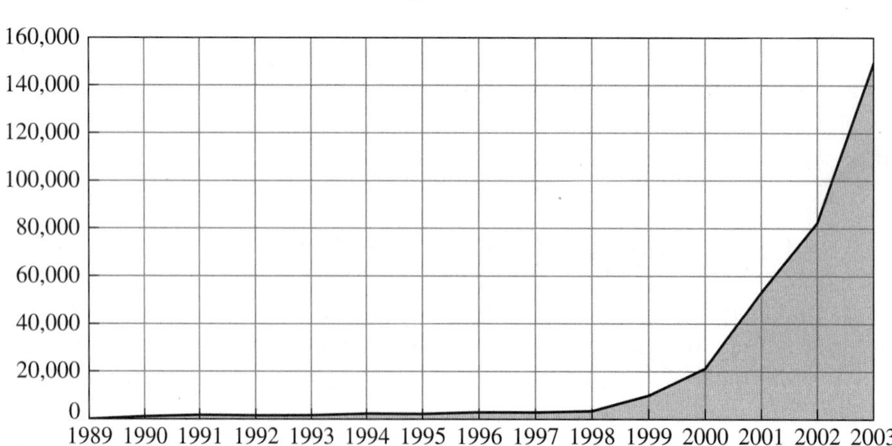

Security incidents reported to CERT.

problem, with the average loss about $200,000. The most recent results reported by various organizations indicate that this 95 percent is still accurate for attempts to breach security, although some industry experts believe successful attempts have fallen off slightly.

Protecting customer privacy also drives the need for increased network security. In 1998, the European Union passed strong data privacy laws that fined companies for disclosing information about their customers. In the United States, organizations have begun complying with the data protection requirements of the **Health Insurance Portability and Accountability Act (HIPAA)** and a California law that provides for fines up to $250,000 for each unauthorized disclosure of customer information.

12.1.2 Recognizing the Problem

For many people, security means preventing unauthorized access, such as preventing an attacker from breaking into a computer. Security is much more than that, however. There are three primary goals in providing security: confidentiality, integrity, and availability. **Confidentiality** refers to the protection of organizational data from unauthorized disclosure of customer and proprietary data. **Integrity** is the assurance that data have not been altered or destroyed. **Availability** means providing continuous operation of the organization's hardware and software so that staff, customers, and suppliers can be assured of having no interruptions in service.

Figure 12-2 identifies some potential threats to a computer center, data communication circuits, and attached computers. In general, your goals in response to security threats are to ensure business continuity and to prevent unauthorized access.

Business continuity planning refers primarily to ensuring availability, with some aspects of data integrity. One concern is **disruptions**, which are losses of or reductions in network service.

Disruptions may be minor and temporary, affecting only a few users. They can be caused by device failures, such as a failing hub or switch, or they can be caused by or result in data destruction. For example, a **virus** (i.e., a malicious program that attaches itself to another program and then propagates copies of itself) may destroy files that users need. Or hardware could be the cause: A hard disk crash could result in needed files being destroyed.

Other disruptions can be catastrophic. Natural (or human-made) disasters such as fires, floods, earthquakes, mudslides, tornadoes, or terrorist attacks can destroy large parts of the buildings and networks in their path. Especially active viruses can overwhelm a network and all its computers.

Unauthorized access relates primarily to confidentiality, but also to integrity, as someone with unauthorized access may change important data. Unauthorized access is often viewed as external attackers gaining access to organizational data files and resources from across the Internet. However, most unauthorized access

Figure 12-2

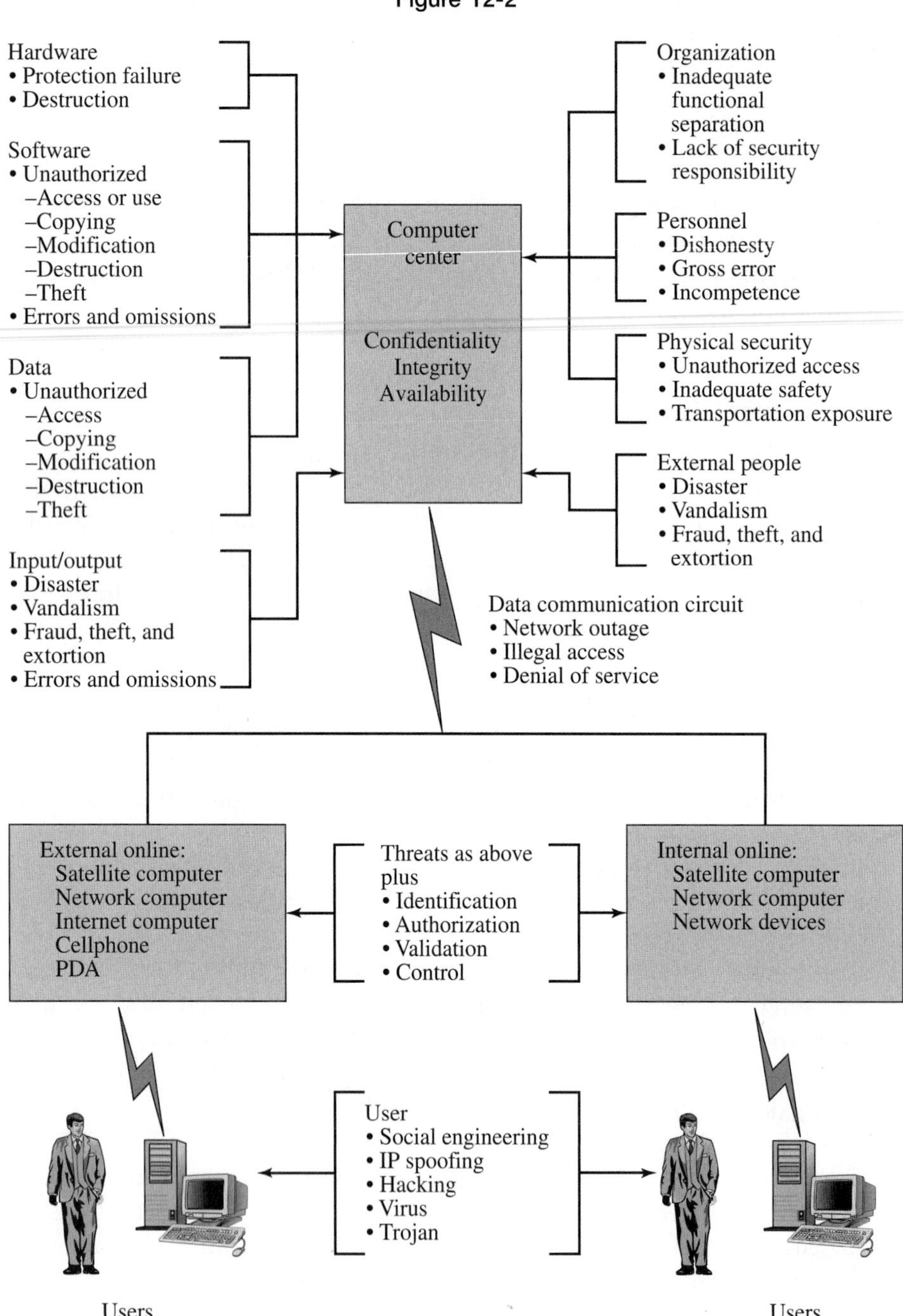
Hardware
• Protection failure
• Destruction
Software
• Unauthorized
–Access or use
–Copying
–Modification
–Destruction
–Theft
• Errors and omissions
Data
• Unauthorized
–Access
–Copying
–Modification
–Destruction
–Theft
Input/output
• Disaster
• Vandalism
• Fraud, theft, and extortion
• Errors and omissions
Computer center
Confidentiality
Integrity
Availability
Organization
• Inadequate functional separation
• Lack of security responsibility
Personnel
• Dishonesty
• Gross error
• Incompetence
Physical security
• Unauthorized access
• Inadequate safety
• Transportation exposure
External people
• Disaster
• Vandalism
• Fraud, theft, and extortion
Data communication circuit
• Network outage
• Illegal access
• Denial of service
External online:
Satellite computer
Network computer
Internet computer
Cellphone
PDA
Threats as above plus
• Identification
• Authorization
• Validation
• Control
Internal online:
Satellite computer
Network computer
Network devices
User
• Social engineering
• IP spoofing
• Hacking
• Virus
• Trojan
Users
Users

Types of risks.

incidents involve employees, if not as the attacker, then as the source for passwords or other information.

Unauthorized access might have only minor effects. A curious intruder might explore the system, gaining knowledge that has little value and perhaps leaving behind some sort of calling card. A more serious intruder might be a competitor bent on industrial espionage who attempts to gain access to information on products under development or the details and price of a bid on a large contract. Worse still, the intruder could change files to commit fraud or theft or could destroy information to injure the organization.

12.1.3 Assessing Security Risks

One key step in developing a secure network is to conduct a risk assessment. This assigns levels of risk (i.e., how likely various risks are to occur and the amount of damage they could cause) to various threats to network security by comparing the nature of the threats to the controls designed to reduce them.

Identifying Network Assets

You start assessing security risks by identifying **network assets**, which are any things of value on the network (hardware or software). Probably the most important asset on a network is the organization's data. Typical assets are listed in Figure 12-3.

Figure 12-3

Hardware	• Servers, such as mail servers, web servers, DNS servers, DHCP servers, and LAN file servers • Client computers • Devices such as hubs, switches, and routers
Circuits	• Locally operated circuits such as LANs and backbones • Contracted circuits such as MAN and WAN circuits • Internet access circuits
Network software	• Server operating systems and system settings • Application software such as mail server and web server software
Client software	• Operating systems and system settings • Application software such as word processors
Organizational data	• Databases with organizational records
Mission-critical applications	• For example, for an Internet bank, its website is mission-critical

Types of assets: DNS = Domain Name Service; DHCP = Dynamic Host Control Protocol; LAN = local area network; MAN = metropolitan area network; WAN = wide area network.

Network assets.

Next, you consider the costs related to the assets. For example, suppose someone stole a database server worth $8,000. The computer and software could be replaced easily enough, and that problem would be solved in a few days. Let's take it a step further. Suppose the stolen database contained archival records for a hospital. Even if the data could be recovered from backups, the cost could easily run into millions of dollars from lawsuits alone resulting from the possible disclosure of confidential information. If the attacker were able to steal or corrupt the backups, the costs would quickly magnify, including the costs to research and reenter all that information manually.

An important type of asset is a **mission-critical application**, which is an information system that is vital to the survival of the organization. It is an application that should not be permitted to fail, and if it does fail, the network staff needs to drop everything else to fix it. For example, an Internet bank has no brick-and-mortar branches, so its websites are mission-critical applications. If they crash, the bank cannot conduct business with its customers.

Once you have a list of assets, they should be evaluated based on their importance. There will rarely be enough time and money to protect all assets completely, so it is important to focus the organization's attention on the most important ones.

Identifying Threats

A **threat** to a data communication network is any potential adverse occurrence that can do harm, interrupt the systems using the network, or cause a monetary loss to the organization. Threats may be listed in generic terms, such as theft of data or destruction of data, but it is better to be specific. In your descriptions, you should use actual data from the organization being assessed, such as theft of customer credit card numbers or destruction of the inventory database.

After you identify the threats, you can rank them according to their probability of occurrence and their estimated costs. Figure 12-4 summarizes common threats and their likelihood of occurring, along with typical cost estimates, based on several surveys (primarily the 2005 CSI/FBI Computer Crime and Security Survey).

These survey results are taken from a number of different businesses, and the threats and possible costs for any particular type of business can vary. These results are meant to provide general guidelines. An Internet bank, for example, is more likely to be a target of fraud and to suffer a higher cost if it occurs than a restaurant with a simple website.

When considering possible threats, most people first think about unknown attackers breaking into a network across the Internet. This does happen. Unauthorized access by an external attacker was experienced by about 40 percent of all organizations each year through 2005. However, Figure 12-4 identifies

Figure 12-4

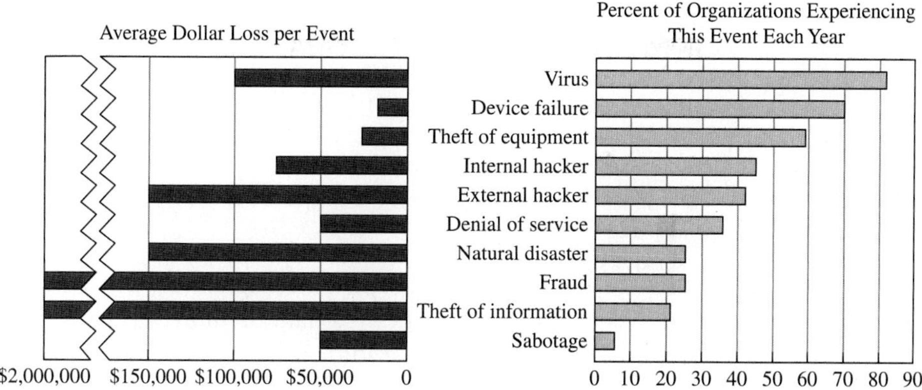

Potential threats to network security.

the most likely event as a virus infection (affecting more than 80 percent of organizations).

Interestingly, more companies suffer unauthorized access by their own employees (about 45 percent) than by outsiders. Unauthorized access and attacks such as data theft, whether from internal or external sources, can have far-reaching consequences. The cost to recover afterward can be very high, both in dollar cost and in terms of bad publicity. Over the years, several major companies have had their networks broken into and have had proprietary information such as customer credit card numbers stolen. Winning back customers can be an even greater challenge than fixing the security breach.

There are two messages you should get from Figure 12-4. First, security threats are expensive. Based on the relative probabilities of the different threats, you can see that the threats to business continuity have a greater chance of occurring than does unauthorized access. The most common threat with fairly high cost is viruses. Still, given the cost of fraud and theft of information, even a single event can have significant impact.

The second important message is that the greatest threat of unauthorized access is not from outside intruders coming at you over the Internet but rather from your own employees. This has been known to be true since the early 1980s, when the FBI first began keeping computer crime statistics and security firms began conducting surveys of **computer crime**, which is any criminal activity involving or directed against computers. However, in recent years, the number of external attacks has increased at a greater rate, while the number of internal attacks has stayed relatively constant. Even external attacks often involve, at least indirectly, internal employees. External attacks are often expedited by compromised **authentication credentials**, supplied by users who haven't used due diligence in protecting their passwords.

12.1.4 Identifying and Minimizing Exposure

Your *exposure* refers to the number of ways in which someone (or something) might gain access to your network. The following are some of the most common risks:

- Network client computers.
- Unprotected servers.
- Remote access servers.
- The Internet.

Network computers are often left unwatched and unguarded when not in use, especially at night. Who's to say that the new janitor didn't apply for the job with the specific goal of stealing corporate information and selling it to the highest bidder? All it might take is someone forgetting to log off at the end of the day. Barring that, many users have very bad security habits, such as "hiding" their password under the keyboard or in the top desk drawer.

Unprotected servers can be another risk. Critical servers should be physically secured—kept under lock and key or other security mechanism—at all times. Data theft or destruction is much easier for someone sitting at the server's keyboard than for someone trying to operate remotely. There have even been cases in which thieves have walked out of the building with servers, or at least their hard drives, tucked under one arm.

Any time you open your network to remote access, you take a calculated risk. When you set up a remote access server, you must put in place security measures to ensure that only authorized personnel have access. The tools available to you vary by operating system but include things like limiting the phone numbers from which calls are accepted, having the server call back to provide access instead of allowing the user to dial in and connect, and requiring secure authentication based on user name and password or other authentication mechanisms.

Even without explicitly configuring remote access, there is a potential risk if your network has any kind of remote point of access. There are literally hundreds of tools available for download from the Internet that let individuals remotely access and control client systems. Even something as simple as Telnet, which lets a user open a command prompt on any remote computer that supports Telnet connections, can be a significant security risk. This is especially true of some free Linux distributions that enable Telnet sessions by default with little or no internal security. Because Telnet is part of the TCP/IP protocol suite and well known to potential attackers, it is recommended that you disable or remove Telnet support whenever possible.

Just as remote access is a known threat, so is connecting to the Internet. As soon as you connect your network to the Internet, you've opened a potential door that **hackers**—individuals trying to break into your system—can start picking away at. Some of these attacks are designed to gain access to the network,

FOR EXAMPLE

Sometimes It's Just Stupidity

This situation is made up, using Busicorp as a fictitious example. It may sound familiar—because it is. There have been multiple cases like this in recent years. However, the names have been changed to protect the innocent (and the stupid).

An employee, overwhelmed by the pressure of end-of-year analysis and reporting, copies some customer files to his laptop. The idea is that he can work on them at home and bring the finished reports back with him in the morning. He dozes off on the train home, and when he wakes up, the computer's missing.

The problem is that those customer records included personal information, such as addresses, Social Security numbers, mothers' maiden names, and so on. In short, the customer records contain all the information that someone needs to steal a person's identity. Within a few days, there is a rash of identity theft reports by Busicorp customers (and even more go undetected for weeks).

Who's responsible? The employee, obviously, is at fault for copying the records to his laptop and not guarding it more carefully. But it doesn't end there. Busicorp is also at fault for not better protecting the data and preventing the employee from copying it in the first place.

and others are designed to bring it down, either crashing the network or tying it up to the point that no one can get access to it.

There are also a number of risks that can follow you home from the Internet. Two of the most common sources of viruses and other malicious programs are files downloaded from the Internet and email attachments. You should never download a file unless you are certain of its source, and even then, you should scan the file for viruses before opening or executing it. One thing that many people don't realize is that most multimedia files are a form of executable file and have become a common mechanism for distributing viruses.

SELF-CHECK

1. Based on industry surveys, what is the most likely source of unauthorized access?
2. What is a *mission-critical application*?
3. What should you consider when assigning levels of risk?

12.2 Implementing User Access Security

Network security begins with user access security. All user access attempts should be authenticated, either with a user name and password or another security mechanism, such as a smart card or **biometric scan** based on characteristics such as the user's thumbprint or retina.

A network is no more secure than its **user accounts**, and user account security should be first and foremost in your mind. You manage access to network resources through a user account and the rights given to that account. You, as the network administrator, are charged with the daily maintenance of those accounts. Common security duties include renaming accounts and resetting forgotten (or compromised) passwords. You can also specify where users can log in, how often they can log in, at what times they can log in, how often their passwords expire, and when their accounts expire.

12.2.1 Managing User Accounts

All NOSs have some method for creating and managing user accounts. Each user should have his or her own account for accessing the network, and the company should have a written policy in place, emphasizing the importance of not sharing account information with anyone else.

In a Windows Active Directory domain, there are two types of user accounts: domain and local accounts. **Domain accounts** give users access to domain resources and are required for domain login. Member computers, both clients and servers, also have **local accounts**. Local accounts don't give the user access to the network but do let users access resources local to the computer. Local administrator accounts give full access to the computer, including configuration information and the permission to install applications.

Active Directory accounts are managed using the Active Directory Users and Computers utility, shown in Figure 12-5. Each user account is contained in an organizational unit (OU) or another domain container.

When you create a user account, you assign an initial password. Typically, the account will be configured to force the user to change the password the first time it's used to log in to the domain.

User accounts are also organized into groups, which are sets of users. Rights and access permissions can be granted individually to users or to a group, in which case they also apply to the group's members.

There are also special user accounts known as **maintenance accounts** because they are used for system and network management and maintenance. The NOS will create one or more of these accounts by default, giving them names like **administrator**, **supervisor**, **root**, or **superuser**, depending on the NOS. These are well-known names, so one of the first things you should do (if possible) is rename these accounts. You can also create additional maintenance accounts, as necessary.

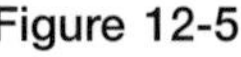

Figure 12-5

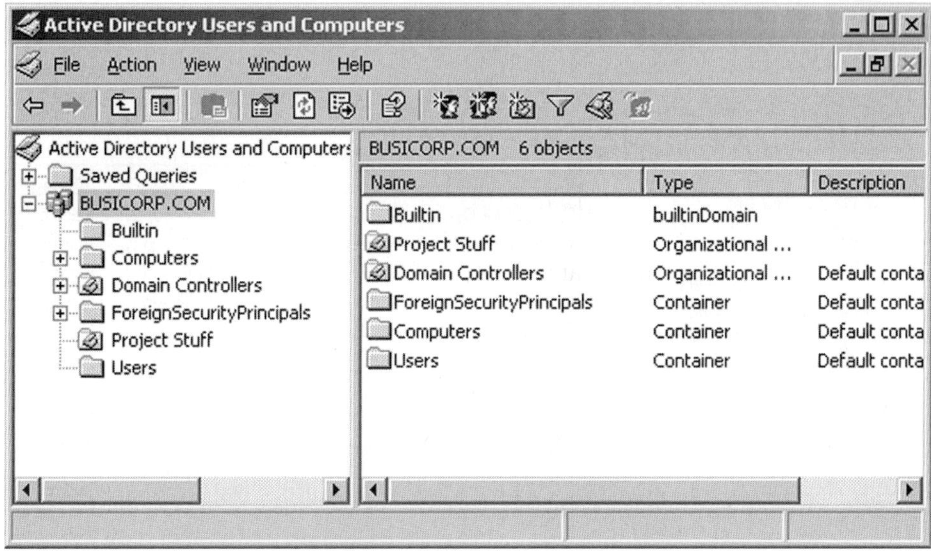

Active Directory Users and Computers.

Users should use these accounts for login only when performing maintenance functions, and they should use standard user accounts at all other times. Why? Think what could happen if you left your desk for an extended time, with the computer logged in as an administrator. The possible result could be devastating.

Windows enables management of maintenance accounts through group membership. There are several predefined groups designed to let users perform specific functions, such as backing up data, managing user accounts, and even administering the network. You can see some of these listed in Figure 12-6. Users should be added to these groups only when they need the additional rights and permissions granted in order to do their jobs.

When a user account is no longer needed (e.g., when the user leaves the company), the account should be either deleted or disabled so that it can't be used for access. The advantage of disabling an account is that it can be renamed and assigned to a new user, making it easy to set up access for the employee's replacement. You should also disable an account if the user will be gone for an extended period, such as on a vacation.

12.2.2 Managing Passwords

Managing passwords involves ensuring that all passwords for user accounts follow security guidelines so that they cannot be easily guessed or cracked, as well as implementing features of the NOS to prevent unauthorized access.

Figure 12-6

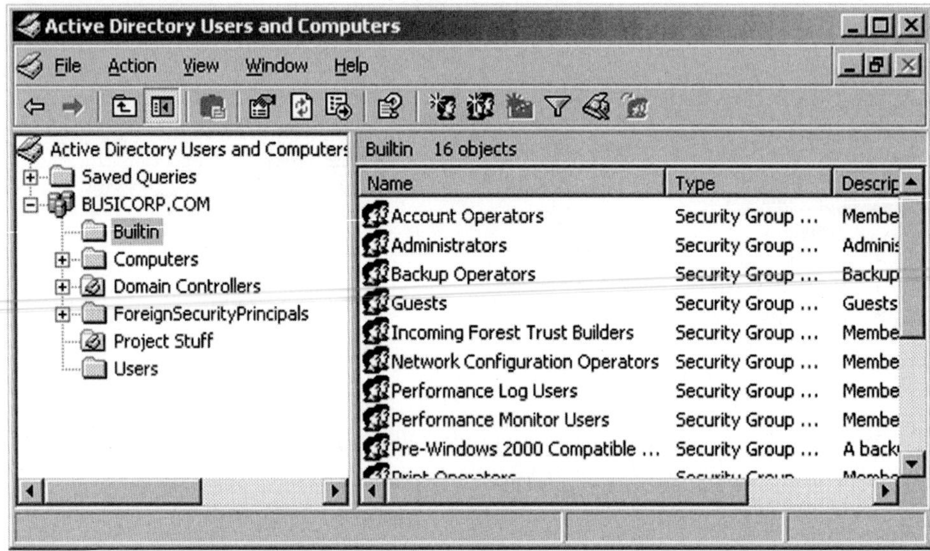

Built-in groups.

Generally speaking, a **strong password** is a combination of alphanumeric and special characters that is easy for you to remember and difficult for someone else to guess. A password should be at least 8 characters, if not more, but generally shouldn't have more than 15 characters so that they are easy to remember. The following are some passwords you should never use:

- ▲ The word *password*.
- ▲ Proper names.
- ▲ Your pet's name.
- ▲ Your spouse's name.
- ▲ Your children's names.
- ▲ Any word in the dictionary.
- ▲ Important dates, such as birthdays, anniversaries, and so on.
- ▲ Any of the above with a leading or trailing number.
- ▲ Any of the above spelled backward.

This is only a partial list of **weak passwords**, but it should give you an idea of what you want to avoid. Most NOSs can be configured to prevent users from using some of them (e.g., using the user name's or the word *password*).

Difficult-to-crack passwords should include a combination of numbers, uppercase letters, lowercase letters, and special characters—that is, not just letters, not just numbers, not just special characters, but a combination of all three.

Special characters are those that cannot be considered letters or numbers (e.g., $, %, ^, #, @). An example of a strong password is tqbf4#jotld. Such a password might look hard to remember, but it doesn't have to be. You may remember the following sentence, which uses every letter in the English alphabet: The quick brown fox jumped over the lazy dog. Take the first letter of each word, put the number 4 and a pound (#) symbol in the middle, and you have a strong password. Here are a few more examples of strong passwords:

- run4!cover
- iron$steel4
- tpwb2m,k? (for "This PassWord Belongs 2 Me, oKay?")

To check passwords, you can use **auditing tools**, such as a **crack program** that tries to guess passwords. If you are using strong passwords, the crack program should have great difficulty guessing them.

All NOSs include functions for managing passwords so that the system remains secure and passwords cannot be easily hacked with crack programs. These functions include automatic account lockouts and password properties such as password expiration. In an Active Directory domain, these functions are set through Group Policy. To have them apply to a domain, you configure password policy through a group policy object (GPO) linked to the domain and include password policies and account lockout policies.

Hackers (and users who forget their passwords) attempt to log in by guessing the password. To ensure that a password can't be guessed by repeatedly inputting different passwords, most NOSs allow an account to be disabled, or locked out, after a set number of unsuccessful login attempts. Once the account is locked, the user cannot log in to that account even if the correct password is entered. This prevents a potential hacker from running an automated script to continuously attempt logins using different character combinations. However, it doesn't prevent an intruder from intercepting the password with specialized tools, so account lockout still leaves some potential security holes. **Account lockout policies** supported by Windows are shown in Figure 12-7.

After a lockout is activated, to log in successfully, the user must ask the network support staff to unlock the account if the NOS doesn't unlock it after a preset period. In high-security networks, it is advisable for an administrator to manually unlock a locked account rather than let the NOS do it automatically. That way, the administrator is always notified of possible security breaches. The problem is, however, that this policy could leave a network more vulnerable to some types of denial of service attacks (discussed in Section 12.3.1).

As a network administrator, you also have control over password policies. The default policies for a Windows Server 2003 Active Directory domain are

Figure 12-7

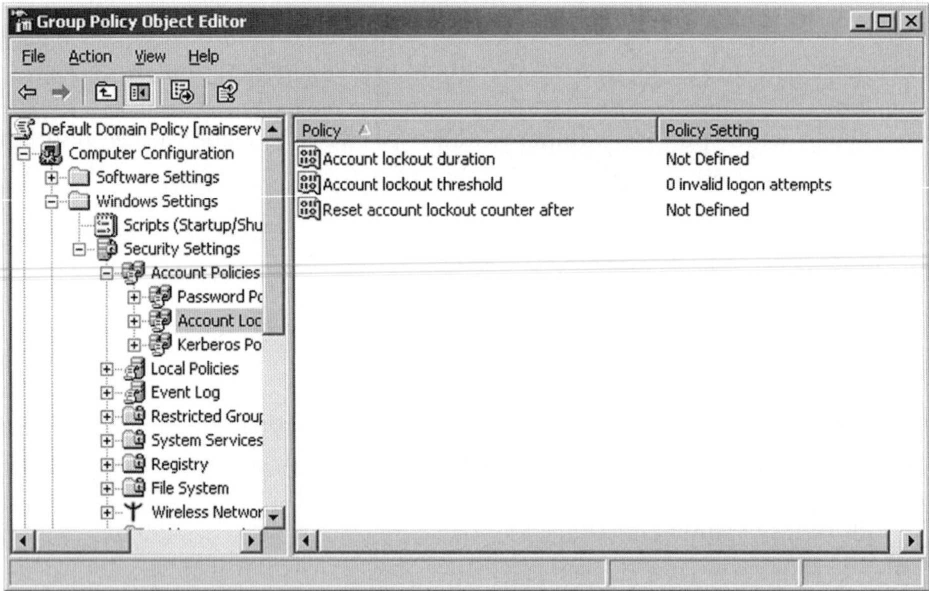

Account lockout policies.

shown in Figure 12-8. The policy settings shown here are for Windows, but most NOSs support the same restrictions, although they might identify them by different names, as described next.

Enforce password history determines how many different passwords will be remembered and prevents the user from reusing passwords. For example, with the setting shown in Figure 12-8, a user would have to come up with at least 25 unique passwords, the 24 remembered passwords plus the current password.

Maximum password age sets password expiration. After the specified period, the password expires and can no longer be used. In Figure 12-8, this is set to 42 days. Most companies use a value between 30 and 60 days. The network will begin warning the user to change his or her password a few days before it expires. Why force changes? The longer a user keeps the same password, the more likely it is to get compromised.

Minimum password age sets the minimum time between password changes. Why? To prevent the user from sneaking past the password history. Even set to a value as short as one or two days, it becomes more effort than it is worth to repeatedly change passwords until the user can get back to using a favorite password.

The user's password must be at least equal to, but can be longer than, the **minimum password length**. Passwords should be long enough to make for secure passwords but not so long as to be difficult to remember.

Figure 12-8

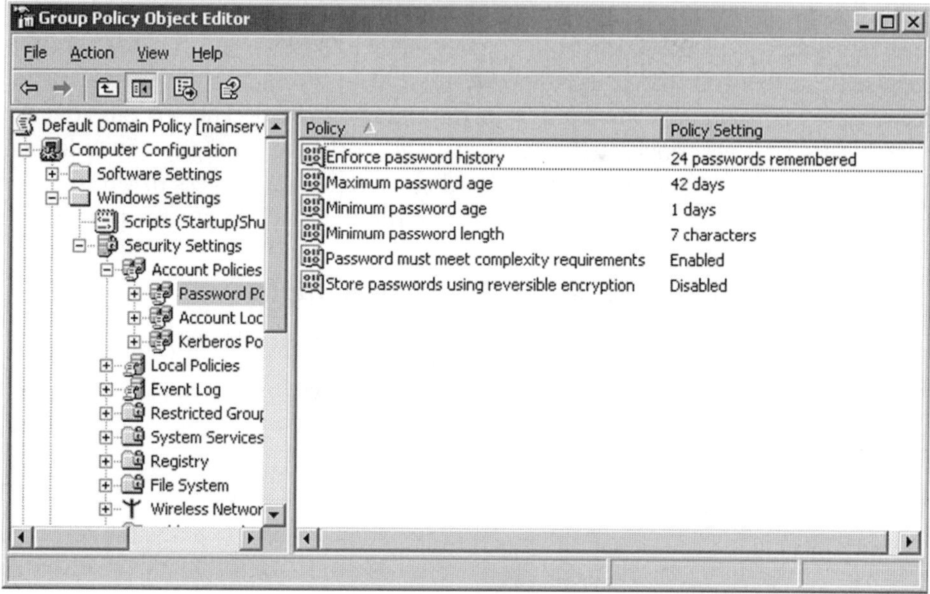

Default password policies.

The **password must meet complexity requirements** policy forces users to use strong passwords. The password must be at least six characters long (unless overridden by a longer value specified as the minimum password length) and include at least three of the following:

- English uppercase characters.
- English lowercase characters.
- Numbers (0 through 9).
- Non-alphabetic "special" characters (e.g., !, @, #, %).

Store passwords using reversible encryption is a policy supported by some NOSs as a default option. Typically, this is disabled in a Windows network and should remain disabled unless required. It is required when using the Challenge Handshake Authentication Protocol (CHAP) and with Microsoft Internet Information Services (IIS) Digest Authentication.

Similar protections are supported for most other NOSs. There is one additional note on passwords specific to Linux systems: With some Linux distributions, passwords are stored by default in an encrypted format in \etc\passwd. Because of the requirements of some commonly used Linux utilities, all users must have access to the **passwd** file. This means that someone could copy the file and decrypt the passwords at his or her leisure. One way to help prevent this is to enable **shadow** passwords, an option supported on most Linux distributions. With shadow passwords, Linux user information is maintained in the \etc\passwd and \etc\shadow files. When you enable shadow passwords, the password is moved from \etc\passwd to \etc\shadow. Instead of an encrypted password, the \etc\passwd file contains the letter *x* in the password field. The \etc\shadow file contains user names, encrypted passwords, and password configuration information, such as time before the next password change. Because access to \etc\shadow requires root privileges, it is difficult to copy the file or decrypt user passwords.

12.2.3 Managing Access Security and User Rights

You can secure files that are shared over the network in two ways:

- ▲ At the share level.
- ▲ At the user (group) level.

Figure 12-9

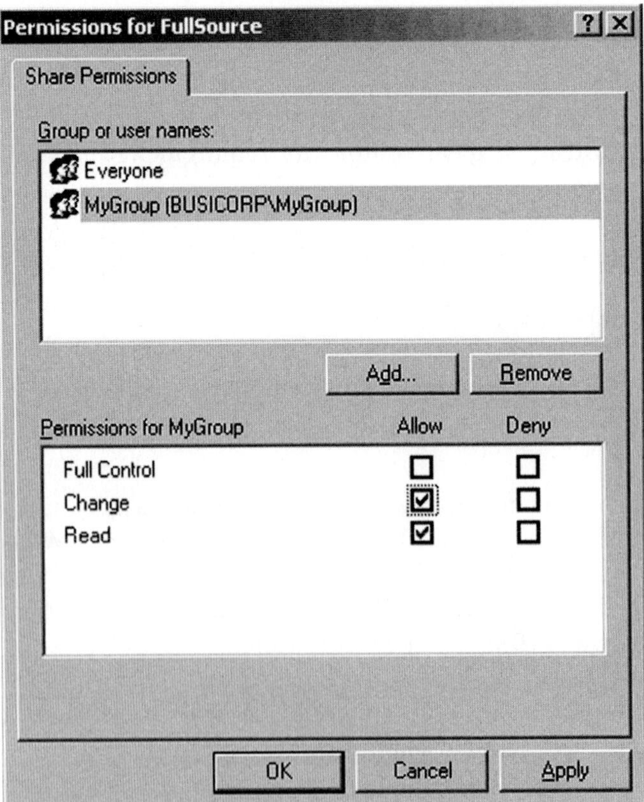

Share permissions.

In a network that uses share-level security, you assign passwords to individual files or other network resources (such as printers) instead of assigning rights to users. This was done in early Windows workgroup configurations as a way to manage security. You then give these passwords to all users who need access to these resources. With this type of security, the network support staff has no way of knowing who is managing the resources.

Current Windows versions and most other NOSs typically use user-level security. Rights to network resources are assigned to specific users or groups. In a workgroup environment, this is managed separately on each computer. In a client/server or directory-based network, permission management is more centralized but can also rely on rights assigned at the computer hosting the resource. Typical file share permissions are shown in Figure 12-9.

One thing to keep in mind is that denied permissions take precedence over granted permissions. If you deny a permission to a user, you can't give the user rights to the resources. If you deny a permission to a group, it is denied to all of the group's members.

You can also manage user rights, which determine what a user can do. One way to assign rights is through group membership in management groups. Individual rights can also be granted to individual users or to groups. A partial list of user rights supported by Windows operating systems is shown in Figure 12-10.

Figure 12-10

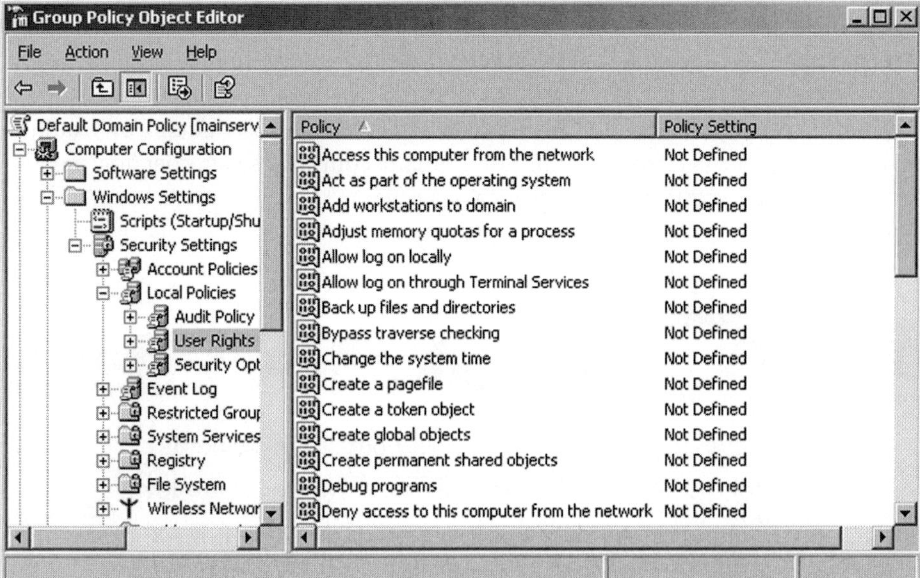

User rights.

FOR EXAMPLE

Understanding the Exceptions

As with most rules, there are exceptions to the guidelines for managing user passwords. Why? Some types of user accounts call for special management procedures.

Some applications and services can be configured to launch in the security context of a user account. One example of this is Microsoft SQL Server. When Busicorp installed SQL Server, the network administrator set up a user account specifically for that purpose. Two months later, SQL Server crashed. More correctly, SQL Server would no longer start. After some investigation, the reason turned out to be rather simple. Take a look at Figure 12-11. Notice that you can override some password restrictions through user properties, including maximum password age. This has been done in Figure 12-11, by checking the Password Never Expires property in the Account Options section.

When the network administrator set up the user account, he forgot one detail: He didn't check Password Never Expires. Two months later, the password expired, the user can't be authenticated, and SQL Server can't start.

These can be set on an individual computer, but more commonly, you set user rights policies for groups of computers through GPOs linked to OUs and, if appropriate, associated with computer groups.

You have a great deal of flexibility when setting user rights. For example, you might set one group of rights for domain controllers, another for member servers, and yet another for client workstations.

SELF-CHECK

1. What are the guidelines for Windows complex passwords?
2. What is the advantage of user-level security over share-level security?
3. Why is it more efficient to manage groups than to manage individual users?

Figure 12-11

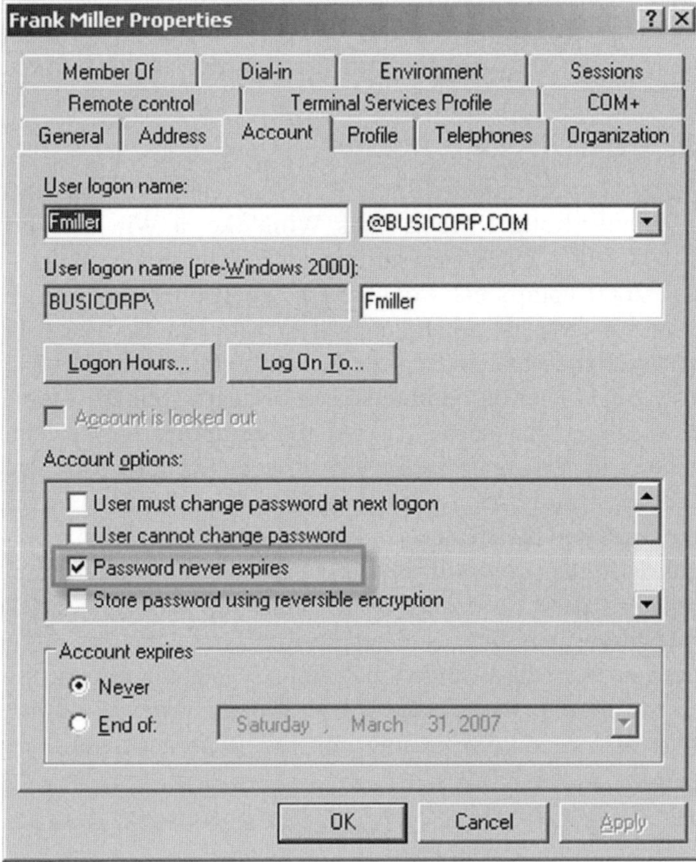

Sample user properties.

12.3 Configuring Network Security

Securing a network involves two general areas: protecting the network and protecting the individual computers on the network. These two areas are very closely related.

The first concern, which we've already discussed, is controlling network access through user authentication, access permissions, and rights assignments. The next is controlling communications into, out of, and through the network. You also need to configure network computers to ensure that they are secure, which sometimes means adding special security programs. This process of making the network and individual computers more secure is sometimes referred to as **hardening**.

What it takes to make a network safe depends on your goals. Is your primary focus keeping the network running efficiently? In this case, you might need to focus on subnetting or configuring collision domains. Worried about keeping information in or out? In this situation, you may need to look at firewalls, which filter network traffic based on various criteria. Worried about someone intercepting data from the network? If so, then encryption might be necessary.

12.3.1 Identifying Network Attacks

Network attacks that are directed by a hacker are called **directed attacks**. One of the first identified attack "tools" was **WinNuke**, a Windows program that sends special TCP/IP packets with an invalid TCP header. Windows 95/98 and Windows NT/2000 computers would crash when they received one of these packets because of how they handled bad data in the TCP header. Instead of returning an error code or rejecting the bad data (Microsoft calls it out-of-band data), it sent the computer to the **blue screen of death (BSoD)**, a terminal failure. Figuratively speaking, the hacker caused the computer to blow up, or to be nuked. Patches and service packs for the affected Microsoft products have long since quelled the threat that out-of-band data once posed, but hackers have continued to fine-tune their attacks.

IP spoofing is the process of sending a packet with a fake source address, pretending that the packet is coming from within the network the hacker is trying to attack. The address can be considered stolen from the hacker's target network. A router (even one that filters individual packets) is going to treat this packet as coming from within the network and will let it pass; however, a firewall can prevent this type of packet from passing into the secured network. Figure 12-12

Figure 12-12

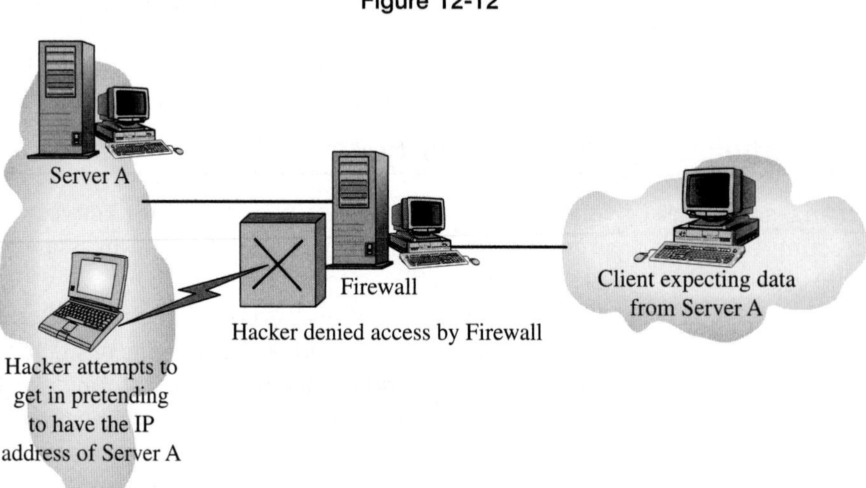

IP spoofing.

shows a hacker attempting an IP spoof. Notice that the hacker with the spoofed IP address is denied access to the network by the firewall.

The **ping of death** is a type of **denial of service (DoS) attack**. A DoS attack prevents any users, even legitimate ones, from using the system. Normally, when you ping a remote host, four normal-sized Internet Control Message Protocol (ICMP) packets are sent to the remote host to see if it is available. In a ping of death attack, a very large ICMP packet is sent to the remote host, whose buffer is flooded by this packet. Typically, this causes a system to reboot or hang. Patches to prevent a ping of death attack from working are available for most operating systems.

A **SYN flood** is another specialized DoS attack. In normal communications, a workstation that wants to open a TCP/IP communication with a server sends a TCP/IP packet with the **SYN flag** set to 1. The server automatically responds to the request, indicating that it is ready to start communicating. Only new communications use SYN flags, and a new **SYN packet** is used only if a user loses connection and must reestablish communications. To initiate a SYN flood, a hacker sends a barrage of SYN packets, and the receiving computer tries to respond to each SYN request for a connection until the victim machine cannot respond to any other requests because its buffers are overfilled. At that point, it rejects all packets, including valid requests for connections. Patches that can help with this problem are available for the various NOSs.

There are also other types of DoS attacks, in which an attacker attempts to disrupt the network by flooding it with messages. One common feature is that most attackers use tools that enable them to put false source IP addresses on the incoming messages so that it is impossible to quickly recognize a message as a real message or a DoS message, making the attack more difficult to prevent.

A **distributed denial of service (DDoS) attack** is even more disruptive than a regular DoS attack. With a DDoS attack, the attacker breaks into and takes control of many computers (sometimes thousands) on the Internet and plants on them software called **DDoS agents**. The attacker then uses software called a **DDoS handler** to control the agents. The handler issues instructions to the computers under the attacker's control, which simultaneously begin sending messages to the target site. In this way, the target is deluged with messages from many different sources, making it difficult to identify the DoS messages and greatly increasing the number of messages hitting the target.

It's important to realize that one of the best ways to prepare against network attacks is to know as much as possible about potential attacks that apply to your network and the OSs in use. **Vulnerability research**, a term that refers to the process of keeping up to date, is an ongoing task. One website that can assist you is SearchSecurity.com, which has online references and searchable database that links you to both security information and utilities. It can link you to tools that help you detect, prevent, and even recover from attacks targeting your network.

12.3.2 Adding Firewalls

When you connect a private network (where only authorized users have access to the data) to a public network (where everyone connected has access to the data), you introduce the possibility for security break-ins. A **firewall** protects a private network from unauthorized users on a public network.

Firewalls are usually a combination of hardware and software. The hardware is typically a computer or a dedicated piece of hardware (often called a black box) that contains two network cards. One network card connects to the public side; the other connects to the private side. The software controls how the firewall operates and protects your network. It examines each incoming and outgoing packet and rejects any suspicious packets. In general, firewalls work by allowing only packets that pass security restrictions to be forwarded through the firewall.

Firewalls can be placed on top of an existing operating system or be self-contained. **Black box systems** are proprietary systems that have external controls and are not controlled by the operating system. Windows supports configuring routers to act as firewalls, plus there are third-party firewalls that run on both Windows and Unix/Linux. Novell makes its own firewall product, BorderManager, which runs on NetWare.

One key feature of firewalls is **packet filtering**, which is the ability of a router or a firewall to discard packets that don't meet certain criteria. Another is **port filtering**, which involves passing or blocking packets based on the port address. The applications that must communicate through the firewall help determine its configuration for port filtering. For example, to support a web server, you typically need to open port 80 and possibly port 443. Port 80 is used with HTTP, which is used by web servers to communicate, and port 443 is used with Secure Sockets Layer (SSL), which is for secure communications.

Many firewalls use **dynamic packet filtering** to ensure that the packets they forward match sessions initiated on their private side. A **dynamic state list** (also known as a **state table**) held on a firewall keeps track of all communications sessions between stations inside the firewall and stations outside the firewall. This list changes as communications sessions are added and deleted. Dynamic state lists allow a firewall to filter packets dynamically.

In dynamic packet filtering, only packets for current (and valid) communications sessions are allowed to pass. Someone trying to play back a communications session (such as a login) to gain access would be unsuccessful if the firewall were using dynamic packet filtering with a dynamic state list because the data sent would not be recognized as part of a currently valid session. The firewall would filter out (or "drop") all packets that don't correspond to a current session, using information found in the dynamic state list. For example, say that a computer in Network A requests a Telnet session with a server in Network B. The firewall in between the two keeps a log of the communication packets that are sent each way.

Figure 12-13

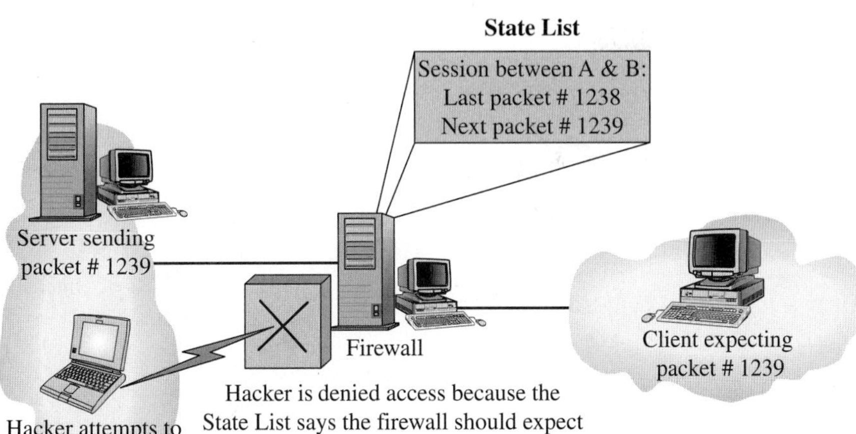

Dynamic packet filtering.

Only packets that are part of this current communication session are allowed back into Network A through the firewall.

Figure 12-13 shows a failed attempt to infiltrate a network that is protected with a dynamic state list. Notice that the hacker attempted to insert a packet into the communication stream but failed because the packet did not have the correct packet number. There are ways around this, but a detailed discussion of hacker techniques is beyond the scope of this chapter. The firewall was waiting for a specific order of packets, and the hacker's packet was out of sequence.

Firewalls are often configured as part of a **demilitarized zone (DMZ)**, also called a **perimeter network**, which is an area protected by one or two firewalls. When used on the intranet to isolate a segment, it is called a screened subnet. One standard DMZ setup has three network cards in the firewall computer, as shown in Figure 12-14. The first goes to the Internet. The second goes to the network segment where the aforementioned servers are located, the DMZ. The third connects to your company intranet.

People outside your network primarily access your web servers, FTP servers, and mail-relay servers, so you should place them in the DMZ. When hackers break into the DMZ, they can see public information only. If they break into a server, they are breaking into a server that holds only public information. The corporate network is not compromised. Also, no email messages are vulnerable because only the relay server, a waypoint for transferring the message, can be accessed. All actual messages are stored and viewed on

Figure 12-14

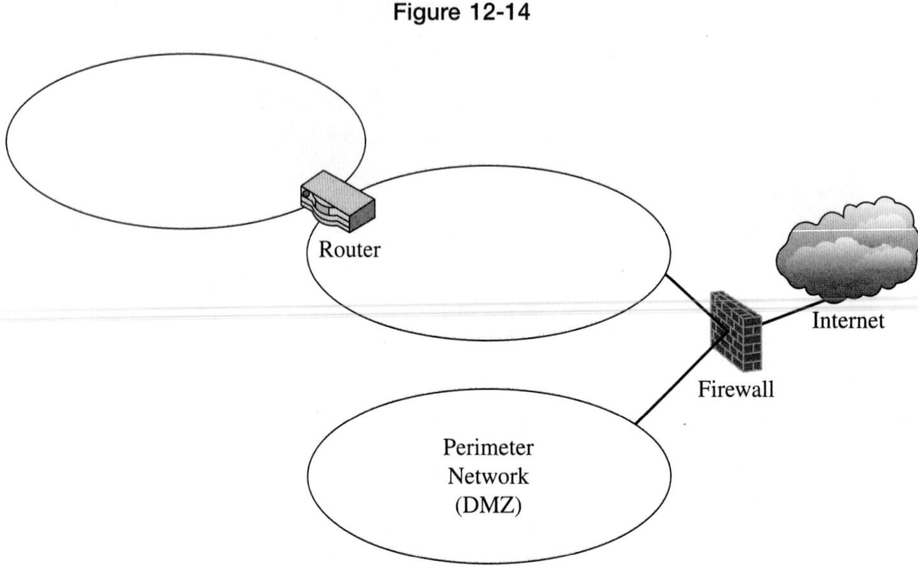

A DMZ with one firewall.

email servers inside the network. As you can see in Figure 12-14, the email router, the FTP server, and the web server are all in the DMZ, and all critical servers are inside the firewall.

Another common configuration is to use two firewalls (see Figure 12-15). One sits between the internal network and the perimeter network, and the other sits between the perimeter network and the Internet. Traffic destined for the internal network must pass through two networks.

The exact configuration you use depends on your particular network support and protection requirements.

12.3.3 Adding Encryption

Encryption is the process of encoding data, and **decryption** is the process of decoding encrypted data. Encrypted data are sent over a network and decrypted by the intended recipient. Generally speaking, encryption works by running the data (represented as numbers) through a special **encryption formula**, or **encryption algorithm** (where the value used in the encryption is called a **key**), used to encrypt and decrypt the data. The National Security Agency (NSA) has classified encryption tools and formulas as munitions since 1979 and therefore regulates them. The NSA does not want unfriendly nations, terrorists, and criminals to use encrypted communications to plan crimes and go undetected.

One way to measure an encryption algorithm is by its **bit strength** (i.e., key length). Until 1998, only software with 40-bit strength and less could be

Figure 12-15

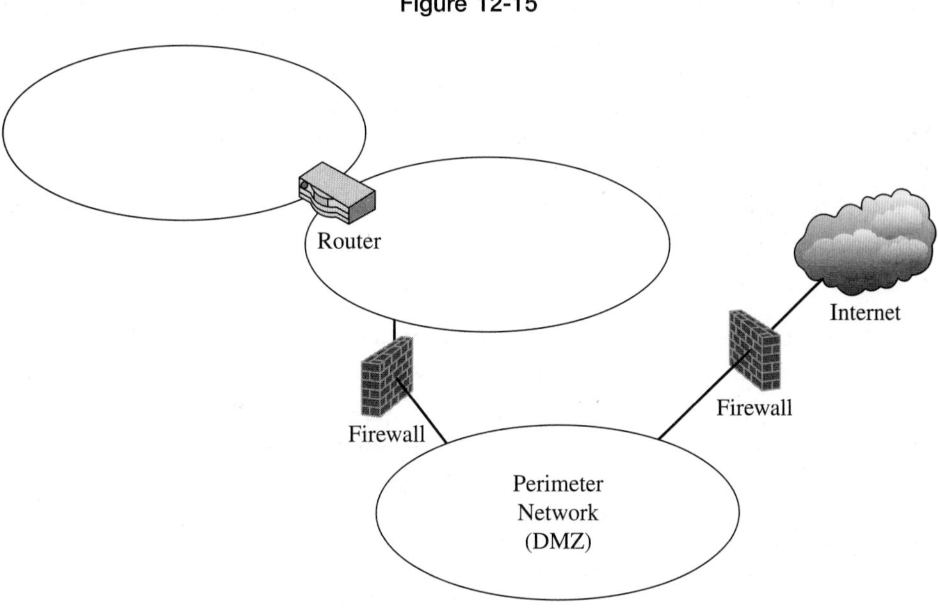

A DMZ with two firewalls.

exported. That limit has been increased to 56-bit strength and then 128-bit strength by special consideration of the U.S. Department of Commerce.

In internal networks, some encryption is necessary, such as when communicating with a secure server. This can be done automatically by many modern NOSs and server applications. Encryption is also used by many email systems, giving the user the option to encrypt individual or all email messages. Third-party software packages can provide data encryption for email systems that don't natively have the ability to encrypt. Encryption is also typically used for data transmission over VPNs to keep the data private when using the Internet to connect remote users securely to internal networks. Finally, encryption has become important with the advent of e-commerce, online banking, and online investing. Buying products and handling finances online would not be possible if the data sent between all involved parties over the Internet were not encrypted.

Encrypting Data

The encryption process involves comparing each character of data against a key. For example, you could encrypt the following string of data in a number of ways:

```
The quick brown fox
```

For sample purposes, let's use a simple letter-number method. In this method, each letter in the alphabet corresponds to a particular number. (You may have used this method as a kid when you got a decoder wheel in your Cracker Jack or breakfast cereal box.) If you use a straight alphabetic-to-number encryption (for example, A=1, B=2, C=3, and so on), the data translate into the following:

```
20 8 5 17 21 9 3 11 2 18 15 23 14 6 15 24
```

You can then transmit this series of numbers over a network, and the receiver can decrypt the string by using the same key in reverse. From left to right, the number 20 translates to the letter T, 8 to H, 5 to E, and so on. Eventually, the receiver gets the entire message:

```
The quick brown fox
```

Most encryption methods use much more complex formulas and methods than this. The sample key used here is about 8 bits long; some keys are extremely complex and can be a maximum of 128 bits long. The larger the key (in bits), the more complex the encryption—and the more difficult it is to crack.

To encode a message and decode an encrypted message, you need the proper encryption key or keys. An encryption key is the table or formula that defines which character in the data translates to which encoded character. Encryption keys fall into two categories: public and private.

Using Shared Key Encryption

In **shared key encryption**, also known as **symmetrical key encryption**, both the sender and receiver have the same key and use it to encrypt and decrypt all messages.

IBM developed one of the most commonly used private key systems, called **Data Encryption Standard (DES)**. In 1977, the United States made DES a government standard, defined in the **Federal Information Processing Standards Publication 46-2 (FIPS 46-2)**.

DES uses lookup table functions and is incredibly fast compared with public key systems. A 56-bit private key is used. In a challenge to break the DES, several Internet users worked in concert, each tackling a portion of the 72 quadrillion possible combinations. The key used in the challenge was broken in June 1997, after searching only 18 quadrillion keys out of the possible 72 quadrillion. The plain-text message read, "Strong cryptography makes the world a safer place."

Using Public Key Encryption

Public key encryption uses two keys to encrypt and decrypt data: a public key and a private key (see Figure 12-16). The receiver's **public key** is used to encrypt a message to the receiver. The message is sent to the receiver, who can then decrypt the message by using the **private key**. This is a one-way communication. If the receiver wants to send a return message, the same principle is used.

Figure 12-16

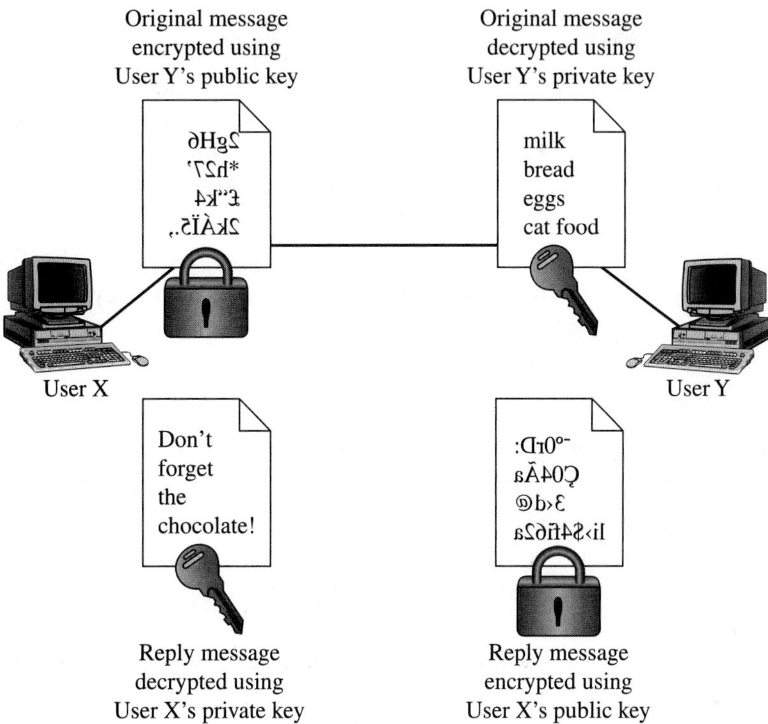

Public key encryption.

The message is encrypted with the original sender's public key (the original sender is now going to be the receiver of this new message) and can be decrypted only with the private key.

Rivest, Shamir, and Adleman (RSA) encryption is a public key encryption algorithm named after the three scientists from the Massachusetts Institute of Technology (MIT) who developed it. They created a commercial company in 1977 to develop **asymmetrical keys** and received several U.S. patents. Their encryption software is used in a number of networking products.

You might have heard the term *certificate* in the context of security and encryption. Basically, a **certificate** is issued to a company, computer, or person and proves they are who they say they are. Windows (and other NOSs) have the ability to generate certificates for internal use or for testing communications. For identification to the world at large, you need to obtain a certificate from an accepted **certificate authority**. You might do this, for example, if you have a public e-commerce site so that your customers can validate who you are. Along with identifying information, the certificate has a specific lifespan and is valid only during that period.

12.3.4 Implementing Wireless Security

While we're talking about network security, we should spend a little time looking at wireless security. Wireless networking has become a popular option because it is inexpensive and easy to configure. One problem, however, is that most default configurations leave gaping holes in network security. In the best case, all that happens is someone "borrows" your signal for free Internet access. In the worst case, the connection gives someone time to hack into your network undetected and unobstructed.

You secure a wireless network through wireless access point (WAP) configuration parameters and by implementing **Wired Equivalent Privacy (WEP), Wi-Fi Protected Access (WPA),** or 802.1x as security mechanisms.

Configuring the WAP

There are literally hundreds of different WAPs, and each uses a different method to configure its internal software. An example is shown in Figure 12-17. For the most part, WAPs follow some general patterns.

You need to configure a WAP's IP address scheme to match your network's. Some important parameters include the following:

- **SSID:** This is the name of the wireless network that this access point will advertise. In a network with only one WAP, you can think of the SSID as the "name" of the access point. A WAP comes with a default SSID, usually based on the manufacturer's name, and usually well known by people looking for a WAP to link into. One of the first things you should do is change the SSID. If you want to keep the network secure, you should also disable SSID broadcasting, as shown in Figure 12-17, to prevent the WAP from announcing itself.
- **Operating mode:** WAPs can operate in either Access Point mode or Bridging mode. Access Point mode allows the WAP to operate as a traditional access point to allow a wireless client transparent access to a wired network. Two WAPs set to Bridging mode provide a wireless bridge between two wired network segments and filter traffic by MAC address.
- **Password:** Every WAP has some kind of default password that is used to access the WAP's configuration. For security reasons, you should change this as soon as you are able to connect to and configure the WAP.
- **Wireless channel:** 802.11 wireless networks can operate on different channels to avoid interference. Most wireless WAPs can be set to work on a particular channel from the factory, so for security reasons, you should change the channel as soon as you can.

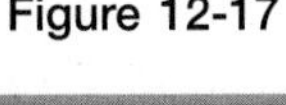

Figure 12-17

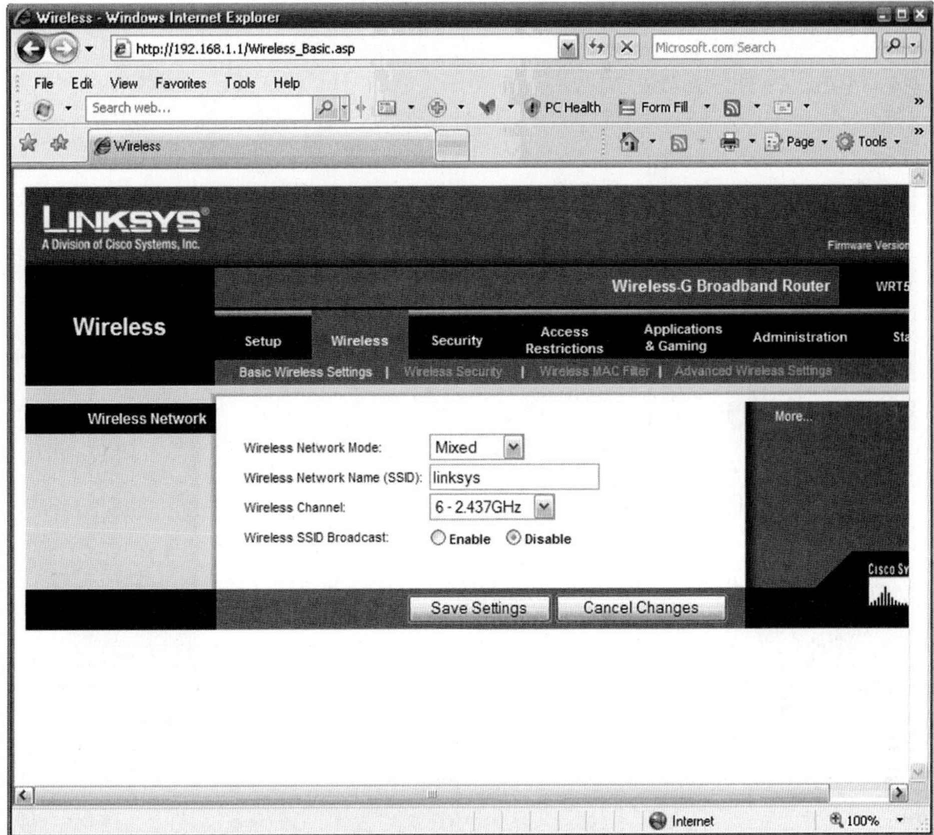

WAP configuration parameters.

WAPs can also support WEP, WPA, and 802.11x to further secure the network. Some support a combination of these.

Wired Equivalent Privacy (WEP) provides basic security for a wireless 802.11b or 802.11g LAN. The WEP protocol is used to encrypt data being transmitted over a wireless 802.11b network. It is a lower-layer security protocol that encrypts the data before transmission, using an algorithm known as **RC4**. To encrypt the data, a string of characters known as a key is used. The key is made up of a random number known as the **initialization value** plus a string of text chosen by the administrator or user that sets up WEP on a device, as shown in Figure 12-18. The keys used to encrypt the data stream are usually 40, 64, or 128 bits long.

Wi-Fi Protected Access (WPA) is a standard that improves on the original design of WEP. It was designed to be compatible with WEP-enabled hardware

Figure 12-18

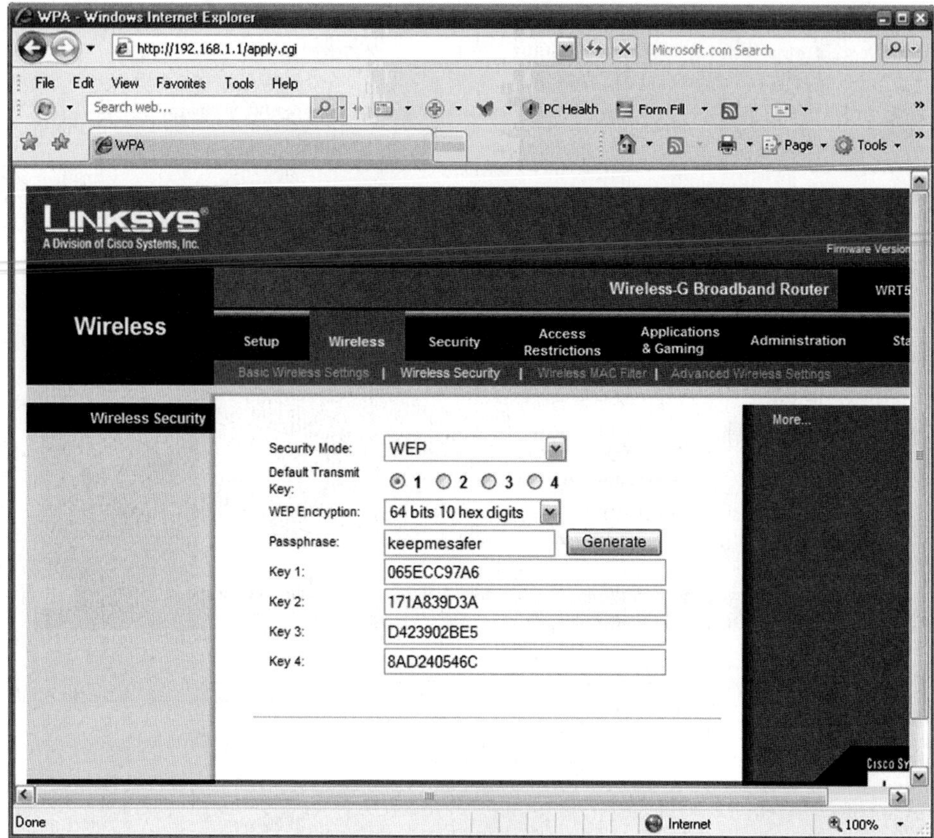

WEP configuration.

and software and can usually be implemented with a simple software upgrade. In order to provide this enhanced security, WPA adds two main components (see Figure 12-19): TKIP and user authentication. **Temporal Key Integrity Protocol (TKIP)** encrypts the keys so they are more difficult to intercept by an eavesdropper. WPA's user authentication uses the Extensible Authentication Protocol (EAP), which is a form of public key encryption, to ensure that the user using the wireless network is a valid user.

The **802.1x** standard is an open framework designed to support multiple authentication schemes. Before a client (known as a **supplicant** in 802.1x parlance) can communicate on a wireless network, it asks the WAP (known as an **authenticator**) for permission to enter and provides its credentials. The WAP passes those credentials to a centralized authentication server (e.g., a RADIUS server).

Figure 12-19

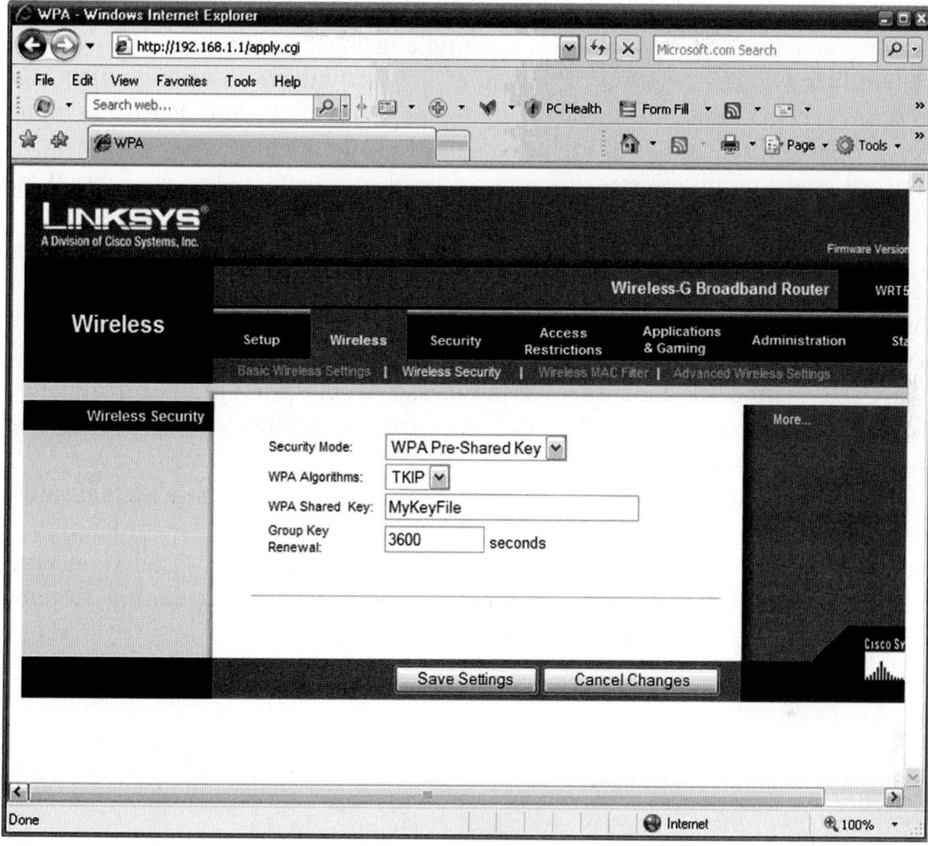

WPA configuration.

The server sends back an accept message to the access point if the authentication method is successful, and the access point allows the user to connect to the wireless network. It is important to note that 802.1x allows no access to any wireless ports of any kind (except for 802.1x/EAP during authentication) until the user is authenticated. Also, encryption is not required for use with 802.1x. It is an authentication method only, but it can provide significant security measures, even without WEP keys.

Some manufacturers have added RADIUS authentication as an authentication option with or without 802.1x, using their own nonstandard implementations. With this type of authentication, you must provide the RADIUS server's IP address, port, and either a shared key or a WEP encryption key.

12.3.5 Using Auditing and Logs

Client OSs and NOSs have different tools built in that help monitor system and network activity. Two key areas are auditing and logs.

Auditing is the process of watching key activities you've identified and recording, depending on how it is configured, successful and failed attempts. Commonly audited activities include user login attempts, changes to system or network security, and attempts to access critical or sensitive files. Available Windows **audit policies** are shown in Figure 12-20.

Perhaps the best way to understand the role of audits in network security is to consider an example. Say that you have a set of sensitive data files in a secure directory. Users should be able to view the files but not modify or delete them. You configure access permissions to limit user access, but you also want to know if any user attempts to delete any of the files. You set up auditing to track failed delete attempts on the files. If a user does try, the attempt, along with a time stamp and user name, is recorded.

Logs give you a way of reviewing what's been happening on a system. Most operating systems and applications keep a variety of logs. For example, installation logs record what happened during OS or application installation, and error logs keep track of detected errors. Windows family operating systems keep one set of logs available for easy access, collectively known as **event logs**

Figure 12-20

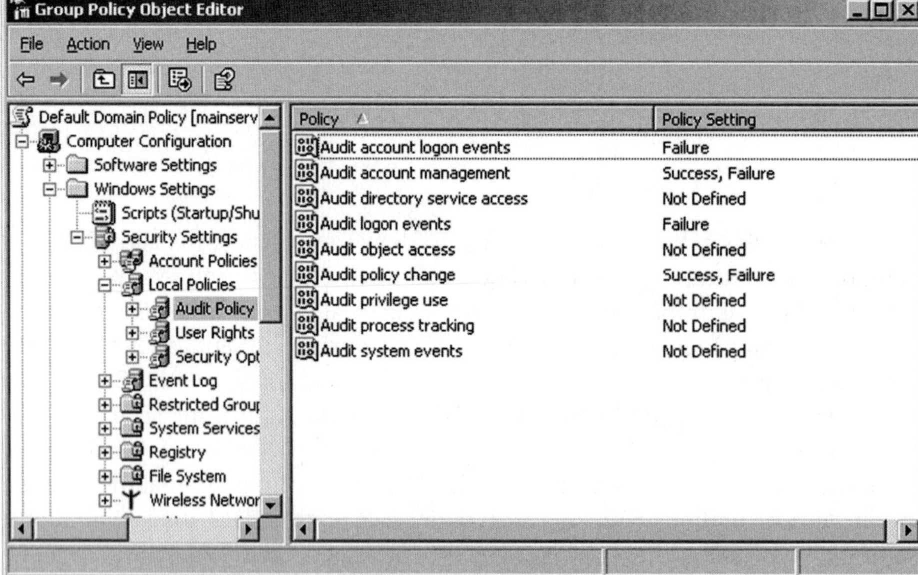

Windows audit policies.

Figure 12-21

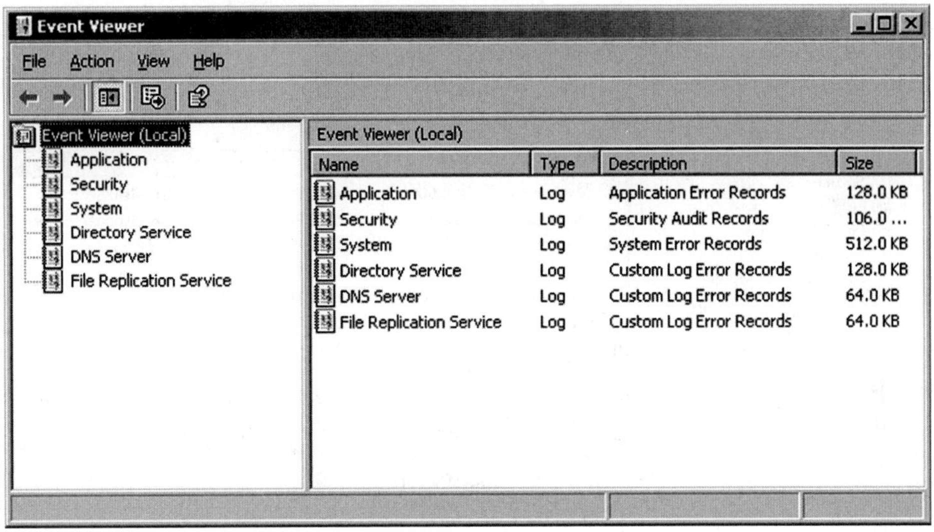

Windows event logs.

(see Figure 12-21). They are accessible through the Event Viewer, which is part of the administrative tools.

The logs you see depend on how your computer is configured and the applications it supports. Log entries include informational messages, warnings, errors, and successful and failed audit entries. The logs, at minimum, include the following:

- **Application log:** The **application log** records application-related messages for applications that support the functionality (e.g., Microsoft SQL Server).
- **System log:** The **system log** records system-related messages related to system hardware, the operating system, and system services.
- **Security log:** The **security log** records security messages, including audit success and failure entries. You must be an administrator to view the security log's contents.

Other logs vary by computer. A domain controller has a directory service log that records Active Directory events. A computer configured as a DNS server has a DNS service log. Some applications even add their own logs, although most write information to the application log.

In Figure 12-22, you see the contents of the system log. Entries with an "i" are informational—things such as the normal starting and stopping of various

Figure 12-22

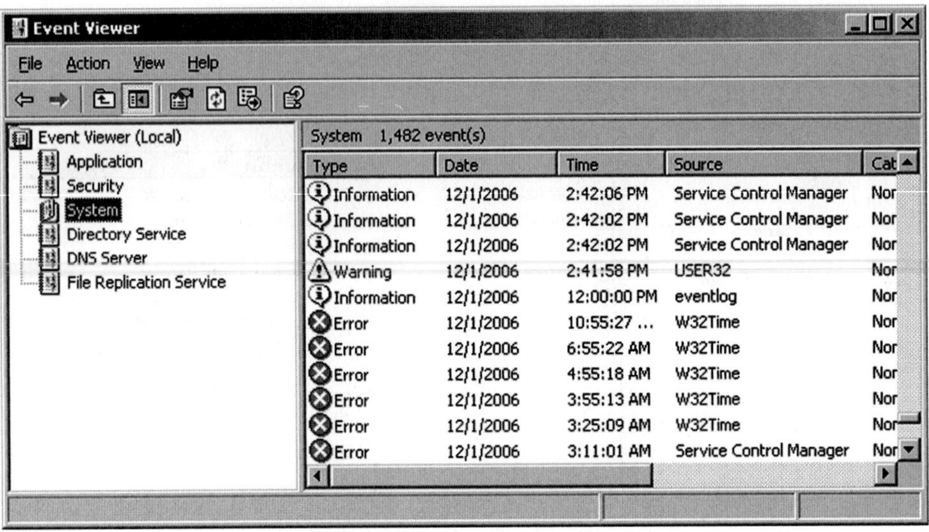

Sample system log entries.

services. Warnings are indicated by an exclamation point (!). These events aren't critical, but you should review them because they could represent a problem that could get worse. An "X" indicates an error, such as a failing device or a service that failed to start.

FOR EXAMPLE

All by Ourselves

Busicorp is worried about corporate espionage. The company has a large research and development (R&D) department that needs occasional access to the rest of the network, but other departments should be prevented from peeking around in R&D servers and clients. One way to accomplish this is to set up a screened subnetwork like the one shown in Figure 12-24. To do this, you set up a subnet and deploy all the R&D computers. You install a firewall between that subnet and the rest of the company intranet.

Once the firewall is in place, you have control over traffic into and out of the screened subnet. You can set up different types of filter criteria, as necessary, including setting different criteria on incoming and outgoing traffic. For example, you could limit incoming traffic so that the only traffic allowed is that generated as a response to a message issued from inside the screened subnet.

Figure 12-23

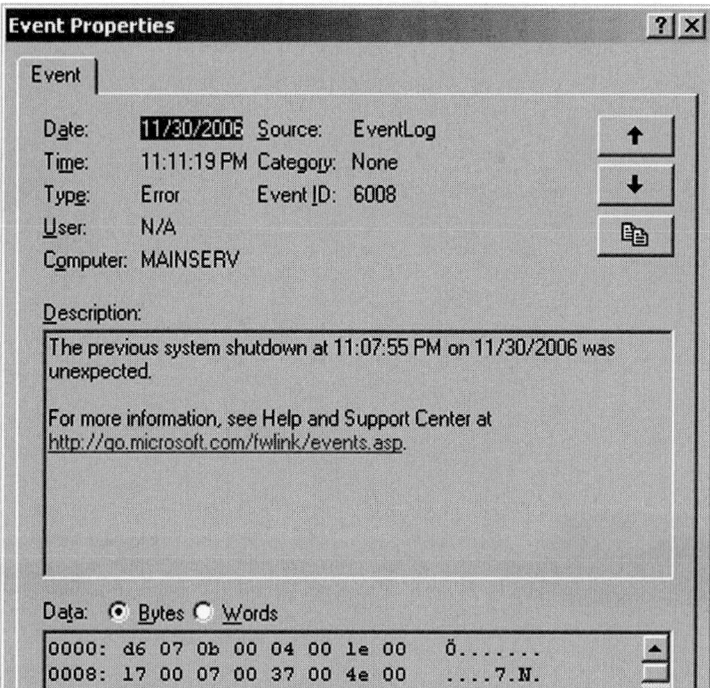

A detailed log entry.

It's common to see a series of errors occurring over a short period of time. These are due to **cascading failures**, where one failure directly results in another. For example, if a service fails to start, any services that depend on that service will also fail to start. Each of these failures will write an error to the system log.

You can open individual entries to get information about that entry. Take a look at the example in Figure 12-23. The exact contents of the error will vary.

It's important that you review the contents of each of the event logs periodically, watching especially for warning and error entries. You may also want to save a log's contents to provide a security trail.

Keep in mind that the use of logs is not unique to Windows. The Windows logs are provided here as representative examples, but similar logs are available on all current NOSs. When supporting a specific NOS, you should research the available logs and the procedures for enabling and configuring auditing.

Figure 12-24

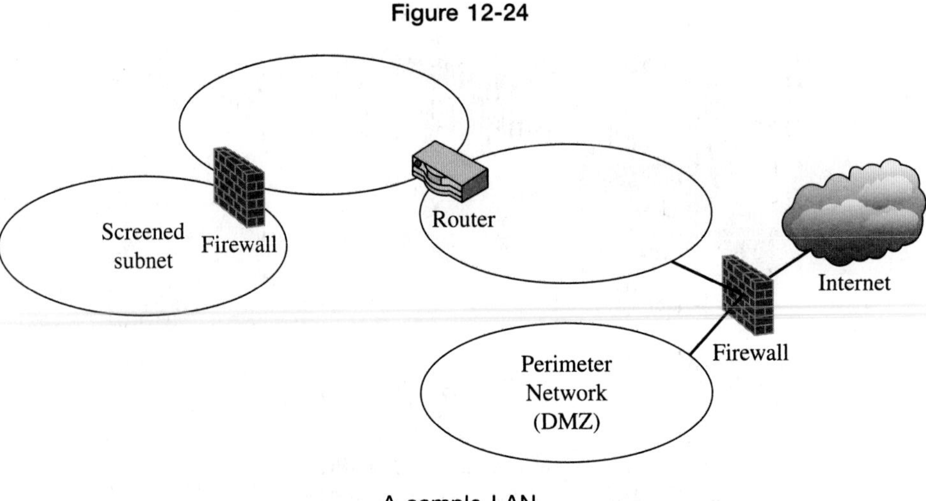

A sample LAN.

SELF-CHECK

1. What typically happens during a DoS attack?
2. What typically happens during a DDoS attack?
3. From an operational standpoint, what is the difference between shared key and public key encryption?

12.4 Configuring Computer Security

Part of securing a network is securing the computers on the network. There are several types of malicious software waiting to infect unprotected computers, including viruses, worms, and Trojans. Other potential risks include spyware, which gathers information about your activities, and adware, which makes you more susceptible to pop-up ads.

12.4.1 Understanding Malicious Software

Special attention also must be paid to avoiding malicious software, sometimes called **malware**, such as viruses. Some malware is harmless, such as nuisance messages, but other malware is serious, causing destruction of data. A virus can be recognized by its **signature**—code within the virus by which it can be identified—but a virus may be able to change its appearance as it spreads, making detection more difficult.

Most viruses attach themselves to other programs or to special areas of disks. As the files execute or are accessed, the virus spreads. Macro viruses, viruses that are contained in documents or spreadsheet files, can spread when an infected file is opened.

A **worm** is a special type of virus that spreads itself without human intervention, copying itself from computer to computer. Worms spread when they install themselves on a computer and then send copies of themselves to other computers, usually by email or through security holes in software. Part of the concern with worms is that they can quickly spread themselves across the Internet and to any connected computer, which makes them difficult to contain or remove.

A **Trojan**, or **Trojan horse**, is a program that appears to be one thing but is actually another. When you execute the program, it does its damage. A Trojan could easily erase disk partition information, causing you to lose all the information on a disk, before you have any idea what's happening. The only good thing about a Trojan is that it can't spread itself. The victim has to actively download and copy and then execute the program.

A **rootkit** is a program that hides itself, as well as other programs, files, and even running processes, from the operating system. The rootkit itself isn't the risk; the programs and files that the rootkit is hiding are the problem. Rootkits are used with various forms of malware to prevent antivirus programs from detecting and removing them. They can also open a backdoor into a system, providing a way for someone to sneak in.

Spyware collects information about a user's activities, such as files opened, programs run, and websites visited. It is sometimes used to track employees' activities. Some types of spyware are rather malicious, not only collecting information but also sending it to a collection site. Spyware of this type is sometimes used to steal sensitive information such as credit card numbers.

Adware is normally not dangerous, but it can be annoying. It acts something like a beacon, advertising your computer's existence and location to the Internet. Adware causes an ongoing flow of pop-up ads and browser windows to open spontaneously on the desktop. Adware usually infects a computer by enticing the user to visit (or be redirected to) a website that **pushes** (which is like downloading, but initiated by the source) the adware onto the user's computer.

12.4.2 Protecting Network Computers

The following guidelines apply to both networked and stand-alone computers that connect to the Internet, computers that dial in to another computer, or computers to which files are copied from removable media. One key to avoiding malicious software and preventing the spread of viruses is to not copy or download files of unknown origin—or at least to check every file you do copy or download. The same goes for email attachments. If you don't recognize the source, you shouldn't open the attachment.

Another key to avoiding malware is to install antivirus software on every computer. There are several different packages available, supporting different feature sets and working with various degrees of success. As a general rule, it's usually best to go with a well-known manufacturer. What about the features you need? At minimum, your antivirus software should be able to scan the computer for viruses, both the hard disk and memory, after it installs. You should be able to configure the software to run periodic scans to keep the hard disk clean, and it should support on-demand scanning, like the scan shown in Figure 12-25. It should also scan both the message content and attachments of both incoming and outgoing email messages.

A critical concern is how extensive a database of malware signatures an antivirus program has and how often it is updated. Some experts estimate that as many as 10 new viruses appear each day. Identifying virus signatures and keeping antivirus software updated is a constant struggle. This is one area where manufacturers cooperate with one another, sharing information with each other about emerging threats.

Figure 12-25

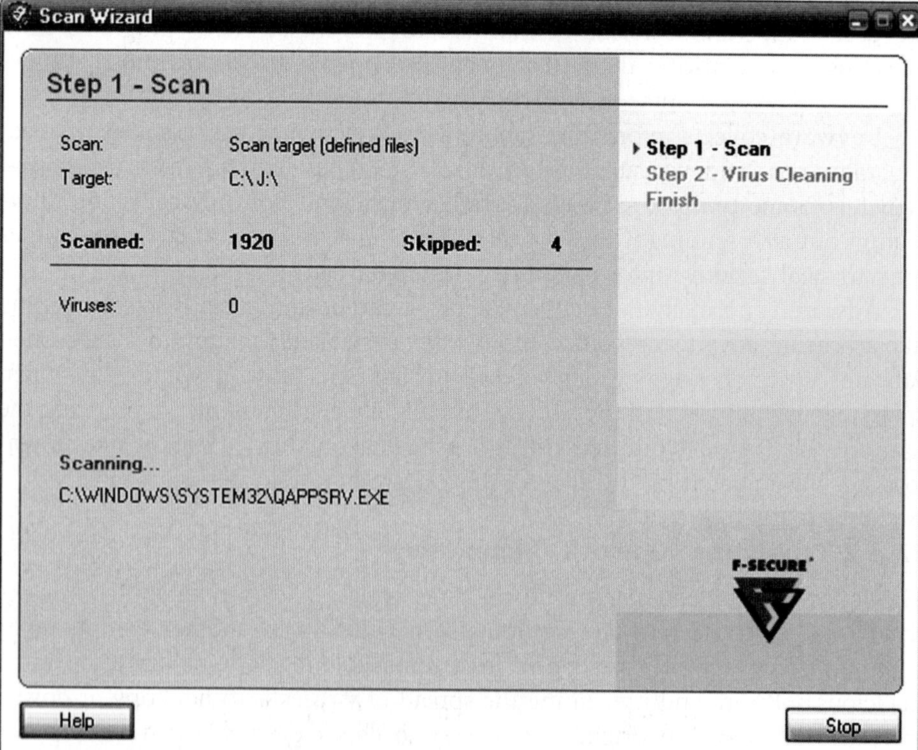

An antivirus scan.

FOR EXAMPLE

The Sony BMG Copy Protection Scandal

For most of the public at large, the first introduction to the term *rootkit* came about as a result of the outcry over an action taken by Sony BMG music, commonly known as the Sony BMG CD copy protection scandal. Here's what happened.

Starting in 2005, Sony BMG placed a rootkit on some of its music CDs. When someone played the CD on a computer running Windows, the rootkit installed on the computer. Actually, there were two different programs used, placed on a total of about 100 different titles. The problem is that Sony didn't warn anyone about what it was doing. There was no specific mention on the CD packaging or the CD itself other than some vague language about security rights management.

Sony's goal was copy protection, a way to prevent customers from sharing the music from the CDs on the Internet. The actual result was quite different. The rootkit opened several security holes, making the computers more susceptible to viruses and interfering with computer operations. Not only that, lawsuits were brought against Sony BMG, claiming that the rootkit itself violated the software license under which it was developed.

An outcry ensued, and Sony BMG released a utility that supposedly removed the rootkit. What it actually did was unhide the files and unmask the rootkit, but it didn't remove it. Sony BMG finally released a utility to completely remove the rootkit and all associated files. It also recalled the CDs on which the "protection" was installed, paying retailers to remove them from their shelves. Despite this action, Sony BMG still had to deal with suits brought in Texas, California, and New York, not to mention the customer satisfaction issues.

Why mention this cautionary tale? If you aren't careful, some of the actions you take in pursuit of security can go too far, especially if they affect networks or computers outside your network. You also need to realize that the threats are constantly evolving as hackers look for new and more efficient methods of attacking their targets. That means that you, as a network administrator, need to keep up to date on emerging threats.

Most antivirus products currently on the market include the antivirus program as part of a security suite that includes features such as these:

- A firewall that lets you set filter parameters for that computer.
- Intrusion detection software that warns you when another computer tries to connect to your computer.

▲ Browser monitoring software that warns you of suspicious activities, such as attempting to redirect you to another website or trying to download a file to your computer.
▲ Spam filters to detect and block unwanted email.
▲ Application controls that prevent one program from launching another without your knowledge.

Most manufacturers and computer dealers install some version of antivirus software, usually one with a license that expires in six months to a year, on new computers. Many of the large ISPs, especially those offering high-speed Internet access, offer security suites at no charge to their subscribers. Why? Avoiding virus infections and other attacks is good business for the ISP, too. Not only that, offers of those kinds of additional perks make for satisfied customers in a competitive market where word of mouth is often the most efficient advertising.

Some of these same security components are also included with current operating systems, although they are not necessarily enabled by default. Windows XP Service Pack 2, for example, added a private firewall. Most Linux distributions can be configured with a local firewall to filter traffic into or out of the computer. There are also a wide variety of security tools that can be downloaded from the Internet, either free or at very low cost. However, you must exercise caution. Some of these are merely benign and ineffective, not giving you anything more than a good feeling about your computer. Others are much more malicious in nature, little more than delivery mechanisms for viruses and Trojans.

SELF-CHECK

1. What are the most common types of malicious software?
2. What is the potential risk from adware?
3. Why is it important that an antivirus program update its signatures?

SUMMARY

In this chapter, you were introduced to issues related to network and computer security. You learned about the need for risk assessment and the types of risks you might face. You learned about user account, password, resource access, and user right management, including why it is more efficient to manage security by group than by individual users. You learned about common types of network attacks and how to use firewalls to protect a network, including a couple of options for configuring perimeter networks. You learned a few basic facts about using encryption to protect your data. You also learned about using auditing and system logs to monitor network security. Finally, you learned about malicious software and antivirus programs that are used to find and remove it from your computer.

KEY TERMS

802.1x
Account lockout policies
Administrator
Adware
Application log
Asymmetrical keys
Audit policies
Auditing
Auditing tools
Authentication credentials
Authenticator
Availability
Biometric scan
Bit strength
Black box system
Blue screen of death (BSoD)
Business continuity planning
Cascading failures
Certificate
Certificate authority
Computer crime
Computer Emergency Response Team (CERT)
Confidentiality
Crack program
Data Encryption Standard (DES)
DDoS agent
DDoS handler
Decryption
Demilitarized zone (DMZ)
Denial of service (DoS) attack
Directed attack
Disruption
Distributed denial of service (DDoS) attack
Domain account
Dynamic packet filtering
Dynamic state list
Encryption
Encryption algorithm
Encryption formula
Enforce password history
Event log
Federal Information Processing Standards Publication 46-2 (FIPS 46-2)
Firewall
Hacker
Hardening
Health Insurance Portability and Accountability Act (HIPAA)
Initialization value

Integrity
IP spoofing
Key
Local account
Maintenance account
Malware
Maximum password age
Minimum password age
Minimum password length
Mission-critical application
Network asset
Packet filtering
passwd
Password must meet complexity requirements
Perimeter network
Ping of death
Port filtering
Private key
Public key
Public key encryption
Push
RC4
Rivest, Shamir, and Adleman (RSA)
Root
Rootkit
Security breach
Security log
Shadow
Shared key encryption
Signature
Spyware
State table
Store passwords using reversible encryption
Strong password
Superuser
Supervisor
Supplicant
Symmetrical key encryption
SYN flag
SYN flood
SYN packet
System log
Temporal Key Integrity Protocol (TKIP)
Threat
Trojan horse (Trojan)
Unauthorized access
User account
Virus
Vulnerability research
Weak password
Wi-Fi Protected Access (WPA)
WinNuke
Wired Equivalent Privacy (WEP)
Worm

ASSESS YOUR UNDERSTANDING

Go to www.wiley.com/college/ciccarelli to evaluate your knowledge of network security fundamentals.
Measure your learning by comparing pre-test and post-test results.

Summary Questions

1. Which of the following is an example of a strong password?
   (a) dictionary
   (b) bluegreen2
   (c) cu&tin=bronze
   (d) ahtraM
2. Which of the following could be used to detect someone trying to guess a user's password?
   (a) account lockout
   (b) password history
   (c) password age
   (d) reversible password encryption
3. Which of the following encryption algorithms are used with WEP security?
   (a) DES
   (b) RC4
   (c) RSA
   (d) DHA
4. Which of the following refers to a network segment isolated for security reasons?
   (a) WPA
   (b) DES
   (c) TKIP
   (d) DMZ
5. Which of the following is a malicious application designed to monitor and record a user's activity on a computer?
   (a) spyware
   (b) rootkit
   (c) worm
   (d) signature
6. A Trojan horse is a program that appears to be one thing but is actually another. True or false?

7. Unauthorized access is most often the result of an incursion by an individual from outside an organization. True or false?
8. Which of the following requires you to store passwords using reversible encryption?
   (a) EAP
   (b) CHAP
   (c) MS-CHAPv2
   (d) WPA
9. Ping of death is an example of which of the following?
   (a) malware
   (b) WinNuke attack
   (c) DoS attack
   (d) SYN flood
10. Which of the following might an attacker employ to make a DDoS attack difficult to detect or block?
   (a) IP spoofing
   (b) dynamic filtering
   (c) WinNuke
   (d) a DES algorithm
11. You can deploy publicly accessible computers within a network segment configured as a perimeter network. True or false?
12. You suspect that a device driver failed to initialize during system startup. Which Windows event log should you check?
   (a) application
   (b) security
   (c) directory service
   (d) system
13. You want to limit traffic into and out of your network to ports 80 and 443. What type of device should you deploy?
   (a) firewall
   (b) NAT server
   (c) switch
   (d) bridge
14. Based on CERT surveys, what is the most prevalent risk to computers deployed on a network that is connected to the Internet?
   (a) unauthorized access by employees
   (b) unauthorized access by outside attackers

(c) virus infection
(d) hidden spyware

15. A smart card is an example of a biometric device. True or false?

Applying This Chapter

1. For the following questions, assume that you are the network administrator for the sample network shown in Figure 12-26.

   Your network has experienced several problems, including virus infections and attempted break-ins. You are reconfiguring the network to improve network security.

   (a) What are the potential points of access to your network?
   (b) Your company has two public web servers. Where should they be deployed?
   (c) Why?
   (d) You want a record of failed attempts to log in locally to a secure member server. How can you obtain this?
   (e) The member server is running Windows 2000 Server. Where should you check to see if there have been any login attempts?
   (f) If you want to configure Network A as a screened subnet, what do you need to do?

Figure 12-26

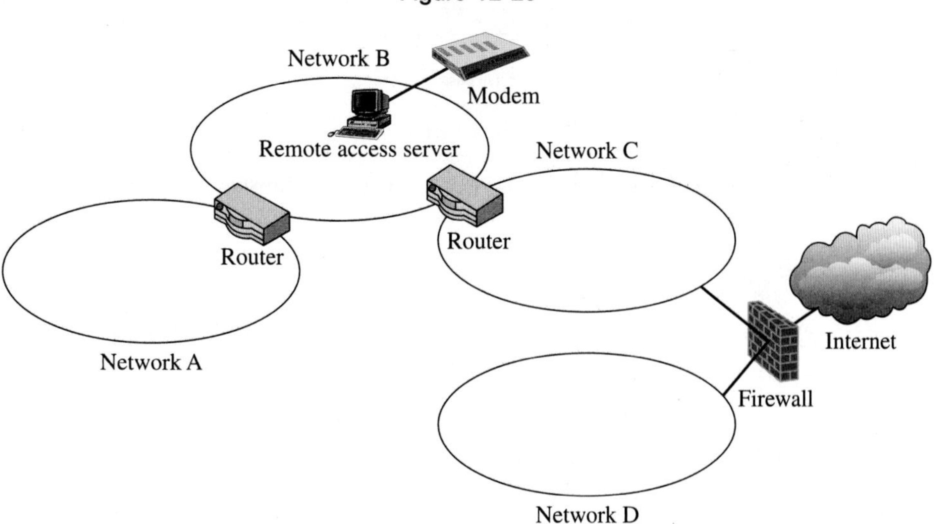

A sample network.

2. The following questions refer to the password policies shown in Figure 12-27.

   Password policies for the Busicorp domain are shown in Figure 12-27. These policies apply to all domain computers.

   (a) What is the minimum password length?
   (b) How often must users change passwords?
   (c) How can you override this so that you never have to change a user's password?
   (d) How can you increase the time a user must wait before changing his or her password?
   (e) Which of the following values could a user could enter as a valid password?

▲ ThisIsMyPassword
▲ il2ra0t
▲ abcABC123#
▲ 44o%45%0
▲ tQbFjOtF2times
▲ $#@@47&!%

Figure 12-27

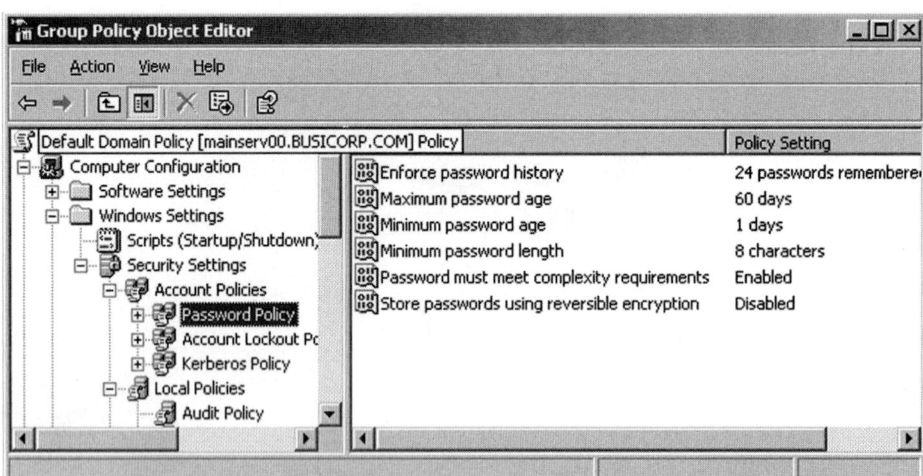

Busicorp domain password policies.

YOU TRY IT

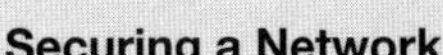

Securing a Network

You were recently hired as the network administrator for Busicorp. The network is a routed LAN with three subnetworks connected in a mesh configuration, using three Linux computers configured as routers. The network is set up as a single Windows Active Directory domain.

You plan to add a WAP to one of the subnets to make it easier to support laptop computers. A single WAP will have sufficient range to cover the office and beyond to the street outside. You are concerned about external access to your network and want to make the wireless subnet as secure as possible.

You have a mail relay server and a web server that you want to deploy so that they are isolated from the internal network by a firewall. You also want to protect them from the Internet with a second firewall.

1. The web server supports an e-commerce application through which customers can purchase and download documents. Why should you install on the web server a certificate from a recognized certificate authority?
2. Why should you deploy the web server on a perimeter network instead of one of the internal subnets?
3. You have been authorized a budget to make improvements to network security. You want to make sure that you use the money as efficiently as possible. What two things should you do first?
4. Why should you do these two things first?
5. You disable SSID broadcast on your WAP. What else can you do to make it more difficult for someone to locate and identify your WAP?
6. Your WAP supports WEP and WPA. Which should you use?
7. Why?
8. Sketch your network. Show the location of the firewalls, routers, web server, and the Internet.

GLOSSARY

10Base2 A bus topology Ethernet network that uses thin coaxial cable. Also known as Thin Ethernet or Thinnet.

10Base5 A bus topology Ethernet network that uses thick coaxial cable. Also known as Thick Ethernet or Thicknet.

10Base100 A logical bus topology that uses a 100Mbps physical star topology.

10BaseT A logical bus topology that uses a 10Mbps physical star topology.

10GBaseT A standard for 10Gbps Ethernet using UTP cable.

802.1 LAN and MAN Bridging and Management A standard that defines how a networking device determines the path to connect to a LAN or MAN.

802.1p A standard that specifies how Layer 2 switches can prioritize traffic and perform dynamic multicast filtering.

802.1Q A standard that defines VLANs.

802.1x A wireless security standard method for authenticating users.

802.2 LLC A standard that defines the upper level of the Data Link layer of the OSI model.

802.3 CSMA/CD A standard that defines an access method used by Ethernet, based on carrier sensing by multiple computers with equal access to the network and collision detection and recovery.

802.3x Fast Ethernet A standard that defines 100Mbps Ethernet.

802.3z Gigabit Ethernet A standard that defines 1Gbps Ethernet.

802.4 Token Bus A bus-based token-passing method not currently used in LAN applications.

802.5 Token Ring The IEEE standard that describes Token Ring.

802.6 Distributed Queue Dual Bus (DQDB) A MAN standard for using two parallel cables in a bus topology.

802.7 Broadband LANs A standard that defines broadband transmissions over a LAN using a full duplex medium and multiplexed signals.

802.8 Fiber-Optic LANs and MANs A standard for recommended LAN and MAN configurations based on fiber-optic cable configurations.

802.9 Integrated Services A standard that defines a unified access method offering integrated services for public and private backbone networks.

802.10 LAN/MAN Security A standard for assigning unique SAIDs for LAN and MAN network security.

802.11 Wireless LANs A set of standards that defines wireless networking and speeds up to 54Mbps.

802.11a The first high-speed wireless standard. Extends 802.11. 802.11a defines transmissions that utilize the 5GHz frequency band with 54Mbps of wireless throughput. The standard is not commonly used.

802.11b The basis for most of the early wireless devices. 802.11b uses the 2.4GHz frequency band for communication and allows for up to 11Mbps of throughput to be transmitted.

802.11g A wireless standard that uses the 2.4GHz frequency bank, like 802.11b, although transmitting at up to 54Mbps. Most 802.11g devices support and provide connectivity to 802.11b devices on the network because they are communicating within the same frequency band.

802.11n A wireless standard currently under development.

802.12 High-Speed LANs A standard that defines support for 100Mbps signal transmission using the demand priority access method.

802.14 Cable TV A standard that defines digital communication services over cable television networks.

802.15 WPANs A wireless networking standard that is similar to the Bluetooth peripheral connection standard.

802.16 WiMAX A set of high-speed wireless communication standards.

802.16d Fixed WiMAX A high-speed wireless communication standard that is sometimes used for MAN connections or to connect public Wi-Fi WAPs to a central point for communication with the Internet.

802.16e Mobile WiMAX A high-speed wireless standard designed as an alternative for cell phones and computer hardware.

A record *See* address record.

Acceptance stage The phase in the standardization process in which the final definition is produced and the authoritative parties agree on the solution.

Access layer The network technology—typically the LAN or remote access connection—closest to the user.

Access method *See* access protocol.

Access point A central connection point for wireless computers that also supports connecting to a wired network.

Access protocol A protocol that operates at the Data Link layer of the OSI model and defines access to the physical network media. Also known as an access method.

Account lockout policies Policies controlling account lockout configuration parameters.

Acknowledgement (ACK) A special packet type sent by a receiving system to acknowledge successful receipt of one or more datagrams.

Acknowledgement number *See* acknowledgement.

Active Directory Microsoft's directory-based network architecture.

Active Directory Users and Computers A Windows Active Directory utility used to manage organizational units, users, groups, computers, and other domain objects.

Ad hoc mode A wireless network topology in which wireless devices communicate directly with each other. Also known as peer-to-peer mode.

Address record A DNS record that maps a host name to an IP address. It is the most common type of DNS record. Also known as the host record.

Address Resolution Protocol (ARP) A TCP/IP protocol that provides a device's MAC address, based on its IP address.

Address scope A set of addresses that is available for assignment through DHCP.

Addressing How computers uniquely identify each other on a network.

Administrator A user name often associated with a maintenance account that has unlimited access to a computer or network. *See also* supervisor, root, and superuser.

Adware Software that makes a computer more easily locatable by and more susceptible to pop-up and other online ads.

Agent An SNMP component that collects MIB information and delivers it to the management console.

Alert A response to a Windows performance threshold value being met or exceeded.

Alias record *See* canonical name (CNAME) record.

American National Standards Institute (ANSI) A U.S. standardization organization that accepts standards developed by other organizations and publishes them as American standards and coordinates development of voluntary national standards that comply with international recommendations.

Apache web server A popular open source web server.

AppleTalk A high-level protocol developed and used by Apple.

AppleTalk Address Resolution Protocol (AARP) An AppleTalk protocol used to retrieve a computer's physical address for packet delivery.

AppleTalk Data Stream Protocol (ADSP) A protocol that is responsible for establishing connections, sequencing, and packet flow control.

AppleTalk Filing Protocol (AFP) A protocol that supports file sharing, file transfer, and end-user printer sharing.

AppleTalk Session Protocol (ASP) A protocol that provides OSI model Session layer services.

AppleTalk Transaction Protocol (ATP) A protocol that provides reliable transport services between computers and applications.

Application layer (DoD and Internet models) The DoD and Internet model layer that is equivalent to the OSI Application, Presentation, and Session layers. Also known as the Process layer.

Application layer (OSI model) The OSI model layer that provides end users and applications access to the network through protocols and utilities.

Application log A Windows event log that maintains entries related to application events.

Archive bit A bit associated with a data file. When set, it indicates that the file has changed and needs to be backed up.

ARCNET A low-level network protocol. It was an early OSI layer 2 networking protocol that is now seen in legacy networks only.

Asymmetrical DSL (ADSL) The most common type of DSL in current use. ADSL includes a voice circuit and upstream and downstream circuits that operate at different speeds.

Asymmetrical keys The public and private keys used in public key encryption.

Asynchronous Transfer Mode (ATM) A packet-switched network standard communication method that provides improved performance compared to X.25 and is scalable up to 39Gbps.

Attenuation Loss of signal strength over distance.

Attribute Directory objects' properties.

Audit To track and record network activity, usually in regard to user activity.

Audit policies Windows policies used to control auditing.

Auditing The process of watching key activities and recording specific successful and failed activities.

Auditing tools Utilities designed to automatically review and test network security.

Authentication The process by which a user proves they are who they say they are to the network operating system.

Authentication credentials Information or a security device used to authenticate a user's access to a network, most commonly based on user name and password.

Authentication method A means to validate a network user's identity.

Authenticator A term that refers to a WAP during 802.1x authentication.

Authoritative server A server with primary responsibility for a DNS zone to which DNS table updates are made and used as the source for updating other copies of the zone table.

Automated software delivery *See* electronic software distribution.

Automatic failover A failover process in which an error is detected automatically, and the configuration switches over to the redundant server without administrator intervention.

Automatic Private IP Addressing (APIPA) A means by which a computer running Windows can assign itself an address if it is unable to lease one from a DHCP server.

Automatic repeat request (ARQ) A stop-and-wait transmission method used by DCF.

Availability A term that refers to providing continuous operation of an organization's hardware and software so that there is no interruption of service.

Average circuit traffic The network's usual traffic requirements.

B channel An ISDN data channel that carries 64Kbps.

Backbone network (BN) A large, central network that can be used to connect LANs to form MANs, and also connect other backbone networks, MANs, and even WANs.

Back-end authentication Authentication performed behind the scenes by an authentication server.

Backoff The delay during CSMA/CD transmissions between the detection of a collision and a device's attempt to re-send the data.

Backup destination A location at which backed-up data is stored.

Bandwidth A term used to describe a frequency range or the capacity of a data transmission.

Baseline values Values collected for comparison against later performance statistics.

Baselining The process of collecting performance baseline information.

Basic rate interface (BRI) An ISDN configuration that has two B channels and one D channel.

Best-effort transmission A term used to refer to the connectionless transmission method used by IP.

Bindery An authentication method used by NetWare servers prior to NetWare 4.

Biometric device A device that uses physical features, such as a fingerprint or retinal pattern, to authenticate network users.

Biometric scan A security scan based on a user's identifiable physical characteristic.

Bipolar signaling An encoding method that uses voltages that vary between plus and minus voltage levels to represent 1s and 0s.

Bit strength A measure of encryption strength based on the number of bits in a key.

Black box system A proprietary system in which you know what a system does but not the hardware or software it contains.

Blue screen of death (BSoD) A visual indication of a stop error. You must reboot the computer to clear the error.

Bluetooth A wireless peripheral connection standard.

BNC connector A Bayonet-style connector used when connecting an Ethernet NIC to a 10Base2 network.

BOOTP enabled A router that is configured to pass DHCP broadcasts.

BOOTP forwarding A router configuration option that enables routers to pass DHCP broadcasts.

Bottlenecks Network or computer components responsible for loss of performance.

Bridge A network communication device used to connect physical networks and provide a level of filtering between the networks.

Bridging loop A condition in which packets are continually passed between bridges without ever reaching the destination computer.

Broadband ISDN (B-ISDN) A high-speed digital ISDN that uses ATM circuits carrying data at either 155.52Mbps or 622.08Mbps.

Broadcast Traffic that is effectively addressed to every device on a network segment.

Broadcast domain A set of nodes configured to receive broadcasts as a group.

Brouter A network communication device that combines the functionality of routers and bridges.

Building-block process A network design process based on the concept that networks that use a few standard components are less expensive in the long run than networks that use a wide variety of components.

Bus topology A physical topology in which all devices connect to a single main cable.

Business continuity planning Ensuring availability and integrity; keeping the business running when disruptions occur.

Cable segment A physical cable section.

Caching Local storage of network resources. Cached files are refreshed, updating either the local copy or the network copy, depending on which has the most recent changes, when a user connects to the network.

Canonical name (CNAME) record A record that is used to map duplicate host names to a single IP address.

Capacity planning The process of estimating the size and type of network circuits needed.

Carrier-Sense Multiple Access/Collision Avoidance (CSMA/CA) An access method used on Wi-Fi networks that is similar to the CSMA/CD used on Ethernet networks, except that it makes more of an effort to avoid collisions between transmitting devices.

Carrier-Sense Multiple Access/Collision Detect (CSMA/CD) An access method used on Ethernet networks that gives all devices equal access to the network.

Cascading failures A situation in which one failure is the direct cause of other failures. Cascading failures are seen after a service fails, causing any dependent services to also fail.

Cell A fixed-size packet.

Certificate A secure identifier issued to a company, computer, or person that proves they are who they say they are.

Certificate authority An organization or a software service that can grant certificates.

Challenge Handshake Authentication Protocol (CHAP) An industry-standard authentication protocol that uses a challenge and response authentication method.

Channel service unit (CSU) A dedicated circuit network connection device.

Checksum A value used to verify that a datagram has not changed during transmission.

Circuit The path over which network devices communicate.

Circuit loading A term that refers to the amount of traffic a circuit must carry.

Circuit-switch network A communication network that uses a cloud architecture and includes POTS and ISDN.

Cladding Reflective material that helps bend light waves as they travel through a cable.

Class A method of organizing available IPv4 addresses for assignment.

Class A A network address classification that defines, by default, up to 127 networks with up to 16,777,214 hosts each.

Class B A network address classification that defines, by default, 16,384 networks with up to 65,534 hosts each.

Class C A network address classification that defines up to 2,097,152 networks with up to 254 hosts each.

Class D Network addresses set aside for multicast broadcast applications.

Class E Network addresses set aside for experimental use.

Classful network A network that is subnetted to define the boundary for the network and host bits.

Classless interdomain routing (CIDR) An alternate way of defining and specifying network addresses, using the format *network_address /network_address_bits*.

Clear to send (CTS) A signal sent by a WAP to inform a computer that it can send data.

Client operating system Software that enables a computer to act as a network client and access shared resources.

Client Services for NetWare (CSNW) A Microsoft-developed NetWare client that runs on Windows client computers. CSNW supports versions prior to NetWare 5 and IPX/SPX (NWLink) communications only.

Client/server network A network model that closely matches the mainframe network model, with servers providing resources to the network and clients consuming resources. A defining feature of this type of network is centralized security control. Also known as a server-based network.

Cloud architecture A connection architecture in which you know your connection points but not the communication path inside the cloud.

Coaxial cable (coax) The first type of networking media used in Ethernet LANs. Coax is constructed from one central copper wire that is covered with a plastic insulator, called a dielectric, and shielded from interference by foil wrapping or braid. The outer jacket that protects the cable is either PVC or plenum.

Collision A transmission error that occurs when two or more computers attempt to transmit at the same time on a bus topology network.

Collision domain An area within an Ethernet network in which all devices in the domain compete for the cable, which may result in collisions.

Common Management Information Protocol (CMIP) A management protocol developed in response to and as an alternative to SNMP.

Common name A specific object name by which an object is recognized. The common name must be unique within its context.

Communication protocol *See* network protocol.

Complex password A user password that is designed to be difficult to guess, typically requiring at least three of the following: uppercase letters, lowercase letters, numbers, and non-alphanumeric characters.

Compression Control Protocol (CCP) A PPP subprotocol that manages data compression.

Computer crime Criminal activity involving or directed against computers.

Computer Emergency Response Team (CERT) A group established by the U.S. Department of Defense to respond to computer security problems.

Computer Management A Windows local management utility.

Conduit Metal or plastic pipe used to contain cable.

Confidentiality A term that refers to protection of organization data from unauthorized disclosure.

Configuration management Management of the network's hardware and software configuration.

Connection The process of having two computers recognize each other and open a communication channel.

Connectionless transmission A transmission method in which the receiving system does not acknowledge the receipt of data.

Connection-oriented transmission A transmission method in which the receiving system acknowledges received data.

Context A directory object's location in the directory.

Convergence Integration of voice, video, and data communication.

Core layer The innermost part of a network, which connects distribution layer networks, as with WAN connections.

Cost A measurement based on an algorithm that is used to determine the best route to a destination.

Cost assessment The third step in the building-block design process, in which the relative costs of available technologies are considered.

Counter-rotating rings Dual rings in a ring topology where the token circles the ring in a clockwise direction on one ring and in a counterclockwise direction on the other ring.

Crack program A program designed to identify weak, easily compromised passwords.

Crossover cable Cable that is wired so that the transmit and receive pairs are reversed between the two ends.

Crosstalk The electromagnetic interference that occurs when the electrical signal on one wire changes the electrical properties of a signal on an adjacent wire.

Customer premises equipment (CPE) Communication equipment installed at the customer's location.

D channel An ISDN control channel that carries 16Kbps or 64Kbps.

Data communications Movement of computer information from one point to another.

Data compression The act of physically shrinking data to minimize the amount of data transferred over a network.

Data encryption The process of using algorithms to modify data to prevent anyone except the sender or intended recipient from reading the data.

Data Encryption Standard (DES) A private key encryption system originally developed by IBM.

Data Link layer (Internet model) The Internet model layer equivalent to the OSI model Data Link layer.

Data Link layer (OSI model) The OSI model layer responsible for managing the transmission circuit in the Physical layer, performing error detection and correction, and formatting data packets as frames for transmission. Includes the Logical Link Control (LLC) and Media Access Control (MAC) sublayers.

Data over Cable Service Interface Specification (DOCSIS) The current dominant standard for cable modem digital communication services.

Data presentation A method of ensuring that data sent to a recipient is in a format that the recipient can process.

Data rate The speed at which data can be sent across a network.

Data separation The process of inserting markers into data packets to enable a conversation to continue after loss of packets or other communication errors.

Data service unit (DSU) A dedicated circuit network connection device.

Datagram Term used to refer to data packets at the OSI network level or equivalent level in other network models. Also known as a segment.

Datagram Delivery Protocol (DDP) An AppleTalk protocol that provides best-effort delivery of network data transmissions.

DDoS agent Software placed on a computer that enables it to be used as a message source in a DDoS attack.

DDoS handler Software used during a DDoS attack to control the agents.

De facto standard A standard developed through use and application and that is generally accepted but has no official standing.

Decapsulation A process in which header and trailer information is put through at the destination device, leaving just the original data.

Decentralized resource sharing Term referring to sharing resources from peer servers and individual user's computers rather than from centralized sources.

Decryption The process of decoding encrypted data.

Dedicated circuit network A connection method in which you lease circuits from common carriers at a flat rate.

Dedicated server A network server that operates as a server only. It does not include an interface for running client applications.

Demand priority access method An access method that puts the responsibility for managing and controlling transmissions on the hub, allowing for higher-bandwidth transmissions between devices.

Demilitarized zone (DMZ) A protected area of a network between the internal network and the Internet that is bounded by one or two firewalls. Also known as a perimeter network.

Denial of service (DoS) attack An attack that attempts to disrupt a network or its servers by flooding them with packets.

Department of Defense (DoD) model A four-layer working model based on the TCP/IP protocol suite. Its development was originally funded by the U.S. Department of Defense. Also known as the TCP/IP model.

Desirable requirements Network requirements identified through needs analysis as items that should be included in the network design.

Desktop management A term that is sometimes used to refer to electronic software distribution.

Desktop Management Interface (DMI) An emerging ESD software standard.

Destination address A 32-bit address field that identifies the host that should receive a datagram.

Determinant access method An access method that lets you track and predict the path that data will take through a network (i.e., Token Ring).

Device driver Software that enables a computer's operating system to communicate with and control devices such as network adapters.

Device number A dynamically assigned unique computer address in an AppleTalk network.

DHCP proxy A computer that is configured to forward DHCP broadcasts through routers.

DHCPACK A message sent by a server to acknowledge the client's acceptance of an address lease that includes the valid address lease and, possibly, optional TCP/IP configuration settings.

DHCPDISCOVER A message sent by a client to start the IP address lease process.

DHCPNACK A message broadcast by a DHCP server to cancel a lease offer.

DHCPOFFER A message returned by a DHCP server offering a valid IP address lease to a requesting client.

DHCPREQUEST A message sent by a client to accept a DHCP lease offer and, at the same time, inform any other servers that their offers were declined.

Dialog control The process of determining which device participating in data communication will transmit at a given time and controlling the amount of data sent in a transmission.

Differential backup A backup in which changed files, as indicated by the archive bit, are backed up. The archive bit is not reset by the backup.

dig A Unix/Linux command that is equivalent to the nslookup command. *See also* nslookup.

Digital signaling technique *See* encoding method.

Digital subscriber line (DSL) A technology that uses existing copper telephone lines to carry digital signals at higher speeds.

Digital transmission Transmission of binary electrical or light with only two possible states, 1 or 0.

Directed attack An attack that is under the direct control of a hacker.

Directory information tree (DIT) An X.500 standard hierarchical structure.

Directory object A directory services network entity, such as a user or computer.

Directory service A feature of a network operating system that enables users to find network resources.

Directory services network A centralized network architecture model that provides support for centralized user, security, and resource management. Also known as a directory-based network.

Directory-based network *See* directory services network.

Disk duplexing A RAID 1 configuration based on two hard disks being connected to different disk controllers.

Disk mirroring A RAID 1 configuration based on two hard disks being connected to the same disk controller.

Disk queue Disk operations waiting to be processed.

Disk striping with parity *See* RAID 5.

Disruption Interruptions of or reductions in network service.

Distributed coordination function (DCF) A media access method in which a device must physically listen before transmitting. Also known as physical carrier-sense method (PCSM).

Distributed denial of service (DDoS) attack A DoS attack in which the attacker controls multiple attacking systems.

Distribution A downloadable or otherwise distributable set of Linux installation files for a specific Linux flavor and kernel version. Most distributions include a suite of preinstalled applications.

Distribution layer The part of the network that connects the access layer to the rest of the network, as with a backbone network.

DIX cable *See* drop cable.

DNS table A DNS mapping file that contains DNS records.

DNS zone An administrative division of DNS names for maintaining name resolution.

Domain A logical security boundary in a directory-based network.

Domain account A Windows Active Directory user account used for domain authentication and resource access authorization.

Domain controller A directory-based network server responsible for maintaining the directory of network objects and managing user authentication and authorization.

Domain member A directory object assigned to a domain, typically referring to a user or computer.

Domain Name System (DNS) A TCP/IP protocol used for mapping of IP addresses to host names.

Domain tree A group of hierarchically related domains.

Dotted-decimal The decimal representation typically used for IP address and subnet mask values consisting of four decimal values separated by decimal points or "dots."

Double current signaling The European name for bipolar signaling.

Downstream circuit A circuit that carries traffic from a carrier or an ISP to a customer.

Downtime A period of time during which a network is unavailable to users, typically unplanned.

Draft standards Standards that have not yet made it through the full acceptance process.

Drop cable A Thicknet Ethernet device connection cable. Also called a DIX cable.

Dual boot A computer configuration in which you can choose the operating system used to start the computer.

Dumb terminal A device consisting primarily of a screen and keyboard and used to connect to a mainframe computer.

Dynamic DNS DNS service that supports automatic DNS table updates.

Dynamic Host Configuration Protocol (DHCP) A protocol and service used to provide IP addresses and TCP/IP configuration parameters.

Dynamic packet filtering A firewall filtering method that passes packets that match sessions initiated on the internal network.

Dynamic routing Automatically generating a route that can adjust to network conditions.

Dynamic service discovery A method for recognizing resources made available by network servers on an IPX/SPX-based network.

Dynamic state list A list of communication sessions between stations inside and outside the firewall that is maintained on the firewall. Also known as a state table.

EAP-Transport Layer Security (EAP-TLS) An EAP protocol extension designed for use with smart cards for authentication.

Echo request A TCP/IP message that requests a response from the host receiving the message.

Economies of scale Cost savings resulting from consolidation or the ability to purchase in bulk at a discount.

eDirectory The current version and implementation of Novell's NDS.

Edition A way of describing product variations for a specific Microsoft server product and version.

Electromagnetic interference (EMI) A source of interference resulting from a strong magnetic field.

Electronic software distribution (ESD) A process by which software and updates are distributed automatically to network computers. Also known as automated software delivery and sometimes desktop management.

Electronics Industries Alliance/Telecommunications Industry Association (EIA/TIA) A standards body that defines UTP cable category standards.

Encapsulation The process of adding information to data as it passes through the layers.

Encoding method The way that information is represented on a network for digital transmission as voltage levels or current changes. Also called the digital signaling technique.

Encryption The process of encoding data.

Encryption algorithm Values used for data encryption. Also known as an encryption formula.

Encryption Control Protocol (ECP) A PPP subprotocol that handles negotiating encryption methods.

Encryption formula *See* encryption algorithm.

End-user support resources First-level support, consisting primarily of user documentation.

Enforce password history The number of passwords a system will remember and prevent a user from reusing.

Enterprise network A large network that contains multiple servers and typically integrates wide area links.

Ethernet A low-level network protocol that is currently the protocol most commonly used. Ethernet is a common term for the IEEE 802.3 networking standard; this is the standard most commonly used for PC networks.

EtherTalk Link Access Protocol (ELAP) An AppleTalk protocol that provides the equivalent to 802.3 physical access.

Event log One of several event logs that the Windows family operating systems keep to give you a way of reviewing what has been happening on a system.

Executioner The current router when the TTL field counts down to zero.

Extended star topology A physical topology that uses two or more connected hubs. Sometimes also called star-bus topology.

Extensible Authentication Protocol (EAP) An industry-standard way of adding additional authentication protocols.

Extensible Markup Language (XML) A data format used for formatting data for transmission using defined schemas, similar in format to the HTML used for webpages.

Extranet A network that uses Internet technologies to enabled users outside an organization to connect to the network.

Failover The process of switching over to a redundant computer.

Fault A term that refers to the error reported when data cannot be found in memory.

Fault tolerance The ability of equipment or network resources to continue operating even after a failure.

Federal Information Processing Standards Publication 46-2 (FIPS 46-2) A U.S. government publication that defines DES as a government standard.

Fiber Distributed Data Interface (FDDI) A fiber-optic dual-ring networking scheme.

Fiber-optic cable A transmission medium that uses glass or plastic fibers to carry light (laser) signals.

File and Print Services for NetWare (FPNW) A Microsoft server application that makes Microsoft file and printer shares available to NetWare IPX/SPX clients.

File server A server that stores data and software that can be used by computers on the network.

File Transfer Protocol (FTP) A protocol, a service, and an application that provides reliable file transfer between TCP/IP hosts.

Firefighting A term that refers to reacting to network problems as they arise rather than relying on planned network management activities.

Firewall A network security device that filters traffic into and out of a network or subnet.

Fixed wireless *See* wireless DSL.

Flow control Communication control that prevents a computer from being overwhelmed by the number of messages it receives.

Forest A logical group of domains.

Formal standard A standard developed by an official industry or government body.

Fragmented datagram A datagram that has been divided into smaller datagrams for transmission.

Frame A data packet that has been formatted for transmission.

Frame relay A transmission method that transmits data faster than X.25 but slower than ATM; it does not include any error control.

Frequency range A set of radio frequencies available for a specific purpose or application.

Frequently asked questions (FAQs) Common problems and their remedies.

Full backup *See* normal backup.

Full duplex communication Two-way data communication that allows both ends of a conversation to transmit simultaneously.

Fully qualified domain name (FQDN) A name made up of a host name prepended to a domain suffix.

Gateway A network communication device used to connect dissimilar networks and devices.

Gateway Services for NetWare (GSNW) A Windows server application that enables a Windows server to act as a gateway, giving Windows clients that do not run a NetWare client access to NetWare resources. GSNW supports versions prior to NetWare 5 and IPX/SPX (NWLink) communications only.

Gauge A measure of wire thickness.

get command A command used by an SNMP management console to retrieve information from a device.

Get Nearest Server (GNS) An IPX/SPX protocol that is used to locate the nearest server providing a specific service.

GNS response A message sent by a server in response to a GNS message, requesting the nearest server providing a specific service.

GNU public license The specific open source license that applies to most Linux distributions.

Group policy object (GPO) An Active Directory method for defining and distributing policy configuration information throughout the directory or to specify groups of users or computers.

Hacker A person who attempts to break into a computer system.

Half duplex communication Two-way data communication in which communication is restricted so that only one device at a time can transmit.

Handshaking The process a computer uses to establish a connection.

Happy macked A term referring to a Mac operating system that can be loaded and run from a single floppy diskette.

Hardening The process of making a network or computer more secure.

Head Term used to refer to a terminating device that acts as a signal source or destination.

Header Packet information added to describe the packet, including source and destination computers.

Health Insurance Portability and Accountability Act (HIPAA) A law passed in the United States that defines requirements for protecting patient data.

Heterogeneous networking Environments that have a mix of hardware platforms, operating systems, and server applications.

Hidden cost Network operational costs that are not readily apparent.

Hidden node problem A situation in which a wireless client at one end of a WAP's range is not able to detect a client at the other end of its range.

High-level protocol A communication protocol operating at the hardware level that controls communication requirements such as message formatting and establishing a connection between computers.

Hop A router passed during packet routing.

Hop count The count of the routers crossed by a packet.

Horizontal cross-connect A dedicated pathway for running cable through a building.

Horizontal relationship The relationship between the same OSI model layer in two different network devices.

Host In TCP/IP terminology, a network device.

Host address A unique computer address on a network segment in a TCP/IP network.

Host record *See* address record.

Host-based network A network architecture based on a mainframe or other host computer with connected terminals.

HOSTS A text file used for host name resolution.

Host-to-Host layer (DoD model) The DoD model layer equivalent to the OSI model Transport layer. Also known as the Transport layer.

Hot redundancy A redundant configuration with duplicate hardware, software, and data, in which the data is kept in sync with the primary server to allow for immediate failover.

Hot-swappable A device that can be replaced without powering off.

Hub A connection device used to connect network cables as a central connection point.

Hybrid fiber coax (HFC) A cable network that uses both fiber-optic and wired coaxial cable.

Hybrid network A network architecture based on a combination of standard network architectures.

Hybrid topology A physical topology that combines two or more standard topologies.

Hypertext Transfer Protocol (HTTP) A protocol that is used to access HTML files (i.e., webpages) over the Internet or through an intranet, allowing for rapid, reliable data exchange.

IBM data connector A square, hermaphroditic connector used with STP cable in Token Ring applications.

Identification of choices stage The phase in the standardization process in which various solutions are proposed and optimum solutions are selected.

ifconfig A TCP/IP utility that can be used to view and manage IP address and configuration information. This is the Unix/Linux version of the command. *See also* ipconfig.

Impedance A measurement of opposition to varying electrical current.

Incremental backup A backup in which changed files, as indicated by the archive bit, are backed up. The archive bit is reset by the backup.

Induction The process through which moving electrical current causes a voltage on a nearby wire.

Infrastructure Transmission media and network devices that make up the physical structure of a network.

Infrastructure mode A wireless topology in which wireless devices connect centrally to a WAP.

Initialization value A WEP encryption key that is based on a random number and text string.

Institute of Electrical and Electronics Engineers (IEEE) A U.S. standards organization that develops various technical and nontechnical standards but is best known for its LAN standards.

Integrated Services Digital Network (ISDN) A circuit-switched network communication method that combines voice, video, and data communication.

Integrity The assurance that data has not been altered or destroyed.

Intelligent hub An Ethernet hub with an on-board processor that can perform various functions.

Intermediate object Objects at the midlevels in a directory structure that are used to contain and organize other objects.

International Organization for Standardization (ISO) A standards body made up of national standards organizations in member countries that develops data communication technical recommendations.

International Telecommunications Union (ITU) A standards organization that makes worldwide recommendations related to telephone, telegraph, and data communication interfaces.

International Telecommunications Union–Telecommunications Group (ITU-T) A standards-setting organization made up of public- and private-sector organizations that operate computer or communications networks or build software and equipment for them.

Internet The worldwide network of networks.

Internet Authentication Service (IAS) A Microsoft implementation of RADIUS technology.

Internet Control Message Protocol (ICMP) A management and troubleshooting protocol that provides support through error and control messages.

Internet Corporation for Assigned Names and Numbers (ICANN) The organization that is responsible for maintaining IP network address and domain name registrations.

Internet Engineering Task Force (IETF) An open-membership standards organization that develops and publishes standards for the Internet.

Internet layer (DoD model) The DoD layer equivalent to the OSI model Network layer.

Internet model The informal five-layer model that most closely matches current network hardware and software.

Internet Protocol (IP) A protocol that provides for network identification through addressing and connectionless delivery of packets.

Internet Protocol Security (IPsec) An industry-standard security protocol that provides encryption and authentication for L2TP VPN connections.

Internet service provider (ISP) A company that provides Internet access to businesses and individuals.

Internet time A term that refers to the need for companies to be able to rapidly evolve as the industry and customer expectations change.

Internetwork Packet Exchange (IPX) The IPX/SPX Network layer protocol used with NetWare versions 2 through 4.3.

Intranet A LAN that uses Internet communication technologies such as web services.

IP Control Protocol (IPCP) A PPP network control protocol that manages and configures TCP/IP over PPP support.

IP spoofing The process of sending packets with a fake source address.

IP version 4 (IPv4) The current IP version, which uses a 32-bit addressing scheme.

IP version 6 (IPv6) A new IP version that uses 128-bit addresses and provides a larger address pool.

ipconfig A TCP/IP utility that can be used to view and manage IP address and configuration information. This is the Windows/MS-DOS version of the command. *See also* ifconfig.

IPX/SPX A high-level proprietary protocol that was originally the only protocol supported by Novell's NetWare networks.

ISDN modem *See* terminal adapter.

Java Virtual Machine A software component that enables an operating system to run Java language applications.

Kerberos A highly secure industry-standard authentication method. Developed for Unix and supported on most current NOSs as an authentication method.

Kernel An operating system core.

Kevlar Material used in fiber-optic cable to strengthen the cable to protect the glass fibers.

Key A value used for data encryption.

Keychain A Macintosh operating system feature that supports local caching of online (Internet) passwords.

Keyed set A cable connector pair constructed so that it can be inserted only one way (i.e., cannot be reversed).

Label A value used to identify an object type or an attribute, represented as a one- or two-character abbreviation.

Latency Network performance delays.

Layer 2 Forwarding (L2F) The Cisco Systems protocol on which L2TP is based.

Layer 2 Tunneling Protocol (L2TP) An industry-standard VPN connection protocol.

Leaf object Directory objects directly representing directory network entities such as users and computers.

Legacy network A network based on existing networks with older, usually out-of-date, network technologies.

Level 1 support staff Personnel responsible for handling minor problems, typically by phone or through email messages.

Level 2 support staff Personnel responsible for resolving more serious problems than and who are more skilled and experienced than Level 1 staff.

Level 3 support staff Personnel responsible for resolving serious problems, often requiring on-site resolution, who are more skilled and experienced than Level 2 staff.

Light-emitting diode (LED) A light source typically used with fiber-optic cable.

Lightweight Directory Access Protocol (LDAP) A TCP/IP authentication protocol.

Link Control Protocol (LCP) A PPP subprotocol used to communicate between PPP hosts and clients to negotiate communication parameters.

Linux An operating system designed to look and act exactly like Unix but distributed through open source licensing.

Listen before transmit method A transmission method in which the device listens to check that no other device is transmitting before attempting to send data.

LLC type 1 An LLC connectionless communication service.

LLC type 2 An LLC connection-oriented communication service.

LMHOSTS A text file used for NetBIOS name resolution.

Local account A user account used by the local computer for authorization and resource access authentication.

Local area network (LAN) A relatively small network of computers, printers, and other devices covering a small geographic area.

Local loop circuit The connection between a carrier's central office and a customer.

LocalTalk Link Access (LLAP) Apple's combined Physical and Data Link layer protocol, which uses a daisy-chain wired bus network.

Logical address An address assigned to a computer through networking software to uniquely identify it in an internetwork.

Logical bus A logical topology in which data travel in a linear fashion from the source to all destinations.

Logical Link Control (LLC) The OSI Data Link sublayer that provides the interface between the media access method and Network layer protocols.

Logical network design The goal of the needs assessment design phase, which consists of a statement of the required network elements.

Logical ring A logical topology in which data travel in a ring.

Logical topology A description of how devices on a LAN communicate and transmit data.

Login script A series of commands that execute when a user logs in or a computer starts up.

Long DDP A DDP version used to send packets between different networks when routing services are required.

Long-haul transmission lines Telephone lines designed to carry traffic over long distances.

Loopback A communication test in which a computer sends an echo request to itself.

Low-level protocol Hardware-level communication standards definitions, including signal strength, data formats, and so forth.

LPD/LPR TCP/IP protocols that support network printer access in a Unix/Linux network environment.

MAC address A network device address that is hard-coded on the NIC as six pairs of hexadecimal digits as a globally unique identifier. Also known as the physical address.

MAC address filtering A WAP security method that allows or blocks wireless clients based on the MAC addresses encoded on their NICs.

Mac OS 8 A Macintosh operating system that used Internet Explorer as its default browser and included Java Virtual Machine support.

Mac OS 9 A Macintosh operating system version that added multiuser configuration support and a network browser.

Mac OS X The current Macintosh operating system version, which added improved color and graphics support and native PDF file format support. OS X is based on a Unix kernel.

Macintosh Plus An Apple computer that offered an early version of peer-to-peer networking.

Mail exchange (MX) record A DNS record used to identify a mail server.

Maintenance account A user account created for the explicit purpose of performing maintenance tasks.

Malware Malicious or annoying unwanted software.

Managed hub An Ethernet hub that supports remote management and monitoring.

Management console SNMP management software's user interface or the computer on which the management software is installed.

Management information base (MIB) A collective term for all management information objects on a network.

Manchester encoding A unipolar signaling method used by Ethernet to represent digital data in which the signal changes from low to high (1 bit) or high to low (0 bit).

Mandatory requirements Network requirements identified by needs analysis as items that must be included in the network design.

Manual failover A failover process that requires administrator or operating intervention, typically because it is necessary to synchronize the data on the redundant server.

Maximum password age The maximum time between password changes.

MD5–Challenge Handshake Authentication Protocol (MD5-CHAP) A protocol designed for testing and troubleshooting EAP connections.

Media Access Control (MAC) The OSI Data Link sublayer responsible for connection to the physical media and the physical address.

Media access method A physical network access method and control.

Member server A directory-based network resource server.

Mesh topology A physical topology in which each device connects to every other device on the network. Also known as net topology.

Meta directory A directory of directories that enables interconnection of directory trees.

Metropolitan area exchange (MAE) Smaller NAPs created to link regional ISPs whose networks come together in major cities.

Metropolitan area network (MAN) A high-speed internetwork of LANs deployed in a metropolitan area.

MIB file A file that details how to access an object and that contains information about the object and how to manage it.

Microsoft Challenge Handshake Authentication Protocol (MS-CHAP) The Microsoft version of the CHAP authentication protocol that passes LAN Manager and NT LAN Manager (NTLM) hashes in parallel.

Microsoft Challenge Handshake Authentication Protocol version 2 (MS-CHAPv2) An enhanced CHAP version created by Microsoft with security enhancements over MS-CHAP.

Microsoft Point-to-Point Encryption Protocol (MPPE) An encryption protocol that provides encryption for PPTP VPN connections.

Minimum password age The minimum time that must pass between password changes.

Minimum password length The minimum length of a password.

Mission-critical application An information system that is vital to an organization.

Mixed mode A wireless communication option supported by some WAPs that enables the device to work with both 802.11b and 802.11g at the same time.

Mode In network topologies, a wireless topology.

Modem A device that enables computers to communicate over dial-up telephone lines.

Multicast A broadcast method that supports broadcast to a defined set of hosts.

Multihomed A TCP/IP host configured with multiple IP addresses.

Multimode fiber Fiber-optic cable that supports multiple concurrent communication signals.

Multiplexer A device that combines multiple signals on a single carrier.

Multiplexing A signaling method that uses multiple signals divided by time or frequency over a single channel.

Multipoint version A wireless DSL configuration that is designed to enable ISP to support wireless customer connections as an alternative to DSL or cable modem connections. Also known as point-to-multipoint version.

Multiserver network A network that implements multiple servers in various roles.

Multistation access unit (MAU) A central hub connection device used in a Token Ring network.

Multitasking Support for running concurrent applications.

Multivendor environment A network environment in which components and services are purchased or leased from multiple vendors.

Name Binding Protocol (NBP) An AppleTalk protocol that maps device names to network addresses.

Name resolution The process of mapping IP addresses to Internet host names.

Name server (NS) record A DNS record that identifies a DNS server.

Narrow and deep A term used to describe the building-block design strategy as having a narrow range of technologies used deeply (i.e., over and over) throughout an organization.

Narrowband ISDN (N-ISDN) BRI and PRI ISDN configurations.

National ISP One of the ISPs that operate at the topmost level of the Internet and is responsible for transferring messages inside and between countries.

National Science Foundation (NSF) The organization originally responsible for management of the Internet.

NDS tree An NDS hierarchical directory structure.

Needs analysis The first step in the building-block design process, which is the process of understanding current and projected future network requirements.

Net topology *See* mesh topology.

NetBEUI A high-level protocol originally used on Microsoft networks.

NetBIOS An API command set used to control lower-level network services and node-to-node data transfers.

NetWare At one time, the most popular NOS, which controlled almost all of the PC network market share. The last version released was NetWare 6.5.

NetWare Core Protocol (NCP) An IPX/SPX protocol that provides services in support of client/server connections.

Network Computers connected in such a way that they can communicate with one another.

Network access point (NAP) A top-level Internet data exchange point maintained and operated by commercial communication enterprise or a common carrier.

Network adapter A device that enables a computer to physically connect to a network.

Network address An address used to identify a network segment for routing purposes.

Network administrator An individual who is responsible for network management and support.

Network architecture A way of describing the logical design of a network.

Network asset Any hardware or software of value on a network.

Network control protocol (NCP) A PPP protocol that enables PPP to support various network protocols.

Network discovery The process by which a network design tool identifies the component already present on an existing network.

Network File Services (NFS) Unix services that support file sharing over a network.

Network interface card (NIC) A device that enables a computer to physically connect to a network.

Network Interface layer (DoD model) The DoD layer equivalent to the OSI Data Link layer.

Network layer (Internet model) The Internet layer equivalent to the OSI Network layer.

Network layer (OSI model) The OSI model layer responsible for network logical addresses and routing control.

Network management The process of operating, monitoring, and controlling a network to ensure that it works as intended and provides value to its users.

Network management system (NMS) A network monitoring device that uses hardware and software to monitor and maintain a network.

Network Monitor Microsoft's network monitoring application.

Network number The network address in an IPX address.

Network operating system Software that enables a computer to act as a network server and provides a management interface.

Network operations center (NOC) A physically secure location for storage of network hardware.

Network protocol A protocol suite operating at the Network layer of the OSI model and higher. Also known as a communication protocol.

Network sniffer A device designed to collect network performance information and capture and log network packets. Also known as a packet sniffer or protocol analyzer.

Network terminator (NT-1 or NT-2) An ISDN connection device that acts like a hub for ISDN connections.

Network topology The physical network design, which describes how network devices connect.

Network-centric A directory-based network design in which users log into the directory to access resources rather than authenticating to individual servers.

Next-Generation Internet (NGI) A new, higher-speed Internet currently under experimental development.

Nexus point The point where several lines of communication come together.

NFS Gateway A Novell product that provides Unix clients access to shared file resources.

Node A uniquely identifiable network device.

Nonreturn to zero (NRZ) A bipolar signaling method that uses voltages that vary between +5 volts and –5 volts, without resting at 0 volts.

Normal backup A backup operation that backs up all specified data and resets the archive bit as each file is backed up. Also known as a full backup.

Novell Directory Services (NDS) Novell's X.500-based hierarchical network directory service, similar to Windows Active Directory.

nslookup A TCP/IP utility that is used to retrieve information from, test, and manage name servers. The same command is supported on both Windows and Unix/Linux.

NT LAN Manager (NTLM) A Windows authentication method that supports authentication for down-level Windows clients.

NWLink The Microsoft equivalent to the IPX/SPX protocol.

Object (1) A directory-based network entity. (2) SNMP management variable.

Object model A network model in which all network models are treated as objects that can be clearly defined and described.

Octet An 8-bit byte value.

Ohm A unit of measurement for resistance or impedance.

Open Directory A Mac directory-based networking model.

Open Enterprise Novell's current networking product, which runs on a SUSE Linux base.

Open source license A software distribution license under which you can modify the software but must distribute the source code with the modified software.

Open Systems Interconnection (OSI) model A framework that defines the way in which information passes up and down between physical hardware devices and the applications running on user desktops.

Optical carrier (OC) level A standard for measuring SONET communication services.

Organizational unit (OU) A directory services container used to organize and hold other directory objects.

OS/2 An IBM desktop operating system similar to Windows.

OS/400 An IBM minicomputer operating system.

Overflow A condition where a destination system is sent more information than it can receive and process.

Overlay network A wireless network that operates in parallel with and overlapping a wired network.

Packet A block of data formatted for transmission over a network.

Packet assembly/disassembly device (PAD) A packet-switched network connection device.

Packet filtering The ability of a router or a firewall to discard packets that don't meet certain criteria. This is a key feature of firewalls.

Packet sniffer *See* network sniffer.

Packet-switched network A cloud architecture carrier network that uses a fixed-rate connection plus per-packet charges to determine charges.

Paging The process of moving data between system RAM and a swap file.

Partitioned data A subset of the data contained in a database.

passwd The default Linux password file.

Password Authentication Protocol (PAP) An authentication protocol that passes a user name and password as clear text.

Password must meet complexity requirements A Windows password policy that forces users to use stronger passwords.

pathping A TCP/IP utility used to track a packet from one host to another, including any routers along the way. This is a Windows command-line command.

Peak circuit traffic A network's maximum traffic requirements.

Peer layer communication Network communication that relies on a horizontal relationship.

Peer server A computer configured to act as both a client and a server.

Peering A term that refers to free message and data exchange between ISPs at the same hierarchical level.

Peer-to-peer mode *See* ad hoc mode.

Peer-to-peer network A network architecture in which each computer can act as both a server and a client.

Performance baseline Performance information used as a point of comparison for network and computer performance analysis. It often includes both typical and peak performance values.

Performance Monitor A Microsoft Windows monitoring application; now called System Monitor.

Performance monitoring The process of collecting performance information about a network or individual computers.

Perimeter network *See* demilitarized zone (DMZ).

Personal computer (PC) Refers generically to a personal desktop computer that includes its own processor, memory, and local storage.

Phase 1 An AppleTalk version that supports one physical network with one logical network (zone).

Phase 2 An AppleTalk version that supports one physical network with one or more logical networks (zones).

Physical address *See* MAC address.

Physical carrier-sense method (PCSM) *See* distributed coordination function (DCF).

Physical layer (Internet model) The Internet model layer equivalent to the OSI model Physical layer.

Physical layer (OSI model) The OSI model layer responsible for the rules that define data transmission and the physical structure of cables and connectors.

Physical network design The result of the technology design process, which identifies the network hardware and software needed, typically as design diagrams.

Physical topology The physical structure of a network, which describes how connections are made between computers.

ping A TCP/IP utility that is used to test host-to-host communication. The same command is used for Windows and Unix/Linux.

Ping of death A type of DoS attack that sends oversized ping packets to the target computer.

Plain old telephone service (POTS) A term referring to the dial-up telephone network.

Plenum Teflon-based, fire-retardant cable insulation.

Podcast Self-contained files that can be played back on a computer or media player.

Point coordination function (PCF) A wireless transmission method that uses RTS and CTS to control transmissions. Also known as virtual carrier-sense method (VCSM).

Point of presence (POP) The place at which an ISP provides services to its customers (i.e., the customers' connections to the ISP).

Point-to-multipoint version *See* multipoint version.

Point-to-Point Protocol (PPP) A protocol that is used for remote connections over a variety of connection methods and that supports multiple network protocols.

Point-to-Point Protocol over Ethernet (PPPoE) A communication protocol that encapsulates PPP frames inside Ethernet packets.

Point-to-Point Tunneling Protocol (PPTP) A Microsoft-developed protocol that is used for VPN connectivity.

Point-to-point version A wireless DSL configuration used to directly connect two locations to each other.

Polling process The process by which an NMS device collects data.

Polyvinyl chloride (PVC) A plastic commonly used as cable insulation.

Port filtering Involves passing or blocking packets based on the port address.

Port number A number that is used to identify the source or destination application during data communication.

Portable Document Format (PDF) The de facto standard document format, originally developed and licensed by Adobe.

POSIX A Unix application development standard.

Presentation layer (OSI model) The OSI model layer responsible for formatting data for display to the user and for transmission on the network.

Primary DNS sever An authoritative server for a DNS zone.

Primary rate interface (PRI) An ISDN configuration that supports up to 23 64Kbps B channels and one 64Kbps D channel.

Print job A document that has been prepared and is ready to print.

Print queue A temporary storage location for print jobs waiting to print. Also known as a print spooler.

Print server A server that provides a network with shared printer services and queues jobs for printing.

Printer Access Protocol (PAP) An AppleTalk protocol that supports shared and network printers.

Private address An address that can be used for addressing LANs but cannot be used on the Internet.

Private key An encryption key known to the receiver only in public key encryption.

Process layer (DoD model) The DoD model layer that is equivalent to the OSI Application, Presentation, and Session layers.

Promiscuous mode A mode of operation that allows a network adapter to intercept and read the complete contents of any packet on a network.

Protocol Rules and standards that define network communication.

Protocol analyzer *See* network sniffer.

Protocol number (IP header) An IP header field that describes the type of protocol used in the datagram following an IP header.

Protocol stack The protocol software components running on a computer.

Protocol suite A set of related protocols that support network communication at the Network and higher layers of the OSI model.

Public key An encryption key used by the sender to encrypt data and based on the receiver's private key.

Public key encryption Encryption based on separate sender and receiver keys.

Public switched telephone network (PSTN) A telephone network and infrastructure that includes the standard dial-up phone network.

Push The process of transferring data from a source to a destination, where the transfer is initiated by the sender, without receiving a request from the receiver.

Quality of service (QoS) Features and services to improve communication, such as direct control over bandwidth use and the setting of relative priorities for packets.

Raceways Dedicated pathways for running cable through a building.

Radio grade (RG) A specification for coaxial cable used for network applications.

Radio-frequency interference (RFI) A source of interference that results from radio-frequency transmissions.

RAID 1 A fault-tolerant configuration based on two hard disk drives, with both containing the same data. Data is protected in the event of the failure of a single hard disk. *See also* disk mirroring and disk duplexing.

RAID 5 A fault-tolerant configuration based on three or more hard disks in which data and parity information are striped across the hard disks. Data is protected in the event of the failure of any one hard disk. Also known as disk striping with parity.

RC4 An encryption algorithm used with WEP.

Red Hat A popular commercial Linux distribution.

Redundancy (1) Duplicate data paths. (2) Duplication of resources.

Redundant array of independent (or inexpensive) disks (RAID) A disk configuration that provides improved disk performance, disk fault tolerance, or both.

Redundant system Systems that duplicate resources provided by primary network systems.

Regional carrier A regional telephone company.

Regional ISP A midlevel ISP that operates between national and local ISPs and provides services directly to some larger companies.

Reliable transport method A term that refers to communication sessions using connection-oriented transmissions.

Remote access server A network server that supports remote client connections.

Remote Authentication Dial-in User Service (RADIUS) A centralized authentication method.

Repeater A network device that amplifies a data signal. A repeater is used to connect network cable segments to extend a network.

Request for Comments (RFC) Documents by which the Internet is defined and through which Internet standards are published. All RFC documents are available from various websites for download and viewing.

Request for proposal (RFP) A thumbnail sketch of network requirements that is used to obtain general vendor recommendations and bids.

Request to send (RTS) A signal sent by a computer wishing to send data to a WAP for authorization to send.

Resource server Any server that provides shared resources to a network.

Return to zero (RZ) A bipolar signaling method that always returns to 0 volts after each +5 volts or –5 volts level representing a data bit.

Reverse Address Resolution Protocol (RARP) A TCP/IP protocol that returns an IP address based on the device's known MAC address.

Ring In The inbound port used for connecting two MAUs.

Ring Out The outbound port used for connecting two MAUs.

Ring topology A topology in which the stations are connected in a ring and in which the data flows in a circle, from station to station.

Rivest, Shamir, and Adleman (RSA) A public key encryption algorithm.

RJ-45 A modular jack used for network connections.

RMON A remote monitoring function supported by some devices and used with an SNMP management console to reduce traffic requirements.

Root (1) In the context of bridges, the main bridge in a network. (2) In the context of a hierarchical directory structure, the top-most level. (3) In a Novell directory information tree, the top level of the tree. (4) In the context of user accounts, a name that may be given by the network operating system to a special user account known as a maintenance account that has unlimited access to a computer or network.

Root domain The uppermost domain in a domain tree and the root of the domain hierarchical structure.

Rootkit A program that can hide itself, along with other programs, files, and processes, from the operating system, antivirus software, and other security software.

Route Path information between a source and destination computer.

Router A network communication device used to connect two or more networks.

Routing The process of directing packets through the correct routers in an internetwork to ensure delivery to the correct destination network and device.

Routing and Remote Access Service (RRAS) A Microsoft service that supports routing, remote access, and VPN access.

Routing Information Protocol (RIP) A protocol used by IPX/SPX routers to share routing tables and route information, including information about networks to which the router is directly connected.

Routing protocol A network communication language used to control routers and, in some cases, route selection.

Routing table A table stored in memory on a router that keeps track of known networks and the appropriate port to use to reach each network.

Routing Table Maintenance Protocol (RTMP) A protocol used to manage AppleTalk routers and routing tables.

Samba A Unix/Linux SMB emulation.

Scale out The process of improving performance by deploying additional servers.

Scale up The process of improving performance by upgrading server hardware resources.

Scaling The process of increasing resources available to a NOS, a server application, or other resource until it meets your needs.

Schema Rules defining objects and their attributes in a directory structure.

Screened subnet A subnet that is isolated from the rest of a physical network by a firewall.

Secondary DNS server A server that contains a copy of a zone database that is periodically updated from the primary DNS server.

Security association identifier (SAID) A unique identifier used by the 802.10 standard for LAN and MAN security management.

Security breach A computer incident that includes somehow bypassing or avoiding security measures.

Security log A Windows event log that maintains entries related to security events and requires administrator-level permissions for access.

Segment (1) A physical network division within a larger physical network. (2) Term sometimes used to refer to datagram fragments.

Sequenced Packet Exchange (SPX) An IPX/SPX Transport layer protocol that provides connection-oriented delivery service, packet sequencing, and flow control.

Serial Line Internet Protocol (SLIP) An older access protocol originally designed for use with Unix computers. SLIP passes user names and passwords as clear text.

Server A specialized computer that provides resources to a network.

Server application Specialized application that runs on server NOSs and provides resources or special services to network clients.

Server Message Block (SMB) A Microsoft Windows protocol that supports resource access.

Server operating system Software that enables a computer to act as a network server and share resources with a network. A server operating system traditionally also offers a standard user interface.

Server-based network *See* client/server network.

Server-centric A network design in which users must log in separately to each server to access resources.

Service Advertisement Protocol (SAP) An IPX/SPX protocol used for dynamic service discovery.

Service profile identifier (SPID) An NT-1/NT-2 unique identifier.

Service set identifier (SSID) A text string that identifies a WAP to wireless clients.

Session accounting A process which ensures that the correct party receives the bill when billing by session time or data volume.

Session initiation A process that arranges for the desired and required services between session participants.

Session layer (OSI model) The OSI model layer responsible for initiating, maintaining, and terminating logical sessions between computers. Also manages dialog control and data separation.

Session termination An orderly way to end a session, as well as a means to abort a session prematurely.

set command A command used by an SNMP management console to manage device configurable parameters.

Shadow A file in which passwords are stored when shadow passwords are enabled.

Shallow learning curve A term that refers to ease of learning because of associations to something that the learner already knows.

Shared key encryption Encryption based on a single key used for both encryption and decryption.

Shared multipoint circuit A circuit design in which several customers connect to the same circuit to share the available bandwidth.

Share-level security A security method used in peer-to-peer networking, with access permissions based on password-protected resource shares.

Sharing A term that refers to making resources (specifically file and print resources) available to network clients.

Shell A Unix/Linux command-line interface.

Shielded twisted-pair (STP) cable Cable that contains multiple pairs of wires that are twisted periodically and covered with a foil or braid shield.

Shiva Password Authentication Protocol (SPAP) An authentication protocol that passes a password using a reversible encryption format.

Short DDP A DDP version used to send packets to computers on the same network.

Signature The code within a virus by which it can be identified.

Simple file sharing A Windows XP file sharing method in which all workgroup members have the same access permissions.

Simple Mail Transfer Protocol (SMTP) A protocol in the TCP/IP protocol suite that is used to send email.

Simple Network Management Protocol (SNMP) A TCP/IP protocol for remote configuration, monitoring, and management.

Simplex communication One-way (broadcast) communication, with information moving from the sender to the recipient(s) only.

Simulation A mathematical technique for simulating real-world network conditions based on variable parameters.

Single point of failure In the context of networking architectures, a term that refers to a resource that, when it fails, causes the network as a whole to fail.

Single sign-in A security system in which a user is given access to all network server resources after signing in once with a user name and password.

Single-mode fiber Fiber-optic cable that carriers a single transmission signal. It is the type of fiber most commonly used for networking applications.

SMA connector A screw-on fiber-optic connector.

Smart terminal A connection device that has on board memory and processing capabilities.

Socket The combination of an IP address and port number used for defining connections for connection-oriented communications.

Source address A 32-bit IP header field that identifies the host that sent a datagram.

Source routing A routing method in which the path to the destination is specified explicitly by the source device.

Spanning Tree Protocol (STP) A protocol used by bridges to decide whether to forward a packet.

Specification stage The phase in the standardization process in which problems to be addressed are identified and nomenclature is developed.

Spooler file A file that acts as a print queue and contains print jobs waiting to print.

Spooling The process of queuing print jobs.

Spyware Software that monitors, records, and sometimes sends out computer activity, usually without the user's knowledge.

Standardization process The three-phase process through which standards are developed. *See also* specification stage, identification of choices stage, and acceptance stage.

Star topology A physical topology in which all the network devices connect to a central point.

Star-bus topology *See* extended star topology.

Star-ring topology A physical topology that connects multiple MAUs to each other.

Start of authority (SOA) record A DNS zone record that describes the zone and the authoritative server. A zone can have only one SOA record.

State table *See* dynamic state list.

Static routing Manually configuring a route that does not change unless it is manually updated.

Store passwords using reversible encryption A Windows password policy that should be left disabled unless required (e.g., when using CHAP for authentication).

Straight tip (ST) connector A fiber-optic connector similar to a BNC connector.

Strong password A password that is designed to be difficult to guess or crack.

Subnet A physical network division within a larger physical network. Also known as a subnetwork.

Subnet mask A value used with an IP address to identify the network and host portions of an IP address.

Subnetting The process of dividing a network address into smaller networks.

Subnetwork address The network address portion of an IP address after subletting.

Subscriber connector (SC) The most popular and easiest-to-use fiber-optic connector, recognizable by its square tip. SC connectors are typically used in a keyed pair.

Superuser A Unix or Linux user account that has unlimited access to a computer or network.

Supervisor A user name often associated with a maintenance account that has unlimited access to a computer or network. *See also* administrator, root, and superuser.

Supplicant An 802.1x term that refers to a client needing authentication.

SUSE A Linux distribution acquired, maintained, and sold by Novell, including a suite of server applications that run on SUSE.

Swap file Disk space set aside to emulate computer memory. A swap file is used to supplement memory.

Switch A connection device similar to a hub but more sophisticated, including functionality that enables it to control and manage data transmissions.

Switched hub An Ethernet hub that integrates OSI layer 2 switch technology.

Switched Multimegabit Data Service (SMDS) A packet-switched server that is under development.

Symmetrical key encryption Encryption based on a single key used for both encryption and decryption.

SYN flag Bits internal to a SYN packet carrying status and other information.

SYN flood A DoS attack that uses a flood of SYN packets.

SYN packet A packet used when initializing a TCP/IP communication session.

Synchronous Digital Hierarchy (SDH) The name under which SONET is marketed.

Synchronous Optical Network (SONET) An ANSI-standard high-speed U.S. fiber-based communication network.

System 1 The first Macintosh operating system version.

System 6 A Macintosh operating system that introduced color.

System 7 A Macintosh operating system version that introduced the use of TrueType fonts, multitasking, virtual memory, and sharing resources to the network.

System 7 Pro A Macintosh operating system version that introduced built-in email support, speech recognition, and the keychain.

System log A Windows event log that maintains system hardware-, operating system-, and service-related entries.

System Monitor A Microsoft Windows monitoring application; previously called Performance Monitor.

Systems Management Server (SMS) Microsoft's SNMP management console product.

Systems Network Architecture (SNA) An IBM proprietary network architecture used with IBM mainframe computers.

T1 The standard T-carrier circuit for carrying voice and data.

T-carrier circuit Most common type of dedicated circuit service.

TCP/IP model *See* DoD model.

Technology design The second step in the building-block design process, in which available technologies are examined and assessed to determine their appropriateness in meeting network requirements.

Telecommunications The transmission of voice and video (images and graphics) as well as data; usually implies longer distances.

Telnet A TCP/IP protocol and application that provides terminal emulation.

Temporal Key Integrity Protocol (TKIP) An encryption algorithm used to encrypt keys used with WPA.

Terminal adapter (TA) An ISDN client device that performs the same role as a network adapter for ISDN connectivity. Also known as an ISDN modem.

Terminator A passive device attached to each end of a coaxial cable in a bus topology to absorb the signal when it reaches the end of the line.

Thick Ethernet *See* 10Base5.

Thicknet *See* 10Base5.

Thin Ethernet *See* 10Base2.

Thinnet *See* 10Base2.

Threat Any potentially adverse occurrence that can harm a network or its data, interrupt network services, or cause a monetary loss.

Threshold A target value used as reference to determine whether an activity or a performance counter is out of expected tolerance.

Ticket A unique identifier issued to a user during Kerberos authentication.

Time to Live (TTL) An IP header field whose value is used to limit the lifespan of a datagram based on the number of routers (hops) it crosses.

Token A data packet used for data transmission in a Token Ring network.

Token Ring (1) A low-level network protocol. (2) An access method developed by IBM and used with a single-ring topology. Device access is managed by use of a rotating token.

TokenTalk Link Access Protocol (TLAP) An AppleTalk protocol that provides the equivalent of 802.5 physical access.

Topology *See* physical topology and logical topology.

Total cost of ownership (TCO) Network costs, including the costs of hardware and software and the costs involved in maintaining and managing the network.

traceroute A TCP/IP utility that is used to track a packet from one host to another, including any routers along the way. This is a Unix/Linux command.

tracert A TCP/IP utility that is used to track a packet from one host to another, including any routers along the way. This is a Windows command-line command.

Traditional network design process A network design process based on lengthy, detailed analysis that often requires up to two years to complete a design.

Trailer Packet information added to the end of a packet that helps identify transmission errors.

Transmission circuit A data communication path, including the source and destination devices as well as the transmission media.

Transmission Control Protocol (TCP) A protocol that provides connection-oriented packet delivery services, including error checking and sequence numbering, with the destination device responding with a receipt on packet delivery.

Transmission Control Protocol/Internet Protocol (TCP/IP) A high-level protocol suite developed for use on the Internet and currently the de facto standard PC network protocol.

Transmission media The media that carry network signals, either copper wire, fiber-optic line, or radio transmission.

Transport layer (DoD and Internet models) The DoD and Internet model layer equivalent to the OSI model Transport layer.

Transport layer (OSI model) The OSI model layer responsible for handling end-to-end communication issues and establishing, maintaining, and terminating connections between computers.

Transport mode An IPsec mode in which the data portion of a packet is encrypted for host-to-host communications.

trap command A command used by SNMP to force an object to notify the management console based on system failures or performance problems.

Trivial File Transfer Protocol (TFTP) A TCP/IP protocol used for acknowledged file transfers over the Internet.

Trojan horse (Trojan) A program that is expected to do one thing but actually does something else. The name is a reference to classical Greek literature.

TrueType fonts Automatically scalable fonts used with Mac and Windows.

Tunnel mode An IPsec mode in which the entire IP packet is encrypted and then encapsulated in another IP packet for host-to-host, host-to-network, and network-to-network communications.

Turnpike effect A situation in which network use exceeds original estimates simply because the network and its services are available to the users.

Twisted-pair cable Multiple-conductor copper wire cable similar to telephone cable with periodic twists in the wire to improve transmission quality.

Type numbers IBM STP category numbers.

Typeful context A directory object's location, including an object's organization and its OU structure, but not including the object's name.

Typeful distinguished name An object's complete context and name.

Typeless context A shorthand method for describing an object's context or name and context, but written without labels.

Unauthorized access Access by unauthorized personnel that violates confidentiality and integrity.

Unipolar signaling A signaling method in which the voltage is always positive or negative.

Unix Network operating system developed in part by Bell Labs that has a 32-bit kernel and is command-line based, but capable of having a graphical interface.

Unshielded twisted-pair (UTP) cable Cable that contains multiple pairs of wires that are twisted periodically to minimize interference.

Uplink port A port used for connecting two hubs.

Upstream circuit A circuit that carries traffic from a customer to a carrier or an ISP.

Uptime A reliability rating based on the percentage of time that the resource will be available to the network.

Urgent Pointer field A TCP header field that is used to identify higher-priority data that is interrupting a lower-priority transmission.

User account A user identified to a computer or network.

User Datagram Protocol (UDP) A protocol that provides connectionless packet delivery services that send packets without any type of error checking, sequence numbering, or guarantee of delivery.

Value In the context of network directories, the information stored in an attribute.

Vampire tap A Thicknet cable tap that pierces the dielectric to connect to the inner core.

Variable-length subnet masking (VLSM) A subnetting option in which variable-length subnet masks are used instead of all subnets having the same subnet mask.

Vertical relationship A relationship between two adjoining layers in the OSI model.

Very-high-data-rate DSL (VDSL) Asymmetrical DSL currently under development and designed to carrier high-speed traffic over shorter distances than standard ADSL.

Virtual carrier-sense method (VCSM) *See* point coordination function (PCF).

Virtual LAN (VLAN) A LAN in which devices are logically configured to communicate as if they were attached to the same network.

Virtual private network (VPN) An encrypted, secure, private communication path over a public carrier.

Virus A program that attaches itself to another program or file and spreads by attaching itself to other files when the host file is opened or run.

Voice over IP (VoIP) The technology on which Internet-based telephone services are based.

Vulnerability research The process of keeping up-to-date about current risks and network attack tactics.

WAN switch A connectivity device specific to LANs and used to connect to long-haul transmission media.

Warm redundancy A redundant configuration with duplicate hardware and software but where data on the redundant hardware is not kept in sync with the primary server.

Weak password An easily guessed password.

Web browser Software that enables a computer to render and display documents published from a web server.

Web server A network server that stores documents and graphics published to the Internet.

Web services Specialized applications that run on web servers and provide services to clients over the Internet.

Wide area network (WAN) LANs connected over a large geographic area, traditionally defined by a LAN connected through the switched telephone network.

Wi-Fi Protected Access (WPA) A wireless security standard that uses TKIP and user authentication.

WildPacket's EtherPeek A network monitoring application.

WiMAX The commercial name for the 802.16 high-speed wireless communication standards.

Window field A TCP header field that identifies the numbers of segments that can be sent before the source host expects an acknowledgment from the recipient.

Windows Backup A Microsoft Windows backup utility.

Windows for Workgroups 3.11 An early Microsoft Windows version that supported peer-to-peer networking.

Windows Internet Naming Service (WINS) A service that is used for automated NetBIOS name-to-IP address resolution on a Windows network.

Windows Services for Unix (SFU) A Windows add-on available from Microsoft that provides additional Unix (and Linux) client support from Windows servers.

winipcfg A GUI-based IP address and configuration management program supported on legacy Windows systems.

WinNuke An early hacker program that sent TCP/IP packets with invalid header information.

Wired Equivalent Privacy (WEP) A security scheme that can provide basic security for 802.11b and 802.11g networks.

Wired network A network in which the computers connect through physical cables, either wires or fiber-optic cables.

Wireless access point (WAP) A central access point for wireless computers that also passes data to and from a wired network.

Wireless DSL A wireless communication method that requires line-of-sight communication between communication transmitters. Also known as fixed wireless.

Wireless Ethernet A term used to refer to the 802.11 wireless standards.

Wireless LAN (WLAN) A LAN that uses radio frequency transmissions to communicate instead of cable media.

Wireless mesh A wireless topology made up of transmission points with overlapping ranges.

Wireless network A network in which the computers use radio-frequency transmissions to communicate.

Wireless personal area network (WPAN) A short-distance wireless network that can include mobile devices such as laptops, PDAs, cell phones, and pagers.

Wish-list requirements Network requirements identified through needs analysis as items that users would like to have included in the network design but that aren't really necessary.

Workgroup A logical peer-to-peer network grouping.

Workgroup name A name used to uniquely identify a workgroup on a network.

World Wide Web A term that refers to the collection of web servers on the Internet.

Worm A self-propagating form of malicious software.

X Window A popular Unix GUI.

X.25 The oldest packet-switched service in current use.

Xerox Network System (XNS) An early network protocol used as the basis for the development of many current network protocols.

Zone A logical network division in an AppleTalk network.

Zone file A DNS mapping file that contains the DNS records for a specific zone.

Zone Information Protocol (ZIP) An AppleTalk protocol that is responsible for tracking network numbers and zones.

INDEX